Practitioner Series

Springer
London
Berlin
Heidelberg
New York
Barcelona
Hong Kong
Milan
Paris
Singapore
Tokyo

Other titles in this series:

The Project Management Paradigm
K. Burnett
3-540-76238-8

The Politics of Usability
L. Trenner and J. Bawa
3-540-76181-0

Electronic Commerce and Business Communications
M. Chesher and R. Kaura
3-540-19930-6

Key Java
J. Hunt and A. McManus
3-540-76259-0

Distributed Applications Engineering
I. Wijegunaratne and G. Fernandez
3-540-76210-8

Finance for IT Decision Makers
M. Blackstaff
3-540-76232-9

The Renaissance of Legacy Systems
I. Warren
1-85233-060-0

Middleware
D. Serain (Translator: I. Craig)
1-85233-011-2

Java for Practitioners
J. Hunt
1-85233-093-7

Conceptual Modeling for User Interface Development
D. Benyon, T. Green and D. Bental
1-85233-009-0

Computer-Based Diagnostic Systems
C. Price
3-540-76198-5

The Unified Process for Practitioners
J. Hunt
1-85233-275-1

Managing Electronic Services
A. Gronlund
1-85233-281-6

Ammar Attoui

Real-Time and Multi-Agent Systems

Translator: Suzanne Ingram

Ammar Attoui
Department of Computer Science, University of Savoie, France

Translator
Suzanne Ingram
Gosport, Hampshire, UK

Practitioner Series ISSN 1439-9245

ISBN 1-85233-252-2 Springer-Verlag London Berlin Heidelberg

British Library Cataloguing in Publication Data
Attoui, Ammar
Real-time and multi-agent systems. – (Practitioner series)
1. Real-time data processing 2. Distributed operating systems (Computers) 3. Multiprocessors 4. Parallel processing (Electronic computers) 5. Real-time data processing – Case studies 6. Distributed operating systems (Computers) – Case studies 7. Multiprocessors – Case studies 8. Parallel processing (Electronic computers) – Case studies
I. Title
004.3'381
ISBN 1852332522

Library of Congress Cataloging-in-Publication Data
Attoui, Ammar, 1957-
[Systèmes multi-agents et le temps réel. English]
Real-time and multi-agent systems / Ammar Attoui ; translator: Suzanne Ingram.
p. cm. -- (Practitioner series)
Translation of: Les systèmes multi-agents et le temps réel.
Includes bibliographical references and index.
ISBN 1-85233-252-2 (alk. paper)
1. Real-time data processing. 2. Intelligent agents (Computer software) I. Title. II. Practitioner series (Springer-Verlag)

QA76.54.A88 2000
004'.33--dc21 00-026568

Ouvrage publie avec l'aide du Ministère français charge de la Culture

Typesetting: Elaine Bingham, 30 Wentworth Road, Dronfield, UK
Printed and bound at Athenæum Press Ltd, Gateshead, Tyne and Wear, UK
34/3830-543210 Printed on acid-free paper SPIN 10681492

Series Editor's Foreword

This book is a translation of the accomplishment of the French engineer Ammar Attoui, who has set out to bring together the works of computer scientists and automotive engineers. Computer scientists have worked on the same type of systems as automotive engineers, but have used different designs, methods and tools. The former call the resultant systems "real-time systems", and the latter call them "discontinuous event systems". Today, telecommunications systems of increasing performance, and increasingly powerful multi-task operating and real-time systems offer the possibilities of the development of distributed structure applications organized in a group of asynchronous entities which communicate by the exchange of messages and events. Hence, combining the cultures of computer science and automotive engineering is essential to gain the benefits of unifying their techniques and methods in order to realize this potential.

The absence of the global state in distributed systems, which is a result of the absence of a shared memory and unique repository, makes communication via messaging the sole means which can be used under any circumstances. Agents are conceptual communicating entities. The book presents the methods and techniques which are necessary for the concrete implementation of the idea of an agent as an autonomous and reactive computing entity. Multi-agent systems are composed of a set of specialized entities communicating on behalf of a global application. The entities can be reactive agents (which react to external events in order to maintain control), processing agents (which implement the processes or computations on the incoming data flow that then produces the outgoing data flow) or cognitive agents (which also contain a knowledge base used to initiate inferences).

The book presents the different aspects of multi-agent distributed systems and real-time computing systems. It brings together the principal theoretical and experimental notions on multi-agent systems in three fields of application: distributed systems and applications, parallel scientific theory and real-time systems and industrial computing. For each field, the approach taken is to present the problems and the basic concepts, tools and techniques currently used in the development of applications in their respective fields. Four complete case studies, each taking a chapter, are used as examples, thus making the material more accessible to practitioners.

Ray Paul

For those who read French, a version of the VALID environment, and the source code from this book, can be found at: http://iutweb.u-clermont1.fr/limos-ia

Foreword

IT and computers have held an important place in the history of technological development which has taken place during the twentieth century, particularly during the second half of the century. This is as much a result of hardware, where the enormous progress in electronics and architecture has allowed us to build machines of increasing performance, as it is a result of methods and models, placing at the users' disposition hardware and tools which are increasingly efficient and user-friendly.

Over the last 50 years alone, we have progressed from the first computer operated using vacuum tubes and card decks, to transistors and batch processing, and then on to integrated circuits and multi-programming. We have advanced via monoprocessing and monoprocesses to multiprocesses and then on to parallel, concurrent and distributed multiprocessors. During this time, methods have developed from machine language towards procedural languages, then to a higher level with functional, logic and object-oriented languages, etc.

At a time when communication and information play an increasingly important role in everyday life, and affect everyone, when communication networks form part of the daily routine, when people increasingly demand the immediate achievement of results, where the machine needs to be increasingly more intelligent, real-time and reactive systems have a lot to offer. By combining the abilities of both the computer scientist and the electronics engineer, this field is rapidly developing and within this context, the ability of an agent to have its independence, its own life, so that it can develop itself and react rapidly to a dynamic environment is fundamental in real-time applications.

This book lies within a field which encompasses the technological development of real-time systems. Specializing in distributed systems, the author explains the different techniques, and involves us in his knowledge by way of case studies which are essential for our complete understanding of the mechanisms. In general, too many books provide us with a purely technical explanation, occasionally accompanied by several comprehension exercises. Rarely, unlike in the following pages, does this comprise of complete case studies which act as examples. This is one of the outstanding qualities of this book.

This publication is aimed at researchers, teachers and students of technological subjects, such as computer science. University has the role of developing not only researchers and teachers, but also those who, for the most part, will go on to work in companies. It is therefore important that their training be both general enough to allow them to adapt quickly to the future advances in technology, and close enough to present technologies to give them a good understanding of the world which will be theirs for a large part of their life. It is for this reason that over 50 per cent of post A-Level students go on to read technological studies. At present, in France, this path is not being followed to its capacity, and is not yet fully integrated. In contrast to classical studies, technological studies are often followed over two years (Technical Institute, School of Engineering), but four or five year courses, which run in neighbouring countries (Germany, Belgium, Holland, England, Sweden etc.) do not exist. However, the rapid development of technologies and their increasing complexity makes these studies necessary. Where training is concerned, it is therefore difficult to say exactly which disciplines have the most need for the techniques explained in this book; however, all of the technological studies which teach real-time and multi-agent systems, will benefit greatly.

I would like to finish these few words by thanking Ammar Attoui for having allowed me to write the foreword of his text, and for the educational efforts which led him to write this book.

Jean-Louis Imbert
University Professor
Head of the IT department
Auvergne University
Clermont-Ferrand

Preface

This book presents a summary of the principal theoretical and experimental notions on multi-agent systems in three fields of application: distributed systems, parallel scientific theory and real-time computing. On the subject of general problems and base concepts, it is aimed as much at University students (College of Engineering, Degrees, Masters in Computing and Mathematics, Automatics etc.) as well as PhD students. It is also directed towards teachers, researchers and engineers who wish to master parallel and distributed programming in the development of applications or systems which exploit the potentials of parallelism offered by the materials available (parallel computers, micro-computers, high-turnover communication networks, methods of acquiring deported data, deported intelligent actuators etc.).

This book derives its origin from a distributed systems and real-time computing course which was given to the students of the three Clermont-Ferrand Schools of Engineering (ISIMA, C/U/S/T, IFMA) and those doing their postgraduate diploma in computer science.

This book responds to a general need. Its contents cover the different aspects of multi-agent distributed systems and real-time computing systems. In comparison to the diverse range of books currently available, its originality lies in the attempt to bring together the three key fields of computer science today: distributed systems and applications, parallel scientific theory, and real-time systems and industrial computing. The common denominator in these three fields is without doubt the concept of an agent which is an intelligent entity and essentially reactive. In this book, the reader, whether a beginner or not, will find the ideas, the designs and the tools necessary to effectively master the study and design of a multi-agent application in one of these three fields. In contrast to other books which deal with multi-agent systems at the design and theoretical level (which only describe the theoretical and fundamental elements), I have tried to present to the readers, through the different chapters, the methods and techniques which are necessary for the concrete implementation of the idea of an agent as an *autonomous and reactive computing entity.*

My intention in writing this book has been to allow the readers to have the necessary hindsight to understand and take part in the development of real-time systems, notably in industry.

I am indebted to the people who have directly contributed to this book, and thank them. I would also like to thank all those who have contributed indirectly in an anonymous and collective way. I thank all the researchers and students who have contributed both directly and indirectly to this book, and particularly the PhD students at the Université Blaise Pascal II, and the third year engineers at the three Clermont-Ferrand Schools of Engineering: A. Hasbani, X-B. Lecoq, H. Maouche, T. Nugeyre and O. Schram.

Ammar Attoui

Contents

Introduction xv

1. Problems Encountered with Distributed Systems 1
 1.1 Definition of a Distributed Multi-Agent Application 1
 1.2 Development of Remote Processing Systems 5
 1.3 Architecture of Remote Processing Systems 10
 1.4 Distributed Applications 14
 1.5 Distributed System Properties 21
 1.6 Activity Management in a Distributed Context 25
 1.7 Process Synchronization and Resource Management 35
 1.8 Validation Protocols for Global Applications 47
 1.9 Fault Tolerance, Security and Protection 53
 1.10 Conclusion 53

2. Interaction Models 55
 2.1 New Generation Distributed Software Architecture 56
 2.2 Event-Oriented Concurrent and Distributed Programming 57
 2.3 Massively Parallel Processors and Distributed Programming 57
 2.4 Basic Principles of Distributed Programming 62
 2.5 The Method of Analysis for a Multi-Agent Application 66
 2.6 Communication Channels 67
 2.7 Elements of a High-Level Distributed Programming Language 69
 2.8 Anonymous Communication 75
 2.9 Hoare Monitors: High-Level Synchronization and Communication Tools for Parallel Machines with a Global Memory 78
 2.10 The Corba Norm 87
 2.11 Conclusion 100

3. PVM: Parallel Programming Tools 103
 3.1 PVM Presented 103
 3.2 PVM Installation 105
 3.3 The User Interface or PVM Primitives 109

4. Distributed Programming under Unix 125
4.1 Unix and the Client–Server Model 125
4.2 Unix Tools for Distributed Data-Processing 126
4.3 IP Interfaces 130
4.4 TCP and UDP Data Transmission Protocols 132
4.5 Unix Tools for Distributed Programming 134
4.6 Sockets 147
4.7 Conclusion 174

5. Principles of Real-Time Data-Processing 175
5.1 Structure and Function of an Automated System 175
5.2 Combinatorial Automated Systems 180
5.3 Sequential Automated Systems 181
5.4 The GRAFCET: Synthesis Tool for Industrial Automated Systems 182
5.5 Technological Options for the Implementation of the Command Part 183
5.6 Digital Control Systems for Processes 185
5.7 The Need for an Adapted Specification Methodology 185
5.8 Process Dynamics 190
5.9 Periodic and Aperiodic Tasks 194
5.10 Basic Functions of Real-Time Kernels 199
5.11 Local Industrial Networks 201
5.12 The Development Environment of VxWorks Real-Time Applications 215
5.13 The Environment of a Multi-Agent Real-Time Application 224
5.14 Tools for the Development and Co-verification of Embedded Systems 231
5.15 CORBA Telecommunications 233

6. Prolog III and Real-Time System Engineering 239
6.1 Impact of Formal Specifications on Software Development 240
6.2 Reminder of Discrete Event Systems 252
6.3 Prolog III and the Study of Simple Real-Time Systems 256
6.4 Specification Methodology of Complex MSS Systems 269
6.5 Conclusion 296
6.6 Project 1: Modelling Distributed Systems 297

7. Parallel Image Processing 307
7.1 Presentation 307
7.2 Implementation 309

8. Client–Server Applications under Unix 319
8.1 Presentation 319
8.2 Implementation 322
8.3 Mini Project 1: "An Event Management System" 327

8.4 Mini Project 2: "A VxWorks Version of the Temporal Constraint Manager" 329
8.5 The Sources of the Temporal Constraint Management System 329

9. Control of a Product Processing Chain 343
9.1 Functioning 343
9.2 Analysis and Specification using the SA/RT (SA/SD) Method 344
9.3 Design and Implementation of the Command Part 362

10. Management of Persistent Objects 375
10.1 Presentation 375
10.2 The Object Manager (OM) 376

Appendix 1: Problems with Hardware-Software Layer Coupling in a Data-Processing System 403
A1.1 The Target Machine 403

Appendix 2: Basic Principles of Peripheral Handlers 417
A2.1 Presentation 417
A2.2 General Notes on Programming 419
A2.3 Communication between the Kernel and the Handler 420
A2.4 Installation Procedure of a New Handler under Unix 422

Appendix 3: Process Management 425
A3.1 Introduction 425
A3.2 Scheduler Implementation Principle 426
A3.3 The Scheduler and the Internal Synchronization of Handlers..... 428

Appendix 4: Management of the Central Memory 431
A4.1 The Part Supported by Hardware 431
A4.2 The Paging Mechanism 432
A4.3 The Segmentation Mechanism 433
A4.4 Characteristics of Segment Systems 433
A4.5 386 Selectors 435
A4.6 Segment Descriptors 435
A4.7 The Part Supported by the Kernel 436

Appendix 5: Introduction to Prolog III 439
A5.1 Functioning of a Logic Program 439
A5.2 Prolog III 442
A5.3 Accepted Expressions 443
A5.4 Conclusion 445

Bibliography 447
Index 457

Introduction

Distributed systems are of interest mainly because of their capacity to tackle complex problems in distributed systems, and to propose sound, responsive solutions. These applications, devised and structured according to the classic approaches of modular programming, generally lead to a centralized monolithic architecture, organized around a principal program which manages the function calls. The execution of the whole is supported by one single process. This is yesterday's computing. Today, applications provide interconnection possibilities using telecommunication systems of increasing performance, and increasingly powerful multi-task operating and real-time systems. These possibilities considerably favour the development of distributed structure applications organized in a group of asynchronous entities which communicate by the exchange of messages and events. Distributed programming involves applications which implicate several interconnected computers (distributed systems) as well as applications on one single computer (multi-task event-oriented applications).

Furthermore, the standardization of communication methods at all levels of a business, from the terrestrial network in the workshop to the local network (Ethernet) in administrative buildings which runs the different business services, has been the catalyst that has brought together two different cultures and communities. Computer scientists and automatics engineers have, until now, worked on the same type of systems, but used different designs, methods and tools. This leads to systems which are called *real-time systems* by the former and *discontinuous event systems* by the latter. Combining these two cultures and unifying their techniques and methods has now become a necessity. The management and real-time tracking of the different services within a company imposes a hierarchic interconnection between its different internal communication systems. This induces exchanges between the applications belonging to extremely heterogeneous information technology environments such as the applications responsible for manufacturing procedure control, computer-aided manufacturing management applications, computer-aided design (CAD) applications, information technology applications for quality control management applications, etc. This poses problems related to real-time systems, including interrupt capacity, reactivity, time management and so on. The two fields of expertise must guarantee that each of their applications have a reasonably high degree of interoperability despite the diverse upgrades of each application, and the constraints of the information technology environment.

This book aims to bring together the three key areas of current and future technology, which are distributed systems and applications, parallel scientific computing and real-time systems, and manufacturing data processing.

The applications in these three fields are composed of several processes where agents work together by interchanging messages or events. If the nature and purpose of the applications differ, then the design and implementation problems within the three fields show distinct similarities. These are the structuring and outlining of the application in terms of the communicating agents, carrying out interchanges between the different agents by developing the means of command execution and the communication potentially available.

For each field we have used the same approach, which involves presenting the problems and the basic concepts, tools and techniques currently used in the development of applications in their respective fields.

Several reliable implementations of complex systems are analysed and presented as a whole. These systems may serve as reference models for the design and implementation of applications in these three fields.

The combination of these three fields homogenizes both the implementation problems, and the standardization of the solutions and concepts which, following a division induced by related peculiarities, was previously considered unique to every type of problem.

Furthermore, those readers who only study classic sequential programming will, with this book, be able to learn distributed multi-agent programming. It primarily covers programming and development tools of today and tomorrow.

This book addresses university students (School of Engineering, degree, Masters in Computing, Mathematics etc.) as well as PhD students on the subjects of general problems and basic designs. It is also aimed at teacher-cum-researchers wishing to study parallel and distributed programming in order to implement the applications or systems which make the most of the parallelism potential offered by the available hardware (parallel machines, microcomputers or Unix stations connected via a local area network, portable terminals, high-throughput communication networks, means of acquiring deported data, deported intelligent actuators).

Finally, we want to heighten the reader's awareness, especially trainee computer scientists, of the importance of having knowledge in both information technology and electronics. We feel that a computer scientist with insufficient knowledge of electronics and automatics will have difficulties in learning and mastering the complex systems. The systems and technology of the twenty-first century are mainly characterized by miniaturization and an unprecedented software-hardware integration rate. The boundary between classic electronics and traditional information technology is gradually disappearing. The appearance on the market of programmable circuits, and their large-scale use has inspired future engineers and specialists to ensure they have the largest possible spectrum of information technology and electronics knowledge. Owing to programmable circuits, a function provided with a new system to design can be implemented by classic (software) programming or by microprogramming using a programmable circuit (hardware). To this end, systems which are increasingly *responsive*, require a *global approach to analysis and development*, in which the assignment decisions of the different functions of the new systems intervene at a late stage in the development cycle.

This same discussion is also aimed at the automatics and electronics engineers, who, in a similar way, are obliged to integrate into their spectrum of abilities the study of a number of more or less neglected techniques and computing methods such as:

- Analysis and specification methods which are used to gain the abstraction power necessary in the study of complex systems which are, as we remember, the consistent integration of a group of hardware and software components. As we have already indicated, in the development process of complex systems, especially real-time systems, the decision to implement a data function using either hardware or software appears at a late stage in the development cycle.
- The development and implementation of information technology systems, such as operating systems, compilers, networks, etc. For example, the development of a card for a specific system, which is designed to process images in real-time, requires its designers to have a knowledge based in electronics, but also the knowledge of information technology.

On the other hand, technological development requires that everyone have a broad knowledge base in the area of engineering sciences. Potentially, the collection of abilities will be such that the identification and separation of abilities, as is the case today, will be more difficult to achieve.

Particular attention is paid to real-time computing. The rapid development of production methods, especially the integration of embedded information technology systems (microprocessor-based cards), has definitively lowered the barrier which separated what was formerly called manufacturing information technology and classic information technology. The specification of control and management systems for automated production systems and manufacturing processes generally follow rules and methods which are the result of a direct collaboration between the computer scientists and the electronics engineers. Automated production systems are a particular example of distributed systems subject to temporal and operational constraints. With the integration of embedded information technology systems in the production methods, electronic regulating modulators no longer control the regulation and control of manufacturing processes. It can now be done using high performance information technology tools and methods, which are able to take into account the environmental constraints of such systems.

The first chapter presents the concepts and basic ideas that we feel are indispensable to the study and the implementation of distributed systems. The intrinsic characteristics of these systems mean that the methods or techniques used in centralized systems are no longer directly applicable to these systems by simple extrapolation or adaptation. The absence of the global state, which is a result of the absence of a shared memory and unique repository, makes communication via messaging the sole means which can be used, under any circumstances, as much by the different components of the distributed execution system (resource allocation, remote program activation, validation of distributed applications, etc.) as by the distributed applications themselves (application protocol: a group of messages used to bring together and synchronize the different actions of the activities or agents of the distributed application). The delays caused by communication (public data transport networks, local area networks or simply switched network lines) and particularly the huge number of software layers crossed by the messages both on their departure and their arrival, have a direct impact on the global performance of these systems. On the other hand, the design and implementation of each distributed or real-time application must take into account all of these determining factors.

In the second chapter, we are primarily interested in distributed programming which represents the highest abstraction level. It allows the masking of the mechanisms and system tools available for the remote activation of agents or processes, communication and for process synchronization. It is the indispensable user interface which aids the development and implementation of distributed applications.

Chapter 3 presents the basic principles of a parallel programming tool used mainly by scientific researchers for the implementation of parallel computing applications. The abstraction level of this tool makes it a practical means with which to learn multi-agent distributed applications.

Chapter 4 will be dealing entirely with client–server models. The Unix tools required for the implementation of applications, depending on the model, are described.

Chapter 5 will concentrate on the basic concepts of manufacturing data processing and real-time systems. We start by outlining the characteristics of these systems, and will then introduce the specification method SA-RT (Structured Analysis-Real-Time). We will end this chapter with a presentation of the principles which underlie the workings of the real-time executive. The real-time executive VxWorks will act as an illustration of this.

Chapter 6 will start with a brief presentation of the different techniques and methods of formal specification. Following this we will present a method which is used for the specification and validation of concurrent systems in general, and real-time systems in particular. The theoretic basis used gives it the ability required to take better account of the intrinsic characteristics of concurrent systems, and aids in the verification of their properties as well as the validation of their performance before passing on to the implementation phase. An implementation of the validation process will be proposed, along with the programming language with Prolog III constraints. A version of this specification and validation of a real-time systems environment has been the subject of numerous presentations and demonstrations at national and international conferences (IEEE Real-Time Systems Symposium, San Antonio, USA; CIMPRO'94 Rugers' Conference on Computer Integrated Manufacturing in the Process Industries, New Jersey, USA;

IEEE International Workshop on Rapid System Prototyping, Grenoble, France; 5e Congrès International de Génie Industriel: Grenoble, France, etc.) and in specialized publications (*Integrated Manufacturing Systems Engineering*, Chapman & Hall, 1995).

Chapter 7 presents the first case study on the design and implementation of a simplified image handling application. This has been introduced to show how to use the PVM parallel programming tool (mentioned in Chapter 3) to design and develop a distributed application composed of several specialized handling agents. This application could serve as a basis for more sophisticated image handling applications.

Chapter 8 presents a second case study which uses Unix tools to implement the client–server model introduced in Chapter 4, taking into account the temporal constraints. This system may be used to implement distributed *soft real-time* applications where the temporal requirements are not too good.

Chapter 9 shows a third case study which is an implementation of the notions and concepts introduced in Chapter 5. It includes a real-time application for the management and handling of an automated distribution system of photographic films, which is composed of several different agents (reactive agents, handling agents, expert agents). The analysis and specification of the command part of this system is made using the SA-RT method. It is a variant of this method which gives it the ability to take into account certain architectural considerations at a very delicate stage of the analysis process. This renders this analysing process more deterministic and certainly more realistic. A discussion on the opportunity of the use of SA-RT in the analysis of the requirements and specification of this system is also put forward. Finally, the main steps of an implementation, first with a programmable automaton, then with a real-time executive, are given.

Finally, Chapter 10 presents a fourth case study. This involves the implementation of a persistent object management system (data) manipulated by real-time applications. This is a tool which considerably facilitates the implementation of multi-agent applications and zone abstraction which manipulates persistent objects and data (databases, rule bases etc.).

The diagram overleaf suggests some possible reading paths depending on the reader's subjects.

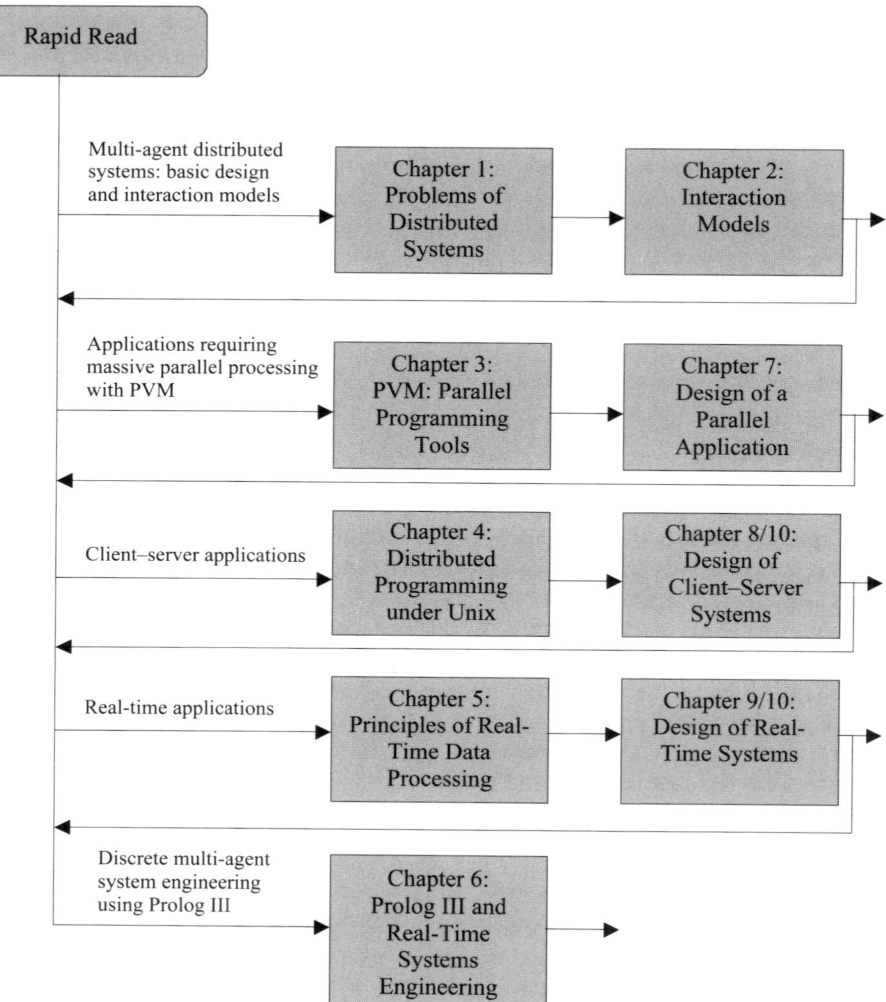
Rapid Read
Multi-agent distributed systems: basic design and interaction models
Chapter 1: Problems of Distributed Systems
Chapter 2: Interaction Models
Applications requiring massive parallel processing with PVM
Chapter 3: PVM: Parallel Programming Tools
Chapter 7: Design of a Parallel Application
Client–server applications
Chapter 4: Distributed Programming under Unix
Chapter 8/10: Design of Client–Server Systems
Real-time applications
Chapter 5: Principles of Real-Time Data Processing
Chapter 9/10: Design of Real-Time Systems
Discrete multi-agent system engineering using Prolog III
Chapter 6: Prolog III and Real-Time Systems Engineering

1. *Problems Encountered with Distributed Systems*

The aim of this chapter is to enable readers to understand more fully the problems inherent in distributed or shared systems, as well as the different solutions and techniques either currently used or which are still being studied. In general, software programs now have new interconnection possibilities using telecommunication systems of enhanced performance, and increasingly sophisticated mobile informatics terminals. These possibilities considerably increase the quantity of available information, as well as the functionality that is available to the numerous different users with a wide variety of requirements. This poses several problems. Users could have real difficulties in effectively benefiting from all these services depending on their specific requirements. The developers need to ensure that their programs can interoperate in heterogeneous data processing environments, and guarantee the continuity of this interoperability, despite the diverse development of software and environmental constraints.

Conversely, the application domains for these software packages are increasing in complexity, and often show rapid change. Their availability underlies a constant, multi-task activity. This poses problems related to real-time systems: interrupt capacity, reactivity, time management etc. This chapter aims to throw the necessary light on the different problems caused by the design of these distributed real-time systems. These are primarily the techniques used in the implementation of distributed applications, processing and data distribution, the management of conflicts between the different activities or agents of shared applications, the management of resources shared by multiple users within a distributed environment, global validation etc.

1.1 Definition of a Distributed Multi-Agent Application

Multi-agent systems developed within the field of Distributed Artificial Intelligence (DAI) are interesting mainly because of their ability to overcome complex problems using a distributed method, and to offer concrete, working solutions. Several studies have recently considered applying multi-agent systems to the decision-making problems of manufacturing systems. These latter are, by their very nature, generally composed of several components, where it is necessary to integrate several functions (control check, manufacturing management, scheduling etc.) and where the decisions need to take place at several levels. However, it must be stipulated at this point that the notion of an agent is not necessarily linked to distributed artificial intelligence. It is therefore important to note that, on the one hand, solving a complex problem in a distributed manner, whatever its nature (standard data processing problems, problems encountered with numerical computation or simulation, running the manufacturing process: flexible circuit etc.), remains the easiest means of understanding agents. On the other hand, the expert system approach need only be considered and used if the knowledge within a given field is very scattered and complex, and is not sufficiently structured to become the subject of standard modelling and problem-solving in the form of an algorithm. In this case, distributed problem solving composed of a set of specialized entities in one part of the cognitive field represents a natural alternative. It must be noted that the cognitive approach should be avoided in situations where the problem can be resolved using the standard procedural approach, for obvious efficiency and performance-related reasons.

With distributed problem solving, resorting to the expert system approach to implement an entity does not have to be systematic. The field of expertise of each agent is actually more restricted, which considerably facilitates its modelling and implementation. A solution based on an expert system, using a large knowledge base can be advantageously replaced by distributed problem solving composed of several expert entities, specialized and implemented according to either the procedural or cognitive approach, depending on the complexity of the task and the knowledge held by each entity.

Faced with a complex problem and abstraction caused by the application field, it is generally preferable to resolve them using distributed means, by dividing them into sub-problems which are more easily overcome and solved. The processes and computations relating to the sub-problems are interdependent and are modelled by *conceptual communicating entities* called agents.

Notion 1 Agent

This is a conceptual entity involved with analysing, structuring and implementing the processing of a complex problem.

In general, every complex application lends itself to refinement and structuring in the form of a series of specialized functional entities each with a precise task, where expertise and knowledge are relatively limited. This occurs independently of the means and techniques necessary for their implementation. This definition also encompasses the *natural agent*, a particular type of agent principally used in certain artificial intelligence applications.

Notion 2 Natural Agent

This is an agent with auto-learning capabilities (the ability to increase knowledge by the addition of rules, arising from changes in its environment and the events which can occur).

In this book we pay particular attention to the tools, the techniques and design and implementation methods of a set of interacting entities, rather than in the semantics and functions of a particular type of agent.

These important points are specified in order to avoid all confusion. We are therefore able to give several definitions which concern the notion of the agent and its role in an application composed of a set of active communicating agents.

We can identify three types of agents, which can be used to structure and refine a complex application and a set of specialized entities: reactive agents, processing agents and cognitive agents.

Notion 3 Reactive Agent

This is an agent with the ability to react to external events in order to maintain either the behaviour and control of a piece of hardware, of which it is the commanding entity, or the supervision and co-ordination of the activities of a set of agents for which it is the controlling agent (controlling part of a multi-agent application).

Notion 4 Processing Agent

The role of this agent is to implement transformations, which are the processes or computations carried out on the incoming data flow to produce the outgoing data flow. It ensures the execution of an algorithm, however complex (the operative part of a multi-agent application).

At another level, manufacturing or artificial intelligence applications may integrate intelligent agents called *cognitive agents.*

Notion 5 Cognitive Agent

This is an agent which contains not only data and procedural methods, but also a knowledge base, and which can also initiate inferences on its own knowledge base and those of others of the same type.

A cognitive agent plays the role of an expert system in a well-defined field, which the procedural approach does not allow to be resolved easily. With this in mind, Chapter 6 presents a global approach to the analysis and design of both reactive and cognitive agents. Chapters 5 and 9 present the fundamental concepts for the analysis, structuring and implementation of real-time applications principally composed of reactive agents, processing agents and, in certain cases, cognitive agents.

The development of a multi-agent system requires the support of analysis, design, implementation and maintenance tools. Software engineering presents several solutions relevant to the development cycle of information systems, but hardly touches on the problems linked to *distribution*, to *interconnections* that are often cyclic, and to *autonomy*. Chapter 6 presents concrete solutions to these problems.

Finally, to reinforce the notion, several current definitions, which will be useful to help understand the rest of the book, follow.

Ferber (1993) defined the *multi-agent system* as being an artificial system composed of a set of autonomous interactive agents that communicate to achieve a common goal. The basic entity, which is the agent, is either a real or abstract entity that pursues an individual objective and is capable of acting on itself, and on the surrounding environment, usually populated by other agents. Each entity has a partial representation of this environment and can communicate with the other agents. Its behaviour is the result of its observations, its knowledge and its interactions with the environment and the other agents. It is equally capable of learning and therefore increasing its knowledge.

Agents are composed of three parts:

Input interface	Expertise Cognitive Internal state variables	Output interface

The expertise part contains the knowledge that represents the processes and actions that an agent is capable of carrying out, which are described in the form of rules. It also contains the state variables that characterize the status of the agent. The input and output interfaces ensure communication with the external environment; this communication occurs by way of an interchange protocol. The state variables, which are visible from the exterior of the agent, are managed by these interfaces.

Following the points set out above, concerning the classification of the agents into three distinct types according to their role in the system to be used, we have outlined below a less restrictive definition of a multi-agent system.

Notion 6 Multi-Agent Systems

This is a system which is composed of a set of specialized entities communicating on behalf of a global application (global function or common aim). The entities can be reactive agents, processing agents or cognitive agents, depending on their role.

This identification and classification of agents is important. It allows us to clearly define the necessary context for the study of each type of agent. In other words, it enables us to specify the group of tools or methods most appropriate for agent analysis, specification and design.

The three types of agents exhibit the same structure, shown above, but differ in the expertise and cognitive part. Reactive agents are generally sequential or combinatorial processes which react in response to input events. Processing agents are simple computation agents. The expert, knowledge-based parts are implemented by a more or less complex algorithm. They are capable of calculating the output data from the input data. Finally, in cognitive agents, the expert, knowledge-based part is usually made up of rules and facts that are operated by an inference engine.

The expertise part of each agent depends on the application field and its complexity, the agent's role, etc. Because of this, it seemed inappropriate to make the distinction between the three types of agents at a later stage of this book. We recall that we are principally interested in the different design and implementation techniques of distributed applications in general, and the implementation of *interactions* between their different components. These could be reactive agents, processing agents or cognitive agents. For these, we start by first presenting the development of data processing systems in general; these form the basis and the implementation platform of these applications. It is important to clearly outline the difficulties and design problems of this type of distributed application, independent of the field of interest. The solutions to these problems remain sufficiently general for them to be used in several application fields, where the distributed approach allows the objectives to be reached naturally in terms of simplicity, performance, reliability and robustness etc.

Notion 7 Agent Implementation

This is the entity used in a host data processing system as execution time support for the agent processing: a process, a task or an activity.

1.2 Development of Remote Processing Systems

The combination of time sharing and multi-programming in the third computer generation (1965–80), notably in the CTSS (Compatible Time Sharing System, developed at the Massachusetts Institute of Technology on IBM's operating system for the 7094 in 1962), was a decisive stage in the development of man-machine interaction, and the optimization of the use of machine resources. With the preceding computer generation, direct access to the machine was not possible. The only means of developing and running the programs was batch processing. Consequently, the development cycles were long and very costly in terms of man hours and machine time.

Notion 8 Time Sharing

This is the technique used in operating systems to simultaneously run several user programs in a quasi-parallel manner. This is done by sharing the central processing unit (CPU).

This way of organizing the processing, which was a direct consequence of the facilities that gave rise to second-generation operating systems, induced chronic under-use of the machine resources.

If the CTSS is the precursor of multi-task operating and time-sharing systems, MULTICS (MULTiplexed Information and Computing Service, 1965), the work of the researchers at the MIT and the Bell Labs, remains without a doubt the most well-known multi-user operating and time-sharing system of its type. It forms the basis of the principal designs and techniques used in current operating systems, especially Unix. It is therefore the true forerunner of multi-user operating systems based on the concepts of processes and descriptors (system object containing the information necessary for the management of system objects: processes, files, and so on).

With the appearance of the first versions of MULTICS, the development of the real-time concept became directly linked to the notion of multi-programming and remote processing, the aim being to increase the number of potential users of computer centres, and to optimize the use of resources. This development took place in four distinct stages which are described below: the connection of remote terminals to a data processing system, the use of concentrators, the use of front- and back-end processors, and the general computer networks and communication systems.

1.2.1 Connection of Remote Terminals

Figure 1.1 gives the overall architecture of the very first third-generation computer installations. Generally, these installations were composed of a fairly powerful machine, which could be accessed by a number of local or remote users via the telephone network.

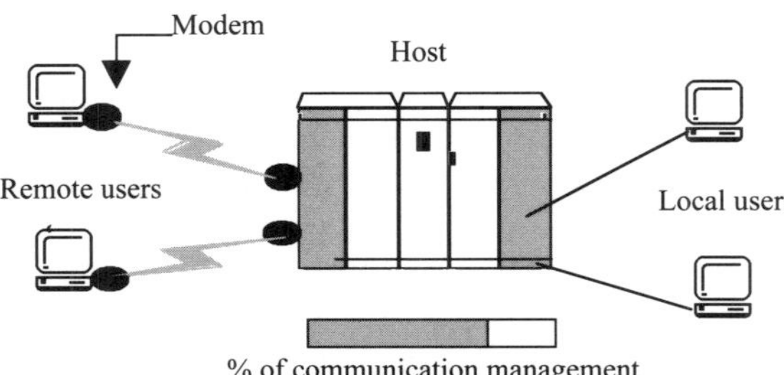

Fig. 1.1 Architecture of a multi-user installation.

It is important to note that, for this type of configuration, the operating system devotes a large part of its load (shaded part of Fig. 1.1) to the management of communication lines, the corresponding transmission procedures and interrupts. The time dedicated to the management and operation of programs was relatively small. This situation was essentially characterized by a system overload, which considerably limited the number of potential users of the installation.

1.2.2 The Use of Concentrators

In order to reduce the machine load, especially that used for the management of communication lines and the corresponding communication procedures, a new piece of equipment was introduced, which was primarily dedicated to this task, as shown in Figure 1.2.

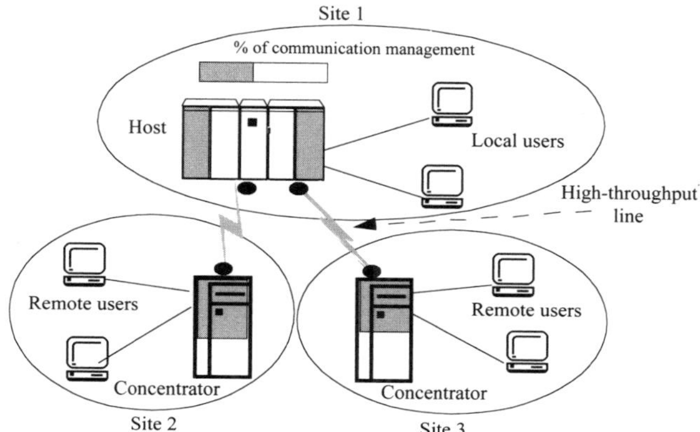

Fig. 1.2 The use of concentrators.

Concentrators are dedicated mini-computers, with a specialized operating system for managing communication lines and traffic or flow (local pre-processing: line multiplexing, flow concentration, management of transmission errors, and so on). With the spectacular technological development of microprocessors and microprocessor cards, concentrators have evolved into a single piece of data processing equipment, scarcely bigger than a single modem.

It is clear that this type of configuration is perfectly suited to standard real-time applications – banking systems, reservation systems, etc. – as they are essentially centralized systems.

1.2.3 The Use of Front- and Back-End Processors

The main aim of earlier architecture was to relieve the CPU of the burden of direct management of the communication lines of remote users. However, it still exhibits a star architecture. The CPU must still devote part of its time to managing communication with local terminals and particularly the concentrators. This time is directly charged to the time used to execute the programs. Thus, despite a significant increase in the number of potential CPU users, and the substantial increase in the overall performance of the CPU, the number of users remained relatively limited compared to its true capacity.

To totally unload the management of communication lines from the CPU, and to consequently allow an increase in the number of system users without reducing performance, another system was introduced whose role was to take charge of total communication management between users. This is indicated in Figure 1.3.

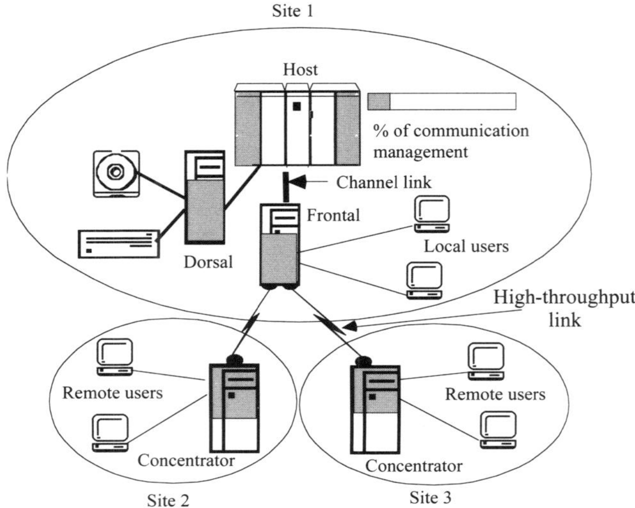

Fig. 1.3 The use of front-end processors for the management of communication lines.

A direct consequence of this distinct separation between program management and communication management functions, was an increase in CPU throughput in terms of the number of programs terminated per second. At the same time, the number of potential users of the installation increased perceptibly. The front-end processor can be compared to an input/output processor. The link between the CPU and the front-end processor is a channel device, a very high throughput connection (bus).

The front-end processor is also a system (usually a microcomputer) with a medium-sized central memory and an operating system which specializes in the management of communication lines, message storage and error management. It is important to note that standardization at the character representation level was not done at this stage (two encoding families: ASCII on 7 bits and EBCDIC on 8 bits as well as control characters specific for each family of terminals).

To separate the application level from the communication level, and thus to relieve the applications of the tedious task of handling the terminal-specific details, the job of constructing the specific bit strings that represents the characters (especially the control characters) for each type of terminal was assigned to the front-end processor level.

However, the CPU was not completely relieved of input/output management from the local peripherals: disk unit, archiving unit, printer etc. To obtain an architecture where each part of the system is specialized for a particular function (notably the CPU would be solely dedicated to the execution of programs), a further system was introduced called the "back-end processor". This was used for the management of all local input/output operations. This is the architecture that is usually used in supercomputers.

The three first stages in the development of remote processing systems were mainly concerned with star-type structures. Although this type of architecture enabled the implementation of real-time applications using the *transactional communicating model* (which will be introduced later), it did not allow the implementation of *distributed* real-time applications. Since the 1980s, we have been witnesses to the spectacular development of another type of remote processing system structure, which represents a historic turn in the development of data processing systems: computer networks.

1.2.4 General Computer Networks

In contrast to the preceding structure, general computer networks allow a user with a terminal and a modem to connect to several geographically isolated *host* systems.

Notion 9 Computer Networks

This is a group of systems interconnected by a communication system (specialized transmission lines, data transmission networks, etc.).

Notion 10 Data Transmission Networks

A group of machines (mini-computers) dedicated to the transmission and routing of data packets between the nodes (terminals, machines etc.) connected or subscribing to the network.

Information interchange between these machines is always possible. As Figure 1.4 indicates, a clear distinction needs to be made between computer networks, which are a set of interconnected machines, and data transmission networks, which are a group of machines called nodes (usually mini-computers). These latter are dedicated to the transmission and routing of data packets between two points in the network (two hosts, a terminal and a host etc.). A program, Pa, on site 1 is in a position to send messages to another program, Pb, active on site 2. With this new structure for remote data processing systems, it is possible to implement real-time distributed applications.

The ability to connect two active programs on two separate machines has opened the way to the development of a new generation of applications called distributed applications. These are essentially characterized by:

- distributed control over several geographically isolated machines;
- the exchange of information between several applications.

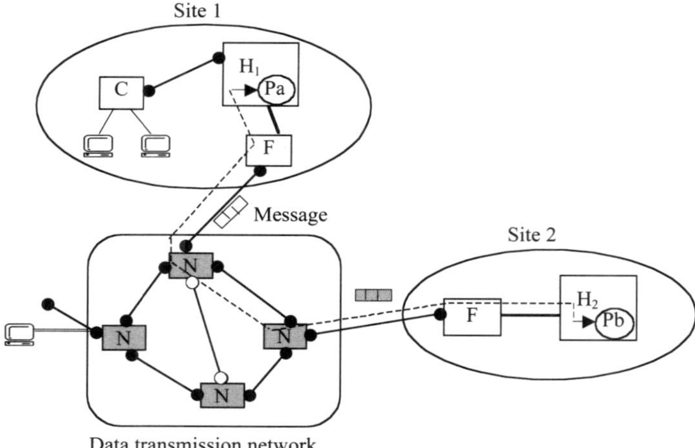

Fig. 1.4 Computer networks.

The next stage, which resulted directly from the introduction of data transmission networks, saw the introduction of a new type of computer network, for which the geographical spread is usually limited to a single site, namely local area networks (LANs). The constraint of the geographical spread in return allowed a higher data transmission speed to be obtained – 10Mbits or more. Several topologies exist: linear (Ethernet) or ring (token network) (Fig. 1.5). LAN's facilitate the implementation of multipoint data interchanges, where several communicating entities are involved. In a LAN, processing machines (large machines or mini-computers), workstations (microcomputers), and passive resources (printers, plotters etc.) are all interconnected.

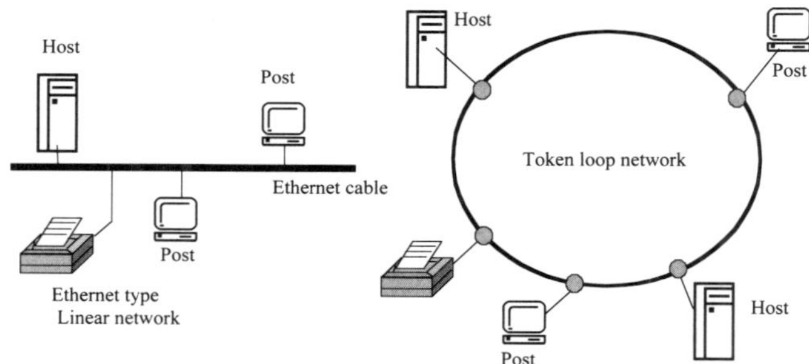

Fig. 1.5 Local area networks.

1.3 The Architecture of Remote Processing Systems

As we have seen over the last few sections, distributed systems, which form the necessary basis for the use of real-time systems in general, are the result of an integration of two fields: information technology (the manufacturers) and telecommunications (the PTT – Public Telephone and Telecommunications), as shown in Figure 1.6.

At the outset, this integration was more or less compromised by fierce competition among the different manufacturers who, until the beginning of the 1980s, adopted a deliberate strategy for the interconnection of internal hardware. Each manufacturer launched on to the market a complete range of homogenous information technology hardware: CPU, hard disk units, tape drives, printers, terminals, etc. Of course, each manufacturer imposed its own standards, protocols and communication procedures, as well as a specific architecture for teleprocessing systems. For example, DIGITAL proposed an architecture based around its DECNET network, IBM data processing systems based it on SNA (System Network Architecture) etc. However, other manufacturers took the initiative of proposing heterogeneous data processing system architectures. Among these manufacturers, was CII with DSA (Distributed System Architecture) which could support the interconnection of SPS7 machines, MINI6 mini-computers, DPS8 machines and up to 68 terminals.

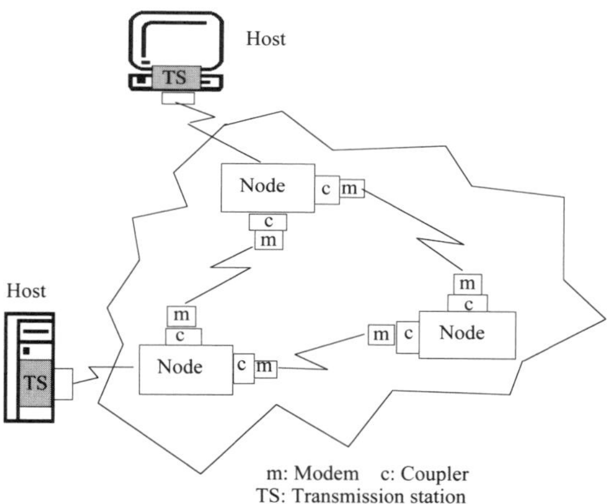

Fig. 1.6 Different hardware and software components of a teleprocessing architecture.

This situation did not last for long. Even the most powerful manufacturers quickly realized that their own survival depended on the facilities they had to offer their clients to support the hardware of the other manufacturers. The spectacular technological advance in the field of information technology and telecommunications, and the strong competition which prevailed during this period forced certain manufacturers to specialize in specific equipment (printers, terminals, communication equipment etc.) in order to survive. This specialization enabled them to become the strongest in their field and, as a result, they forced others to open up to their hardware. However, the interconnection of heterogeneous hardware could not be done without a minimum number of common rules being respected, especially at the connection interface level and the procedures or protocols surrounding data interchange. In this way an international standards committee was formed (ISO). Its sub-committee SC-16 was concerned with the architecture of open systems. The primary aim of SC-16 was to define architecture, and then to offer interconnection standards (Figs 1.7 and 1.8).

Notion 11 Co-operation Protocol

A collection of dialogue and synchronization rules embodied in messages and the corresponding procedures for interpreting them.

The ISO model architecture is made up of seven layers, with the entities at each level using a specific co-operation protocol.

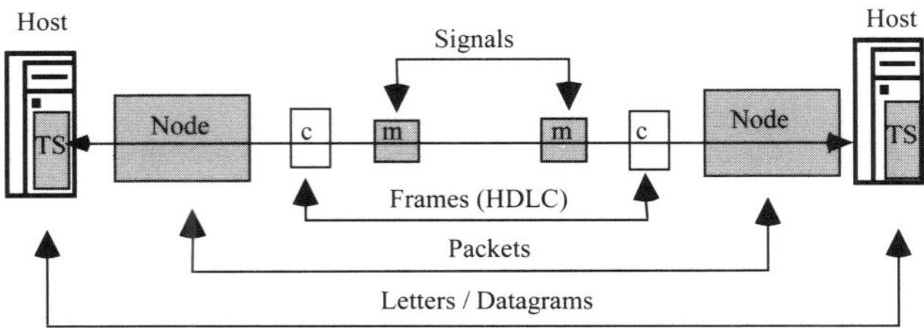

Fig. 1.7 Different levels of interchange protocols.

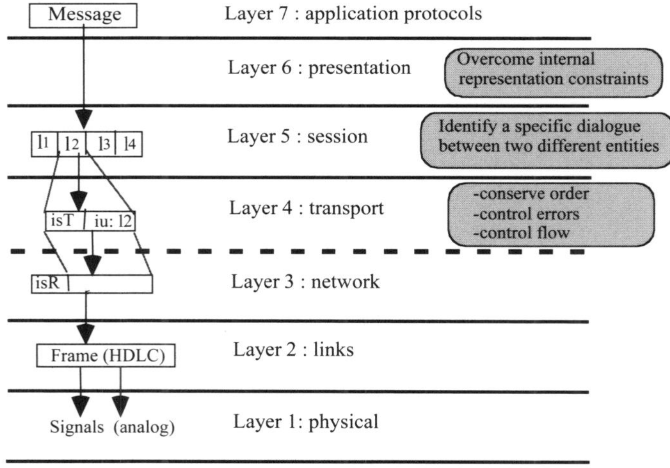

Fig. 1.8 The different layers of the ISO model.

Between two layers there exists a communication interface, which offers a collection of services implemented at level L-1 and used by level L.

- The *application layer* of the ISO model contains the protocols for communication between the different entities active in a distributed application as shown in Figure 1.9.

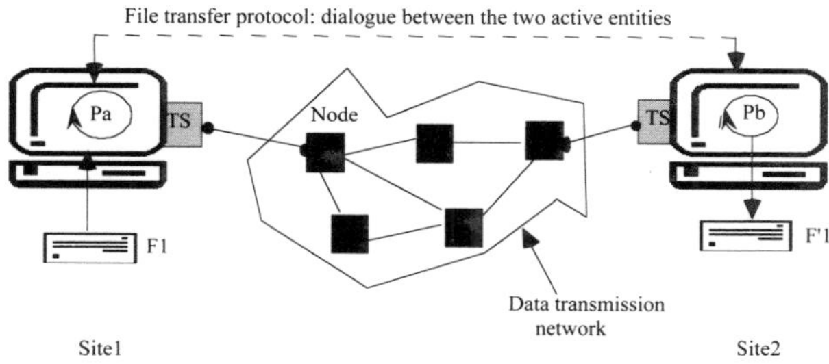

Fig. 1.9 Example of a distributed application.

- The *presentation layer* of the model combines the rules to enable two machines, using two different internal information representations, to communicate. For example, on certain machines the integers are represented by 16 bits, while on others they are represented by 32 bits.
- The *session layer* enables a virtual link (virtual channel) to be established between two communicating remote entities. The protocol for this layer is called "end to end" because it guarantees the order of the messages interchanged and includes procedures that allow communication to be re-established at the place where it was interrupted, in case of a fault.
- The *transmission layer* essentially brings about the multiplexing and the optimization of the existing links between the different sites (Fig. 1.10).

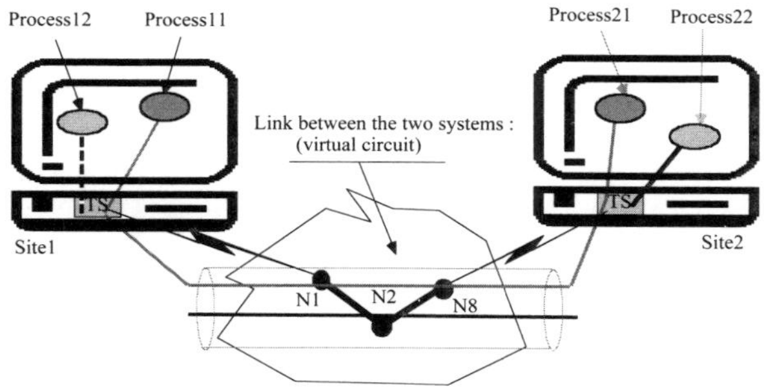

Fig. 1.10 Role of the transmission layer of the ISO model.

- The *network layer* has the role of transmitting the packets from one point to another, and establishing virtual links between the sites (X25 virtual circuits). Various fixed or adaptive routing techniques are used depending on the nature of the network.
- The *link layer* manages data interchange between two points via the intermediary of a transmission procedure (HDLC).

- The *physical layer* serves to generate and transmit the physical or electrical signals (the analogue signal is the carrier) which represent binary information interchanged between two components. An element of information (a bit or a series of bits) is obtained by acting on one or more of the carriers characteristics (frequency modulation, amplitude modulation, etc.). The physical medium can be either an electrical cable or an electro-magnetic wave in the case of wireless transmissions.

For more information on these different layers, the reader is advised to refer to the bibliography (CFIP, 1991; Comer, 1992; Ghernaouti, 1990; Coulouris *et al.*, 1993).

1.4 Distributed Applications

Notion 12 Distributed Application

A set of active programs (processes, tasks or agents) executed on one or more remote machines, which communicate by the interchange of messages on behalf of the same global application.

In a distributed application, there is a division of global application control between different communicating entities and data distribution between the different sites. There is, of course, a certain correlation between the different parts of the distributed data, related to the semantics of the global application, because it is the same application. This being the case, we can ask: what are the distribution criteria?

One important aspect that encourages distribution, is *modularity*, the breakdown of the global application into modules. Modularity essentially encourages local processing (agents) inside the modules. It represents an altogether natural approach for the structuring of these applications by taking into account their intrinsic properties. Although it promotes interaction between the different modules, these interactions remain the *exception*, compared to local processing. In other words, it involves the breakdown of the global application into a number of more or less autonomous modules. It is this autonomy which will allow the distributed execution of these different modules. We note in passing, and from the above definition, that this design model of distributed control applications can be used to implement applications on one site as well as those on several different sites:

- On the same machine and using event-driven or concurrent programming: different processes implement different modules or agents. The concurrent execution model is favoured over the sequential execution model. This tends to be a generalized approach, given the rapid technological advance of machines (microcomputers, workstations, etc.) and the current orientation towards multiprocessor platforms. This evolution also encompasses operating systems, which are becoming increasingly efficient at supporting multi-task operations.

Even the microcomputer operating systems (OS/2, Windows-NT, Windows 95) no longer form the exception to this gradual tendency.

- On several machines the means of communication between the different computers, either a public data transmission network such as TRANSPAC, a LAN of the Ethernet type, or even simple RTC lines, provides the mechanism for interactions between the different modules. However, these interactions remain relatively unusual compared to local processing.

In general, the data distribution is based on one of the following three criteria:

- *geographic*: this is the most common (for example banking systems);
- *organizational*: this is naturally linked to the preceding criteria (the data processing system of a company);
- *functional*: the distribution or sharing of a certain number of functions (office automation systems).

In the following sections, several examples are given which are sufficiently representative of this type of distributed application, and which also play an integral part in our daily life.

1.4.1 Banking Systems

Modularity is the essential element of these systems. At each hierarchic level, with the exception of the highest, the module that manages the services provided has simply been duplicated (Fig. 1.11).

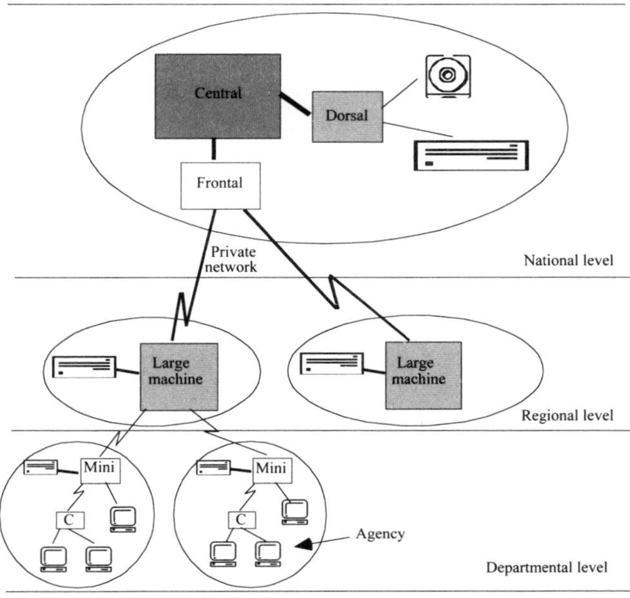

Fig. 1.11 The architecture of banking systems.

The lowest level module corresponds to the processing of a standard or automatic workstation of a branch of a bank. Because local processes are preferred to interactions, the consultation and updating of local accounts can take place in real-time. In contrast, updates of non-local accounts are stored at the level of each branch in the local log. During the night, they are transferred to the central installation, which carries out the updating procedure for the data files of each branch before opening time.

In this application, we note that the criterion which was the directing element in carrying out the modular refinement was a purely *geographical* criterion. To each local branch there corresponds a module, which contains the usual functions (crediting an account, debiting an account, credit transfer between two accounts, account advice and so on). Ninety per cent of the processes are carried out in the local branch. For each region there is a corresponding regional office, which is responsible for carrying out a number of services on behalf of local branches in the region: cheque printing, printing monthly client account statements, etc.). The central banking system is found at the national level, where global operations are carried out, such as updating the files of different branches, transferring funds between banks, archiving etc.

It is evident that seat reservation systems (such as for aeroplanes and trains) follow the same rules and partitioning criteria, that is the distribution of processing power according to geographical criteria, and preference towards local processing. The principal characteristic of this type of system is the ease with which we are able to insert or remove modules. As a general rule, the incorporation of new sites into the system has no effect on overall functioning, and the same applies to the failure or removal of a site.

1.4.2 Office Automation Systems

Modularity in this type of system is of an entirely different nature from that used in the preceding systems, which lend themselves perfectly to the simple hierarchic duplication of identical modules on several sites. Geographical scale is less important for office automation systems, and modularity can be compared to the availability of several *common independent functions* on the LAN (Fig. 1.12): archiving (through an archive server), printing (through a common laser printer) etc.

In general, workstations (microcomputers or Unix stations for the scientific community) connected on a LAN, support a certain number of generic software applications (word processing, spreadsheets, database management systems, etc.), as well as more specific software packages (for example, CAD software and management and compatibility applications).

These workstations therefore share common equipment or processing resources, either hardware or software. Sharing processing resources is particularly characteristic of software that operates in client–server mode.

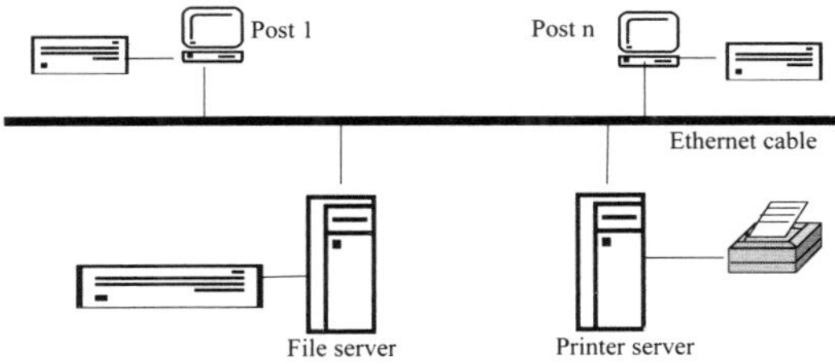

Fig. 1.12 Common functions on a local area network.

1.4.3 Data Processing Systems within a Production Company

This type of system is composed of several different information sub-systems interconnected by a LAN (Fig. 1.13). Each sub-system is responsible for managing the data for a service or particular unit of the company at a given site. It is therefore logical that a correlation should exist between the processes and data of different sub-systems.

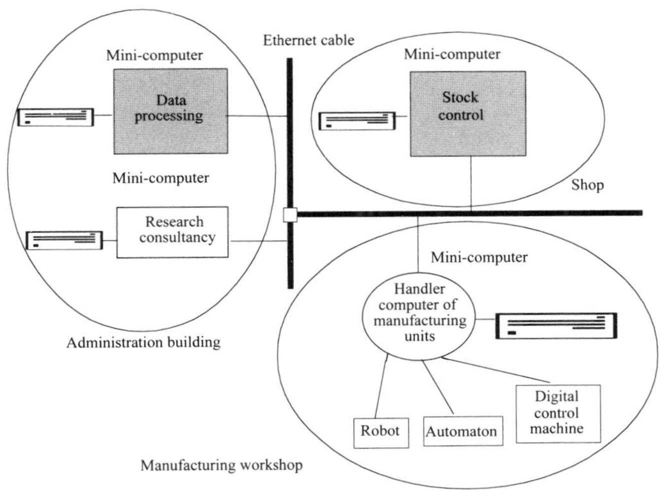

Fig. 1.13 The organization of the data processing system of a production company.

The LAN supports a number of machines, which are dedicated to specific processes. The data processing computer supports the management of payroll, accounting, billing and order processing applications etc., among others. The development department uses a machine which runs the software for CAD, computer aided drafting, computer aided manufacturing management and production scheduling and planning applications, etc. Recall that there always exists a correlation between the data from different parts. As a consequence, the redundancy of some common data is inevitable in this type of system. For example, the intersection of the data from the information processing and stock control systems is not empty (orders, etc.). What is more, the names and designations of the product range are also data shared between the research department information sub-system and that of the workshop. This latter ensures the supervision and control of automated means of production. Finally, there also exists a direct correlation between data managed at the level of the stock control computer and the other computers. It is clear that these shared parts pose a number of problems concerning the maintenance of their consistency and their integrity. In Chapter 4, we will see how the client–server model brings an elegant solution to the implementation of the interactions between the different data parts within an enterprise, and also guarantees global consistency of the information system, at a lesser cost.

1.4.4 The Design of Distributed Information Systems

The design of a distributed information system must conform to the rules laid out earlier, that is, to encourage local processing and make access to remote data the exception. Three approaches are used to access data on separate sites.

1.4.4.1 The Information Warehouse Approach

An initial solution to using data resident on a remote site involves retracting the data necessary for the execution of local processes (part of a file, a link of a relational database, a series of semantically linked files or relations, data corresponding to one view on a database etc.). Following the execution of local processing (enquiry and updating), the data is retransmitted to its original site. This solution poses a number of problems, notably the maintenance of data consistency when several sites are using it simultaneously. The interlocking technique is a possible solution, but one which needs to be adjusted to the desired degree of parallelism. Parallelism between the different user sites of data on a particular site depends essentially on the level of *granularity* (size of the object to process) used for interlocking the data. The larger the granularity (interlocking the whole of the file, relation, or even the database in its entirety), the more restricted the parallelism between the user sites. Large granularity poses fewer problems where maintaining the consistency of the data is concerned. There is less risk of interference from operations carried out on the data by the different sites. Compared to large granularity, small granularity (interlocking of a file write, a tuple space of a relationship, or even a field, etc.) poses more problems in guaranteeing data consistency, as the risks of interference and concurrent access are greater. It requires the use of relatively complex concurrent access techniques. However, it does allow the considerable growth of parallelism between the user sites. It is important to note that the use of this approach on the client–server model simplifies these problems considerably, and brings greater flexibility to the implementation of dialogue between local processing and the management of remote data. Local processors are called “clients”. In order to obtain the data, they send requests to their manager called the “server”. This model will be the object of a more detailed description in Chapter 2. At the site where the data originates, a single process or agent handles data access, as indicated in Figure 1.14.

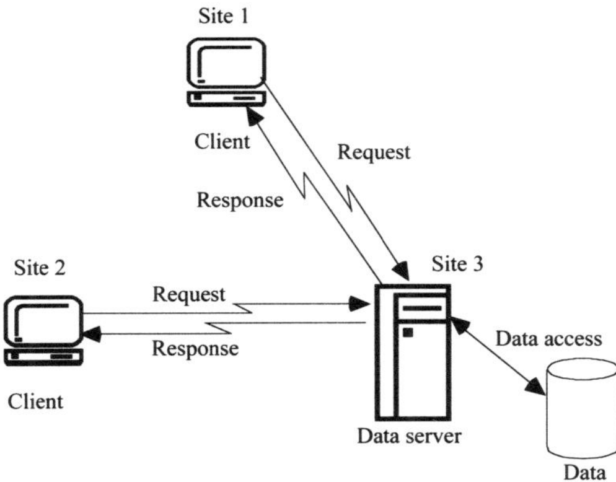

Fig. 1.14 Implementation of the information warehouse approach using the client–server model.

This is by the far the most interesting approach, which excites the interest of different researchers and users of real-time and distributed data processing systems. In contrast to the previous approach, the processes are carried out on the data site itself. A first solution consists of sending the processes to the site in question.

This solution is mainly used for the interrogation of remote databases (the user sites send SQL requests for example, and collect the results). However, another more natural solution exists, which involves linking to the data at each site all the operations or programs (transactions) possible on this data.

1.4.4.2 The Transactional-Communication Approach

This is made up of interrogation and updating operations. The basic principle of this approach consists of capturing the data on each site, using a set of transactions or programs that are the only means of using and manipulating this data. Enthusiasts of the object-oriented paradigm find in this model a concrete application of the notion of data encapsulation and protection via the intermediary of a class of objects, which provides a set of methods or primitives. This protection by data encapsulation has been one of the principal and natural motivations for using the transactional-communication approach in a distributed context. The number of transactions associated to local data is not fixed, and may increase with time. The only rule to be respected is the encapsulation rule: *the only possible access routes to local data are those which use the transactions or programs provided.* In this case, remote access to this data involves sending a request to the local site to ask for the execution of one of the available transactions. On the data site, a server receives the requests and creates the processes to execute the transactions requested (Fig. 1.15). The dialogue can therefore commence between the created agent and the client. Note that in this approach the processes (or transactions) are executed on the site where the data is found. In contrast to this, in the information warehouse approach, the data is brought to the client's site for consultation or modification, and then returned to its original site if it has been updated.

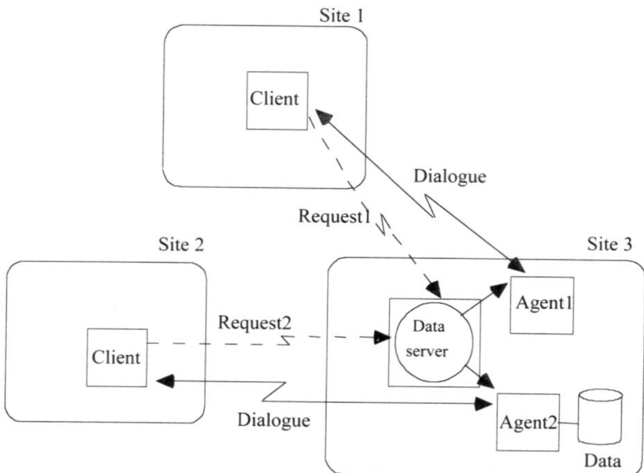

Fig. 1.15 The implementation of transactional systems with the client–server model.

This approach assumes that the application designers have sufficiently identified, during the design stage, the different transactions or programs that might be used on the data held at the site. Furthermore, the programs must be known to all future users and visible to them.

1.4.4.3 *The Distributed Data Base Approach*

In this approach, the Distributed Data Base Management System (DDBMS), or the Distributed File Management System (DFMS), brings a level of global abstraction which enables them to mask for the users, the physical distribution of the data or files. The user does not have to worry about problems concerning the location of the distributed data. He has a global view (for example, the overall schema of the distributed database) of the data, as a result of which he can write the requests. The DDBMS maintains an identical catalogue on each site, which brings together all the existing local database schemas. These latter form the distributed database. When a user on a given site submits a request (called a global transaction), the DDMBS divides up the global transaction into a number of local transactions (SQL requests which bear local databases), depending on the location and identification information contained in its catalogue. It then sends these local transactions to their corresponding site and gathers the results. This understandably requires the program itself to be sent (local request) to the site where it needs to be executed. This approach assumes that the following problems can be solved:

- the heterogeneity of local DDBMS or DFMS;
- the refinement of global requests into local requests;
- the representation and modelling of the overall view of the distributed database.

1.5 Distributed System Properties

The complexity of the software for this type of system, composed of several different functional layers (ISO model), and the technical problems inherent in the use and interconnection of a large number of pieces of hardware, have for a long time held back the development of distributed systems.

Notion 13 Properties of Distributed Systems

There is a cause and effect type of relationship between software and hardware in distributed systems. The absence of shared memory and transmission delays represent the most significant technical problems. They are at the core of implementation difficulties encountered with distribution systems.

The complexity of interconnected equipment in a distributed system explains that of the corresponding layers of software. The absence of global memory creates the absence of a global state in the distribution system. Equally, transmission delays represent another important characteristic of distributed systems that must never be neglected during the study and design of a system or application of this nature.

In the following chapters we will endeavour to highlight the impact of these properties on the implementation of these systems. We start by outlining the advantages of distributed systems, which were the determining factors in their development, as well as their disadvantages.

1.5.1 Advantages

The advantages of distributed systems are without doubt numerous, and to a large extent offset the impact of their disadvantages. The principal recognized advantages for this type of system are listed below.

- *Security.* The applications are designed following a modular approach that enables data to be encapsulated (isolated) in order to protect access to it more effectively.
- *Reliability.* Reliability at the level of availability is a major element in favour of distributed systems. If one site crashes, the others continue to function. For certain types of distributed applications, this situation generally leads to the *duplication of critical data* to enhance the robustness of the system. However, this duplication leads to a problem which is more specific to distributed systems, the problem of managing multiple copies of files.
- *Flexibility.* The preceding examples, especially the banking systems, accurately reflect the degree of flexibility of these systems. The addition or removal of a site, machine or workstation is a standard operation, and has no effect on the efficient functioning of the system as a whole.

- *Performance to price ratio.* At equal power and performance levels, a distributed configuration consisting of microcomputers, with one playing the role of file server, is clearly cheaper than a star configuration constructed around a large or even a mini-computer. It is evident that the cost of maintaining this latter configuration is prohibitive compared to that of microcomputers, which now form part of consumer electronics.

1.5.2 Disadvantages

Distributed systems present a certain number of disadvantages inherent in their actual structure, and the slowness of communication has doubtless been the main disadvantage. This essentially concerns the public data transmission network. Despite the level of reliability of these networks (TRANSPAC) and the transmission speeds that they promise, they remain relatively slow compared to the computation speed of the machines. On the other hand, network fluctuations triggered by traffic (network congestion), especially during peak periods, have direct repercussions on the performance of applications using their services, particularly real-time applications. Recall the problems caused by a long wait for confirmation when you use a bankcard to carry out payments in the shops on a Saturday afternoon. This problem is overcome by local networks that have sufficiently elevated transmission speeds (10Mbits/second). In the present state of things, technological advancement in this field, especially since the appearance of ATM technology, is such that it is now possible to reach 100Mbits/second. It is clear that in terms of speed, such performance introduces certain constraints on the geographical scale of the network.

1.5.3 The Absence of Shared Memory

One of the technical problems that has had a direct impact on the architecture of distributed systems and the complexity of their software is the absence of shared memory. This situation arises from the lack of a global state in a distributed system. In centralized systems, synchronization and communication between the different active tasks or processes is still possible using standard synchronization tools such as semaphores. Furthermore, the operating system of one machine, whose role is to manage and optimize the use of the physical or logic resources available (CPU, memory, hard disk, printers, compilers, files, etc), has at all times an overall view of all events occurring within the system and of the state of business of the resources. As a result, it is in a position to take adequate decisions to improve the management of its resources. All the information related to the state of progress of the processes, and the status of the resources is stored and maintained by the operating system in unique data structures (process tables, file descriptors and so on). Using this method, each event (release of a resource, status change of a process, termination of an input/output operation on which a process is jammed, use of a semaphore (*a system object used to manage concurrent access to shared objects*) by a process, deadlock between processes etc.) is immediately recorded and processed by the operating system, as indicated in Figure 1.16.

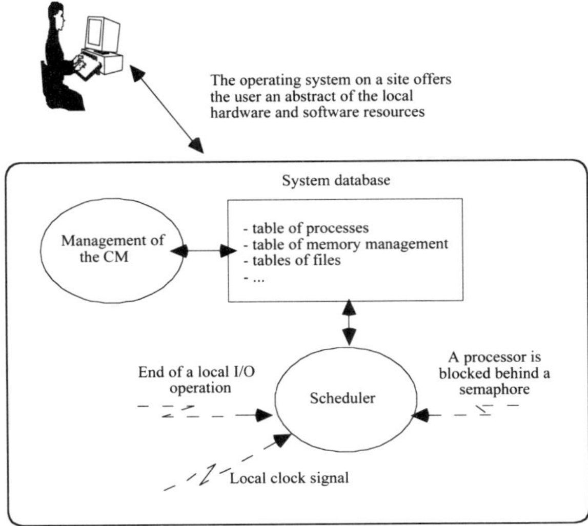

Fig. 1.16 On one site, the operating system provides an abstraction of the local resources.

If the same reasoning is to be applied to a shared system, that is to provide the user with an idea of the global management of shared system resources located on several machines at different sites, we immediately face the problem of the *absence of global state* in the shared system. Global management of the resources of a shared system requires the formation of a decision sub-system (global scheduler, global manager of all the memory banks of the different sites, file manager for all the local files on the different sites, etc.).

There are two possible approaches to implementing a resource manager:

1. A centralized implementation that gathers the management of shared system resources into one place: one site will hold a privileged role and manage the system data structures for all the sites. This is difficult to achieve for various reasons:

   - the reliability of the global system depends on that of the privileged site;
   - there is the risk of the traffic towards this site being too high. This is because each time an event occurs at a site, this site must inform the privileged site by way of a message;
   - the performance is a function of the transmission speed of the data transmission network, which remains relatively slow compared to the site execution speed (Fig. 1.17).

2. An implementation distributed by the duplication of the decisional subsystem. This solution is scarcely more encouraging. To enable each site to make a local decision, but one which also concerns the global state of the shared system, it is necessary to maintain the consistency of the different sub-systems.

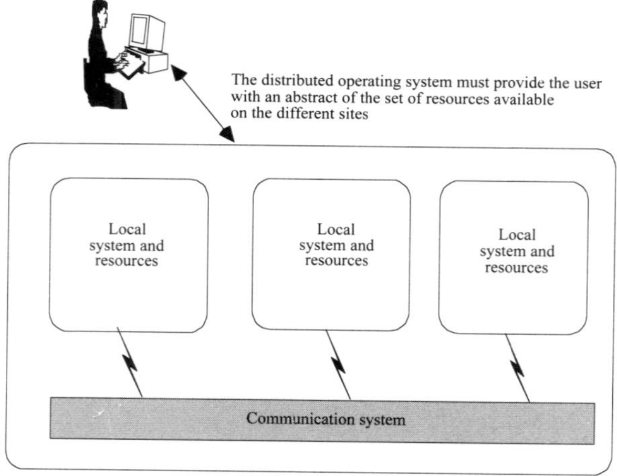

Fig. 1.17 A shared operating system.

In this last case, the global state of the shared system is composed of the union of all of the different local states. Reconstruction of the global state on each site triggers the regular exchange of messages between the different sites in order to broadcast each event that occurs. At any moment, therefore, the sites have an image approaching that of a global state as a result of message transmission delays (Fig. 1.18). In this figure, the observation points, which may correspond to the end of the execution of each current statement, are specific to each system. Furthermore, two clocks made by the same person from the same production method, and which tick at the same frequency, will eventually diverge.

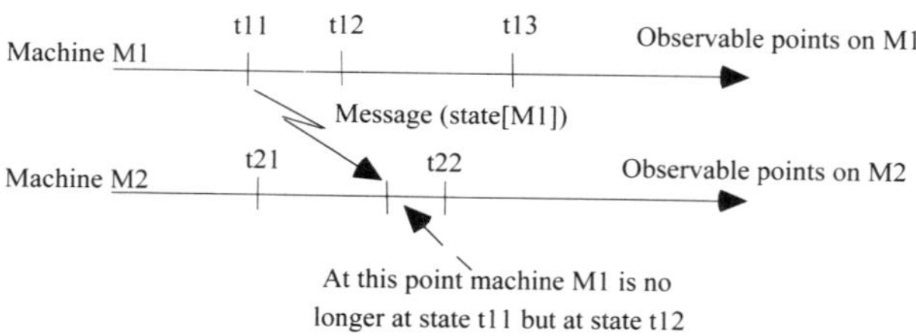

Fig. 1.18 Shift in the vision of events introduced by transmission delays.

Whatever the case, the approach used must first take into account the nature of the data transmission system (Ethernet network, public transmission network, specialized lines) and its speed, the degrees of operation reliability required, and expected performance, before choosing between a solution using total distribution or centralization, or even a compromise between the two. In the following sections, we provide several solutions which could serve as a basis for the design of a distributed system.

1.5.4 Transmission Delays

In this section we illustrate the effect of transmission delays in a shared system, on the global status of the system as a whole. Figure 1.19 shows two processes, P_1 on site 1 and P_2 on site 2, which communicate on behalf of a file transfer application.

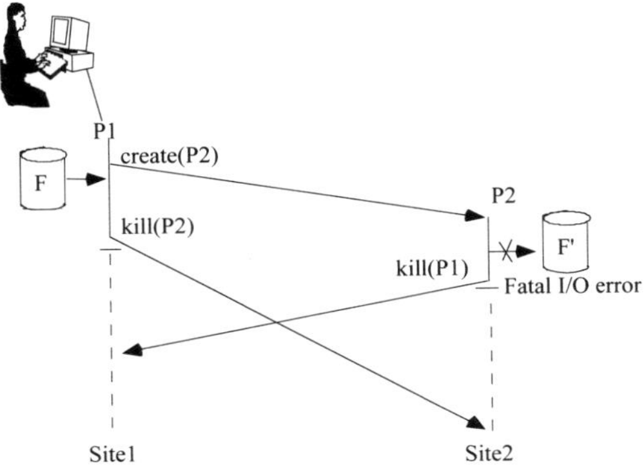

Fig. 1.19 The impact of transmission delays on global decision-making.

It could be implied that following a fatal input/output error on site 2, the local system decides to terminate P_2. However, P_2 communicates with P_1 to effectuate the transfer of file F on site 2. As a result, the site 2 system sends a message requesting that the site 1 system terminate the execution of process P_1. In the meantime, on site 1, and before the message from site 2 arrives, the user decides to terminate process P_1. In its turn, the local system sends a message to terminate P_2 which, as we remember, no longer exists. This results in an embarrassing situation for the two local systems. What will be the subsequent message to give to the two messages on the two implicated sites? It is clear that this form of dysfunction would be rapidly detected if a global observer were present surveying events on both sites.

We note that these transmission delay problems are enhanced if the remote site, or even one part of the network crashes and isolates the site in question (formation of two sub-networks).

1.6 Activity Management in a Distributed Context

An activity (a transaction or an agent), represents the execution of a process on one machine on a given site, by a process under the control of the local operating system. In a shared system, the execution of a global application, which involves several activities on several different sites, is carried out in three distinct phases:

1. remote activation of processes;
2. dialogue and synchronization between separate processes;
3. global termination and validation of the actions of all activities.

We will study the different problems that the implementation of each of these three phases could encounter, and present several techniques and solutions. The activity, process, agent or transaction of the term will be used when the execution of a process or a program on a given site is involved.

1.6.1 Distributed Execution Control Structures

Since distributed systems first started to excite interest within the research community, several techniques and solutions have been proposed and tested. Some have remained at the experimental stage, others are now in operation in certain commercialized systems. Among distributed execution control structures we remember in particular the structures presented below. Readers are warned that the textual formality used to describe distributed applications is purely virtual. We have introduced it only to facilitate the understanding of the concepts presented.

1.6.1.1 Migration

> **Notion 14 Migration**
>
> *This is a process execution control technique that enables a process that has just been executed on a given site, to be transferred to another separate site.*

Migration can be seen as the equivalent of the <GOTO> command of programming languages in sequential execution, and is unique where branching (no backtracking) is concerned. Figure 1.20 presents the distributed execution of an application using this control structure.

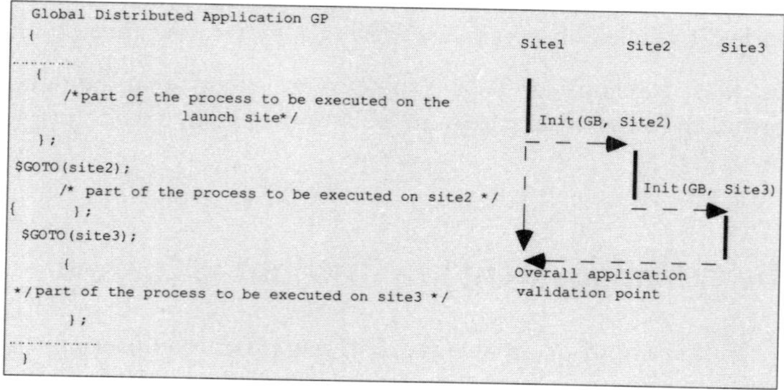

Fig. 1.20 An example of distributed using the migration principle.

Incidentally, this form of control structure could prove to be an efficient means of reserving seats on journeys carried out over several stages or towns.

This approach raises the following questions:

- Is it the same process which starts its execution on site 1, and which is then transferred as a whole to the next site? This solution can only be envisaged if the operating systems of different sites are compatible or homogeneous. However, how can the identification problems of these processes be resolved? Several solutions to the problem will be presented in the following sections.
- Or, on the other hand, is it that once the execution of the part of the application concerning a site is terminated, the process requests the creation of a new process on the next site and transfers the rest of the application to it before terminating itself? In this case, how can the validation of the global application (global transaction) be achieved?

Finally, we note that in this execution model, control is totally distributed, and involves weak coupling between the processes.

1.6.1.2 Remote Procedural Control (RPC)

This model of agent interaction (activities) is clearly present at the interaction that exists between a call program and a subroutine called in the sequential execution model. When a process requires an activity to be triggered on another site, it is suspended until the latter completely terminates its execution.

In an application which uses this type of distributed execution control structure, control is centralized at the level of the process or agent initiator (a perfect analogy of a main program). Coupling is therefore very strong (*synchronous mode*) between this process and the other remote processes. As a result, there is an absence of parallelism between the different activities of the global application (Fig. 1.21).

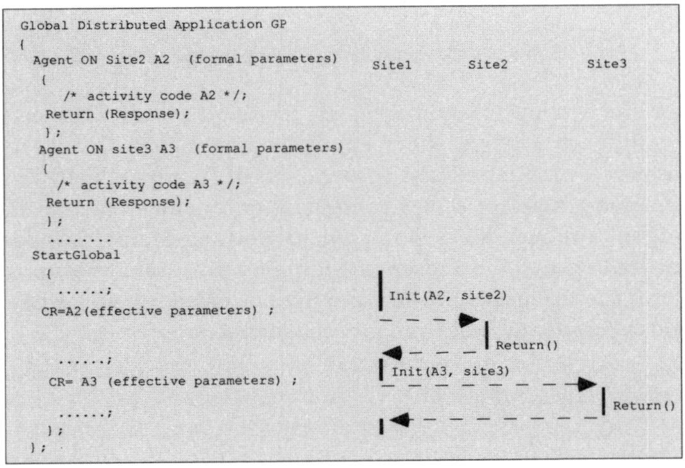

```
Global Distributed Application GP
{
  Agent ON Site2 A2  (formal parameters)
   {
     /* activity code A2 */;
    Return (Response);
   };
  Agent ON site3 A3  (formal parameters)
   {
    /* activity code A3 */;
    Return (Response);
   };
   ........
  StartGlobal
   {
    ......;
   CR=A2(effective parameters) ;

    ......;
    CR= A3 (effective parameters) ;

    ......;
   };
};
```

Site1 Site2 Site3

Init(A2, site2)

Return()

Init(A3, site3)

Return()

Fig. 1.21 Example of a distributed application using the RPC control structure.

1.6.1.3 Co-routines

A consequence of using the preceding control structure is strong coupling between the different agents. As a result, each time the process initiator (which controls and co-ordinates the execution of all the distributed application tasks) wishes to execute another operation on the same site (site 2 for example), and on behalf of the same global application, this is expressed by the creation of a new process to support its execution. The co-routine model was introduced to considerably reduce the number of processes implicated in the same distributed application, notably in the preceding case, namely the execution of several operations on the same site on behalf of the same global application (Fig. 1.22).

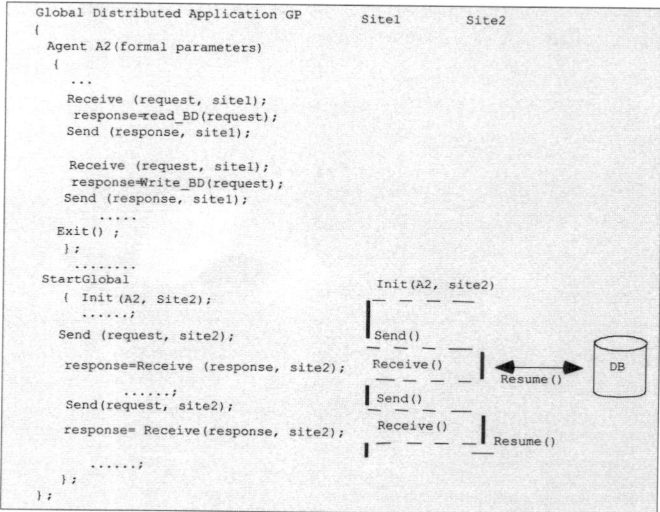

Fig. 1.22 Example of an application built using the co-routine model.

An agent on site 1 triggers another agent on site 2 (Init). This latter remains suspended until the agent on site 1 explicitly prompts it. Once it is active, it executes the process requested and suspends itself (typify) while waiting for the next dialogue. On receipt of a new prompt, it is re-launched from the point at which it finished. Although it is still in asynchronous mode, in this model only one process is created on site 2 to execute the different processes or actions requested by the agent on site 1. This is in contrast to the earlier RPC model, where a process is created and subsequently destroyed for each interaction.

1.6.1.4 Parallel Execution Model

In the two earlier execution models, coupling between the processes is strong, especially in the RPC model. To authorize weak coupling, which promotes a largely independent development in parallel with the different agents, the distributed system must provide the necessary means to authorize the triggering of several agents in parallel and on different sites: the `fork ()` primitive (Fig. 1.23).

This is a more general model. It supports strong coupling (synchronous execution) as well as weak coupling (asynchronous execution). Figure 1.23 shows true parallelism between agent A2 on site 2, agent A3 on site 3 and the principal agent on site 1 before the latter uses the "Wait" primitive to wait for the termination of A3. The Wait primitive is a blocking primitive introduced at the end of synchronization.

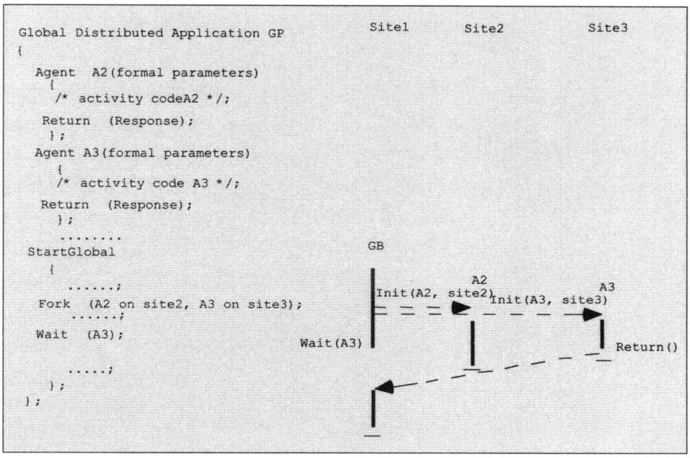

```
Global Distributed Application GP
{
  Agent  A2(formal parameters)
    {
    /* activity codeA2 */;
   Return  (Response);
    };
  Agent A3(formal parameters)
    {
    /* activity code A3 */;
   Return  (Response);
    };
    ........
 StartGlobal
   {
     ......;
  Fork  (A2 on site2, A3 on site3);
     ......;
  Wait  (A3);

     .....;
   };
};
```

Site1 Site2 Site3
GB
Init(A2, site2) A2
Init(A3, site3) A3
Wait(A3)
Return()

Fig. 1.23 Example of an application using parallelism in the execution of activities.

1.6.2 Triggering a Remote Activity

We have just seen four possible structures for execution control in a distributed context. They all require the remote triggering of activities or agents. Triggering a remote activity comes back to requesting the execution of a program or a subroutine on a remote site via the activation of a process. We have simplified this request by using *Init* in the preceding figures. To enable this remote triggering, it is necessary to define the nature of the remote processes by providing the following information:

1. identification of the program to be executed;
2. identification of the site on which the execution will be carried out;
3. the context of the initial execution or call parameters.

The program to be executed can be identified using two methods: static or dynamic.

1.6.2.1 Static Connection and Identification Processes

Following the compilation of one of the preceding global applications, identifiers of the activities used in the program serve to identify, on their respective sites, the processes created to carry out their execution (Init[A3, site 3]). This solution is only valid in instances where these agents (processes) or activities are used by one single, unique global application (preceding scenarios). However, in a distributed context, an activity or process is often designed to be used by several global applications at once (e.g. seat reservation transactions). This assumes that these tasks are already predefined (compiled and ready to be executed) and resident on a site. Global application simply activates them with the appropriate call parameters as shown in Figure 1.24.

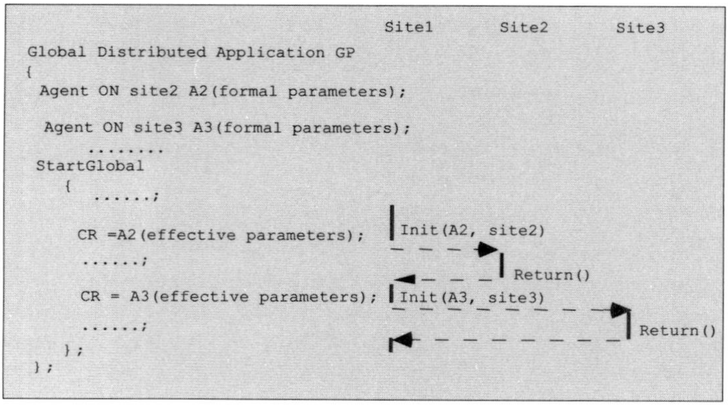

```
                                              Site1        Site2        Site3
Global Distributed Application GP
{
 Agent ON site2 A2(formal parameters);

 Agent ON site3 A3(formal parameters);
    ........
 StartGlobal
   {
    ......;

    CR =A2(effective parameters);    | Init(A2, site2)
                                      - - - ->|
    ......;                                   | Return()
                                      <- - - -
    CR = A3(effective parameters);   | Init(A3, site3)
                                      - - - - - - - - ->|
    ......;                                              | Return()
                                      |<- - - - - - - - -
   };
};
```

Fig. 1.24 The use of predefined activities.

This solution requires each initiator site (called the superior site) of the global user application of an activity on another site, to know the exact external identifier of this activity. The problem involves the visibility of the available activities on a site by the global applications. A solution is to maintain on each site a table of the tasks that are available on all the sites.

Furthermore, because we are in the distributed context, every alteration in the identification of a task on the site of residence will result in the propagation of this modification on all the other sites available to the user. This is the familiar problem of updating of multiple copies.

A more elegant solution involves allocating a unique logic identifier called a "network name" to the different precompiled tasks. This consists of the number of a local port and the number of the resident site, and is a more flexible solution, especially where the identification of a task by the site users is concerned. Each site is therefore not obliged to know the external task identifier. This is of more use when there is an alteration in the name of the task on the resident site. It also allows the robustness of the distributed system to increase when a small breakdown on the site occurs (instantaneous break in current, disconnection of a piece of equipment following an accident etc) or following a decision from the local scheduler (detection of a deadlock), an activity has been destroyed to be triggered again very rapidly. The dialogue between the new process, which supports the execution of the activity, and the other sites, is not affected. A possible implementation of this solution is based on the use of a correspondence table:

Site1 Correspondence table

Known name of the activity	Network name	
	Port No	Site No
A2	6	Site2
A3	19	Site3
. . .		

Site3 Correspondence table

Network name		Known name of the activity
Site No	Port No	
Site2	6	A2
Site3	19	A3
		. . .

1.6.2.2 Dynamic Connection and Identification of Processes

Another solution for this remote activity identification problem involves transmitting not the identification of the activity, which is not known at the time of the call, but the activity code (program). In Figure 1.24, *Init* is used to transmit the code for activity A2 to site 2, and the code for activity A3 to site 3. On site 2 (and site 3 respectively) the code is received and a process is created to execute it (after it has been compiled). Just after the creation of the process, the identifier of this is transmitted to site1.

A direct application of this solution is the request for and upgrade of distributed databases. A global request (for example an SQL request) which focuses on the data resident on several sites can be refined in a series of local requests that will be sent to their respective sites (Fig. 1.25). This can also play a certain role in the implementation of distributed applications on the heterogeneous area networks.

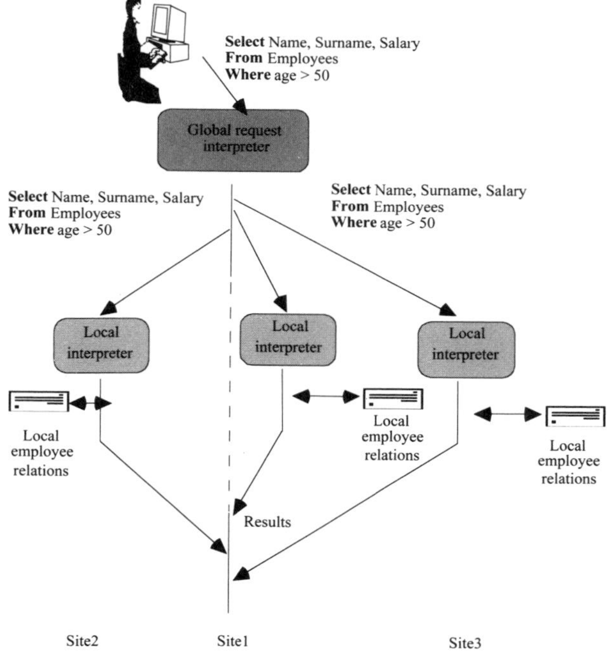

Fig. 1.25 Launching remote activities by transmission from the program source.

To conclude this section, we note that the implementation of an activation called a remote activity can be carried out according to the diagram proposed in Figure 1.26. On each site a component of the Distributed Execution System (DES) is responsible for intercepting requests to trigger activities on the local site. This involves the *Listener* process, which is permanently active (a DAEMON process for the Unix Terminal). For each *Init* message it receives, it creates a new local process to execute the activity requested. The *Init* message is part of the distributed execution protocol. DES can be considered as a global application the same as the other applications (user programs) which use these services.

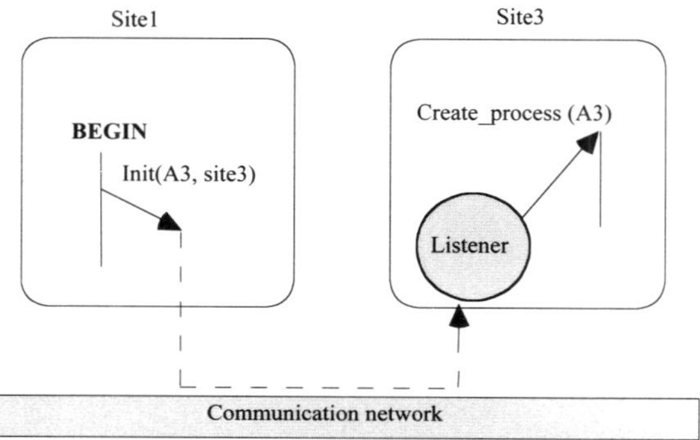

Fig. 1.26 The execution of a remote activity.

1.6.3 Dialogue Management between Two Communicating Entities

Dialogue management between communicating entities of a distributed application poses the following problems:

- the definition of the context of the exchanged messages or the protocol of the distributed application;
- the identification of different remote schedulers or processes.

We remember that a distributed application is a set of co-operating activities or processes, this co-operation is carried out by the exchange of messages. For each distributed application there is a specific communication protocol. A group of messages and their rules of interpretation embody this protocol. These messages represent the data flow and control carried via a communication system between the application process. As a result, the design of distributed applications primarily consists of the definition and identification of different activities/agents. Following this it is necessary to define the different messages exchanged by defining their format and semantics. Activities integrate the different rules of message interpretation, conforming to their semantics.

The remote activation of different tasks is carried out using one of the execution models or control structures mentioned above. The exchange of messages between tasks must also follow a model of communication and co-operation between processes. This second problem concerns the identical semantics of the application. The different interaction and co-operation problems between processes, which could be used to construct a distributed application, as well as the different communication models which could be used to enable the co-operating activities to communicate, are subject to a more detailed study in Chapter 2. In this section, we give an example of an application and the corresponding protocol, so as to better identify the problems posed by the development of distributed applications. This includes an example of a file transfer application.

Example of a File Transfer Application

The analysis of system requirements has uncovered the existence of two communicating activities: the emitter and the receptor. When the user triggers application FT (imagine the use of FTP on Unix or Kermit on other systems), two activities are created to achieve the dialogue between the two sites involved (Fig. 1.27).

Notion 15 The Structure of a Distributed Application

This is defined as a set of activities or agents and a co-operation protocol, which embodies the interactions between the application agents.

This assumes that all the messages, as well as their format (code part and data part) have been clearly defined. The interpretation rules of these messages are integrated in the two activities. A rule indicates the actions to be triggered when a message is received.

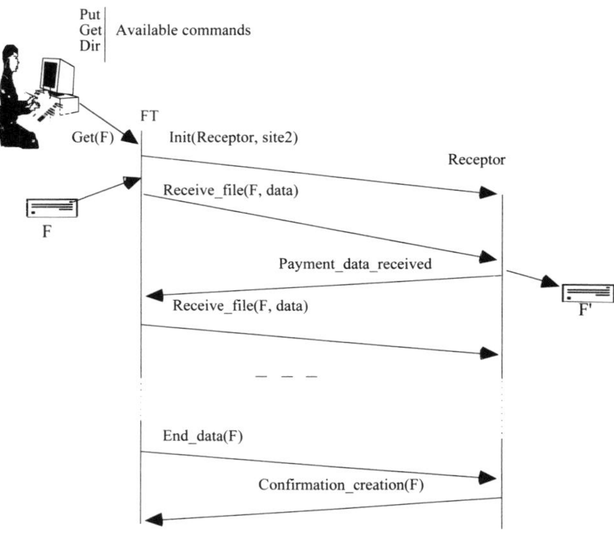

Fig. 1.27 The exchange diagram of a File Transfer Protocol.

The identification of a dialogue between two communicating activities can take place following two possible approaches:

- Either it is the remote site that sends the message in response to the system message *Init* – the local number of the process that was created to execute the requested activity. In this case, subsequent dialogue could be established between the two activities using the process number. *Init* must provide the process number supporting the activity initiator;
- Or network names are used (input/output parts). A network name is associated to each of these two activities, either dynamically or statically depending on the establishment of dialogue (see Unix Sockets, Chapter 4). This problem increases the prerogatives of the session layer of the ISO model. Chapter 4 gives a possible solution to this Unix socket problem. We note that in certain dialogue cases, it is preferable to manage the different global application process identities at the level of the application layer as indicated in Figure 1.28. This requires a *triangular* dialogue, which is difficult for the session layer to control. When A_1 requests the creation of activity A_3 on site 3, A_1 transmits to it the identity of A_2 on site 2 in its initial context. This identity could be the local process number or a network name (socket). From this point, A_3 can enter into dialogue with A_2 on behalf of the global application.

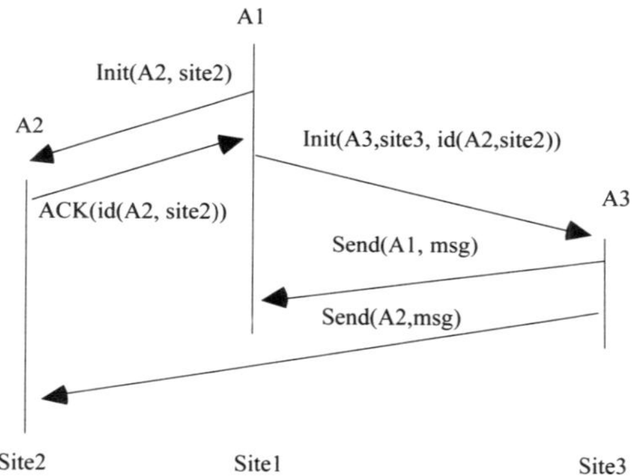

Fig. 1.28 Example of triangular dialogue.

1.6.4 The Global Termination and Validation of Distributed Applications

In a case where one of the active entities of a distributed application encounters difficulties in continuing its processing, its termination must lead to the termination of all other communicating entities. In other words, when an activity on a given site terminates its processing, it can only validate its actions locally if all the other distributed application activities have also successfully terminated their processing. This therefore needs a dialogue and a co-ordinated global action to validate the distributed application. To determine the solution to offer the global application, a validation protocol, executed when the activities have reached their termination point (end of processing), is essential. The different types of validation protocol will be discussed in Section 1.8.

Notion 16 Global Validation of Distributed Applications

A distributed application involves several remote communicating entities. Each of these entities carries out a specific process on local data. To guarantee distributed data consistency, the synchronization and termination of all remote entities, with the help of a validation protocol, is essential.

1.7 Process Synchronization and Resource Management

Within a distributed context it is important not to confuse communicating processes, which execute activities on behalf of an identical global application, with concurrent processes. This latter represents a set of processes belonging to different global applications, which are in competition or conflict for the acquisition and use of a shared resource (file, record, printer, central memory or CPU on a particular site, etc.).

Notion 17 Communicating Processes

These execute activities on behalf of the same global application, and use a specific co-operation protocol to manage the interactions between these activities.

Notion 18 Concurrent Processes

These are processes belonging to diverse global applications, which compete for the acquisition of a shared resource.

In this section we are primarily interested in management problems concerning concurrent access to shared resources in a distributed context. The arguments for the principal solutions to this problem will also be put forward. Within a distributed context, which is essentially characterized by the absence of a global state (a direct consequence of the absence of a shared memory), the standard solutions and techniques which are valuable in a centralized context are, at least directly, useless. The following are no longer possible: the implementation of critical sections using basic synchronization tools such as semaphores; HOARE monitors (monitors will form the subject of detailed description in Chapter 2); synchronous expression paths or any other synchronization tool of another nature. In a distributed context, each solution must be based either on scheduling processes on all sites, or on synchronization via message exchanges.

Notion 19 Critical Section

This is a part of the process code that regroups the instructions that manipulate a shared object (common global variable, file database, I/O port etc.). The critical section must be executed in mutual exclusion.

Notion 20 Process Synchronization in a Centralized Context

The execution (entry into) a critical section by a process is regulated by a synchronization tool (e.g. semaphore) which guarantees that only one process is active in that section at any one time (mutual exclusion).

Notion 21 Process Synchronization in a Distributed Context

This relies mainly on either process scheduling or global synchronization carried out principally by the exchange of messages.

Over the following sections we offer several basic concepts to aid the reader in understanding the rest of the chapter. A detailed study of the problems surrounding process synchronization and scheduling in a distributed context can be found in Raynal (1983, 1991, 1992).

1.7.1 Implementation of Total Order

Notion 22 Total Order

A presiding link between the different processes in a distributed system is total if the scheduling is strictly on all sites. It is only partial if there can exist two processes on two different sites with the same range.

One solution to establishing total order between the different processes is to use time stamps – dates. Each time a new process is created, it is given a time stamp (its date of birth). If, for one reason or another, the operating system needs to make a decision in order to resolve a conflicting situation (deadlocking, for example), it can choose one process from those in conflict by exploiting the age criterion. For example, to resolve a fatal deadlock situation, it can choose the youngest process (in the distributed system) and terminate it. This scheduling method could be used to return upgrades in the same order on the different copies of a duplicate file etc. Simplified, this date of birth will be associated to the global application. *All communicating processes for this application will inherit the same date or time stamp.*

A time stamp in a distributed context can be achieved in several ways. One of these is the implementation of local counters by synchronization (Fig. 1.29), or via a circulating token as indicated in Figure 1.30.

The solution, using local event counters, involves maintaining and incrementing a counter on each site at each significant event. Incidentally, the launch of a new global application on a site represents a significant local event that must be stored locally and diffused to other sites to enable them to upgrade their counters. On receipt of the value of a counter, each site executes the *same algorithm*. This algorithm compares the value received to the value of its own counter. In the case where its own counter has a value inferior to that of the counter received, it adds the received value to its counter increased by one unit. Counters are not all that is required to establish total order. At a given instant, two sites can have identical counters (same value), and as a result they can use them simultaneously to date two new global applications. These latter will therefore have the same time stamp (same age). This is partial order. To impose total order, the time stamp must be composed of the value of a local counter and the site number (Fig. 1.29).

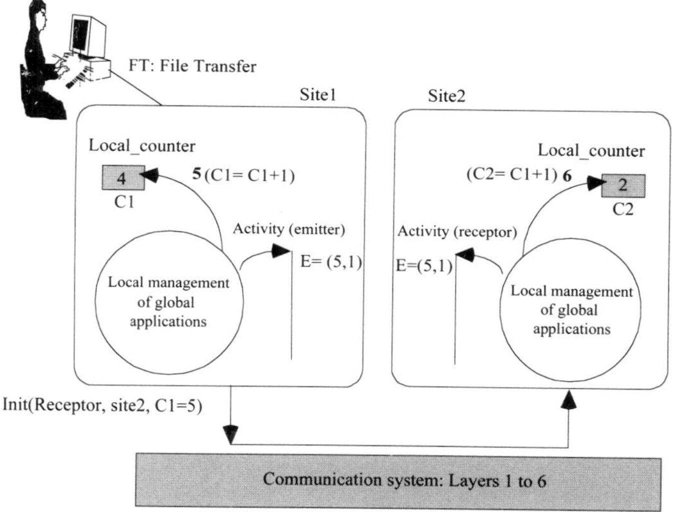

Fig. 1.29 Time stamp with local counters.

The solution, which involves a circulating token, is much simpler. A logic counter circulates between the different sites situated in a *virtual ring*. A site can only date an event (launch a new application for example) when it has a token. In this case it increases the token by one or several units if it needs to date several events at a time, and transmits the token to the next site (Fig. 1.30). Although this technique may seem easier to undertake, it does have several problems:

- each site must wait for the token to pass before it can time stamp events;
- what are the actions to be carried out if a site crashes when in possession of a token, or if a token is lost?
- under what conditions can a new site be inserted? etc.

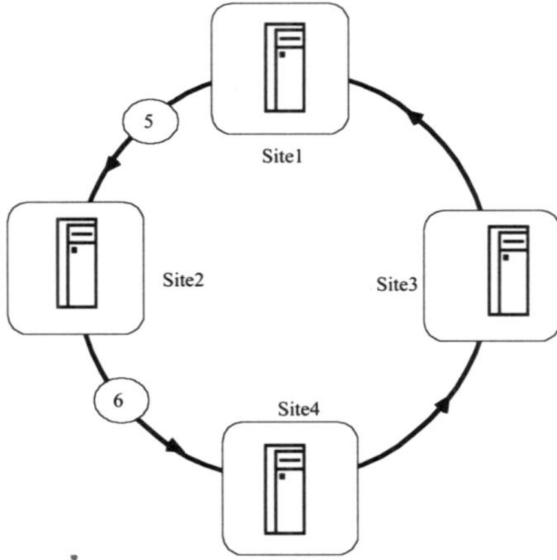

Fig. 1.30 Time stamps with a token.

The answers to these questions, as well as a detailed discussion of the problems caused by the implementation of total order in distributed systems can be found in Raynal (1983, 1991, 1992).

1.7.2 The Allocation of Resources in a Distributed Context

In a centralized context, several techniques have been suggested and used successfully to manage system resources.

Notion 23 Resource

This is a system object to which is associated a set of rules for the user (the authorized operations of the object: reading, writing etc.) and rules surrounding sharing which indicate the authorized access methods (exclusive access, shared access or both of these) depending on the nature of the object.

For each resource or class of resources there is usually an associated *descriptor.* Among other things, this contains state variables, a list of processes which possess the resource and a list of blocked processes awaiting the resource. Simplified, for each resource or class of resources there is a corresponding *scheduler.*

Notion 24 Resource Scheduler or Resource Manager

This is a set of functions and data structures which contain the necessary information for the management of the resource or group of identical resources (descriptor). The functions manipulate the descriptor by mutual exclusion to guarantee the consistency of its contents.

Within a centralized context, the operating system must ensure at all times that a deadlock situation does not occur. This occurs when process A possesses resource R1 and requests resource R2. Meanwhile, a second process B possesses resource R2 and requests resource R1. To detect this type of situation, the operating system must maintain a wait graph. This is a graph where the nodes represent the processes awaiting a resource. An arc indicates that process P_i is blocked behind a resource held by the process of the other extremity P_j (Fig. 1.31).

Figure 1.31 indicates that process P4, which was active, has requested a resource already held by P1, which is itself blocked by P2. As a result, a cycle is created in the graph that indicates the existence of a deadlock within the system.

The continuation of the wait graph, and the detection of deadlocks is made possible by the existence of a shared memory. The different primitives or input points (system functions used by processes to manipulate a particular resource) of system resource schedulers have access to the graph, and as a result can efficiently upgrade it (using mutual exclusion). The operating system kernel has a global view of events that are produced within the system.

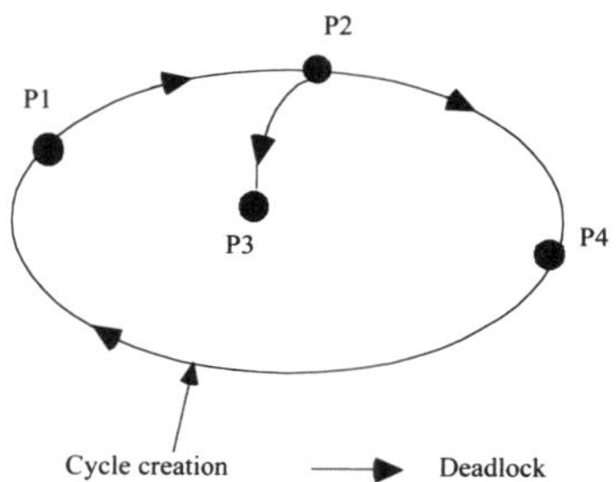

Figure 1.31 A wait graph.

Recall that there exist two abstraction levels in a distributed context. First, the global level, where abstraction of all the distributed resources is brought to the user (to clarify to the user the scheduling and management of resources across the sites). Secondly, on each site, the local operating system must manage the processes and resources resident on the site (Fig. 1.32) either on behalf of global applications, or on behalf of local applications or programs.

A schedule request for a global resource is translated by the Distributed Execution System (DES) for local schedule requests (addressed to local schedulers) as well as local resources which form part of the composition of the global resource.

Notion 25 Distributed Execution System (DES)

This is a module (kernel) for the management of resources and processes duplicated across the sites of the distributed system. These generally form a sub-layer of the local operating system.

There is therefore the local schedule synchronization problem to resolve. Two approaches are possible: centralized management of the global state of the resources, or distributed management of the resource state via the maintenance of a partial representation.

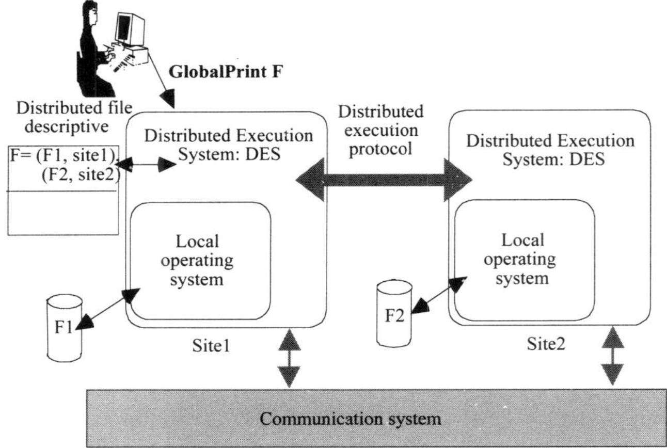

Fig. 1.32 The interaction between the DES and the local operating system.

1.7.2.1 Centralized Management of the Global Resource State

This approach looks at taking the solutions used in centralized systems and applying them to the management of distributed resources. It is brought back to the centralized system by maintaining a unique representation of the global state of the resources. Two techniques may be used to do this:

1. The scheduling of global resources occurs on a single privileged site, which can then maintain a wait graph. Each schedule request is translated by sending a request (message) to this site. The main disadvantage of this technique is the large number of messages used. This can trigger a considerable increase in traffic on the network and lead to its saturation. It is clear that the solidity and reliability of this solution depends directly on that of the privileged site. A renewal site can always be anticipated (a solution in tandem).

2. A circulatory token may be used which contains a description of the state of the resources and the wait graph. The sites are distributed following a virtual ring. A given site can only carry out the schedule operation if it possesses a token. The main disadvantage of this solution is the absence of parallelism between the different sites. On the other hand it is imperative to find a solution to the problems posed by reconfiguring the ring if it collapses, the reintroduction of a site or the loss of a token.

It is important to note that the two techniques present a degree of interest especially on a local network where there is considerable throughput and where transmission delays remain reasonable when compared to the processing speed. Their implementation is simplified using message broadcasting.

1.7.2.2 Decentralized Management of the Global Resource State

This allows the different local schedulers to make a global decision from a partial representation of the resource state. In order to do this, the synchronization of different schedulers becomes essential to try to reconstruct the global state as accurately as possible. The absence of synchronization between the different sites can lead to a global deadlock state, despite the absence of a local deadlock as shown in Figure 1.33.

In this example, the global application `transfer (C1, C2, S1)` which carries out fund transfers (the sum S1) between two accounts (account C1 on site 1 and account C2 on site 2) has been initiated on site 1. This has created two activities or agents: `credit (C1, S1)` on site 1 and `debit (C2, S2)` on site 2. Simultaneously, another global application, `transfer (C2, C1, S2)`, has been initiated on site 2. This has also initiated the activity `credit (C2, S2)` on site 2 and `debit (C1, S2)` on site 1.

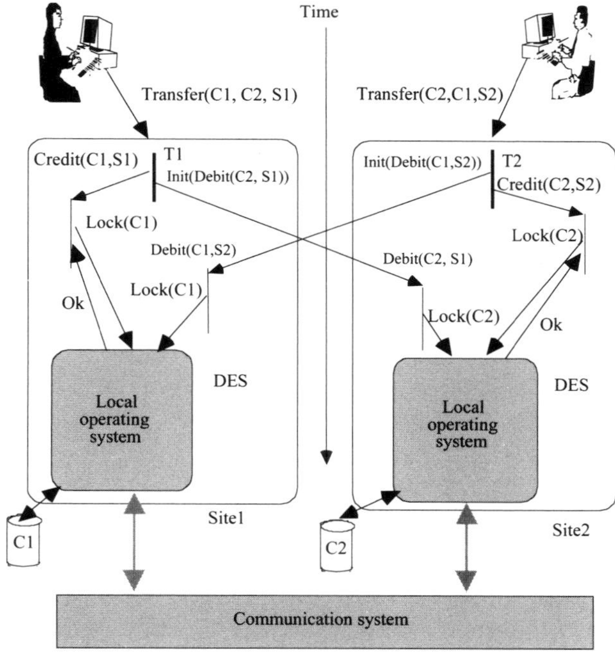

Fig. 1.33 Example of a global deadlock.

On each site, the wait graph indicates that there is no local deadlock:

- Site 1: `Debit(C1, S2)` ....▶ `Credit (C1, S1)`: Credit to interlock (save) account C1 primarily;

- Site 2: `Debit(C2, S1)` ⋯⋯▶ `Credit (C2, S1)`: Credit to interlock, account C2 primarily.

As mentioned earlier, the communicating activities of the same transaction:

```
Transfer(C1, C2, S1) = (Credit(C1, S1), Debit(C2, S1))
```

and

```
Transfer(C2, C1, S2) = (Credit(C2, S2), Debit(C1, S2))
```

must co-ordinate and synchronize their termination to ensure data consistency on the different sites. This operation is carried out using a validation protocol (see Section 1.8). The activities remain active until they receive the order to terminate and definitively validate their data. Consequently, `Debit(C1, S2)` on site 1 can only liberate C1 if the global application `Transfer(C2, C1, S1)` has been validated. It is the same for `Transfer(C1, C2, S1)`. If there was a global observer to draw up the wait graph between global applications, we would arrive at the following situation:

```
Transfer(C1, C2, S1) ◀————▶ Transfer(C2, C1, S2)
```

There is therefore a cycle in the graph which clearly shows the existence of a global deadlock between the two global applications. This is where the necessity of synchronization between different sites via the exchange of messages, enabling them to detect a specific situation originates. Several techniques exist to carry out this co-ordination between the local schedulers.

- *Ignore the deadlocks*: This technique involves giving a TimeOut for each global application. If the time expires before the application (the different distributed activities) has terminated its execution, it can be assumed that a global deadlock results. In this case, the initiator site (*superior site*) of the global application decides to abandon it. Similarly, it requests the termination of all of its activities. It can re-launch them at a later date. The advantage of this mechanism is that it is easy to implement, however, it is difficult to evaluate and fix a TimeOut in a distributed context. The value retained must take into account the transmission delay factor, which is subject to traffic fluctuations on the data transmission network. Incidentally, IBM's CICS Transaction Server uses this technique.

- *Detection-recovery methods:* This technique uses the wait graph in an attempt to prevent the formation of a state within this graph, thus a deadlock is avoided. Where centralized management is used, implementation is immediate and the manipulation operations of the graph can be integrated into the bodies of different primitives or entry-points of resource schedulers. With decentralized management, however, the actions of different local schedulers must be co-ordinated via the exchange of messages in order to allow them to reconstitute the global wait graph. The solution used must also enable the *optimization* of the number of messages used. Several researchers have attempted to apply various solutions to this problem by proposing algorithms which fit this condition. Figure 1.34, for example, shows one of these theoretical algorithms which enables the number of messages to be considerably limited. This algorithm involves only sending the message that the conflict is occurring (an activity which requests a resource already held by another activity) if the activity which provoked the conflict did not originate at the site where the conflict has been detected. This is the case with activity A1 on site 1, and activity A2 on site 2. The global component of the scheduler sends a message containing the local wait graph to the activity's original site. Site 1 is then able to detect a global deadlock, having received a message from site 2. It must therefore make a decision to unlock the situation by requesting that 1 of the 2 global applications is abandoned (recovery). The time stamps of different applications could be used to determine which application is abandoned – the oldest, the youngest etc. – depending on the global aims of the system.

- *Prevention-avoidance methods:* A deadlock situation always develops following the dynamic allocation of resources. A global application can only start the execution if all of its activities distributed across the different sites have obtained all of the resources required. It is evident that this solution is very difficult to achieve in a distributed context. Determining *a priori* the needs of each global application is unclear, hence the tendency towards the other more realistic techniques, which involve predicting or avoiding the formation of states in the wait graph.

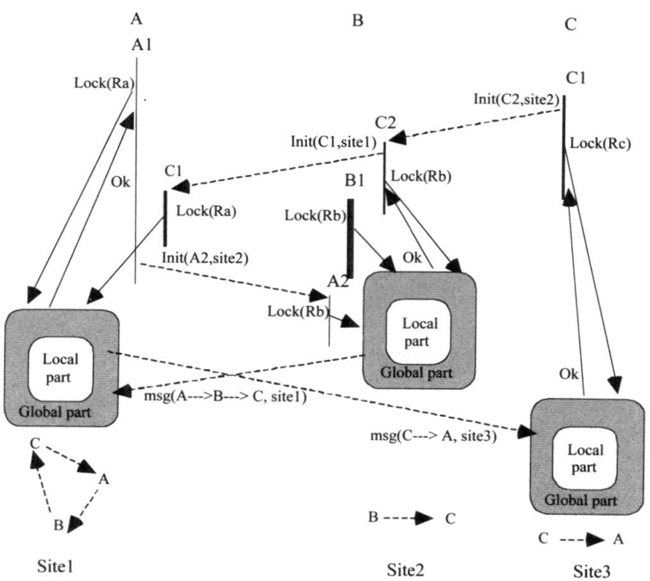

Fig. 1.34 Decentralized detection-recovery.

Among the techniques advocated and used in the prevention-avoidance method, we present techniques which involve limiting the length of the waiting string in the graph, and scheduling, using time stamps.

Where the first technique is concerned, if we examine its one management rule, which is to limit the length of the waiting string to one on each site in order to make a global decision locally, the risk of a deadlock between two global applications remains high. We actually end up with two global applications: A = {(A1, site1), (A2,site2)} and B = {(B1,site1), (B2,site2)}. On site 1, A1 possesses a resource that B1 requests, this gives rise to the creation of an arc between B1 and A1 (B1 –→ A1). On site 2, B2 possesses a resource which A2 requests (A2 → B2). A deadlock between the two applications exists despite the constraint in the length of the waiting chain being one at each of the two sites. To avoid this type of situation, it is necessary to prevent one global application from waiting on another. Therefore, on one site the resource scheduler must make the distinction between the schedule requests emitted from the local programs, and those emitted by the activities which work on behalf of a global application. The following diagram shows how this can be applied to site 1:

```
Program_Local11 → Program_Local12 → Program_Local13 → A1
```

This is an authorized sequence; the following sequence, however, is unauthorized:

```
B1 → Program_Local11 → Program_Local12 → Program Local13 → A1
```

Where the second sequence occurs, it is necessary to abandon and terminate the application that has come into conflict with the waiting application. However, is it necessary to terminate activity B_1 only and then launch it again after a specific time period has elapsed, or must we do the opposite and abandon and re-launch the global application B?

Other algorithms exist for the implementation of techniques based on scheduling with the help of time stamps: the WAIT-DIE algorithm, the DIE-WAIT algorithm, the WOUND-WAIT algorithm. The basic principle is to orient and schedule the wait graph using time stamps. When a conflict is detected, it is possible to select the application to be terminated according to its age (time stamp). In the following section, we will assume that all the applications have the same time stamp. This is the date of birth of the global application. We will use the notion Ai,ei(R) to designate activity i belonging to the global application A, for which the time stamp is (ei). Ai,ei(R) triggers the formation of an arc between the two corresponding processes: (Bj,ej → Ai,ei(R)). The system therefore applies the following algorithm:

The WAIT-DIE algorithm

If ((ei) < (ej) (that is to say Ai,ei is older than Bj,ej)
Then Ai,ei(R) must wait; Bj,ej is terminated and all of its resources are released;
If not Ai,ei(R) is terminated (because Bj,ej is the oldest).

This algorithm prevents deadlocks as it does not allow the older applications to become trapped behind the younger applications. So, with the two preceding examples, A = {A1,site1), (A2,site2)} and B = {(B1,site1), (B2,site2), it could be assumed that A's time stamp is smaller than B's time stamp (A is older then B). In this case:

- On site 1: B1 → A1 is authorized.
- On site 2: A2 → B2 is not authorized, and as a result, site 2 requests site 1 to terminate application A. This enables B1 to recover the resource held by A1.

The two other algorithms offer solutions, which at first resemble this algorithm. *They all base the scheduling and orienting of the wait graph on time stamps.* Finally, we note that the role of concurrent access control on a site is to *supervise the interference* between the actions of the different activities, so that the result of their passage, from the aspect of the *consistency of the resources content*, is the same as that of the sequential execution of the concurrent activities. The possession of serialization is fundamental.

Notion 26 Serialization

This ensures that the effects of the actions of different concurrent activities on shared data (shared resources) are equivalent to the sequential execution of these activities.

Serialization enables the consistency of the resource contents to be maintained, and it can be guaranteed if the different activities are made to respect the two phases of the following process:

- the first part of the activity code contains different instructions for reserving the different resources used (calls to the `Lock()` primitive);
- the second part contains the actual processing of the activity.

It appears that these activities or transactions are therefore well formed: two phase interlocking.

The release of resources occurs when the activity reaches its *termination point.*

Notion 27 The Termination Point

This indicates the end of the processing (computation) part of an activity, and prepares the activity for the final validation phase.

This principle is very efficient and enables deadlocks to be easily avoided if all the activities request the reservation of the different resources on a site, in the same order. For example, if there exist three shared resources on site 1: A, B and C, any use of these resources by the concurrent activities must respect the following order of reservation: A, B and C as indicated in the following diagram:

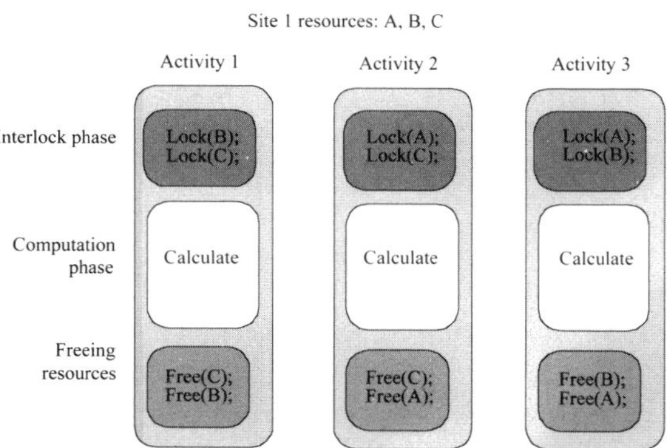

In this way, any *local deadlock* situation is avoided. However, implementation is not as simple as could be expected. Either it is the responsibility of the programmer to specifically manage the reservation requests and release of resources, which is not easily achieved, or it is the responsibility of the compiler to identify the resources and to insert the different reservation and release calls into the right places (beginning and end of a code).

Another approach leaves the different activities to be executed in the normal manner until their termination (the OPTIMIST approach). After their termination, the system checks that there was no interference with the results. Where there was interference, it proceeds to cancel the activity as well as the results (undo the processing). In the case of logic resources such as files, databases or any other structure with shared data, the system must be able to undo the result of an activity by returning to the resource the value that it had before the activity occurred and increased it. This operation is only possible if the different activities which share the resource *use a copy* or *an image* of the resource. It is once the activity has terminated its execution that the system attempts to recopy the value of the image into the original version. It is therefore said that the system has validated the actions of the activity, or that the activity has reached its *validation point.*

Notion 28 Validation Point

This indicates that the effects of the actions of an activity are valid and are therefore ***permanent****: the activity can no longer be cancelled.*

The system stores this validation in a filing system called a *log.* For each activity, the log contains a record, or several records linked together, which contain:

1. its identification (name, time stamp etc) for each resource handled;
2. the image (value) before the activity has passed;
3. the image after;
4. a record which represents the validation point if the activity has successfully terminated its execution, if not, a cancellation record.

The validation record clearly indicates that there has been no interference from other activities, or that no event has occurred which has disturbed its execution (semantic error, system crash, fatal deadlock, etc.). Where there has been interference with other activities, cancelling the result simply involves cancelling the image recopying operation, and a cancellation record being written into the log.

The log is an essential component in the life of a local system. It is also used when a crash occurs to initiate the restart procedure. This procedure consists of bringing the different resources in use when the crash occurred, into a single, consistent state. The local system records in its log all the events which occurred before the crash, especially the activities which were in the process of being executed. *These are the activities which did not reach their validation point.* If the crash affected the persistent storage support (hard disk) of the resource contents or their state variables, by searching the log from the beginning and coming up with a saved version, it would be possible to re-run the actions of the different activities which *reached their validation point.* The activities which were in the process of execution are simply cancelled.

To conclude, the validation of an activity or a program on a site does not pose any particular problems. *It comes down to the simple operation of writing into the log a validation record.* This is not the case for global applications which incorporate several activities on different sites. Validation of the global application must go through the validation of all of its activities. This global validation problem forms the object of study in the following section.

1.8 Validation Protocols for Global Applications

Figure 1.33 shows the problems inherent in concurrent access which can arise during the execution of different components of a global application. Other problems could also compromise the smooth running execution of a global application:

- *Semantic errors:* one of the activities of the global application contains a logic or design error (division by zero, exceeding the limits of a table, etc.) that was not detected during the design phase of the tests.
- *Faults:* faults can affect one of the sites where one of the activities of an application is being executed, as well as the data transmission network.

For these reasons, the different sites implicated in the execution of global application activities *must communicate via a validation protocol, to ensure the atomicity of the global application.*

Notion 29 Atomicity

This guarantees that all the actions of an activity are either executed or cancelled if the activity encounters an event which calls into question the outcome of its execution. This is the "all or nothing" approach.

Atomicity is a property which guarantees that all global application activities are terminated correctly (the global application is valid), or if for whatever reason, one of the activities was unable to succeed and terminate its processing, all the other activities are cancelled. The absence of such a protocol would have disastrous consequences on the efficient functioning and integrity of the distributed system. If, following the cancellation on a site of one of two global "transfer" application activities, (credit or debit) due to an access conflict, the other activity had not been cancelled due to lack of communication between the two sites, the modification of an account (credit or debit) results, and the other account remains unchanged. The validation point of a global application, notably an application carrying out updating operations on distributed data, *can under no circumstances be assimilated at its termination point*, as was the case with one activity on a site.

To implement this validation protocol, we can contemplate the encapsulation of the global application code and that of its components by two primitives (Fig. 1.35):

- *BeginAgent:* Among other things, this is responsible for writing into the local log a declaration record of a new activity or agent;
- *EndAgent:* This has the role of synchronizing local validation with that of other components of the global application, following one of the validation protocols presented below.

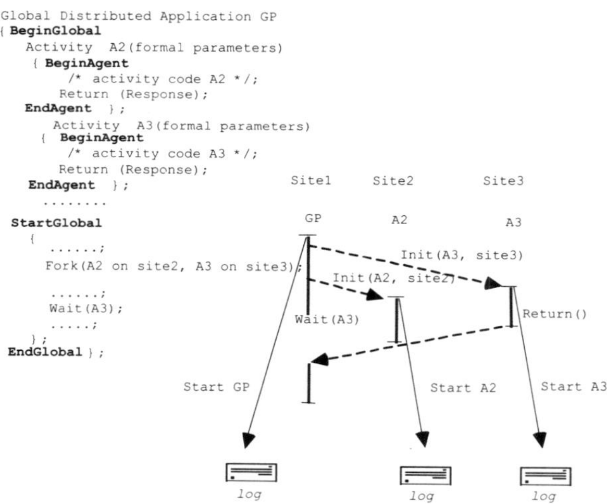

Fig. 1.35 The encapsulation of activities in view of a global validation.

Control of the execution of a global validation protocol can either be distributed or centralized. In this latter case, one of the sites implicated in the execution of the global application must play the role of the *superior site* which will trigger and supervise the execution of the global validation protocol. Generally, it is the site on which the global application has been initiated which takes this role (site 1 in the example in Fig. 1.35).

In certain cases, however, notably if the execution model used is a migration model, it is more natural that the last site in the chain plays this role (Fig. 1.36).

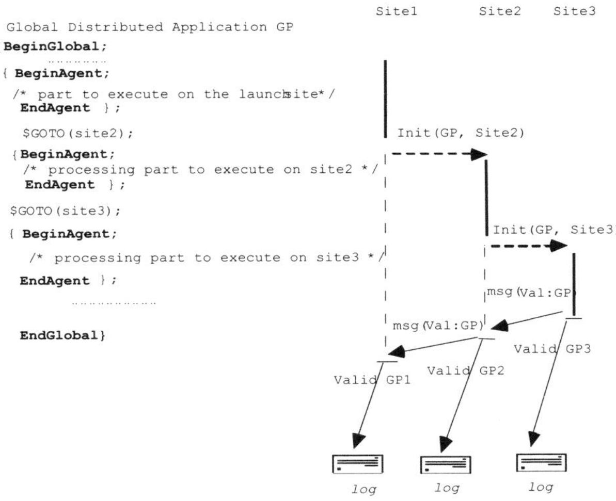

Fig. 1.36 Triggering of the global validation procedure: migration instances.

1.8.1 Decentralized Control Validation

The decentralized control global validation procedure does not require supervision. Each global application activity which terminates its execution, that is, reaches its validation point (*End Agent*) broadcasts a termination message to the other activities.

Each activity can only validate its results (write the validation record into the log) if it has received a termination message from all of the other activities in the global application (Fig. 1.37). This assumes that each activity knows all of its links.

This type of control of the global validation procedure uses $n \times (n - 1)$ messages where n is the number of sites implicated. It is clear that this solution relates more to implementation on the local broadcasting network (Ethernet).

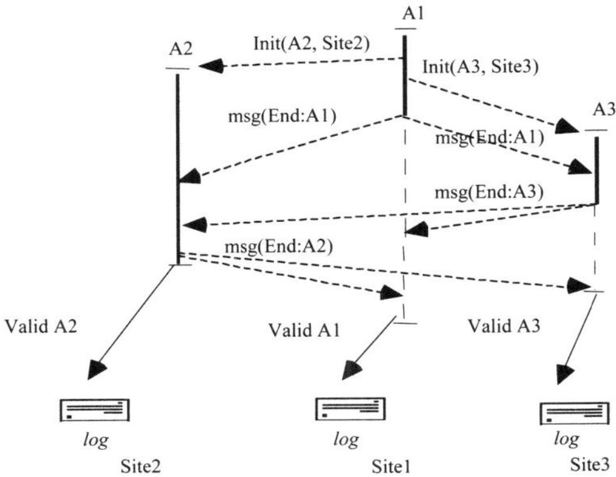

Fig. 1.37 Decentralized control validation.

1.8.2 Centralized Control Validation

The centralized control global validation procedure incorporates a privileged site, the superior site, which makes the decision to trigger and supervise global validation (Fig. 1.38).

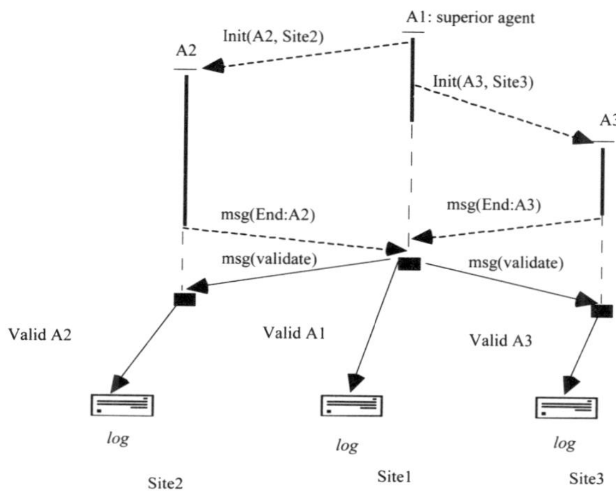

Fig. 1.38 Centralized control validation: 1-phase protocol.

It is noted that the activities pass through three distinct states:

- *Active:* in this state, the activity reserves the different resources and carries out its processing (computation phase). The resources acquired during this stage can be released if the activity enters into conflict with other concurrent activities or following an error or a site crash. In this state, it is still possible *to cancel the activity* and to request that the other sites cancel the communicating activities.

- *Wait validation*: when the activity passes into this state, it is said to be in a *grey zone*. In this zone, *the local site can no longer make decisions locally* involving the outcome to give to the activity. The only decision it can make is one which can only be taken in direct collaboration with the sites of other communicating activities (validation protocol). Notably, the site can no longer cancel the activity to free its resources if another concurrent activity blocks it by forming a cycle in the wait graph (deadlock). The site must choose one concurrent activity to terminate or wait for the outcome of the activity in question. In other words, in this phase of *undetermined duration* (depending on the reaction speed of the supervisor agent, transmission delays, and so on) the activity *monopolizes* all of the resources acquired during the computation phase.

- *Validation*: in this phase the local site has received the order to validate the local activity, which enables it to *write into the log the record of validation.* In this respect, it is important to underline that *the validation point of the global application is assimilated to the validation point of the superior agent.* For reasons of security, the superior agent must first write its record of validation into the log before sending validation orders to the other sites (Fig. 1.38). In doing this, if the superior site crashes just before it sends its messages, during the restart phase, it can restart the transmission of these messages. In this type of situation, the other sites can still enquire from the superior site about the outcome given to the local activity following a fault in the grey zone.

In the following text, three global validation protocols are presented. Each protocol carries with it a *degree of excess robustness or reliability* towards site faults. Generally, this robustness is expressed by the use of a number of higher messages.

1.8.3 0-Phase Validation Protocol

There does not exist a grey zone in this protocol. As soon as a communicating activity reaches its termination point, it takes the decision to locally validate its results without waiting for an explicit order from the superior agent. This is called the "auto-validation protocol" (Fig. 1.39). Where updating is concerned, this protocol does not guarantee the consistency of distributed resources. Consequently, it can only be used by applications which deal uniquely with remote consultations (remote interrogation of a database, an account, a descriptor, etc.).

1.8.4 1-Phase Validation Protocol

To guarantee the consistency of the content of the resources (data), distributed according to the applications which use them in upgrade mode, it is necessary to synchronize the local validation procedures of different communicating activities (Fig. 1.38). This validation protocol uses two types of messages:

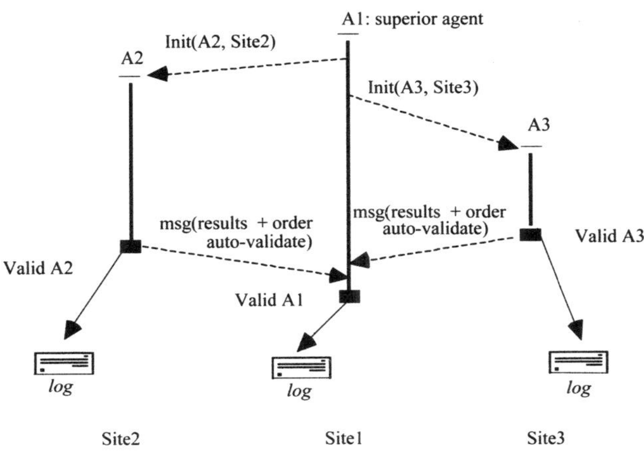

Fig. 1.39 Diagram of a 0-phase validation protocol.

- *msg(end):* this message is sent by the communicating activities to the superior agent to inform it that they have reached their termination point and that they are entering into the grey zone to await the validation order;
- *msg(validate):* this message is used by the superior agent to request the sites of the communicating activities to validate their actions (render their modifications or actions permanent) by writing the validation record into the log.

This protocol presents the major disadvantage of submitting the different communicating activities to *variable duration grey zones*, and could be fairly lengthy.

1.8.5 2-Phase Validation Protocol

This protocol introduces *supplementary synchronization* between the different sites, the aim being to *shorten* the duration of the grey zones. It also allows *the consequences of a crash to be minimized* during this period (Fig. 1.40).

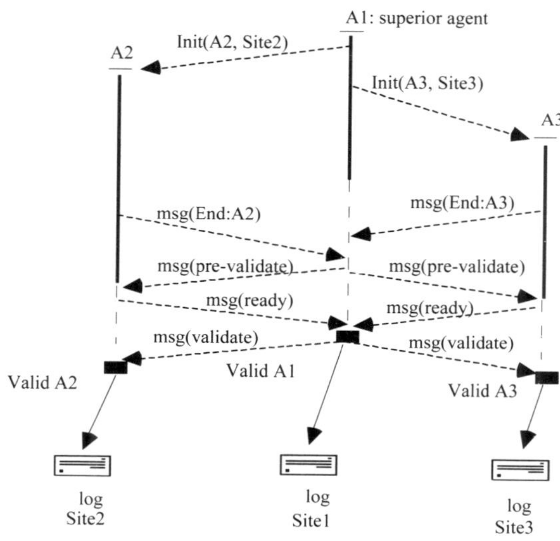

Fig. 1.40 Diagram of validation using the 2-phase protocol.

It is clear that this protocol is more costly in terms of messages; however, it enables a reduction in the duration of the grey zone. This zone starts just after reception of the *ready* message. A direct consequence of this solution is that the local site can always cancel the local activity for reasons mentioned earlier, which allows it to *release* the activities resources (especially where a fault has occurred after the *pre-validation* message has been sent). We also note that with this protocol, the grey zones of different communicating activities have gradually become the *same duration* again.

Other global validation protocols of a superior level exist. They are more complex and more costly (with a higher number of messages) and have the ability to better resist the different site crashes. Incidentally, the 3-phase validation protocol allows higher resistance to superior site faults by imposing a replacement site (*substitute site*). This substitute site must receive the different messages exchanged in the same way as the superior site, and when a fault occurs it can then take over from it. This type of protocol is essentially used in critical real-time applications (sensitive industrial process control systems, aeroplane or spacecraft supervisors, etc.).

1.9 Fault Tolerance, Security and Protection

To guarantee the functional reliability of a data processing system, it is essential that the following factors are taken into account:

- *availability:* the ability of a system to ensure delivery of the required services according to its capabilities. This property is generally established in distributed systems, given the modular character of the different hardware and software components.
- *reliability:* to guarantee the correct functioning with respect to the services required (prevent the occurrence or introduction of errors which may compromise the efficient functioning of the system when delivering a service). The implementation of a reliable system requires the use of a certain set of tools and methods (fault prevention, fault tolerance, fault elimination, fault prediction). The use of formal specification methods enables the verification and validation *a priori* of the specifications of the system components, and with respect to each identified service, and is the best guarantee against faults. Chapter 6 presents our method for the specification and validation of the behaviour of distributed systems in general, and real-time systems in particular. It has the advantage of supporting the formal descriptions of the systems studied, in a semi-graphic formality from which the theoretical foundation finds its roots in the techniques and methods of artificial intelligence and expert systems. The validation of specifications, and especially of global behaviour and temporal constraints, rests principally on the simulation of behaviour by syntactic reduction, which will be explained at a later stage.
- *security:* maintenance of a degree of data confidentiality and integrity to merit the confidence of its users.

1.10 Conclusion

In this chapter we have presented the basic concepts and notions which we feel are essential to be able to correctly understand the study and implementation of distributed systems and applications in general, and real-time multi-agent systems in particular. The intrinsic characteristics of these systems are such that *the methods or techniques used in centralized systems are no longer directly applicable to these systems by simple extrapolation or adaptation.* The absence of a global state, a result of the absence of a shared memory and single referential, makes communication via messages the sole means which can be used, under any circumstance, as much by the different components of a distributed execution system (resource schedulers, remote program activation, validation of distributed applications, etc.) as by the distributed applications themselves (application protocol: all of the messages used to make, communicate and synchronize the different actions of the activities or agents of the distributed application). Delays caused by the communication methods (public data transmission network, local area network or simple RTC lines) and especially the high number of software layers crossed by messages both at the start and on arrival, have had a direct impact on the overall performance of these systems. Consequently, the design and implementation of every distributed or real-time application takes into account all of these determining factors.

If real-time goes hand in hand only with real-time direct access to the contents of a particular resource (database, file, state variable of a device, and so on), all distributed applications are therefore real-time applications. This is not always the case. Real-time applications are, essentially, distributed applications. They are very often subject to time constraints (response time or reaction time, maximum time limit for the execution of an activity or a particular process, periodical triggering of certain processes, etc.) and their processing is evenly oriented. Time constraints increasingly complicate the design of this type of application. Their architecture must be adequately designed. Asynchronous events require concurrent programming for the implementation of different global application agents. If the designer is not sufficiently aware of the problems that these applications pose, particularly their complexity, the results could be very disappointing. This includes the prohibitive cost of development due to the lack of control of the different factors having an impact on the implementation and the exploitation of these systems.

2. *Interaction Models*

As already indicated in the previous chapter, rapid technological progress in the field of information technology resulted in the appearance of new machines on the market. These are essentially characterized by a very modular architecture, and high component specialization. One single machine can carry several active or intelligent components in the same way as the CPU, assembled around a bus. These components may be specialized processors (floating computation coprocessors, direct memory access controllers etc.) or couplers specialized in the control of exchanges between given peripherals (disk controller, video controller, controller of input/output either in series or in parallel, network controller etc.). Each component has the ability to complete the task it has with relative autonomy, and synchronization and communication between the processor and the rest of the components is largely carried out by the exchange of signals or interrupts via the control bus. The data bus and address bus are used to carry out data transfer operations.

Consequently we see that there is asynchronization or weak coupling between the different hardware components of a data processing system. In other words, new hardware is composed of a number of communicating asynchronous hardware components where interactivity is manifested by physical and electrical signal exchanges via the three system buses. To increase the performance of the hardware layer of data processing systems, the same rule that applies to distributed systems has been applied: modularity (agents or activities) and interactions (communication protocols).

However, the increased complexity of basic software (multi-task and real-time operating systems and so on) and utilities (database management systems (DBMS), text processing editors, spreadsheets, scientific computation software, computer-aided design (CAD) etc.), which are increasingly user-friendly, necessitates significant machine resources (central memory, CPU execution speed, permanent storage support etc.). The monolithic architecture of software used up until the beginning of the 1990s, that is, where all the software functions are supported and executed by a single process, has proved to be inadequate and incapable of supporting this new software, and unable to form a link between performance and user-friendliness. Standard monolithic software architecture has been abandoned in favour of a more distributed architecture in order to better understand the design and implementation of these software applications, provide them with a fairly high degree of support, and simultaneously guarantee a reasonable response time in spite of their complexity.

2.1 New Generation Distributed Software Architecture

Software designed using the standard approach is composed of a series of programs or functions that work towards the implementation of a particular task. The execution time and co-ordination of the series is supported by *one single system*. Here, a specific program or function plays a privileged role: the sequencing and supervision of the activation time of other functions following a predefined logic that conforms to the semantics of the application. This function is called the main program. The interaction between the main program and the other functions is mostly carried out by the function call. Data exchange result gathering is carried out either in variables presented in parameters, or in global variables.

Notion 1 New Generation Software

This is a series of communicating processes (tasks) which react in time according to a specific number of internal or external events.

Examples of new generation software are Windows 95 and OS2 data processing systems, as well as the applications that run on these systems. They are the origin of *event oriented programming* which is now becoming standard within the micro-computing world. However, this type of software can be considered as belonging to a particular class of distributed application, where interactions between and the positioning of the different global application agents, restricts them to the host machine. Nevertheless, the main principles for the design and implementation of these ideas remain identical to those of distributed applications.

In light of what has just been stated, it is acknowledged that today's IT systems are mostly composed of highly specialized active or passive entities, which generally communicate via the exchange of messages, events or signals. This is vital for both hardware and software layers. Furthermore, with the appearance on the market of programmable logic circuits (for example the Xelinx family, FPGA, etc.), it is difficult to establish a clear division between hardware and software components, knowing that it is now possible to micro-program software algorithms or functions using circuits, and to interface them directly with the other material components via the bus system. This is called *co-design.*

To conclude, a data processing system is a series of software or hardware entities, organized by abstraction levels into a layered architecture, and capable of interacting or communicating.

In the following sections, particular attention will be paid to the basic principles underlying concurrent and distributed programming. The concepts and notions which will be introduced are not only applicable to the design and programming of distributed systems, but also to the programming of concurrent distributed control applications on the same machine, conforming to the ideas presented above.

2.2 Event-Oriented Concurrent and Distributed Programming

In the early 1990s, the use of concurrent and distributed programming was only essential if the implementation of the application required either apparent or real parallelism. Event programming under Windows 95 or OS2 clearly showed that distributed programming is no longer saved for distributed applications. It is important to note that while event-oriented concurrent programming has started to find its way into the world of standard data processing, it has been the work tool of manufacturing data processing specialists since the appearance of real-time executives (IBM's OS-9 executive for example). Chapter 5 presents the principal notions used within this field for the design and implementation of industrial process control systems, notably automated production systems.

Concurrent programming is used to implement:

- windowing systems on microcomputers or stations (Windows, OS2, Macintosh, XWindows);
- transaction processing in a multi-user DBMS;
- file servers in a network;
- processing or scientific computation which manipulates a large amount of data (image processing, distributed simulation etc.).

This last form of concurrent programming corresponds to parallel programming, which requires a multiprocessor execution platform or a network of microcomputers or Unix stations.

The following text presents the different forms of interaction that can exist between several processes within a distributed context. Each interaction paradigm constitutes an example or an inter-process *communication model*, around which is associated a *programming technique* which can be used to solve a variety of problems.

2.3 Massively Parallel Processors and Distributed Programming

Parallel distributed programming, which uses several small, specialized parallel tasks or agents to solve a complex problem, has become the keystone in the programming of modern systems where demands for improved performance, cost reduction and better productivity have continued to grow. The determining factors that have led to the progressive spread of distributed programming are:

- the appearance on the market of massively parallel processors at increasingly competitive prices;

- the increasingly large scale use of distributed programming for the solution of scientific or more commonplace problems.

Massively parallel processors (MPPs) are the most powerful computers. They use a network composed of several hundred to several thousand central units (CPU) connected to a central memory, which can easily reach hundreds of gigaoctets. MPPs offer colossal computing power and are mainly used to execute large, time-consuming CPU programs such as those which model and simulate climatic conditions, programs which aid the design of aeroplanes and buildings, and the simulation of socio-economic or ecological systems.

As simulation programs become increasingly realistic, so the computing power needed to execute them also increases. This explains in part the position of researchers in the field of massively parallel processors.

A second factor, which has had a direct impact on solving scientific problems, has been the use of distributed programming. *Distributed programming is an approach involving the use of a series of machines connected via a communication network to resolve a complex problem.* As local area networks increase in performance and offer throughput in excess of 100Mbits/second, the combined use of resources available on workstations connected to the network, can easily reach and even surpass the performance of a single massively parallel processor. In certain cases, several MPPs have been interconnected via a local high-throughput network in order to resolve a particular type of problem (simulation).

The common factor between distributed programming and MPPs is without doubt the use of message exchanges as the basic principle of communication and co-ordination between different entities of the application.

Finally, the classification of these machines is outlined according to the Flynn Model. To establish this classification, Michael Flynn exploited the definition of a kernel with the architectural origin of a computer defined by Von Neumann (processing unit, storage space and control unit) in the 1950s to establish four different functioning modes, each representing a class of parallel machines:

- SISD (Single Instruction Stream Single Data Stream);
- SIMD (Single Instruction Stream Multiple Data Stream);
- MISD (Multiple Instruction Stream Single Data Stream);
- MIMD (Multiple Instruction Stream Multiple Data Stream).

In his classification, Flynn principally took into account two parameters; the control of one part, and memory access of another part. Flynn saw storage space as being shared by all the processing units. Multiprocessors can function using all of these modes (with the exception of the SISD mode). To take into consideration the notion of parallel distributed programming, two variations were added to the dictionary relating to computer architecture:

- the SPMD mode which is an analogy of the SIMD mode. The distribution of a shared instruction to all the processing units is replaced by that of a *whole program* which therefore represents a *processing agent* or more precisely an *actor*. All of the units execute the same agent, but on different data;

- the multi-SISD mode which is a variation of the MIMD mode. Instead of sharing storage space with the other processing units, each processing unit has access to a private memory, therefore generating several independent SISD type units.

In general, the SIMD mode is suitable for the architecture of supercomputers. The MISD class has never materialized. A small variation can transform this mode to characterize the "pipeline" model where the control and processing units are divided into levels, each responsible for part of the operation to be executed. The flow of information is continuous. The MIMD mode is generally assigned to parallel machines as it suits the flexibility of the architecture, especially at the level of the memory position in relation to that of processors.

Table 2.1 shows several machines classed using the Flynn model.

Table 2.1: Classification of parallel machines.

Class and memory	System	Manufacturer
SIMD	CM-2	Thinking machines
SIMD	MP-1	Maspar
SIMD	DECmpp	Digital
Distributed MIMD	CM-5	Thinking machines
Shared MIMD	XMP, YMP	Cray
Distributed MIMD	TC2000	BBN
Distributed MIMD	iPSC, PARAGON	INTEL
Distributed MIMD	RS/6000	IBM
Distributed MIMD	nCUBE2	nCUBE
Virtually shared MIMD	KSR1	Kendall Square Research
Shared MIMD	SX2, SX3	NEC
Distributed MIMD	T.NODE	TELMAT
MIMD + SIMD	CONCERTO	TELMAT
Shared MIMD	TR5000, TR7000	TELMAT
MIMD + SIMD	MPP	Cray

2.3.1 Distributed Programming and Heterogeneous Computer Networks

In a massively parallel processor, the processors are identical, have the same processing capacity, offer the same hardware and software resources and use the same communication speeds. This does not apply to a computer network. The interconnected machines can belong to different manufacturers and therefore exhibit notable differences not only at the technological (and therefore hardware) level (CPU speed, communication speed, disk access speed, cache memory, "RISC" internal architecture, etc.), but also at the software level (different architecture and performance of basic software, different compilers and so on).

A programmer, wishing to exploit the available capacity of a computer network, must therefore face a vast array of problems inherent in the intrinsic nature of these heterogeneous systems:

- different hardware architecture;
- internal representation of different data (different format);
- different execution speeds;
- local load for each machine;
- network load and induced fluctuations.

A large selection of hardware technology and architecture is now available on the market, such as:

- standard PC486/586 microcomputers;
- workstations (with a more advanced architecture and offering a high performance level);
- multiprocessor machines with shared global memory;
- multiprocessor machines without shared global memory (transputers: a specific type of microcomputer from the manufacturer Inmos/Telmat);
- supercomputers;
- and a wide range of massively parallel processors (hundreds or thousands of CPUs).

For each of these architectures there is the appropriate corresponding programming method. However, the simultaneous presence of standard sequential machines such as the Von Neumann type, and parallel machines, has further complicated the task of programming. Incompatibility occurs between the binary codes when it comes to compiling a distributed application involving several machines.

Incompatibility of data format on the different machines is an important factor in distributed programming, as the data transmitted from one machine in its internal format is not understood by the receiving machine, hence the importance of the presentation layer of the ISO model. Even in cases where the computer network is composed of workstations with identical internal data representations, heterogeneity subsists because of differences at the central unit speed level. Incidentally, the programmer must prevent tasks placed on the MPP of the network from waiting too long for data coming from other tasks placed on the stations. However, the local load of each machine has a direct influence on the performance of that machine. As well as executing tasks belonging to a distributed application, a workstation also supports the work of other users on the network.

Finally, the overload of a communication network due to the large number of messages in transit, naturally has direct repercussions on message transmission time. Data transmission time becomes critical when a task is suspended while waiting for a message.

In spite of all of these difficulties inherent in the heterogeneity of computer networks, distributed programming offers many advantages:

- by using existing machines, the overall cost of processing remains relatively low;
- performance can be increased by assigning each task to the most appropriate machine (task requiring a specialized processor);
- the productivity of programmers can be increased by using familiar environments (editors, compilers, debuggers) on their individual machine;
- microcomputers and individual stations are generally stable, enabling programmers to rapidly acquire a certain expertise in their use;
- hardware and software resources available on the network are generally on the increase;
- fault tolerance at the user interface level of a system and at the level of programs and user applications is easy to achieve;
- distributed programming facilitates teamwork.

All of these factors contribute to a reduction in the development time of distributed applications, and work towards reducing conflicts in the use of resources, a reduction in costs, and help to find the best implementation possible for a given application. It is with this in mind that the PVM (parallel virtual machine) program came to light. PVM will be described in detail in Chapter 3.

2.3.2 High-Throughput Networks and Distributed Programming

Workstations today offer computer power to the order of several tens of millions of instructions per second, and experts in the field foresee a noticeable increase in this power in the immediate future. Consequently, once these machines are interconnected via a high-throughput network, they produce an overall computing power that is generally sufficient to resolve a large number of problems using many computations.

In order to be efficient, distributed programming requires a very rapid means of communication. Since the start of the 1980s, network transmission speed has increased dramatically (Fig. 2.1).

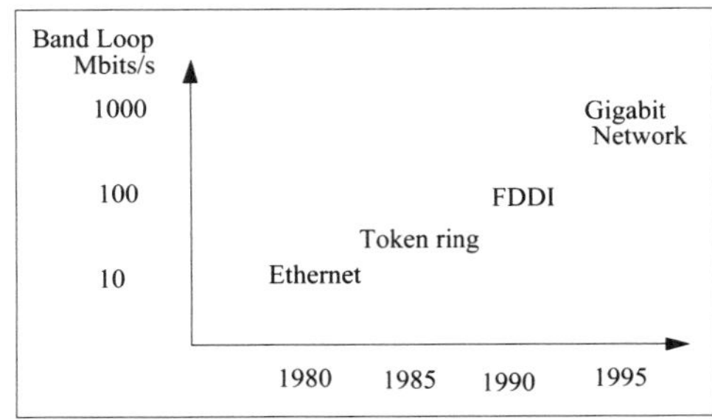

Fig. 2.1 The development of network speeds.

Among the huge technological advances in the field of communication networks can be found:

- Ethernet: this is the name given to the famous local data transmission network invented by Xerox PARC. Ethernet is technology involving the transmission of packets of data by broadcasting, using distributed access control. The speed is 10 Mbits/second;
- FDDI (Fiber Distributed Data Interface): FDDI is a token network at 100Mbits/second which uses optical fibres as physical support for transmission between stations;
- HiPPI (High-Performance Parallel Interface): HiPPI is a parallel communication bus that can reach 800 Mbits/second with 32 parallel lines, and 1.6Gbits/second with 64 lines. The majority of top-of-the-range machines available on the market have the HiPPI interface. It is a point-to-point communication structure;
- SONET (Synchronous Optical NETwork): SONET is a series of optical signals which are multiples of a basic signal with a speed equal to 51.84 Mbits/second called OC-1, OC-3 (155.52 Mbits/second) and OC-12 (622.08 Mbits/second);
- ATM (Asynchronous Transfer Mode): ATM is a transmission, multiplexing and routing technique offering a high level of flexibility. ATM is a connected protocol that uses fixed size packets with 5 octets for the header of the packets and 48 octets for the data.

This technological advance in the field of communication networks promises high level throughputs with less latency and indicates that distributed programming will be trivialized in the immediate future. As a direct consequence of this development, an increasingly large number of universities, private or public research laboratories and businesses within the financial, tourism and transmission sectors, have resorted to distributed programming to solve their problems.

2.4 Basic Principles of Distributed Programming

We start this section by outlining the definition of a distributed program.

Notion 2 Distributed Program

This is a multi-agent application with a hierarchical structure composed of several processes (tasks) communicating by the exchange of messages via a means of communication. For each identified distributed program interaction, each process involved is either a filter process, a client process, a server process or even an actor process.

Four basic process models therefore exist which can be used to *manufacture* a distributed program and determine the *operational scope* of each agent: filter processes, client processes, server processes and actor processes.

Notion 3 Interaction

An interaction is determined by the nature of the exchanges, communication and the structural relationships between the different agents involved.

An agent is a conceptual entity that is identified in the analysis phase of a multi-agent system. This entity is destined to accomplish a particular function within the application (community). In this phase, no choice of implementation needs to be made. It is in the design and implementation phases that the basic process models (shown above), can be used to decide the nature of the process which will serve as *support* to the conceptual agent, and the formal scope within which it is going to develop.

In the same way as a human society, an agent society (multi-agent applications) must be ruled by a set of regulations and laws which are designed to *organize and structure the society to guarantee its lasting quality and coherency.* As a result, it is important to clearly define for each agent, an abstraction taken from its nature (reactive, cognitive, or processing): the manner with which it will interact and collaborate with the other agents of the application.

2.4.1 Filter Processes

A filter process carries out transformations of the data input flow before transmitting them to the output flow (Fig. 2.2). This is the *transformation* process.

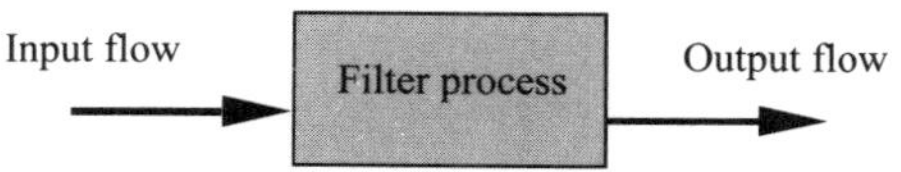

Fig. 2.2 Filter process.

For example, several Unix commands are filters; the *tbl* command for the formation of programs, and *troff* for documents etc.

2.4.2 Client and Server Processes

A client process is the caller for the delivery of a service from a server process. *It initializes a request that triggers a reaction from the server.*

A server process is a reactive process; it waits until a request arrives. These requests involve the services that are available and offered to several clients. Process servers are *continuously active processes* (the Unix DAEMON).

A file server on a network is a classic example of this type of process. In this case, the user applications for file data managed by this server are client processes (Fig. 2.3).

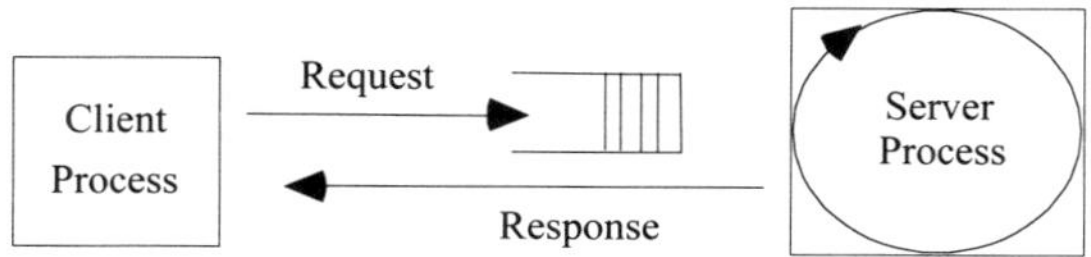

Fig. 2.3 Client–server interaction.

2.4.3 Actor Processes

Actor processes are a collection of identical processes (*executing the same algorithm*) which communicate to provide a service, a computation or a result. In general, this actor community periodically carries out message exchanges to distribute the intermediate results. For example, two actor processes could be used to guarantee the coherency of two copies of a file on two different sites (Fig. 2.4). As the two actors execute the same algorithm (application of local and remote upgrades in the same order, application of time stamps with upgrade broadcasting), in the absence of requests the two copies end up identical.

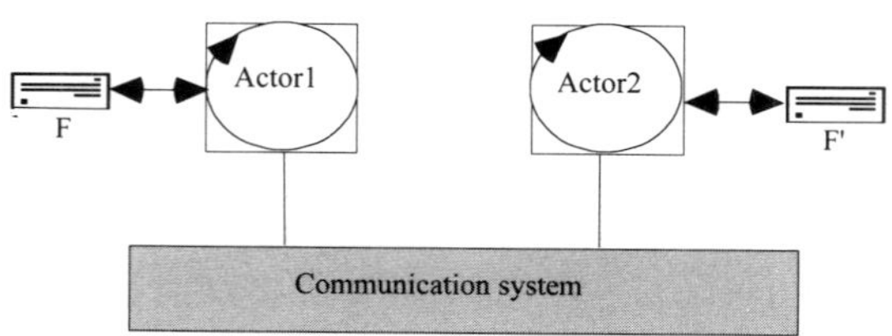

Fig. 2.4 The use of two actors for the management of multiple copies.

Image processing on a parallel machine is another example of how this type of process is used. The image is divided into a specific number of identical parts, which are distributed to each actor for processing (e.g. filtering). All of the parts are then reassembled to reconstitute the original image (Fig. 2.5).

The paradigm of actors can actually be divided into two categories; the master–slave model and the tree model of actors.

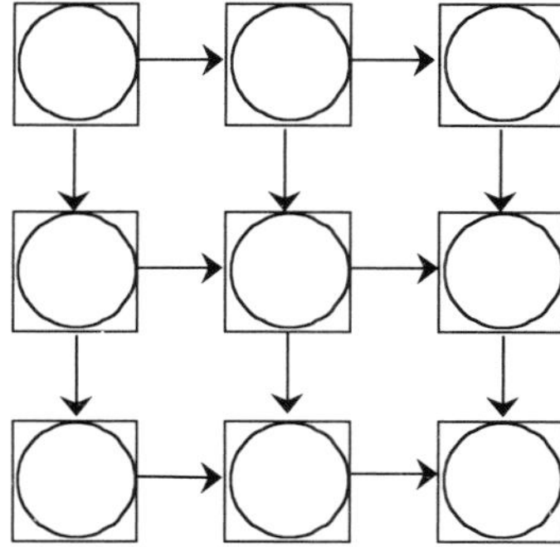

Fig. 2.5 The use of actors for the implementation of parallel processing.

2.4.3.1 The Master–Slave Model

The master–slave model (Fig. 2.6) is a model where one of the agents (processes), called the *master*, has the specific role of controlling the creation and initialization of the other actors called the *slaves*. It must also ensure the collection and display of the results, and sometimes the supervision of the execution time of the slave actors.

The slave actors execute the same algorithm and receive data, dynamically or statically, from the master to process at the time of their creation. *The number of actors is fixed and known in advance.*

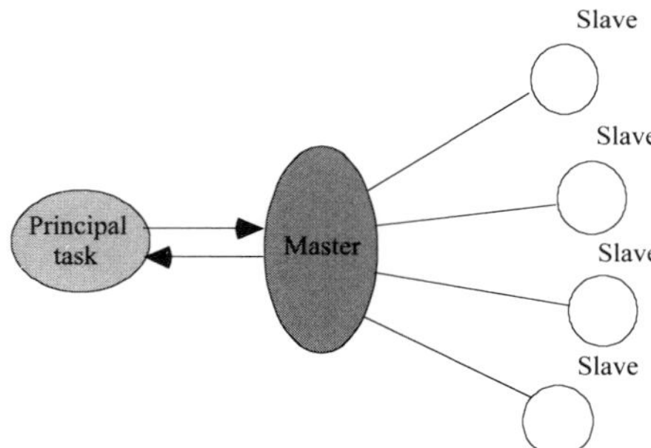

Fig. 2.6 The master–slave model.

2.4.3.2. The Tree Model of Actors

In this model, *the actors are created dynamically as the processes progress in the form of an arborescence* (Fig. 2.7) where there is a father–son relationship between the different actors. Although this model is rarely used, it suits applications where the number of data partitions to be processed is not known in advance. The example of sorting in Section 2.7.2 illustrates this model.

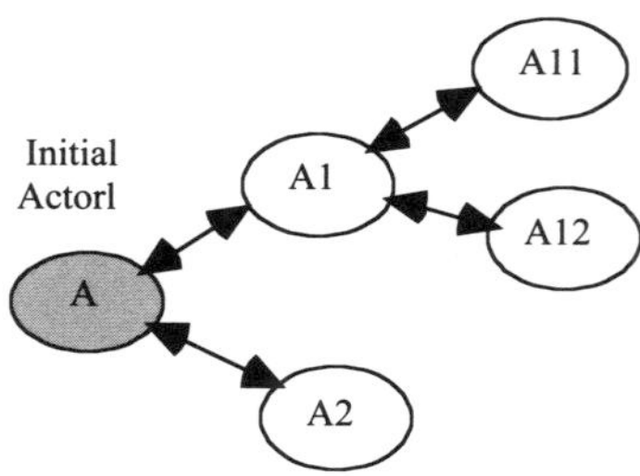

Fig. 2.7 The tree model of actors.

2.5 The Method of Analysis for a Multi-Agent Application

The refinement of a distributed application in terms of agents, and the identification of interactions according to one of the interaction models described above can be carried out using two approaches: data-oriented refinement or functional refinement at the abstraction level. The main aspects of the two approaches are outlined in this section. Data-oriented refinement is mainly used in distributed scientific calculation applications on massively parallel processors. Functional refinement at the abstraction level is more general. Several methods currently in use are based on this approach, such as SA-RT (Structured Analysis – Real Time), UML (Universal Modelling Language), OMT (Object Modelling Technique), etc. The SA-RT method will be presented in Chapter 5. Chapter 7 gives an example of the actual use of SA-RT in the analysis and specification of the command part of an automated parts distribution system, which is a real-time system.

2.5.1 Data-Oriented Refinement of a Distributed Application

This approach assumes that the entire problem requires the application of a process or transformation on one or more data structures that *lend themselves perfectly to finer partitioning*. Each of these small partitions must also undergo *the same transformations* or processes as the initial structure. For example, consider the problem of adding two vectors $A[1...N]$ and $B[1...N]$ to produce the resulting vector $C[1...N]$. If we consider that P processes have been assigned this application, then data partitioning involves the allocation of N/P elements corresponding to the resulting vector. This partitioning can be carried out statically when each processor knows in principle (at least via the N and P intermediates) the part of the overall structure to which it is allocated. This partitioning can also be carried out dynamically. Where this occurs, a control process (such as the master process) is responsible for allocating partitions to the processes as soon as they become available.

In all cases, the application agents are clearly identified as well as the corresponding interaction model:

- static partitioning → master–slave model;
- dynamic partitioning → master–slave or actor tree model.

2.5.2 The Functional Refinement of Distributed Applications

Although data-oriented refinement methodology is suitable for computation problems (usually scientific) manipulating the data structures which are well adapted to this process, it is difficult to apply it to other types of more standard problems. For these problems, the simplest method is to conduct application refinement in functions or units, ensuring that each has a precise task. This is a standard approach that will be recognized by most readers.

In general, complex distributed applications use several subroutines or different functions:

- either on the same data (MPSD – Multiple-Program Single-Data);
- or in pipeline mode: transformation chain;
- or, in certain cases, in a way which does not obey any particular order or organization of exchange between different functions.

As we have already mentioned, readers not familiar with this type of approach can turn to Chapter 5 for more details on the basic principles and concepts, and Chapter 7 for an example of how this approach is used in the study of a real-time system.

In the following section, we analyze the design and implementation tools used in distributed multi-agent applications, especially the tools necessary for the implementation of agents and the different interactions. Particular interest will be paid to the definition of basic concepts that are needed to support a distributed programming language. Such a language must be at a high abstraction level to *free* the application programmer from providing process management details and using low-level communication tools. These are extremely tedious, and are the root cause of many serious errors, as we will see in Chapters 3 and 4. Nevertheless, the tools presented in these two chapters serve as a basis for the implementation of a distributed programming language based on the concepts introduced in the following sections.

2.6 Communication Channels

A distributed programming language must be supported by a mechanism that enables interactions between the processes of a distributed application. This medium is called a channel.

Notion 4 The Communication Channel

This is either an abstraction at the level of the seventh layer (application) of the ISO model, of a physical inter-machine communication mechanism (data transmission networks, telephone lines). Or, simply, the abstraction of an intra-machine communication mechanism (pipes, mailboxes, files, Unix sockets, global variables, etc.).

Figure 2.8 shows an example of interactions between the processes of a multi-agent application using a communication channel, according to the above definition. A distributed multi-agent application is, in essence, an application with a hierarchical structure covering several abstraction levels. Consequently, the communication channels must be of different load or visibility to respect the natural protection levels (encapsulation principle) which exist within the application.

Therefore, a channel can be:

- *Global*, and consequently visible by all of the shared application processes (e.g. channel C in Figure 2.8), independent of the geographic locality of the site of the host machine;
- *Local* to a group of processes (e.g. channel A). In this case, it is only visible to the processes of this group and eventually to their internal processes at the inferior level.

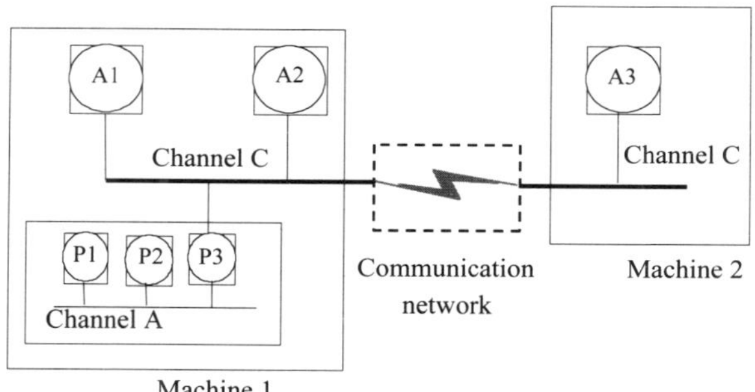

Fig. 2.8 A channel: the implementation of interactions between processes.

This structure enables the same rules of declaration, load and visibility to be applied to the channels as the variables in the standard structure programming languages (C language). As a result, a channel becomes an object in the same way as other objects (variables, constants, functions, etc.) are manipulated within a program.

Among the other properties or attributes of a channel, a communication channel can be *uni-directional* or *bi-directional*, *asynchronous* or *synchronous*. An asynchronous communication channel has an unlimited capacity, the *communications are non-blocking*. The declaration of a synchronous communication channel in a distributed application introduces *strong coupling* between the entities communicating via this channel, notably the introduction of a synchronization point. The transmitter is suspended until the point at which the receptor extracts the message. Nevertheless, asynchronous communication channels are more flexible mechanisms and are more easily realized. In the rest of this chapter, we concentrate mainly on this last mechanism.

2.7 Elements of a High-Level Distributed Programming Language

The concepts and notions introduced in this section serve to enrich the communication mechanisms already supported by programming languages authorizing pseudo-parallelism or true parallelism. ADA (Bal *et al.*, 1989) and Concurrent C (Gehani and Roome, 1992) use the rendezvous mechanism to enable communication and synchronization between tasks. In LYNX (Bal *et al.*, 1989) communications are mainly carried out using the remote procedure call (RPC). Lastly, LINDA and Concurrent PROLOG (Bal *et al.*, 1989) use shared variables as a means of communication. OCCAM (Inmos Ld, 1988) enables point-to-point transmissions between live entities. You will recall that a transputer machine is a machine comprised of a network of processors from which the instruction set has been voluntarily reduced for reasons of efficiency, and given a local internal memory. A communication device intermediary interconnects all of these processors. Intuitively, we can consider a transputer machine as being a distributed system where the machines involved are reduced to transputers. This type of hardware structure presents several characteristics of the distributed system, notably the absence of a shared memory. The primitives which will be introduced are more general, and are not answerable to any existing language, either at the syntactical level, or at the semantic level. They are used to present the basic principles underlying distributed programming languages in the widest sense, independent of any hardware structure. We believe that a distributed programming language must satisfy the following fundamental property:

Notion 5 Fundamental Property of a Distributed Programming Language

A distributed programming language must be free from hardware specifications and must be situated at the level of the seventh layer of the ISO model.

The notions introduced in the following sections can easily be directly or indirectly integrated into the compiler, with the help of a pre-processor or translator, and into a standard programming language such as C or C++. Nevertheless, a rapid method of using these notions consists of creating a pre-processor from a higher level layer for the PVM tool which, despite the possibilities it offers, is still hard for non-specialist users to understand, especially students. This tool will form the object of a detailed description in Chapter 3.

2.7.1 Asynchronous Channels

The following format is used to depict an asynchronous channel:

```
Channel <Channel_identifier> [(<lists_types_fields)];
```

The list of types must be used in cases where the messages which the channel must carry are structured or featured and have a fixed length. The interaction and transfer unit is the message as a whole. A channel is assumed to be perfect. This hypothesis implies that each implementation of this mechanism must respond to the following requirements:

- reliability: every message sent arrives at its destination (delivered);
- absence of errors: the content of the messages is not altered;
- conservation of the order of messages on arrival.

The reader will recognize the intrinsic properties of the "end to end" communication protocol under these constraints.

The following examples are used to illustrate the use of this instruction:

- `1- chan input(char);`

input is a channel which allows the exchange or flow of characters.

- `2- chan disk_access (int cylinder; int block; int nb_characters; char[80] buffer);`

disk_access establishes a method of communication between the disk driver and the user layers.

Recall that the range or visibility of a channel compared to the distributed application process is almost identical to that of the variables compared to the waits and functions of a standard program. In Figure 2.9, channel A is visible to all of the processes on the same level (P_1, P_2, P_3). On the other hand, channel B is visible to process code P_3, and processes P_{31} and P_{32}. This being the case, it involves a simplified hypothesis which imposes a vertically descending visibility on the processes. This hypothesis, however, is perfectly justified to maintain the encapsulation principle of complex applications. A given process could comprise a specific number of internal communicating processes that are not visible at the superior level (e.g. processes P_{31}, P_{32} and P_3). Figure 2.9 also shows the general architecture of the distributed application.

By definition, only one process owns a channel. It is the only one authorized to receive or extract messages from the channel. Once a channel is declared, its nature will depend on the number of transmitter processes:

- When the channel is *used for the reception of one process only*, the channel is called the process entry-point. There can be any number of transmitters. In this case, the channel is seen as the mailbox of the owner process.
- When the channel *possesses one transmitter and one receptor only*, the channel is called the link channel between the two processes (*pairwise*) communication.

```
Channel A;
Process P1 { ...} ;
Process P2 { ... };
Process P3
     { Channel B;
       Process P31 ;
        Process P32 ;
        ....;
     };
     .... ;
```

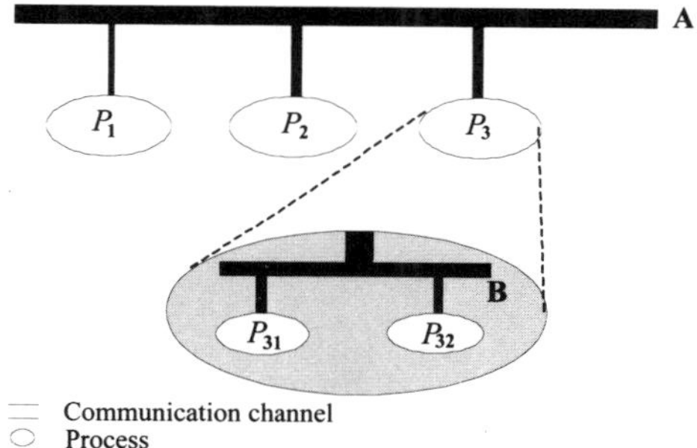

Fig. 2.9 The architecture of a distributed application.

Channel owner identification can either be static, by bringing a slight extension to the declaration instruction to include the identifier of the owner process, or it is left under the charge of a pre-processor or compiler. This is dependent on whether this mechanism is integrated to a compiler or is essential to locate the different instructions relative to the mechanism, and replace them with calls to library functions. The second solution has the advantage of being easy to implement.

2.7.2 Channel Manipulation Primitives

From the point at which a channel is declared in a distributed application, it provides the different potential processes of the application likely to use the channels, with adequate primitives to realize an effective exchange. Three primitives are essential:

```
1- send <ch_ident> (<expr1..., exprn>).
```

Exp_n elements must be identical to the types in list *<lists_types_fields>* used in the declaration of the channel. This is a non-blocking primitive. A process will always be able to submit a message to a channel. A channel can be thought of as a queue with infinite length.

```
2- receive <ch_ident> (<var1...varn>);
```

<var_n> represents a zone or a buffer where a message taken from a channel will be deposited. This is a blocking primitive in cases where the channel is empty.

3- **empty** <ch_ident>

is a boolean function which prevents a process from waiting on `receive` when the channel is empty.

The example shown in Figure 2.10 shows a filter process with an asynchronous communication mechanism. It uses two channels; `input` for the incoming stream of data and `output` for the outgoing stream of data. The first channel transmits the stream of characters, while the second transmits structured messages; lines of characters.

```
#define maxline 80;
channel Input(char c);
channel output(char l[ maxline] );
FilterProcess character_lines ()
 { char line[ maxline] ;
     int i = 0;
     while (StopCondition)
   { while (line[ i] <> CR and i <= maxline)
     receive Input(line[ i++] ;
     send Output(line);
     i = 0;
   };
 };
```

Fig. 2.10 An example of a filter process.

A filter process is one that processes the input data stream to produce the output data stream. Consequently, the filter process in the example transforms the incoming stream of characters into an outgoing stream of lines. Figure 2.11 shows another example of a parallel sorted application. It is constructed using the actor tree model.

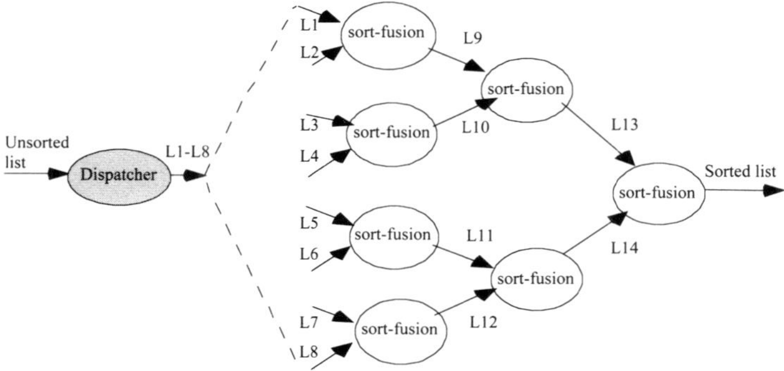

Fig. 2.11 The architecture of a parallel sorted application.

This is composed of a network of actors that execute the same sorting algorithm. Each actor receives two sorted lists from the input data stream, which it merges into one sorted list that forms the output stream. The actor code is given in Figure 2.12. The "dispatcher" process feeds the first level of actors by cutting up the initial list into a set of lists which represent the monotony encountered depending on the arrival order in the input stream. The size of these lists can be limited to a single element. The first level of actors later provides the second level with the necessary lists, and this continues to the final level, which is comprised of a single actor. If N_i is the number of actors on level i, then: $N_{i+1} = N_i / 2$ if N_i is even, otherwise $N_{i+1} = N_i / 2 + 1$ if N_i is odd, will be the number of actors at level $i + 1$. The onus is on the "dispatcher" process to create first level actors (call to the `createActor(F[0, A])` primitive, each time that it encounters two monotonies (the L indicator takes the value of 1).

In the solution presented, each *merger* actor is only responsible for creating the actor of the following level if it is of the even range:

```
if (p) {createActor(F[in, j+i]); d=i}.
```

Furthermore, the instruction:

```
if (L) send input[0,A][0](E1) else send input[0,A][1](E1)
```

enables the breakdown of the value received from the "unsorted" input channel of one of the two input channels from the actor on the lower level: a channel by list.

The following line:

```
If (L = 1) {send input[0, A][1] (EOS);A+1; CreateActor(F[0, A]; L=0}
```

enables the implementation of the following actions:

1. `send input[0, A][1](EOS);`: send the "end of stream" character to terminate transmission on the channel;
2. `A+1` increase the counter with the actors to be created;
3. `CreateActor(F[0, A])`: create the next actor;
4. `L=0`: return L indicator to zero to announce a new pair of lists.

The reader will have noticed that a semantic distinction has been introduced to differentiate the declaration of processes from those of actors. This distinction takes into account the methods and considerations of implementation. A particular class of processes called threads, now available under Unix, will support the actors. Under OS2 or Windows 95, the term threads designates this type of process. The difference between a normal process and a thread is found in the quantity of system resources (memory, stack) to ensure their execution. The execution context for a thread is reduced to a strict minimum.

It is important to note that a solution using communicating actors that execute a simple and identical code, is generally of high performance and lends itself easily to CO-DESIGN implementation. When this is the case with a real-time application, it is possible to micro-program the actor code with programmable logic circuits, if the code is relatively simple.

```
#define MaxL 50                     /*max number of lines of matrix of actor identifiers */
#define  MaxC 10                                /* max number of columns in the matrix*/
Input channel [MaxL, MaxC][2](int);    /*channel declaration : 2 per actor: 2 lists to
sort*/
Unsorted channel (int);                      /* declaration of dispatcher input channel*/
fusion F[MaxL, MaxC];            /*declaration of a table of pid's for fusion type actors */
Process dispatcher()
      { int E1 = 0; int E2 = 0;  int A = 0; int L = 0;
        createActor(F[A, 0]);
        receive unsorted(E1);

                                         /*at the worst it cannot exceed MaxL/2 actor sons*/
    while (E1 <> Eos) and (A <=  MaxL /2))
      { while (E1 >= E2)
        {if (L)  send input[A, 0][1] (E1)
               else send input[A, 0][0](E1);
          E2 = E1;
          receive unsorted(E1);
              };
        if (L = 1) {send input[A, 0][1](Eos);
                    A++; createActor(F[A, 0]);  L = 0}
         else {send input[A, 0][0](Eos); L = 1};
   };
              };                                              /*end of dispatcher process*/

  Actor fusion [ i: 1..MaxL, j:1..MaxC]
  {int v1, v2, d;
    p = i % 2;
                                          /* if d is a pair, create an actor of the same line 'i'*/
    if (p){createActor(F[i, j+1]); d = i}
         else d = i - 1;
                                                                      /*read two numbers*/
   receive input[i,j][0](v1); receive input[i,j][1](v2);
  while ((v1 <> Eos) and (v2 <> Eos))
      if (v1 <= v2 ){send input[d,j+1][p](v1);
                  receive input[i,j][0](v1)}
     else {send input[d,j+1][p](v2); receive input[i,j][1](v2)};
        if (v1 = Eos)
       while (v2 <> Eos) {send input[d,j+1][p](v2);
                              receive input[i,j][1](v2)};
        if (v2 = Eos )
        while (v1 <> Eos) {send input[d,j+1][p](v1);
                            receive input[i,j][0](v1)};
        send input[d,j+1][p](Eos);
}                                                                         /*end fusion*/
```

Fig. 2.12 The code of a distributed parallel sorting application using channels.

Finally, implementation of this language occurs inevitably by the use of a process placing algorithm on the network used (transputer network, local microcomputer or workstation network), which has at its disposal a table of the machines or processes available. This table gives an indication of machine identification (hostid), and the load of each machine in terms of processes or placed actors etc.

It is clear that these concepts and the notions introduced up until now are not sufficient in themselves to take responsibility for a fairly wide range of distributed applications. Present and future data processing essentially involves archetypal real-time systems, whose principal characteristic is reactivity in relation to their natural environment. To complete the possibilities offered by the concepts introduced, the following section proposes a communication mechanism whose novel feature enables communicating entities to communicate with each other without knowing each other. This mechanism has the distinctive feature of overcoming the problems inherent in identifying the entities of an application. This is done by extending the notion of communicating via channels. The approach proposed here enables any process to receive and extract messages from a visible channel, and it involves the principle of anonymous communication, which is introduced in the following section. This mechanism also aids the implementation of many-to-many communications and message broadcasting.

2.8 Anonymous Communication

In this model a channel is a means of communication authorizing dialogues (*point-to-point communication*) for entities which know each other, as well as *multi-point communications* between entities which do not know each other (anonymous communications). In the latter case, a process that does not know its partners, must be able to indicate to the channel the format of the messages it wishes to receive. In this type of anonymous communication, the channel filters and sends to the process callers all the messages which conform to the format that they have specified. Figure 2.13 shows the use of the anonymous communication principle for communication between processes. In this example, process P_2 does not know the identity of the process server for the B_1 base. To be able to communicate with it, it sends an identification demand to the channel. Process server P_3, which requested that the channel send all messages with the format *"Client C requests connection to the base B_1 server"* to it, will intercept this message to state its identity.

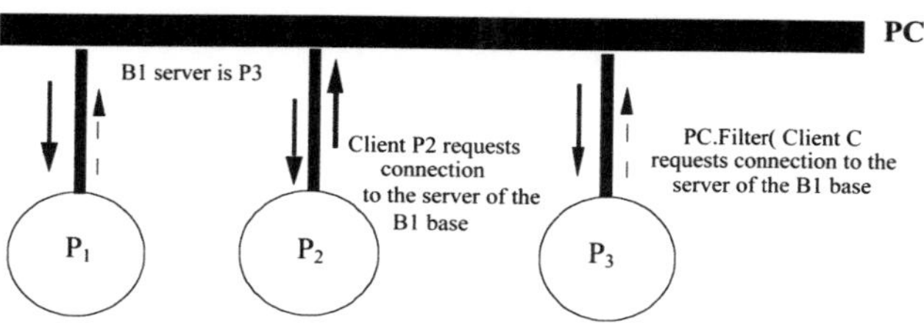

Fig. 2.13 Anonymous communication between processes.

It is important to note that in this anonymous communication model *the processes are identified by the service requested*, and not by any identifier. The advantage of such an approach is to offer greater flexibility in programming, especially concerning the time availability of a certain number of services according to events.

In Figure 2.14, for example, the body of process P_3 contains the declaration of an object with the message format `connection`. A signal type software event and a message queue object are associated to an object of this type. When the PC channel detects a message in the format indicated, it activates the corresponding event and deposits it in the queue, while removing the envelope. Only the useful syntactical entities are saved (in the example shown in Fig. 2.13, *C* is the useful syntactical entity). The direct read-out in the queue is blocking. In P_3, an interception handler is associated with the software event `connection`. Every time the PC channel activates the event, process P_3 is re-routed to execute the handler. A software event that is not intercepted by a handler is lost. The `Get` method, associated with the queue of a channel, triggers a new activation of the signal if the queue is not empty.

In this model, a process is an object which possesses, among other things, an object of the type *message queue*, where it can receive messages which are addressed directly to it (point-to-point communication). In Figure 2.13, process P_1 has sent a message directly to process P_3 via the PC channel.

```
#include <Channel.h>
#include <Process.h>
#include <Event>
#include <Handler>
...
PC Channel;

Process P1 {...
      PC.Put("select balance from account where name='DUPONT'", P3);
      };
          ...
 Process P2 {...};
 Process P3
      { Frame connection;
        Handler DeclineIdentity{Item *msg;
              connection.Fifo.get(msg);
              PC.Put("Server of B1 is P3 for" msg[1])
              };
        PC.Filter ("Client C requests connection to the server of
the B1 base", connection);
        ON connection.event DeclineIdentity;
          ...
        DO::                                                  /* loop*/
              {Message *msg;
                ....;
               me.Fifo.get(msg);
                                                    /* message processing*/
              };
      };
```

Fig. 2.14 Example of a distributed application outline.

2.8.1 Implementation Elements for Anonymous Communication Models

We have adopted the client–server approach to implement a prototype of the distributed communication and execution model. There exists a site channel administrator and in distributed cases, sites are organized according to virtual ring architecture. The administrator is composed of two dedicated servers: an intrasite communication server and a potential network server for intersite communications (Fig. 2.15).

The local server has the role of supervising and co-ordinating communications between local processes. When a process sends a message, the local server places it in the destination process queue, if it is local. Should this happen, it submits it to its network server who will take responsibility for its transmission to the next network server in the ring. The network server unburdens the local server of the management of intersite communications.

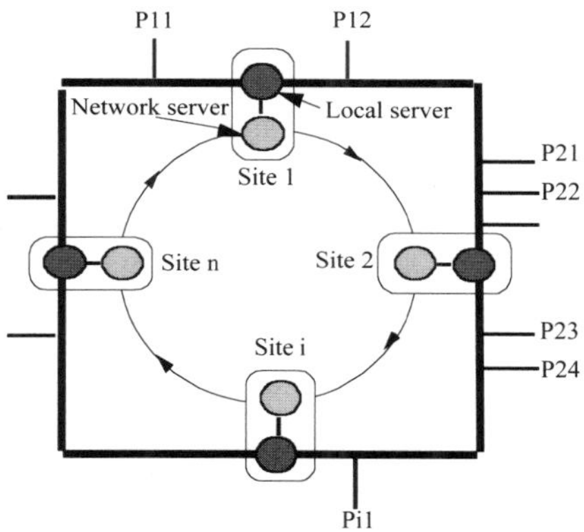

Fig. 2.15 Logic architecture of a distributed communications administrator.

When the network server receives a message from the local server, this message is for a process which is unidentified locally, but which could exist on another node. In this case, the network server transmits the message to its successor. In the case where it receives a message from its predecessor, there are two possible outcomes:

- it is an anonymous message. It verifies that the local processes have demanded its interception. In this case, it transmits a copy to the local server before reinserting it into the ring. It is the responsibility of the server who initiated the message to remove it from the ring after a complete turn;
- it is an identified message. If the destination process is a local process, it deposits it into the queue. In the opposite case, it transmits it to its successor.

2.9 Hoare Monitors: High-Level Synchronization and Communication Tools for Parallel Machines with a Global Memory

We have decided to introduce Hoare monitors in this section because they serve as basic implementation tools for server processes on parallel machines with shared global memory. They also realize communication channel administration on this type of machine, as was indicated in the preceding section (installation of anonymous communication). The use of monitors to a similar end on a single processor unit machine, under Unix for example, is not totally devoid of sense. On the contrary, monitors are the tools of high-level synchronization. They are more powerful than semaphores, and error risks are therefore relatively low.

Notion 6 Semaphore

This is an object system used to manage concurrent shared object access (a shared variable for example). A process wishing to gain access to an object protected by the semaphore u, executes the P(u) primitive. It executes V(u) when it releases it.

A u semaphore is composed of a variable counter u, a process queue and two atomic primitives $P(u)$ and $V(u)$ which respectively serve to decrease and increase the u counter via mutual exclusion. Before using a semaphore, its u counter must be initialized to a value which indicates the number of processes authorized to *simultaneously access* the object: 0 for a synchronization (rendezvous) semaphore, 1 for a mutual exclusion semaphore, n for an object which can be shared by n processes at a time (a read-out file for example). The u counter must be greater than or equal to zero. When it is zero, the execution of the $P(u)$ primitive by a process, triggers its suspension and its placement into the queue of a semaphore, because u becomes negative ($u < 0$). It will be reactivated when one of the processes, while being used by the object, executes $V(u)$ (u becomes greater than or equal to zero: $u \geq 0$) to release it. It is clear that forgetting to execute the $V(u)$ primitive following the release of the object can lead to a difficult situation, primarily waiting processes suspended in the queue of a semaphore, if the capacity of the semaphore (initial value) is equal to 1.

The basic principles of synchronization tools have been studied across a number of academic problems. The most well known is without doubt the reader–writer problem, for which it is difficult to find a priority solution with semaphores. For this type of problem it is necessary to use a queue for each condition of the problem. A semaphore solution is always possible but far too complex, especially for the management of transitions from one queue to another. To simplify the solution and for the implementation of complex problems involving priorities between different classes of processes, Brinch Hansen in 1973 and Hoare in 1974 introduced another design and synchronization tool at a higher abstraction level than semaphores: *monitors*.

Notion 7 Monitors

This is a syntactic entity (a module) which groups together synchronization variables and shared resources with the procedures which manipulate them.

A monitor avoids the dispersion of access operations to the shared variables (*P*() and *V*())in the process code. By definition, variables declared in the monitor can only by accessed by the procedures of the monitor. Among these procedures, some are internal within the monitor, others can be called from the exterior. These make up the monitor *entry points*.

Two types of synchronization are defined within a monitor:

- mutual exclusion arrived at by a default between the monitor processes. This is analogous to mutual exclusion between critical regions associated with the same variable;
- the explicit definition of synchronization variables, called condition variables, to which three primitives can be applied: `Wait`, `Signal` and `Empty`.

`Wait` expresses the wait on conditions by blocking the processes which execute this primitive in the queues associated with each condition. The `Empty` primitive tests if the queue related to a condition is empty. The `c.signal` primitive releases a process (if there is at least one) which was waiting on condition *c*. So that mutual exclusion is always tested, the process which executed the instruction `c.signal` finds itself waiting as long as there are processes active in the monitor. Each time a process is released (at the end of a procedure or execution of a `Wait` instruction), the monitor checks that there are no longer any waiting processes following a `signal` instruction, before introducing a new process waiting at an entry point. If not, one of these processes is reawakened to be executed.

The general structure of a monitor (resource allocator) is given below:

```
Monitorname: MONITOR
     begin ...declaration of data local to the monitor
     primitive primname (...formal parameters...);
     begin ... primitive body ...end;
     ... declarations of other primitives local to the monitor;
     ... initialization of local data of the monitor
     end;
```

It is important to note that a monitor can be compared to the class notion.

Notion 8 Class

This is a data structure (type of data) to which is associated a series of methods (functions) which form the only means to access and manipulate its contents (encapsulation principle). A class object is an implementation of this latter principle.

The only difference is in the execution of the class methods in the object approach, and primitives in the monitor paradigm. In monitors, mutual exclusion is *a default.* It is provided by the system (see the following section). In the object approach, the programmer using synchronization tools such as semaphores must *explicitly write* the management of concurrent access to the different objects of a class. It is, however, impossible to associate one semaphore to each class object, especially when the size is important, which is why other techniques are used, such as interlocking the whole class (the semaphore is associated with the class and not with the objects). On the other hand, a monitor has the same granularity as an object in a class. However, it is acceptable to design *generic monitors* which can be realized.

2.9.1 The Implementation of Monitors using Semaphores

To guarantee mutual exclusion between the different primitives of a monitor, a mutual exclusion semaphore initialized to 1 needs to be associated to the monitor: *mutex*. In this case, ***P(mutex)*** must be the first instruction to be executed on each monitor primitive. ***V(mutex)*** must be executed at the end of each primitive:

```
Primname(…formal parameters…);
begin P(mutex);
     begin… primitive body… end
V(mutex);
end;
```

When a process uses `signal` to trigger a condition on which another process is waiting, this process must wait until the resumed process permits it to proceed with its execution. We therefore introduce to each monitor, a second semaphore, *urgent* (initialized to 0), on which signalling processes suspend themselves by the operation ***P(urgent)***. Before achieving mutual exclusion, each process must test whether any other process is waiting on *urgent*, and if so must release it with a ***V(urgent)*** instruction.

We therefore need to count the number of processes waiting on *urgent*, using an integer *urgentcount* (initialized to 0). Thus, each exit from a monitor primitive should be coded:

```
Primname(…formal parameters…);
begin P(mutex);
begin… primitive body… end
if (urgentcount >0) V(urgent) else V(mutex);
end;
```

Finally, for each condition local to the monitor, we introduce a semaphore `condsem` (initialized to 0) on which a process desiring to wait suspends itself (in the corresponding queue) until the condition is resolved. This is done by executing a *P*(`condsem`) operation. We also need a count to enable the process triggering the condition to know if other processes are waiting on the condition. This is realized by the integer variable `condcount` (initialized to 0). In this case, `cond.Wait()` may now be implemented as follows:

```
Condcount:=condcount+1;
If urgentcount>0 then V(urgent) else V(mutex;
P(condsem);
Condcount: = condcount-1;
```

It is obligatory that a process must exit mutual exclusion before suspending itself.

The corresponding call to the `cond.signal()` primitive must respect the following sequence:

```
Urgentcount: = urgentcount + 1;
If condcount > 0 then {V(condsem) P(urgent)};
urgentcount: = urgentcount - 1;
```

The following sections show several examples which use the techniques and solutions introduced above for the implementation of monitors.

2.9.2 The Semaphore Solution to Read–Write Problems

You will recall that the Read–Write problem as specified by Hoare, respects the synchronization rules shown in Figure 2.16.

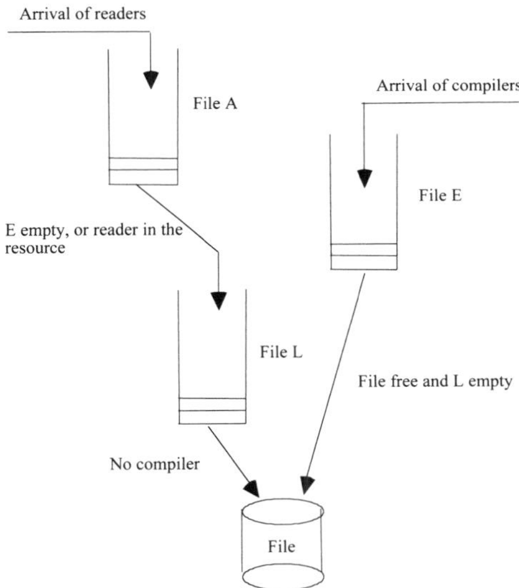

Fig. 2.16 The Hoare problem.

We now go back to the solution using semaphores. These serve as a departure point for the other solutions. In this solution:

- semaphore `E` ensures exclusive access in writing. It is initialized to 1. `P(E)` is used before each write and `V(E)` at the end. This semaphore is also modified by the first reader (to know if it is authorized) and by the last (to free access);

- semaphore `L` ensures the indivisibility of counting operations of the number of readers (the *readercount* variable is defined to this effect).

```
Reader                              Writer
P(L);                               P(E);
readercount+1;                      writer();
if readercount=1) P(E);             V(E);
V(L);
reader();
P(L);
readercount-1;
if readercount=0 V(E);
V(L);
```

It is important to note that this solution instils priority to readers over writers able to bring about the *starvation* or deprivation of writers.

2.9.3 Monitor Solution to Read–Write Problems

The monitor version of the preceding solution is as follows:

```
File manager MONITOR;
begin readercount: integer;
busy:Boolean;
OKtoread, OKtowrite: condition;
begin initialization of global monitor variables;
readercount =0;
Busy =0;
primitive startread;
     begin if busy, OKtoread.wait;
          readercount:= readercount+1;
          OKtoread.signal;
     end startread;
primitive endread;
     begin readercount:= readercount-1;
          if readercount =0 then OKtowrite.signal;
     end endread;
primitive startwrite;
     begin ;
          if readercount!0 or busy then OKtowrite.wait;
          busy:= true;
     end startwrite;
primitive endwrite;
     begin busy:=false;
          if not Oktoread.Empty; then Oktoread.signal;
          else Oktoread.signal;
     end endwrite;
end;
```

It is clear that this solution is incomplete compared to the problem presented in Figure 2.14. The following sequence provides a possible solution, which takes into account all of the synchronization rules introduced by Hoare.

```
File manager MONITOR;
     Begin;
        Waitwrite:integer =0;
        Runwrite:integer =0;
        Waitread:integer =0;
        Runread:integer =0;
A, L, E, CONDITION;

Primitive Startread;
Begin if (waitwrite busy) AND (runread busy);
        Begin A.wait; A.signal;
        End;
     If (waitwrite busy;
        Begin waitread +1;
        L.wait;
        Waitread-1;
        L.signal;
     End startread;
 Runread+1;
End;

Primitive endread;
     Begin runread-1;
        If (runread =0) AND (waitread =0);
        E.signal;
End;

Primitive startwrite;
Begin   if (waitwrite busy) OR(runread busy);
        OR (waitread busy);
     Begin waitwrite+1;
        E.wait;
        Waitwrite-1;
        End;
     Runwrite+1;
     A.signal;
End startwrite;

Primitive endwrite;
     Begin runwrite-1;
        If (waitread busy)L.signal;
            Else E.signal;
End endwrite;
End;
```

2.9.4 Example of the Implementation of a Synchronous Communication Channel

For simplification reasons, we have restricted the size of messages to one character. The example can be applied to messages of any size. All that is required is the use of a pointer table of character strings, the use of `malloc()` to allocate memory space for new messages, and `free()` for its release and return. The code for the channel monitor manager is simple enough not to require any other explanation.

```
Lostream:MONITOR;
Begin        buffer:char;
     Short clount =0;
     Nonempty,nonfull:condition;
Primitive send(char x);
Begin        if count=1,then nonfull,wait;
     Buffer: =x;
     Count: =1;
     Nonempty.signal;
End send;
Primitive receive char*x;
Begin        if count=0 then nonempty,wait;
     X: =buffer;
     Count: =0;
Nonfull.signal;
End receive;
End lostream;
```

The reader could give a more general version of this monitor (a synchronous channel):

- with a size *N* cyclic buffer;
- with a dynamic buffer by using the `malloc()` and `free()` primitives.

2.9.5 Server Processes and Monitors

A server process can be compared to an active monitor. Their shared properties are as follows:

- they are resource managers in the same way as monitors are;
- they are provided with local variables to memorize the states of the resources they manage;
- they introduce a series of requests (services) for access to these resources;

The analogy between the two paradigms is identical for these three points; however the similarities end there. The differences between monitors and process servers are as follows:

- servers are *active* processes (DAEMON under Unix);
- monitors are *passive* (the entry points, which are functions, are executed by the caller processes);
- clients communicate with the server via messages;
- clients communicate with the monitor via call procedures;
- a predicate is associated to each monitor if no client is in the process of executing one of these processes (Fig. 2.17).

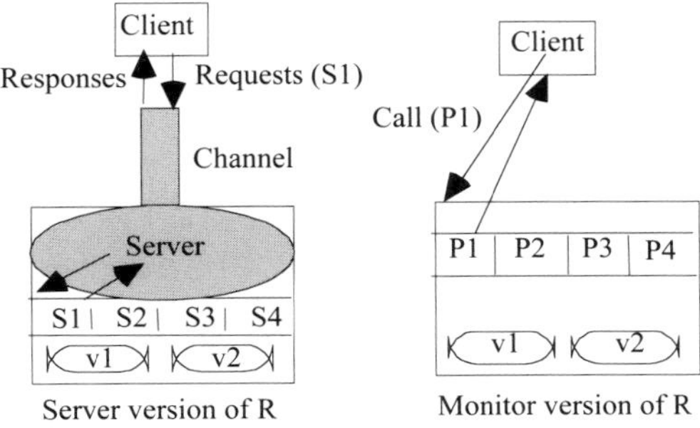

Fig. 2.17 Monitor and server version of a resource manager.

Figure 2.18 shows the monitor version of a resource allocator. Figure 2.19 shows the server version.

```
#define Maxunit 10                                  /* max number of resources*/
int units[maxunits] = 0;                             /*table of unit descriptors*/

                                                     /* internal service functions*/
int take ()
      {int i;
        for(i=0; i++; i <= Maxunits)
            if (units[i] == 0) {units[i]= 1; return(i)};
      };
return (int r)
      { units[r]= 0; };
      MONITOR allocator_R;
                                                     /* monitor predicate*/
      {[Alloc: available >= 0 ^ (available > 0) ==> empty(free)];
         int available = Maxunits;
         CONDITION free;
        Acquire ( int * id)
              { if (available == 0)free.wait()
                   else available--;
                 id = take ();
              }
        free ( int id)
              { return (id);
                 if( empty (free)) available ++
                   else free.signal();
              }
      }                                              /*end of monitor*/
```

Fig. 2.18 Monitor version of a resource allocator.

```
#define ACQUIRE 0
#define FREE1
#define Maxunits 10
#define Nbclients 100
int units[maxunits] = 0;                    /*table of unit descriptors*/
int FIFO[Nbclients];
                                       /*management of unit descriptors*/
int take ()
     {int i;
      for(i=0; i++; i <= Maxunits)
           if (units[i] == 0) {units[i]= 1; return(i)};
     };

return (int r)
     { units[r]= 0; };

                        /*Manage the queue of clients waiting for a unit */
short empty()
 { short R=0; int i; for(i=0; i++; i<= Maxunits); if (FIFO[i] <>
       0) R= 1}; return (R);
 };
insert( int e){     /* enables the number or the index of the client to be inserted into the
FIFO queue*/};
remove (){           /*enables the number of a client to be removed from the FIFO queue*/
channel request (int index; short type; int id);
channel response[1..NbClients] (int);

Allocator Process ()
     { int available = Maxunits; int index; short type; int idunit;
     while(TRUE)
     {
       receive requsts (index, type, idunit);
       case type in
          ACQUIRE:{if (available >0)
                             { available --; idunit = take();
                                send response[index] (idunit)}
                         else  insert( index);
                  }
          FREE:   {if (empty ()==0) { available ++; return (idunit}
                          else { index = remove();
                               send response[index](idunit)}}
     }
     }
Client Process [i: 1..NbClients]()
     { int idunit;
         /* acquire a unit of resource class R */
          send requests (i, ACQUIRE, 0);
          receive response[i] (idunit);
        /* resource use*/
        /* free the resource*/
          send requests(i, FREE, idunit);
     }
```

Fig. 2.19 Server version of an allocator for a class of identical resources.

Examination of the code of these two versions clearly shows that the monitor version remains the easiest to specify and by far the easiest to read. Recall, however, that monitors can only suit *centralized solutions* on one processor unit or multi-computers with a global shared memory. On the other hand, the distributed client–server solution does not rely on a hardware platform. The server offers its services to processors both on the same machine and on remote machines. The client–server version uses a structured message communication channel associated to the server. A client who needs a resource, sends an allocation request to the server in the `acquire` format. The request also contains the client transmitter process number. The server will use this number to transmit a reply through its own channel. There is therefore a specific channel which corresponds to each client, enabling it to receive the responses from the server. The descriptors (numbers) of units are regrouped into a table of "units".

When the server receives an allocation request from a client with an "index" number, if a descriptor is available, the number of the corresponding unit is transmitted to this client on its own channel (`response[index](idunit)`). Should this happen, the client number is stored in a queue managed by the FIFO technique. When a unit is released, (receives a `RELEASE` request), the server checks if the queue is empty. If it contains client numbers waiting for a unit, it removes a client number using the FIFO technique and directly transmits to it the number of the unit that has just become free. If the queue is empty, it upgrades the unit descriptor.

2.10 The Corba Norm

The Internet has been at the origin of the changes that we see in international exchanges, particularly *commercial exchanges.* It has also given second wind to object-oriented programming. In the field of data transmission method standardization, the Internet has contributed largely to the introduction of new mechanisms, such as browsers and distributed application models, which clearly indicate how technology oriented objects can be applied in a *shared global (intergalactic) context.* Distributed objects represented state of the art technology in 1997, following the emergence of three different tendencies:

- The acceptance and rapid dependency of users to thread objects, such as Sun Microsystems products which use *Java.* It is now even easier to produce and manipulate objects which represent natural processing platforms.
- The appearance in companies of a new real mode vision based largely on the notion of *components* and architecture of object-oriented applications. This principle, which involves connecting or progressively adding new functions, is applied to a wide range of hardware and applications, from *Netscape Navigator* to *Oracle's Webserver* etc. The original idea involves picturing the architecture of all of the functional components of a company as *being the same:* this is the application *interoperability* principle.

- The ultimate unifier of these applications and hardware is without doubt the uniform, intergalactic *software bus* CORBA (Common Object Request Broker Architecture: Fig. 2.20) (see Chauvet, 1997; Orfali *et al.*, 1996; Mowbray and Zahavi, 1995; Sessions, 1996; Object-Oriented Concepts Inc., 1998). CORBA enables every object to locate and interact with any other object on any other network, without having to know its geographical position: CORBA enables the implementation of applications without being concerned with communication problems. With CORBA the implementation of true distributed applications interoperable on a global scale is, in this way, in the process of becoming reality.

Notion 9 Software Bus (ORB)

This is a group of modules and software libraries which enable any object (application) to locate and integrate with any other object on any other network, without having to know its geographical position or the type of communication network.

The notion of objects is appealing. Distributed objects can contribute to the *unification and harmonization* of application architectures, a direct consequence of which is an increase in software productivity and the compatibility of execution platforms. Designers can easily develop, use or reuse the components of applications or distributed software, which interact independently of hardware or software platforms and the network. The objects enable the designer to add important functions, such as remote interactive access using a Java terminal and real-time active objects.

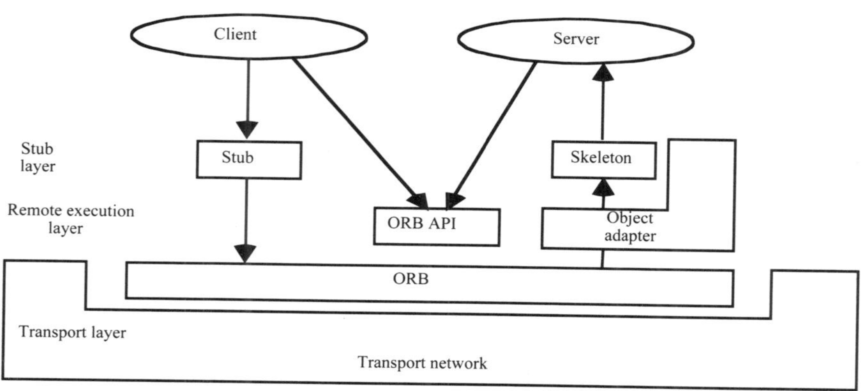

Fig. 2.20 The CORBA model.

2.10.1 From the RPC Model to CORBA Distributed Objects

Two basic models marked the end of the 1980s: the *client-server architecture model*, which is itself based on the *remote execution model, RPC* (remote procedure call). During this period, object-oriented programming was mostly supported by the C++ language. The software became one of the more determining factors in the global performance of the system, more so than the hardware or the communication network. In spite of these two basic models, distributed system software architecture still remains subject to serious constraints. In the RPC remote execution model, the caller process (client) assumes that the server uses *the same communication protocol, the same language*, and is supported by *an identical system environment.* The two co-operating entities communicate via network addresses (sockets). With the CORBA model, the entities will be able to communicate using *object references* (Fig. 2.21).

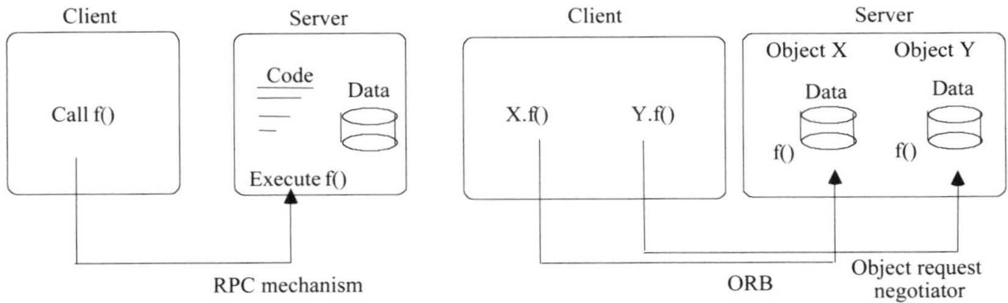

Fig. 2.21 The RPC mechanism and method execution mechanism.

We are currently witnessing major changes in the construction of distributed application architecture. The basic distribution principles of the client–server model are combined with the perspectives of a new abstraction called *distributed-object computing*, which uses the services of an intergalactic object bus (Fig. 2.21).

Figure 2.22 reflects the different components required to implement an intergalactic bus to CORBA standards. It is important to note that the bus is built using two protocols: GIOP and IIOP. The GIOP protocol (general inter-ORB protocol) is a generic transmission request protocol which ensures the interconnection of the CORBA bus. It defines a common data representation (CDR), a format of interoperable object references (IOR), and a group of object request transmission messages (Request, Reply, etc.). This generic protocol must be instanced on the network used. For example, the IIOP protocol is the specialization of GIOP over TCP/IP.

2.10.2 OMG-IDL (Interface Definition Language)

This enables the specification of types manipulated by a set of distributed applications in the form of a contract. A contract therefore shows the communication protocol between the manufacturers and the service users, while at the same time separating the interface and the establishment of objects. The main use of an IDL contract is to render transparent the problems related to the interoperability, heterogeneity and physical location of objects.

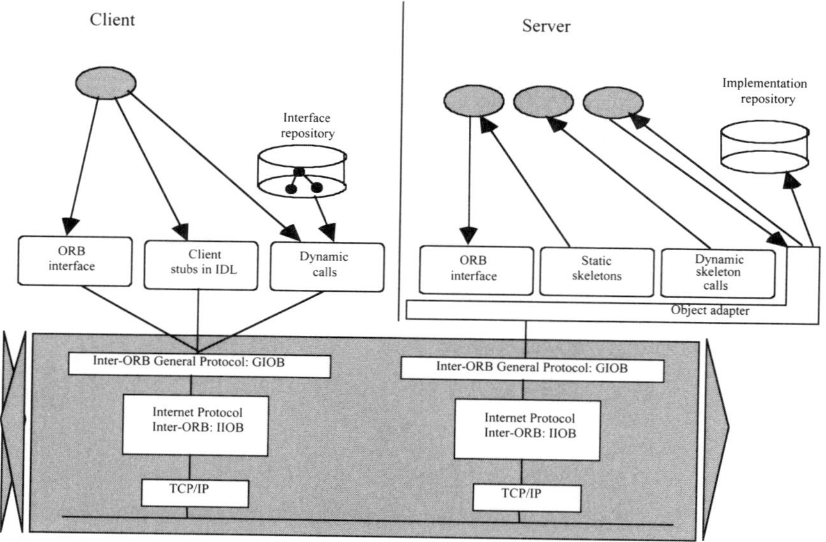

Fig. 2.22 The overall architecture of a CORBA ORB 2.0.

Notion 10 IDL Contracts

This is a specification of object (method signatures) and data types (attributes) manipulated by a set of distributed applications. It enables object interface and establishment to be separated, which ensures the independence of client applications and the server application from the software and hardware infrastructure, forming a connection across the software bus.

The use of the IDL contract to link a client application which solicits the services of a server, is indicated by the contract being shown in IDL stubs (or SII – static interface invocation) in the client's programming environment, and in IDL skeletons (or the SSI – static skeleton interface) in the manufacturer's programming environment (Fig. 2.23). Chapter 10 presents several simple ideas for the implementation of a software bus, especially the implementation of stubs (Fig. 10.5).

The stubs are automatically formed by the IDL language compiler. They encapsulate the necessary code for the construction of requests which will be carried by the bus, then delivered to the IDL skeletons which will delegate them to the server.

Notion 11 IDL Client Stubs

These provide the static interfaces which have the role of proxy on behalf of a remote server object. They allow the requested operation, as well as its parameters, to be encoded and decoded, into a known message format to transmit to the server. At the server end, the stubs are called skeletons.

The stubs also enable *include* files to be included in the messages; these are needed to enable the execution of the method requested by a higher language (C, C++ etc.). Thus, they render themselves completely transparent to the underlying protocols and data packaging problems. To obtain a remote service, *a method must be called from the program.* The services are defined with the help of the IDL language, and the client and server stubs are generated by the IDL compiler. It is compulsory for a client to possess one IDL stub for each interface that it uses on the server.

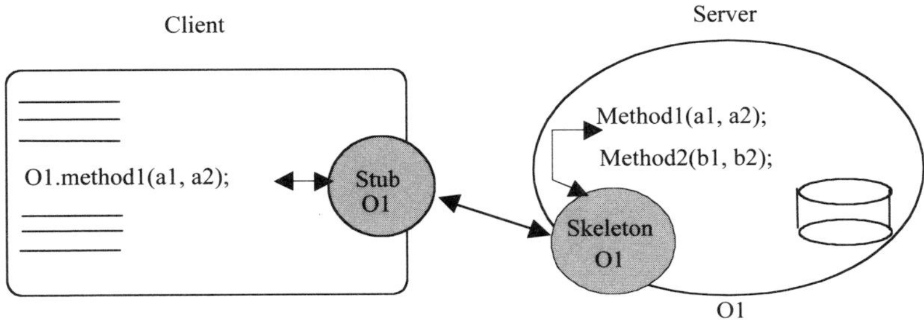

Fig. 2.23 Transparency of the physical locality between the client and the server.

2.10.3 The Different Bus Libraries or Interfaces

Dynamic Invocation Interfaces (DII)

CORBA proposes API (primitive) standards to consult the metadata which define the service, generate the parameters, emit the call and collect the results (Fig. 2.24).

Interface Repository APIs

The interface repository (interface dictionary) is a database that holds the executable versions of interfaces defined in IDL. Consequently, APIs are CORBA primitives which enable the interrogation and update of this database.

The ORB Interface

This is a set of CORBA service primitives which enable the conversion of an object reference into a string of characters and *vice versa.*

Server IDL Stubs

Server IDL stubs manufacture the static interfaces (written in IDL) for each service exported by the server.

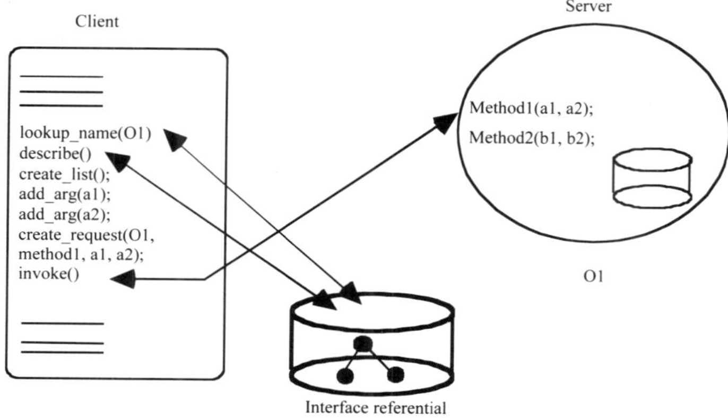

Fig. 2.24 Dynamic invocation primitives for remote objects.

Dynamic Skeleton Interface (DSI: CORBA 2.0)

In contrast to ordinary compiled skeletons, which are defined by a particular class of objects (an establishment for each method declared), dynamic skeletons are more generous and allow the management of incoming method calls to components that do not possess skeletons.

The Basic Object Adapter (BOA)

The BOA plays the role of an active manager (lookout process) which enables the necessary execution environment to be produced to instance server objects, and communicates to them the demands of the clients. It attributes object identifiers (object references) or ID to the different server instances.

Notion 12 The Basic Object Adapter (BOA)

This is the abstract CORBA receiving entity (installation), enabling an object to understand how to manage and interpret object references, to know the current installation associated with an object, to know how to delegate requests to objects at their installation, and to know how to activate an installation for an object if one does not exist.

The Basic Object Adapter enables the isolation of the bus of different technologies able to act as support for the installation of the welcoming entity. There are several types of adapters:

- POA (Portable Object Adapter): the installation of objects is realized by objects which have a programming language;
- BOA (Basic Object Adapter): receiving entities are indicated by system resources (processes).

- LOA (Library Object Adapter): the installation code for objects is stored in full libraries in the client application memory;
- OODA (Object-Oriented Database Adapter): the receiving structure is an object-oriented database.

The basic object adapter is situated above the communication centre. It is responsible for the administration and management of the classes (databases: implementation repositories) that it supports, and their execution instances. Several of the services provided by the adapter are shown below:

- Recording new server classes in the implementation repository.
- Activating an object by creating a new process, or a new thread in an existing process, or by using a thread or a process which already exists:
  - the activation process to a shared server (one process supports several objects at the same time);
  - the activation process to a non-shared server (a process/object);
  - the activation process to a method server (a process/method);
  - the activation process to a persistent server (a unique process or scheduler manages the activation of each object).
- Generation and management of repository object.
- Service broadcasting.

The Implementation Repository

This is a database system which holds information on the classes that a server supports, instanced objects and their ID. It contains other information relating to audit books, security and other administrative data.

The ORB Interface

This is a set of system primitives for local services.

Shared Object Facilities (service utilities)

These utilities are necessary for the implementation of interoperability between objects. They offer a dynamic, constant view of the environment:

- *Naming facility:* enables objects to be located using their name (i.e. the white pages of the telephone directory);
- *Selling facility*: advertises available objects (i.e. yellow pages);
- *Life facility:* enables objects to be created, moved and destroyed;
- *Events facility:* management of events (asynchronous mode) between objects;

- *Transaction facility:* management of transaction atomicity;
- *Parallel access facility, persistence facility etc.*

2.10.4 Distributed-Object Computing

It is clear from the preceding sections that the client–server model currently used for the implementation of distributed applications in companies, will undergo a radical change. The concept of *bilateral interactions* in the client–server model, which is supported by the remote procedure call, will be replaced by the concept of *distributed facilities*. From then on, in a distributed system, the client will be able to emit *facility requests* and not *processing requests*.

2.10.5 Rollout for the Implementation of a CORBA Application

The following example shows how to implement a simple distributed service using CORBA. The aim of the service is to enable clients to archive (historical) messages (important events) in a unique object. This facility is supported by a simple CORBA object representing a journal. In the following sections, we show the different stages currently used to implement a CORBA application. The code given involves the CORBA ORBacus bus (Object-Oriented Concepts Inc., 1998) that has the advantage of being free. Nevertheless, the application remains easily applicable to other buses.

2.10.5.1 The Definition of an IDL Contract

In this stage, an object-oriented method (i.e. UML) is used to identify the different objects (components) of the application from specifications. In this case, we have only one object: `journal`. The interface of this facility (CORBA object) is defined in independent programming language (IDL-OMG) as follows:

```
#pragma prefix "llp.fr"     /*definition of the organization specifying the IDL contract*/
#module journal {                 /*regrouping of definitions common to one service*/
typedef string Content                    /*defines the design content of a message*/
typedef sequence<Content> OfMessages                              /*set of messages*/
     typedef string Identifier          /*defines the identifier design of a message*/
     typedef enum Nature {                          /*enumeration of message types*/

ordinary, secret, topSecret
     } ;
     typedef short Year ;                         /*a year is coded by a 16-bit integer*/
     enum Month {                                            /*enumeration of months*/
January, February, March, April, May, June, July, August,
               September, October, November, December
     } ;
     typedef unsigned short Day ;           /*a day is coded by an integer of 16bits
                                            unsigned*/

     struct Date {                          /*structure definition the notion of date*/
```

```
            Day the_day ;
            Month the_month ;
            Year the_year ;
      }
      struct Message {               /*information associated with an archived message*/
            Identifier ident ;                                        /*its identifier*/
            Nature type ;                                                   /*its type*/
            Date stamp ;                                                   /*its stamp*/
            Content valueMessage ;                                       /*its content*/
      } ;
   interface historical {
      readonly attribute string word;
      exception ExistsAlready { Identifier ident ;};
      void stocker(in Message the_message) raises (ExistsAlready);
      Message ReadMessage (in Identifier ident) raises (Unfound) ;
      TheMessages listMessages() ;
   };
   } ;
```

The application contract is grouped together in the journal module. The `historical` interface provides the `word` attribute, which informs on the content of the journal and the operations used to store, read and list messages. The `ExistsAlready` exception allows the signalling of an exceptional case that occurs when a message, which already exists in the journal, is deposited. The `Unfound` exception is generated when an attempt at reading a message fails.

The section of this contract on pre-compilers (see Chapter 10) enables the automatic generation of stubs and skeletons using a given signal language: C++, Java, COBOL etc.

2.10.5.2 Journal Installation

The `journal` object will be implemented by a Java class. It could, of course, be implanted with another language such as C++; however, the projection of the IDL contract for the journal by the pre-compiler produces the Java package `fr.llp.journal`. The installation of the contract using a Java class `historicalInst` therefore goes through a specialization (legacy) of the `abstract_historicalInstBase` class generated by the pre-compiler. This latter class contains the basics for implanting the journal. Consequently, the installation of the journal amounts to implanting the attribute and the IDL operations. We use a simple table to store the messages of the journal. The reader could use serialization or Java DataBase Connectivity (JDBC) Java libraries to realize a persistent version of the journal. We also assume that the reader is familiar with the Java language.

```
Public class historicalInst extendfr.llp.journal._historicalInstBase
{
protected String the_word ;          /*installation of the word attribute protected*/
 java.util.Hashtable messages ;                         /*installation of messages*/
public historicalInst (String the_word)
{
     this.the_word = the_word ;
     this.messages = new java.util.Hastable() ;
 }
```

```
public String word ()
{
     return this. the_word ;
}

public void stocker(fr.llp.Journal.Message message)
     throws fr.llp.Journal.historicalPackage.ExistsAlready
{
     if (this.messages.containsKey(message.ident) )
throw new fr.llp.Journal.historicalPackage.ExistsAlready(message
ident) ;
     this.messages.put(message.ident, message) ;
}
public fr.llp.Journal.Message ReadMessage( String identif)
          throws fr.llp.Journal.historicalPackage.Unfound
{
fr.llp.Journal.MessagePT(fr.llpJournal.Message)this.message.get(ide
nt)
      if (PT == nil)
          throw new
fr.llp.Journal.historicalPackage.Unfound(ident) ;
     return PT
}
public String [] listMessage()
{
     String [] OfMessages = new String[this.messages.size()] ;
     Int i = 0 ;
     For (java.util.Enumeration elt = this.messages.keys() ;
     elt.hasMoreElements() ; i++) {
          OfMessages[i] = (String) elt.nextElement() ;
          }
     return OfMessages;
      }
 }
```

It is important to remember that this code is totally applicable to other CORBA/ Java installations, both source and binary.

2.10.5.3 Implementation of a Client Application

This involves a processing example (client) which triggers the operations of an object journal. The client displays the wording of the journal, adds a "`secret`" type message and displays the contents. It is clear that this process is completely independent of any installation and physical location of the journal. It is also possible to use the C++ process on the Java installation, or vice versa.

IDL interfaces are represented by Java interfaces (`fr.llp.journal. historical`). Any invocation of IDL operations must use the notation aimed at calling Java methods. IDL structures are represented by Java classes, and are dynamically allocated. Similarly, the standard Java mechanism is responsible for IDL exceptions. Finally, IDL enumeration is represented by classes that contain a static form attribute, one for each element of the enumeration. This class also contains an operation for conversion into an integer (value):

```
static   void    ProcessClient(fr.llp.journal.historical
      historical)
             throws Exception

String [] MONTH = {"Jan ", "Feb", "Mar", "Apr", "May", "Jun",
"Jul", "Aug",, "Sep", "Oct", "Nov", "Dec"} ;

String word = historical.word() ;
System.out.println("Journal Word : " + word) ;

Fr.llp.journal.Message      message      =         new
fr.llp.journal.Message() ;
message.ident = "XM08TR" ;
message.type = "secret" ;
message.stamp = new fr.llp.journal.Date( (short)1,
                        fr.llp.journal.Month.January, (Short) 2000)
                  ;
try {
    historical.stocker( message) ;
} catch (fr.llp.journal.historicalPackage.ExistsAlready attention)
{
  System.out.println("ATTENTION : Year 2000 has already gone") ;
}

String [] identMessages = historical.listMessages()
;
For (int i=0, i < messages.length ; i++) {
     message                                          =
historical.readMessage(identMessages[i]) ;
     System.out.println("Identifier :       "           +
message.ident) ;
     fr.llp.journal.Date d = message.stamp ;
     System.out.println("Date of message : "            +
d.the_day + " " +
     MONTH[d.le_month.value()] + " " + d.the_year) ;
     System.out.println("Identifier :       "           +
message.ident) ;
}
 }
```

Now that client processing has been described, the client itself remains to be created. The design of the client, in the same way as that of the server, is mainly based on the ORB interface. This interface, which models the CORBA bus, is made up of a set of primitives that enable the behaviour of the bus to be controlled, the creation of access objects and the manipulation of the different components of the bus, the conversion of the IOR (interoperable object reference) of an object reference into a string of characters and vice versa (i.e. object_to_string and string_to_object) and to obtain "recognized" object references (i.e. list_initial_services and resolve_initial_references). Finally, the initialization of the bus or ORB object is also carried out by a primitive of this interface: ORB_init.

The main model for a client application is as follows:

1. Initialize the CORBA bus by creating the ORB object; (1)

2. Obtain the object references used by the client application ; (2)
3. Client processing and use of obtained objects; (3)

In this case, the final code for the client application is:

```
Import fr.llp.Journal.*

Public class ClientJournal
{
     public static void main(String args[]) {

       try {
                    /*initialization of CORBA bus for a client process*/
                                  /*creation of ORB system objects*/

org.omg.COBRA.ORB orb = org.omg.COBRA.init (args, null);    (1)

                  /*Instantiation of a Java stub referencing the object repertoire*/
     org.omg.CORBA.object objet = orb.string_to_object(arg[0]);
(2.1)
     historical journal = historicalHelper.narrow (objet)
     (2.2)
     ProcessClient (journal);
     (3)

/*It is necessary to intercept the exceptions generated by the bus primitives, in case of problems*/
     } catch(org.omg.CORBA.SystemException e) {
        System.err.println(" Error System : " + e) ;
 }
}
}
```

Note that in the IDL/Java projection, the `narrow` operator of the `historical` interface was stored in the Java class `historicalHelper` and not in the `historical` Java interface, because a *Java interface cannot contain the code.*

2.10.5.4 Server Implementation

In a general way, server programming always follows the following format:

1. Initialization of the CORBA bus which results in the creation of the ORN object;
2. Initialization of the object adapter;
3. Creation of object installation(s);
4. Recording of the installation(s) near to the object adapters;
5. Broadcast of client application object reference(s);
6. Wait for object requests.

The application of this main format to our case gives:

```
Import fr.llp.Journal.*
Public class serverJournal
{
```

```
public static void (String args[])
 {
   try {
/*Initialization of the CORBA bus for a server process*/
/*Creation of ORB and BOA system objects.*/
     org.omg.COBRA.ORB orb = org.omg.COBRA.init (args, null) ;
     (1)
     org.omg.COBRA.BOA boa = org.BOA_init (args, null) ;
     (2)

/*Creation of the Journal object*/
     historicalImp journal = new historicalImpl("llp") ;
     (3)+(4)

/*Obtain the IOR of the object in text format*/
     String stringIOR = orb.object_to_string (journal) ;
     (5)

/*Place the server process in wait for requests coming from the CORBA bus*/
     boa.impl_is_ready(null)
     //(6)

/*It is necessary to intercept the exceptions generated by bus primitives, in case of problems*/
     } catch(org.omg.CORBA.SystemException e) {
      System.err.println(" Error System : " + e) ;
  }
}
```

The ORB initialization operation is found in the `org.ormg.CORBA.ORB` class and not in the `org.ormg.CORBA` package because a Java package cannot directly contain a Java method.

2.10.6 Several ORBs

We end this chapter with a non-exhaustive list of several ORBs.

IONA Orbix

Orbix2.0 (1995) provides a C++ interface for CORBA1.2 (interface repository, installation repository, IDL pre-compiler and elementary object adapter, static calls, dynamic method calls, etc.) and is supported by several platforms. Orbix is implemented in the form of two libraries, one for the client and the other for the server. It also includes a server activation *daemon*. It uses TCP/IP as a transmission layer.

OBJECTBROKER

Digital's OBJECTBROKER2.5 is conformed to Microsoft's CORBA and OLE/COM. It is mainly used in financial establishments, and uses TCP/IP and sockets. It provides all the functions of CORBA1.2: interface repository, installation repository, IDL pre-compiler, object adapter, static or dynamic method calls, C interface and

CORBA naming facility. It is supported by several platforms: Windows, MacOs, OS/2, SunOS, HP-UX, AIX etc.

SOM

IBM's SOM (System Object Model) is available in a product called SOM Objects 2.1. It is probably the most important CORBA ORB on the market due to its direct relation with OpenDoc. It provides the object bus that conforms to CORBA, which supports OpenDoc, and is delivered with each copy of OS/2 Warp, MacOs and AIX. It is produced by CI Labs and Novell on all versions of Windows, SOM will become the first ORB installed in bulk. SOM2.1 is based on CORBA1.2.

DOE

DOE (Distributed Objects Everywhere) from Sun is based on CORBA1.2, and is executed on Sun platforms on TCP/IP.

ORB Plus

ORB Plus1.0 from HP is a CORBA1.2 ORB that uses the RPC mechanism of DCE and TCP/IP. It will only execute under HP-UX.

2.11 Conclusion

In this chapter, we have tried to make the reader aware of the problems which currently form the subject of advanced research, especially those posed by high level distributed programming languages. The aim is to enable the user to write an application in terms of concurrent processes communicating through the exchange of messages via communication channels. Location of the different processes as well as the physical methods used to realize communication channels, need no longer be one of the problems to resolve to be able to implement the distributed application.

From this point of view, we have presented the different interaction models that could help the user to efficiently structure and organize the different entities of the application. To this end we have proposed a distributed programming formalism which can act as a basis for the implementation of this type of language. Several indications of the tools and means which can be used to reach this aim have been provided, and we have also shown that for concurrent distributed programming on one processor unit or multiprocessors, Hoare monitors remain a powerful tool to express the synchronization and management of concurrent entry points. This is on condition that a single transcoder, whose application rules have been declared, is implemented. These monitors may be used effectively to establish specific introduced concepts, especially channels. This does, however, involve a simple proposition to facilitate the programmer's task, challenging neither the efficiency nor the idea of other tools and techniques (sockets, semaphores, shared segments, Unix pipes and so on).

Chapter 3 will be devoted to the presentation of an existing distributed programming tool: PVM (Parallel Virtual Machine). PVM is a series of primitive libraries that can be used in a standard programming language (C, Fortran, etc.) in the field of distributed application development. PVM enables the user to see a network of Unix machines interconnected as one large parallel machine. This tool has the distinctive feature of being available free for several versions.

In Chapter 4, we will present a more standard use of the client–server model with the help of Unix sockets. The sockets represent a communication tool between processes (IPC) available under Unix. This presentation will be completed in Chapter 7, with an example of the application type: "establishment of a temporal constraints manager for real-time applications". However, these sockets remain a *low-level tool*, the same as semaphores. They require much *attention*, and more *precision* to be able to accurately realize a distributed application with this tool.

3. *PVM: Parallel Programming Tools*

PVM started out as a research project initiated in 1989 by Oak Ridge National Laboratory (ORNL) in the United States. Since then, the project has taken another turn, and other organizations and research laboratories have become involved (ORNL, University of Tennessee, Carnegie Mellon University and Pittsburgh Supercomputing Centre at Emory University, Atlanta). The research carried out on this project is funded mainly by the research programme in applied mathematics by the American Energy Research Laboratory, the American Department of Energy, the American National Foundation for Science and Tennessee State. This series of software tools is available free to the world scientific community, in the interests of scientific research.

3.1 PVM Presented

PVM (parallel virtual machine) is a series of software tools aimed at facilitating multi-agent distributed programming on heterogeneous Unix machines (sequential, parallel or supercomputers), interconnected via a network. These machines can be PCs under Linux or SCO, Unix stations, or even parallel computers or supercomputers connected up to the network. PVM enables the user to see all of the machines as if they form the CPU (processor) network of a huge virtual multiprocessor computer lacking a shared global memory (Fig. 3.1), similar to transputer machines. Each Unix machine in the network is called the *host* of the virtual parallel machine. It will therefore be possible to share the processes of an application requiring a large computation (large simulation programs, multi-agent distributed applications in A.I, image processing applications, complex multimedia applications, etc.) between the different machines available on the network. In this chapter, the term virtual machine will designate this series of interconnected machines.

PVM proposes primitives for:

- initialization and automatic triggering of tasks on the virtual machine;
- establishing communication between tasks;
- synchronization between tasks, etc.

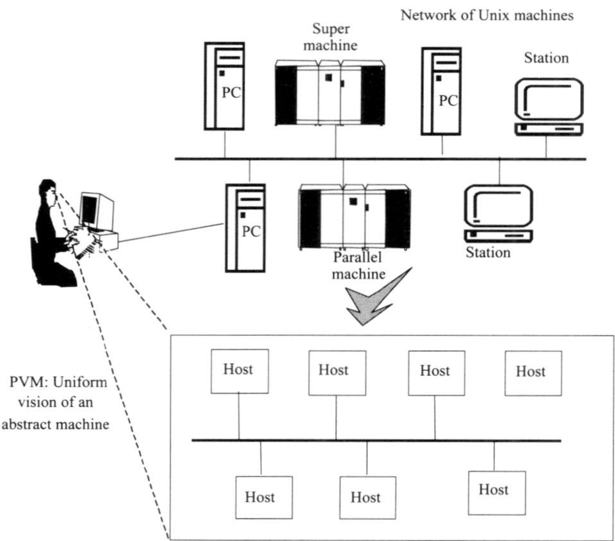

Fig. 3.1 Parallel virtual machines.

With PVM, a task constitutes the unit of refinement of a distributed application. Recall that a distributed application is composed of a series of tasks or agents communicating via the exchange of messages. Each task fulfils a specific function conforming to the general semantics of the distributed application. PVM offers facilities which allow the implementation of the majority of interaction and execution models seen in the preceding chapters (Fig. 3.2).

PVM supports heterogeneity at the application, machine and network levels. In doing this, it enables the tasks of an application to profit from the available architecture, to find the best possible organization and structure for the application. This particularly occurs with the allocation of tasks with high CPU time consumption to machines within the network which possess the required capabilities. PVM supports all types of necessary data conversion to allow the exchange of data between machines using different internal representations (words, integers, floating points). It also enables the interconnection of *hosts* to the virtual machine using different network types (Ethernet, token, packet transmission: Transpac, or simply line series). A PVM system is composed of two parts:

1. The distributed execution kernel (see DES in Chapter 1). This is supported by a DAEMON Unix process: pvm3 or simply pvmd. This process is present or duplicated on all hosts of the virtual machine. The pvm3 kernel was designed in this way so that any Unix system user could install it without difficulty on this machine.

2. User interface or PVM primitives library (libpvm.3). This contains the routines or functions that can be used in user programs to create tasks and establish communication between them, to co-ordinate and synchronize tasks and for

the modification of the virtual machine, etc. It is clear that editing application links or user programs must be done using this library. This exists in various programming languages, especially C and Fortran77.

When a user wishes to execute a PVM application, they must first create a PVM machine with the `PVM` command by pointing out its *host* machines. The PVM application can then be triggered from any *host* machine within the virtual machine.

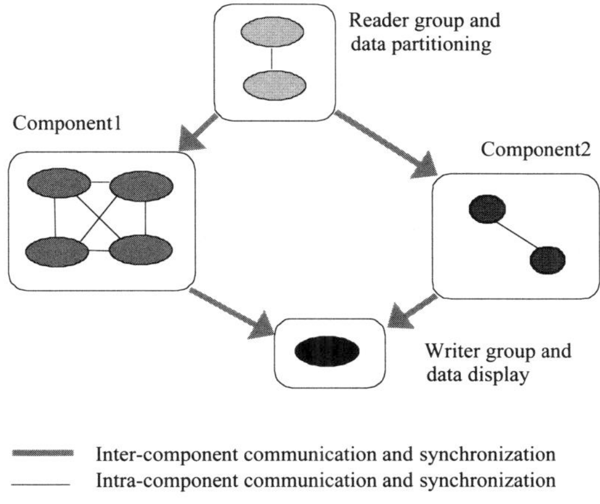

Fig. 3.2 PVM execution model.

It is important to note that several virtual machines, and consequently several PVM applications belonging to different users, can exist together on the network.

Before presenting the different PVM possibilities, the following section outlines the principal characteristics of PVM version 3: PVM3.

3.2 PVM Installation

As we have already mentioned, any Unix machine user has the option to install PVM. This operation is therefore not the privilege of the super user (the system administrator). However, only one person is needed to install PVM for all of the potential machine network users. Figure 3.3 gives the name used by PVM to designate the execution platforms or the machines supported by PVM3.3.

3.2.1 How to Obtain PVM

There are several ways of obtaining PVM software and the corresponding documentation. The user guide, PVM3 sources, "man" pages, XPVM and other annexe tools are available on *Netlib*. Netlib is a distribution service for software available on the Internet. By sending e-mail to: netlib@ornl.gov with the message: "send xnetlib.shar from xnetlib" an X-Window interface is received which enables the user to:

- access Netlib;
- cover the arborescence of all of the available software tools;
- automatically gather software.

PVM_ARCH	Machine	Operating system
AFX8	Alliiant FX/8	
ALPHA	DEC Alpha	DEC OSF-1
BAL	Sequent Balance	DYNIX
BFLY	BBN Butterfly TC2000	
BSD386	80386/486 Unix box	DSDI
CM2	Thinking Machine CM2	Sun front-end
CM5	Thinking Machine CM5	
CNVX	Convex C-series	
CNVXN	Convex C-series	Native mode
CRAY	C-90, YMP	UNICOS
CRAY2	Cray-2	
CRAYSMP	Cray-S-MP	
DGAV	Data General Avion	
E88K	Encore 88000	
HP300	HP-9000 model 300	HPUX
HPPA	HP-9000 PA-RISC	
I860	Intel iPSC/860	Link-lrpc
IPSC2	Intel iPSC/2 860 host	SysV
KSR1	Kendall Square KSR-1	OSF-1
LINUX	80386/486 box	LINUX
MASPAR	MASPAR host	
MIPS	MIPS 4680	
NEXT	NeXT	
PGON	Intel Paragon	link-lrpc
PMAX	DECstation 3100, 5100	Ultix
RS6K	IBM/RS6000	AIX
RT	IBM RT	
SGI	Silicon Graphics	IRIX 4.X
SGI5	Silicon Graphics	IRIX 5.1
SUN3	Sun 3	SunOS 4.2
SUN4	Sun 4, SPARCstation	SunOS 4.2
SUN4SOL2	Sun 4, SPARCstation	Solaris 4.2
SYMM	Sequent Symmetry	
U370	IBM 370	AIX
UVAX	DEC Micro Vax	

Fig. 3.3 Hardware platforms supporting PVM.

Another way involves connecting to the ftp server cs.utk.edu pub/xnetlib in *anonymous* mode and collecting this interface. Otherwise, use the "Mosaic" or "Netscape" navigation software on the Internet to access the following w3 server: http://www.epm.ornl.gov/pvm/.

Once the source files (about 1 Moctet) have been downloaded, it is necessary to decompress and install them, which is a relatively simple procedure. For more information on this procedure the reader can refer to the PVM user manual.

3.2.2 Creation of a Virtual Machine

PVM uses a particular daemon process called "pvm" as a process of control and supervision of virtual machines (Fig. 3.4), and is better known under the process name of "PVM console". This process enables the user to launch a virtual machine, to question the machine status, and to modify the configuration or structure of a machine. It is the interpretation of the commands of the virtual machine which, overall, reminds the user of Unix commands.

The console process can be activated and deactivated several times without affecting the functioning of the machine or the active applications.

Once activated on a network machine, the *pvm* process checks if the kernel process *pvmd* is active on this machine. If it is not active, it automatically launches the configuration options and the list of hosts of the virtual machine using *pvmd*. The following command is used to launch the *pvm* process:

```
pvm [hostfile]
```

Once activated, the PVM console process attaches its prompt (welcome string):

```
pvm>
```

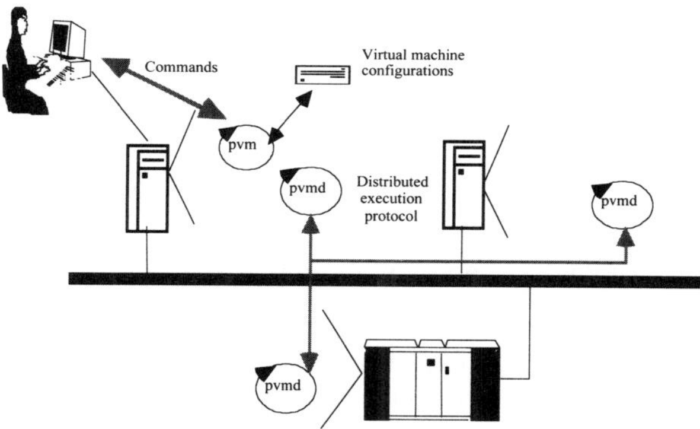

Fig. 3.4 The daemon process of a PVM virtual machine.

From this point, it can accept a certain number of commands. Among these commands are found:

- `add` <list_hostnames>: enables the addition of specified hosts to the virtual machine;
- `conf`: provides the list of hosts for the virtual machine;
- `delete` <list_hostnames>: eliminates the hosts from the machine lists;
- `halt`: terminates all the PVM process and those composed of *pvm* and stops PVM;
- `kill`: enables a process to be terminated;
- `ps-a`: provides the list of all the active PVM processes;
- `spawn` <options>: initializes the execution of a PVM distributed application; Among the options are found:
  - `count`: the number of tasks the application has, this is 1 by default;

- (host): the host where execution must start. Any machine on the network can do this by default;
- (pvm_arch): the type of machines which must be selected;

For more information of the different pvm options, see the PVM user manual.

To end this section, here are several indications of the contents of the *hostfile* file. This file contains the list of hosts that make up the initial configuration of a virtual machine. It also holds information on the *host* machines that the user can also add to the configuration if they wish (the use of the pvm add command). It is important to note that *only one person may install PVM for all of the potential network users. But each user must define the configuration of their own virtual machine according to the specific requirements of their application*, using the *hostfile* intermediate. Figure 3.5 shows the contents of a *hostfile* file, which describes one configuration for a virtual machine.

Several options are available. Among these are:

- **lo**=userid: enables the user to define another login for a machine. By default, it is the login that was used on the initial machine which will be used.
- **so**=pw: indicates to PVM that it must request the password for this machine. This option is mostly used in cases where the user has several logins and passwords on the network machines. PVM uses the Unix command rsh() to remotely launch pvmd daemons. Where pw is specified, PVM uses the rexec() command.
- **dx**=pvm_access_path: this indicates the access path of the PVM index if the location by default has not been retained on this machine.
- **ep**=search_index: provides the list of indexes to search to find the files of programs to be executed.
- **Sp**=value: gives the execution speed of the machine.

```
# the comment lines start with #
ipsc dx=/home/attoui/pvm3/i860/pvmd3
sp.isima.fr  lo=attoui so=pw

# the specification of options is done using the * character
* ep=/home1/ammar/problem1
libd1.univ-bpclermont.fr
libd2.univ-bpclermont.fr

# replace the default options with specific options
for the following machines
* lo=ammar so=pw ep=problem1
isma.isima.fr
jil.univ-bpclermont.fr

# machines to add later are specified
with the character &
& pc1.isima.fr ep=problem1
& sungi01 dx=/usr/local/bin/pvmd3
```

Fig. 3.5 Definition of one configuration of a virtual machine.

3.3 The User Interface or PVM Primitives

In this section we give a summary of the PVM primitives. We follow the same structure as that used in the user manual for PVM version 3.3. The primitives will be introduced in order of functionality and type.

In PVM, the task identifier (*tid*) is provided by the local PVM kernel. This is a perfect analogy with the idea of a process descriptor under Unix and its identifier (*pid*). However, there is a substantial difference between the two types of descriptors. The PVM task descriptor has information on the location of the process in the virtual machine. This facilitates the management of message routing and communication.

Figure 3.6 shows a simple example of a PVM program (*hello1*) which proves the basic concepts of PVM programming. This program is designed to be activated manually by the interpretation of commands. It starts by attaching the *tid* (task identifier) of the task (`pvm_mytid()`). It then launches the execution of another program called (*hello2*), using the `pvm_spawn()` primitive. If the activation of this latter is carried out correctly, *hello1* calls for the blocking `pvm_recv()` primitive to await a message from *hello2*. Having received this message, *hello1* attaches its *tid* to the message received. The content of the message is extracted and decompressed by the intermediary `pvm_upkstr()` primitive. Finally, *hello1* leaves the PVM environment by executing the `pvm_exit()` primitive.

```
        /* program Hello1.c  */
#include "pvm3.h"

main()
{
int cc, tid, msgtag;
char buf[ 100] ;

printf ("In am the tid task= t%x\n",
pvm_mytid());

cc = pvm_spawn("Hello2", (char**)0, 0, "",
1, &tid);

if (cc == 1) {
    msgtag = 1;
    pvm_recv(tid, msgtag);
    pvm_upkstr(buf);
    printf("a message of:%x\n, tid, buf);
    } else
    printf("impossible to activate
    hello2\n");
pvm_exit();
}
```

```
        /* program hello3.c
#include "pvm3.h"

main()
{
int ptid, msgtag;
char buf[ 100] ;

ptid = pvm_parent();

strcopy(buf, "hello from the
machine");
gethostname(buf + strlen(buf), 64);
         msgtag = 1;
pvm_initsend(PvmDataDefault);
pvm_pkstr(buf);
pvm_send(ptid, msgtag);

pvm_exit();

}
```

Fig. 3.6 A simple example of a PVM application.

In the *hello2* program, which is the slave of *hello1 (activated by hello1)*, the first action involves obtaining the *tid* of its master (*hello1*) by using the `pvm_ parent()` primitive. It then requests the name of the machine on which it is running, and transmits it to *hello1* with the three successive calls:

- `pvm_init()` to initialize the transmission buffer,
- `pvm_pkstr()` to transform the character string into an independent intermediate form (network format) of the internal representation format of each machine and to place it in the transmission buffer.
- `pvm_send()` to deliver the message to the destination processes specified by ptid by designating the message with a number "1".

All PVM primitives have been written in C. C++ applications can use these primitives, as can Fortran applications (Fortran 77), which use them to cross the interface provided by PVM. This interface enables correspondence to be established between Fortran arguments and their equivalent in C language. It also takes into account the representation of character strings in Fortran, and the denomination conventions used by the different Fortran compilers to call C functions. In the following paragraphs the C interface will be used. The Fortran interface can be found in the PVM user manual.

3.3.1 Control of Distributed Execution under PVM

Control of the execution of tasks on a PVM distributed application is carried out using a set of primitives. These primitives especially enable Unix processes to declare themselves to the local PVM kernel in order to become one of the PVM tasks of a distributed application, or, alternatively, to leave the PVM environment. These primitives form the subject of the following description.

3.3.1.1 Declaration of a Task

The declaration of a task is carried out with the help of the `int tid = pvm_mytid(empty)` primitive.

The `pvm_mytid()` primitive permits a Unix process to enter into the PVM environment from the point when it is first used, and to generate a unique *tid* if the process has not been initialized with the `pvm_spawn ()` primitive. It sends back the *tid* of the call process and can be used several times.

It is important to note that all PVM primitives, and not only the `pvm_mytid()` primitive, permit the insertion of a Unix process into the PVM environment if the process has not previously been integrated.

The `int info = pvm_exit (empty)` primitive informs the local PVM kernel that the process has left PVM. The call process is not terminated, it can continue to process the same as any other Unix process.

3.3.1.2 The Launch of Actors

The `int numt = pvm_spawn (char *task, char **argv, int flag, char *where, int ntask, int ntids)` primitive is used to launch `ntask` copies of the executable file `task` on the virtual machine. The reader will have noticed that this primitive represents the available means under PVM for the implementation of the actor paradigm presented in the preceding chapter. `argv` is a pointer on a `task` call argument array which obviously ends with the character NULL. If `task` does not take a call argument, `argv` contains the character NULL. The *flag* witness is used to specify the options. Some of these options are as follows:

- `PvmTaskDefault` PVM chooses where it must launch the execution of agents;
- `PvmTaskHost` the argument `where` specifies the host where the argument will be initiated;
- `PvmTaskArch` the argument `where` specifies the hardware platform for the execution;
- `PvmTaskDebug` execute these processes in debug mode;
- `PvmTaskTrace` the call of PVM primitives in these actors generates a trace;
- `PvmHostCompl` launch the actors on further set of hosts;

On the return, `num` contains the number of actors successfully launched, and in this case the `tid` array contains their `tids`. Should this happen, `num` contains an error code if no actors have been launched. In cases where the initialization of certain actors has failed, the corresponding error codes are placed in the last positions (`ntask - numt`) of the `tid` array. Note in passing that this primitive can be effectively used to launch actors on multiprocessor machines.

Finally, the `int info = pvm_kill (int tid)` primitive serves to kill the PVM task identified by `tid`. It cannot be used to kill the caller process. This process can be killed by using the PVM `pvm_exit ()` primitive followed by the Unix `exit()` primitive.

3.3.1.3 Information on the Execution of Distributed Applications

To control the execution of its distributed application, the programmer must be able to gather a certain amount of information on the different processes implicated. The main PVM primitives used to do this are shown below.

The `int tid = pvm_parent (empty)` primitive enables the `tid` of the process which created the caller actor to be obtained. PVM resends the system value `PvmNoParent` if the actor or task was not created by `pvm_spawn()`.

To obtain a status word on a PVM task identified by its `tid`, it is necessary to use:

```
Int pstat = pvm_pstat(int tid)
```

This resends the `PvmOK` value. If the task is not active, it resends the `PvmNoTask` value. Finally, if the `tid` is invalid it resends the value `PvmBadParam`:

```
Int mstat = pvm_mstat (char *host)
```

This primitive is used to find out if a *host* (PvmOK) is active or inaccessible (PvmHostFail). This information is especially useful to provide the distributed application with a relatively high degree of fault tolerance:

```
Int info = pvm_config(int *nhost, int *narch, struct hostinfo
**hostp)
```

This primitive examines information on the virtual machine which contains the number of hosts (nhost), the number of different data formats (narch), and a pointer on a structure array (hostinfo) whose size is equal to nhost. Every input contains the tid of pvmd, the name of the *host*, the type of machine and the relative speed of the central unit of the hosts compared to the other hosts in the configuration.

```
Int info = pvm_tasks(int which, int *, struct hostinfo **taskp)
```

This primitive is used to gather information on the active tasks on the machine. Using the *which* value, information can be obtained on all tasks (*which* = 0), on the active tasks on a host (which = tid of *pvmd* of the host), or simply to obtain information on one particular task (which = the tid of the task).

The number of tasks is examined in ntask. The ntask size taskinfo array contains one input for each task that it contains: the tid of the task, the *pvmd*, the tid of the parent process, the status word of the task, the name of the executable file (PVM does not know the names of the tasks launched manually).

```
Pvm dtid = pvm_tidtohost (int tid)
```

This primitive enables the user to recognize the host on which a task is active.

3.3.2 The Dynamic Configuration of Virtual Machines

The following two PVM primitives,

```
Int info pvm_addhosts(char **hosts, int nhost, int *info)
Int info pvm_delhosts(char **hosts, int nhost, int *info)
```

permit the *dynamic* upgrading of the configuration of virtual machines during the execution of applications, by adding or removing a series of machines whose names are given in the hosts array.

3.3.3 The Implementation of Interactions between Tasks

In PVM, the transmission of a message is carried out in three distinct phases:

- The first stage involves initializing (activating) a buffer by calling the primitive pvm_initsend() or pvm_mkbuf().
- In the second stage, the data to be transmitted must be compressed using the compression operations available under PVM (pvm_pk*()) depending on their initial type.

- Finally, it is only in the third stage that the effective transmission of data is implemented using the `pvm_send()` or `pvm_mcast ()` primitive.

Message reception is carried out using a blocking or non-blocking reception primitive, the receptor task must then decompress the message. It is only after decompression that the extraction primitives for messages coming from the reception buffer can be used. They enable the extraction of any message, or messages coming from a particular source. Lastly, it is possible to extract messages which carry a particular witness, or messages which carry a witness originating from a particular source.

3.3.3.1 Managing Message Buffers

To initialize a transmission buffer it is necessary to use the following primitive:

```
Int bufid = pvm_initsend(intencoding)
```

The `encoding` parameter enables specification as to the nature of coding to be used. The different possible options for `encoding` are:

- `PvmDataDefault`: the standard data exchange format, XDR (abstract representation of data independent of machines and manufacturers; this is sometimes called "network format": see Chapter 4) is used by default as PVM does not automatically know if the message concerns a compatible machine or a heterogeneous machine. In cases where the user knows that he needed to send the message to a remote task being carried out on a compatible machine which recognizes the native format of the data to be transmitted, he can save time by omitting the coding procedure by using the `PvmDataRaw` option;
- `PvmDataRaw`: this option indicates to PVM that no coding is needed, and that the data must be transmitted in their current format;
- `PvmDataInPlace`: the data is left in its place, to avoid the costs incurred by compression. The buffer only contains the size of the data and a pointer on the zone where it is initially stored.

We note that PVM gives the user the option of managing several emission buffers within its application. We will leave the reader to find out the corresponding primitives in the PVM user manual.

3.3.3.2 Data Compression

PVM uses a series of primitives to carry out the compression of data to be transmitted, and the dual primitives for the decompression of data on its reception (Fig. 3.7).

The first argument of these primitives is a pointer towards the first element to compress. The second argument indicates the total number of array elements to compress. As for the third argument, it indicates the next elements involved in the operation. A value equal to 1 indicates that compression involves a close vector of elements. A value equal to 2 indicates that all the other elements are compressed separately.

Type	Compression	Decompression
byte	pvm_pkbyte(char *cp, int nitem, int stride)	pvm_upkbyte()
complex	pvm_pkcplx(float *xp, int nitem, int stride)	pvm_upkcplx()
double rpl	pvm_pkdplx(double* zp, int nitem, int stride)	pvm_upkdplx()
double	pvm_pkdouble(double *dp, int nitem, int stride)	pvm_upkdouble()
real	pvm_pkfloat(float *fp, int nitem, int stride)	pvm_upkfloat()
Integer	pvm_pkint(int *np, int nitem, int stride)	pvm_upkint()
long	pvm_pklong(long *np, int nitem, int strid)	pvm_upklong()
short	pvm_pkshort(short *np, int nitem, int str e)	pvm_upkshort()
char	pvm_pkstr(char * cp)	pvm_upkstr(char *cp)

Fig. 3.7 Data compression and decompression primitives.

3.3.3.3 Emission and Reception of Elements

PVM proposes two types of data emission primitives:

- `Int info = pvm_send(int tid, int msgtag)`

  With the help of the preceding primitives (buffer initialization and data compression), this primitive provides the message prepared in the buffer with a number given in the `msgtag` argument and immediately transmits it to the PVM task for the identifier *tid*.

- `Int info = pvm_mcast(int tid, int msgtag, void *vp, int cnt, int type)`

  This primitive enables the two preceding compression and transmission operations to be regrouped into one indivisible operation. The `type` argument indicates the type of data to be transmitted, contained within the `vp` vector. The dual function is :`Int info = pvm_precv();`

  PVM proposes several methods to receive messages within a task. The following primitives can be used to receive any message received in the buffer, abstraction is carried out during transmission: `pvm_send` or `pvm_mcast`.

- `Int bufid = pvm_recv(int tid, int msgtag)`

  The caller task is blocked until the arrival of the identifier message (number) `msgtag`. The message must be emitted by the task identifier `tid`. If the task wishes to receive all messages which arrive, it must give the value –1 to `msgtag` or `tid`. It creates a new reception zone in the active reception buffer and places the received message into it (returns the identifier of the new buffer in `bufid`). Following the arrival of the current message, the storage zone of the preceding message is emptied unless it is specifically requested to be saved using the `pvm_setrbuf()` primitive.

- `Int bufid = pvm_nrecv(int tid, int msgtag)`

  In contrast to the preceding primitive, this is *non-blocking*. It can be used several times to find out if a message has arrived or not. The conditions for reception are identical to those of the preceding primitive.

- `Int info = pvm_trecv(int tid, int msgtag, struct timeval *tmout)`

  To prevent a task waiting indefinitely behind the `pvm_recv()` primitive for example, PVM offers another `pvm_trecv()` primitive which provides the user with the ability to specify the maximum wait time (watchdog timer). If the specified time runs out before the message has arrived, the task is revived to retake its execution and take a decision accordingly.

- `Int info = pvm_bufinfo (int btid, int *bytes, int *msgtag, int *tid)`

  This primitive is used to obtain information on the message which has just arrived, notably to find out its number or mark (`msgtag`), its emitter (`tid`), and its size (`bytes`).

To conclude this section, we note that PVM offers a function which enables the user to modify the conditions for the selection and filtering of messages on reception. The `pvm_recvf(int(*new) (int buf, int tid, int tag)` primitive enables the user to offer its own filtering function which can be any level of complexity. Recall that by default, filtering operates the `tid` of the message emitter and identifier (`msgtag`). The reader has by now made the link between the possibilities offered by this primitive, and the notion of anonymous communication introduced in the preceding chapter.

Figure 3.8a gives a brief example of the use of certain primitives already introduced, notably the creation of several tasks or actors, and the implementation of a communication protocol by message exchange. This involves a unique program, once launched under Unix with the number of actors to create as arguments. It starts by recuperating its `tid (montid = pvm_mytid)`, and checking that it is the father of the actors it is going to create `(tidparent = pvm_parent())`. This check is essential given that the father and the actors (sons) execute the same code or program. The next stage for the father involves creating the actors (sons) with the help of the `pvm_spawn()` primitive:

```
info = pvm_spawn(argv[0], (char**)0, PvmTaskDefaults, (char*)0,
ntask, son).
```

Under Unix, `argv[0]` always contains the name of the activated program. In our case, `argv[1]`contains the number of tasks to be activated. The final stage for the father is restricted to waiting for a message coming from whichever son whose argument `tid` of `pvm_recv()` is equal to –1. However, it indicates that it does not request the filtering of messages carrying the `y` mark or indicator (`MSGSON = msgtag` argument). When a message arrives, the father is reactivated and requests information on the message to find out its emitter and mark, before decompressing it and displaying its characteristics.

As for the sons, they execute the same program but only the part of the code which is reserved for them. Once active, an actor son starts by initializing a transmission buffer (`pvm_initsend()`), and then indicates to PVM the compression procedure to use with `pvm_pkint(&montid,1,1)`before transmitting its message with `(info = pvm_send(tidparent, MSGSON))`. The message will be marked or will carry the mark `MSG-SON`. It is important to note that the argument of the `pvm_initsend()`

primitive is `PvmDattDefault` because not only does the father not know on which type of machine his sons will be activated, but neither has he specified in the `pvm_spawn()` primitive, the type of execution platform. On the contrary, he leaves the PVM to choose the target machine: `PvmTaskDefault`.

The general structure of the application is given in Figure 3.8b.

```
/* Example of a Communication Program between Tasks*/
#include <pvm3.h>
#define MAXACTORS   20              /* maximum number of actor sons to create*/
#define MSGSONS      11             /*value to identify the messages to join*/
main (int argc, char* argv[])
{
int ntask = 3;                      /*number of tasks to create, by default 3 */
int info;                           /*return code for PVM primitives*/
int montid; int tidparent;
int actor[MAXACTORS];               /*actor son tid table*/
int i, data, buf, lg, tag, tid;
montid = pvm_mytid();               /*know the tid of the task*/
if (montid < 0) {
        pvm_perror(argv[0]);        /*in case of error display message */
        return -1;                  /* stop the execution*/
        }
tidparent = pvm_parent();           /* find the tid of the task parent*/
if ((tidparent < 0) && (tidparent != pvmNoParent)) {
        pvm_perror(argv[0]);
        pvm_exit();
        return -1;
        }
                                    /*I have no parent therefore I am the father */
if (tidparent == pvmNoParent) {
        if (argc == 2) ntask = atoi(argv[1]);
                                    /* find the number of sons to create*/
        if ((ntask < 1) or (ntask > MAXACTORS)) {pvm_exit(); return 0;
}                                   /* create actor sons*/
         info = pvm_spawn(argv[0], (char**)0, pvmTaskDefault,
              (char*)0, ntask, actor);     /* display the actor son tid*/
        for (i = 0; i < ntask; i++)
             if (actor[i] < 0) printf ("%d", actor[i]);
                 else printf("t%x\t", actor[i]);
        putchar('\n');
                                    /* ensure the sons are created*/
        if (info == 0) {pvm_exit(); return -1;}
                                    /* the father awaits the sons message only*/
        for (i = 0; i < ntask; i++){
                                    /* receive a message coming from any son*/
            buf = pvm_recv (-1, MSGSON);
            if (buf < 0) pvm_error("appel ^ recv");
            info = pvm_bufinfo(buf, &lg, &tag, &tid);
            if (info < 0) pvm_perror("appel ^ pvm_bufinfo");
            info = pvm_upkint (&data, 1, 1);
            if (data != tid) printf("impossible that that could
happen!\n");
            printf("length %d, Tag %d, Tid t%x\n", lg, tag, tid);
            }
```

```
        pvm_exit();
        return 0;
        }
                                                    /* I am an actor son*/
info = pvm_initsend(PvmDataDefault);
if (info < 0){pvm_perror("call^ pvm_initsend"); pvm_exit(); return -
1;}
info = pvm_pkint (&montid, 1, 1);
if (info < 0) {pvm_perror("appel ^ pvm_pkint"); pvm_exit(); return -
1;}
        info = pvm_send(tidparent, MSGSON);
        pvm_perror("call^ pvm_send"); pvm_exit();
return -1;
}
pvm_exit();
}
```

Fig. 3.8a Example of an actor creation program.

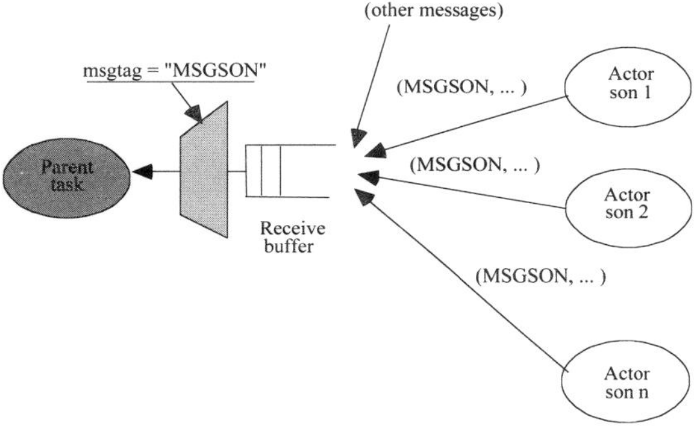

Fig. 3.8b Structure of the *hello* program.

3.3.3.4 Notification and Transmission of Events

The following primitive:

```
int info = pvm_sendsig(int tid, int signum)
```

enables a task PVM to send a signal numbered `signum` to another task PVM identified by its `tid`.

To request the PVM to inform the caller task of the completion of certain events, it is necessary to use the following primitive:

```
int info = pvm_notify(int what, int msgtag, int cnt, int tids)
```

The following are different values for `what`:

- `PvmTaskExit`: to indicate the exit of a task from the PVM system;
- `PvmHostDelete:` to warn the task of the removal of a machine;

- PvmHostAdd: to warn the task of the addition of a machine.

The tids array is used to indicate the list of tasks to watch. When a task using pvm_exit() (TaskExit), is killed following a host crash or executes itself, (HostDelete), the task which is called pvm_notify will be warned of the event which triggered the destruction of the task. Tids is empty when the HostAdd event is carried out. If a host supporting the execution of task A crashes at the point where another task B has requested the PVM that it is informed of the termination of A and its exit from the PVM system, then B will be notified of the indirect termination of A which is a direct consequence of the crash of the host in question.

The following example shows how a task can terminate another task and also how a task can be warned of the end or the destruction of another task. In this example, the main part of the preceding Hello program is used again, involving the creation of actor sons. The only difference lies in the use of the

```
info = pvm_notify(PvmTaskExit, TASKKILLED, ntask, actor)
```

primitive, after the creation of sons by the parent task to be warned by the PVM system of the termination of actors (sons). This termination could be normal following the use of the pvm_exit() primitive, or abnormal if the actor son is killed. To trigger this event, the parent task will ask the PVM to kill one of the actor sons by calling the pvm_kill() primitive. The actor in the middle is chosen to be killed (info = pvm_kill(son[ntask/2])).

```
    /* Example of event notification*/
#include <pvm3.h>
#define MAXACTORS   20                  /* maximum number of actor sons created*/
                                        /*value to mark the notification messages*/
#define TASKKILLED 11
int
main (int argc, char* argv[])
{
int ntask = 3;                          / number of tasks created, by default 3*/
int info;                               /*return code of PVM primitives*/
int montid;
int tidparent;
int actor [MAXACTORS];                  /*tid table of actor sons*/
int i, tidkill;
int tid;
char *argv[5];
montid = pvm_mytid();                   /*know the tid of my task*/
if (montid < 0) {
     pvm_perror(argv[0]);               /*in case of error display message*/
     return -1;                         /* stop execution*/
     }

tidparent = pvm_parent();               /* find the tid of the task parent*/
if ((tidparent < 0) && (tidparent != pvmNoParent)) {
     pvm_perror(argv[0]);
     pvm_exit();
     return -1;
```

```
    }
                              /* I have no parent therefore I am the father*/
if (tidparent == pvmNoParent) {
                                        /*find the number of sons created*/
    if (argc == 2) ntask = atoi(argv[1]);
            if ((ntask < 1) or (ntask > MAXACTORS))
                    {pvm_exit(); return 0; }
                                                    /* create actor sons*/
            info = pvm_spawn(argv[0], (char**)0, pvmTaskDebug,
                              (char*)0, ntask, actor);
                                              /* display the actor son tid*/
             if (info != ntask) { pvm_exit(); return -1;}
    for (i = 0; i < ntask; i++)
            printf("t%x\t", actor[i]); putchar('\n');
                     /* request to be notified if an actor son is terminated*/
            info = pvm_notify (PvmTaskExit, TASKKILLED, ntask,
actor);
           if (info < 0) {pvm_error("notify");; pvm_exit();
return -1;}
                                              /* kill the environment actor */
          info = pvm_kill(actor[ntask/2]);
          if (info < 0) {pvm_error("kill"); pvm_exit(); return -
1;}

                                                     /*await notification*/
         info = pvm_recv (-1,TASKKILLED);
          if (info < 0) {pvm_error("recv"); pvm_exit(); return -
1;}
           info = pvm_upkint (&tidkill, 1, 1);
           if (info < 0)  pvm_error("appel ^ pvm_upkint");

                                 /*this must involve the environment actor*/
         printf(Actor t%x tu•: \n", tidkill);
         printf(environment actor t%x \n", actor[ntask/2]);
         pvm_exit();
         return 0;
         }

                                                      /* I am an actor son*/
sleep (63);
pvm_exit();
return 0;
}
```

Fig. 3.9 Example of a PVM application using notifications.

3.3.4 The Dynamic Regrouping of Tasks

This mechanism of regrouping tasks within a logical unit called a group or component, is not directly supported by PVM primitives. A "libgppvm3.a" library annexe must be used (during the compilation and editing of links) if the application intends to use this mechanism to regroup the different tasks into units or groups during execution (Fig. 3.2). A group server is activated to manage the groups created and the intra or inter-group interactions. The primitives related to the groups enable every PVM task to join a group, and to broadcast a message to the tasks of a different group. In general, the following primitives can be used by any PVM task.

- `int inum = pvm_joingroup(char *group)`: creates a new group with the name *group* and integrate the caller task into this group. It sends back the instance number of the task in the group (*inum*). This number is unique within the group, and enables a task to be singled out within a group (related address).
- `int info = pvm_lvgroup(char *group)`: allows a task to leave a group.
- `int tid = pvm_gettid(char *group, int num)`: enables the `tid` of a task to be obtained from the name of its group and its instance number.
- `int inum = pvm_gsize(char *group, int tid)`: provides the instance number of a task within a group.
- `int size = pvm_gsize(char *group)`: permits a task to recognize the number of elements in a group.
- `int info = pvm_bcast (char *group, int msgtag)`: this primitive gives the message the number specified by `msgtag` and broadcasts it to all the task members of the group named *group* with the exception of the emitter task. If the tasks rejoin the group during the broadcast of a message, this message is not delivered to them. On the other hand, tasks which leave a group a message broadcast will receive a copy of this message.

Example of a Distributed Application under PVM

This is a computation program for the diffusion of heat across a conducting wire described in Gesit *et al.* (1994). It uses a simple differential equation for the propagation of heat in a wire:

$$(A_{i+1,} - A_{i,j}) \,/\, \Delta t = (A_{i,j+1} - 2^*A_{i,j,} + A_{i,,j-1}) \,/\, \Delta^{-2}$$

with $A_{i,j}$ = heat at the co-ordinates (i,j); and initial conditions and borders:

$$A(t,0) = 0, A(t,1) = 0$$

$$A(0,x) = \text{ in}(\pi^*x) \text{ with } 0 \leq x \leq 1$$

The model used to implement this parallel program is the master–slave model. To calculate the propagation of heat in this wire, the wire is divided into five sections (Fig. 3.10). Each section is attributed an actor slave (*heatSlave.c*) which the master *heater.c* created. Consequently, each actor slave is responsible for calculating the propagation of heat in its section using the above formula. At each stage of the calculation, the actor slaves exchange the temperature at the borders of their section.

In the *heater.c* program a "solution" array is used to store the solution for the diffusion of heat at each point. The *heater* starts by creating the actors, it then calculates the initial data. The initial temperature of either end of the wire is fixed at zero. The principal process is therefore executed four times, each time with a new Δt value. A counter is used to calculate the time passed for each stage. The initial data is transmitted to the *heatSlave* actors. The master transmits the initial data to each slave as well as the `tid` of its two neighbouring actors (the actor on the left and that on the right). The actors use the two `tids` to communicate to their neighbours information concerning the borders of their section.

After the transmission of initial data, the master awaits the results calculated by the slaves. When these results arrive, they are regrouped into the "solution" matrix. The elapsed time is also calculated.

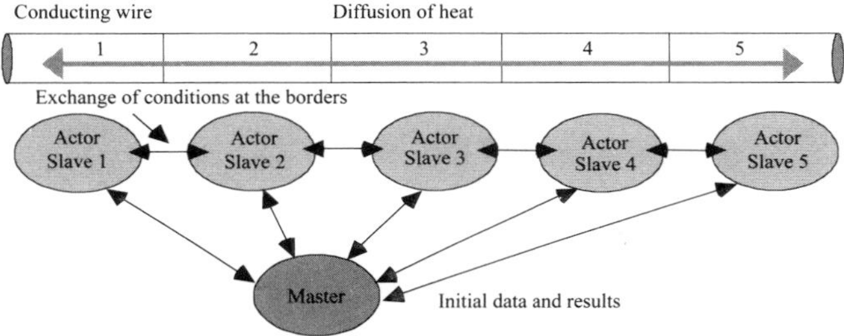

Fig. 3.10 Computation by several actors of the diffusion of heat in a wire.

The program for the master process is given in Figure 3.11.

/* program master:heater.c */

```
#include "pvm3.h"
#include <stdio.h>
#include <math.h>
#include <time.h>
#define SLAVE"heatSlave"
#define Nactors   5
#define NBETAPE   100
#define  PLOTING 10
#define  SIZE  1000

int nb_part  = SIZE/ Nactors;

main {
int montid, actor[Nactors], i, j;
int right, left, k, l;
int stage= NBSTAGE;
int info;
double init [SIZE], solution[[NBSTAGE][SIZE];
double result[NBSTAGE*SIZE /Nactors], detlax2;
double delta[4];
time_t t0;
int time[4];

delta[0] = 5.0e-1;
```

```
delta[1] = 5.0e-3;
delta[2] = 5.0e-6;
delta[3] = 5.0e-9;

montid = pvm_mytid();                    /* request access to the PVM system*/


                                              /* creation of actor slaves*/
info = pvm_spawn(SLAVE, (char **)0, PvmTaskdefault, "", Nactors,
actor);


                                              /* creation of initial data*/
for (i = 0; i <SIZE; i++)
     init[i] = sin( M_PI * ((double)i / (double)(SIZE - 1)));
init[0] = 0.0;
init[SIZE-1] = 0.0;


                              /* execute the process four times for each*/
                                                   /*new value of delta*/
for (l = 0; l < 4; l++) {
     deltax2 = (deltat[l] / pow(1.0 / (double) SIZE, 2.0));
     time(&t0);                  /* initialize a time counter for this process*/
     time[l] = 10;
                              /* transmit the initial data to the slaves with */
                                           /* the indications of vicinity*/
     for ( i = 0; i < Nactors; i++) {
          pvm_initsend(PvmDataDefault);
          left = (i == 0) ? 0 : actor[i-1];
          pvm_pkint (&left, 1, 1);
          right= ( i == (Nactors-1) ? 0 : actor[i+1];
          pvm_pkint(&right, 1, 1);
          pvm_pkint( &stage, 1, 1);
          pvm_pkdouble(&deltax2, 1, 1);
          pvm_pkint( &nb_part, 1, 1);
          pvm_pkdouble(&init[nb_partT*i], nb_part, 1);
          pvm_send(actor[[i], 4);
          }


                                                   /* await the results*/

     for ( i = 0; i < Nactors; i++) {
          pvm_recv(actor[i], 7);
          pvm_upkdouble(&result[0], nb_part * NBSTAGE, 1);


                                            /* update the solution table*/
          for ( j = 0; j < NBSTAGE; j++)
                for (k = 0; k < nb_part; k++)
                     solution[j][nb_part*i+k] =
result[wh(i,j)];
          }
                                               /* stop the time counter*/
          time(&t0);
          time[l] = t0 - time[l];


                                         /* store the results in the files */
          store_data ();
     }
```

```
                                              /* kill the actor slaves*/

    for (i = 0; i < Nactors; i++) pvm_kill(actor[i]);
    pvm_exit();
}
 int store_data ()
{                                  /* define according to the storage method chosen*/
}
int wh(int x, int y) {
return (x*nb_part + y);
}
```

Fig. 3.11 The master process program.

The *heatSlave* program in Figure 3.12 has the role of calculating the propagation of heat across the wire. It is made up of a infinite loop into which it receives all of the initial data and effectuates several iterations to calculate a solution based on this data. For each iteration, and before starting the computations, it exchanges data with its neighbours across the borders of its section. After the calculation has been made, it transmits the partial results to the master process.

```
/*program of actor slaves: heatSlave.c */

#include "pvm3.h"
#include <stdio.h>

int nb_part;
main() {
int montid, right,left, i, j, master;
int stage;
double *init, *A;
double rightData, leftData, delta, leftSide, rightside;

                                              /* rejoin the PVM system*/
montid = pvm_mytid();
master = pvm_parent();

                                              /* receive data from the master*/
while(1){
    pvm_recv(master, 4);
    pvm_upkint(&left,, 1, 1);
    pvm_upkint(&right, 1, 1);
    pvm_upkint( &stage, 1, 1);
    pvm_upkdouble( &delta, 1, 1);
    pvm_upkint( &nb_part, 1, 1);
    init = (double *) malloc(nb_part*sizeof(double));
    pvm_upkdouble(init, nb_part, 1);
                                    /* copy the initial data into work table A*/
    a = (double *) malloc(nb_part * stage * sizeof(double));
    for (i = 1; i < nb_part; i++) A[i] = init[i];

                                              /* carry out the calculation*/
    for ( i = 0; i < nb_part; i++) {
```

```
                        /* exchange the information at the borders with neighbours*/
                                          /*send to the left, receive from the right*/
        if (left!= 0) {
          pvm_initsend(PvmDataDefault);
          pvm_pkdouble(&A[wh(i,0)], 1, 1);
          pvm_send(left, 5);
          }
        if (right!= 0) {
          pvm_recv(right, 5);
          pvm_upkdouble(&rightdata, 1, 1);
                                          /* send to the right, receive from the left*/
          pvm_initsend(PvmDataDefault);
          pvm_left, 6);
          }
        if (left!= 0) {
          pvm_recv(left, 6);
          pvm_upkdouble(&rightdata, 1, 1);
          }
                                                      /* do calculations for this stage*/

        for ( j = 0; j < nb_part; j++) {
          leftside = (j == 0) ? rightside: A[wh(i, j+1)];
          rightside =
              (j == nb_part - 1)) ? rightside: A[wh(i, j+1)];
          if ((j==0) && (left== 0)) A[wh(i+1, j)] = 0.0;
          else
            A[wh(i+1, j)] =
            A[wh(i,j)]+delta*(rightside -2*A[wh(i,j)]+leftside);
            }
    }
                                                      /* send results to the master*/
       pvm_initsend(PvmDataDefault);
       pvm_pkdouble(&A[0], nb_part*stage, 1);
       pvm_send(master, 7);
    }
                                                           /* by security measure*/
    pvm_exit();
}
int wh( int x, int y)
{ return (x*nb_part +y);
}
```

Fig. 3.12 Programming slave actors.

4. *Distributed Programming under Unix*

The client–server model is without doubt the model best adapted for the implementation of applications within a distributed context, given the flexibility and relationship between the simplicity of software development and the ease of their maintenance. The users' need for access to remote data or services continues to grow, and the interoperability between applications engendered by this makes this model a tool and a basic reference to reach these objectives. However, we must not lose sight of the fact that this model has become a standard in this field, which is partly due to Unix and especially to the communication and process management tools that this data processing system provides in a centralized or distributed context.

4.1 Unix and the Client–Server Model

As we have already indicated in the first two chapters, the main interest in this model resides in the type of interaction that it has, and its considerable simplification, for installation problems. The use of the client–server model for the development of distributed applications notably reduces the problems related to the initialization of distributed applications, and the management of global resources, in situations where the different co-operating entities are clearly identified:

- the requester programs of one or more services called clients;
- the server which is the process provider of a service, known among clients.

The server process is responsible for the management of the necessary resources to implement the services offered.

The model particularly enables the *proliferation* of processes within a distributed system. In contrast to other distributed execution models, the client–server model limits the number of processes to those of the server on the site of the resource(s) controlled by the server. Recall that in a distributed application based on the remote procedural call (RPC) technique, each program user must remotely trigger a process on the resident site of the resource in order to be able to execute the program or transaction which corresponds to the service requested (Fig. 4.1).

Every remote access to an available server therefore necessitates the creation of a new process with all the problems of synchronization and adjacent concurrent access management.

In this chapter, we propose to initiate readers in system programming according to the client–server model, and to make them aware of the essential tools and techniques required for such an exercise. We start by a short outline of the Unix tools necessary for the manipulation of processes in a distributed context.

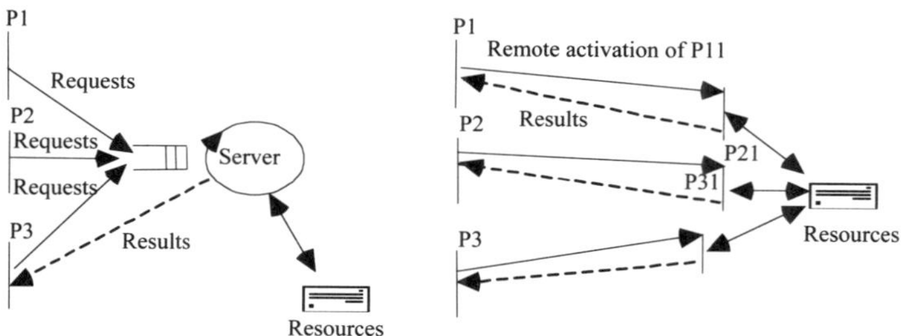

Fig. 4.1 Comparison between the client–server model and the RPC model.

An approach is now presented for the development of applications for the client–server model that is used in Chapter 7 in the study and implementation of a management system for the persistence of object oriented languages, C++ as it happens. This system is composed of three closely linked sub-systems: a persistent object manager, an event manager, which offers the user a high-level synchronization and communication mechanism, and a time constraint manager. This latter is essential for the development of distributed applications subject to time constraints. Our aim is to show at which point the client–server model reduces the problems of design and implementation of systems as complex as those presented in this study.

4.2 Unix Tools for Distributed Data Processing

TCP/IP is without doubt the origin of the remarkable developments that have taken place in the field of distributed data processing over the last five years, and forms the cornerstone of the information highways already in operation on the Internet. In the following section, we touch upon the main areas of the TCP/IP protocol, to enable the reader to understand the rest of the chapter. The amateur in this field, however, may benefit from reading more specialized publications on TCP/IP (Comer, 1992).

4.2.1 The TCP/IP Protocol

TCP/IP is the product of a DARPA (Defence Advanced Research Project Agency) project for the Department of Defence in the United States, created in 1980, and integrated into the UNIX BSD4.2. Figure 4.2 gives the relationship between the layers of the ISO model and those available on the Internet. The outermost layer predefines applications called Internet services, which the user can activate directly using a Unix machine. Among these services, the reader will almost certainly have already used the Unix command `mail` to send or receive electronic mail, the `ftp` command to send or collect files, `telnet` to remotely connect to a Unix machine, etc. This layer corresponds to layers 5 to 7 of the ISO model (session, presentation and application). The next layer integrates the two basic protocols, TCP and UDP, used to implement applications at a superior level (`mail`, `ftp`, `telnet`, `rcp`, etc). TCP (transmission control protocol) is a data transmission protocol in connected mode (end to end protocol). In contrast, UDP (user datagram protocol) is a data transmission protocol in connectionless mode. TCP is generally used if reliability of communications between the application entities is the overwhelming criteria. UDP is used where transmission speed constitutes the determining element within an application.

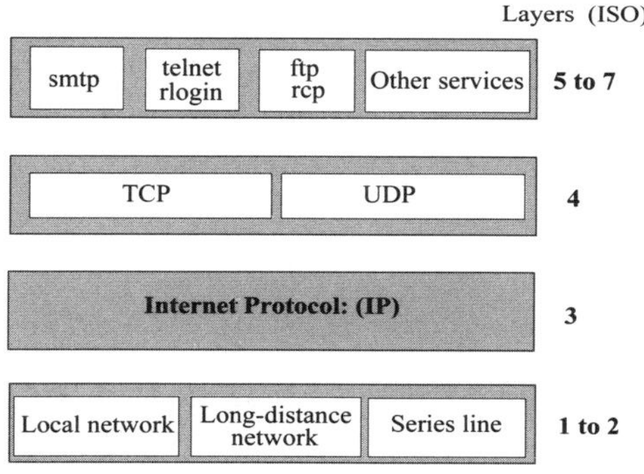

Fig. 4.2 The different layers of the Internet.

The IP layer supports the Internet protocol for the transmission of data packets between two pieces of IT equipment. This is a network protocol. The last layer supports the drivers needed to access the different types of physical support for data transmission: local networks, remote networks or simply a lines series.

The main aim of the Internet is *network interconnection* (Fig. 4.3). It would otherwise be unthinkable to so easily construct information highways, which are already a reality. This way, it would be possible to allow two machines (M1 and M2) in two local, geographically remote networks, to communicate with each other, whatever the physical means linking the two networks may be, as shown in Figure 4.3. Incidentally, we note that more than 500,000 machines throughout the world are already interconnected via the Internet (TCP/IP).

4.2.2 The Designation and Addressing of Machines on the Internet

The Internet uses a two-level addressing system. The first level is used to address a given network among all of the interconnected networks, the second level enables the designation of one machine within a network. The addresses handled by this mechanism are therefore logic addresses. There also exists another form of address, the physical addresses, which are an integral part of the local Ethernet network.

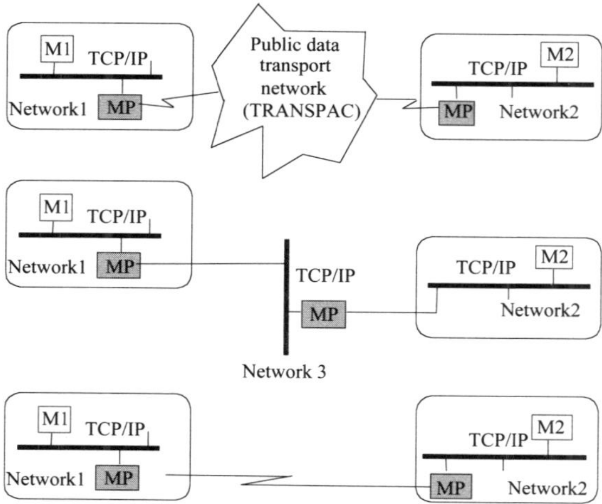

Fig. 4.3 The interconnection of networks via the Internet.

4.2.2.1 *Ethernet Addresses*

Each Ethernet card is given a physical address called an *Ethernet address*. This is unique and is determined by the manufacturer: if one machine (usually one which acts as a link between two networks) supports two Ethernet cards, it possesses two physical addresses (one for each network).

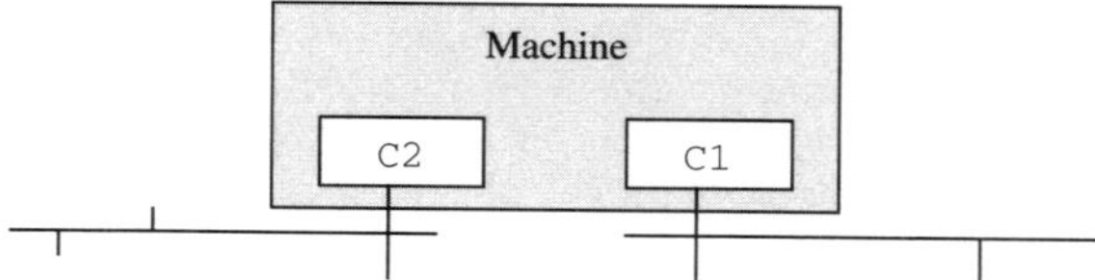

4.2.2.2 *IP Addresses*

In a network, a machine is designated by a unique 32 bit logic address called an *Internet address*. Each machine is given a logic address composed of two fields: the network address and the address of the machine within the network:

Nevertheless, the interconnected networks do not have to use the same addressing mechanism for the different machines. The size of the two fields varies depending on the class of the network. In other words, the greater the potential number of machines on the network, the larger the *Machine Address* field. The standard TCP/IP has, however, designated three classes of networks, and as a result three types of addresses:

- *Class A:* The structure of the corresponding address is as follows:

Given the size reserved for the *Machine Address* field, it is clear that this class of network concerns networks where the number of machines is very high.

- *Class B:* For this class of network, the two fields are identical. This comes from a medium sized network.

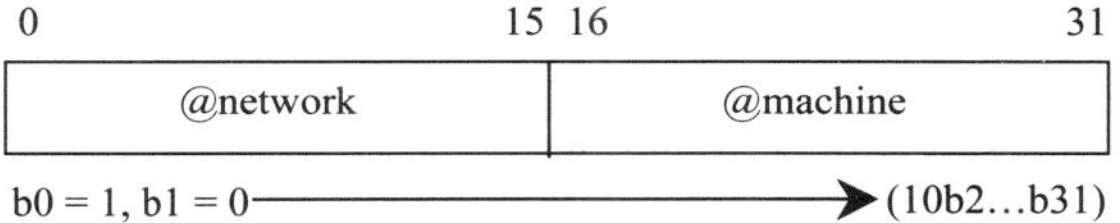

- *Class C:* In this class the number of machines is relatively low:

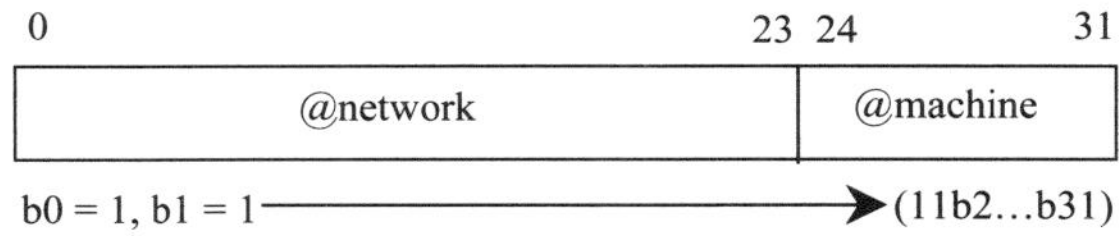

In contrast to the Ethernet address, which is invisible to the user, the IP address is visible, especially to TCP/IP application programmers. On each Unix machine, this address is stored in a system file called '/etc/host'. This also contains the addresses of known machines. Figure 4.4 shows the contents of this file for a machine called 'isma'.

```
192.54.142.37 isma.isima.fr     isma  loghost  mailhost   dumphost
104.45.10.1  libd3.univ-bpclermont.fr
```

Fig. 4.4 The contents of the host system file.

For each machine declared, each line of this file gives its Internet address (192.54. 412.37) and its symbolic name (isma). The first concerns the machine itself, the other lines are used to declare the known local or remote machines.

The establishment of communication between two machines is carried out using not only the IP address, but also the IP interfaces according to the physical means of data transmission.

4.3 IP Interfaces

The protocol used at the IP layer level is a network level protocol for the exchange of datagrams (packets), in a connectionless manner. Consequently, it does not guarantee the arrival of messages at the right port. The structure of a datagram is shown here:

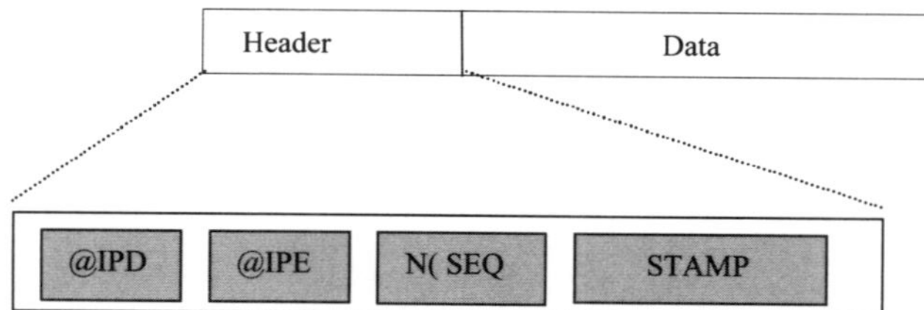

IP interfaces ensure the management of protocols specific to each type of physical network. Figure 4.5 below shows the different stages of cutting and transforming a message to be transmitted from machine x to machine y on a local Ethernet network. The message is cut into fragments of a fixed size (p1, p2,...pm). A packet is made up from each fragment, which contains a header and a data part. The header encloses the Internet address of the emitter machine 1x, and the receptor machine 1y.

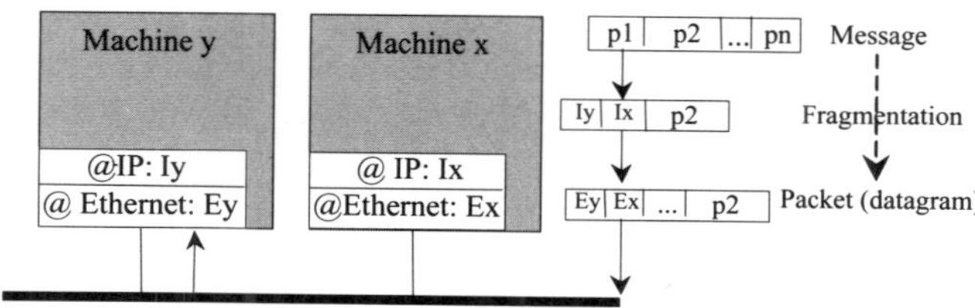

Fig. 4.5 The different stages of transmission of a message between two machines.

To render communication effective, two specific protocols are necessary to implement the transformation of IP addresses into physical Ethernet addresses:

1. The Address Resolution Protocol (ARP). If machine x wishes to communicate with machine y:
    - Either it already knows the physical address (Ethernet) from previous communication;
    - Or it does not know the address, in which case the IP interface sends an Ethernet broadcast frame (11...1):

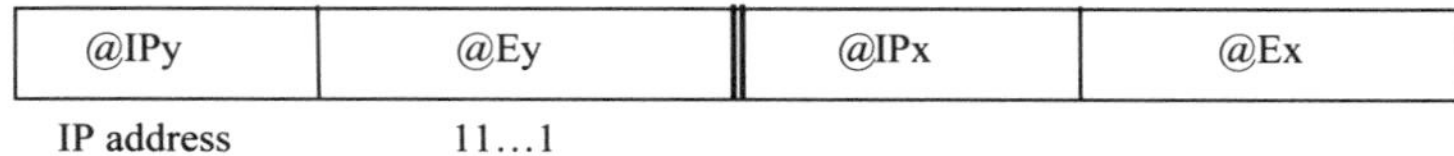

Machine y recognizes its Internet address and will send its Ethernet address to machine x.

2. The Reverse ARP (RARP). This protocol enables a station without a disk, which does not know its own Internet address to demand it by broadcasting a specified Ethernet message on the network. Only one machine (RARP server) is authorized to reply to this type of message.

As we have already shown, the lowest layer contains the drivers or the interface needed to manage the different physical access cards for the support of the communication used. There exists one interface for each type of support:

- IP/X.25 Interface. This interface decompresses the packets of 576 octets sent by the IP protocol into packets of 128 octets which is the maximum size for X.25 packets.
- Serial Line Internet Protocol (SLIP) Interface. This enables Internet family protocols to be used on asynchronous lines managed by the RS232/V24 protocol.

4.3.1 Datagram Routing

When communication involves two machines on the same network (Fig. 4.6), it is said to be an intra-network communication, and routing is limited to the execution of the procedure concerned with the resolution of the previous address, which enables the two machines to communicate (Fig. 4.5).

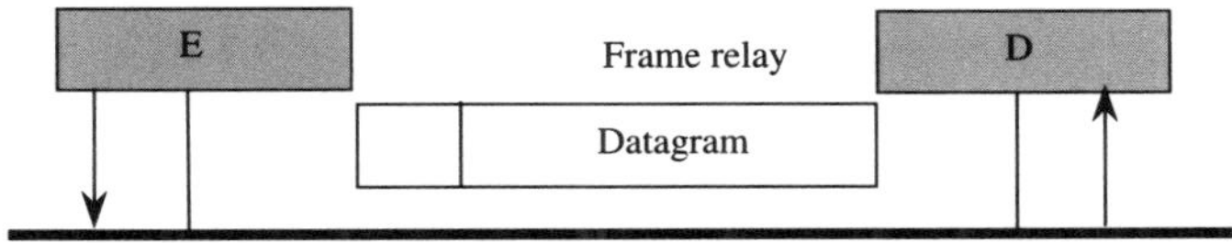

Fig. 4.6 Intra-network communication.

However, when communication involves two machines from two different networks, routing is controlled by intermediate link machines (Fig. 4.7). To summarize, in comparison to the preceding case, the LM_1 machine will detect that there is a packet addressed to another machine which is not part of the network, and will send its physical Ethernet address. LM_1 has a routing table which enables it to use the IP address to determine the link machine (LM_2) to which it sends machine E's messages. LM_1 determines to which physical interface it is to send the packets. LM_2 is a link machine which has the same functions as LM_1. This continues until the messages arrive at the correct port.

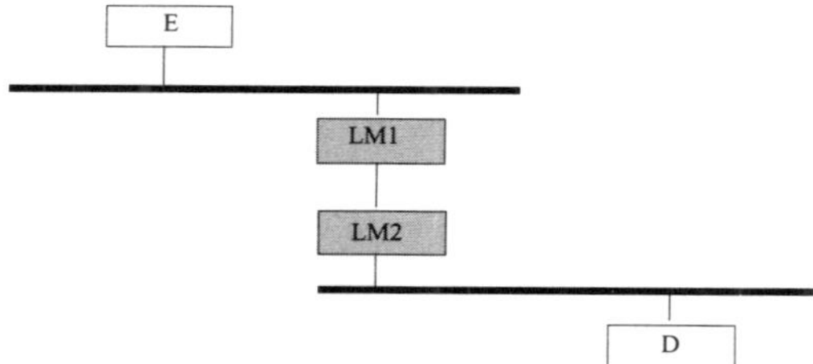

Fig. 4.7 Inter-network communication.

As we have already indicated, the IP protocol is responsible for the management of physical interfaces and connectionless packet routing. It is not an end-to-end protocol. This characteristic is introduced by protocols of the layer above: TCP and UDP.

4.4 TCP and UDP Data Transmission Protocols

The aim of the TCP/IP layer is to facilitate the communication (interaction) between activities (processes) on remote machines. To enable this, two protocols are present at the level of the transmission layer: TCP and UDP. These protocols use network addressing to design a given process. They introduce a separation between the identity of processes and the service that they ensure. A process is identified by a network address called a "port", or a "socket" in Unix terminology. On each machine there are a set of ports identified by integers (Fig. 4.8).

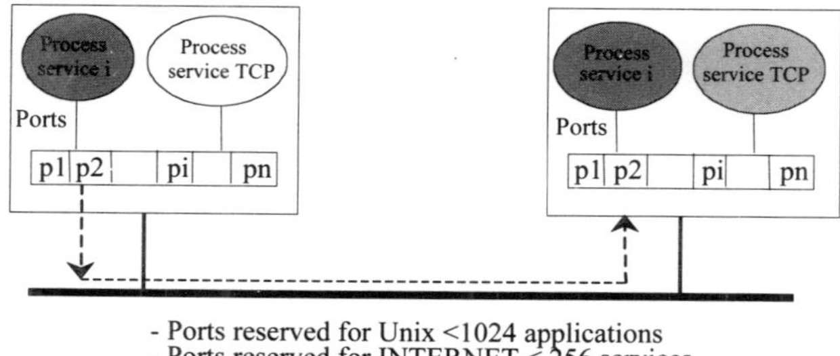

Fig. 4.8 The use of ports to identify an interaction between two processes.

A Unix socket can be compared to a telephone socket which serves as a point of entry into the telephone network. The connection of a telephone is all that is required to establish communication. The telephone number corresponds to the Unix socket number.

Notion 1 Socket

This is a system object to which a process can connect in order to send or receive data. Only one process at a time owns (or is linked to) a socket (a telephone number is given to one subscriber only).

The structure of packets used by protocols is shown below:

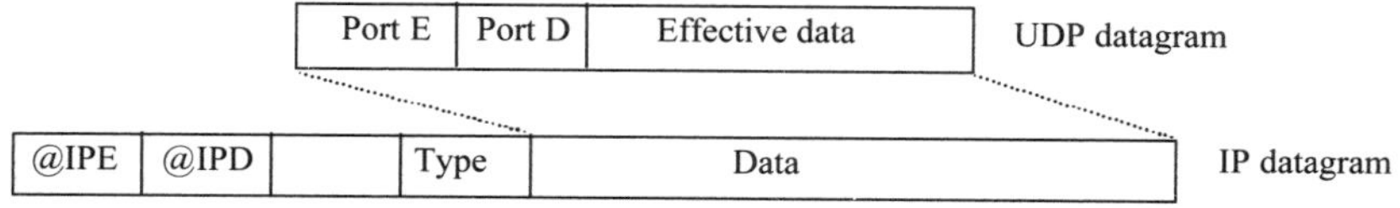

4.4.1 *The User Data Protocol (UDP)*

This enables one activity to send messages to another activity in connectionless datagram mode.

4.4.2 *The Transfer Control Protocol (TCP)*

This involves a connection-oriented transport layer protocol which offers a reliable service for the transfer of octet flow: end-to-end protocol. It has the following properties:

- unit of transfer : TCP segment (packet);
- services provided ("type" field of the TCP segment):
  - request to open a connection;
  - expedition: urgent messages or forced message sending;
  - reception with the possibility of directly accessing an urgent message;
  - closure of a connection.
- reserved ports:
  - FTP:21;
  - TELNET:23.

It is important to note that all of the high level standard services proposed within the Internet function use the *client–server* model. Each service is identified by a *port* (socket) on each machine. There are three types of service:

1. Standard service (available on any Internet implementation).
   - FTP (file transfer protocol): enables a file transfer session to be established between two machines from different systems. FTP uses TCP and TFTP (trivial FTP) uses UDP: transmission of small files;

- SMTP (simple mail transfer protocol) enables e-mail exchange between remote machines. SMTP uses TCP;
- TELNET (terminal network protocol) enables a terminal physically connected to a given system to be transformed into a "logic" terminal of another remote terminal.

2. General services (potentially available).
   - `NFS:` enables file distribution (new application);
   - `XDR:` enables the standard representation of objects (new presentation);
   - `RPC:` enables remote procedure calls (new session);
   - `X-WINDOW:` Uses Internet protocols to enable the management of windows on bitmap screens on a network;
   - `TALK:` enables the establishment of dialogue between two users;
3. Unix services.

The remote Unix execution commands (remote commands): rlogin, rsh, swho, rcp and so on.

4.5 Unix Tools for Distributed Programming

In the previous chapters we have presented the fundamental properties of distributed applications, and the principal characteristics of high level programming languages. Unfortunately, if distributed programming languages exist they are in the form of a simple prototype. Chapter 3 was dedicated to the PVM tool which remains a reference in the field of distributed programming. This has the particular feature of being able to provide several libraries of the basic functions used for the development of distributed applications, and not a language as such. Nevertheless, the reader will certainly have observed that *the basic mechanisms used to implement the PVM system were Unix mechanisms.* The kernel process of PVM, "`pvmd`", is none other than a Unix process. PVM communication primitives mainly operate Unix communication tools, that is, the sockets of the client–server model. In this paragraph, we outline the Unix tools required to implement applications using the client–server model, especially mechanisms offered by Unix to establish communication between processes on the same machine or on different machines. Over the following pages we assume that the reader understands the basic concepts of the C language.

In general, the structure of two Unix processes communicating via one of the communication methods offered by this mechanism follows the diagram shown in Figure 4.9. The structure of these processes conforms to the general form of distributed applications (see Chapter 1), which are made up of three phases: the initialization phase, the dialogue phase and the termination phase.

The initialization phase is indicated by the `connection_IPC()` function. It uses one of the Unix communication mechanisms called IPC (inter-process communication) to establish communication with another process. This latter must use a similar function. Once the link between the two processes is effective, the dialogue can commence. The `disconnection_IPC()` function is used to terminate the link between the two processes. It is a model which we recommend that our readers follow scrupulously. Experience has shown us that every other structure is a source of errors or difficulties, notably during correction and program test phases.

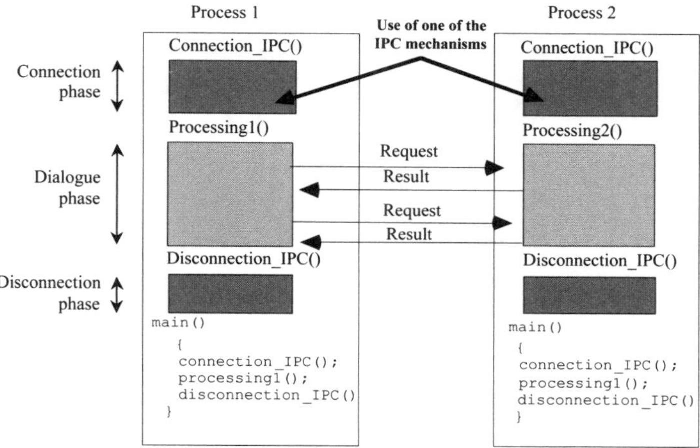

Fig. 4.9 The general form of two Unix communication processes.

4.5.1 The Creation and Manipulation of Processes from a Program

Under Unix, it is important to distinguish two types of processes. On the one hand, the processes involved in the implementation of a *distributed intramachine* application that uses Unix communication methods, and can be *independent* (a user (client) process which uses the services of a daemon system process (server)), and on the other hand processes belonging to the same *lineage* (same family). These processes possess the same father process (Fig. 4.10). They belong to the same principal application and are therefore connected to the same terminal for the same user.

Incidentally, if a user executes the following line of commands from shell:

%date | lpr

this triggers the creation of a process to execute the "date" command and a second process to execute the "lpr" printing command. The two processes are the direct descendants of the "csh" welcome process, and they communicate via a communication pipe: the exit of the first is linked to the entrance of the second.

An execution space for these processes (pool) is allocated to each user connected to the system. These are generally linked in order of descendants. This *descendants link* enables the son processes to inherit the content of the father process (environmental variables, open file descriptors, shared segments, semaphores etc.). This, to a certain extent, facilitates the transmission of initial conditions between the father and the sons, and the sharing of certain common objects which could serve as a means of communication between the two processes (pipes, shared segments, semaphores, files).

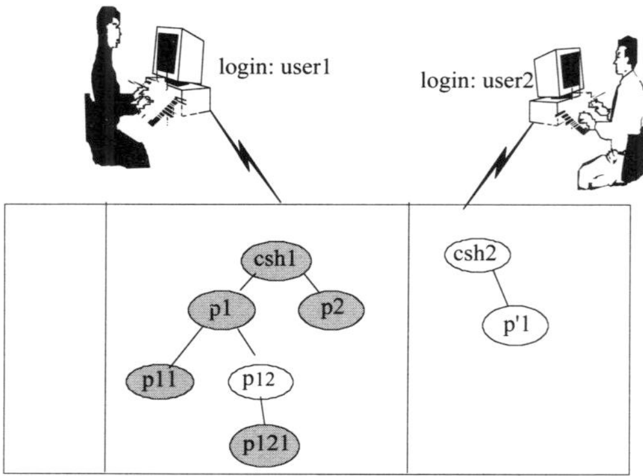

Fig. 4.10 Relations between processes in a Unix system.

It is clear that two processes belonging to two different pools are independent processes. Under these conditions, the means of communication between processes from the same descendants are not valid, and it is necessary to use other more generous means of communication and synchronization. Before presenting the two types of communication mechanisms between Unix processes, we will first present the different means of manipulating the processes from a program.

The creation of processes from a program is carried out using the intermediary of one of the four following primitives: `fork()`, `exec()`, `system()` and `popen()`.

The `fork()` *Primitive*

This primitive is the archetypal means used in the creation of son processes from a program on a Unix machine. The son process is the replica or the exact copy of the image of the father (same code segment, same data segment, same environmental variables, open files, objects used by the father) when the primitive was called. The execution side is, of course, different. After the `fork()` the two processes have a different life span: they usually execute different parts of the program (code segment). The only way the two processes can identify each other is by the value returned by the `fork()` primitive. This is non-existent in the son's code; however, it is equal to the PID (process identification) of the son in the father's code. Figure 4.11 gives an example of the creation of son processes with the `fork()` primitive. After duplicating the father's image, primarily the code segment, the system places the value 0 into the memory zone associated with the `pid_son` variable in the code of the son, and places the PID of the son into the memory zone associated with the pid_son in the code of the father. Following the return of the fork() primitive, the two processes will be able to select the part of the program to be executed.

The reader will have understood that the use of this primitive is limited to distributed and concurrent (same machine) applications where there is a moderate number of co-operating processes.

```
#define  CONST_shared  100
int  VAR_SHARED
Father_processing  () {
...
}
Son_processing  () {
....
}

main() {
int pid_son;
....

switch(pid_son = fork())
     case -1 printf" execution problem with the fork()
             primitive");
                exit(2);
                break;

     case 0 printf("I am the son process, my pid is: %d",
getpid());
 Son_ processing  ();
               exit(0);
               break;

      default  : printf( "I am the father");
                Father_processing  ();
                exit(0);
                break;

}
```

Fig. 4.11 Creation of a process with the fork() primitive.

The exec() *Primitive*

This primitive has the advantage of enabling the recovery of the father's code with that of the executable file provided in parameter. Consequently, following the execution of a fork(), this primitive can be used to replace the code of the father with that of the executable file. It is a means of executing one program from another. There are several variations of this primitive (execl(), execlp(), execle()...). Each one brings additional facilities concerning the location and call arguments of the file to be executed. Figure 4.12a shows an example of the creation of actor processes with this primitive. The role of the father is to create ten files which contain data for the actor son processes. It then creates the actors and transmits to them the relevant number. Each actor collects its number which enables it to identify its data file, process the contents of the file and generate the result in a file always identified by the number of the actor. As soon as an actor son terminates, the father starts to collect the results. Then it terminates.

Note that the father has used the wait() synchronization primitive, which allows the father process to wait for the termination of the son process. This is a form of elementary synchronization. Before blocking this primitive, the father can execute a specific process. A pseudo-parallelism exists where there is weak coupling between the father and the son (asynchronism).

```
                              /* father.c */
 #define NB_ACTORS 10

int pid_terminated;
union wait statut;

generate_data_actors (int i){
    .....
}
process_results_actors(){
......
}
main() {
int pid_son;
int i;
....

for (i = 0; i < NB_ACTORS; i++)
  generate_data_actors(i);

for (i = 0; i < NB_ACTORS; i++)

switch( actors[ i] = fork())

                        exit(2);
                        break;

        case 0 :  strcopy(numActor, i);

                       exit(0);
                       break;

pid_terminated = wait (&statut);
for (i = 0; i < NB_ACTORS; i++)
 process_results_actors(i);

}
```

Fig. 4.12a Creation of processes with the `fork()` and `exec()`: master process.

```
      /*son.c  */
process_m_file() {
....
}

main(int argc, char *argv[ ])
{ int i;
  i = atoi(argv[ 1] );
  printf"I am the actor: %d,i");
 process_name_file();
exit(0);
}
```

Fig. 4.12b Creation of processes with the `fork()` and `exec()`: slave process.

The `system()` *Primitive*

Strong coupling between father and son (synchronous execution) is carried out via the `system()` primitive intermediary. This enables the execution of one program from another with a wait for the termination of the son process. It is as if the father had called the `wait()` primitive just after the execution of the `exec()` primitive, in the scenario shown in Figure 4.12.

The `rexec()` *Primitive*

We have just seen the main Unix primitives used for the creation of processes from a program on the same machine, but essentially, a distributed application can involve local processes on the same machine, and remote processes on different machines. Figure 4.13 shows how we can create a process on a remote site where the IP number (`e_site`) of the corresponding machine is known, to execute the command present on that machine (command).

Communication with the remote process can take place using a port number returned by `rexec()`. This method of communication will be described in the following paragraphs. We are particularly interested in Unix primitives required for the implementation of `connection_IPC` and `disconnection_IPC` functions of our implementation model for processes co-operating under Unix. We start by presenting a mechanism for intramachine communication which is very often used because of the similarities it has with files; this is made up of Unix "pipes". We will then present a more universal communication mechanism to establish communication between activities which can either run on the same machine or on different machines. This involves sockets.

```
//***************************************************************
//
//  Role : - creation of a process on a remote site
//
// Input:        -site on which the process will be created
//               -the complete route of the program to execute
//***************************************************************

void createRemoteProcess(char *e_sites, char *command)
{
struct serve *serve;// structure used for the port number
int sockerr;          // control socket resent by rexec

// search for the port number associated to rexec
serve = getservbyname("exec","tcp");

// call rexec
rexec(&e_site, serve->s_port, USER, PWD, command, & sockerr);
}
```

Fig. 4.13 Creation of a remote process.

4.5.2 Asynchronous Input/Output Operations

It is important that an application designer using the client-server model knows the difference between blocking input/output (I/O) operations provided automatically by the Unix kernel, and non-blocking I/Os which are available at the specific request of processes. Unix is a multi-task, multi-user operating system. Consequently, blocking I/O operations form the basic mechanism operated by the scheduler to share the central unit between the different processes. As soon as a process makes an I/O request, it is suspended for the benefit of another process in the "ready" state in search of the central unit. Blocking I/O operations do not generally place current applications, particularly client processes, at a disadvantage. It is the same principle as standard sequential programming. On the other hand, for the implementation of server processes, the risks of compromising the performance of the server are quite high if only blocking I/O operations are used. When a server process launches an I/O operation (read on a listening socket, write on a service socket, etc) it is necessary to give it the potential ability to continue to carry out other processes in parallel (process another waiting request for example) (Fig. 4.14). When the I/O operation is terminated, the system informs the server of the event; it is then able to process it.

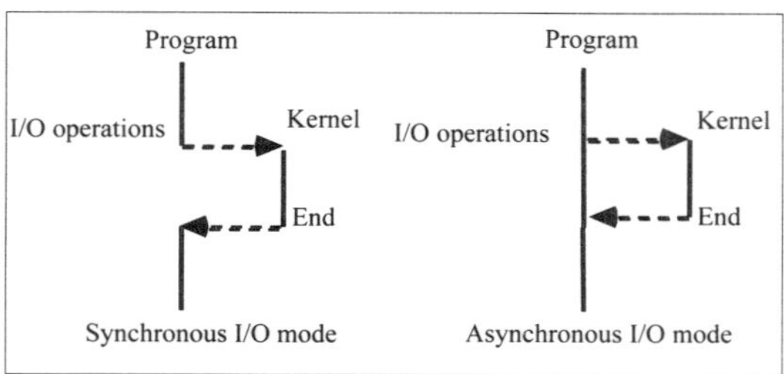

Fig. 4.14 Blocking and non-blocking I/O operations.

Figure 4.15 gives a simple example of a management program for the displacement of graphics on a screen. The user must intervene to alter the direction of the object (for example, H for Higher, R for Right, E for End). After having selected the asynchronous I/O mode, the program carries out a reading. If a character is available, it requests it to change the direction, if not, it continues to advance the object in the same direction. We leave it up to the reader to imagine the situation which results if the I/O operations were blocking.

```
#include <fcntl.h>
#include <stdio.h>
#include <sys/ioctl.h>
advance(){

}
change_dir(char d) {
   /* change the direction of the object*/
}
....
main()
{ int fd;           /* file descriptor*/
   int on=1, off=0;      /* variable for ioctl() */
   char buf;
   fcntl(0, F_SETFL, O_NDELAY I fcntl(0, F_GETFL, 0));  /* I/O non
blocking */
 while (buf <> FIN))
   if ( read(fd, buf, 1)  == 0 ) advance()
       else change_dir(buf);
   fcntl(0, F_SETFL, -O_NDELAY&fnctl(0, F_GETFL, 0)); /* I/O blocking */
   printf("you want to quit");
   if ( read(0, buf, 1))<0)  printf("Error");
   exit(0);
}
```

Fig. 4.15 An example of the use of non-blocking I/O operations.

4.5.3 Software Interrupts

One of the fundamental concepts which enters into the design of a server process is taking account of events in asynchronous mode. In other words, it is necessary to allow a process to intercept events in its immediate environment (system kernel, other processes, external peripheries and so on) without imposing an active blocking wait which will take up CPU time and prevent the server process from carrying out other, more urgent, processes.

Unix suggests the use of *handlers* or logical signal interception routines, whose functioning principle is identical to that of hardware interrupts. In this way the processes are able to ask the kernel to alert them when an I/O operation is completed on a file. This enables asynchronous I/O operations to be implemented without a non-blocking reading loop (Fig. 4.15). All that is required is to combine a *handler* with the SIGIO signal so that the process will be warned when the event occurs (Fig. 4.16).

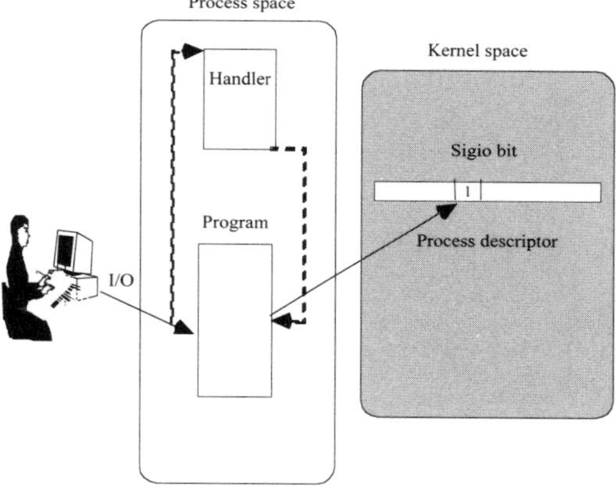


```
        /* Asynchronous I/O on stdin  */
#include <signal.h>
#include <fcntl.h>
Handler_sigio()
{ char buf [ 80] ;
  int nboct;
  nboct= read(1, buf, sizeof(buf));
  buf[ nboct] = '\0';
  printf("buffer received %s\n", buf);
};
main()
{ signal(SIGIO, Handler_sigio);/*positioning the handler*/
fcntl(0, F_SETOWN, getpid())/*authorize the receipt of SIGIO*/
fcntl(0, F_SETFL, FASYNC); /*position the asynchronous   O's*/
I/ for ( ; ; )
 }
```

Fig. 4.16 Management of signals under Unix.

There are 31 predefined signals under Unix. The table in Figure 4.17 lists all of these signals, as well as the default behaviour of processes in their presence. The default behaviour indicates the outcome of the life of a process if it has not been combined with a *handler* to intercept the signal. For example, if a process receives the SIGKILL signal via the intermediary of a *handler*, when it has not foreseen its interception, the process is killed. On the other hand, if an event such as SIGURG is not specifically intercepted, it does not affect the execution of the receptor process.

Figure 4.16 shows that for each system process, Unix associates a 31-bit vector (one bit per signal). The bit is positioned at each occurrence of the signal. If a *handler* is declared by a signal on its arrival, the kernel verifies the existence of the *handler* and the process is re-routed to execute the *handler* before continuing in sequence. The absence of the *handler* triggers a default behaviour (the process is generally killed). It is the `signal()` primitive which enables a *handler* to be combined with a signal.

Number	Signal	Event	Default behaviour
1	SIGHUP	end of session	process termination
2	SIGINT	interrupt: touch <esc>	process termination
3	SIGQUIT	interrupt: touch <quit>	killed: image memory generated
4	SIGILL	illegal instruction	killed: image memory generated
5	SIGTRAP	trace mode	killed: image memory generated
6	SIGIOT	IOT instruction	killed: image memory generated
7	SIGEMT	EMT instruction	killed: image memory generated
8	SIGFPE	arithmetical exception	killed: image memory generated
9	SIGKILL	termination	process termination
10	SIGBUS	bus error	killed: image memory generated
11	SIGSEGV	memory protection violation	killed: image memory generated
12	SIGSYS	call system error	killed: image memory generated
13	SIGPIPE	writing in a tube without reader	killed: image memory generated
14	SIGALRM	triggering clock alarm	process termination
15	SIGTERM	termination signal	process termination
16	SIGUSR1	signal available to define	process termination
17	SIGUSR2	signal available to define	process termination
18	SIGCHLD	termination of son	ignored
19	SIGPWR	reboot following a break	ignored
20	SIGWINCH	redimensioning the window	ignored
21	SIGURG	urgent data on socket	ignored
22	SIGIO	surveilled event realization	process termination
23	SIGSTOP	suspension request	suspension
24	SIGTSTP	external suspension request	suspension
25	SIGCONT	reactivation request	ignorance
26	SIGTTIN	reading the terminal backwards	suspension
27	SIGTTOU	writing to the terminal backwards	suspension
28	SIGVTALRM	virtual clock	process termination
29	SIGPROF	clock	process termination
30	SIGCPU	maximum CPU time disposed	killed: image memory generated
31	SIGXFSZ	maximum size of queue	killed: image memory generated

Fig. 4.17 The different Unix signals, version SYSTEM V.5.

Finally, to complete this section assessing events under Unix, it is important to note that there exists a simple way to search or poll for the arrival of an event, without forcing the process to enter into a loop of non-blocking reading operations. This involves the use of the `poll()` primitive (Fig. 4.18). The form of search carried out by this primitive enables an event to be intercepted on a descriptor (reading on a descriptor, writing on a descriptor etc.). It is a primitive currently used in the design of writing Unix server or *daemon* processes.

```
#include <poll.h>
#include <stropts.h>
#include <stdio.h>
#define fdio 0
#define fdip 4
main()
{  struct pollfd fds[ 2] ;
   char buf[ 80] ; int i;
   for ( ; ;)
       { fds[ 0] .fd=fdio; fds[ 1] .fd=fdip;fds[ 0] .events=POLLIN;fds[ 1] .events=POLLIN;
         fds[ 0] .revents=0;fds[ 1] .revents=0;
         switch (poll(fds,2,6000))
            { case 0:  /* timeout */
                              fprintf(stout, "timeout \n"); exit(0);
              default:
                             /* stdin*/
                if (fds[ 0] .revents == POLLIN){
                for (i=0; i< sizeof(buf); i++){ read(fdio,  &buf[ i] ,1);
                       if (buf[ i] =='\n')break}
                   else     /* file */
                if (fds[ 0] .revents == POLLIN){
                for (i=0; i< sizeof(buf); i++){ read(fdio,  &buf[ i] ,1);
                       if(buf[ i] =='\n')break} ;
                 buf[ i+1] ='\0'; fprintf(stdout, buf received%s \n", buf);
         }}
```

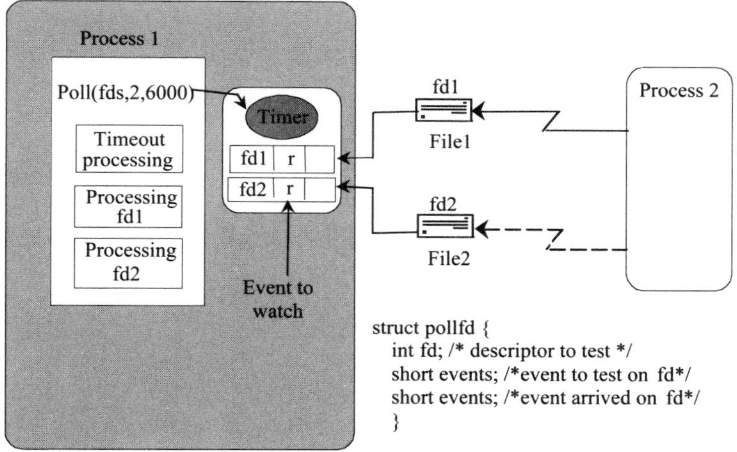

Figure 4.18 The Unix polling principle.

4.5.4 Pipes: An Intra-machine Communication Method

Unix offers several communication and synchronization mechanisms (IPC) on the same machine. There are two groups of mechanisms: the first involves mechanisms whose use is identical to that of files: pipes and named pipes. The second mechanism groups strings of messages (BAL), semaphores and shared segments (Unix System V).

Pipes are rapid, unidirectional methods of communication between processes on the same machine. They include special files present in the central memory for performance reasons. Consequently, file manipulation primitives remain valid for pipes. The unit of storage in pipes is the character, which makes up the *character flow*. The creation of a pipe is carried out using the `pipe()` primitive.

There is a noticeable difference between pipes and files. Two descriptors are associated to a pipe instead of one, as is the case with files. One of the descriptors will be used for writing in the pipe, and the other for reading (Fig. 4.19). The two descriptors are being shared by the two processes communicating via this pipe (one of the two processes has inherited from the other, which is the father process for the pipe descriptors), this therefore imposes the use of an elementary communication protocol between the write process and the read process:

- The write process must close the descriptor with a read-out;
- The read process must close the descriptor with a write.

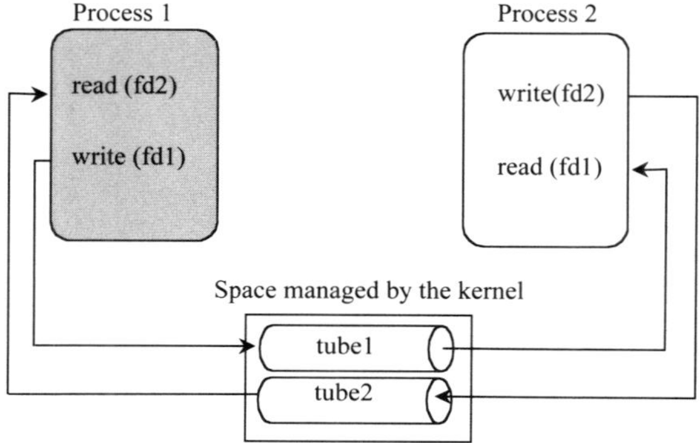

Fig. 4.19 The use of pipes as a means of communication.

Figure 4.20 shows the implementation of the client–server model on the same machine by using pipes as a means of communication. This example illustrates the numerous aspects of the client–server model, especially those concerned with the communication between several processes in the completion of a complex task and its functional or modular refinement into more or less independent sub-tasks.

To enable readers to find the structuring model for a distributed application (Fig. 4.9) based on the client–server model, we have linked (with the same background colour) the parts which have an identical function in the client code (Fig. 4.20a) and the server code (Fig. 4.20b).

```
#include <stdio.h>    /*shared file.h */
#include <fcntl.h>
#include <sys/types>
struct request { structure of a message of a request*/
       short code;
       char parl[ 80] ; part2[ 80] ;
      }
```

```
#include "shared.h"
int  lfd, efd;  /* pipe descriptors*/
main()  /* Client process*/
{    connection_IPC();
 clientProcessing();
     disconnection();
}
```

```
connection_IPC ()
{  int tube1[ 2] ; /* descriptors tube1 */
    int tube2[ 2] ; /* descriptors tube2 */
    int code;
    char arg1 [ 10] , arg2[ 10] ; /* temporary variables*/
/* creation of two tubes to communicate bidirectionally*/
    if (tube (tube1) <0)  II tube(tube2) < 0) printf("error");

/* create a server process by fork() */
    switch( fork()) {
                case 0:  /* son*/
                          /* close the descriptors not used */
                       close(tube1[ 1] );
                      close(tube2[ 0] );
                          /* launch the server process*/
                  sprintf(arg1, "%d", tube1[ 0] );
                  sprintf(arg2,"%d", tube2[ 1] );
   code = execl("server", "server", arg1, arg2,  (char *)0);
              lfd=tube2[ 0] ; efd= tube1[ 1] ;
                default:  /* father */
                           /* close the descriptors not used*/
                        close(tube1[ 0] );
                        close(tube2[ 1] );
              }
}
```

```
Processing Client()
{ struct request *req;
   req->code= 0; /* code add */
   req->par1="MAXLINE";
   req->par2="100";
  /* send the request to the server*/
   code= write(efd,req,sizeof(*req));
  /* receipt of return code*/
    code= read(lfd, req, sizeof(req));
  if (req->par1="0") printf("succes")  else printf("fail");
   /* search request*/
   req-> code= 1; /* code lookup*/
   req->par1="MAXLINE";
    code=write(efd,req,sizeof(*req));
    code=read(lfd,req,siezof(req));
 if(req->par1 != "0") printf("replacement value %s", req->par1);
}
```

```
disconnection()
       int code;
  {          close(lfd);
            close(efd);
          /* wait end of execution of son*/
               wait (&code);
                 exit(o);
  }
```

Figure 4.20a Implementation of the client–server model with pipes: client part.

```
#include "shared.h"
#define MAXHASH 100
 struct nlist { /* type of input in the table of  symbols*/
                       char *name, * def;
                        struct nlist *next; };
  static struct nlist * hashTab[ MAXHASH] ;
int lfd, efd;  /* tube descriptors*/
main (argc, argv)
int argc; char ** argv;
{  connection( argv[ 1] , argv[ 2] );
 serverProcessing(();
   disconnection();
}
```

```
connection_IPC (argv1, argv2);
 char *argv1, *argv2;
{     lfd = atoi(argv1);
       efd = atoi(argv2);
}
```

```
ServerProcessing  ();
{   int code;
     struct request req;
       /* receipt of a request*/
     code = read (*lfd, req,sizeof(req));
     switch (req->code) {
           case 1      /* search request*/
                             req->code= 3; /* result code*/
                             req->par1 = NULL;
                              tmp = lookup(   req->par1);
                             if (temp)    req->par1= temp->def;
                             code = write( efd,req,sizeof( req));
           default:     /* request to add a new element*/
                             req->code = 3;
                             req->par1 = add( req->par1, req->par2);
                             code =write( efd,req,sizeof( req));}
}
```

```
hash (s)    /* function of hashing*/
char *s     /* transform a chain into an integer*/
{     int hashval;
      for (hashval =0; *s != '\0'; )
              hashval   += *s++;
      return (hashval % MAXHASH );
}

struct nlist  *lookup (s) /* search for s in the table*/
 char *s;
{    struct nlist * np;
      for ( np= hashtab [ hash(s)] ; np != NULL; np = np-> next)
         if ( strcmp(s, np->nom) ==0 )
              return ( np);    /*  found*/
          return( NULL);
}

char *add(name, def)
  char *name, * def;
{  struct  nlist * np; char *lookup(); int hashval;
   if (( np = lookup(nom)) == NULL) { /* does not exist*/
        np = (struct nlist *) alloc (sizeof(* np));
       if (np == NULL) return (NULL);
        sprintf ( np->nom, %s, nom);
         hashval = hash( np->name); np->next = hashtab[ hashval] ;
         hashtab[ hashval] = np;
     } else free(np->def);  /* exists already*/
         sprintf(np->def, %s, del); return (NULL);
 }
```

```
disconnection ();
{ close (lfd);
   close(efd);
   exit(0);
```

Figure 4.20b Implementation of the client–server model with pipes: server part.

It represents all that can be found in management programs of the symbolic reference tables of a pre-processor or a compiler. Take the `#define` C language instruction, for example. When the pre-processor encounters a line such as

`#define YES 1`, the YES chain as well as its value of 1 are stored in a table. Later on, when YES appears in an instruction such as `X = YES`: the X variable takes the value of 1.

Table management (the addition or search for a name) is carried out by a server process. The client process is the compiler. The communication protocol between the two is very simple and is limited to the two following messages:

Client processes		*Server process table references*
Add s, t	⇒	(Record the name s and its replacement value t in the table).
	⇐	(Code: 0 success, 1 error).
Look up s	⇒	(Search for s in the table).
	⇐	(Result: 0 if it does not exist, otherwise its replacement value).

It is important to note that a pipe can only allow processes from the same system to communicate. To enable independent processes from different system to communicate, *named pipes* must be used. Different from ordinary pipes, named pipes are identified by an outside name for the same reasons as files. The example given in Figure 4.20 can therefore serve as a basis from which to implement a database server or a file server in a machine.

Enough about the use of named pipes as a means of communication between independent processes. There is another more efficient means: sockets, which are described in the following section.

4.6 Sockets

The BSD 4.2 Unix version was the first to include TCP/IP in the kernel of an operating system, and to offer a programming interface for these protocols: *sockets.* Sockets are an API (application program interface) or an interface between application programs and network layers. The term "socket" describes both a library of network interfaces and the extremity of a communication channel (communication point or port) via which a process can emit or receive data. This communication point is designated by a *variable integer,* which represents its *descriptor* in the same way as the descriptor represents a file opened by the process. It is important to note that this descriptor has to be *local* to the process (S1, S2 are variable descriptors of sockets local to the P11 process in Figure 4.21). Consequently, it is not visible from the outside and therefore not visible to other processes. Sockets enable the establishment of Unix inter-machine and intra-machine communications.

There are two types of sockets (Fig. 4.21):

- AF_UNIX type sockets, which only allow intra-machine communication;
- AF_INET type sockets, which only allow inter-machine communications.

The principles surrounding the use and manipulation of these two types of sockets are found in its identical main features. The development and perfection of distributed applications can be carried out first on a Unix machine using AF_UNIX type sockets. A distributed version of the application can be obtained this time using AF_INET sockets.

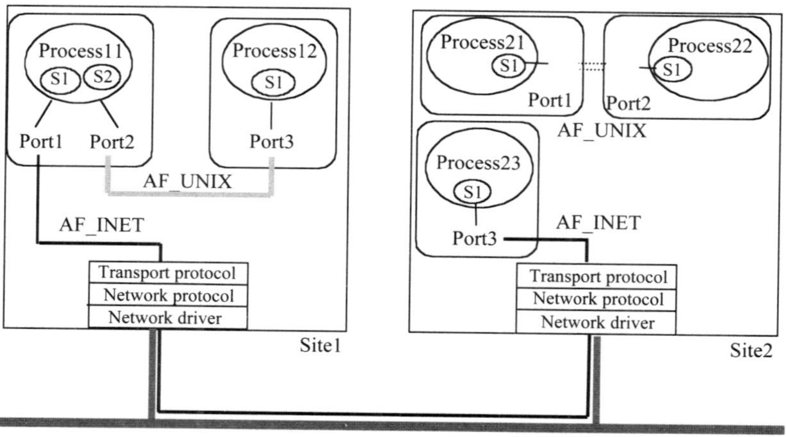

Fig. 4.21 Sockets: a universal communication mechanism.

To establish communication between two processes, at least one of the two processes must have a visible communication port (recall that under Unix there is a list of communication ports identified by their numbers). Each communication port represents a *fixed address* within the system. A process that asks to be *re-attached* to this fixed address, could receive datagram link establishment requests. Furthermore, the two processes could then request the creation of a socket. The socket enables them to indicate the type of data transmission protocol (TCP/IP: SOCK_STREAM or UDP: SOCK_DGRAM) to use and the field (geographical range) of authorized communication (AF-UNIX for network communications). When the chosen protocol is the TCP/IP protocol, and therefore a SOCK_STREAM type socket, the link between the two processes is permanent – a virtual channel between the two processes (connected mode). On the other hand, if the protocol used is the UDP protocol, there does not exist a permanent virtual link between the two processes. The order of message reception by an extremity can be totally different from that used by the emitting extremity to transmit them (connectionless mode).

Depending on the connection mode used, several rules must be followed to enable two processes to communicate via sockets. Figure 4.22 gives the dialogue protocol between a client process and a server process in connected mode. Both the server and the client start by requesting the creation of a socket with the `socket()` command, to have access to the kernel's data transmission service. The `socket()` primitive sends a local socket descriptor to the process, as mentioned above. The server must then request the re-attachment of the socket to a communication port visible to other processes, before tuning in to the socket for potential connection requests from client processes using the `listen()` primitive. A client requests the establishment of a link or virtual channel using the `connect()` primitive. If the server accepts the link establishment with a client using the `accept()` primitive, dialogue can then commence between the two processes. The virtual channel established can then be closed at the specific request of one of the two primitives with the `close()` primitive.

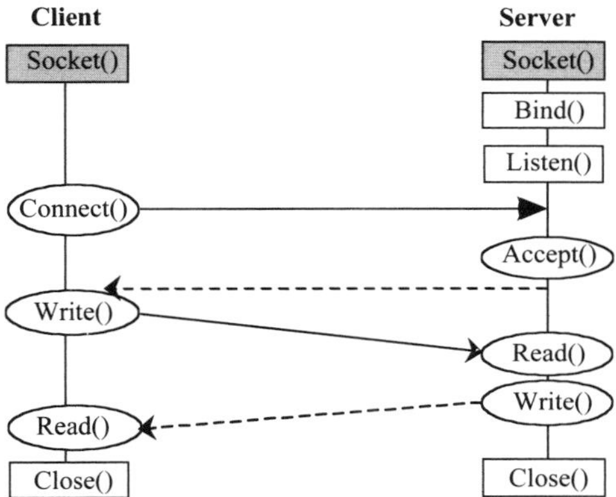

Fig. 4.22 Dialogue protocol in connectionless mode.

Figure 4.23 gives the dialogue protocol between a client process and a server process in connectionless mode. In this mode, the implementation of dialogue between two processes requires fewer system primitives, and does not need the creation of a virtual channel. A client process which has requested the use of transmission layer services (UDP protocol) by specifying the exchange field with the `socket()` primitive, can send datagrams to any server in the field in question using the `sendto()` primitive, if it knows the re-attachment port (visible address). As for the server, after attachment to a port, it can receive any message emitted towards this port using the `recvfrom()` primitive.

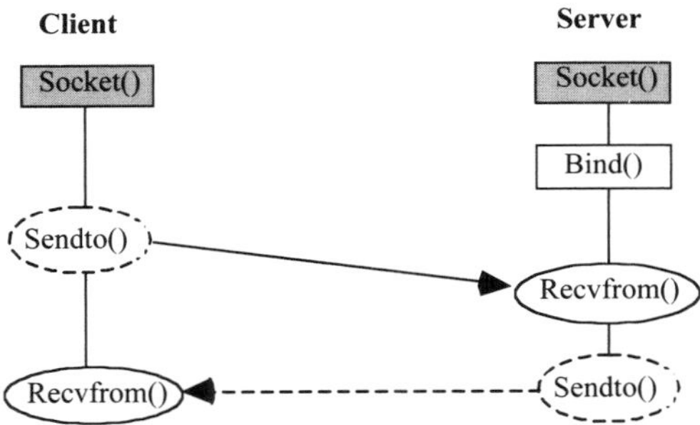

Fig. 4.23 Dialogue protocol in non-connected mode.

At this stage, it is important to note that if the exchange field is the AF_UNIX field (the machine), the port used by a process for socket attachment is limited to a simple external file name. Effectively, every independent machine process that knows the name of this file can enter into communication with the process which used it as a fixed address.

4.6.1 Client–Server Applications in "AF_UNIX Connected Field" Mode

The following distributed application shows the client–server interaction from Figure 4.19, this time with sockets as the means of communication, limiting the exchange field to the machine. *The client and server processes are, of course, independent processes.* In this implementation, we have followed our structuring model for the code of processes communicating under Unix. We have also linked the code of the two processes to enable the readers to locate and compare the different functional parts of the two processes. We have also continued our approach which involved isolating the instructions related to the declaration and creation of a communication means in a separate part of the process code. In this case, it is a virtual communication channel between the client and the server. This declaration follows the example below in terms of an *automaton* (use of a pre-processor for high-level formalism: Chapter 2):

- definition of an attach port of a channel owner process (server);
- definition of the type of messages exchanged within this channel;
- definition of the reading and writing primitives on the channel;
- definition of the opening and closing primitives of the channel.

The content of the functions `connection_IPC()`, `processing_server()` or `processing_client()` and `disconnection_IPC()` is explained.

The reader will judge the readability and clarity of the content of the `processing_server()` or `processing_client()` function as a direct consequence of our method. The application designer focuses all his efforts on writing unique processing methods for each process.

It is well known that the `accept()` primitive returns the socket descriptor of a *different* service from that of the listening socket. This facility has been introduced to give the server process the option of creating a son process and delegating to it responsibility for the interaction (dialogue) which has been accepted. This enables the global performance of the server to increase substantially. *The duplication of the server process again poses standard problems of the sharing and management of concurrent access to shared resources.* If this solution must be used, we advise our readers to adopt the monitor approach (see Chapter 2) for the management of shared resources. For implementation purposes, it is enough to simply alter the `processingServer()` function. The new version of this function must resemble the following code:

```
{int nsock;
for(;;)
     {
```

```
        nsock = accept(sock,(struct sockaddr*)0,(int*)0);
        if(fork() == 0)
                        processingRequest(nsock);
        }
    }
```

It is always possible to improve this version by recovering the server code. It is sufficient to create a file which contains the `processingRequest()` function, and to load it after the `fork()` call using the `exec()` primitive or one of its variations.

➢ Implementation of the Server for the Table of References with AF_UNIX Type Sockets on a Single Machine in Connected Mode

```
                                    /*Server Process*/
#include <sys/types.h>
#include <sys/socket.h>
#include <sys/ioctl.h>
#include <unistd.h>
#include <stdio.h>
#include <fcntl.h>
#include <errno.h>
#include <sys/un.h>
#include <string.h>
#include <bstring.h>
#include <malloc.h>
#define MAXHASH 100
```

```
/****CHANNEL DEFINITION****/

#define SPATH "/tmp/usocket"                        /*server port*/
                                        /*format of channel messages*/
int sock;                                           /*server socket*/
struct request {
         short code;
         char par1[10], par2[10];
         };

/****WRITING IN THE CHANNEL****/
int writes(register int sock, register char *pbuf, register int noc)
{
int nrest, nwrite;
nrest = noc;
while (nrest > 0) {
        nwrite = write(sock, pbuf, nrest);
        if (nwrite < 0) return(nwrite);
        nrest-=nwrite;
        pbuf+=nwrite;
        }
return(noc-nrest);
}

/****READING FROM THE CHANNEL****/
int reads(register int sock, register char *pbuf, register int noc)
{
int nrest, nread;
nrest = noc;
```

```
while (nrest > 0) {
        nread = read(sock, pbuf, nrest);
        if (nread < 0) return(nread);
        else if (nread==0) break;
        nrest-=nread
        pbuf+=nread;
        }
return(noc-nrest);
}

/****CHANNEL CREATION****/

connection_IPC()
{
int nsock;
struct sockaddr_a server;
int len;

/*Creation of a socket*/
sock = socket(AF_UNIX,SOCK_STREAM,0);
alink(SPATH);
bzero(&server, sizeof(server));
server.sun_family = AF_UNIX;
strcpy(server.sun_path,SPATH);
len = strlen(server.sun_path) + sizeof(server.sun_family);
bind(sock,(struct sockaddr*)&server, len);

/*Tuning in to entering connections*/
listen(sock,5);
}
/****CHANNEL CLOSURE****/
disconnection()
{
printf("disconnection \n");
close(sock);
}

/****END OF CHANNEL DECLARATION****/
```

```
struct nlist {
         char *name, *def;
         struct nlist *next;
         };
static struct nlist *hashtab[MAXHASH];
hash(char s)                                   /*function of hash*/
{                                              /*transform a chain into an integer*/
int hashval;
for (hashval=0; *s != '\0' ;)
        hashval += *s++;
return(hashval % MAXHASH);}
struct nlist *lookup(char *s){                 /*search for s in the table*/
struct nlist *np;
for {*np->next = *hashtab[hash(s)]; np != NULL; np = np->next)
        if (strcmp(s, np->name) == 0)
                return(np);                    /*found*/
return(NULL);}
```

```
char *add(char *name, char *def){
 struct nlist *np;
int hashval;
if ((np = lookup(name)) == NULL) {
       np = (struct nlist*)malloc(sizeof(*np));
       if(np==NULL) return(NULL);
       sprintf(np->name, "%s", name);
       hashval = hash(np->name);
       np->next = hashtab[hashval];
       hashtab[hashval] = np;
else free(np->def);
sprintf(np->def, "%s", def);
return(np->name);}

processingRequest(int nsock){
int code;
struct request req;
struct nlist *time;
code = reads(nsock, (char *)&req, sizeof(req));

switch(req.code) (
       case 1 :
               printf("processing request : element search \n");
               req.code = 3;
               strcpy(req.par1, "search");
               time = lookup(req.par1);
               if (time) req.par1 = time->def;
       code = writes(nsock, (char *)&req, sizeof(req));
break;
       default :
req.code = 3;
               strcpy(req.par1, "add");
               strcpy(req.par2, "12345");
               req.par1 = add(req.par1, req.par2);
               code = writes(nsock, (char *)&req, sizeof(req)); }
}

/****SERVER PROCESSING****/
serverProcessing ()
{int nsock;
for(;;)
       {
       nsock = accept(sock, (struct sockaddr*)0,(int*)0);
       processingRequest(nsock);
     }
}

/****MAIN PROGRAM****/
main()
{
connection_IPC();
serverProcessing ();
disconnection();
}
```

➢ Implementation of the Server for the Table of References with AF_UNIX Type Sockets on a Single Machine in Connected Mode

```
/*Client Process*/

#include <sys/types.h>
#include <sys/socket.h>
#include <sys/ioctl.h>
#include <unistd.h>
#include <stdio.h>
#include <fcntl.h>
#include <errno.h>
#include <sys/un.h>
#include <string.h>
#include <bstring.h>
```

```
/****CHANNEL DEFINITION****/
#define SPATH "/tmp/usocket"                    /*server port*/
int sock;                                       /*client socket*/

                                                /*format of channel messages*/
struct request {
        short code;
        char par1[10], par2[10];
        };

/****WRITING IN THE CHANNEL****/
int writes(register int sock, register char *pbuf, register int noc)
{
int nrest, nwrite;
nrest = noc;
while (nrest > 0) {
        nwrite = write(sock, pbuf, nrest);
        if (nwrite < 0) return(nwrite);
        nrest-=nwrite;
        pbuf+=nwrite;
        }
return(noc-nrest);
}

/****READING FROM THE CHANNEL****/
int reads(register int sock, register char *pbuf, register int noc)
{
int nrest, nread;
nrest = noc;
while (nrest > 0 ) {
        nread = read(sock, pbuf, nrest);
        if (nread < 0) return(nread);
        else if (nread==0) break;
        nrest-=nread;
        pbuf+=nread;
        }
return(noc-nrest);
}
```

```
/****CHANNEL CREATION****/
connection_IPC()
{
struct sockaddr_a server;
int len;
                                        /*socket creation*/
sock = socket(AF_UNIX,SOCK_STREAM,0);

                                        /*place character string at zero*/
bzero(&server, sizeof(server));
server.sun_family = AF_UNIX;

                                        /*character string copy*/
strcpy(server.sun_path,SPATH);
len = strlen(server.sun_path)+ sizeof(server.sun_family);

                                        /*server connection*/
connect(sock,(struct sockaddr*)&server,len);
}

/****CHANNEL CLOSURE****/
disconnection()
{
printf("disconnection \n");
close(sock);
}
/****END OF CHANNEL DECLARATION****/
```

```
/****CLIENT PROCESSING****/
clientprocessing()
{
int code;
struct request req;

                                        /*request to add an element*/
req.code = 0;
strcpy(req.par1, "MAXLINE");
strcpy(req.par2, "100");
printf("req.code = %d \n",req.code);
printf("req.par1 = %s \n",req.par1);
printf("req.par2 = %s \n",req.par2);
printf("Processing request 1 \n");
if((code = writes(sock, (char *)&req, sizeof(req))) == -1) {
        perror("writing problem");
        }
printf("code write : %d \n", code);
code = reads(sock, (char *)&req, sizeof(req));
if((code = writes(sock, (char *)&req, sizeof(req))) == -1 {
        perror("reading problem");
        }
printf("code read : %d \n", code);
printf("req.code = %d \n",req.code);
printf("req.par1 = %s \n",req.par1);
printf("req.par2 = %s \n",req.par2);
if (strcmp(req.par1, "add")==0)
```

```
        printf("success. req.par1 = %s \n", req.par1);
else printf("fail. req.par1 = %s \n",req.par1);
printf("End of request processing 1 \n");

                                                    /*search request*/
req.code = 1;
strcpy(req.par1, "MAXLINE");
printf("req.code = %d \n",req.code);
printf("req.par1 = %s \n",req.par1);
printf("processing request 2 \n");
code = writes(sock, (char *)&req, sizeof(req));
if((code = writes(sock, (char *)&req, sizeof(req))) == -1) {
        perror("writing problem");
        }
printf("code write : %d \n", code);
code = reads(sock, (char *)&req, sizeof(req));
if((code = writes(sock, (char *)&req, sizeof(req))) == -1) [
        perror("reading problem");
        }
printf("code read : %d \n", code);
printf("req.code = %d \n",req.code);
printf("req.par1 = %s \n",req.par1);
if (req.par1 != NULL)
        printf("replacement value %s \n",req.par1);
else printf("no replacement value %s \n",req.par1);
printf("end of processing request 2 \n");
}
/****END OF CLIENT PROCESSING****/
```

```
/****MAIN PROGRAM****/

MAIN()
{
connection_IPC();
clientProcessing();
disconnection();
}
```

4.6.2 Client–Server Applications in "AF_INET Field Connected" Mode

To fully understand the network connection procedure with AF_INET sockets, we look at the content of two client and server connection functions "`connection_IPC()`". The client starts by recuperating the IP address of the machine on which the server process lies, using the `gethostbyname()`primitive, which takes the name of the machine as a parameter. It then calls the `socket()`primitive to obtain a description of a socket in the network field (AF_INET) using TCP/IP (SOCK_STREAM) as a transmission protocol. The following instruction involves the initialization of the `sockaddr_in` type server structure to zero. This structure will contain the information required to transmit to the server host kernel to establish connection with the server process; the field (`server.sin_family`), the server port number (`server.sin_port`) and the Internet address of the server host (`server.sin_addr`). At this point, the reader must pay particular attention to the use of the `htons()` instruction to transform the port number, which is an integer, into an independent network representation with the internal format of the machine which runs the client. If transmitting strings of characters does not pose any major problems, the machines all use the same ASCII table, numerical quantities (integers, real numbers), which must be used carefully as we have already seen in Chapter 3. A set of primitives are available and enable coding to be carried out in an independent abstract representation of machines before emission and decoding into local format after reception. Incidentally, the dual `htons()` primitive (**h**ost **to** **n**etwork) is `ntohs()`. The next stage of the procedure to establish connection with the server involves calling the `connect()` primitive with the necessary information concerning the address of the remote process, which is contained in the "server" structure. If the execution of this latter primitive is carried out successfully, a link (virtual channel) is established between the socket of the client process and the socket of the remote server.

```
connection_IPC()                                                    /*Client*/
{struct sockaddr_in server;
hp = (struct hostent*)gethostbyname(NAME_HOST);
sock = socket(AF_INET,SOCK_STREAM,0);
bzero(&server, sizeof(server));
server.sin_family = AF_INET;
bcopy((char*)hp->h_addr, (char*) &server.sin_addr, hp->h_length);
server.sin_port = htons(PORT);                               /*network format*/
connect(sock,(struct sockaddr *)&server,sizeof(server));}
```

➢ Implementation of the Server for the Table of References with AF_INET Type TCP Sockets on a Network in Connected Mode

```
/*Server Process*/

#include <sys/types.h>
#include <sys/socket.h>
#include <sys/ioctl.h>
#include <unistd.h>
#include <stdio.h>
#include <fcntl.h>
#include <errno.h>
#include <netdb.h>
#include <netinet/in.h>
#include <string.h>
#include <bstring.h>
#include <malloc.h>
#define SPATH "/tmp/usocket"
#define MAXHASH 100
```

```
/****CHANNEL DEFINITION****/
#define PORT 6259

/****MESSAGE STRUCTURE****/
struct request {
               short code;
               char par1[80] ,par2[80];
```

```
                };

char *host;
struct hostent *hp;
int sock;                                              /*SERVER SOCKET*/

/****WRITING IN THE CHANNEL ****/
int writes(int sock, char *pbuf, int noc)
{
int nrest, nwrite;
nrest = noc;
while (nrest > 0) {
                nwrite = write(sock, pbuf, nrest);
                if (nwrite < 0) return(nwrite);
                nrest-=nwrite;
                pbuf+=nwrite;
                }
return(noc-nrest);
}

/****READING FROM THE CHANNEL****/
int reads(int sock, char *pbuf, int noc)
{
int nrest, nread;
nrest = noc;
while (nrest > 0) {
                nread = read(sock, pbuf, nrest);
                if (nread < 0) return(nread);
                else if (nread==0) break;
                nrest-=nread;
                pbuf+=nread;
                }
return(noc-nrest);
}

/****CHANNEL OPENING****/
connection_IPC()
{
        struct sockaddr_in server;
/****Socket Creation****/
sock = socket(AF_INET,SOCK_STREAM,0);
bzero(&server, sizeof(server));
server.sin_family = AF-INET;
server.sin_addr.s_addr = INADDR_ANY;
server.sin_port = htons(PORT);
bind(sock,(struct sockaddr *)&server, sizeof(server));
                                        /*place in touch with incoming connections*/
listen(sock,5);
}

/****CHANNEL CLOSING****/
disconnection_IPC(){
                close (sock);
}
/****END OF CHANNEL DECLARATION****/
```

```
struct nlist {
               char *name, *def;
               struct nlist *next;
               };
static struct nlist *hashtab[MAXHASH];
hash(char s)                                        /*hash function*/
{                                    /*transform a string into an integer*/
int hashval;
for (hashval=0; *s != '\0' ;)
              hashval += *s++;
return(hashval % MAXHASH);
}
struct nlist *lookup(char *s)
{
                                                /*search for s in the table*/
struct nlist *np;
for (*np->next = *hashtab[hash(s)]; np != NULL; np = np->next)
              if (strcmp(s, np->name) ==0)
                     return(np);                            /*find*/
return(NULL);
}

char *add(char *name, char *def)
{
struct nlist *np;
int hashval;
if ((np = lookup(name)) == NULL)
{
       np = (struct nlist*)malloc(sizeof(*np));
       if(np==NULL)return(NULL);
       sprintf(np->name, "%s", name);
       hashval = hash(np->name);
       np->next = hashtab[hashval];
       hashtab[hashval] = np;
       }
else free(np->def);
sprintf(np->def. "%s", def);
return(np->name);
}
Requestprocessing (int nsock)
{
int code;
struct request req;
struct nlist *temp;
code = reads(nsock, (char *)&req, sizeof(req));
switch(req.code)
        {
        case 1 :
               req.code = 3;
               strcpy(req.par1, "NULL");
               time = lookup(req.par1);
               if (time) req.par1 = time->def;
 code = writes(nsock, (char *)&req, sizeof(req));
               break;
       default:
               req.code = 3;
```

```
                    strcpy(req.par1, "add");
                    strcpy(req.par2, "12345");
                    req.par1 = add(req.par1, req.par2);
 code = writes(nsock, (char *)&req, sizeof(req));
                         }
}
```

```
/****SERVER PROCESSING****/
serverProcessing()
{
int nsock;
/****SERVER DETACHMENT****/
close (0); close(1); close(2);
if ((i = open("/dev/tty")) > -1{
        ioctl(i,TIOCNOTTY,0); close(i);
}
while(1)
         {
         nsock = accept(sock,(struct sockaddr*)0,(int*)0);
         requestProcessing (nsock);
         }
```

```
main()
{
connection_IPC();
serverProcessing(sock);
}
```

- **Implementation of the Server for the Table of References with AF_INET Type TCP Sockets on a Network in Connected Mode**

```
/*Client Process*/
#include <sys/types.h>
#include <sys/socket.h>
#include <sys/ioctl.h>
#include <unistd.h>
#include <stdio.h>
#include <fcntl.h>
#include <errno.h>
#include <netdb.h>
#include <netinet/in.h>
#include <string.h>
#include <bstring.h>
```

```
/****CHANNEL DEFINITION****/
#define PORT 6259                           /*communication port*/
#define HOST_NAME "isma"                    /*host server*/

/****MESSAGE STRUCTURE****/
struct request {
         short code;
         char par1[80]; char par2[80];
         };
```

```
char *host;
struct hostent *hp;
struct hostent *gethostbyname();
int sock;                                              /*Client socket*/

/****CHANNEL WRITING****/
int writes(int sock, char *pbuf, int noc)
{
int nrest, nwrite;
nrest = noc;
while (nrest > 0) {
        nwrite = write(sock, pbuf, nrest);
        if (nwrite < 0) return(nwrite);
        nrest-=nwrite;
        pbuf+=nwrite;
        }
return(noc-nrest);
}

/****READING FROM A CHANNEL****/
int reads(int sock, char *pbuf, int noc)
{
int rest, nread;
nrest = noc;
while (nrest > 0) {
        nread = read(sock, pbuf, nrest);
        if (nread < 0) return(nread);
        else if (nread==0) break;
        nrest-=nread;
        pbuf+=nread;
        }
return(noc-nrest);
}

/****CHANNEL OPENING****/
connection_IPC()
{
struct sockaddr_in server;

hp = (struct hostent*)gethostbyname(HOST_NAME);
sock = socket(AF_INET,SOCK_STREAM,0);
bzero(&server, sizeof(server));
server.sin_family = AF_INET;
bcopy((char *)hp->h_addr, (char *) &server.sin_addr, hp->h_length;
server.sin_port = htons(PORT);                          /*f. network*/
connect(sock,(struct sockaddr *)&server,sizeof(server));
}

/****CHANNEL CLOSURE****/
disconnection_IPC()
{
close(sock);
}
/****END OF CHANNEL DECLARATION****/
```

```
/****CLENT PROCESSING****/

clientProcessing()
{
int code;

struct request req;
req.code = 0;
strcpy(req.par1, "MAXLINE");
strcpy(req.par2, "100");
code = writes(sock,(char *)&req,sizeof(req));
code = reads(sock,(char *)&req,sizeof(req));

printf("req.code = %d \n",req.code);
printf("req.par1 = %s \n",req.par1);
printf("req.par2 = %s \n",req.par2);

if(req.par1 == "0")
          printf("success \n");
else printf("fail \n");

req.code = 1;
strcpy(req.par1, "MAXLINE");

code = writes(sock,(char *)&req,sizeof(req));
code = reads(sock,(char *)&req,sizeof(req));

printf("req.code = %d \n",req.code);
printf("req.par1 = %s \n",req.par1);

if(req.par1 !=NULL)
        printf("replacement value %s \n",req.par1);
}
```

```
main()

/****MAIN PROGRAM***/
{
connection_IPC();
clientProcessing();
disconnection();
}
```

Where the server is concerned, the procedure for establishing connections between the client processes is just as simple. It starts by creating a tuning socket by specifying its characteristics (field: AF_INET, type: SOCK_STREAM). It then prepares the descriptor for the network address (attachment point) on which the server will carry out the attachment with the `bind()` primitive. After this operation the server facilities will become accessible to all client processes in possession of the descriptor for its network address (field: AF_INET, type: SOCK_STREAM, port: 6259). The number of the server port is of course stored in network form.

After attachment, the server tunes into the socket linked to its network address, to accept the connection demands carried out by the client processes using the `connect()` primitive.

```
Connection_IPC()                                          /*server*/
{
     struct sockaddr_in server;

/****socket creation****/
sock = socket(AF_INET,SOCK_STREAM,0);
bzero(&server, sizeof(server));
server.sin_family = AF_INET;
server.sin_addr.s_addr = INADR_ANY;
server.sin_port = htons(PORT);
bind(sock, (struct sockaddr *)&server, sizeof(server));
/*tuning in of incoming connections*/
listen(sock,5);
}
```

We end this section by giving the network version of the preceding application, this time in datagram mode.

➢ Implementation of the Server for the Table of References with AF_INET Type TCP Sockets on a Network in Datagram Mode

```
/*Server Process*/
#include <sys/types.h>
#include <sys/socket.h>
#include <sys/ioctl.h>
#include <unistd.h>
#include <stdio.h>
#include <fcntl.h>
#include <errno.h>
#include <netdb.h>
#include <netinet/in.h>
#include <string.h>
#include <bstring.h>
#include <malloc.h>
#define MAXHASH 100
```

```
/****CHANNEL DEFINITION****/
#define PORTS 6259
#define PORTC 6260
#define HOSTS_NAME "isma"
#define HOSTC_NAME "sp"

/****MESSAGE TYPE****/
struct request
{
          short code;
          char par1[80] ,par2[80];
          };

struct sockaddr_in server;
struct sockaddr_in client;
```

```
char *host;
struct hostent *hp;
int sock;                                    /*server tuning socket*/

/****WRITING IN THE CHANNEL****/

int writes(int sock, char *pbuf, int noc);
{
int nrest, nwrite;
nrest = noc;
while (nrest > 0) {
        nwrite = write(sock, pbuf, nrest);
        if (nwrite < 0) return(nwrite);
        nrest-=nwrite;
        pbuf+=nwrite;
        }
return(noc-nrest);
}

/****READING FROM THE CHANNEL****/
int reads(int sock, char *pbuf, int noc)
{
int nrest, nread;
nrest = noc;
while (nrest > 0)
 {
        nread = read(sock, pbuf, nrest);
        if (nread < 0) return(nread);
        else if (nread==0) break;
        nrest-=nread;
        pbuf+=nread;
        }
return(noc-nrest);
}

/****CHANNEL OPENING****/
connection_IPC()
{

/****Socket Creation****/
sock = socket(AF_INET,SOCK_DGRAM,0);
bzero(&server, sizeof(server));
server.sin_family = AF-INET;
server.sin_addr.s_addr = INADDR_ANY;
server.sin_port = htons(PORT);
bind(sock,(struct sockaddr *)&server, sizeof(server));

/*Preparation of client network address*/
hp = (struct hostent*) gethostbyname(NAME_HOSTC);
sock = socket (AF_INET<SOCK_DGRAM,0);
bzero(&client, sizeof(client));
bcopy((char *)hp->h_addr,(char *)&client.sin_addr,hp->h_length);
client.sin_family = AF_INET;
client.sin_port = htons(PORTS);
)

/****END OF CHANNEL DEFINITION****/
```

```
struct nlist {
        char *name, *def;
        struct nlist *next;
        };
static struct nlist *hashtab[MAXHASH];
hash(char *s)                                  /*hash function*/
{                                    /*transform a string into an integer*/
int hashval;
for (hashval=0; *s != '\0' ;)
             hashval += *s++;
return(hashval % MAXHASH);}
struct nlist *lookup(char *s)                  /*search for s in the table*/
{
struct nlist *np;
for (*np->next = *hashtab[hash(s)]; np != NULL; np = np->next)
             if (strcmp(s, np->name) == 0)
                   return(np);                              /*find*/
return(NULL);
}
char *add(char *name, char *def)
{
struct nlist *np;
int hashval;
if ((np = lookup(name)) == NULL)
 {
      np = (struct nlist*)malloc(sizeof(*np));
      if(np==NULL) return(NULL);
      sprintf(np->name, "%s", name);
      hashval = hash(np->name);
      np->next = hashtab[hashval];
      hashtab[hashval] = np;
      }
else free(np->def);
sprintf(np->def. "%s", def);
return(np->name);
}
```

```
serverProcessing )
{
int code;
struct request req;
/*struct nlist *time;*/
int len;

len = sizeof(client);
code = recvfrom(sock, (char *)&req, sizeof(req), 0, (struct sockaddr
*)&client, &len);
switch(req.code)
             {
             case 1 :
             req.code = 3;
             strcpy(req.par1, "NULL");
             time = lookup(req.par1);
             if (time) req.par1 = time->def;
       code = sendto(sock, (char *)&req, sizeof(req), 0,
             (struct sockaddr *)&client, len);
```

```
                break;
                default:
                req.code = 3;
                strcpy(req.par1, "add");
                strcpy(req.par2, "12345");
                req.par1 = add(req.par1, req.par2);
        code = sendto(sock, (char *)&req, sizeof(req), 0,
                                (struct sockaddr *)&client, len);}
}
```

```
main()
{
connection_IPC();                                    /*server processing*/
while(1)
        serverProcessing();
}
```

➢ Implementation of the Server for the Table of References with AF_INET Type TCP Sockets on a Network in Datagram Mode

```
/*Client Process*/
#include <sys/types.h>
#include <sys/socket.h>
#include <sys/ioctl.h>
#include <unistd.h>
#include <stdio.h>
#include <fcntl.h>
#include <errno.h>
#include <netdb.h>
#include <netinet/in.h>
#include <string.h>
#include <bstring.h>
```

```
/****CHANNEL DEFINITION****/
#define PORTS 6259
#define PORTC 6260
#define HOSTS_NAME "isma"
#define HOSTC_NAME "sp"

/****TYPE OF MESSAGES ****/
struct request
{
          short code;
          char par1[80];
          char par2[80];
          };
struct sockaddr_in server;
struct sockaddr_in client;
char *host;
struct hostent *hp;
struct hostent *gethostbyname();
int sock;                                            /*Client socket*/
```

```
/****WRITING IN THE CHANNEL****/
int writes(int sock, char *pbuf, int noc)
{
int nrest, nwrite;
nrest = noc;
while (nrest > 0) {
        nwrite = write(sock, pbuf, nrest);
        if (nwrite < 0) return(nwrite);
        nrest-=nwrite;
        pbuf+=nwrite;
        }
return(noc-nrest);
}

/****READING FROM A CHANNEL****/
int reads(int sock, char *pbuf, int noc)
{
int rest, nread;
nrest = noc;
while (nrest > 0) {
        nread = read(sock, pbuf, nrest);
        if (nread < 0) return(nread);
        else if (nread==0) break;
        nrest-=nread;
        pbuf+=nread;
        }
return(noc-nrest);
}

/****CHANNEL OPENING****/
connection_IPC()
{

sock = socket(AF_INET,SOCK_DGRAM,0);
bzero(&client, sizeof(client));
client.sin_family = AF_INET;
client.sin_addr.s_addr = INADDR_ANY;
client.sin_port = htons(PORTC);
if (bind(sock, (struct sockaddr *)%client, sizeof(client))==-1) {
        printf("connection problem \n");
        }
/*Server network address preparation*/
hp = (struct hostent*)gethostbyname(HOSTS_NAME);
bzero(&server, sizeof(server));
bcopy((char *)hp->h_addr, (char *)&server.sin_addr,hp->h_length;
server.sin_family = AF_INET;
server.sin_port = htons(PORTS);
}
/****END OF CHANNEL DEFINITITION****/
```

```
clientProcessing()
{
int code;
struct request req;
int len;
len = sizeof(server);
```

/*add request*/

```
req.code = 0;
strcpy(req.par1, "MAXLINE");
strcpy(req.par2, "100");
code = sendto(sock,(char *)&req, sizeof(req), 0, (struct sockaddr
*)&server, len);
code = recvfrom(sock,(char *)&req, sizeof(req), 0, (struct sockaddr
*)&server, &len);
if (strcmp(req.par1, "add")==0)
                printf("success. req.par1 = %s \n",req.par1);
else printf("fail. req.par1 = %s \n",req.par1);
printf("end of processing erquest 1 \n");
```

/*Search request*/

```
req.code = 1;
strcpy(req.par1, "MAXLINE");
code = sendto(sock, (char *)&req, sizeof(req), 0, (struct sockaddr
*)&server, len);
code = recvfrom(sock, (char *)&req, sizeof(req), 0, (struct sockaddr
*)&server, &len);
if(req.par1 !=NULL)
        printf("replacement value %s \n",req.par1);
else printf("no replacement value %s \n",req.par1);
printf("end of processing request 2 \n");
}
```

```
main()
{
connection_IPC();
clientProcessing ();
disconnection();
}
```

4.6.3 Exchange of Structured Messages

In Chapter 3, we encountered the problem of exchanging structured messages, and the techniques proposed by PVM. These techniques mostly use the facilities of Unix mechanisms and tools on the subject. Recall that the problem involves enabling two entities being executed on two different platforms or machines, to be able to exchange messages. In other words, it will be necessary to use a data representation that will allow the two entities to overcome the constraints of internal representation specific to each machine. We have already seen that two remote processes under Unix must use the `htons()` or `ntohs()` primitive to transmit or receive the port number, which is a numeric quantity. The `htons()` primitive enables the number of the port to be encoded in a network representation (abstract) independent of any hardware platform. The other extreme must simply effectuate the inverse operation, decoding to extract the original value.

In this section, we show several elements of the XDR (eXternal Data Representation) protocol defined by SUN Microsystems to enable the exchange of structured messages in a representation independent of any internal representation. XDR takes the form of a library of primitives which ensure the two principal functions of encoding (transition into network representation) and decoding (transition into the local internal representation). The base concept of the XDR protocol is the *XDR flow*. There are two types of XDR flow:

- XDR_ENCODE type flows used by the emitter process for carrying out the internal representation–external representation transition;
- XDR_DECODE type flows which ensure the inverse function.

In reality, the creation of an XDR flow is obtained by creating a memory zone where the encoding or decoding operation would take place. It is on the data deposited in this memory zone that the encoding and decoding primitives will operate (Fig. 4.24).

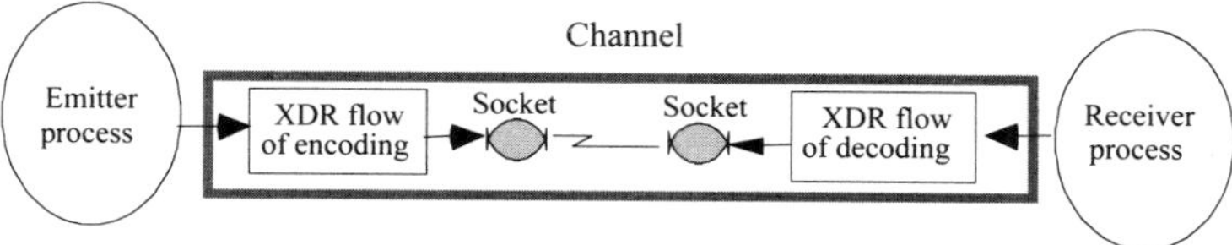

Fig. 4.24 Exchange of structured messages.

The creation of an XDR flow is carried out using the `xdrmem_create()` primitive. During the creation, it is necessary to indicate the type of flow (XDR_ ENCODE or XDR_DECODE). Depending on the type of data, it is then necessary to use the corresponding encoding/decoding function:

Type	XDR transformation function
char	xdr_chart
int	xdr_int
unsigned int	xdr_u_int
short int	xdr_short
unsigned short	xdr_u_short
long int	xdr_long
unsigned long	xdr_u_long
float	xdr_float
double	xdr_double
character string	xdr_string()
octet array	xdr_bytes()
object array	xdr_array

It is important to note that according to our approach to structuring distributed applications, an XDR flow must be specific to a channel. In all of the preceding examples, we have not taken into account the problem of possible incompatibility of the internal representations between the machine supporting the client process and the machine supporting the server. In the following example, we have taken the preceding version of the client–server in connected mode in the AF_INET field, and modified the channel definition in the two processes (only the first part of the code is shown below, the second part remains unchanged). In the `server()` processing or `client()` processing part, it is necessary to use `writeChannel()` or `readChannel()` to send or receive messages of the *struct request* format, without worrying about the nature of the execution platform of the two communicating entities.

➢ Implementation of the Server for the Table of References with AF_INET Type TCP Sockets on a Network, in XDR Connected Mode

```
/*Server Process*/
#include <sys/types.h>
#include <sys/socket.h>
#include <sys/ioctl.h>
#include <unistd.h>
#include <stdio.h>
#include <fcntl.h>
#include <errno.h>
#include <netdb.h>
#include <netinet/in.h>
#include <string.h>
#include <bstring.h>
#include <malloc.h>
#include<rpc/types.h>
#include<rpc/xdr.h>
#define MAXHASH 100
```

```
/****CHANNEL DEFINITION****/

#define PORT 6259
#define SIZE   (1 +   80 + 80)

/****MESSAGE STRUCTURE****/
struct request {
        short code;
        char par1[80] ,par2[80];
        };
XDR xreq_E;                         /*emit XDR flow pointer*/
XDR xreq_R;                         /*receive XDR flow pointer*/
        char zone[SIZE];            /***memory support flow*/
char *host;
struct hostent *hp;
int sock;                           /*server socket*/

/*Encoding request*/
xdr_request( XDR *xptr, struct request prt)
{
 return(xdr_short(xptr, &ptr->code)
        && xdr_array(xptr, &ptr-par1,80, 1, xdr_char)
        && xdr_array(xptr, &ptr-par2,80, 1, xdr_char)
};

/****WRITING IN THE CHANNEL ****/
int writes(int sock, char *pbuf, int noc);
{
int nrest, nwrite;
nrest = noc;
while (nrest > 0) {
        nwrite = write(sock, pbuf, nrest);
```

```
        if (nwrite < 0) return(nwrite);
        nrest-=nwrite;
        pbuf+=nwrite;
        }
return(noc-nrest);
}

int writechannel int nsock, struct request *message){
 if (! xdr_request( &xreq_E, &message)){
         printf("encoding problem"); exit(2);}
 writes(nsock, char *)&zone, SIZE);
}

/****READING FROM THE CHANNEL****/
int reads(int sock, char *pbuf, int noc)
{
int nrest, nread;
nrest = noc;
while (nrest > 0) {
        nread = read(sock, pbuf, nrest);
        if (nread < 0) return(nread);
        else if (nread==0) break;
        nrest-=nread;
        pbuf+=nread;
return(noc-nrest);
}
int readchannel int nsock, struct request *message){
 reads(nsock, char *)&zone, SIZE);
 if (! xdr_request( &xreq_E, &message)){
         printf("decoding problem"); exit(2);}
}

/****CHANNEL OPENING****/
connection_IPC()
{
        struct sockaddr_in server;

/*Socket Creation*/
sock = socket(AF_INET,SOCK_STREAM,0);
bzero(&server, sizeof(server));
server.sin_family = AF-INET;
server.sin_addr.s_addr = INADDR_ANY;
server.sin_port = htons(PORT);
bind(sock,(struct sockaddr *)&server, sizeof(server));

/****CREATION OF XDR FLOW ****/
xdrmem_create(&xreq_E, &zone, SIZE XDR_ENCODE);
xdrmem_create(&xreq_R; &zone, SIZE XDR_DECODE);

/*Tuning in of incoming connections*/
listen(sock,5);
}
/****CHANNEL CLOSURE****/

disconnection_IPC()
{
```

```
close (sock);

                /****DESTRUCTION OF XDR FLOW ****/
xdr_destroy(%xreq_E);
xdr_destroy(%xreq_R);
}

/****END OF CHANNEL DECLARATION****/
```

➢ Implementation of the Server for the Table of References with AF_INET Type TCP Sockets on a Network, in XDR Connected Mode

```
/*Client Process*/
#include <sys/types.h>
#include <sys/socket.h>
#include <sys/ioctl.h>
#include <unistd.h>
#include <stdio.h>
#include <fcntl.h>
#include <errno.h>
#include <netdb.h>
#include <netinet/in.h>
#include <string.h>
#include <bstring.h>
#include<rpc/types.h>
#include<rpc/xdr.h>

/****CHANNEL DEFINITION****/
#define PORT 6259                               /*communication port*/
#define HOST_NAME "isma"                        /*host server*/
                                                /*size zone of XDR flow*/
#define SIZE   (1 +   80 + 80)

/****MESSAGE STRUCTURE****/
struct request {
               short code;
               char par1[80]; char par2[80];
               };
XDR xreq_E;                                     /*emit XDR flow pointer*/
XDR xreq_R;                                     /*receive XDR flow pointer*/
       char zone[SIZE];                         /***memory support flow*/
char *host;
struct hostent *hp;
struct hostent *gethostbyname();
int sock;                                       /client socket in emission*/

/****ENCODING REQUEST****/
xdr_request( XDR *xptr, struct request prt){
 Return(xdr_short(xptr, &ptr->code)
       && xdr_array(xptr, &ptr-par1,80, 1, xdr_char)
       && xdr_array(xptr, &ptr-par2,80, 1, xdr_char)
};
/****WRITING IN THE CHANNEL****/
int writes(int sock, char *pbuf, int noc);
{
```

```
int nrest, nwrite;
nrest = noc;
while (nrest > 0) {
        nwrite = write(sock, pbuf, nrest);
        if (nwrite < 0) return(nwrite);
        nrest-=nwrite;
        pbuf+=nwrite;
        }
return(noc-nrest);
}
int writechannel int nsock, struct request *message){
 if (! xdr_request( &xreq_E, &message)){
         printf("encoding problem"); exit(2);}
 writes(nsock, char *)&zone, SIZE);
}

/****READING FROM THE CHANNEL****/
int reads(int sock, char *pbuf, int noc)
{
int nrest, nread;
nrest = noc;
while (nrest > 0) {
                nread = read(sock, pbuf, nrest);
                if (nread < 0) return(nread);
                else if (nread==0) break;
                nrest-=nread;
                pbuf+=nread;
return(noc-nrest);
}
int readchannel int nsock, struct request *message){
 reads(nsock, char *)&zone, SIZE);
 if (! xdr_request( &xreq_E, &message)){
         printf("decoding problem"); exit(2);}
}

/****CHANNEL OPENING****/
connection_IPC()
{
        struct sockaddr_in server;
hp = (struct hostent*)gethostbyname(HOST_NAME);
sock = socket(AF_INET,SOCK_STREAM,0);
bzero(&server, sizeof(server));
server.sin_family = AF-INET;
bcopy((char *)hp->h_addr, (char *)&server.sin_addr, hp->h_length);
server.sin_port = htons(PORT);                                  /*f. network*/
connect(sock,(struct sockaddr *)&server, sizeof(server));

/****CREATION OF XDR FLOW ****/
xdrmem_create(&xreq_E, &zone, SIZE XDR_ENCODE);
xdrmem_create(&xreq_R; &zone, SIZE XDR_DECODE);
}

/****CHANNEL CLOSURE****/
disconnection_IPC()
{
close (sock);
```

```
/****DESTRUCTION OF XDR FLOW ****/
xdr_destroy(%xreq_E);
xdr_destroy(%xreq_R);
}

/****END OF CHANNEL DECLARATION****/
```

4.7 Conclusion

We have now learnt the essentials of the Unix tools and mechanisms necessary for the development of distributed applications in general, and specifically applications using the client–server interaction model. As we have already pointed out, this presentation does not prevent the reader, who does not yet know these mechanisms, from using the Unix instruction manual, from better understanding the functions of the different primitives introduced, and especially from having a more detailed description of the different call parameters of these primitives. During the writing of this part of the chapter, our objective was to give the reader a precise idea of the tools used in the implementation of distributed applications under Unix. Therefore, to further the study and comprehension of these mechanisms, the reader should refer to either the Unix manual, or more specialized publications (Rifflet, 1990; Gabassi and Dupuoy, 1992).

5. *Principles of Real-Time Data Processing*

With the current economic competition, businesses must improve the productivity and quality of their manufactured products. They are increasingly obliged to adopt the automated production tool as the single alternative to increase and promote the global competitiveness of their products. Furthermore, production tool flexibility has become a necessity to enable the business to adapt and diversify its products, and therefore increase its reactivity on the market.

A modern business is essentially characterized by the real-time management and monitoring of the different services. This imposes a hierarchical interconnection between the different information systems and the different internal communication systems of the business, in order to favour the exchanges between the applications belonging to extremely heterogeneous data processing environments: handling and driving applications of manufacturing processes, computer aided manufacturing management, computer-aided design (CAD), data processing applications for quality control management, management applications for client commands etc. The availability of these applications underlies a constant and eventually multi-task activity. This raises problems related to real-time systems: interruption capacity, reactivity, time consideration, etc. In a modern company, automation affects all levels: administration, workshop and production lines, logistics and transmission etc. The interconnection of all of these activities and corresponding data processing systems ultimately replaces the field of distributed and real-time systems (see preceding chapters).

In this chapter particular attention is paid to the tools and methods used for the design and implementation of control applications for automated industrial processes. These applications are essentially multi-agent or multi-task. They are also subject to temporal constraints, which must be taken into consideration by the tools and methods used to develop this type of application.

5.1 Structure and Function of an Automated System

An automated system is composed of two main parts: the *operative part* (process) or physical process, and the *command part* (Fig. 5.1)

Notion 1 Operative Part

This is made up of a set of components, usually mechanical, whose aim is to implement a particular transformation process such as soldering, drilling parts, etc. The displacement and physical control of these low-level passive methods is provided by actuators, such as electrical motors, jacks etc., which form an integral part of the operative part.

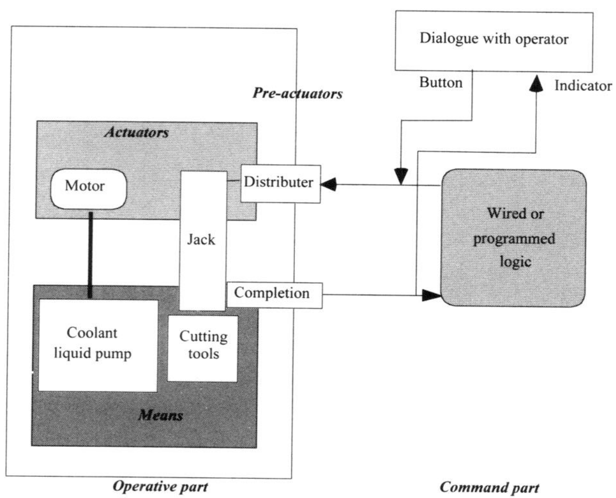

Fig. 5.1 Overall structure of an automated system.

The interface between the operative part and the command part is formed by *pre-actuators* for:

- the command of actions (distributors, contactors etc.),
- or for the acquisition of signals generated by the sensors which take into account (record) the development of the status of the operative part (end sensor, optical sensor, pressure sensor etc.).

Notion 2 Record

These are signals generated by sensors, and which represent the information operated by the command part. They take account of how the status of the operative part develops.

Notion 3 The Command Part

This is the logical control of the operative part. It can either be hardwired or programmed (digital control of physical processes).

The command part varies depending on the nature of the physical process, especially in terms of its complexity, the degree of automation needed, and the implementation methods. As we have already indicated, the command part is interfaced with the operative part using pre-actuators and sensors. It also integrates the dialogue interface with the operator, to seize instructions on the functioning and display of certain parameters on the status of the operative part. Several degrees of automation can be distinguished, which correspond to different functioning modes: surveillance mode, operator guide mode and command mode.

Notion 4 Surveillance Mode or Open Loop Structure Systems

The command part acquires information on the functioning and behaviour status of different parts of the physical process, and displays them on the operator consoles.

In certain simple cases, the sensors are directly linked to warning lights and indicators on the instrument panel.

The command part of this type of system does not act directly on the operative part (Fig. 5.2).

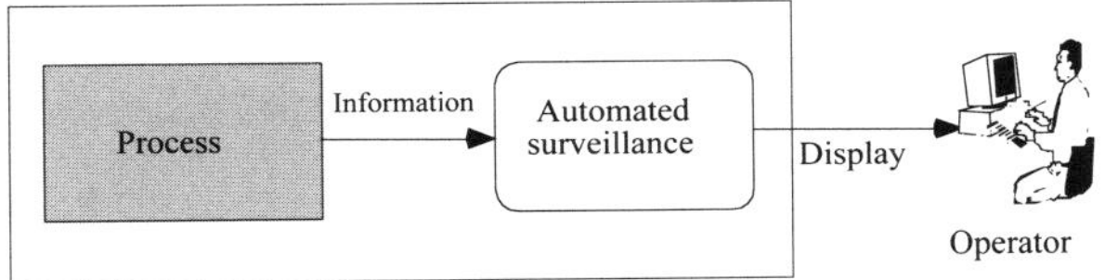

Fig. 5.2 Structure of a system in surveillance mode.

In surveillance mode, all of the decisions concerning the actions to be carried out on the operative part (opening a safety gate, stopping a motor etc.) are made and implemented by the operator. The command part is totally neutral or passive.

There is a second functioning mode, called the operator guide mode (Fig. 5.3), where before undertaking an action on the operative part, the operator transmits its orders to the command part which functions in open loop compared to the operative part. In terms of information coming from the process, the command part a plan of action to the operator.

Notion 5 Operator Guide Mode

The command part is used to acquire and process information in a reasonably complex manner before giving the operator the actions to be carried out on the command part.

In this mode, it is the operator who closes the loop by sending the necessary commands to the operative part. This configuration gives the operator certain assistance. The processing part of the command can be quite complex depending on the degree of intelligence required.

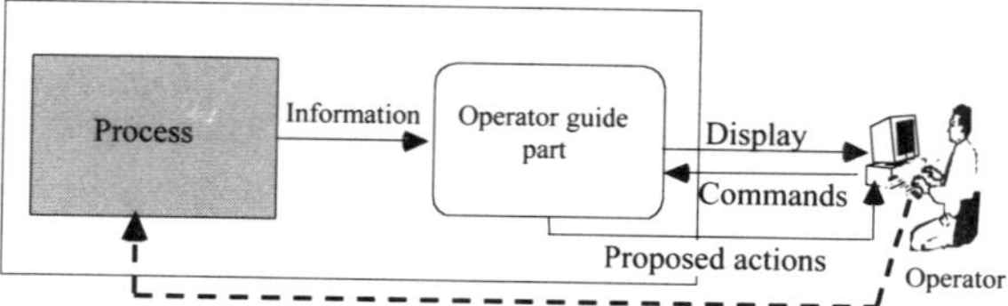

Fig. 5.3 Structure of a system in operator guide mode.

Finally, there is a third functioning mode called the "command mode" (Fig. 5.4) which became widespread in line with technological advance, especially with the appearance of a new generation of high performance sensors and actuators, increasingly powerful programmable automaton, and as a result of the use of embedded real-time systems which are true data-processing systems (microprocessor cards and user-oriented packages) capable of supporting process command applications to any degree of complexity (computers on board aeroplanes, space shuttles, etc.).

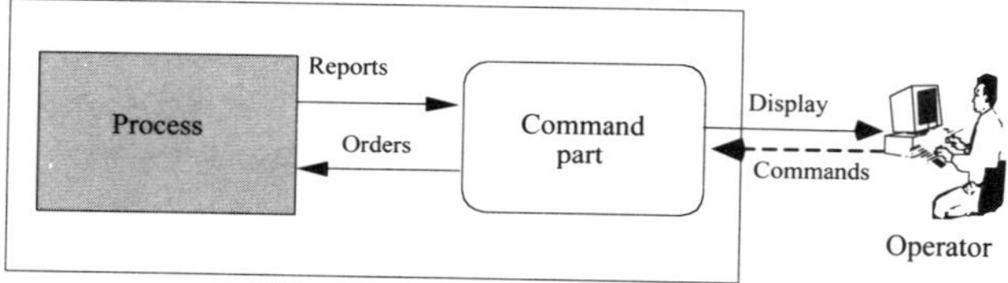

Fig. 5.4 Structure of a system in command mode.

Notion 6 Command Mode

The command part is responsible for collecting, processing and sending commands to the operative part using a closed loop structure.

The command part carries out *three main tasks* in this mode:

- *Command task:* generates orders from records coming from the operative part and orders given by the operator, before transmitting them to the operator part.
- *Security task:* the role of this task is to ensure installation and user security. It must inform the operator of every event which could compromise the efficient functioning of the systems, and the security of the personnel (open loop surveillance: alarm, fault signals, real-time display of the different sensitive installation parameters). It must potentially set in motion emergency actions (in closed loop: emergency stop, etc.).
- *Control task:* this enables production information concerning the qualitative or quantitative aspects (inspections, checks, decision help, etc.) to be generated. This information is given to the team leader to increase operations and production quality.

The command part is generally composed of a processing unit (microcomputer, embedded micro-processor cards, programmable automaton), an operator console and the different couplers and interfaces necessary for the efficient functioning of the system. Recall that the sensors as well as the actuators are integrated into the operative part. The sensors provide the records and the actuators transform the orders into effective actions. Figure 5.5 shows an example of an automated control system whose main task is to maintain the level of the tank between two thresholds: the lower level *B* and the higher level *A*.

A level sensor enables the system to adjust the electromagnetic gate via the actuator *V* to refill the tank. If, during this phase, the level rises above the tolerable threshold level, a sensor signal generates a priority alarm signal.

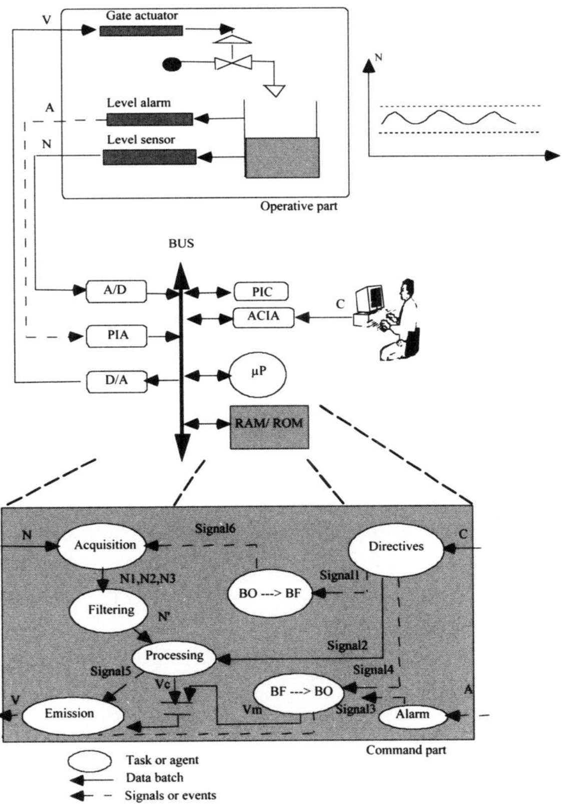

Fig. 5.5 Example of a programmed automated system.

Notion 7 Architecture of a Digital Control System

This is composed of group of communicating parallel tasks supported by a data-processing system (automaton, computer (industrial PC) or micro-processor card etc.).

5.2 Combinatorial Automated Systems

For this type of automated system, the command part is limited to a simple standard base combinatorial system (Fig. 5.6) where logical functions are implemented using one of three well-known technologies:

- *Electromechanical technology* where variables are indicated by an open or closed contact (relays, sequencers, contactors).
- *Electronic technology* where the transistor functioning in blocked/saturated mode constitutes the base element for the implementation of variables and functions of automation (sequencers, integrated circuits, etc.).
- *Pneumatic technology* where variables and functions are indicated by air pressure.

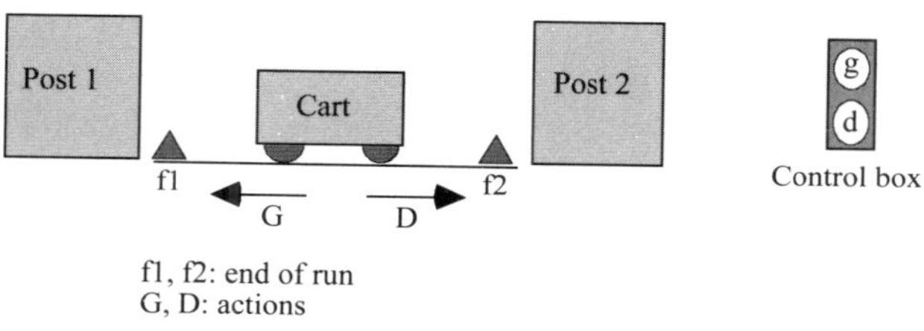

Fig. 5.6 Example of an automated combinatorial system.

Figure 5.6 represents a remote control cart. When pressure is exerted on a button on the control box, the chariot moves in the chosen direction until it reaches the end of the road (a sensor, a bump). The logical implementation diagram for the command part is given in Figure 5.7.

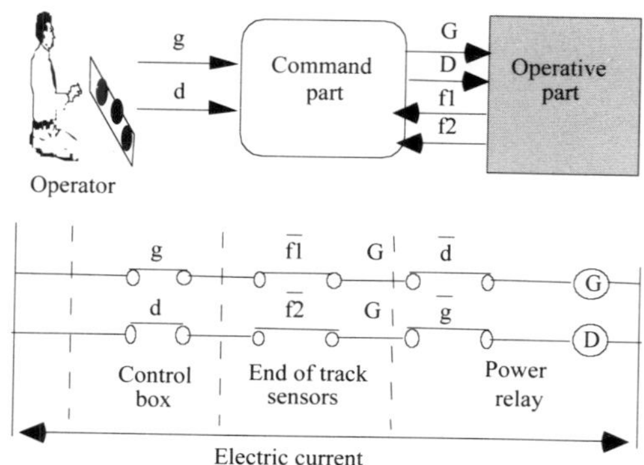

Fig. 5.7 Implementation principle for the command part of the cart.

Notion 8 A Combinatorial System

This is a system where a combination of the vector of the output variables corresponds to one single combination of the vector of the input variables. The output does not rely on the former system (its internal status).

5.3 Sequential Automated Systems

In comparison to combinatorial systems, the output of sequential systems depends not only on the system input, but also on the output values at the preceding instant. The following diagram represents such a system:

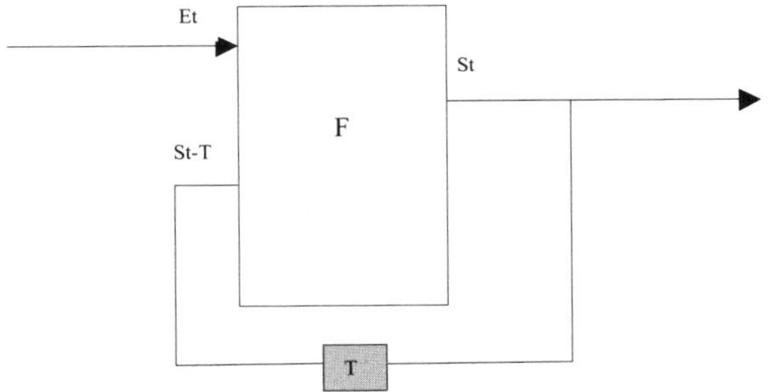

Notion 9 A Sequential System

This is a system for which the output variables depend on the history of the system (its internal status and the values of input variables) and on the input variables. It must be given a memory element to be able to memorize the preceding status.

The equation used to establish the system output in terms of the input can be written as follows:

$$S_{t+T} = F(E_t, S_t).$$

If T is time period, the system is called *synchronous*; in the opposite case, it is called *asynchronous*. In the latter case, T takes any value.

5.4 The GRAFCET: Synthesis Tool for Industrial Automated Systems[1]

The tool used essentially for the synthesis and specification of the command part of automated systems is the GRAFCET. It was proposed in 1977 by AFCET (Association Française pour le Cybernétique Economique et Technique). It was then standardized and broadcast across France by the ADEPA (Agence pour le Développement de la Production Automatisée). It enables the accurate *graphic description* of the behaviour of an automated system. Figure 5.8 gives the specification of a sequential version of the command part of the cart from the preceding example. In this new version, the control box contains a single button "a". At the push of this button, the cart must carry out a return trip from the position that corresponds to the end of the road "f1".

The basic elements of the GRAFCET are:

- *Stages* (0, 1, 2), to which *actions* are associated ([1, D], [2, G]);
- *Transitions* (t1, t2, t3), to which are associated *logics* ([t1 to f1], [t3, f1]), which are logical conditions that concern the external variables (operative part) or internal variables (command part). The completion of a transition occurs when all of the stages above are active and the associated logic is true;
- *Oriented links*, which link the stages to the transitions and indicate the evolution direction of the command part simulation.

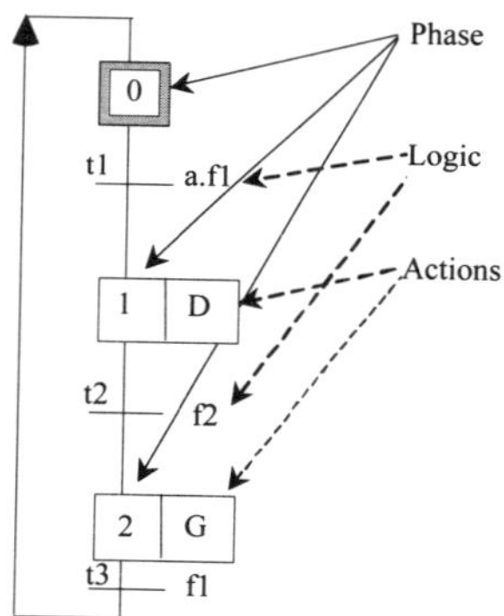

Fig. 5.8 GRAFCET of the sequential version of the cart.

In the GRAFCET in Figure 5.8, stage 0 represents *the initial state* (the relaxed state or waiting to be switched on). A GRAFCET enables the following to be explained:

- unique sequences (there is only one path between two states);

[1] GRAFCET: Graphe de Command d'Etat Transition.

- simultaneous or structural sequences (between two given states there can exist two different paths which are carried out in parallel according to their conditions for selection);
- sequence selections;
- temporal constraints on logics or on actions (delayed actions);
- conditional actions, upheld actions;
- cyclic functions;
- cycle anti-repetitions, etc.

Incidentally, in the GRAFCET in Figure 5.9, the t/2/20s logic associated with the t3 transition will only be true 20 seconds after the activation of stage 2, the loading of the cart. The execution of the loading action need only commence after the end of a 10 second time interval. Finally, the execution of the unloading action, P, of stage 4 only lasts a maximum of 12 seconds, as it is a delayed action. The case study in Chapter 9 gives the practical details on the different possibilities offered by the GRAFCET formalism, especially its use in the analysis and design of real-time systems.

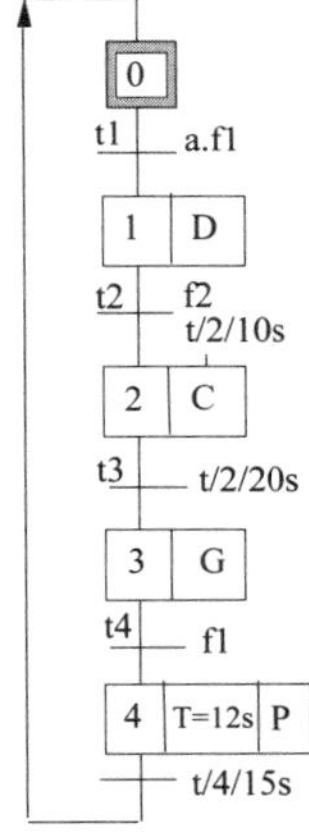

Fig. 5.9 Expression of temporal constraints on actions and transitions.

5.5 Technological Options for the Implementation of the Command Part

The examples presented in the previous sections clearly show that there exist several possible technological tools and methods for the development of the command part of an automated system. There are actually two possible solutions for the design of the command part:

- *A hardwired solution:* using any one of the three technological principles (electromagnetic technology, electronic technology, pneumatic technology);
- *A programmed solution:* which uses one of the following data processing systems as support: industrial programmable automaton (IPA), industrial computer or embedded computer (microprocessor card for VME frame).

The choice of final solution must take into account *four* types of criteria currently allowed:

1. *Functional criteria,* which enable the determination of the degree of automation complexity required (performance required in terms of precision and speed, the number and type of I/O sockets, volume, nature and level of data processing).
2. *Technological criteria,* which aim to specify how the system will integrate into its environment:
   - characteristics of sensors and actuators;
   - energy sources;
   - geographical or geometric configuration;
   - conditions of the operative part–command part links;
   - characteristics of the surrounding environment (temperature, dust, static, vibrations, etc.).
3. *Operational criteria,* which enable the intrinsic characteristics of the operative part to be taken into account, especially the consideration of some of the following factors:
   - Spatio-temporal factors (complexity and geographical disposition of the operative part as well as the interdependence of its different sub-routines, the prospects of development and extension over time);
   - Impact factors on production. This particularly involves the accurate specification of the behaviour and role of the command part in two functional regimes: the *normal regime* (handling, control and surveillance) and the *layered regime* (emergency stops, occasions, etc.);
   - Factors linked to the maintenance of the installation (the equipment accessibility, storage of spare parts).
4. *Economic criteria,* which are related to the costs (acquisition cost, implementation cost etc.).

To conclude, we accede that a programmed solution (numeric process command) will be accepted in the case where a hardwired logical solution is not wanted for various reasons (see the above criteria), notably as a result of the *complexity* of the operative part. In the rest of this book, we focus on the design and implementation problems of a programmed solution for the command part of an automated system. The study of other hardwired logical solutions lies beyond the scope of this publication; however, readers interested in this last category of systems can look at Asch *et al.* (1991) and Bernard *et al.* (1979).

5.6 Digital Control Systems for Processes

Digital control systems are usually characterized by:

- the possibility of processing *several control loops*;
- the possibility of the design and implementation of *complex* regulation or control *algorithms*;
- the possibility of implementing *tendency analysis* processing, to improve the quality and productivity of automated systems, and to help in the surveillance and rapid identification of faults, and therefore increase the reliability of the system;
- *easily adaptable* control systems following technical modifications at the level of the operative part, or modifications carried out on the command part to integrate other functions;
- the use of a *real-time kernel* (multi-task system) for multiplexing and interlacing several tasks which constitute the command part;
- the possibility of conducting the *simulation,* implementation and tests in the research laboratory, *independently of the operative part*;
- the reliability of diagnostics with the possibility of automating the tests because the problem produced by the components (hardwired command part) no longer exists;
- the *compatibility* of data between the different hierarchical levels of the automated system;
- the use of a real-time kernel enabling interrupts to be processed for the management of random, unpredictable events;
- the control of two physical process categories (operative part): the *slow dynamic processes* and the *fast dynamic processes.*

5.7 The Need for an Adapted Specification Methodology

The GRAFCET is a very powerful graphical representation tool which perfectly suits the specification of the command part of sequential automated systems. When the command part presents a *fairly complex structure* (operative parts composed of several identical or non-identical geographically distributed modules) (Fig. 5.10), where several independent and parallel tasks must exist together, the GRAFCET is insufficient, alone insofar as it is only able to express a *very localized function.* With complex automated systems, where they are true *distributed systems*, a *global* and *hierarchical* analysis and specification *strategy* or approach of the command part becomes indispensable. In this global approach, and for want of a integrated formalism for the specification of control aspects, the GRAFCET can be used in a localized manner, conforming to the functional separating imposed by the approach. Among these most frequently used methods is the *SA/RT* method.

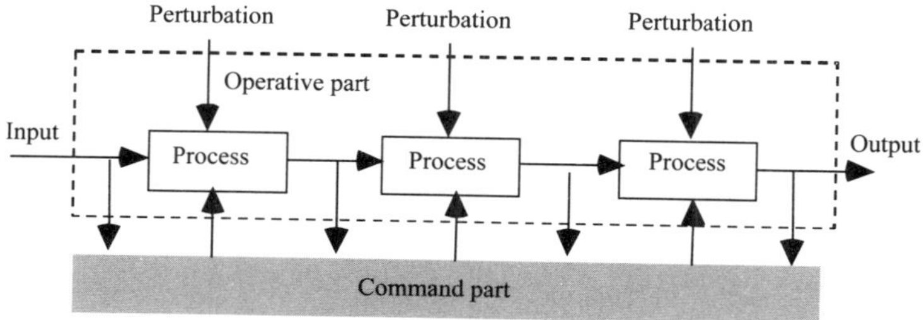

Fig. 5.10 Complex industrial process.

Complex automated systems of the new generation, especially automated manufacturing systems, use a combination of digital or hardwired controls displaced to the physical module level (control), and digital controls to a more global level (supervision). This approach is made possible due to the appearance on the market of displaced logic sensors and actuators. Furthermore it is easy to design a complex system, such as the assembly of intelligent modules capable of executing specific tasks in a largely autonomous manner.

5.7.1 Introduction to the SA/RT Method

This is the *descending analysis by abstraction level method*, of systems studied, which is applicable to software and hardware systems, or both. It advocates two different stages:

1. The elaboration of the requirements model which aims to display the different system functions (tasks) as well as the data and control flow, independently of any technological consideration or design constraints. This is undertaken by obtaining a set of hierarchical data flow diagrams (DFD) and control flow diagrams (CFD) (Fig. 5.11), accompanied by different specification files for transformation or control processes.
2. The elaboration of an architecture model which aims to clarify design limitations, technological or otherwise, namely the type of physical means necessary to implement a given interaction: data flow or control flow, choice between the software or hardware implementation of a process or a DFD function, etc. It is also a question of studying the problems of performance, adaptability or flexibility of the system in terms of extensions, security problems, the technology of the signal platform, the implementation language, the maintenance requirements, the degree of conviviality and both ergonomic and user interface problems, etc.

The first stage concerns system analysis and functional refinement. The second phase involves the architecture and the interfacing of the new system with its environment. This second phase is rarely used, however, (even contested) given that it intervenes late on in the analysis and specification cycle. As Chapter 9 shows, certain details of the system environment can be taken into consideration very early on to facilitate the analysis process, and make it more deterministic. This second phase is not referred to again in this section, the reader will find a complete study of a real-time system which uses this method in Chapter 9.

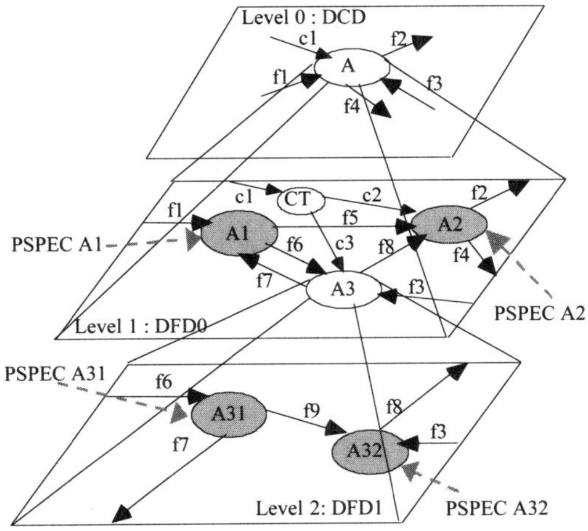

Fig. 5.11 Descending analysis of digital control systems.

The basic tools of the method are:

- *Data flow diagrams* composed of transformation processes and data flows. These show how each process (task) transforms its input flows into output flows. If, at a given level, there is a simple transformation process, a PSPEC (A1, A2, A31, A32) specification file is attached to it, which outlines the main areas of the processing algorithm applied by the process to transform the input data flow into output data and control flows. In the opposite case it involves a complex process, and must form the subject of another level of refinement (A, A3). The DFD at level zero is called a data context diagram (DCD), and clearly indicates *the interaction* of the command part with the different components of the operative part (the sources and the wells). The analysis and specification process is in this way *repeated* and will stop when there are no longer any complex processes to refine.

- *Control flow diagrams* which recapture the hierarchical architecture (network of data transformation processes) displayed by the different DFD of the system, and replacing data flow with control flow. Nevertheless, it is not essential to separate the corresponding DFD and CFD. One single diagram can be used just as effectively to display data flow and control flow. This is called the *transformation diagram* (TD): Figure 5.11, level 1. Control flows are signals which represent the occurrence of particular events over time. They also represent discrete synchronization and external (coming from the operative part: status of a particular variable or component) or internal control data (messages exchanged by the different transformation processes with the aim of synchronization and control). Similar to DFD, the CFD at level 0 indicates control signal flows at the highest abstraction level (generic flows) exchanged at the highest level. The descending refinement principle can be applied to transformation processes as well as data and control flows.

Once the different DFC are displayed, a particular process, called a control process must be associated to each CFD (represented by a dashed circle). This is done using a control process specification file (CSPEC). The synchronization, control and sequencing of transformation process activation is described using a control specification tool such as the state-transition diagram, finite state automatons, GRAFCET or any other similar tool. Given the hierarchical nature of the systems obtained using this method, the control process will only be associated to a given DFD if its transformation processes necessitate centralized control and synchronization. For each system studied, it is therefore possible to opt either for totally distributed control in the image of distributed data-processing systems (communication between the different processes by the exchange of data and control messages) without a global memory, or centralized control where a particular process fills the role of co-ordinator (*the control process represents the command part of transformation processes*). Transformation processes therefore constitute the operative part controlled by the control process, from where the idea of using GRAFCET to specify the control process originates. However, we must not lose sight of that fact that for complex automated systems the combined use of these two approaches is inevitable.

5.7.2 Example of System Specification using SA/RT

This involves a regulatory system previously shown in Figure 5.5. The system specification manual indicates:

- a level N measure of liquid every second;
- calculation of the average of the last three measures every three seconds;
- computation and emission of the command;
- the operator can modify the instructions in real-time;
- the operator can move in real-time from the open-loop mode (OL) to the closed-loop mode (CL) and vice versa;
- the operator can modify the manual command;
- the alarm triggers a CL==>OL commutation and imposes a manual command.

Figure 5.12 shows the level 0 diagram representing the data context diagram (data flow in unbroken lines) and the control context diagram (control flow in broken lines). It displays the interaction with its environment of the objective function to be implemented (*control and supervision*). Note that for this system, there exists an entity which acts a flow *source* and *sink*: the process. The operator is a flow source.

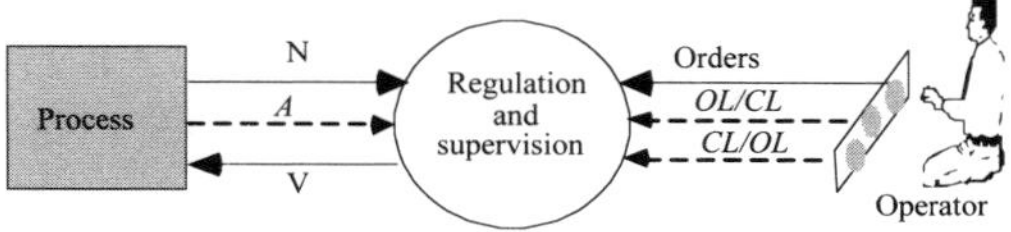

Fig. 5.12 System context diagram.

Figure 5.13 gives the TD for level 1 (refinement of the objective function) and level 2.

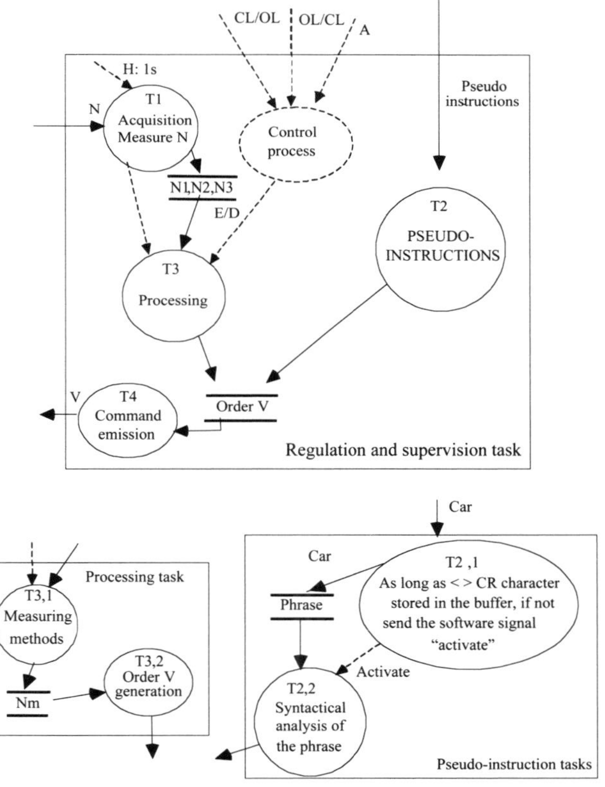

Fig. 5.13 Example of the descending refinement of a command system.

Figure 5.14 shows the control process CSPEC, which is relatively simple. At the start, the system is in a closed loop state (automatic control). It passes from the closed loop state to the open loop state (manual control) on a specific command from the operator, or on an alarm coming from the process. Chapter 9 gives a complete example of the analysis and specification of the implementation part of an automated system. "D" for deactivate a task and "A" for activate a task.

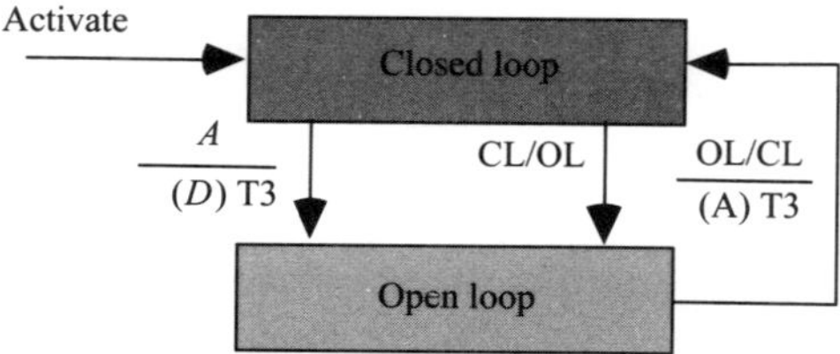

Fig. 5.14 State-transition diagram for the control process.

To guarantee the efficient functioning of the system, an order of priority between the tasks must be established: T1 > T4 > T2.1 = T3 > T2.2.

The following section presents the different notions which concern the fundamental properties of real-time systems and real-time executives.

5.8 Process Dynamics

The example in the preceding section displayed the *modular* and *distributed* character of processing in a digital control process system. Nonetheless, this structuring in parallel and communicating tasks (completely supported by a single processing unit (centralized case) or distributed over several processing units geographically separated and interconnected via a local industrial network) poses *specific problems linked to the nature of the process to control and command.* This not only involves the *process reactivity speed* and the temporal constraints induced, but also all of the usual problems of communication and co-operation between tasks. The solutions to the co-ordination and co-operation problems between distributed application agents already presented in the first chapters, remain valid in this context. However, these techniques and methods must take into consideration the idea of the reactivity and dynamics of the physical process. There are two types of process: slow dynamic processes and fast dynamic processes. The architecture of the command part will, to a large extent, depend on this intrinsic property of the process.

Notion 10 Process Dynamics

This is the response time of the operative part, or its reaction speed. It characterizes the speed of the changes in the state of the process.

5.8.1 Slow Dynamic Processes

Notion 11 Slow Dynamic Process

This is a physical process whose reactivity is relatively slow in comparison to the execution time of the command system tasks.

The speed of the processing unit (CPU), which is the physical support of the digital control system, is faster than the industrial process. The time separating two consecutive events coming from the process is relatively high compared to the execution speed of the CPU. In this case, the architecture of the digital control can be indifferently *monolithic* (standard programming: a single program which calls sub-programs) or *multi-task distributed*. Looking at the example in Figure 5.15, the command part can be implemented in two ways. The first comes down to a single standard program which executes an infinite loop for polling the process and corresponding process execution variables (Fig. 5.16a).

The second is an implementation following a multi-agent architecture (Fig. 5.16b) where the activation of tasks can be carried out on the arrival of a signal or hardware interrupt originating from the process. The command part must maintain the level of liquid in the reservoir between B and H by acting on the electromagnetic gate V. It must also maintain the temperature of the liquid between two limits (low threshold, high threshold) by acting on the relay R of the electric resistance of the heater. This is a continual process.

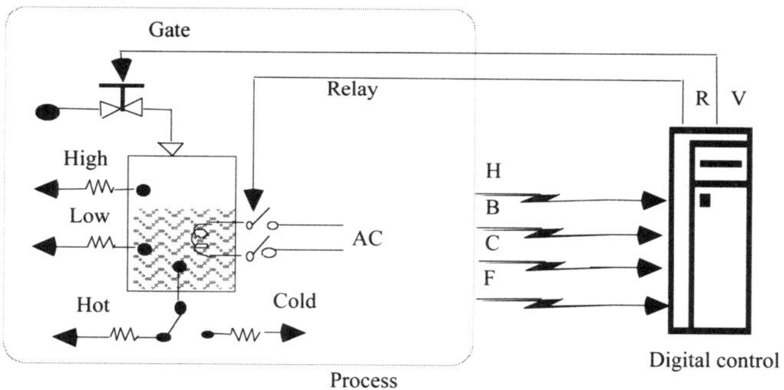

Fig. 5.15 An example of a slow dynamic process.

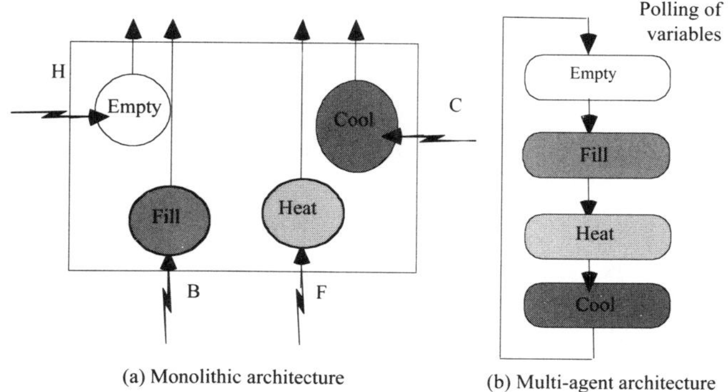

Fig. 5.16 Architecture of the command part of the process.

Nevertheless, we advise the reader to adopt, wherever possible, the multi-agent solution as this offers a degree of *modularity, maintenance,* and *flexibility,* especially in the event of major system development. Such a solution is easy to construct, maintain and configure. It facilitates separated programming and the collaboration between several members of a team of programmers. Lastly, it ensures the *recycling* of the different components or modules of the system.

The tasks of a distributed solution, for slow dynamic systems, can be non-pre-emptive.

Notion 12 Pre-Emption

This involves temporarily suspending a T1 task in the process of execution, to benefit a higher priority task. Once this latter has terminated, or is waiting behind an event, either the T1 tasks takes up its execution again, or another task at the same level of priority as T1 is activated.

To guarantee process quality control in terms of *precision, rate* and *stability,* it is sensible to look at cases where each task will be executed after the others in order to ensure that it does not compromise the properties mentioned above. Figure 5.17 shows an execution diagram over time for the tasks shown in Figure 5.15. We note that the onset and execution of the FILL task follows the arrival of signal (hardware interrupt) B, and was delayed until the HEAT task terminated its execution. The same occurs for the EMPTY task, which was activated after the end of the COOL task.

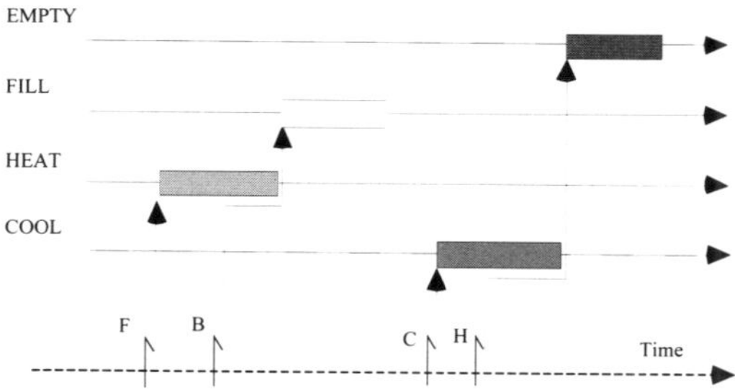

Fig. 5.17 The use of non-pre-emptive tasks for slow processes.

In cases where a monolithic architecture (single unit processor) has been retained to guarantee the correct regulation of a process, the Shannon theory on signal sampling must be rigorously adhered to:

- The sampling frequency of an S signal must be higher than the highest S frequency;
- The processing time *Ti* by the computer of a control loop must be less than the sampling period *T*;
- Where there are several control loops, (multiplexing), it is necessary to satisfy the following condition: $T1 + T2 + \ldots + Tn \leq T$.

5.8.2 Rapid Dynamic Processes

Notion 13 Rapid Dynamic Process

This is mainly characterized by high-level reactivity of the operative part, maintained over a period of time. The architecture of the command part can only be a distributed multi-agent or multi-task architecture.

For this type of system, the command part must be in a position to react rapidly to and process any event originating from the process, before the appearance of other events which will render them void.

On the other hand, it is imperative to use the task pre-emption technique to guarantee correct control of the process. The use of the task pre-emption technique must always be accompanied by attributing a priority to the different parallel tasks.

To satisfy the principal constraint of rapid dynamic process control systems, namely a very short event processing time, it is necessary to give a *deadline* to each task of the command part.

Notion 14 Deadline

This indicates the time period which must elapse between the appearance of the event trigger for the activation of a task, and the effective end of the task execution. This is a time constraint on the execution of a task.

This is an important property of real-time systems. The scheduler for the real-time executive which supports the execution of the parallel tasks of the command part, mainly operates the *priority* level of each task and their *deadline*, to attempt to guarantee the coherent and stable execution of the command part. The study of the fundamental properties of the executives, or real-time kernels will form the subject of Section 5.10. Figure 5.18 shows the execution diagram for the task of the command part of the process shown in Figure 5.15, that we have deliberately assumed is rapid dynamics. We have also established priority between the different tasks. In the diagram, the HEAT task has been suspended in preference to the FILL task, which has a higher priority. The execution of the EMPTY task has been deferred until the COOL task, which has a higher priority, has terminated its execution.

We end this section by presenting several important characteristics of the multitask digital control of rapid dynamic processes:

- Prioritization enables the establishment of an *order relationship* between the tasks and not a precedence relationship.
- The deadline or the time constraint on the execution of a task is determined independently of the other tasks. It is defined according to the task specifications and environment.

- To keep to the deadlines, the task priorities must be *dynamic* and *increasing* over time.

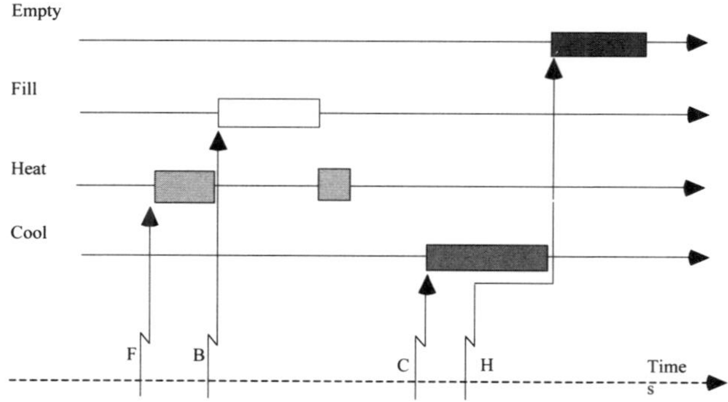

Fig. 5.18 Execution diagram with pre-emption and priority between tasks.

5.9 Periodic and Aperiodic Tasks

An automated digital control process is a distributed application composed of communicating, parallel tasks or agents. The execution platform is generally a micro-processor card with an optimal operating system to guarantee extremely high performance. This type of multi-task operating system is called *the executive* or *real-time kernel*. It is usually micro-programmed, and its principal function consists of:

- managing the *simultaneous execution* of digital control system tasks;
- providing the *communication means* and the necessary *synchronization* to these communicating tasks;
- *guaranteeing the deadlines* of application time limits.

In most cases, real-time executives are equipped with a series of software or hardware counters and timers. These enable watchdog timers to be implemented, which are triggered at a specified time. They also enable several different period clocks to be installed etc.

In Figure 5.13, we observed that digital control is composed of:

- Tasks which execute internal processes (*T*2, *T*3);
- Tasks which *poll* the external variables periodically (variables associated with sensors integrated to the physical process) to acquire their value (*T*1);
- Tasks which are activated by the occurrence of a hardware interrupt (signal) coming from the process.

5.9.1 Periodic Tasks

Tasks which ensure an interface with the industrial process to periodically acquire the values of a variable provided by a sensor are called *periodic tasks.*

Notion 15 A Periodic Task

This is a fixed period cyclic task. Upon each activation, its execution must terminate before the next clock interrupt which relaunches it.

If a digital control system is composed of several periodic tasks, which is usually the case, the condition necessary to guarantee the time limits and the periodicity of each task by the real-time executive is:

$$\sum_{i=1}^{n} (Ri/Ti) < 1 \tag{5.1}$$

where Ti is the period of task i; Ri is the maximum execution time of task i and n is the number of tasks in the system.

The control system designer must define the period for each periodic task, and choose a real-time executive that uses a scheduling policy to guarantee the verification of the constraint in equation (5.1). Periodic tasks are tasks synchronous in relation to their clock.

Since 1973, Lui and Layland (see also Colette, 1996) have suggested an approach for a feasibility study for the scheduling of real-time application tasks. This approach is based on the RMA method (rate monotonic analysis) and the theory of rate monotonic scheduling. RMA was originally used for *totally pre-emptive* periodic systems, *without interactions between tasks.* RMA is a method that enables the identification of the conditions which guarantee the correct functioning of a pre-emptive multi-task system, even in the worst cases. It enables a priority level to be given to each task according to its period. The level of priority is inversely proportional to the duration of the task period: the priority is particularly high when the period is shorter. Lui and Layland therefore suggest a formula (theory) which guarantees the scheduling of real-time application tasks if the following condition is satisfied.

Notion 16 Schedulable Real-Time Systems

These are real-time systems composed of periodic tasks and without interactions, which satisfy the following condition:

$$\sum_{i=1}^{n} (R_i/T_i) \leq n \times (2^{1/n} - 1) \tag{5.2}$$

To take into account the true requirements of real-time applications, and therefore be free from the restricting hypothesis introduced in condition (5.2), namely, the system tasks are without interactions (unrealistic conditions), Lui and Layland suggested a second variant of their theory, this time adapted to the scheduling of synchronized tasks. This variant requires that the *priority inversion* problem inherent in these types of synchronized task systems should be resolved using the priority ceiling protocol (PCP).

Notion 17 Priority Inversion

This is a phenomenon which could occur when a priority task waits behind a lower priority task which possesses a common resource required by the higher priority task.

The phenomenon of priority inversion could drive the system to help an *intermediate priority* task. Consequently, the risks of exceeding the period of the higher priority task become very real.

To pre-empt this type of situation, several protocols have been introduced and used by real-time executives to maximize the number of times priority inversion occurs in the system. The PCP protocol is one of these, and consists of:

- giving each shared resource and the whole real-time application (the group of tasks) a pre-emption level;
- resource blocking is only possible if its pre-emption level is higher than that of the real-time application, or if the task which demands the blocking of the resource in question is using the highest priority resource;
- blocking tasks see their priority temporarily increased.

The second variant (below) of the Lui and Layland theory (schedulable synchronized tasks) is only valid if this protocol is used by the real-time executive.

Notion 18 Schedulable Synchronized Tasks

A real-time application with synchronized tasks is schedulable if and only if the following condition is satisfied for each task i:

$$R_1/T_1 + R_2/T_2 + \ldots R_i/T_i + A_i/T_I \leq n^*(2^{1/i} - 1) \quad (5.3)$$

In this formula, A_i represents the maximum wait time for task i which is the sum of the critical phases of lower priority tasks.

5.9.2 Aperiodic Tasks

Notion 19 Aperiodic Task

This is a non-cyclic task activated either by the arrival of an interrupt coming from the operative part, or by a software signal emitted by another communicating task.

Aperiodic tasks are *asynchronous tasks*. They can be compared to true software signal interception handlers or interrupts. Interrupts are physical signals generated by all or nothing_sensors.

Managing the arrival of external events relies on the use of a *polling* task which checks the implementation of each event occurrence. Even this type of dedicated task, however, poses scheduling problems. If an aperiodic event arrives soon after the polling task notices its absence, the polling task must wait a complete period before being picked up and processed. To enable aperiodic events to be picked up, while remaining in the context of periodic tasks, and to therefore exploit the theories presented earlier, the notion of the *sporadic server* was introduced.

Notion 20 The Sporadic Server

This is a periodic task whose activation period must be accurately calculated according to its mean response time to an external event, and to which the second theory of schedulable synchronized tasks must be applied.

At the end of this chapter we will present several techniques to show the interception and implementation of these servers.

Incidentally, prototype tools for real-time systems by RMA analysis, such as the Pert software, are available on the market. This integrates the different RMA computation algorithms, which enables us to determine rapidly, using a graphical description of real-time system tasks and resources, if the system is schedulable, and to evaluate its performance. It also offers the possibility of automatic creation of the sporadic server, the simulation of aperiodic events, the generation of scheduling graphs, the analysis of distributed applications, etc. For more details on the RMA method, the reader can look up Lui and Layland.

Figure 5.19 gives an example of the physical process (automatically regulated heater) with three control loops:

- The first control loop, *R*1, involves keeping the fuel level constant. The corresponding *T*1 task is a periodic task for the *H*1 period. It uses a level (*N*) sensor that it polls cyclically to pickup the current fuel level. It can act on the electromagnetic gate (*V*).
- The second loop, *R*2, is controlled by the periodic task *T*2 for the period *H*2. This task polls the temperature sensor (*T*) to acquire the heater temperature. This temperature must be maintained at a precise interval. It controls the *V*1 gate to increase the fuel input.
- The third control loop manages the arrival of water. The corresponding task *T*3 for the period *H*3 can act on the *V*3 gate. The *D* sensor provides the current throughput.

There is no aperiodic task for this digital control, the system is a slow dynamic process system.

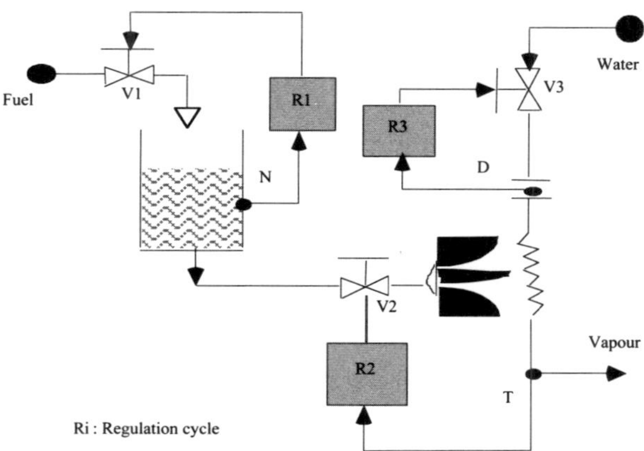

Fig. 5.19a Principle of the heater architecture: operative part.

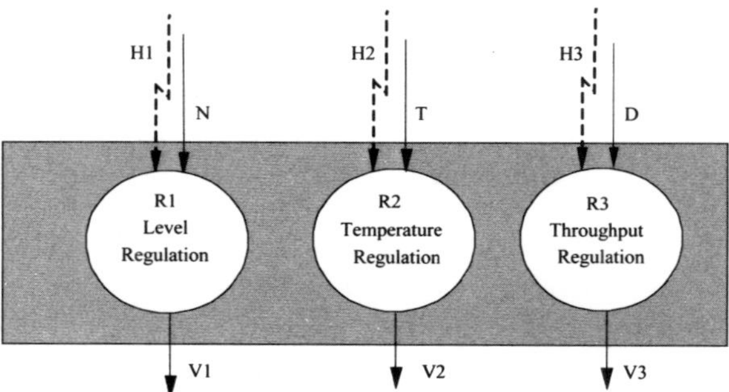

Fig. 5.19b Principle of the architecture for the digital control of the heater.

Figure 5.20 shows a task execution diagram. The real-time executive must carefully operate the period of each task to guarantee their periodicity, and end the execution of the current task before the next period. At *t*1, it has delayed the execution of *R*1 and *R*2 in favour of *R*3 which has a very short period. It has then helped *R*1 which has been able to terminate its processes. In contrast, when *R*2 was activated, it was quickly abandoned in preference of *R*3, etc.

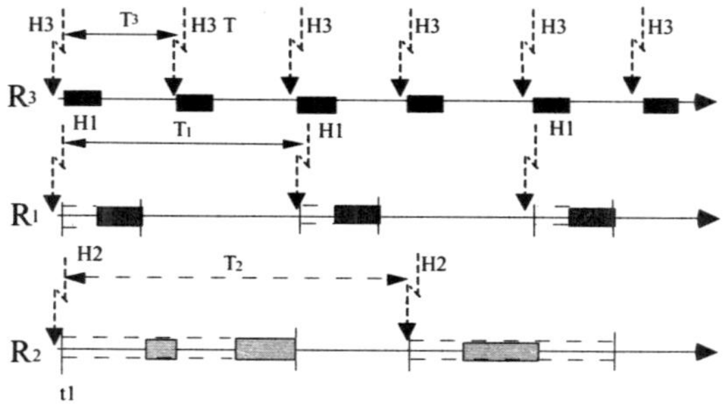

Fig. 5.20 Execution diagram of periodic tasks.

5.10 Basic Functions of Real-Time Kernels

In this section we attempt to provide a succinct presentation of the basic functions of a real-time executive. Readers already familiar with this type of system can move directly to the following section, which presents an approach using artificial intelligence techniques and tools for the study and engineering of parallel systems.

In the first chapters we presented a set of techniques and tools for developing multi-agent distributed applications. As we have just shown in this chapter, the digital control of automated processes is essentially carried out by multi-agent distributed applications. From here on we can ask ourselves whether the tools and environments presented in the first four chapters, especially the Unix operating system and its tools, do not enable these systems to be supported.

Before answering this question, first remember the principal properties of applications and real-time systems. Essentially, a real-time system is used to ensure the efficient management of external events coming from its environment (the operative part). It must react and process *asynchronous events* (interrupts). The objects that it is responsible for controlling or managing in its environment, are interdependent objects or components (a production line made up of several manufacturing posts (modules).

Real-time systems are systems which are characterized by a fairly high processing speed. They must react rapidly to an event or an external interrupt. Consequently, it is imperative that the time taken up by internal processing should be as short as possible so that the system is ready to intercept new external event occurrences. Especially when the operative part is dynamically rapid. A real-time system is deterministic; a late response to an event is a false response. It can compromise the rate, security, coherence and synchronization of the system as a whole and of its environment.

If the digital control (real-time system) of a process is not supported by an automaton or an industrial computer, it is generally embedded, and consequently is integrated in the operative part (telephone switchboards, faxes, printers, digital control machines, robots, vehicle, train and plane control and supervision systems, etc.). Data processing resources available to execute the command part are thereby limited (reduced size central memory, almost non-existent permanent storage methods, etc). The functions of operating systems (such as VxWorks, Lynx/OS etc) which support embedded real-time applications are reduced to a strict minimum: interrupt management, task management and scheduling, inter-task synchronization and communication, and basic, low level I/O operations. Figure 5.21 shows a table comparing a VxWorks real-time application development environment and the standard Unix operating system.

5.10.1 Functions of a Real-Time Kernel

A real-time kernel offers a minimum set of optimized primitives (interface user). The functions of a real-time executive are:

	VxWorks	Unix
Priority sequencing	*	
Rapid and deterministic context switching	*	
Rapid and deterministic response to interrupts	*	
Rapid and deterministic communication principles	*	
The ability to interlock a task in execution	*	
The ability to connect tasks to interrupts	*	
The ability to share data easily	*	*
The ability to freeze a CM application	*	
The ability to directly access I/O ports	*	

Fig. 5.21 The comparison between the VxWorks real-time executive and Unix.

- *The multi-task:* a direct consequence of the asynchronous character of real world events. This is important to enable the parallel execution of several tasks or processes.

- *Pre-emptive scheduling:* there is a natural order of precedence between events, which must be respected by the task scheduler at the time of CPU allocation. Within the policy of execution with priority and pre-emption, the tasks possess a priority. At a given instant, the highest priority task that is ready, is authorized to use the CPU.

- *Rapid and flexible communication and synchronization mechanisms:* in an RT system there are several parallel tasks which execute on behalf of a single application (digital control of a process). Consequently, it is important that the executive provides a set of communication tools between rapid tasks. The kernel must also provide synchronization mechanisms for resource sharing, and the implementation of critical sections.

- *The communication (link) between the tasks and the interrupt interception handlers:* acknowledging the interrupts coming from the outside world is carried out by interception handlers which make up the interface between the tasks and components of the real world.

- *Fixed performance (deterministic):* an RT executive must be optimized for the highest performance cases. A kernel which enables the constant execution of a given function in 50 milliseconds is appreciated more than an executive which has a mean execution time of 10 milliseconds; but sometimes takes 75 milliseconds.

- *Special considerations:* as demand on RT executives increases, it is important to consider the impact of the RT kernel requirements to support increasingly complex functions: multiprocessor processing, integrated ADA, RISC architecture processors, etc.

In light of this presentation, it emerges that only one standard operating system, Unix for example, can be used to support a real-time system. Standard operating systems are extremely resource greedy, because their aim is not only to optimize the use and sharing of machine resources, but also to offer the users certain user-friendliness. They are very risky compared to real-time, and are not optimized, as is the case with real-time executions. Furthermore, they are not designed to be easily stored in read only memory (PROM, EPROM, etc). They can be used in embedded systems.

5.10.2 Internal Structure of a Real-Time Kernel

For a programmer, a real-time executive is none other than a set of usable program functions.

Notion 21 Real-Time Kernel

This is a set of functions available in the form of primitives that can be used from a programming language (in general, the C language or the assembler).

The primitives provide:

- the management of task execution;
- synchronization between tasks;
- the management of software signals;
- the management of interception handlers of interrupts coming from the physical process;
- the management of temporal constraints.

A task is composed of an executable *program*, an execution *stack* and a *descriptor* which contains the obligatory descriptive and dynamic information for the management of its execution in the system (TCB: task control bloc) (Fig. 5.22).

5.10.3 Task Scheduling

Tasks must respect an order of precedence during CPU allocation. The use of the pre-emptive scheduling with priority policy introduces a priority relationship between the tasks. The CPU is allocated to the task which possesses the highest priority and which is ready (not blocked or suspended) (Fig. 5.23). The scheduler intervenes each time a task becomes ready and its priority is higher than that of the current task: *pre-emption* of this latter (task C was suspended to the benefit of the higher priority task B which, in turn, was suspended to aid the higher priority task A). The kernel proceeds to change the context to save the elements needed to resume the execution of the suspended task (ordinal counter, stack register, work register, etc.), and replaces them by those of the chosen task. Saving the context of the current task is carried out in its descriptor (TCB). Restoring context to the task to be activated can also be done from its TCB.

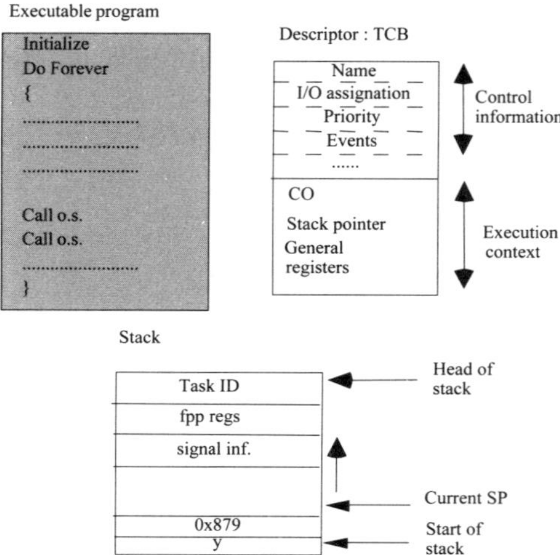

Fig. 5.22 Task components.

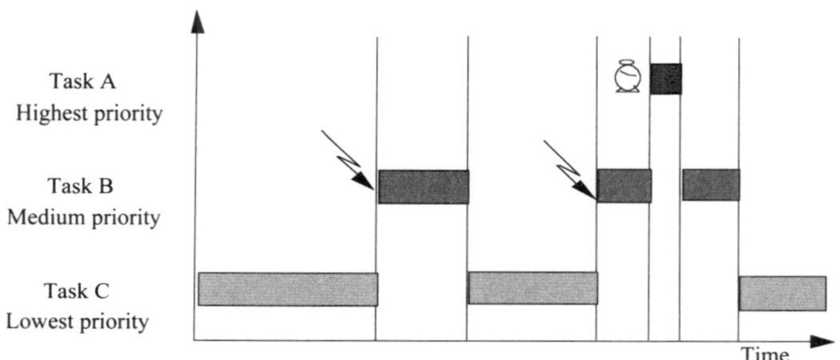

Fig. 5.23 Task pre-emption.

The duration of the context change operation must be very short. The kernel carries out this operation using a *scheduling algorithm*, which mainly exploits task priority. In general, real-time executives propose priorities running from 0 to 255. The priority is specified at the moment of task creation, and can be modified during the execution. Incidentally, the most well-known scheduling algorithm uses the *round-robin* policy:

- All tasks with the same priority are executed *in turn* during the same quantum and in a *cyclic* manner.
- A task will complete its quantum after pre-emption.

During their life in the system, and at a given instant, the tasks possess one of the following states:

- *Active:* the current task possesses the CPU;

- *Ready:* the task is waiting for the CPU and possesses all of the resources that it needs;
- *Blocked:* the task is blocked behind a semaphore or queue;
- *Dormant:* the task has been stopped for a determined length of time (temporization);
- *Suspended:* the task is awaiting a resource.

5.10.4 Methods of Communication and Synchronization between Tasks

Multi-task applications require means of communication, and synchronization is necessary to enable true resource sharing. The communication and co-ordination between tasks is essential (Fig. 5.24) to accomplish the control function.

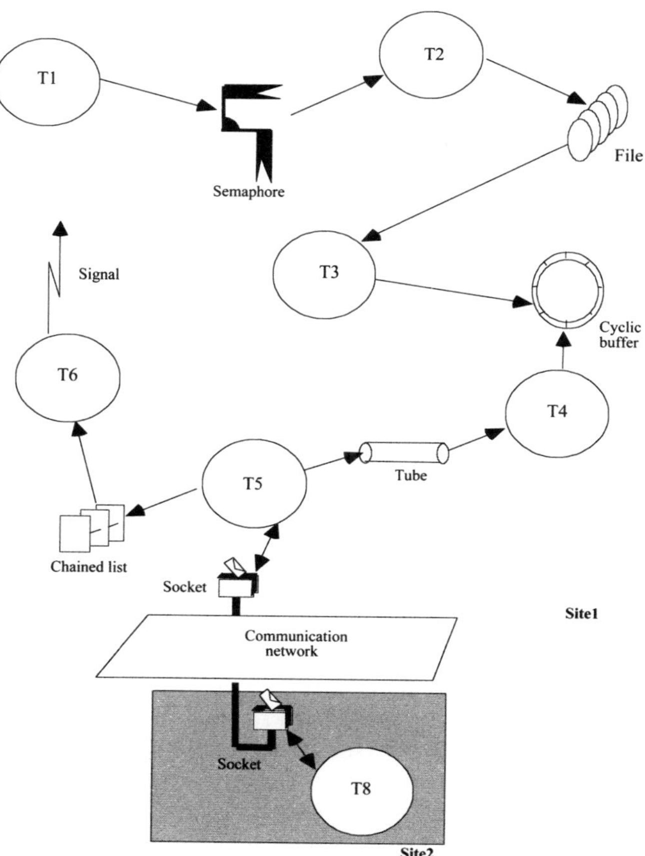

Fig. 5.24 Example of a multi-agent real-time type of application under VxWorks.

Tasks of a real-time application can easily share data stored in a *shared addressable space.* However, the structure of shared data presents the problem of *parallel access.* Under these conditions it is imperative to use a control and synchronization tool such as semaphores, as well as means of communication. It is the responsibility of the programmer to give each shared data structure the adequate parallel access control tool, and especially to make good use of it when writing different parts of the application code. As we have already indicated in Chapter 2, semaphores generally remain low-level synchronization tools, which are very often the source of functioning errors and anomalies if the strict rules for their use are not respected (see Chapter 2).

To reassure our reader, real-time executives propose other more elaborate means of communication between communicating tasks, which do not require the *explicit control* of parallel access by the programmer. Among those available (Fig. 5.24) in the majority of real-time kernels, we particularly mention mailboxes, string lists, cyclic buffers and communication tubes. In reality, the kernel associates a semaphore to each of these communication methods and takes charge of its management.

5.10.5 Re-entrance in Real-Time Executives

In multi-task systems, the re-entrance of the code plays a primordial role in the design and implementation of real-time applications.

> **Notion 22 Re-entrance**
>
> *A handler is a re-entering handler if it can be simultaneously called by several tasks without conflict. Only the handler code is shared, the data remains private for each execution (the data and stack segments are private to each calling task).*

Re-entrance is a property which enables a considerable reduction in the size of software, and also facilitates its maintenance. It is obligatory that the shared codes are re-entering. All of the real-time executives available on the market offer this possibility. The example in Figure 5.25 shows that a single handler (control procedure) is used to simultaneously control the four arms of the articulated mechanical structure (manipulator arm). The conflicts provoked by the simultaneous use of a handler by several tasks manifest themselves during access to the global or static variables. A simple and effective means to resolve this problem involves using the stack variables. The articulation number (Fig. 5.25) is a call parameter for the handler which is stored in the stack. The multi-task real-time executive duplicates and manages the variables of a shared handler in the execution stack of the calling task. Only the code is effectively shared. The variables and data are therefore local to the execution context of each task.

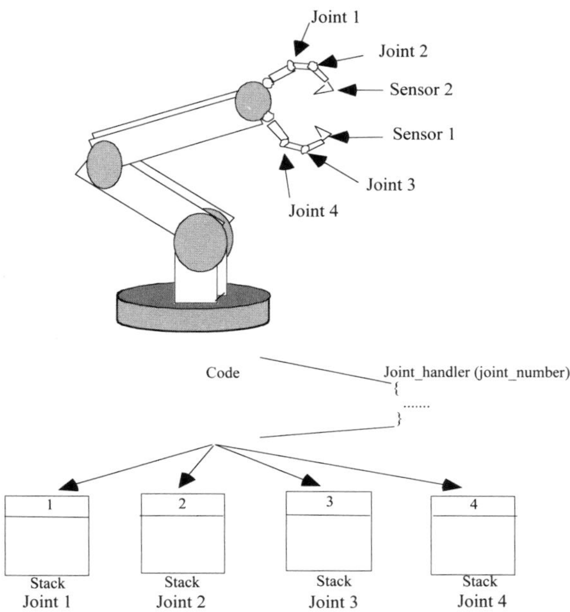

Figure 5.25 Re-entrance management by real-time kernels.

5.10.6 Exceptions, Interrupts and Timers

Software signals or events were initially used to resume the service after the occurrence of an exception or even an error. However, this concept was rapidly generalized to use it as a means of *synchronization* and *communication* between tasks, especially in a real-time context. Tasks can associate an interception handler to each signal declared by the user, or each signal available in the system (see Chapter 4). Certain system signals are reserved for hardware exceptions (bus errors, illegal instructions, dividing by zero, error instructions in floating commas, etc.). Figure 5.26 shows the main aspects of processing a signal by the system, when it arrives.

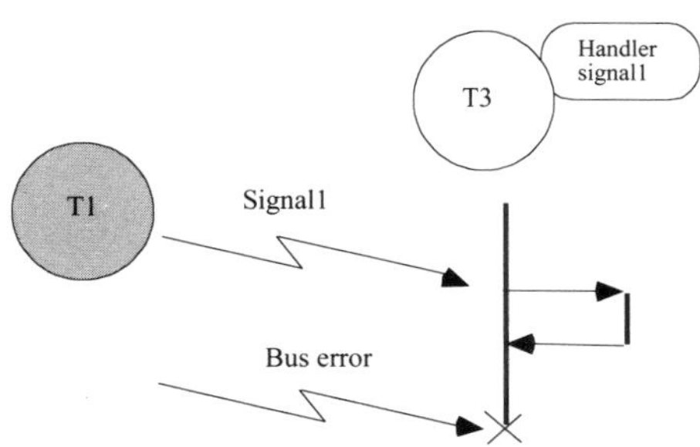

Fig. 5.26 System software signal processing.

Interrupts are critical events in real-time, generated by the operative part. Interrupts therefore signal an exterior stimulus, and trigger *asynchronous state changes.* For greater efficiency in processing interrupts, C handlers can be associated to interrupts. When an interrupt arrives, the kernel executes the following actions:

- Intercepts an interrupt: immediately triggers the change of the execution stack to use the stack system which is reserved for this reason (all interrupts use the same execution stack);
- Saves the ordinal counter in the stack;
- Executes the interrupt interception handler (*handler: interrupt service routine - ISR*).

These actions are entirely supported by the hardware layer. An ISR handler must satisfy the following properties:

- an ISR is not authorized to block;
- it cannot be suspended;
- it cannot be deferred;
- it cannot use a semaphore;
- it cannot call a function susceptible to blocking;
- it is not authorized to effectuate I/O operations except via tubes.

The body of an ISR must be as small as possible. It leaves the task in charge of the processing which takes the most time, is less critical and rarer.

Interrupts are vectored to enable the system to take charge rapidly. The address of each handler is stored in the entrance associated with the corresponding interrupt of the interrupt vectors table. Figure 5.27 shows the order of execution of handlers and tasks in the system.

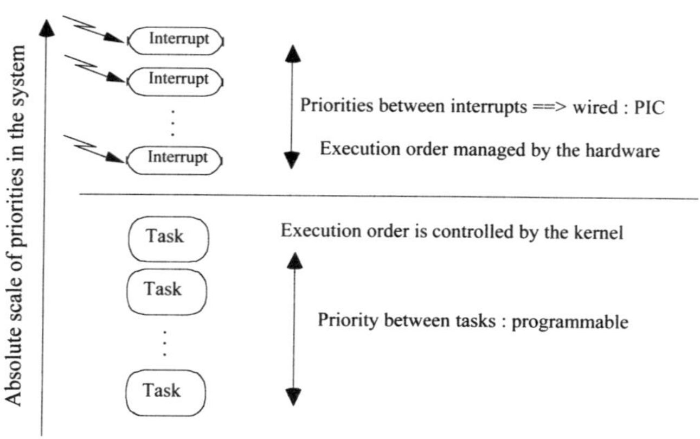

Fig. 5.27 Execution priority between handlers and tasks.

It is important to note that interrupts always cause the pre-emption of tasks whatever their priority. The handlers form the interface between the operative part and the tasks of the command part. Figure 5.28 gives the communications allowed between tasks and the handlers.

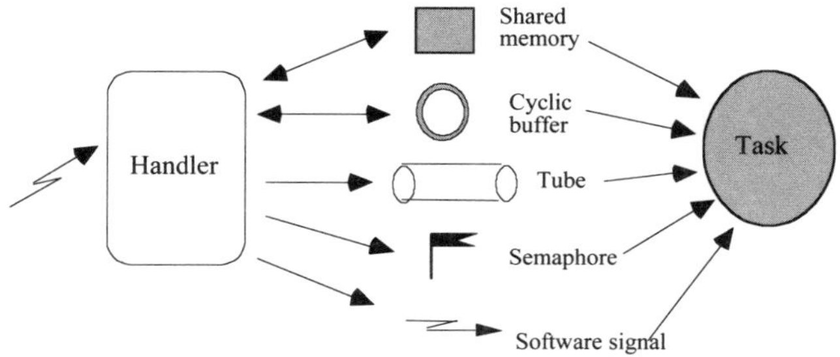

Fig. 5.28 Methods of communication between tasks and ISR handlers.

Finally, to enable the tasks to carry out the periodic polling of external variables belonging to the operative part, (periodic tasks), especially sporadic servers, and to suspend themselves for periods while waiting an event, (maintain temporization), etc., real-time kernels use *timers*. These enable the association of a deadline to C handlers. When the deadline expires, the handler is executed. The C handler is subject to the same conditions as the ISR.

5.11 Local Industrial Networks

In today's factories, data transfer is organized around specialized, hierarchical networks (Fig. 5.29).

Level 0 corresponds mainly to two types of exchange:

- the exchange of "synchronization" type data between the different data processing command systems (automaton or micros) which each ensure the control of a functional part (a manufacturing process) of the physical process;
- the exchange of "report" or "process" type data between the modules of the physical process and the control systems (automaton, micros, hardwired regulators).

The exchange messages are short and there are few stations. Moreover, the response time must be compatible with the dynamics of controlled processes.

- *Level 0* contains the bus or terrestrial network. This constitutes the lower level of the hierarchy. It establishes physical links between the processor unit and the physical variables of the operative part which are indicated by *sensors* or *actuators*. In a continuous process, the terrestrial network (terrestrial bus) provides the link between pressure, temperature and throughput sensors etc, and the control unit supporting the command part: programmable automaton, computer (micro). In an automated manufacturing process, it links together position sensors, counters, speed variators, bar-code readers, robot controllers, programmable automaton, etc.

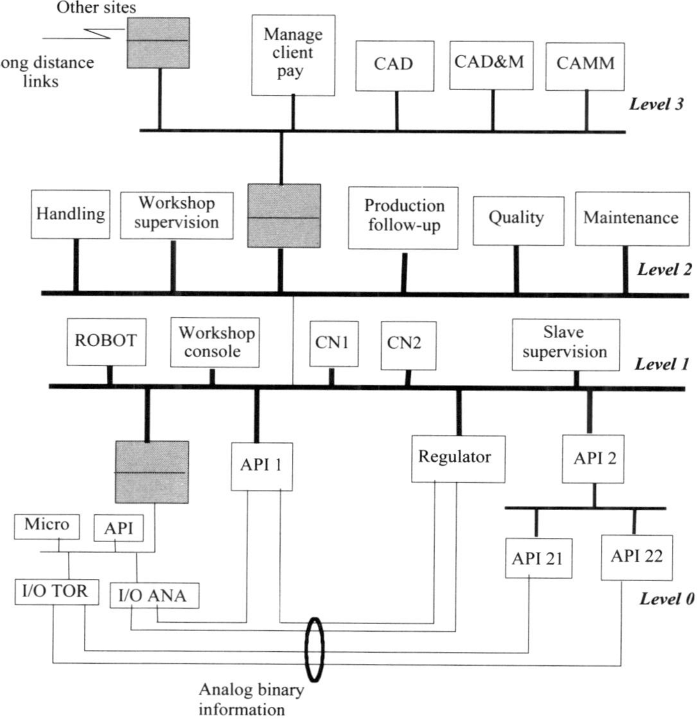

Fig. 5.29 Transmission hierarchy within a company.

- *Level 1* is essentially involved with the modular implementation of complex processes following distributed control and architecture. It groups together the data processing command systems of a production line, or a complete operative section which is composed of several physical processes (loading robot, drilling post, conveyor belt, etc). The synchronization information exchanged between the different systems is relatively weak. The communication speed must be sufficiently elevated to guarantee the coherent and stable synchronization of the different modules of the operative part.

- *Level 2* enables all of the information related to production, maintenance or quality control to be centralized (control and supervision room). The management of changes to the manufacturing program, and the remote loading of machines and automaton of the inferior level also takes place at this level. If the volume of information exchanged at this level remains relatively weak compared to level 3, the transmission speed must be relatively high to guarantee real-time control of the installation. The local industrial networks FACTOR and MAP are currently used to ensure this level of communication.

- *Level 3* constitutes the general level of the business, where the management, design aid, maintenance records and production balance sheets are held. It consists of the research, method and compatibility sectors etc. The volumes of data exchanged are very high, but the communication time is not critical. Ethernet or TOP networks match perfectly.

In the following sections we will concentrate particularly on Level 0.

Level 0 Link Techniques

Two solutions are possible:

- A standard solution using a *terrestrial bus* where each actuator and sensor is linked to the control unit by a point to point link (a physical line).

  Today, every designer of programmable automaton (API), of digital command control systems, sensors and intelligent digital actuators, proposes their own terrestrial bus with communication protocols responding to specific standards (Fig. 5.30).

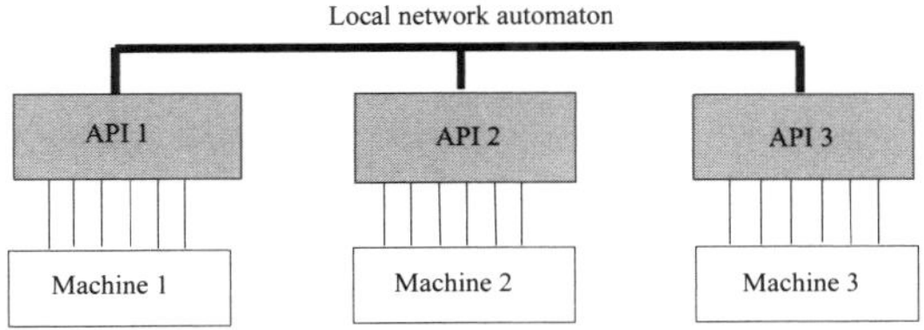

Fig. 5.30 Local automaton network.

  The Télémécanique TELWAY network and the April JNET network are examples of local *proprietary* networks.

- A more elaborate solution using a unique digital transmission support authorizing multi-point links, such as coaxial or fibre optic cable (Fig. 5.31). This solution has the advantage of *considerably simplifying the cabling* of the workshop, *increasing the modularity* of systems by displacing smaller and smaller stations. It also enables the increasing accuracy of transmissions, and the remote interrogation of transmitters for remote regulating or autodiagnostics. This type of network is called an open network because it applies to the interconnection of heterogeneous equipment (heterogeneous network).

In contrast to standard architecture using a terrestrial bus, in a terrestrial network solution a new constraint must be taken account of to link a new piece of equipment to the network: *the equipment must transmit digital signals.*

Analogue signals at the standard 4-20 milliamps are not accepted. It is clear that this type of network favours the use of the new generation of *intelligent* sensors or actuators.

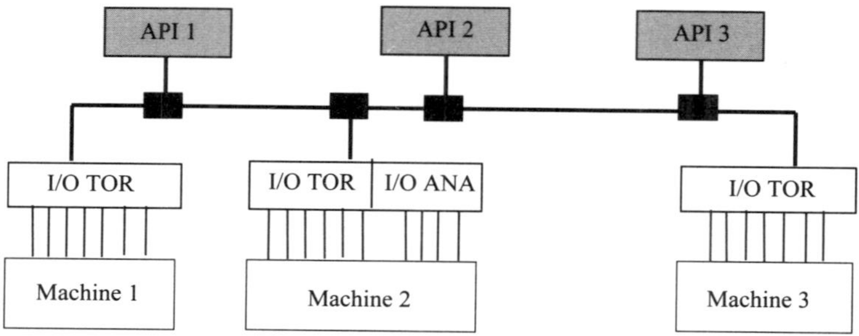

Fig. 5.31 Terrestrial network.

5.11.1 The FIP Terrestrial Network

The FIP concept (factory information protocol) was formed in September 1982 with the formation of a work group "Réseaux Locaux Industriels" by the Ministère de la Recherche et de la Technologie.[1] In March 1987, the "CLUB FIP" was officially born, an association which continues today to bring together European manufacturers, users and research laboratories. Its principal objectives are the promotion and broadcasting of concepts, national and international standardization, the study of procedures and conformity tests and demonstrations.

5.11.1.1 Motivation Techniques

The "Livre Blanc FIP" defines a decentralized system with the following phrase: "It is a system in which there must exist at each level a *unique element*, hardware or software, which is *essential* to the *correct* functioning of the system."

This is a definition which matches that of a distributed system and the notions and concepts introduced in Chapter 1.

The contribution which FIP could bring is as follows:

1. A considerable *improvement* in functioning reliability due to its services which offer:
   - the availability of information (repeated in spread manuals);
   - data coherency (information which is *unique*, common and *shared* by all subscribers simultaneously);
   - reliability (by potential hardware *redundancy*);
2. A major structural *modularity* authorizing the installation or the suppression of hardware and software resources without interfering with the rest of the system.

---

[1] Ministère de la Recherche et de la Technologie: the Minister for Research and Technology, however, there is no real equivalent in the United Kingdom.

3. The *increasing access to information* by *broadcasting* the information to all of the subscribers linked to the bus (a distributed database).
4. A set of *service facilities* such as design, tuning, maintenance, etc.
5. The adaptability of *spatial* and *functional* development without challenging the operative part of the installation.

5.11.1.2 Economic Motivations

The structured design of systems which leads to functional separation using the "one function = one piece of equipment" principle results in an increase in the cost of hardware compared to centralized systems. The cost is largely compensated by a substantial reduction in the cost of studies whose means and methods become repetitive. Moreover, FIP enables an improvement in the costs of cabling (the bus link will be replaced by wire-to-wire links), installation, start-up installations and maintenance.

5.11.1.3 Interconnection Model

Figure 5.32 gives an example of the FIP topology currently found. It involves a network composed of a single segment of cable of a maximum length of 500 m, to which up to 32 subscribers can be connected. The length of the adapter between the passive socket and the subscriber must not be more than 3 m. The junction box ensures the conversion of signals for a connection from the bus, to *N* point-to-point links particularly destined for sensors and actuators. It also acts as an isolator. The repeater links two segments of cable and re-emerges on a cable similar to the first but regenerating the signal. It also enables the length and consequently the number of subscribers on the network to be increased. It is important to note that it is possible to install an *arborescent structure* to *n* segments in a star format around a principal segment.

Figure 5.33 shows an example of the use of FIP in an industrial installation.

This installation is composed of two simple processes:

- One process to regulate the temperature of the oven and the level of fuel in the tank, with real-time supervision, synoptic display and remote control of the fuel and coolant gates.
- One reflex process which enables the passage of a part to be detected by an inductive sensor, and the oven door to be opened. Notice that the two pressure and temperature sensors are *intelligent integrated logic sensors*, which authorize their direct connection with the FIP bus. This *displaced* intelligence therefore enables the increased credibility of measurements by *autodiagnostics*, *autosurveillance, autoadaptability* as well as taking into account the large effect of interference. It also authorizes remote control, remote loading and help with repairs.

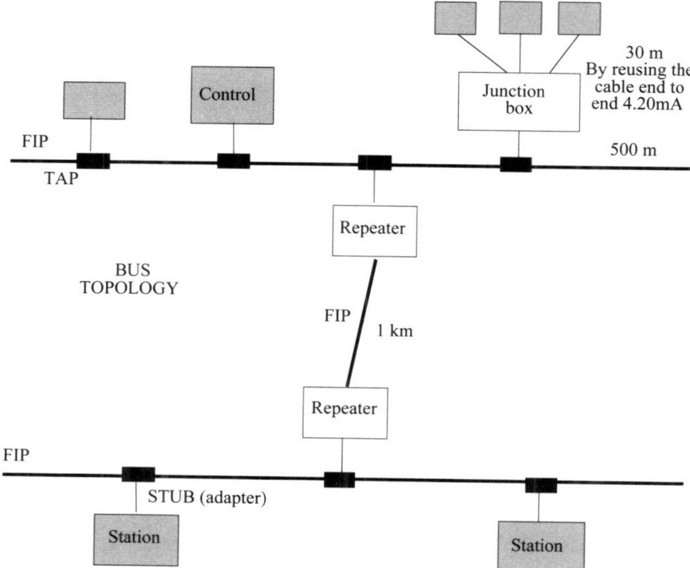

Fig. 5.32 Example of FIP typology.

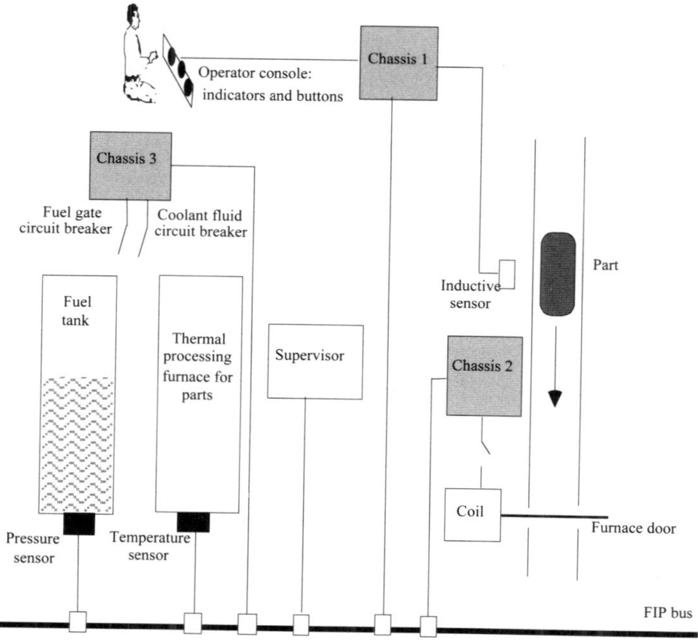

Fig. 5.33 Thermal processing furnace for metal parts.

5.11.2 The Principal Services of the FIP Model Application Layer

In this section we give a brief insight into the options offered by the application layer of the global FIP model (Fig. 5.33). The detailed study of the different layers of this model falls outside the scope of this book; however, the interested reader can study WorldFIP (1995a, b).

The global FIP model enables the command part (workshop, factory, production line, flexible cell etc.) of a complete installation to be modelled in the form of *agents* or communicating processes. The command part represents a distributed application according to the definition introduced in Chapter 1.

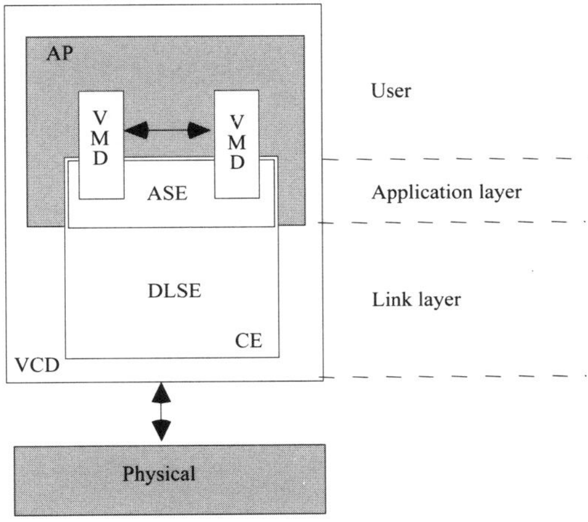

Fig. 5.34 Structure of virtual communication devices.

In the global FIP model, each piece of equipment in the command system is represented at the level of the command system by a virtual image in the form of a *virtual manufacturing device* (VMD). All VMDs of an application associated to a command system device make up an application process (AP). An application process associated to a communication entity (CE) is a virtual device for communication (VDC). It is this abstract entity which provides the user with the application service elements (ASE) to be able to communicate with other VDCs.

The application service elements are composed of two application entities (AE):

1. managing periodic and aperiodic data services (MPS);
2. manufacturing message services (SUB-MMS: MMS kernel). These services represent the link between the command part and the operative part of an installation.

In the application layer of the FIP, the implementation of interactions or the exchange of information between APs is carried out by the access intermediary for the variables, by analogy with data processing programs (tasks or processes) sharing the global variables.

> Every station likely to receive or transmit information is modelled and represented by an FIP variable. Even within a station, a variable is represented by an abstract object which possesses its own attributes. They describe the principal characteristics of the station.

They must associate to a variable:

- a *name* by which it will be identified and used;
- a *type* (boolean, integer, etc.) which specifies the nature of data flow exchanged with the station;
- an application level *address* to be referenced;
- a *status* of validity (in production or in reception of data flows).

The manipulation of FIP variables is carried out using a set of methods (service layer applications) which are:

1. reader services (value and associated status);
2. writing services (value updating);
3. indication services for the emission or reception of a variable on the network.

Finally, the variables used for an agent or a command process (AP) can be any of the following:

- LOCAL INTERNAL when it involves variables (stations) specific to an AP. They do not need to exchange via the network.
- LOCAL IMPORTED for variables produced by the remote AP and rendered accessible and locally visible in an AP by the services of the AE-MPS entity.
- LOCAL EXPORTED, which enables an AP to export variables and make them visible to other AP variables produced locally.

Incidentally, the "MPS" service offers the user a set of reader primitives (Fig. 5.35) for variables locally visible (private or imported):

1. A-READ.Rq for the formulation of a request to read a variable;
2. A-READ.Conf, for the response.

For example, you can write in a supervision agent in Figure 5.35, if the C-Temperature variable has been declared as an integer:

A-READ.Rq (C-Temperature);

and receive a confirmation

A-READ.Conf (350, OK Refresh).

To conclude, the concepts introduced by the FIP model facilitate the implementation of the command part of an installation according to *a multi-agent distributed architecture*. They follow the general definitions of distributed systems, particularly enabling concepts to be standardized between two communities: computer scientists and automation specialists. The services offered by the application layer of the FIP model bring considerable comfort to the developer for the modelling and development of the different entities and interactions between them.

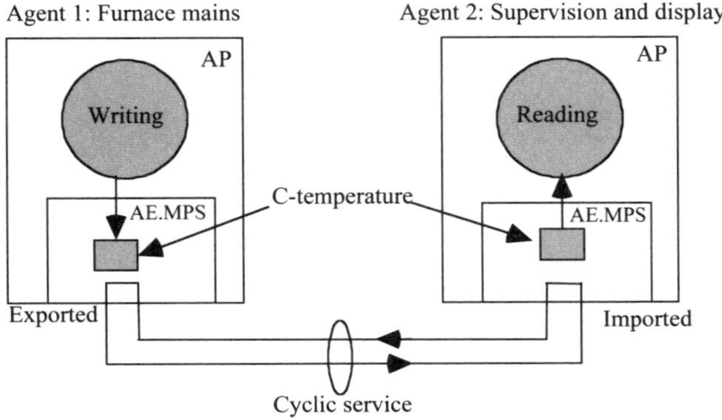

Fig. 5.35 Example of the implementation of the access to variables.

Chapter 6 presents an approach for the modelling and specification of real-time systems which conforms to the concepts of distributed systems in general, and which facilitates the design of a command process application following the concepts introduced by the FIP.

To complete this chapter, we present the different tools and services offered by the development environment for VxWorks real-time applications. Recall that the support of a command system can be a *programmable automaton* or a *computer* (micro). To be able to properly manage the different parts of the physical process, especially the random character of events, and the asynchronism which follows, the computer must be equipped with a sufficiently high performance, optimized multi-task operating system (real-time executive). The rapid dynamics of certain industrial processes require data processing systems to take immediate control of different events, and to process in minimum time periods to ensure coherent and efficient reactivity. Furthermore, real-time executives offer the possibility of implementing embedded command systems, by using specialized microprocessor cards, where the real-time executive and command applications are programmed into ROM or EPROM type memory circuits ("promable").

5.12 The Development Environment of VxWorks Real-Time Applications

The development environment of VxWorks real-time applications is a *reference* in this field, especially for the industrial development of this type of application. It offers a development crossed with Unix (Fig. 5.36), namely the use of real-time targets (embedded cards), a Unix development post (workstation) and host/target connections via a network. It is a high performance real-time executive whose principal characteristics are as follows:

- very rapid and determinist micro-kernel;
- I/O compatible with Unix;
- independence towards the bus and microprocessors;
- supports industry standards (POSIX, ANSI C);
- modular;
- commutation of determinist context : 6 ms;
- latency time to interrupts : 5 ms;
- give/take of a semaphore : 2 ms;
- pre-emption invalidation : 1 ms.

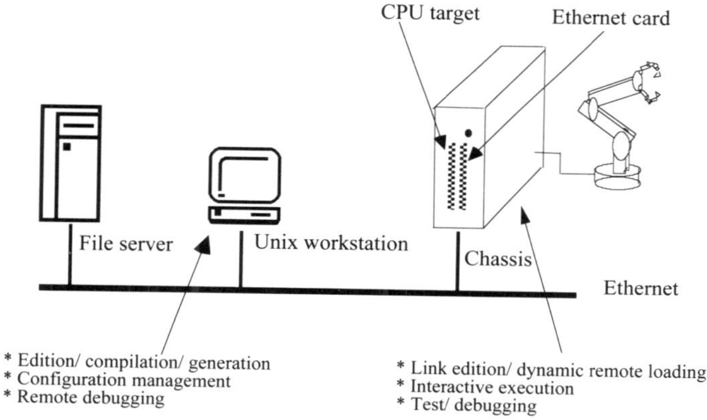

Fig. 5.36 The VxWorks environment.

The internal architecture of VxWorks is given in Figure 5.37. In this architecture, we notice that the real-time executive is called Wind (inside the grey part). It is limited to the basic functions: task management, clock management, management of communication tools and synchronization between tasks, management of signals and interrupts. The external layers do not concern the kernel. They provide the communication network, file management and a set of development tools (compilators, debuggers etc.).

5.12.1 Task Management

The Wind kernel enables the deterministic management and commutation of tasks. It uses sequencing or scheduling based on priority (256 levels). It is pre-emptive and suggests several scheduling algorithms according to the nature of the target application and the time constraints. It is characterized by an interrupt management facility and a weak latency time to pre-emption which is manifested by very limited execution time at the kernel level. Recall that from the point of view of the user, a real-time kernel is seen in the form of a set of usable primitives from a C program or an assembler. In the following sections, we cite only the available primitives with several comments. If the reader wishes to know more, they can refer to the VxWorks user manual (1992).

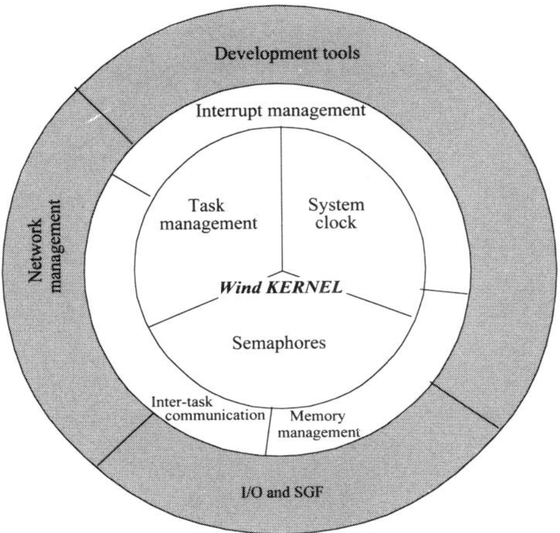

Fig. 5.37 The architecture of the VxWorks environment.

1. Task creation and activation primitives
   - `taskSpawn():` the creation and activation of new tasks
   - `taskInit():` the use of a new task
   - `taskActivate():` the activation of a task already initialized.
2. Scheduling policy control primitives
   - `kernelTimeslice():` allocation and scheduling using the round- robin policy
   - `taskPrioritySet():` change the priority of a task
   - `taskLock():` avoid the pre-emption and reactivation of the task ⇒ lock the task in the CM
   - `taskUnlock():` unlock the task.
3. Task suppression primitives
   - `exit():` terminate the execution of a caller task and free the memory
   - `taskDelete():` terminate the execution of a task and free the memory

- `taskSafe()`: prevents the task from being killed by other tasks. This protection is vital, especially when the task finds itself in a critical section
- `taskUnsafe()`: withhold the protection.

4. Task control and execution primitives
   - `taskSuspend()`: suspend the execution of a task
   - `taskResume()`: continue the execution of a task
   - `taskRestart()`: restart the execution of a task after it has started
   - `taskDelay()`: suspend a task for a certain number of clock turns.
5. Primitives for gathering information on a task in a system
   - `taskIdlistGet()`: obtain ID lists of tasks active in the system
   - `taskInfoGet()`: obtain information related to a task
   - `taskPriorityGet()`: examine the priority of a task
   - `taskRegsGet()`: examine the records of a task
   - `taskRegsSet()`: position the records of a task
   - `taskIsSuspended()`: check if a task is suspended
   - `taskIsReady()`: check if a task is ready
   - `taskTcb()`: obtain a pointer on the TCB of a task.
6. Management identification of tasks primitives
   - `taskName ()`: give the name of a task corresponding to an ID
   - `taskNameTold()`: search for the ID of a task corresponding to a name
   - `taskIdSelf()`: send the ID of the caller task
   - `taskIdVerify()`: verify the existence of the specific task.

5.12.2 Example of Task Creation

This involves an application which starts with the creation of three tasks. After five seconds, it is destroyed. For this example, the mother task is thrown from the command interpreter, and the daughter tasks display the message "hello" and their external identification. They then enter into an infinite loop until the application or mother task destroys them (Fig. 5.38).

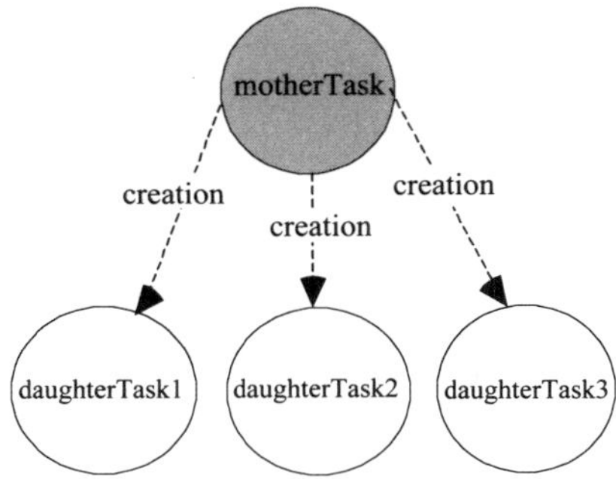

Fig. 5.38a Example of the creation of tasks under VxWorks.

```
#include "vxWorks"
int tid1, tid2, tid3;                                    /* ID of daughter tasks*/
void daughterTasks();

motherTask ()
{
                                                  /* creation of 3 daughter tasks*/

    tid1= taskSpawn ("daughterTask1", 100, 0, 2000, daughterTask);
    tid2= taskSpawn ("daughterTask2", 100, 0, 2000, daughterTask);
    tid3= taskSpawn ("daughterTask3", 100, 0, 2000, daughterTask);

                                  /*leave the daughter tasks to execute for 5 seconds*/

    taskDelay(sysClkRateGet()*5);

                                                      /* destroy daughter tasks*/

    taskDelete(tid1);
    taskDelete(tid2);
    taskDelete(tid3);
}

void daughterTask()
{
                                                                /* infinite loop*/
  while(TRUE)
  {printf("Hello, it is the task: %s/n",taskName(taskIdSelf()));}
```

Fig. 5.38b Application code.

5.12.3 Inter-task Communications

Because a real-time application is essentially a multi-agent or multi-task distributed application, the real-time executive must provide easy to use communication mechanisms. These must be high performance so as not to compromise the global performance of the application, and therefore guarantee meeting deadlines and temporal constraints.

The following can be found among the mechanisms and tools supported by Wind:

- shared memory which enables simple data sharing;
- semaphores – a tool of mutual exclusion and synchronization;
- messages files and pipes for intra-machine message communication;
- sockets and RPCs for inter-task and inter-machine communication;
- software signals or events for exception management.

Semaphores

There are three types of semaphore supported by Wind as indicated in the table below:

Type	Utilization
Binary	General: for synchronization or mutual exclusion
Mutual exclusion	Priority inheritance problem, controlled destruction
Counting	To control several copies of a resource

Semaphore Management Primitives

- `SemBCreate():` allocation and initialization of a binary semaphore
- `SemMCreate():` allocation and initialization of a mutual exclusion semaphore
- `SemCCreate():` allocation and initialization of a counting semaphore
- `SemDelete():` withholding of a semaphore
- `SemTake():` P(s)
- `SemGive():` V(s)
- `SemFlush():` free all the tasks blocked behind a semaphore.

Message Queue Management Primitives

- `msgQCreate():` allocation and initialization of a message queue
- `msgQDelete():` destruction of a message queue
- `msgQSend():` writing a message in a queue
- `msgQReceive():` reading a message from a queue.

Pipe Manipulation Primitives

The creation of a pipe is carried out using the following primitive:

- Status = pipeDevCreate("/pipe/name", max_msgs, Max_size).

The pipe created in this way usually becomes an I/O *device*, and consequently, the standard manipulation primitives for I/O devices can be used for these pipes: `write()`, `read()`, `close()`, `select()`.

Signal Management Primitives

- `sigvec()`: position and interception handler for a `signal`
- `kill()`: generate a signal
- `sigsetmask()`: mask a signal
- `sigblock()`: block a signal.

5.12.4 Interrupt Management

- `intConnect()`: connect a C handler to an interrupt vector
- `intCount()`: send the current imbrication level to the interrupts
- `intLevelSet()`: position the processor interrupt level mask
- `intLock()`: inhibit interrupts
- `intUnlock()`: authorize interrupts
- `intVecBaseSet()`: position the interrupt vector base address
- `intVecBaseGet()`: send the interrupt vector base address
- `intVecSet()`: create an exception vector
- `intVecGet()`: send the exception vector.

5.12.5 Timer Management

- `wdCreate()`: allocation and initialization of a watchdog timer
- `wdDelete()`: suppression of a watchdog
- `wdStart()`: activation of a watchdog
- `wdCancel()`: stop the watchdog counter.

5.12.6 Example of Mutual Exclusion and Synchronization between Tasks

Two tasks of the same application use two global variables, *v*1 and *v*2 to exchange data (communication via shared variables). The program in Figure 5.39 shows a version which fixes tasks in the CM before entering the critical section. Each task asks the system to prevent context changing (scheduling) when it has the lead, which enables it to terminate the loop where it manipulates the variables, after it re-establishes the scheduling.

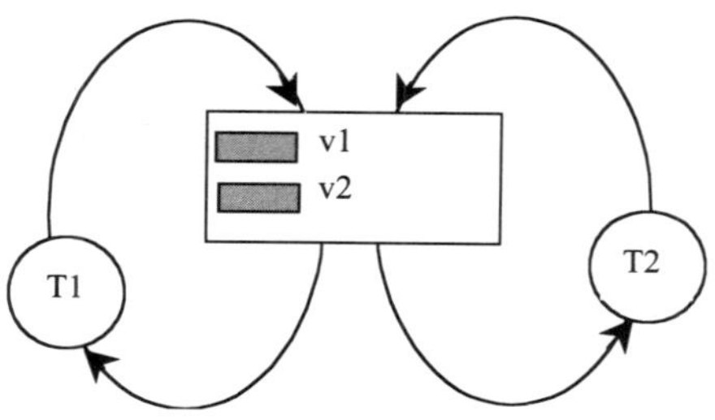


```
int    v1;                                          /* global variable */
int    v2;                                          /* global variable */

task1()
{int counter=0;
FOREVER
      {
      taskLock();                 /* prohibit any change in execution context*/
      v1= counter;
      v2= counter ;
      taskUnlock();                              /* authorize contest change */
      counter++;
      }
}
task2()
{
int idem;
for (;;)
{
      taskLock();
      idem= (v1=v2);
      taskUnlock();
      if (!idem)
      printf("oh!  v1 = %d, v2 =%d",v1,v2);
      taskDelay(1);
}
}
```

Figure 5.39 Example of the use of semaphores under VxWorks.

Figure 5.40 gives another version of the same application, this time using semaphores.

```
int    v1;                                          /* global variable */
int    v2;                                          /* global variable */
SEM_ID  sid;

task1()
{int counter=0;
sid= semMCreate(SEM_Q_FIFO);

FOREVER
      {semTake(sid,WAIT_FOREVER);
      v1= counter;
```

```
        v2= counter ;
        semGive(sid);
        counter++;}
}

task2()
{
int idem;
for (;;)
        {semTake(sid, WAIT_FOREVER);
        idem= (v1=v2);
        if (!idem)
        printf("oh!  v1 = %d, v2 =%d",v1,v2);
        taskDelay(1);}
}
```

Fig. 5.40 Mutual exclusion with semaphores.

Finally, we end this section with an example of the use of signals between tasks. The principal task has the role of creating two daughter tasks, one task which takes on the role of emitter, and the other the role of receptor. The receptor starts by giving signal 30 an interception routine "`sighandler`". It then creates a semaphore before entering into an infinite loop. In this loop, it waits behind the semaphore. The emitter starts by waking the receptor and incrementing the semaphore; it then generates signal 30 which triggers the release of the receptors `sighandler` handler (Fig. 5.41).

```
#define     CPU       MC68020
#include "vxWorks.h"
#include "sigLib.h"
#include "semlib.h"
SEM_ID sid;
int tid1, tid2;
void  emitter();
void receptor();
void  sighandler();

triggerTask ()
{
   tid1= taskSpawn("EMITTER",100,0,2000,emitter);
   tid2= taskSpawn("RECEPTOR",100,0,2000,receptor);
   taskdelay(sysClkRateGet()*100);
   td(tid1);
   td(tid2);
}

void receptor()
{
   SIGVEC vec;
   vec.sv_handler = sighandler;  /* the handler to call when the signal arrives*/
   vec.sv_mask = 0;
   vec.sv_flags  = 0;
   sigvec (30, with, 0);                    /* link the handler signal to signal 30*/
```

```
    sigsetmask (0);                                  /* authorize all signals*/
    sid= semBCreate(SEM_Q_PRIORITY, SEM_EMPTY);
    for (;;)
    {
         semTake(sid,WAIT_FOREVER);
    }
}

void sighandler (sig, code, sigContext);
     int sig;
    int code;
    SIGCONTEXT *sigContext;
    {
        printf ("sig= %d, interrupt pc at the address 0x%x", sig,
code,
                          sigContext->sc_regs.pc);
      }

void emitter()
{
    taskdelay(sysClkRateGet()*25);
    semGive(sid);
    kill (tid2,30);
}
```

Fig. 5.41 The use of signals as a means of communication.

5.13 The Environment of a Multi-Agent Real-Time Application

The global environment of a multi-agent real-time application (Fig. 5.42) is generally composed of:

- objects or variables of the physical process (variables or I/O ports associated with sensors/actuators);
- temporary work variables which are internal and whose life-span is equal to that of the agent which declared them and which uses them;
- persistent variables which are stored on a non-volatile support (hard disk). Their life-span does not depend on the agent that created them. This type of variable normally involves soft real-time applications;
- Network variables for communication with other remote application agents (sockets).

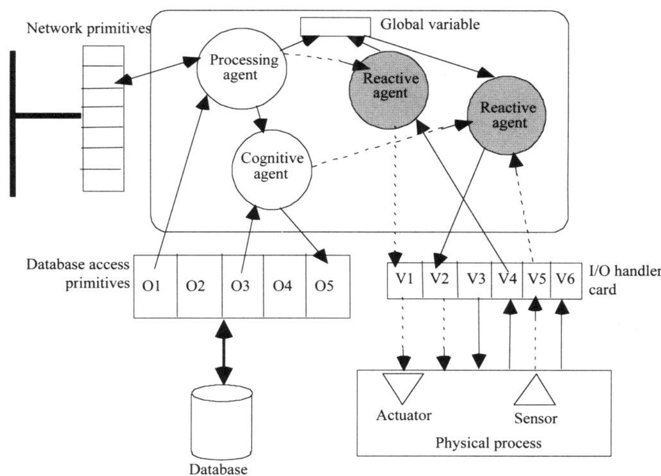

Figure 5.42 Global environment of a real-time multi-agent application.

5.13.1 Analogue/Digital I/O Card Handler

The use of physical process sensors and actuators (variables) is carried out principally using an *input/output card*. There are several types of card offering all-or-nothing I/O, analogue I/O or both. The appendix contains a general introduction to operating systems; it summarizes their basic principles, particularly the problems of coupling between the *hardware layer* and the *software layer*s of a data processing system. These notions are essential for the design and successful implementation of a real-time application. The reader must read the first part of the appendix to gain an idea of the interfacing of an input/output card and the main principles of its handler design.

The main principles of the card handler and its use by the different application agents – for a real-time application which uses an input/output card (Fig. 5.43) to manipulate physical variables of the operative part, which has been implemented using a real-time executive (for example VxWorks) – are given below. We use a fictional I/O card whose programming principles and functions remain similar to cards currently used in industry.

This is a card which takes on the elements of existing real cards. These depend directly on the type of bus used. Incidentally, the E32-DE-IDM-32 card for microprocessor systems is a standard VME P1014-87 A24, D16 interface card, and generates the double Europe format interrupt.

We propose an approach to the design and structure of the handler which is valid for different types of systems and environments.

The card in Figure 5.43 is composed of an emission register enabling it to command up to 32 all-or-nothing actuators. The input register permits access to up to

32 all-or-nothing sensors. The inputs and outputs are isolated (opto-coupled) which generally enables protection and interfacing between the physical lines connected to the process (5-50 volts) and the data processing system host which uses the TTL level. Simplified, the activation of an actuator serves to position the corresponding bit in the emission register. Reading a sensor involves reading the corresponding bit in the register on reception. The handling of the card can be carried out using two methods: *the direct method* and *the asynchronous method.* If the card is capable of generating an interrupt at each modification of input register bit, the second mode can be increased to obtain the interruptible mode.

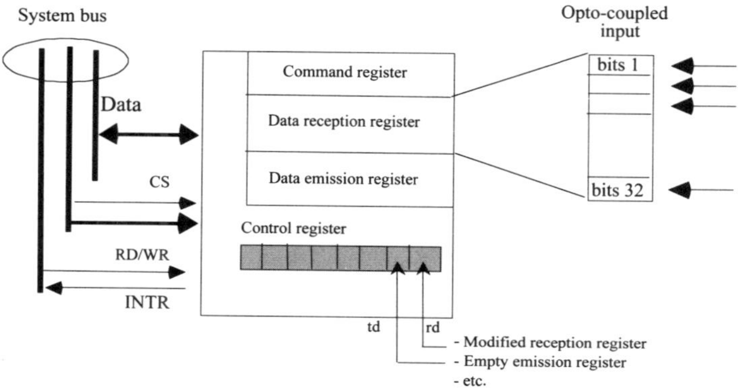

Fig. 5.43 Example of a fictional all- or-nothing I/O card.

The main aspects of an input/output card handler are given below (see the appendix for more details on handlers). We assume that the host system processor is part of the M680x0 family, which enables us to directly address the card registers. In contrast, if the processor is the Intel386 type or above, it is necessary to use the instructions `in()` or `out()` of the corresponding C language to access the input/output space of the machine (registers or ports of different input/output cards).

5.13.2 Direct Mode Handler

The direct mode handler is essentially composed of the following entry-points (functions):

- The *function* which enables the initialization of the card during the launching phase of the host data processing system. It also enables the configuration of different input/output register bits, the initialization of card timers etc.
- All-or-nothing input *reading functions.* This is a function by the all-or-nothing entry.
- The *command functions* of all-or-nothing outputs. This is a function by output bit.

All of these functions must be regrouped in the `include` file to be used by any application which sends input/output via this card.

```
        /*handler file.h of the input/output all-or-nothing card*/
#define ADR_E_S 0x80                    /*basic address of the all-or-nothing I/O card*/
#define ADR_REG_INPUT          ADR_E_S + 1
#define ADR_REG_OUTPUT         ADR_E_S + 2
#define ADR_REG_CONTROL        ADR_E_S + 3
#define ADR_REG_COMMAND        ADR_E_S + 4

                                        /*access masks to the I/O register bits*/
#define bit0           0x00000001
#define bit1           0x00000002
...;
#define bit31          0x80000000

             /*mask to extract the value of bit '0' from the content 'x' of an I/O register*/
#define BIT(~(~0<<1))          /*only bit 0 is equal to 1, a constant independent of the host
                                                                                system*/
#define TRUE 1
#define FALSE 0
void Init_handler (char *command)
 {
             /*this handler entry-point enables the initialization of the card following the
                                                                        utilization mode*/
     *ADR_REG_COMMAND = *COMMAND;
    ...;
    };
short Sensor1 ()                                    /*access to the value of sensor 1*/
    {       char *REG_INPUT = (char *) ADR_REG_INPUT;
    return  (((*REG_INPUT>> 0) & BIT ==TRUE);
    };

short value_sensor2 ()                              /*access to the value of sensor 2*/
    {       char *REG_INPUT = (char *) ADR_REG_INPUT;
    return  (((*REG_INPUT>> 1) & BIT ==TRUE);
    };
...;
short Sensor32 ()                                   /*access to the value of sensor 32*/
    {       char *REG_INPUT = (char *) ADR_REG_INPUT;
    return  (((*REG_INPUT>> 31) & BIT ==TRUE);
    };
...;
void Actuator1(short value1)    /*enables the corresponding bit to be placed at 1 or 0*/
    {if (value) ((ADR_REG_OUTPUT) || = bit1)
    else     ((*ADR_REG_OUTPUT)     && = ~ (bit1))
    };
...;
void Actuator32(short value)    /*enables the corresponding bit to be placed at 1 or 0*/
    {if (value) ((ADR_REG_OUTPUT) ||= bit32)
    else     ((*ADR_REG_OUTPUT)  && = ~ (bit32))
    };
```

The following example shows how this handler can be used in a multi-agent application (Fig. 5.15). A first agent "cmdgate" is used to watch the level of liquid in a reservoir. If the level exceeds the authorized threshold (Sensor1 is True), then the gate is closed (Actuator1) for a certain period of time, and the alarm is simultaneously triggered by signal 30. During this time, the emergency management agent "alarm" (`semGive`) is activated to manage the situation.

```
#define     CPU     MC68020
#include "vxWorks.h"
#include "sigLib.h"
#include "semlib.h"
#include "vxWorks.h"
#include "handler.h"
SEM_ID sid;
Int tid1, tid2;
Void cmdgate();
Void alarm();
Void sighandler();
launchTask()
{    Init_handler();                     /*Initialization of the card following sequences
                                                     recommended by the designer*/
                                                  /*creation of the cmdvanne agent*/
     tidl= taskSpawn("Cmdliquid",100,0,2000,cmdgate);
                                                      /*creation of the alarm agent*/
     tid2= taskSpawn("Alarm",100,0,2000,alarm);
}
void cmdgate()
{
     for (;;)
             if (Sensor1 ()) {
               Actuator1(False);                                 /*close the gate*/
               Kill (tid2,30);                                /*trigger the alarm*/
               SemGive(sid);            /*activate the emergency management agent*/
                                                /*close the gate for a specific time*/
             taskdelay(sysClkRateGet()*100);
              Actuator1(TRUE);                                 /*re-open the gate*/
     }
}
void sighandler (sig, code, sigContext);
     int sig;
     int code;
     SIGCONTEXT *sigContext;
     {
       Actuator2(TRUE);                                       /*trigger the alarm*/
     }
void alarm()
{
     SIGVEC vec;
     vec.sv_handler = sighandler;        /*the handler calls when the signal arrives*/
     vec.sv_mask = 0;
     vec.sv_flags = 0;
sigvec (30, &vec, 0);                           /*link the handler signal to signal 30*/
sigsetmask (0);                                              /*authorize all signals*/
sid= semBCreate(SEM_Q_PRIORITY, SEM_EMPTY);
for (;;)
            {semTake(sid,WAIT_FOREVER);                        /*wait until awakened*/
taskdelay(sysClrateGet()*100);                                     /*temporization*/
Actuator2(FALSE);                                                  /*stop the alarm*/
                                                             / emergency processing*/
                         /*carry out the actions necessary according to the situation*/
     }
}
```

5.13.3 Asynchronous Mode Handler

In the preceding mode, every agent which commands or uses a sensor must regularly poll it to detect status changes. The interrupt mode enables these agents to unload this task. When a value change of a sensor occurs, the agents are warned by a dispatcher which is the sporadic server. This is the handler's internal service routine and not an entry-point. It is an asynchronous solution which introduces weak coupling between the agents and the physical process. The main points of such a handler are given below. In this solution, a signal is associated to every all-or-nothing entry. An agent which wants to be informed of the changes at the level of an entry associated to a sensor must associate a 'handler' or an interception routine to this signal. In this solution, one agent alone can use a signal associated to an all or nothing entry. The reader can easily increase the sporadic server to enable several agents to intercept the same signal (associated to a port, a vector or tid list). It is clear that if the card enables a hardware interrupt to be generated when a change arises in the entry register, the dispatcher can be transformed into a card interrupt routine.

```
                /*file handler2.h*/
#define ADR_E_S 0x80                     /*basic address of the I/O all-or-nothing card*/
#define ADR_REG_INPUT (ADR_E_S + 1)
#define ADR_REG_OUTPUT (ADR_E_S + 2)
#define ADR_REG_CONTROL (ADR_E_S + 3)
#define ADR_REG_COMMAND (ADR_E_S + 4)

#define bit0         0x00000001
#define bit1         0x00000002
...;
#define bit31        0x80000000

                                        /*access masks to the I/O register bits*/
#define bit0         0x00000001
#define sig0         0
#define bit1         0x00000002
#define sig1         1          /*signal associated with the all or nothing I/O entry*/
...;
#define bit31        0x80000000
#define sig31        31
#define TRUE 1
#define FALSE 0
#define POLL_PERIOD 25                   /*poll period for input/output card ports*/
int tid0, tid1,..., tid31;               /*tid of agents associated with each entry*/
void Init_handler (int command)
{        /*this handler entry point enables a card to be initialized depending on the mode of use*/

(*ADR_REG_COMMAND) = command;
            ...;
    };
/*The sporadic server*/
short dispatcher ()                             /*access to the value of sensor 1*/
                                                /*pointer on the data register*/
    {      char *REG_INPUT = (char*) ADR_REG_INPUT;
    for (;;)
```

```
        {
        if (*REG_INPUT * bit0) kill(tid0, sig0);
        if (*REG_INPUT) * bit1) kill(tid1, sig31);
        ...;
        if (REG_INPUT & bit31) kill(tid31, sig31);

    /*The poll period*/
                taskdelay(sysClkRateGet()*POLL_PERIOD);
        };
    void Actuator1(short value)       /*enable the corresponding bit to be placed at 1 or 2*/
        {
                char *REG_OUTPUT = (char *) ADR_REG_OUTPUT;
                if (value) ((*REG_OUTPUT) || = bit1)
                else ((*REG_OUTPUT) && = ~ (bit1));
        };
    ...;
    void Actuator32(short value)      /*enable the corresponding bit to be placed at 1 or 2*/
        {
                char *REG_OUTPUT = (char *) ADR_REG_OUTPUT;
                if (value) ((*REG_OUTPUT) || = bit32)
                else ((*REG_OUTPUT) && = ~ (bit32));
        };
```

Now we are ready to rewrite the preceding example with this new asynchronous version of the handler:

```
/*Asynchronous version of the application*/

#define     CPU     MC68020
#include "vxWorks.h"
#include "sigLib.h"
#include "semlib'h"
#include "handler2.h"
SEM_ID sid;
Void cmdgate();
Void alarm();
Void sighandler();
SEM_ID sig0;
TriggerTask()
{ Init_handler();                 /*Initialization of the card following the sequences
                                              recommended by the designer*/
/*Creation of the cmdgate agent*/
    tid1= taskSpawn("Cmdliquid", 100,0,2000,cmdgate);

/*Creation of the alarm agent*/
tid2= taskSpawn("Alarm",100,0,2000,alarm);
short sensor1_on = FALSE;
void handler_sensor1 (sig, code, sigContext);
    int sig;
    int code;
    SIGCONTEXT *sigContext;
    {
sensor1_on = TRUE;                               /*position the sensor indicator*/
    Actuator1(FALSE);                                            /*close the gate*/
SemGive(sid0);                                         /*awaken the cmdgate agent*/
SemGive(sid);                               /*awaken the emergency management agent*/
```

```
            Actuator2(TRUE);                          /*trigger the alarm*/
}
void cmdgate()
{    SIGVEC vec;
                    /*the handler is called when sensor 1 generates a high level*/
  vec.sv_handler = handler_sensor;
  vec.sv_mask = 0;
  vec.sv_flags = 0;
  sigvec (0, &vec, 0);                   /*link the handler signal to signal 0*/
  sigsetmask (0);                                    /*authorize all signals*/
sid0= semBCreate(SEM_Q_PRIORITY, SEM_EMPTY);      /*private synchronization
                                                                semaphore*/
  for (;;)
  {         semTake(sid0, WAIT_FOREVER);                  /*wait until awoken*/
  taskdelay(sysClkRateGet()*100);          /*close the gate for a specific period*/
            Actuator1(TRUE);                                  /*reopen the gate*/
     }

void alarm()
{
 sid= semBCreate(SEM_Q_PRIORITY, SEM_EMPTY);      /*private synchronization
                                                                semaphore*/
     for (;;)
  { semTake(sid,WAIT_FOREVER);                            /*wait until awoken*/
  taskdelay(sysClkRateGet()*100);                           /*temporization*/
     Actuator2(FALSE);                                       /*stop the alarm*/
                                                         /*urgent processing*/
                 /*carry out the necessary actions depending on the situation*/
     }
}
```

5.14 Tools for the Development and Co-verification of Embedded Systems

A complex embedded system such as that found in satellites and planes etc. is composed of several specific cards. Each card ensures a specific function (telecommunication, signal processing, equipment surveillance, system handling etc). Each card is composed of a hardware part (a Risc microprocessor, an Asic circuit, a DSP signal processor, a standard microprocessor) and a software part (user-oriented package).

If the tools which come under the scope of real-time computer software engineering enable software development projects for this type of system to be seen through to the end, the integration phase of hardware and software remains fairly laborious and costly, and in certain cases, represents up to 50 per cent of the development cycle of the embedded system.

In this section, we aim to make the reader aware of the hardware/software integration problem, and to provide several references to tools currently available which facilitate the development of this type of system, especially those which facilitate the software/hardware integration phase.

The software/hardware integration phase, which is by far the most critical in the development cycle of complex embedded systems, is now facilitated by the return to hardware/software co-verification tools (Fig. 5.44). In this architecture, software and hardware debuggers communicate to enable, from stop points in the code (error), to go back up to the hardware simulator and visualize the forms of corresponding waves and the internal status of each part of the processor (registers, bus, etc.). It is clear that this type of environment is only of interest if the hardware simulator is capable of executing a large number of instructions per second. However, before 1996, these types of techniques and tools only enabled the execution of one instruction per second, which left this type of approach unusable. Since June 1996 (Gross, 1996), two firms specialized in electronic computer-aided design – *Eagle Design Automation* and *Mentor Graphics* – proposed two similar environments which enable the rapid co-verification of complex embedded systems. The execution speeds of the hardware simulators proposed are 5000 instructions per second for Eagle Automation, and 3000 instructions per second for Mentor.

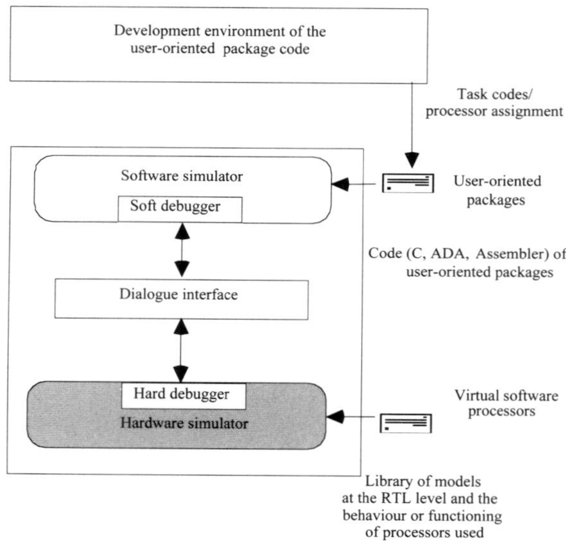

Fig. 5.44 Basic architecture of a software/hardware co-verification environment.

Mentor Graphics has called its environment "Seamless CVE" (for co-verification environment) which enables the user-friendly package to be validated with RTL (register transfer level) and behavioural hardware models. It mostly uses the Microtec software XRAY simulator, hardware simulators QuikSim and Quick-VHDL and the Asic SimExpress emulator from Mentor. It also accepts external simulators such as Verilog XL from Cadence.

The Eagle Design Automation Environment is called *Eaglei.* It is composed of a set of tools enabling the C code of the real-time embedded system to be simulated with microprocessor models called VSP (virtual software processors) and Asic models written in VHD language and in Verilog.

We will not expand any further on the presentation of these two precursor environments. Our aim is to make the reader aware of the hardware/software co-verification problem of real-time systems in general, and complex embedded systems in particular. The reader will note that these two types of tools and environments carry an interesting solution to this problem, and open the way towards more elaborate environments that are able to guarantee almost perfect reliability of complex embedded systems, which remain far from being the first characteristic of this type of system.

5.15 CORBA Telecommunications

In Chapter 2 we introduced the CORBA norm. We also specified that the entity which manages object activation and updating was the BOA (basic object adapter). Consequently, several versions of CORBA using a real-time executive (Lynx OS, VxWorks, etc.) such as BOA have had their time on the market. In this example we speak of CORBA Real-Time.

In this section, we present the propositions of the Object Management Group (OMG), concerning the specifications of the interfaces necessary to implement telecommunication systems, especially all that falls under the control and management of audio/video channels (Ishikawa *et al.*, 1990; Menga *et al.*, 1989). These propositions have the advantage of specifying and categorizing:

- The definition of components which enter into the composition of an audio/video channel, especially:
  - the definition of the interface of objects for the control and management of channels;
  - the definition of the interface of objects for the control of channels associated with the extremity of an individual channel.
- Particularly CORBA interface references for channel control objects. These references are used to designate all channel extremities within the parameters of the channel control operations (methods) defined in these specifications.
- The specifications propose a set of interfaces which give the necessary scope for the implementation of distributed multimedia channels. The principal components of this framework are:
  - virtual multimedia equipment and multimedia equipment, represented respectively by `Vdev` and `MMDevice` interfaces;
  - channels represented by the `StreamCtrl` interface;
  - channel extremities represented by `StreamEndPoint` interfaces;
  - flows and extremities of flows represented by `FlowConnection` and `FlowEndPoint` interfaces;
  - flow equipment represented by the `Fdev` interface.

5.15.1 General Presentation

A channel is a data flow between objects, where a flow is a unidirectional sequence of frames. A channel interface is an aggregation of one or more sources and wells of data flows associated with an object. Data carried by the flows can of course be in any format. This specification emphasizes the applications which process audio and video data exchanged with certain quality of service (QoS) constraints.

The control and management specification of an audio/video channel concerns the following points: the different topologies, multiple flows, description and type, identification and designation of channel interfaces; channel installation and removal; channel modification; channel termination; multiple protocols; the quality of service (Q0S), flow synchronization; interoperability and security.

> **Notion 23 Channel**
>
> *This is a set of modules and software libraries which enable every object (application) to locate and interact with any other object on any other network, without having to know its geographical location or the type of communication network.*

Figure 5.45 shows a channel with a simple flow between two end points of a channel, one acting as a data source, and the other as the data sink. Each channel end is encapsulated and composed of three logical entities:

- *a channel interface control object*, which provides IDL interfaces (for example server 2b) for the control and management of the channel (such as the invocation of operations such as client 2a, on other object servers);
- *a data source or sink object* (at least one per channel extremity), which is the final destination of data flows;
- *a channel adapter*, which transmits and receives data frames on the network.

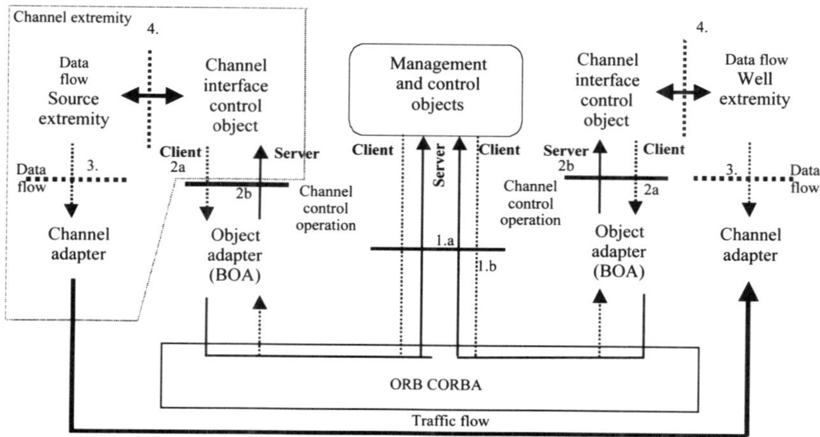

Fig. 5.45 Example of channel architecture.

When a channel is partly cabled (hardware), the source/sink object and the adapter are no longer visible as distinct entities. It is important to note how the channel interface control object communicates with the source/sink object, and perhaps directly with the adapter (interface 4, Fig. 5.45), and also how the source/sink object communicates with the adapter (interface 3). These communications are not covered by the OMG specifications.

Figure 5.46 shows a channel between a microphone (audio source or producer) and a loud speaker (audio sink or consumer).

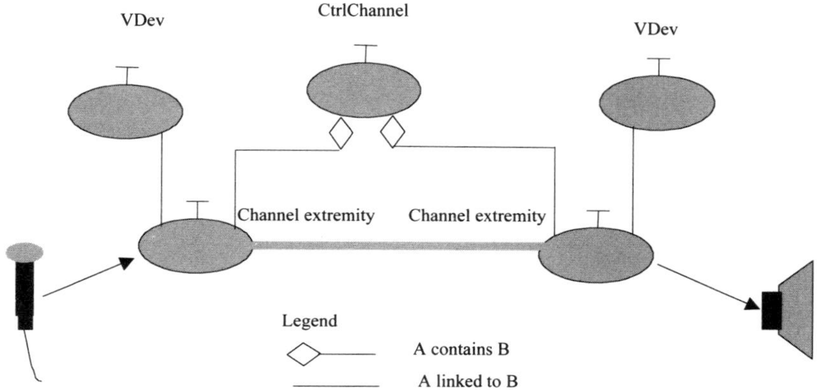

Fig. 5.46 Basic configuration of a channel.

A channel can contain several flows. Each flow transmits data in one direction only in such a way that a flow end is either a source (producer) or a sink (consumer). An operation (method) on a channel can simultaneously involve channel flow integrity for both or just one of them.

A channel end can contain several flow ends which can be source extremities (producer) or sinks (consumers). There must be a CORBA object representing each flow end and a connection flow (the flow itself). A channel can carry several flows in different directions. Furthermore, it is not essential that all flow extremities be used in the channel. When two different flow extremities are linked, we can use a compatibility rule to determine which of the two extremities connects to the other.

5.15.2 Channel Control Interface

The channel control interface `StreamCtrl` is an abstraction of a continuous multimedia data transfer between virtual equipment. It proposes operations to connect multimedia equipment across the channel. If an application requests more complex functions (for example, "`rewind`") it can extend the basic channel interface to support such an operation.

When an application requests a channel between two or more pieces of multimedia equipment, it can specify the quality of service of the channel. A QoS can signify several things and different levels. Incidentally, multimedia equipment which supports video can be affected by the parameter (QoS), the Frame-Rate, and the colour spectrum. This type of QoS will be designated as an application level QoS. A channel will be supported by inferior layer network protocols. The QoS for the network protocol must include parameters such as minimal bandwidth and frequency. This type of QoS will be designated as network level QoS. An application programmer can establish a channel between two pieces of equipment by using the `bind_devs()` operation of the `StreamCtrl` interface:

```
Boolean bind_devs(in MMDevice a_party, in MMDevice b_party, inout
streamQoS the_qos, flowSpec the_spec);
```

An application can connect one equipment source to several equipment sinks. For example, broadcast a video signal:

```
MyStream->bind_devs(cameraDev, nilobject, someQoS, nilFlowSpec);
```

The use of a reference to an empty object in place of parameter `b_party` has the effect of a camera as a source of broadcast: `a_party`. The programmer can also add any number of televisions to the broadcast by using:

```
MyStream->bind_devs(nilobject, TVDev, someQoS, nilFlowSpec);
```

5.15.3 Example of an End-to-End Channel

Figure 5.47 shows the diagram of objects necessary to install an end-to-end videophone channel.

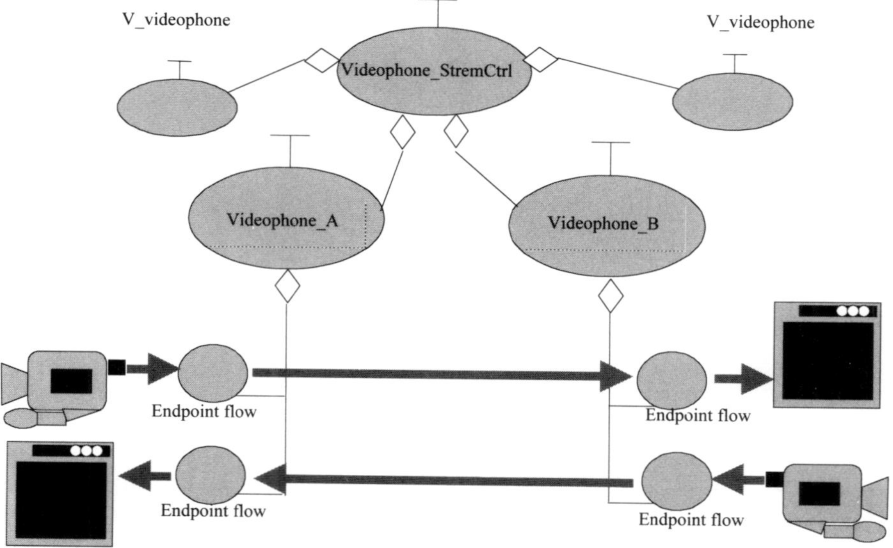

Fig. 5.47 Architecture of an end-to-end videophone channel.

The following fragment of code illustrates the installation of the channel in Figure 5.47:

```
/*C++*/
/*Declaration of local and remote multimedia channel devices*/
videophone_ptr myPhone = ... ;
videophone_ptr JohnPhone = ... ;

/*Declaration channel handler*/
videophone_StreamCtrl_ptr myStream ;
            /*The code in this place for the initialization of the local MMDevice (myPhone*/
...
                                                      /*connect to JohnPhone*/
...
myStream = myPhone->bind(johnPhone, someQoS,
            &wasQoSMet,                               /*QoS has been honoured*/
nilFlowSpec) ;                                        /*link all flows*/
myStream->start(nilFlowSpec) ;
cost << "tap a button to close the channel"<< endl ;
cin>>buf ;
myStream->stop(nilFlowSpec) ;
myStream->destroy(nilFlowSpec) ;
}
```

The reader wishing to increase their knowledge in this field, will find in Ishikawa *et al.* (1990) and Menga *et al.* (1989) all of the object interface specifications for channel control, flow control, QoS parameter control etc, necessary to be able to develop distributed multimedia applications.

6. *Prolog III and Real-Time System Engineering*

The aim of formal specifications is to support software development, and gradually reduce their cost and production time. They also enable program maintenance by providing precise and automatically analysable interfaces.

Formal specification methods are often very technical, and demand a considerable training effort (that must not be confused with the study of the mathematical aspect on which the technique is based), which discourage industrial designers. Several studies are being carried out today on the design of industrial tools for description, validation and implementation, to integrate into work environments adapted to different fields. The existence of adequate software tools should soon see the knowledge of formal methods not as current fashionable methods, but as an essential transformation process.

Much formalism is used today to implement the competition and parallelism between real-time systems. Imagine their relevance relieved sometimes by conviction, while advanced criteria stem from the history of their elaboration. None of them can truly aspire to the presentation of all the facets of the problems studied, as each one favours some to the detriment of others.

The aim of this chapter is first to make the reader aware of the necessity of using a tool or method which ensures coherence of specifications of the dynamics of real-time systems studied, before continuing to the implementation phase. We then propose a global approach to specification and validation which enables certain difficulties inherent in these formal specification methods to be overcome (see the following paragraph). This is a global approach for the engineering of complex real-time systems according to the "multi-agent" paradigm. The principal characteristics of this approach are:

- *The integration of logical and digital specification* (axiomatic/algebraic), seems more appropriate to allow the static description of systems as well as their passage from one state to another (therefore the dynamic description), and constitutes a formal kernel suitable for the approach.
- The approach *respects object-oriented concepts* and *the multi-agent paradigm* for the structuring of the control part of a real-time system, conforming to a global analysis approach. This takes into account the nature of interactions with the components of its environment (the physical process), which are

either sources (generator) or sinks (receivers) of data or exchange control flows.

- Formal specifications are established using a *graphics editor* which masks the details of the formalism and therefore renders them more accessible to non-specialists.
- The verification and validation of the coherence of specifications and properties of the system studied is made possible by simply simulating the dynamics of the system studied using the inference engine of a limited Prolog III programming language;
- The *automatic generation of a specification code* for behaviour simulation is a simple operation which involves decompiling the graphic description towards a pivot language close to functional specification languages. This description in the pivot language acts as a basis for generating the simulation model for the dynamics of a system using Prolog III (phase verification and validation of specifications). It can also be used by transcoders (exportation filters) for the automatic generation of code towards any programming language signal (C, C++, ADA or VHDL) according to the reception platform.
- The study of interactions which exist between the different elements of the system is largely facilitated by the use of the graphics editor.

Figure 6.1 gives the basic principle for this approach. The aim is to avoid processing any implantation (coding) before the global change and behaviour of the systems studied are verified and validated: namely, to conform to the specifications.

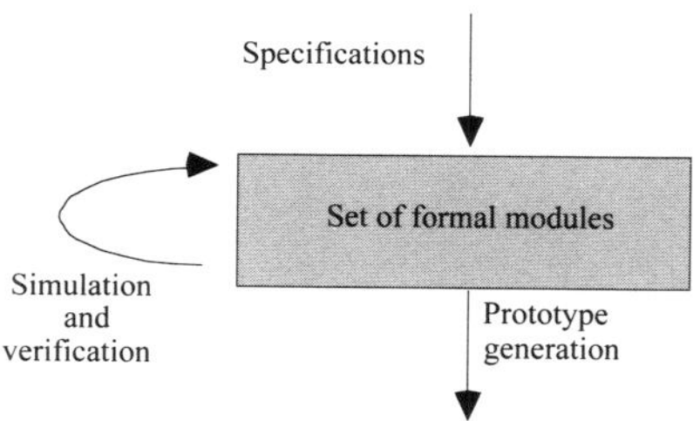

Fig. 6.1 Principle of the approach.

6.1 Impact of Formal Specificatons on Software Development

Towards the end of the 1960s, businesses and research laboratories organized a conference on what has been called the "software crisis".[1] The term "software

[1] Slump of hardware costs and the rapid increase of software costs.

engineering" was therefore introduced, with the aim of reducing the costs of developing extensive software systems, and improving their quality.

The first studies involved detailed analysis of system costs. Final statistics clearly showed that their maintenance (error correction, modification) was at the root of the exorbitant costs of their development (Fig. 6.2):

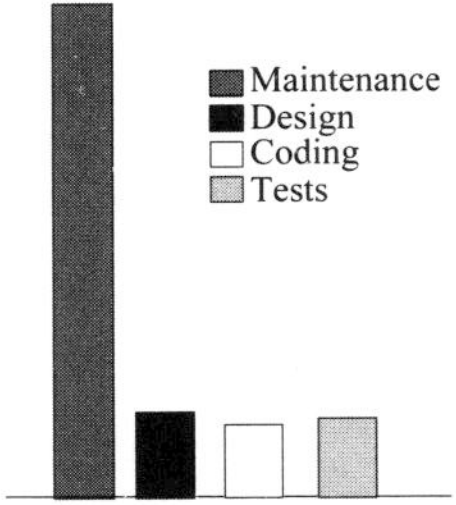

Fig. 6.2 Analysis of the final cost of a large data processing system.

To improve the study and maintenance methods, numerous techniques and approaches were suggested:

- structured programming;
- modular programming;
- systematic programming;
- descending analysis;
- composite analysis etc.

Although these ideas are productive and fundamental, experiments show that they only resolve part of the problem, and that they are inappropriate for larger applications. The main difficulties arise during the analysis and specification phase where we aim to understand and break down the problem before starting to resolve it.

Specifications in natural language thought to be accessible to everyone, turn out to be unsuitable where the contractual base is concerned, because of the ambiguity inherent in natural language.

> Thus follows the importance of a clear and precise specification to enable design errors to be avoided, which are by far the most costly to correct, especially if they are discovered after system installation. This note is all the more relevant when it involves an embedded real-time system.

Although these standard (or semi-formal) methods have brought about substantial improvements (clarity and ease of reading), it is difficult, even impossible to verify the consistency and completeness of requirements expressed using automatic tools. A large investment in terms of man-hours and work is necessary to design the first prototypes alone. In certain critical fields such as real-time embedded (automatic handling and control system of a rocket or plane), the slightest error is fatal. It can result in extensive human and hardware damage. Pragmatic solutions such as tests are unreliable, and are generally difficult to use if they are not carried out with mathematical precision. This is what we advocate in this chapter: precision + simulation.

> It is inconceivable that civil engineering specialists would construct a bridge using approximate functional specification, and then test it by driving cars across it. Yet, it is at this level that most of the specification techniques are currently found in the field of real-time systems.

6.1.1 General Points on Formal Methods

The term "formal methods" groups together *formal specification* and *validated design.*

> **Notion 1 Formal Specification**
>
> *This is based on logic as the foundation theory for modelling dynamics, structures, and installation objects and ideas.*

Formal specifications use *mathematical notations* for problem description, to achieve both precision and concision. By their precision, formal specifications resemble programs more than mathematical wording. However, they are easy to read and understand, but cannot usually be executed on their own on a computer. Their advantages are self-evident, and can be summarized in the following points.

- *They provide a formal document which explains the users problem.* The syntax and semantics of the specification language must be formally defined, in such a way that the signification of a specification can be determined according to the definition of the specification language.
- *They enable formal verifications (evidence),* which help to detect and/or avoid contraindications and ambiguities in the specifications, which enhances the security of the critical functioning of the software.
- *They mathematically study two specifications* so that for example, their equivalence can or cannot be established.
- *They facilitate program writing at a later date.* The specifications can be computer manipulated, and tools can be constructed to aid the designer in the development, comprehension and finalization of both specifications and programs;
- *They facilitate later program maintenance,* with the help of precise, rigorous documentation reference.

A further important aspect of formal methods is *validated design.*

Notion 2 Validated Design

This is the possibility of establishing arguments which, in contrast to tests, will establish program priorities. With the help of formal specifications of the problem, this offers the possibility of arguing about the formal relationships that they have with their programs.

In as much as program writing can automatically, or at least systematically, be done from specifications, its certification could be carried out in two stages:

- *Prove that the specification satisfies the properties* of consistency, completeness etc., which express that certification is consistent, which is enough to efficiently reveal the user's problem.
- *Prove that the transformation of the specification is correct,* that is to say the program obtained satisfies the specification.

6.1.2 Formal Specification Techniques

There are four main approaches to formal specification: axiomatic or logical specifications, algebraic specifications, specifications based on a model and functional specifications.

Notion 3 Axiomatic Specifications

A system is represented by a set of functions whose internal status is hidden. Each function is specified using pre- and post-conditions. A precondition specifies the values on entry into a function, while a post-condition specifies the values when exiting a condition.

This is the simplest form of formal specification. The pre- and post-conditions are in practice *predicates* which can be quantified and whose variables are parameters of the specified function. Predicates are boolean expressions which are true or false. The quantifiers are universal and existential quantifiers of the unit theory. An operator "in" is used to select the unit to which the quantifier applies.

Example of Specification

Either the function log_bin(x: integer) which gives the logarithm of a natural x integer.

The informal description of this function is as follows:

Given a natural integer number. We want to find y so that $2^y = x$.

The corresponding formal or axiomatic description is:

```
Function log_bin(x : integer) return integer;
Pre: x ≥ 1;
```

```
Post: 2^(log_bin(x)) ≤ x and x < 2^(log_bin(x + 1))
Error: log_bin(x) = -1
```

The informal preliminary description describes the binary logarithm by the solution of an equation. On the one hand, it does not take into account the fact that the equation does not have solutions for all of the natural integers; on the other hand the problem of natural integer numbers which are not greater than 2 is ignored.

The formal description is more precise. It fixes the functionality, the field and the range of the logarithm. The characteristic property which states, by using first order logic formalism, that for all integers of one or more, the binary logarithm is the solution of the equation, or, in cases where x is not greater than two, it is the largest number which is an approximation of this equation. This specification treats the case where a precondition is not satisfied; it indicates the error by returning a negative value (–1). The log_bin function user must therefore test the value returned to see if the operation succeeded.

It is important to note that the exclusive use of pre- and post-conditions is only possible with small systems or system components. Large systems often have a notion of status, and in this case this technique is inappropriate. Nevertheless, this approach suits the specification of object dynamics by using logic, but does not suit the description of the structures of these objects. Consequently, to profit from axiomatic specification techniques, this last is integrated to other approaches, especially algebraic specification.

6.1.2.1 The Assertion Method (Based on a Model)

This method was developed by Floyd, Dijksra and Hoare at the end of the 1960s for program verification. Specification by this method relies on the definition of a system model using studied mathematical entities (such as functions, set, etc.), from which the appellation of methods was based on a model.

Notion 4 Specifications Based on a Model

These use notions of status to determine the pre- and post-conditions of a system. The theory of sets is used to enable both the description of system structures, and the dynamics surrounding these structures.

This technique therefore involves bringing all of the structures back to data sets of the same type, and the dynamics to the actions on these sets. This is an appropriate way of enabling the transition from one state to another.

The specification languages which use the approach are numerous. The principal languages already in use in industry are Z and VDM. J.R Abrail and B. Suffrin (Lightfoot, 1991, 1994) developed Z at Oxford University. It is based on the theory of sets, the semantics of which are formally defined. It enables a complete representation of the specifications to be given, and also permits the reuse of these specifications. Below is a brief presentation of VDM.

The VDM Method

VDM (Vienna Development Method) is the name given to a collection of notions and concepts. D. Bjomer and C. Jones developed it at the end of the 1970s in the old IBM research laboratory at Vienna, then improved it during the 1980s (Jones, 1993). VDM is a formal method for the design and specification of data processing systems. It represents one of the most widely used formal methods in the industrial world, as it has reached a level of maturity and acceptance. Like all of the other formal specification methods, it uses mathematical notations, with the aim of increasing concision and precision. The VDM method is carefully defined. It has, for example, enabled the establishment and validity of proof rules for the design stages of programs.

Program Proof in VDM

VDM relies on the basic ideas of proposition computation and the computation of predicates. It introduces a style of specification implicit for functions and programs. The use of implicit specifications enables the level of details of "how" to be abstracted. It therefore represents a means of replying to a function without having to *take into account a particular computation method.* The description of an implicit specification is based on the notion of pre- and post-conditions. A direct definition of the function takes the form of:

$F : T_p \rightarrow T_r$ — p is a parameter and T_p its type;
$f(p) = r$ — r is the result, T_r its type.

It is possible to describe specifications which cannot be satisfied, and it is evident that a specification must avoid such an error. This idea, and the corresponding style of proof, are taken into account, and form the basis of the VDM method.

Informally, to keep the notion of specification, it is necessary to claim that a function, when applied to arguments (a good type) which verify the precondition, provides a result (also a good type) which verifies the post-condition.

A direct definition of a function satisfies the specification if and only if:

$$(\forall p \in Tp,\ pre(p)) \Rightarrow ((f(p) \in Tr) \wedge post(p,\ f(p)))$$

On top of rules that can be cleared of the definition of the direct function, formal proof (also called the obligation of proof of satisfaction) necessitates the well-known rules of the logic of propositions and that of the logic of predicates. The functions to be specified are sometimes not whole but partial (do not always provide a result). In this case, the reason for proving satisfaction is based on the logic of partial functions.

Notion 5 The Notion of Proof in VDM

A definition of a direct function is said to satisfy an implicit specification if, for all of the arguments of the required type which satisfy the pre-condition, the evaluation of the direct definition gives the required result which satisfies the post-condition.

For example, consider the specification of the Sum_n function which calculates the sum of n first natural numbers.

- *The implicit specification* of such a function is as follows:

```
Sum_n(n: N) r : N
pre true
post r = n*(n+1)/2
```

- *The recursive definition* of the direct function is:

```
Sum_n : N) → N
Sum_n = if n = 0 then 0 otherwise n + Sum_n(n - 1)
```

The rules that can be deduced from the direct definition:

$$\frac{}{\text{Sum\_n}(0) = 0} \; ; \; \frac{n \in N; n \neq 0; \text{Sum\_n}(n-1) = k}{\text{Sum\_n}\ (n) = n + k}$$

The corresponding sequential form is:

$$n \in N\, \text{Sum\_n}(n) \in N \wedge \text{post}(n, \text{Sum\_n}(n))$$

Proof of the sequential form can be obtained easily from a demonstration by induction in the logic of propositions.

6.1.2.2 *Algebraic Specifications*

Algebraic specifications use the notion of algebra to simultaneously define data and their dynamics.

> **Notion 6 Algebra**
>
> *Algebra is defined by a set of objects and operations to apply to the elements of this set.*

By analogy, a type defines a set of objects. The dynamic behaviour of these objects can be described by operations which meet certain laws. We can also define algebra, and therefore talk of algebraic specifications of these objects. In algebraic specifications, the notion of abstraction manifests itself by the bias of abstract data types. Informally, an abstract data type (referred to from hereon as ADT) defines a class of data structure, which is characterized by the operations possible on these structures (creation and manipulation operations). In standard languages (C, Pascal, PL/1, and so on), the definition of ADTs is carried out in two stages: a first phase of operation specification characterizing the ADT to be defined, and a second phase of implementation (or of representation) of ADT operations. To avoid this second phase, which is a potential source of errors, new algebraic languages appeared: OBJ (Goguen and Meseguer, 1988); PLUSS, ASL (Wirsing, 1990), SPECTRUM (Broy *et al.*, 1992). GPL (Generic Programming Language) by Bert (1988) and the ASSPEGIQUE system (ASSistance à la sPEcification alGébrIQUE) developed by M. Bidoit and C. Choppy (Choppy *et al.*, 1994), are algebraic specification environments which exist in France.

Notion 7 Algebraic Specification

Algebraic specification is composed of four parts:

- *The first introduction defines the sort of entity that needs to be specified and gives the name of all of the specifications the user will require.*
- *A second part informally describes the operations defined on this type of entity.*
- *A signature part defines the sort and names of algebraic functions. This part describes the syntactic interface of the data structure.*
- *The properties, called "axioms" are described in the fourth part. Axioms describe the abstract semantics of the data structure.*

Operation generally takes on two forms:

- construction operations which *generate* or *modify* entities of the type defined in this specification;
- inspection or selection operations which *evaluate* the attributes as defined in this specification.

The improvement of a sort is the name given to the creation of a new sort through the *inheritance* of operations and axioms of an existing type, and by adding new operations and new axioms.

Example of Algebraic Specifications

This is the "`News`" Unix system (Wirsing, 1993). "`News`" are messages which are automatically sent to each user who has subscribed. Algebraic specification imports USER specifications of users, MESSAGE and BOOLEAN. It introduces a *board* sort and five functional symbols: *empty, send, move, read and seen_all.*

1. Informal Specification

Board is a means of communication where it is possible to send messages. Each user can read messages individually by starting with the first and advancing by one. Five operations are described in this specification.

`empty:`	denotes the empty board;
`send(b,m)`	adds message `m` to board `b`;
`move(b,u)`	advances user `u` from the current message `m` to the next message in the board `b`. After having carried out the operation "`move(b,u)`", the message `m` is no longer accessible by `u`;
`read(b,u)`	gives the user `u` current message on the board. If there is no current message, the result is not specified;
`Seen_all(b,u)`	gives the result as true, if user `u` saw all of the messages on board `b`.

2. *Formal Specification*

```
/*Sort Declaration*/
sort board
import USER, MESSAGE, BOOLEAN;

     empty      :                      → board;      /*designer*/
     send       : board, message       → board;      /*designer*/
     move       : board, user          → board;      /*designer*/
     read       : board, user          → message;    /*selector*/
     seen_all   : board, user          → boolean     /*selector*/

/*Axioms*/
∀ u, u' : user, b : board, m : message;

/*Read properties*/
     (1) seen_all(b,u) = true          ⇒ read(send(b,m),u) = m;
     (2) seen_all(b,u) =false          ⇒ read(send(b,m),u) =read(b,u);

/* send_all Properties*/
(3) send_all(empty,u) =true;
(4) seen_all(send(b,m),u) =false;  ⇒
     (5) eq(u,u') = false   seen_all(move(b,u'),u)= seen_all(b,u);
     (6) seen_all(b,u) = true ⇒seen_all(move(send(b,m),u),u)= true;

/* Move Properties*/
     (7) seen_all(b,u)=false ⇒move(send(b,m),u)= send(move(b,u),m);
     (8) move(move(b,u),u') = move(move(b,u'),u);
```

One of the consequences of analyzing axioms is that once a message has been read by all of the users, it can no longer be accessed. This can be formally expressed by the equation:

```
seen_all(move(...move(send(empty,m),u1),u2)...,one),u) = true.
```

In cases where there are only two users, u1 and u2, the following equation is written:

```
seen_all(move(move(send(empty,m),u1),u2),u) = true.
```

Prototyping specifications with a system such as ASSPEGIQUE enables expressions to be evaluated, such as the left term of the above equation, or to find the solution, if u1 and u2 are unknown.

To conclude, this type of specification has a major advantage: *abstraction*. This leads to relatively easy program design.

6.1.2.3 The Functional Approach

It is extremely difficult to consider programs written in conventional languages as objects, and to design elegant reasoning, in the same way as other mathematical objects. Therefore, the need for a new style of programming and of languages whose semantics will be based more on the notion of function as opposed to the evolution of the state of the machine, soon became apparent. In contrast with *imperative* programming based entirely on assignment operation, we speak of *functional* or *user-oriented* programming (user-oriented alluding to the application of functions to their arguments).

In addition to known advantages of the formal approach, several other advantages are also appreciated for functional methods:

- program recycling is made easier thanks to superior order functions (practical);
- the absence of assignments which do harm to "classic" Pascal family languages;
- the movement of program transformation algorithms towards other more efficient programs;
- the existence of effective functional language oriented computers (such as the Lisp computer).

6.1.3 Verification, Implementation and Recycling

Recall that confidence in data systems is a crucial problem. The probability of a random hardware error (physical) has fallen considerably over the last twenty years, but software design errors still persist.

Software validation tools enable errors to be detected and corrected. They can be placed into two categories. In the first category the following are found:

- *Test and finalization techniques* assess if the particular execution of a program (seen as a "black box") controls a property or not. These techniques which have improved over the years, still lack precision, and are often non-exhaustive. If they are exhaustive, they are very long and costly.
- *Verification techniques* which show the correspondence between the program (or its design) and its specification, using mathematical methods. During the development process by formal transformation, the final stage is the program executed by the user. This program only provides correct results if it is itself a correct solution to the original problem. The control of installation correction is therefore an advantage of formal description compared to semi-formal techniques.

There are a certain number of different proof techniques, but the general principle underlying these techniques is the same.

Example

In the following section we will use the News Unix example again. Note the specification given by (SP). The fundamental idea is to provide "board" type structured specification. To implement this idea, we need to specify the set of users "SET USER", of a "PAIR" specification of the message and set of users, and a LIST specification of lists with elements of the "elem" type, which will change name to process the "PAIR" sort. The specification of LIST must be equipped with the functional symbols "add" and "remove", which enable the respective addition and removal of an element from the list.

The global specification (SP) is obtained by combining the element specifications by using operators present in almost all specification languages. The juxtaposition of two specifications, SP1 and SP2, give (SP1 + SP2), the extension of a specification by new sorts (enrich SP), the exportation of a sort and functional symbols interface (export SP) and changing the name of this (rename SP by r).

```
SP = { expand
     rename LIST by [liste → board, vide → empty, elem → paire]
     + PAIR
     send; move; read; seen_all;
     axiomes  ∀m : message, b :board, u : user, E :all in user
          (1) send(b, m) = add(<m,∅>,b);
          (2) (u ∈ E) = false ⇒ read(add<m,E>,b),u)= If
seen_all(b,u)
                                   then m otherwise read(b,u);
          (3) seen_all(nil,u) = true;
          (4) seen_all(add<m,E>,b) = (u ∈ E);
          (5) (u ∈ E) = false ⇒ move(add (<m,E>,b),u) =
                         If seen_all(b,u) Then
                              If full (E) Then b
                              Otherwise add (<m,E ∪ {u}>,b)
                         Otherwise add (<m, E>, move(b,u))
     end_axioms}
```

Fig. 6.3 Specification of "board" with a new structure.

(SP1) can be considered as an *implementation* of SP.

Notion 8 Implementation of a Specification

(*) An sp specification is implemented by an sp1 (spsp1) specification if spsp1 contains all of the symbols of sp and if sp1 satisfies all of the properties of sp.
(**) If sp is implemented by sp1 and this latter is implemented by sp2 then sp is also implemented by sp2.
(***) If sp1 is implemented by sp2 and sp1 is a sub-specification of sp'1, then an sp'1 implementation is achieved by replacing all of the sp1 occurrences with sp2 in sp'1.

To prove the connection of (SP1), the axioms of (SP) are first checked in the (SP1) specification. Proving the axiom (1) of (SP) involves:

- Axiom (2) of (SP1)

```
(SP1) |—— (u ∈ S) = false ⇒ read(add(<m,E>,u)=
if seen_all(b,u) Then m
otherwise read(b,u);
```

- Case where seen_all(b,u) = true

```
(SP1) |—— (u ∈ S) = false ∧ seen_all(b,u) ⇒
read(add(<m,S>,b>,u) = m;
```

- S = ∅

```
(SP1) |—— (u ∈ ∅) = false ∧ seen_all(b,u) ⇒
read(add(<m, ∅>,b>,u) = m;
```

- Definition of send (1) of (SP1)

```
(SP1) |—— (u ∈ ∅) = false ∧ seen_all(b,u) ⇒
read(send(b,m), u) = m;
```

- *modus ponens*

```
(SP1) |—— seen_all(b,u) ⇒ read(send(b,m), u) = m;
```

The notion of (SP) implementation by (SP1) enables specifications to be described at different abstraction levels; (SP1) is more concrete than (SP). It possesses two important properties enabling both progressive software development and the achievement of appropriate implementation. The implementation notion is transitive, if it is local then it is globally correct (if sp1 is implemented by sp2 and sp1 is a sub-specification of sp'1 then the implementation of sp'1 is achieved by replacing all the occurrences of sp1 by sp2 in sp'1).

> To conclude, sometimes the program proving is at least as complex as the program itself; the effort normally given to the implementation of a proving is generally *greater* than the programming effort. Consequently, program control is actually only profitable for the *critical* areas of large systems.

Even if mathematical control techniques are probably the only efficient method of reaching a sufficient level of confidence, and noticeably reducing the cost of testing, these techniques do not seem to completely guarantee the accuracy of the developments, as the program acting as the controller could itself be incorrect. It is also always possible that the basic underlying axioms are themselves inconsistent. The control process must be completed using accurate tests. Simulators appear to be a suitable way of doing this.

Several approaches have been developed, using models such as status machines, Petri networks, abstract algebraic types and formal software. The associated validation mechanisms are *status examination* and *structural induction*. Other languages closer to programming language implementations have been developed and used with the aim of both expressing the behaviour of systems, and enabling the compilation of descriptions obtained, for example SDL, LOTOS and ESTELLE. The reader can find more information on these approaches in Arnold (1990), Belina and Hogrefe (1988), Courtiat *et al.* (1989), Diaz (1993), Fraser *et al.* (1994), ISO 8807 (1988), ISO 9074 (1989), Sijelmassi and Strausser (1991) and Vigder (1991b).

Now that a brief overview has been given of the fundamentals of the approaches forming the subject of extensive research by the IT community, it is also interesting to see a robotics specialists approach.

The following section gives a presentation of discrete event systems which form the natural environment of real-time systems which are themselves essentially discrete event systems. We then briefly cover the theory of automaton (Max, Plus) which represents an interesting tool for the study of discrete event systems with limited complexity. This involves a tool which is still the object of several research studies. Not only can it easily integrate into the approach presented in this chapter, but we also present the *practical framework* for implementation using the use of the programming language with Prolog III constraints (algorithm Fig. 6.22).

6.2 Reminder of Discrete Event Systems

Discrete event systems (DES) have been the subject of in-depth studies for several decades. It is understood that a DES can be represented by the quadruplet: $S = (T, E, X, \Sigma)$ where T is the time axis, E is the variable interval and X is the set of the trajectories $e(t)$. Σ is the set of events.

6.2.1 Discrete Systems

Notion 9 Discrete Systems

A system is classed as discrete when the variable interval E is discrete. Consequently, all possible evolution of the system can be represented by a sequence: $(\sigma 1,t1)$, $(\sigma 2,t2)$…where $\sigma i \in (E \times E)$.

σi represents the transition of the system at moment ti from one state to the next. $\Sigma = \{\varnothing\}$

In Figure 6.4 (after Jean-Jaques Loiseau):

$$S1 = \{\mathbb{R}+, \mathbb{N}, X1\} \text{ with } X1 = \{e(t)/e(t+1) = 2.e(t)\}$$

This is a simple example of a discrete system, but not discrete events, because $\Sigma = \{\varnothing\}$.

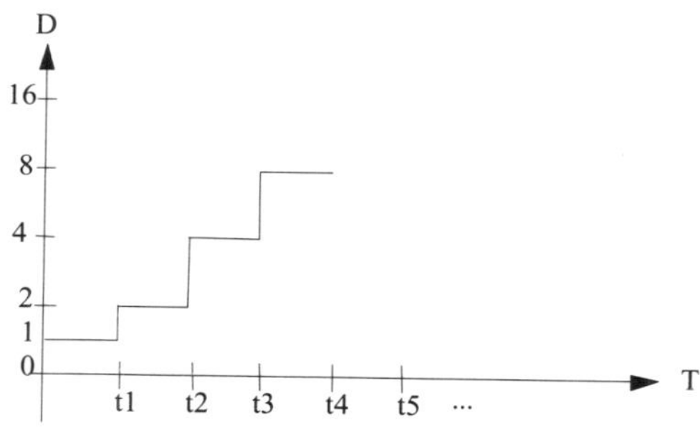

Fig. 6.4 Representation of the development over time of a discrete system.

6.2.2 Discrete Event Systems

Notion 10 Discrete Event Systems

A system is called a discrete event system when the implementation of a transition σ_i is subject to the occurrence of the event $\alpha_i \in \Sigma$.

Incidentally, $S = (\mathbb{R}+, \{e_1, e_2\}, X, \Sigma)$ with:

$X = e(t)$ with $e(t) = e_1$ if α is the last event to happen

otherwise

$e(t) = e_2$ if it is β.

$\Sigma = \{\alpha,\beta\}$.

It is clear that S is a DES as indicated in Figure 6.5:

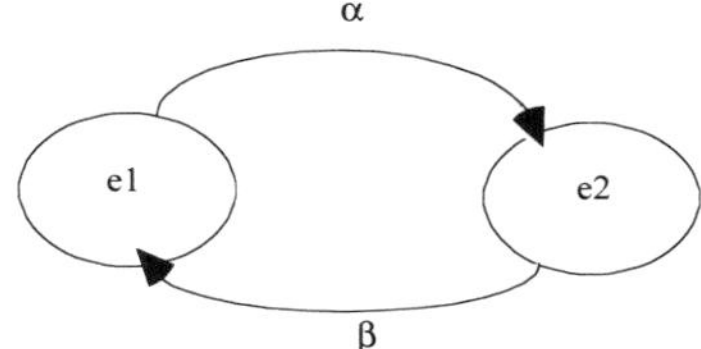

Fig. 6.5 Graphical representation of a discrete event system.

In this example, the system state changes do not really depend on time. The system is in fact either independent of time, and in this case $e(t) \in X \Longrightarrow e(f(t)) \in X$, $\forall$ f increasing, or the time constraints likely to restrict the occurrence of α and β events, are not perfectly understood. Consequently, the different possible paths or advances of the system can be represented by the sequence $\sigma 1 \sigma 2 \ldots$of occurrences and of events. This sequence represents the word $\sigma 1 \sigma 2 \ldots$of Σ^*, with $\sigma i \in \{\alpha,\beta\}$. In this case, a system $S = (T, E, X, \Sigma)$ can be *assimilated* to a language L included in Σ^*. Generally, a word $\omega \in L$ if the sequence of elementary events given by ω corresponds to a possible system behaviour. To study the properties of a system $S = (T, E, X, \Sigma)$, the properties of language L which is included in Σ^* can be studied. In practice it is easier to argue about and study L to directly manipulate S. The discrete event system is therefore an automaton recognizing L. At this stage, it is important to note that this approach, which involves representing a DES by an automaton takes particular interest in the study of *logical behaviour* of this category of systems where an input event (α or β for example) enables one path to be determined out of several possible paths (for example a real-time scheduling module in an automated production system). However, there exists a large class of DES which have a *deterministic* behaviour, such as the use of *predefined* static scheduling in an automated production system. In this second class of DES, certain events can be controlled (Fig. 6.2) and time influences event management. The Max-Plus approach is usually used for modelling this class of system. A DES of controllable events is therefore represented by a date function vector (date stamp) X. An x_i input of the vector is an application:

$$x_i : N \dashrightarrow R\ U\{-\infty\};$$

and $x_i(n)$ is interpreted as the nth occurrence of the event labelled i (i.e. the production date of the nth piece of type i in the automated production system). To enable the reader to better understand the functioning of a Max-Plus automaton, a formal definition of this type of automaton is given below.

6.2.3 Max-Plus Automaton

A finite state Max-Plus automaton on a Σ alphabet is a quadruplet $A = (Q, \alpha, \beta, T)$, where Q is a finite set of states and α, β, T are the applications:

$\alpha : Q \dashrightarrow \mathbb{R}\ U\{-\infty\}$, *period of rest.*

$\beta : Q \dashrightarrow \mathbb{R}\ \mathrm{U}\{-\infty\}$, *period of use.*

$T : Q \times \Sigma \times Q \rightarrow \mathbb{R}\ U\{-\infty\}$ *crossing date of transitions.*

Before going deeper into the theory, and to consolidate the concepts, take the simple example of a system which manages the passage of parts in a machining centre (Fig. 6.6).

The parts are of different types and require a specific operation in the centre (machining range depending on their type). Each operation requires a certain time to complete the change of machining tools.

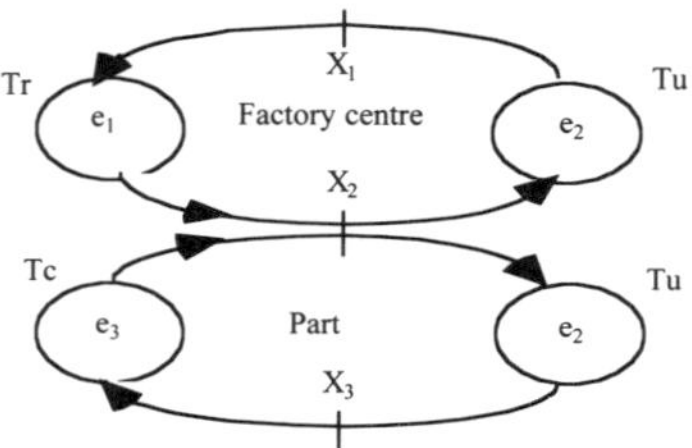

Fig. 6.6 Example of the modelling of a simple system.

This system is composed of three states (Fig. 6.6):

- *e*1: free machining centre; the machining centre remains inactive for a maximum period *Tr*, during which the tool change takes place;
- *e*2: machining centre occupied: maximum duration of a machining operation, *Tu*;
- *e*3: part in convoy; maximum duration of conveyance, *Tc*.

For this example we have:

$Q = \{e_1, e_2, e_3\},$

$\alpha(e_1) = Tr; \beta(e_2) = Tu; \alpha(e_3) = Tc.$

$\Sigma = \{x_2$ ==> allocation of a part to the machining centre,

x_1 ==> freeing of the machining centre,

x_3 ==> end of the machining operation on the part}.

This system can be represented by the transition crossing date vector:

$x_i: X = (x_1, x_2, x_3)$ such that:

$x_1(t)\ \mu\ x_2(t) = Tc$

$x_2(t)\ \mu\ \max(x_1(t-1) + Tr \cdot x_3(t-1) + Tr)$

$x_3(t)\ \mu\ x_2(t) = Tc$

$x_i(t)$ represents the date of the tth crossing of transition x_i. Under this form, this system can be directly implemented in Prolog III with the algorithm in Figure 6.7, as we will see in the following sections. It can, in fact, be integrated into a more global system (production system) as a static scheduling agent (see Section 6.3).

This is a non-linear system. To make it linear in the Max-Plus algebra it could be written:

$x_1(t) = Tc.x_2(t)$

$x_2(t) = Tr.x_1(t-1) \otimes Tr \cdot X_3(t-1)$

$x_3(t) = Tc.x_2(t)$

the binary operation $\otimes$ is the max operator.

More formally, a Max-Plus type automaton A functions in the following manner: a word with length n is a sequence $p = (q_1,\ldots,q_{n+1}) \in Q^{n+1}$. This sequence can also be written in the following format: $p = (q_1\text{-}> q_2\text{-}>\ldots\text{-}> q_{n+1})$. A word (for example an action plan, a schedule etc.) $w = a_1\ldots a_n$ is acceptable or recognizable by A if and only if:

$$\text{weight}(p,w) \equiv \alpha(q_1) + T(q_1, a_1, q_2) + \ldots + T(q_n, a_n, q_{n+1}) + \beta(q_{n+1}) \neq -\infty. \qquad (6.1)$$

This equation can also be written as follows:

$$\text{weight}(p,w) = \text{weight}(q_1 \xrightarrow{a_1} q_2 \xrightarrow{a_2} q_3 \rightarrow \ldots q_n \xrightarrow{a_n} q_n + 1).$$

The multiplicity of the word $w = a_1\ldots a_n$ is the maximum weight of the w recognition sequence, noted:

$$A(w) \equiv \max_{p\in Q^{n+1}} \text{weight}(p,w) = \max q_1\ldots q_{n+1} [\alpha(q_1) + T(q_1, a_1, q_2) + \ldots + T(q_n, a_n, q_{n+1}) + \beta(q_{n+1})]. \qquad (6.2)$$

According to the above, it could be said that automaton A recognizes the function date stamp $w \rightarrow A(w)$. A function date stamp y: Σ --> $\mathbb{R}$ U $\{-\infty\}$ is said to be recognizable if there is an automaton A such as $y(w) = A(w)$. $y(w)$ must be interpreted as the occurrence of event w, with, however, the following hypothesis: $y(w) = -\infty$ *if* w does not produce itself.

The detailed study of this theory falls outside the scope of this book. For more on the theory of Max-Plus automaton, the reader can refer to Gaubert (1994).

To conclude this section, it could be said that discrete systems which are not subject to deterministic problems (no multiple choice on entry/exit to or from a state) are linear, and can easily be modelled by Max-plus automaton. These automatons essentially take care of problems surrounding synchronization and throughput limitation. The classes of systems involved are discrete event systems where time intervenes explicitly. Finally, these systems are represented using a linear equation system where the variables are the time stamps $x_i(t)$ ($x_i(t)$ = date of jth crossing of x_i) and counters $x'(t)$ which provide the number of crossings of x_i.

> Max-Plus automaton can easily integrate into our approach, especially for the design of decision agents.

6.3 Prolog III and the Study of Simple Real-Time Systems

In this section, particular attention is paid to the modelling and behaviour simulation of simple real-time systems with programming language by Prolog III constraints. Primarily, it is necessary to point out that in this section, the systems we are concerned with are simple real-time systems whose global dynamics can be expressed using a single system equation. This limitation leads to a noticeable simplification of the generated simulation program. Given the non-linear character of these systems in general, we propose a simple simulation algorithm based on successive computations over time. This algorithm can act as a basis for the implementation of the automaton theory (Max-Plus) presented in the preceding section. It can also be used for the study of the behaviour of *known systems*. In this case, it is necessary to use a step-by step integration of the equations describing their dynamics, which involves re-writing these regulation equations under an approximate discrete form. Consider the following equation which represents the speed $n(t)$ of an electric motor:

$$F(t, n(t)) = \mathrm{d}n(t)/\mathrm{d}t = (-n(t) + k^{*}v(t)/Tc$$

where n is the speed, t the time, v the tension, k an amplification factor and Tc a time constraint. To resolve it digitally, this equation must be replaced for example, by using the traditional method of trapezoids, by the following equation:

$$N(t_{i+1}) = n(t_i) + \Delta t/2 * (\mathrm{f}(t_i,n(t_i)) + \mathrm{f}(t_i + 1, n\ (t_i + 1)))$$
$$\Delta t = (t_{i+1} - t_i)$$

This re-write introduces an error, because it assumes that the values of $n(t)$ are constant during an interval of time Δt called “computation”.

This type of simple, discrete real-time system can be described by (Fig. 6.7):

- system state variables;
- input data and control flows (input vector);
- output data and control flows (output vector);
- rules and laws for the generation of output flow from input flow (transformation rules). These rules give the different stages required in the form of a set of transformation equations, to generate output flows. For discrete systems (see the definition in the preceding paragraph), this set of equations generally represents a linear system which enables a solution to be found according to the input vector variables and the system state variables.

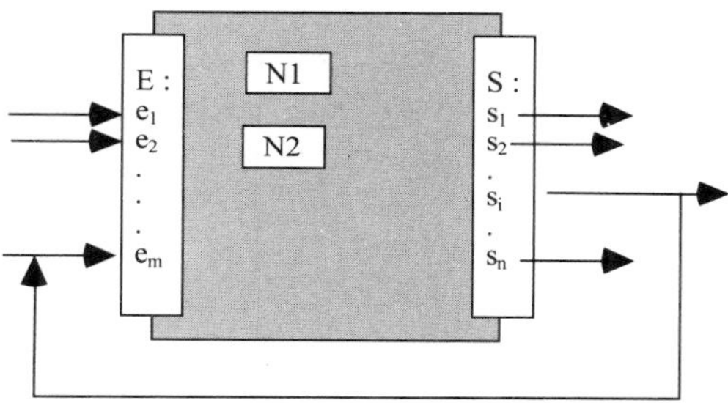

Fig. 6.7 Graphical representation of a system.

The main features of the simple discrete real-time system behaviour-simulating algorithm are given in Figure 6.8.

```
Simulate_Simple_Reactive_System
  {
   t  the simulation running time;
   Dt the calculation step;
   T  the simulation horizon;
   N(t) the vector for the variable states in the
system at time t;
   I(t) vector for the variable input states at time t;
   O(t) vector for the variable output states at time t;
   R set of system equations;
   Z = { E(0), N(0)} initial state of the system;
    t = 0;
   S(0) = f(R, Z); /* activate the rules whose
conditions are verified*/
 As long as t + Dt < T
 Do
         N(t + Dt) = f(E(t), N(t), R);
        S(t + Dt) = f(E(t), N(t), R);
        t = t + Dt.
        E(t) = f(S(t));
 End as long as
  }
```

Fig. 6.8 Algorithm of the simulation of behaviour of simple reactive systems.

In the following sections, we study how this algorithm is applied to two types of simple systems: combinatorial systems and discrete systems where time plays a major part in the equation and their dynamics. First, we approach combinatorial laws of transformation which can be simply expressed in the form of equations. We then extend the scope of our study to discrete systems. We will adopt the same approach which involves proposing a methodology for the analysis, specification and simulation of behaviour with Prolog III, in light of the validation and verification of specifications, for each of the classes of system studied (combinatorial systems, discrete systems).

6.3.1 Modelling and Simulation of the Behaviour of Combinatorial Systems

The modelling and behaviour simulation of combinatorial systems with Prolog III is easier to implement than in the case of sequential systems (see Chapter 5 for the definitions of combinatorial and sequential systems). We will mostly use the example given in Figure 6.9 to introduce the different stages of our approach to the modelling and behaviour simulation of combinatorial systems. This is an example of a combinatorial system used by Colmerauer (1990).

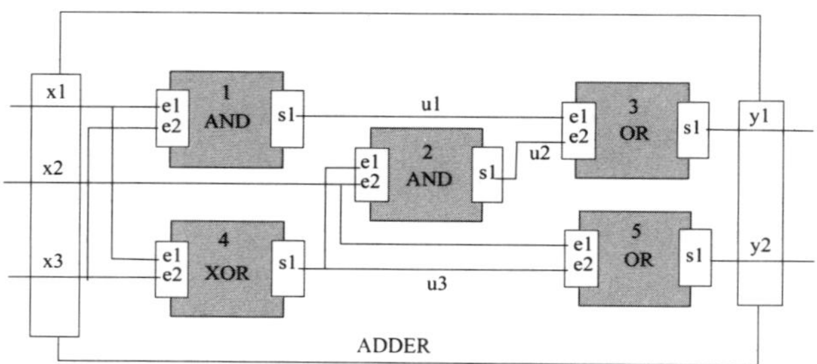

Fig. 6.9 Example of a simple combinatorial system (an adder).

The adder carries out the binary sum of three bits, $x1$, $x2$, $x3$, under the form of a two bit binary number $y1y2$. This circuit is composed of five components numbered 1 to 5 : two "AND" ports, one "OR" port and two "XOR" ports. The interfaces of each component are clearly identified. For modelling with Prolog III, three variables $u1$, $u2$, $u3$ have been introduced to represent the outputs of ports 1, 2 and 4.

In order to enable a better understanding of combinatorial systems, following our approach, we propose a methodology for the modelling and study of this type of system.

6.3.1.1 *Methodology for Combinatorial System Modelling*

A combinatorial system can be defined by the result of the following elements:

<E, S, O, C, T>:

where E is the input data and control flow vector; S is the output data and control flow vector; O is the internal elementary operators vector (logical ports); C is the matrix of connections between the internal flows of the system; and T is the decision table which describes the transformation rules.

The decision table can be used to optimize the system and consequently reduce its complexity. The M matrix can also be exploited to simplify the internal connections of the system (circuit). At this point, it is important to note that these matrices can (must) be generated automatically by a graphics editor, especially for relatively complex systems. The application of our approach on the example in Figure 6.9 therefore gives the results shown in Figure 6.10.

Now that the analysis and specification of a combinatorial system is complete, it would be interesting to generate a Prolog III prototype to study its behaviour. This study can be carried out in two different ways depending on the aims (which are complementary):

1. *diagnostic support* on cases where the system behaviour model acts as a basis for detecting faulty components;
2. *the study of the reactivity and behaviour* of the system according to input data. This study enables the architecture and global behaviour of the system to be checked against the specifications.

6.3.1.2 Diagnostic Support

To be able to generate a Prolog III program which can be used for diagnostic support, we recommend the following approach:

Stage 1: The Identification of the Principal Predicates of the System

- Associate a Prolog III rule to the circuit to be studied, which has the same name (`adder`).
- The parameters for the left part (the head) of the rule are made up of three lists:
  - the list of circuit input variables;
  - the list of circuit output variables;
  - the list of elementary circuit variables which make up the main circuit.

```
Adder(<x1, x2, x3>, <y1,y2>, <c1, c2, c3, c4, c5>) ->
```

Stage 2: Constraints System

- The right part (the queue) of the rule is constituted of two parts:
  - The call to a recursive predicate to determine the faulty element:

```
OneOrMoreFaultyElements(<c1, c2, c3, c4, c5>)
```

E = <x1, x2, x3>;
S = <y1, y2>;
O = <AND1, AND2, AND3, XOR4, XOR5>;
C =

		AND1			AND2			OR3			XOR4			XOR5			Output circuits	
		e1	e2	s1	e1	e2	s1	e1	e2	s1	e1	e2	s1	e1	e2	s1	y1	y2
	e1																	
AND1	e2																	
	s1							u1										
	e1																	
AND2	e2																	
	s1								u2									
	e1																	
OR3	e2																	
	s1																y1	
	e1																	
XOR4	e2																	
	s1				u3											u3		
	e1																	
XOR5	e2																	
	s1																	y2
	x1	x1									x1							
Input	x2					x2								x2				
circuits	x3		x3									x3						

T =

		AND1			AND2			OR3			XOR4			XOR5			Output circuits		Condition
		e1	e2	s1	e1	e2	s1	e1	e2	s1	e1	e2	s1	e1	e2	s1	y1	y2	
	e1																		
AND1	e2																		
	s1							u1											u1 ≡ x1 ^ x3
	e1																		
AND2	e2																		
	s1								u2										u2 ≡ x2 ^ u3
	e1																		
OR3	e2																		
	s1																y1		y1 ≡ u1 / u2
	e1																		
XOR4	e2																		
	s1				u3											u3			u3 ≡ ~(x1 ≡ x3)
	e1																		
XOR5	e2																		
	s1																	y2	y2 ≡ ~(x2 ≡ x3)
	x1	x1									x1								
Input	x2					x2								x2					
circuits	x3		x3									x3							

Fig. 6.10 Description of combinatorial systems by tables.

- *The list of constraints* on the values of the output data flows of different internal elements calculated from the input flows. This is a system of linear equations that Prolog III endeavours to solve at the same time as erasing the questions (aims) asked. These equations are provided by the decision table (grey area of the table in Figure 6.10). Negation (for example ~c1) used in the equations indicates that the output flow from the component is only valid if the component in question is not faulty.

```
{~c1 => (u1 <=>x1& x3),
 ~c2 => (u2 <=>x2&u3),
 ~c3 => (y1 <=>u1 | u2),
 ~c4 => (u3 <=> ~(x1<=>x3),
 ~c5 => (y2 <=> ~(x2<=>u3))
};
```

Stage 3: Design of the Principal Predicate

- The definition of the body of the recursive predicate *OneOrMoreFaulty Elements.* This predicate must respect the hypothesis that one component at the most is faulty:

```
OneOrMoreFaultyElements(P)-> OrOnOneOrMoreFaultyElements(P,p);
OrOnOneOrMoreFaultyElements(<>,0) ->;
OrOnOneOrMoreFaultyElements(<p>.P, p | q) ->
     OrOnOneOrMoreFaultyElements (P, q),
              { p |q = 0};
```

The application of this approach to our example gives the following Prolog III program:

```
PROLOG III, v1.3 December 91 (C)PrologIA 1989-92
>    adder(l,m,n) ->
              OneOrMoreFaultyElements(n)
        {
               l=<x1,x2,x3>,
               m=<y1,y2>,
               n=<c1,c2,c3,c4,c5>,
               ~c1 => (u1<=>x1& x3),
               ~c2 => (u2 <=> x2 & u3),
               ~c3 => (y1 <=> u1|u2),
               ~c4 => (u3 <=> ~(x1⇔x3)),
               ~c5 => (y2 <=> ~(x2⇔u3))
     };
OneOrMoreFaultyElements(P)->
              OrOnOneOrMoreFaultyElements(P,p);
OrOnOneOrMoreFaultyElements(<>,0') ->;
OrOnOneOrMoreFaultyElements(<p>.P, p|q) ->
              OrOnOneOrMoreFaultyElements (P,q),
  { p |q = 0'};
```

The execution of the preceding program from a report (a real circuit response to an input vector E) enables behaviour simulation of the circuit to be carried out and defective components to be detected. Note that the five boolean variables c_i which signify that "component number *i* is faulty" have been introduced.

If examination of the circuit reveals that for the inputs <*x*1,*x*2,*x*3> = <1,1,0> the vector <*y*1,*y*2> = <0,1> is obtained on output, the following question must be presented to the Prolog system to identify the faulty component:

```
>adder(<1',1',0'>, <0',1'>,n);
     {n = <0',0',0',1',0'>}
```

The response to this question clearly shows that it is component *p*4 which is faulty.

6.3.1.3 *Study of Combinatorial System Behaviour*

Another possible use for the above model involves studying the behaviour of a system with the aim of validating its behaviour. In contrast to the preceding case, the different possible configurations of the input vector will be imposed on the system in order to determine if the corresponding output vectors conform to the specifications. The results obtained are part of the results relied upon.

The set of different source configurations $\psi = \{E_1, E_2, \ldots, E\}$ is called a set of scenarios. The Prolog III required to implement this phase is slightly different from the diagnostic support program. This program can be seen as an application of the set of possible input vectors towards the set of possible output vectors. As with the preceding case, we propose the approach below to obtain this program from Table T. This approach involves the following stages:

Stage 1: The Identification of the Principal System Predicate

- Associate a Prolog III rule which has the same name (`adder`), to the circuit to be studied.
- The parameters for the left part (the head) of the rule are made up of three lists:
  - o the list of circuit input variables;
  - o the list of circuit output variables;
  - o the list of internal data flow variables:

```
Adder(<x1, x2, x3>, <y1,y2>, <u1, u2, u3>) ->,
```

Stage 2: Constraints System

- The right side (the queue) of the rule is made up of only one part: the list of constraints on the values of different data flows coming from internal components, calculated from input flows (result function). It is therefore a simple system of linear equations that Prolog III endeavours to solve. These equations are provided by the decision table (grey part of the table in Fig. 6.10).

```
{
    u1 = x1&x3,
          u2 = x2&u3,
          y1 = u1 | u2,
          u3 = ~ (x1 <=> x3),
          y2 = ~ (x2<=>u3)
};
```

The behaviour simulation for the circuit in the preceding example is:

```
Adder(l,m,n) ->
  {
          l=<x1,x2,x3>,
          m=<y1,y2>,
          n=<u1,u2,u3>,
```

```
                  u1  = x1&x3,
                  u2  = x2 & u3,
                  y1  = u1 | u2,
                  u3  = ~ (x1 <=> x3),
                  y2  = ~ (x2<=>u3)
      };
```

The use of this program to study the behaviour of a circuit can be carried out in two possible ways:

1. Interrogate the Prolog program to know the vector result:

```
adder(<1,0,1>, <y1,y2>, <u1,u2,u3>)?
Adder(<1',0',1'>, m,n) ;
adder(<1',0',1'>, m,n) ;
{m = <1',0'>, n = <1',0',0'>}
```

2. Interrogate the program to obtain the input vector when the output vector is known:

```
adder(1, <0',1'>,n) ;
     {1 = <x1_1,x2_1,x3_1>, n = <0',0',u3_1>,
            x3_1 => u3_1,
            x2_1&u3_1 = 0',
            x2_1|u3_1 = 1',
            x1_1&x3_1 = 0',
            x1_1 => u3_1,
            u3_1 => x1_1|x3_1}
```

3. It is also possible to interrogate the system with a possible configuration of the internal flow vector:

```
adder(1, m, <0',1',1'>) ;
{1 = <x1_1,1',x3_1>, m = <1',0'>,
x1_1&x3_1 = 0',
     x1_1|x3_1 = 1'}
```

Finally, it is interesting to generate all the possibilities for the three vectors:

```
adder(1, m, n) ;
 {1 = <x1_1,x2_1,x3_1>, m = <y1_1,y2_1>, n = <u1_1,u2_1,u3_1>,
         u2_1 => u3_1,
         y1_1 => u1_1|u2_1,
         u1_1 => y1_1,
         u2_1 => y1_1,
         u1_1 => x3_1,
         x2_1&y2_1&u3_1 = 0'
         x2_1 => y2_1|u3_1,
         x2_1&u3_1 => u2_1,
         y2_1 => x2_1|u3_1,
         u3_1 => x2_1|y2_1,
         u2_1 => x2_1
         x1_1&x3_1&u3_1 = 0'
         x1_1 => x3_1|u3_1,
         x1_1&x3_1 => u1_1,
         u3_1 => x1_1|x3_1,
         x3_1 => x1_1|u3_1,
         u1_1 => x1_1}
```

This elementary example of a combinatorial system and the simulation of its behaviour with Prolog III shows the strength of this language and the possibilities that it offers for the study of the behaviour of dynamic systems.

Recall that Prolog is a symbolic and logical programming language which mainly manipulates syntactic abstract quantities. Digital processes are rare and are generally implemented by external predefined predicates or external sub-programs written in more conventional languages, such as C language.

The approach presented can be easily generalized, and automated. The generation of a program for diagnostic support or for the simulation of combinatorial system behaviour is rendered systematic and easy to achieve by using tables. The use of a graphics editor to generate the different tables introduced in this section renders the Prolog III system more accessible to users who do not want to invest their time in learning and using logical programming with constraints.

6.3.2 Modelling and Simulation of the Behaviour of Discrete Systems

In contrast to combinatorial systems, discrete systems are essentially *sequential systems* whose state is recursive: the system state at instant t depends on the input and output variables, but especially on its state at instant $t - 1$. A sequential system passes from a stable state to another stable state via a certain number of intermediary states. This recursive development of the system state is easily modelled in Prolog by *recursive predicates*. Modelling a system state will be completely described by the data of three vectors N, E, S (see Fig. 6.11). The coding of this state happens naturally under the form of a list E: <<N>,<E>,<S>>, which is composed of three sub-lists: N, E, S. On the other hand, for the behaviour simulation of discrete systems, it is necessary to take into account the time dimension. To code the simulation time, a variable t must be introduced, positive or zero. The general format of a Prolog III program for the simulation of the behaviour of these systems is the following:

```
state (1, E) ->
 state _initial (E);
state (t, E) ->
 state(t-1, E')
transition (E', E),
{ t> 1};
```

This model indicates that the system state at point 1 is its initial state, and that the system state at point $t \neq 1$ is E if it was in state E', and a transition made it pass from state E' to E. In this model, the part of the Prolog III program specific to each new system will limit itself to writing two predicates:

- the predicate `initial_state (E)`, which will define the state of the system or the initial configuration (that is to say, the value of all of the state variables at instant $t = 1$), by a list of constants;

- the predicate `transition(E1,E2)`, which describes the rules of passage from state E1 (configuration E1) at instant *t*, to state E2 (configuration E2) at instant *t'*, with ($t' > t$). It is clear that all the system equations will be inserted into the tail of this predicate.

Figure 6.11 gives a simple example of a discrete system. This system describes the progressive increase of the pressure level in the gas tank of a nuclear power plant.

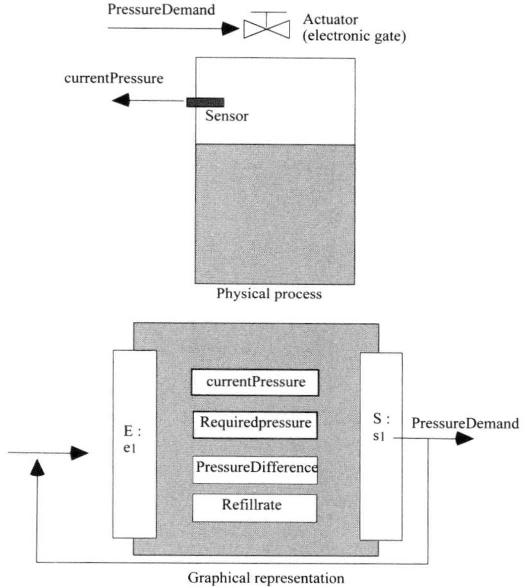

Fig. 6.11 Example of a discrete system.

Note that in this system, we have not used a level sensor to know the current value of the pressure. A displaced logic electromagnetic sluice gate, capable of receiving an instruction and discharging the corresponding amount of gas, was chosen. Each time the pressure falls to 100 bars and for security reasons, linked to a careful internal pressure measurement, taking into account the metal structure of the tank, it is only possible to increase the difference between the actual value and the required value of pressure in the tank every hour. The value required is 2500 bars.

The reader will have noted that the state variables of the system which represent a physical size obtained from a sensor placed at the level of the physical process, are represented by a grey rectangle. In contrast the temporary variables required for the implementation of internal processes in the command part of the system are represented by a normal rectangle. For this system the initial configuration (initial state) is given by the value of vectors E(0), S(0), N(0):

E(0) = <0>
S(0) = <0>
N(0) =<100>.

The analysis table for this problem is given by Figure 6.12.

Rules	T	E e1	N n1	n2	n3		S s1	Actions
	t		n4					
r1	t+1	*	<2500	2500	*	0.5	*	n1(t+1)= n1(t) + s1(t), n3(t+1) = n2 - n1(t+1), s1(t+1) = n3(t+1) * n4, e1(t+1) = s1(t+1).
Initial conditions		0	100	2500	0	0.5	0	

Dictionary

		Name	Description	Type
t		TopClock	Variable indicating the time	control
E: e1		PressureAdded	Amount of pressure to add to each time unit. Unit = Bar	data
S: s1		Pressure_to_Add	Amount of pressure to add to each time unit. Unit = bar	data
N	n1	CurrentPressure	The current pressure in the tank, Bar	data
	n2	RequiredPressure	Maximum pressure reading in the tank unit = bar	data
	n3	PressureDifference	Difference in pressure between the pressure required and the current pressure , Unit = bar	data
	n4	Refillrate	For security reasons, only a percentage of difference in the pressure is to be added	data

Figure 6.12 The analysis table for a tank refill system.

This table indicates that there is only one transition rule. This is principally made up of three parts:

1. The *condition* part of a transition concerns input and state variables. For a transition rule, the input or state variables marked by an asterisk indicate that they do not intervene in the triggering of a transition. A comparison operator followed by a value in the column indicates a condition on the corresponding variable. For variables constant over time, only their value is represented in the corresponding column;
2. The *action* part of a transition indicates the list of actions and operations to trigger if the conditions expressed on the input and state variables are satisfied;
3. The *initial condition* part gives values taken by the different variables of the system at point 0.

The system in Figure 6.11 contains only one transition rule, rule r1. The equivalent of this rule in text format is:

```
Rule R1:
IF (top clock following) AND (CurrentPressure(t) < 2500)
    THEN
```

```
    Do
    CurrentPressure(t+1) := CurrentPressure(t) +
Pressure_to_Add(t);
    PressureDifference(t+1):=DesiredPressure-CurrentPressure(t+1);
    Pressure_to_Add(t+1) := PressureDifference(t+1) * RefillRate;
    PressureAdded(t+1) := Pressure_to_Add
EndDo
EndRule.
```

It is clear from this table that it will be possible to automatically generate the Prolog III simulation program. The main points of the approach used to generate such a program of discrete system behaviour simulation are as follows:

Stage 1: Design a Principal Predicate

- The main program predicate is the state predicate (E,N,S), where E, S, and N are the respective vectors of input variables, output variables and state variables. This is a *recursive* predicate, because to know the system state at time *t*, it is first necessary to calculate the system state at time *t* –1. This is equally dependent on the state of the system at *t* – 2. Consequently, to find the system state at time *t*, it is necessary to go back in time to the initial state and then progressively return until *t*. The general form of this predicate is:

```
State(1,<E>.<N>.<S>) ->
     Initial_state(<E>.<N>.<S>);
State(t,e) ->
          State(t-1,e').
     Transition(e',e)
          ,{e=<E>.<N>.<S>,
           e'=<E'>.<N'>.<S'>,
          t>1
          };
initial_state(<E0>.<N0>.<S0>) ->;
```

The first form of predicate calls the `initial_state` predicate which has the role of providing the system state at time 0. It also constitutes the stop condition for going back in time. In contrast, the second form of predicate calls the `transition` predicate. This guarantees the system to pass from the state at time *t* – 1 to the state at time *t*.

Stage 2: Design of System Transition Rules: The Dynamics

- The predicate which guarantees the passage of the system from the state at instant *t* to another state at instant *t*' can be easily obtained from the table. This predicate contains the rules of passage from one state to another. These rules are expressed in the action part of the table in the form of equations. These equations can then be taken and inserted into the constraint part of the predicate. The transition predicate used in our example is:

```
transition(e,e') ->
     ,{
     e=<E>.<N>.<S>,
     e'=<E'>.<N'>.<S'>,
```

```
        Lists of equations associated with the transition
    };
```

In this way, the Prolog III program for the example in Figure 6.15 is:

```
state(1,<e1>.<n1>.<s1>) ->
     initial_state(<e1>.<n1,n3>.<s1>;
state(t,e) ->
     state(t-1,e')
 transition(e',e)
             ,{e=<e1>.<n1,n3>.<s1>,
             e'=<e1'>.<n1',n3'>.<s1'>,
             t>1
             };
initial_state(<0>.<100,0><0>) ->;
transition(e',e)
             ,{e=<e1>.<n1,n3>.<s1>,
              e'=<e1'>.<n1',n3'>.<s1'>,
             t>1
             };
initial_state(<0>.<100,0>.<0>) ->;
transition(e,e') ->
             ,{
     e=<e1>.<n1>.<s1>,
     e'=<e1'>.<n1',n3'>.<s1'>,
     P_ressureDesired = 2500,
     R_atePressure = 0.05,
     n1' = n1 + s1,
     n3' = P_ressureDesired - n1',
     s1' = n3' * R_atePressure,
     e1' = s1',
     n1' < P_ressureDesired
             };
```

This program can be used to study the development of the system for a given T horizon. Incidentally, if $T = 20$, the following question must be asked:

```
state(t,e){t>=1, t<=20, E= <E>.<N>.<S>};
```

Solving this question gives the following results:

```
>state(t,<e1>.<n1,n3>.<s1>){t>=1, t<=20};
{t = 1, e1 = 0, n1 = 100, n3 = 0, s1 = 0}
{t = 2, e1 = 1200, n1 = 100, n3 = 2400, s1 = 1200}
{t = 3, e1 = 600, n1 = 1300, n3 = 1200, s1 = 600}
{t = 4, e1 = 300, n1 = 1900, n3 = 600, s1 = 300}
{t = 5, e1 = 150, n1 = 2200, n3 = 300, s1 = 150}
{t = 6, e1 = 75, n1 = 2350, n3 = 150, s1 = 75}
{t = 7, e1 = 37.5, n1 = 2425, n3 = 75, s1 = 37.5}
{t = 8, e1 = 18.5, n1 = 2462.5, n3 = 37.5, s1 = 18.75}
{t = 9, e1 = 9.375, n1 = 2481.2, n3 = 18.75, s1 = 9.37}
{t = 10, e1 = 4.6875, n1 = 2490.6, n3 = 9.3750, s1 = 4.6875}
{t = 11, e1 = 2.3437, n1 = 2495.3, n3 = 4.6875, s1 = 2.3437}
{t = 12, e1 = 1.1718, n1 = 2497.6, n3 = 2.3437, s1 = 1.1718}
{t = 13, e1 = 0.5859, n1 = 2498.8, n3 = 1.1718, s1 = 0.5859}
{t = 14, e1 = 0.2929, n1 = 2499.4, n3 = 0.5859, s1 = 0.2929}
{t = 15, e1 = 0.1464, n1 = 2499.7, n3 = 0.2929, s1 = 0.1464}
{t = 16, e1 = 0.0732, n1 = 2499.8, n3 = 0.1464, s1 = 0.0732}
```

```
{t = 17, e1 = 0.0366, n1 = 2499.9, n3 = 0.0732, s1 = 0.0366}
{t = 18, e1 = 0.0183, n1 = 2499.9, n3 = 0.0366, s1 = 0.0183}
{t = 19, e1 = 0.0091, n1 = 2499.9, n3 = 0.0183, s1 = 0.0091}
{t = 20, e1 = 0.0045, n1 = 2499.9, n3 = 0.0091, s1 = 0.0045}
```

According to the results, we note that the system starts to stabilize itself from point $t = 16$. The value of the output vector tends towards zero, and the state variable `CurrentPressure` approaches 2500.

A complex real-time system is linked to its environment by a large number of connections. A real-time system is only significant because it is part of a global system: the connections that it will make with the other sub-systems are essential, they are its reason for being. The state of a system will depend on its preceding state.

6.4 Specification Methodology of Complex MSS Systems

The `transition()` predicate which was introduced in the preceding section enables access to all of the variables of the three vectors representing the system state: <E>, <N>, <S>. It also holds the set of transformation rules of the current system state depending on trigger events and conditions of the rules. We will now study complex reactive discrete event systems, concentrating on a particular class of these systems: automated production systems. Nevertheless, our approach remains valid and applicable to a large number of discrete event systems or real-time systems.

The systems that we will study will be approached in a standard manner as a communication between two coupled sub-systems (see Chapter 5): the physical sub-system (the operative part) and the control sub-system (the command part).

6.4.1 Analysis and Specification of Complex Systems with MSS

Our aim is the specification of the control sub-system, but its analysis cannot be dissociated from that of the physical sub-system. Faced with a given system, it must be capable of clarifying its physical structure and its functioning rules. For complex systems, refinement is essential in order to operate by modules. The MSS method relies on hierarchical refinement by abstraction level which facilitates the study of these systems. Each hierarchical level is composed of two distinct but strongly coupled specification phases.

First Phase: Identification of Physical Sub-System Resources

This phase is made up of the following three stages:

1. Identification of physical sub-system objects or resources. This involves freeing the components of the system studied. This identification concerns availa-

ble objects if it involves studying a system which already exists, or even the resources or objects necessary to construct a new system. This stage may rely on the use of the I/O model or any other simple format (OOA: see Chapter 9);

2. For each object or resource identified during the preceding stage, clearly define its interface in terms of input and output messages and signals (events) (dialogue and communication protocol). The messages involve data flow and signals representing the input and output control flows of the object;
3. For each object, identify the state variables or visible predicates at this level, if there are any. This includes predicates which are necessary to write the control and decision rules at this level. This involves state variables of objects which are used in global synchronization and supervision rules (state of a machine: working, stopped, occupied etc.);
4. For each resource, decide if it is an active type or a passive type of resource.

Notion 11 Active Resources

These are objects with an internal logic invisible at the current refinement level. These objects are able to accomplish one or more tasks in autonomy provided that they transmit the order or corresponding command (robot, digital-operated device, software server etc.).

Active resources are reactive objects which interact with their environment via the exchange of messages and control signals. They represent complex sub-systems the same as the system being studied, and can form the subject of later specific analysis (hierarchical refinement).

Notion 12 Passive Resources

These are objects necessary for the implementation of a particular task or function, but which are not given internal logic which enables them to advance or accomplish actions in an autonomous manner (palettes, factory tools, actuators, sensors, files or any other data storage resource).

The distinction between these two types of objects is liable to considerably facilitate the analysis and specification of digital control during the next phase. Consequently, it is important to have a precise idea of the nature of the components of a system at this stage, before continuing to the next phase.

Second Phase: The Identification of Control Sub-System and Hierarchical Refinement Agents by Abstraction Level.

This phase is composed of the following phases:

1. A *control agent* is associated to each active object or resource. The interface of this agent must contain the data and control flows of the object in question, already identified during the preceding phase (command and use protocol of a

robot, device, software etc). The value of the visible traits or state variables of the object form part of the input data flow of the agent. This latter is the only one authorized to provide the contents of these variables to other agents of the same level, or to the processing rules of the signals of the encompassing system.

2. An access *management agent* must be associated to each passive resource which is accessible and essential for the implementation of the control sub-system. The interface of this agent must contain the data flows (protocol for the use of a database, sensor, actuator etc.).
3. Identify the input and output data and control flows for the control sub-system. This involves control and command flows that the system exchanges with its environment;
4. An *interception rule* (interception handler) is associated to each control flow signal or data flow message entering the system under study. This interception rule can implicate several *control agents* and *management agents* for its processing. It can bring into intervention visible traits of the physical sub-system via their agents. If the interception rule of the processing of a signal or event must bring in a complex logical, as well as the simple synchronization and the command of control agents or management agents, it is advised that an *abstract functional decision object* be linked to it which will be the subject of a later refinement (inferior level). This object is called the *expert agent.* The processing and decision-making concerning such an event relies, in fact, on a certain expertise in a particular field (scheduling algorithm, planning, etc.) These expert agents use their own data and passive resources which are simple information carriers. Rendering these objects passive or this data visible at this level is likely to compromise the readability and ease of comprehension of the decision logic at this level.

Hierarchical Refinement

Each time that a physical resource must be defined, or each time that an expert agent has been introduced, there is good reason to consider it as a new system to study and to which to apply phases 1 and (or) 2. A hierarchical refinement approach is thus introduced.

6.4.2 Example of the Analysis of a Production System

In this example we use the analysis approach presented in the preceding section in view of the specification of a control system of a flexible production unit. This unit can be used for the manufacturing of several types of parts depending on diverse conditions: unit production, medium or large batches. The configuration presented corresponds to a true production unit. It is composed of a machining centre with BOCH digital control, a tower with NUM 1060 digital control, a tri-dimensional measuring device, a wire-guided handling trolley, an initiating post (with a loading and unloading wharf), six storage posts, an operator console (for operator dialogue), and a robot to load the tower (Fig. 6.13). This unit functions as follows:

- The production management system plans the production for a given period (a day, a week) depending on the capacity of the unit and the demands of the client. For example, 30 type A parts and 40 type B parts per day.

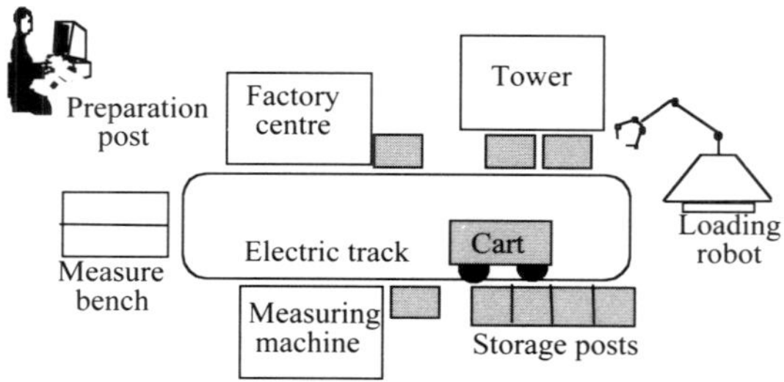

Fig. 6.13 Flexible production unit.

- The scheduling system generates the manufacturing order files which specify the order in which the parts are fabricated, while optimizing a certain number of criteria (i.e. minimizing the time to change tools, or maximizing the occupation time of the machines).
- For each part, an order is displayed on the screen of the operator to request him to place the appropriate part on the palette. Each palette is identified by an electronic label on which up to 8 Koctets can be read or written. This involves reading or writing operation sequences which must be carried out on the part.

The main functions of the system design are:

- *Scheduling* (supported by a computer-aided manufacturing management package): its role is to generate manufacturing order files which will be used by the control function;
- *Control*: its role is to manage the physical system in real-time. This function must control the tasks to execute on the physical system in order to achieve, under optimum conditions, the manufacturing orders. The departure point is the period collection, that is the list of parts to manufacture and their number. This function must then collect further information on the day's manufacturing in the database, For each part, the information is represented in the following format:

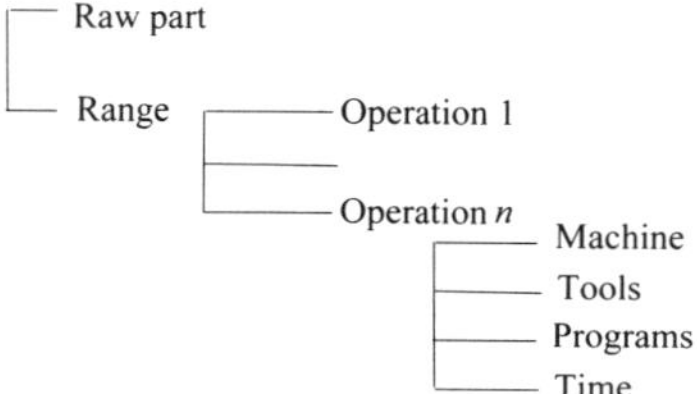

Production scheduling during the day is carried out by optimizing certain criteria: minimizing machine stoppage time, minimizing program changing, minimizing tool changing etc. The control function must also ensure dynamic re-scheduling depending on the state of advance of the manufacture, unforeseen production events (faults, functioning in reduced mode, etc.), the arrival of priority orders etc. According to the manufacture to be implemented, the control function must generate the set of commands to carry out and the order in which they must be executed. To execute machining, the robot must be requested to load the part, load the current program, ensure that the tools are present otherwise request their loading, trigger the execution etc. The control function must send commands to the equipment to implement the actions (stop/start, load programs, change current program, move the trolley from point A to point B, communicate with supervisor, communicate with operator).

- *Supervision* (supported by a software supervisor): this has the role of providing the interface between the operator and the production system. It must collect information either directly on the physical system (sensors), or from other functions, to present them to the operator in different forms: synoptic, tendency curves, historical data. It must also present the status of the production system;
- *Quality management:* its role is to manage the quality of the production system. It operates the manufacturing reports which come from the control and supervision functions. It must indicate the potential anomalies and problems so the control system can correct them (if possible) or stop manufacture. The output from the quality management function can also act as a maintenance management function;
- *Maintenance management:* this function must manage the maintenance of the production system and involve preventative as well as curative actions. It is used as a report on the state of the physical system and manufacturing reports which come from control, supervision and quality management functions.

The application of the above analysis method to this example gives the following stages:

Stage 1

1. Hardware resources:
    - Four towers;
    - Four machining centres;
    - One wire-guided handling trolley;
    - One operator console;
    - Storage banks.

2. Software resources:
   - Computer-aided design and manufacturing software (UNIGRAPHICS);
   - Supervision software (LABVIEW);
   - Database management system (ONTOS).

Stage 2

1. Tower

   Input:

   - Order: change the machine mode (execution mode, loading, unloading...);
   - Order: select current program;
   - Order: load/unload the program;
   - Order: start the machine;
   - Order: stop the machine;

   Output:

   - Data: machine status.

   Physical communication protocol: NUM protocol

2. Robot

   Input:

   - Order: load/unload programs;
   - Order: Start;
   - Order: Stop;
   - Order: execution of movement;

   Output:

   - Data: machine status.

   Physical communication protocol: network protocol FACTOR.

The other components will be studied in a similar manner.

Each active resource has a corresponding control agent, and each passive resource is linked to a management agent as indicated in the table in Figure 6.14.

Nature of the agent	Identified agents
Control	CartAgent, TowerAgent, RobotAgent, FactoryCentreAgent, Control_Agent
Management	PreparationPostAgent, FactoryCentreStoragePostAgent, Tower1StoragePostAgent, Tower1StoragePostAgent, StorageZoneAgent

Fig. 6.14 Table of the different system agents.

It is then standard to conduct a study of the set of agents whose actions are strongly coupled. To that end, another type of agent was introduced, the *unit agent.* The "TowerUnitAgent" is composed of the following agents: `AgentRobot, AgentTower, AgentStorageTower1, Agent StorageTower2`. Figure 6.15 gives the final architecture of the system. Note that for the control sub-system, one agent is defined for the five functions described earlier: SchedulingAgent, ControlAgent, Supervision Agent, MaintenanceAgent, QualityAgent. We also note that the ControlAgent is composed of the agents:

```
InputAgent, TRSchedulingAgent, MachineMeasuringAgent,
TransmissionAgent, TowerUnitAgent, MachiningCentreAgent.
```

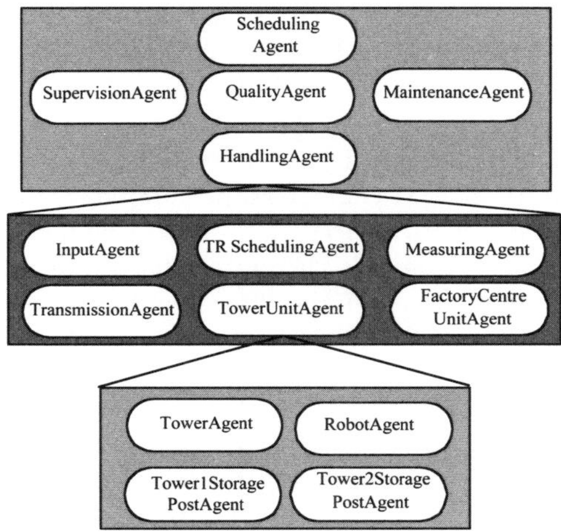

Fig. 6.15 The hierarchical structure of system agents.

The "`TRSchedulingAgent`" and "`InputAgent`" agents are expert agents.

The role of the "`TRSchedulingAgent`" agent is to ensure the dynamic scheduling of the manufacturing unit. It takes account of the manufacturing plan generated by the "`SchedulingAgent`" agent, and of the real state plan (i.e. resource availability, fault occurrences, the arrival of urgent orders etc.).

The "`InputAgent`" agent uses the results from the "`TRSchedulingAgent`" to select the next part to be made. It displays the information on the operator console and writes the sequence of operations to be executed on the palettes electronic label.

6.4.3 The MSS Support Environment

MSS is based principally on the use of a graphics editor as support for phase 2. The main lines of the simulation program generation will be explained in the following section, when the simulation part of the dynamics of discrete event systems with Prolog III will be covered. In the rest of this section, we pay particular attention to the use of such an editor for the analysis and specification of complex real-time systems using the descending approach, as it was earlier called. Recall that for discrete event systems time does not have a great influence, except for the expression of temporal constraints on state transitions. Consequently, the correct editor for this phase must particularly allow objects to be released from the system by respecting its internal hierarchy (relation: system→sub-system) and the different event or messages exchanged (relationship of internal causality or with the user environment).

6.4.3.1 The Formal Scope of MSS

The unit of refinement and specification in MSS is the formal module. A formal module is a formal system which is composed of a quadruplet (Σ, α, S, R). Σ represents the set of function symbols of the module (fundamental syntactic entities). Each function is defined on a well-determined zone. The definition of the zones is an integral part of the design process of module words. Σ is the formal description of the *static part* of a real-time system. The symbol used in Σ are either simple syntactical units such as characters, or complex syntactical units, which obey strict design and use rules. This latter case corresponds to the importation of other formal modules by the module currently being specified. Σ represents what is called the module signature. S is the set of module axioms. In practice, the axioms of a module represent the stable states (initial and final states) of the true system. The axioms of a module are of major importance for the validation process which will be detailed later on. Finally, R is the set of deduction rules (of production or re-writing) of the form [*t*] ==>[*t*'] where *t* and *t*' are terms designed from Σ according to the design process. R is the formal description of the dynamic part of the real-time system. The notation [*t*] designates the representative of the modulo class of identical terms the potential structural axioms, and the sequence [*t*] -> [*t*'] is interpreted as [*t*] becomes [*t*']. For the rules we use the three structural axioms, ACI (associativity, commutativity, identity).

Under these conditions, the rules enable arguments about the state changes in a system, and to draw valid conclusions on its development from typical changes expressed across the rules of R.

For this reason, logic can be placed under two aspects: syntactic, when we are interested in the formal deduction between formulae; and semantic, when we examine the true conditions of the terms. In real-time system specification, it is important to be able to know at any instant its behaviour and development from a given state corresponding to a term. Recall that a real-time system must essentially be a deterministic system.

A formal module is used to generate, filter and reduce the syntactical entities in the phases of the corresponding formal system.

> Simplified, a formal module can be seen as a finite state automaton capable of recognizing and transforming input flow strings which obey a certain syntax to a string in the output flow.

A parallel system will be represented by a set of automaton which all have a large structure of shared data or shared memory as an input flow that we will call the black table or configuration (Fig. 6.16).

This global structure represents the system environment. The automaton simultaneously selects character strings which are found in the configuration and which obey the syntax of their respective grammar.

The following sections will show that formal modules can act as fundamental elements for the formal description and validation of parallel systems (a set of communicating, parallel agents) in general, and specifically real-time systems (parallel systems subject to temporal constraints, user constraints etc.). They are mostly composed of several active entities or agents and in this way are multi-agent systems conforming to the definition that was given in Chapter 1. As we indicated at the beginning of this chapter, the basic idea is to find a model for the formal modules which are capable of being in charge not only of the description of passive elements of a real-time system (structural part) but also the description of its dynamic part (control part). This model must also take account of all of the *synchronization* problems encountered in multi-agent systems (synchronism, asynchronism and parallelism). The management of events and non-determinism inherent in these systems must be explained. In other words, one phrase in the language recognized by a formal module according to this model must reflect the development of the state of the system studied. For each object or system component, the configuration contains (in some internal representation) its state variables with their current value, current events or messages which represent the external stimuli and control messages or internal data in transit. The reduction of a string of the configuration is implemented using the different deduction rules of the module.

> The reduction process of the string is in itself sufficient to represent, simulate and study the development of the system state over time.

At a given instant, the observable state of a multi-agent system is represented by the content of the configuration (the fact base) (Fig. 6.16) which is essentially composed of:

- Identified objects. Each object possesses intrinsic properties; it is in a well-defined state (value of state variables).
- Messages. Messages are generated by external excitations of internal interrupts. The same message can be sent to different objects (configuration is global to the set of formal modules).

During the specification process, any system can be considered, if necessary, as a complex system composed of other systems. The hierarchical refinement process is therefore naturally introduced. A formal model can call for its specification to other formal modules. Later, the notions of the level and visibility (notion of meta-rules in expert systems) will be introduced. A system A is at a level immediately superior to B, if system B intervenes directly in the composition of system A.

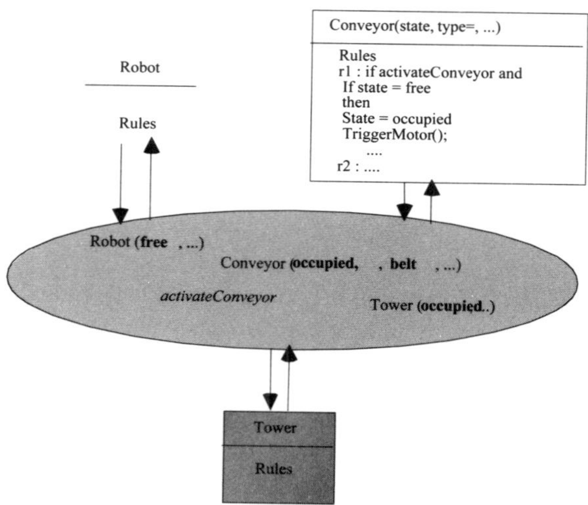

Fig. 6.16 The modelling of parallel systems and their behaviour over time.

Normally system A only knows the traits of systems at its own level which are made visible or public.

To completely define the formalism required, it is necessary to specify the general form of the signature (Σ, α) and re-writing rules of R.

Signature

The elements of the sets Σ, α and R are directly dependent on the system specified. They represent the fact base and inference rules. The fact base describes the properties of a system and the structural relations (assertions and established facts). The rules representing the knowledge, expertise and logic of the system are a standard form used in expert systems: **if** *conditions* **then** *actions*. Figures 6.17 and 6.18 give the textual formalism grammar for the description of multi-agent systems conforming to that presented here. It is more complex (semantically richer) than the usual formalism used to describe expert system because it must not lose sight of the fact that automatic code generation is one of the aims of our approach. To make this process automatic, it is necessary to have enough information on the nature and type of the system objects, the value fields of the different variables and data used, the nature of structural links between the different objects, the emitters and receptors of the different events and messages etc.

Note that the alphabet of the formal module was introduced specifically to enable the recognition of the different components which enter into the design of the system associated with the formal module. It is then necessary to specify the links of inheritance, composition and others which exist between the components of a system: the internal structure. With this in mind, note that only the composition link is of interest to real-time systems in this study. The other links form part of the links which exist in more standard applications (databases, object oriented programming...). Op<_:_/_> represents the object constructor. It indicates the identity of the object to be designed, its type or class, and the list of its traits or state variables with their respective field.

```
                /* System Alphabet*/
Object Type, Attribute, Attributes, Msg, Value, ObjetId, ClassId, AttributeId;

   /* Hierarchies and structural relations between syntactical
entities                          (objets)*/
          SubType ObjetId, ClassId, AttributeId < Value;
                SubType Attribute < Attributes;
              SubType Objet, Msg < Configuration;

     /* Construction process of words and phrases of a formal model*/
        Op < _: _ / _> : ObjetId ClassId Attributes -> Objet;
            Op _ = _ : AttributeId Value -> Attribute;
 Op _, _ : Attributes Attributes -> Attributes [ Assoc, Com, Id= Null] ;
```

Fig. 6.17 Definition of the signature of parallel systems.

The description of a real-time system involves the instantiation of Σ meta-types (Object, Attribute, Attributes, Msg and so on). In other words, it involves defining the objects which it is composed of as well as events or messages likely to affect its behaviour over time. It is clear that the direct manipulation of such formalism is tedious, and in the long run risks challenging the interest of the use of our approach. This formalism is particularly useful, as indicated in the preceding paragraph, for transcoding or automatic code generation. It is therefore not essential to make it visible to the user. A graphics editor can be used to describe the systems studied and the instantiation of different formalism meta-types.

Re-Writing Rules

An agent can be solicited for a service. This solicitation is represented by a message. The effect of a message on an agent is described in a rule. Such a message can only be emitted by agents of the same level or higher. A message can be intercepted by a rule and redirected towards any level. A rule expresses the occurrence of a communication in which *n* messages and *m* agents or objects are involved. All of the agents intervening in a rule must be of the same level. The general form of these rules is given in Figure 6.18.

```
                        /* Syntax */
          M1M2..Mp<O1: C1/ ListAt1>...<Oi: Ci/ListAti>
             <Oj: Cj/ ListAtj>...<Ok: Ck/ ListeAtk>
                             ==>
             <Oj: Cj/ ListAtj>...<Ok: Ck/ ListAtk>
             <Om: Cm/ ListAtm>...<On: Cn/ListAtn>
                        Mq ... Mr [ T]

                       /* Effects */
   M1 messages  ..., Mp are suppressed after the execution of the rule
          The states of objects oj, ..., Ok are modified
Objects O1, ..., Oi which only appear on the left part are suppressed.
              New objects Om, ..., On are created.
             New messages Mq, ..., Mr are created.
               [ T] : is a temporal constraint.
```

Fig. 6.18 General form of re-writing rules.

An object is represented using this syntax by the term <ObjectId: C\listAt>. Object Id is the object identifier. *C* represents the class of the object. ListAt is a list of conditions of the object attributes. Finally, *T* expresses a maximal time constraint.

This general rule format enables all the problems of communication and synchronization between objects to be expressed at a very high abstraction level (declarative level: see logic programming languages such as Prolog).

A rule indicates that the system passes from the state at instant *t* indicated by the left part to the state at instant *t'* defined by the right part. A rule can be activated when all of the messages of the left part are present and when all of the conditions of the object attributes in the right part are satisfied. The rules describe the effects of events associated to messages (transition). Finally, *T* expresses a temporal constraint of transition using one of the following primitives: Before(*t*): *m*, After(*t*): *m*, During(*t*,*t'*): *m* or Within(*t*): *m* (where *t* and *t'* are expressions and "*m*" a message which is generated if the constraint is not satisfied.

Architecture and Interface of a Control Sub-System

To consolidate this phase, we advise the reader to use the graphics editor, the principle of use of which conforms to the ideas stated below. It enables a *descending* description of the control sub-system in terms of agents (Fig 6.19).

At a given abstraction level, the user must describe the state variables or attributes of the corresponding agent (for example, the State attribute of agent A). Level 0 corresponds to the control and supervision sub-system of the system studied. It is called the *global* agent. This agent contains the set of agents associated to resources identified during phase 1 (for example agents O1, O2, O3, O4 are components of the global agent A). The interface of each agent is also described: it is composed of input and output messages and of the visible state variables (e.g., the Number characteristic is a visible attribute of the agent O1). Finally, for each agent the number of instances must be indicated. By default, it is equal to one.

Visible Attributes

To respect the encapsulation principle, the attributes and agents of inferior levels are neither normally visible nor accessible at a given level. However, in many situations, the expression of decision rules requires encapsulated information across state attributes or variables. To enable access to this information, the user must declare the corresponding attributes as visible (public). For example, in Figure 6.19, `Speed` is a visible attribute for the agent O4. For more clarity, an attribute represents a variable of the physical sub-system, indicated by a sensor in the case of automated production systems, or a logic object variable in the case of more standard applications.

Behaviour

In the preceding phase the static aspects of the control sub-system are described in terms of agents and interconnections *between agents*. The sub-system logic remains to be defined. This objective is achieved by assigning a set of rules to each agent which describe how the different events associated with messages modify its state.

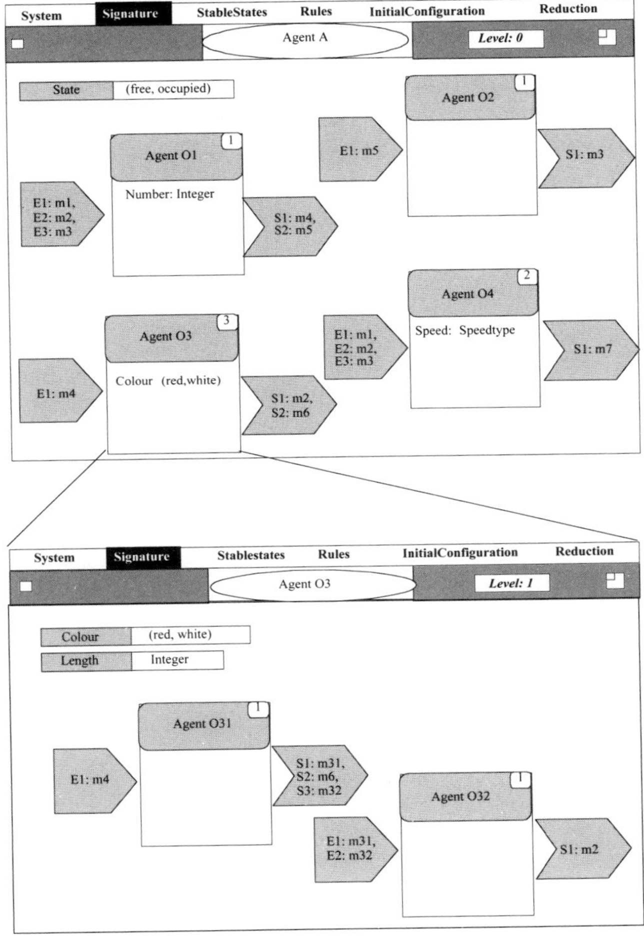

Fig. 6.19 Example of a system description.

First Stage

For each input message, the attributes which condition whether it is accepted are determined. These attributes can be simple attributes of the level agents, or visible attributes of agents intervening in their composition. The effective consideration of a message can in fact be subject to conditions particular to these attributes. For example, the interface of agent A in Figure 6.19 is composed of message m1 on input. The list of conditions on the characteristics which condition the interception of m1 could be the following:

```
{(State = free), (O1.Number>10), (O4.Speed < 50)}
```

Each list enables the object concerned to be grouped into a single rule called a synchronous rule:

```
m1<A:C1A/State=free,…><O1:C1O1/Number>=10>04<:C1O4/Speed<50>
==>.(1)
```

The right part of the rule needs to be completed to specify the effect of the occurrence of the message on the system: modification of the level agent attribute values or the agents composing them, emission of messages or events.

This rule is said to be synchronous because it expresses a global condition which is concerned with the attributes of several agents (objects) of the same level. The rule can only be triggered if all of the conditions are satisfied at the same time. Note that this rule can also be written in the following standard format:

```
IF (A.State=free)AND (O1.Number>=10) (AND O4.Speed<50) THEN …(2)
```

The reader familiar with expert systems will recognize the general form of the expression of knowledge rules. Nevertheless, form (1) is preferred to form (2) because it enables better condition location and encapsulation. All of the conditions necessary to trigger a rule, and relative to the same object are grouped together. Furthermore, other relevant information, such as the agent type, are also linked to the triggering conditions of the rule. This type of information will be particularly useful for the *phase of automatic code generation* of the application in an object-oriented programming language (C++) or other (ADA, VHDL).

Second Stage

In this stage, the messages which represent the same list of conditions are grouped together. The respective right parts are therefore fused to form one single rule. For example, the two rules:

```
m1<A:C1A/State=free,…><O1:C1O1/Number>=10>04<:C1O4/Speed<50> ==>.
RightPart(m1)
m4<A:C1A/State=free,…><O1:C1O1/Number>=10>04<:C1O4/Speed<50> ==>.
RightPart(m4)
```

can be fused into a single rule:

```
m1m4<A:C1A/State=free,…><O1:C1O1/Number>=10>04<:C1O4/Speed<50> ==>
RightPart(m1) RightPart(m4)
```

The fusion is only carried out for *synchronous* rules where m1 and m4 are necessary for the simultaneous execution of RightPart(m1) and RightPart(m4).

Third Stage

The third stage involves determining internal functioning and asynchronous rules. First, following the two preceding stages, there may remain messages which figure in the output interface of an object and which are not generated by any of the rules displayed (for example, message m2 of the object O2 in Figure 6.19). In this case, an expert agent must be associated which generates the messages in question. The possibility of transforming certain synchronous rules into a set of asynchronous rules can then be studied, to increase the degree of parallelism in the system.

The informed reader will have understood that a rule enables the expression of a *system transition law* which takes account of the current state of the system, events which occur and specifies the changes and modifications to be carried out on the system state.

6.4.3.2 An Example of Complex System Specification

As an illustration, we first apply the specification approach to a true system. Then we will outline the main points of the Prolog III code generation process.

Description of the System to be Studied

The example chosen is a workshop (Fig. 6.20).

Type A products enter the machining centre. They pass through milling and then the turning operation. Type B products enter into the system via a conveyor belt. The two parts are then fitted together, then separated to be painted.

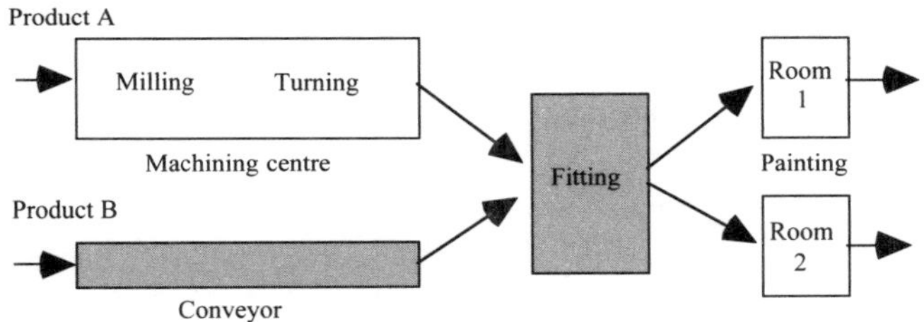

Figure 6.20 Example of a workshop.

The operation time in each centre must correspond to a workshop range (in units of time).

	Milling	Turning	Fitting	Painting
Part Type A	15	22	12	5
Part Type B			12	5

The time on the conveyor belt is estimated at three units. Figure 6.21 gives the hierarchy of system objects according to our methodology.

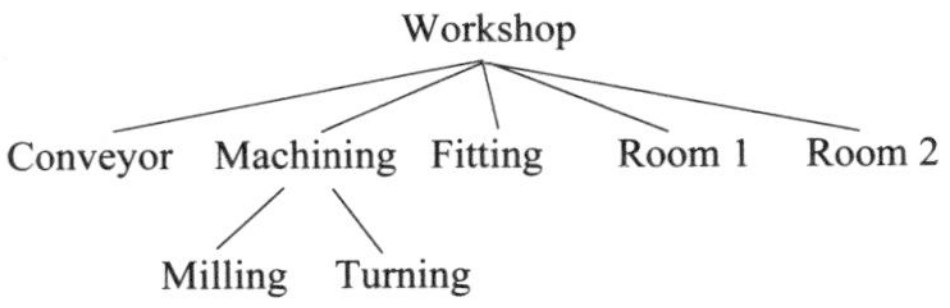

Fig. 6.21 Hierarchy of system objects.

Consider that each centre possesses a state variable called E whose value will be `empty` or `occupied`. This static description of the system is reached using the graphics editor introduced in the preceding section. Each sub-system is associated an agent.

```
- WS for workshop
- MC for machining centre
    - MI for milling centre
    - TU for turning centre
- FI for fitting centre
- PR for painting rooms, with two object instances
    - PR.1
    - PR.2
```

Figure 6.22 gives an example of the description session of this system with the editor.

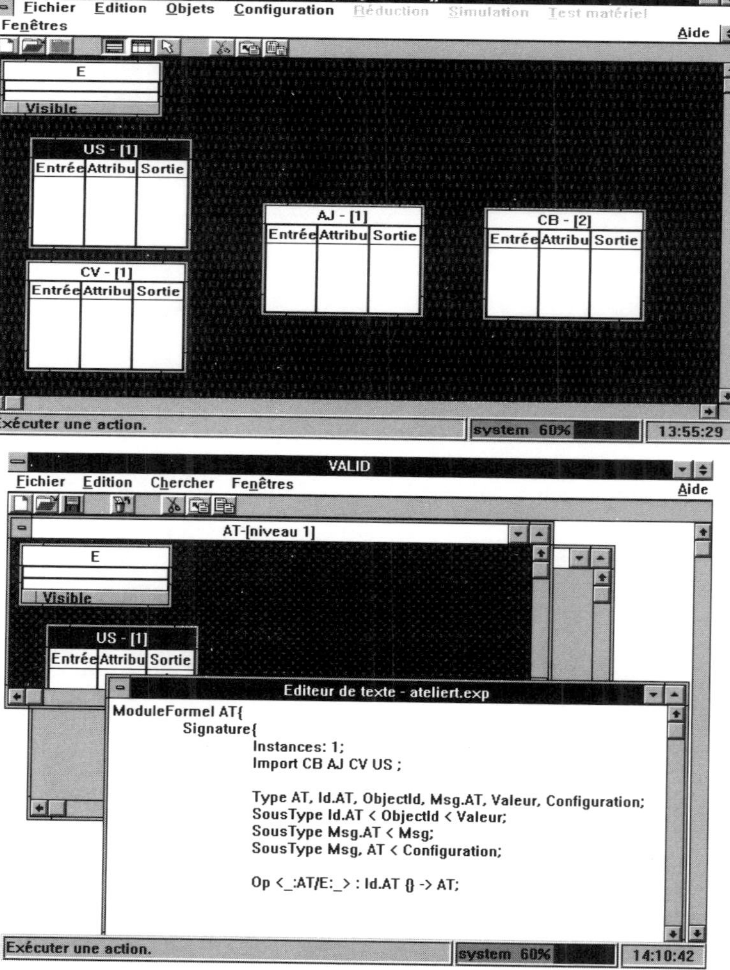

Fig. 6.22 A specification session with the graphic editor.

6.4.3.3 *Pivot Textual Formalism*

From the graphic description of the system, made using the editor, it is necessary to generate a textual abstract description which accurately reflects the composition and structural links between the different system components. It must also provide a precise description of the dynamics of the system by using the deduction or re-writing rules. This description must follow the encapsulation principle and must also be the result of the integration of logical and algebraic specification (axiomatic/algebraic), to enable the static description of systems as well as their passage from one phase to another (hence the description dynamic).

This textual description is not obligatory and the reader wishing to move to the next phase of Prolog III code generation can ignore this part.

The study of a system includes an *abstract representation* or a *model*. This representation is composed of a set of definitions, and a set of relations. The definitions enable the identification of elements constituting the model or the *static part* of the system, and the relations specify the interactions between these elements; the *dynamic part* of a system. Therefore,

> A system is seen as a set of elements in interaction, that it agrees to render explicit by a modelling process.

The fundamental idea is to identify and represent a real world system or entity by a *formal module* (see formal approaches in Section 6.1).

The textual description in the form of formal system modules, introduced earlier (Fig. 6.20) is given in Figure 6.23.

```
Formal Model WS{
Signature {
Instances:1;
Import PR FI CV MC;
Type WS, ID.WS<ObjectID, Msg.WS, Value, Configuration;
SubType ID.WS<ObjectId<Value;
SubType Msg.WS<Msg;
SubType Msg, WS<Configuration;
OP<_:WS/E:_>: Id.WS{}->WS;
Op (contents of_of_value for_):Object Id.WS ObjectId->Msg.WS;
Op (contents of_is_for_):Object Id Value ObjectId->Msg;
Op (put_of_to_): Object Id.WS Value->Msg.WS;
};
Rules{
Var T:Id.WS;
R1:<[T]:WS/E:'empty'>==>(factory input) (conv input <[T]:WS/E:'oqp'>;
R2:(exit)(exit)<[T]:WS/E:'oqp'>==><[T]:WS/E:'empty'>;
    }
}
```

```
FormalModelWS.MC {
Signature{
Instances:1;
Import MI TU;
Type MC, Id.MC, ObjectID, Msg.MC, Value, Configuration;
SubType Id.MC<ObjectId<Value;
SubType Msg.MC<Msg;
SubType Msg.MC<Configuration;
Op<_:MC/E:_>: Id.MC{}->MC;
Op(contents of_of_value for_):ObjectId Id.MC ObjectId->Msg.MC;
Op(contents of_is_pour_): ObjectId ValueObjectId-> Msg;
Op(put_of_to_): ObjectId Id.MC Value-> Msg.MC;
};
Rules{
Var U:id.MC;
R1:(fact input)<[U]:MC/E:'empty'>==> (mill input)<[U]:MC/E:'oqp'>;
R2:(turn output)<[U]:MC/E:'oqp'>==> (B fit input)<[U]:MC/E:'empty'>;
}
}
```

```
FormalModuleWS.MC.MI{
Signature{
Instances:1;
Type MI, Id.MI, ObjectId, Msg.MI, Value, Configuration
SubType Id.MI <ObjectId<Value;
SubType Msg.MI < Msg;
SubType Msg.MI < Configuration;
Op<_:MI/E:_>:Id.MI{}->MI;
Op(contents of_of_value for_): ObjectId Id.Fr ObjectId->Msg.MI;
Op(contents of_is_for_):ObjectId Value ObjectId->Msg;
Op(put_of_to_):ObjectId Id.MI Value->Msg.MI;
};
Rules{
Var F:Id.MI;
R1:(mill input)<[F]:MI/E:'empty'>==> (mill underway)<[F]:MI/E:'oqp'>;
R2:(mill underway)<[F]:MI/E:'oqp'>==>(turn input)
<[F]:MI/E:'empty'>[during(15)];
}
}
```

```
FormalModuleWS.MC.TU{
Signature{
Instances:1;
Type TU, Id.TU, ObjectId, Msg.TU, Value, Configuration
SubType Id.TU <ObjectId<Value;
SubType Msg.TU < Msg;
SubType Msg.TU < Configuration;
Op<_:TU/E:_>:Id.TU{}->TU;
Op(contents of_of_value for_): ObjectId Id.TU ObjectId->Msg.TU;
Op(contents of_is_for_):ObjectId Value ObjectId->Msg;
Op(put_of_to_):ObjectId Id.TU Value->Msg.TU;
};
Rules{
Var T:Id.TU;
R1:(turn input)<[T]:TU/E:'empty'>==> (turn underway)<[T]:TU/E:'oqp'>;
R2:(turn underway)<[T]:TU/E:'oqp'>==>(turn exit)
<[T]:TU/E:'empty'>[during(22)];
}
}
```

```
FormalModuleWS.CV{
Signature{
Instances:1;
Type CV, Id.CV, ObjectId, Msg.CV, Value, Configuration
SubType Id.CV<ObjectId<Value;
SubType Msg.CV<Msg;
SubType Msg.CV<Configuration;
Op<_:CV/E:_>:Id.CV{}->CV;
Op(contents of_of_value for_):Object Id.CV ObjectId->Msg.CV;
Op(contents of_is_for_):ObjectId Value ObjectId->Msg;
Op(put_of_to_):Object Id Id.CV Value->Msg.CV;
};
Rules{
Var V:Id.CV;
R1:(conv input)<[V]:CV/E:'empty'>==>
            (conv underway)<[V]:CV/E:'oqp'>;
R2:(conv underway)<[V]:CV/E:'oqp'>==>(A fit input)
            <[V]:CV/E:'empty'>[during(3)];
}
}
```

```
FormalModuleWS.FI{
Signature{
Instances:1;
Type FI, Id.FI, ObjectId, Msg.FI, Value, Configuration
SubType Id.FI<ObjectId<Value;
SubType Msg.FI<Msg;
SubType Msg.FI<Configuration;
Op<_:FI/E:_>:Id.FI{}->FI;
Op(contents of_of_value for_):Object Id.FI ObjectId->Msg.FI;
Op(contents of_is_for_):ObjectId Value ObjectId->Msg;
Op(put_of_to_):Object Id Id.FI Value->Msg.FI;
};
Rules{
Var A:Id.FI;
R1:(A fit input)(B fit input)<[A]:FI/E:'oqp'>==>
            (fit underway)<[A]:FI/E:'oqp'>;
R2:(fit underway)<[A]:FI/E:'oqp'>==>
            (paint input)<[A]:FI/E:'empty'>[during(12)];
}
}
```

```
FormalModelWS.PR{
Signature{
Instances:2;
Type PR, Id.PR, ObjectId, Msg.PR, Value, Configuration
SubType Id.PR<ObjectId<Value;
SubType Msg.PR<Msg;
SubType Msg.PR<Configuration;
Op<_:PR/E:_>:Id.PR{}->PR;
Op(contents of_of_value for_):ObjectId Id.PR ObjectId->Msg.PR;
Op(contents of_is_for_)ObjectId Value ObjectId->Msg;
Op(put_of_to_):ObjectId Id.PR Value->Msg.PR;
};
Rules{
Var B:Id.PR;
R1:(paint input)<[B]:PR/E:'empty'> ==>(paint underway)<[B]:PR/E:'oqp'>;
R2:(paint underway)<[B]:PR/E:'oqp'> ==>
            (output)<[B]:PR/E:'empty'>[during(5)];
}
}
```

Figure 6.23 Formal description of a workshop.

The example chosen is significant for more than one reason:

- It breaks down several hierarchical object levels (which will enable the multi-level exchange of messages to be displayed);
- It integrates the notion of time in the part manufacturing ranges (implementation and checking of time constraints);
- The symbolic objects "painting room" admits two instances (verification of generic properties by object instantiation).

On the other hand, the relative simplicity of the definition of inference rules and their limited number (two rules per object) can be seen. More complex definitions could have been expected. Recall that this textual form was introduced specifically to facilitate communication between the different modules of an environment of the design of discrete event systems, particularly automatic code generation given the wealth of information that it contains. Under no circumstances should the user directly manipulate such formalism which requires perfect control of the syntax and semantics. If we introduced it, it is purely to draw the readers' attention to the necessity of a complete pivot description sufficiently rich to facilitate the passage between the different phases of the software development cycle.

6.4.4 Simulation of Complex System Behaviour

Conforming to the graphic representation of a system or an agent such as that already introduced in Figure 6.7 and which was consolidated in the editor (Fig. 6.22), a complex system or agent can be represented by Figure 6.24:

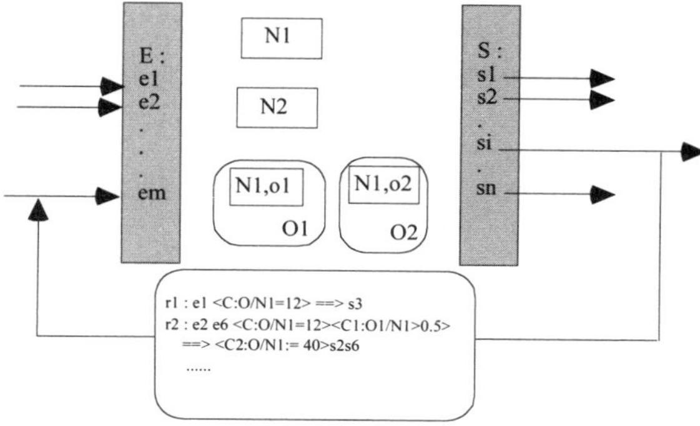

Fig. 6.24 Graphical representation of a complex system.

The only difference compared to Figure 6.7 is the accounting for the visible attributes of composite sub-systems, and the expression of the dynamics of the system using rules. In other words, in addition to its own variables, the system must integrate the visible and therefore accessible variables of its different sub-systems, necessary for the specification of its dynamics. The dynamics of a system are therefore easily expressed using the rules introduced. This definition is recursive and is applied to sub-systems. The new version of the simulation algorithm for complex discrete event systems is given in Figure 6.25.

```
Simulate_Discrete_Event_Reactive_Systems
  {
   T current simulation time;
   Dt the calculation step;
   T the simulation horizon;
   N(t) the vector of system state variables at time t;
   E(t) the vector of input flow variables at time t;
   S(t) the vector of output flow variables at time t;
   R   the set of deduction rules of the system;
   S = { E(0), N(0), NO(0)} initial state of the system;
   O the set of sub-systems
   NO the set of visible sub-system state variables (attributes)
   EO(t) the vector of variables of sub-system input traffic at time  t
   SO(t) the vector of variables of sub-system output traffic at time  t
   t = 0;
   S(0) = f(R, S); /* activate the rules whose conditions have been verified*/
 As long as t + Dt < T
     Faire
    N(t + Dt) = f(E(t), N(t), S(t), NO(t), SO(t), R);
This algorithm is recursively applied to each element of O
    S(t + Dt) = f(E(t), N(t), S(t), NO(t), SO(t), R);
    E(t) = f(E(t), N(t), S(t), NO(t), SO(t), R);
    t = t + Dt.

End as long as
  }
```

Figure 6.25 Simulation algorithm for the behaviour of SED complexes.

Unlike combinatorial and simple discrete systems, complex discrete event systems have a textual description generated in the *pivot* language introduced in the preceding section. Given the complexity and the large number of sub-systems (which are fully complex systems), it is simpler to manage and manipulate a textual description than analysis tables. A global and synthetic view is provided by the editors' graphic description, which is more than sufficient to use for the analysis and comprehension of the system and its structure.

The description in the pivot language particularly acts as a means of communication between the graphics editor and the other components of the environment (simulation code generator for performance evaluation, the Prolog III specification and validation control code, the application code for a real-time executive: ADA, C++...).

Every station likely to receive or transmit information is modelled and represented by an FIP variable. Even within a station, a variable is represented by an abstract object which possesses its own attributes. They describe the principal characteristics of the station.

Compared to discrete systems, it is necessary to:

- Manage the activation of the different sub-systems constituting the global system;
- Include visible variables and sub-systems in the vector state N variables;
- Manage sub-system *internal interconnection* flows.

6.4.4.1 Validation of the Behaviour of Systems Studied Using Prolog III

A simple inference motor (reduction motor) of an order 0 system expert can be used to allow the user to check the specifications developed previously under the graphics editor. Nevertheless, it is preferable to use Prolog III because it is a language which has the advantage of permitting programming with constraints, and considerably facilitates the implementation of temporal constraints on transitions. It also enables structural constraint formulation on the different objects of the system.

Specification validation therefore involves submitting the system description in terms of Prolog agents or objects (facts base) and deduction rules (rule base) to the Prolog III system. Each test session is based on the *scenario* notion.

A scenario is a predicted development of the behaviour of the system from an initial state to a final state (a system state being represented by the values of the attributes of instantiated agents constituting the true system).

The user therefore indicates the states in which the system should be found at the beginning of the scenario (initial state) as well as at the end of the scenario (final state). If it is able, it also shows a list of undesirable system states for this scenario.

It is possible to verify the global behaviour of the system specified but also, in the case of complex systems, to conduct a *validation* increasing by level. In this case it is enough to indicate to the motor the name of the agent to consider as the root (departure point) and, of course, to provide it with a scenario (initial and final stages) adapted to this agent.

Verification involved the control of:

- dead locks: the reduction process can no longer develop and remains blocked in a configuration which is not that foreseen by the user;
- unwanted infinite cycles: the system unexpectedly reduces the same set of rules in a cyclic manner and the motor achieves the maximum number of inferences indicated by the user;
- the impossibility of reaching the final state desired by the user;
- passage via an undesirable state (when the user has provided a list of undesirable states).

6.4.4.2 Generation of Prolog III Simulation Programs

The design of the Prolog III program is limited to the specialization of the generic model in Figure 6.24, for each system agent. To do this, each formal model (or graphic object if a formal intermediary is not used) is linked to a Prolog predicate which carries the same name and whose general form is given in Figure 6.26.

```
SystemName(1,<E>.<N>.<S>) ->
InitialStateSystemName(<E>.<N>.<S>)
        SubSystem1(1,<E1>.<N1>.<S1>)
        SubSystem2(1, <E2>.<N2>.<S2>)
 ...
         SubSystem(1, <En>.<Nn>.<Sn>)
            ,{ <E1>.<N1>.<S1>= F(<E>.<N>.<S>),
    ....
     <En>.<Nn>.<Sn>= F(<E>.<N>.<S>)};

SystemName (t,<E>.<N>.<S>) ->
 SystemName(t-1,<E'>.<N'>.<S'>)
 TransitionSystemName(t-1,<E'>.<N'>.<S'>,<E>.<N>.<S>)

          SubSystem1(t,<E1>.<N1>.<S1>)
 SubSystem2(t,<E1>.<N1>.<S1>)
  .....
 SubSystemn(t,<E1>.<N1>.<S1>)
  ,{ <E1>.<N1>.<S1>= F(<E>.<N>.<S>),
    ....
    <En>.<Nn>.<Sn>= F(<E>.<N>.<S>),
    t>1};

InitialState SystemName (<E0>.<N0>.<S0>) ->;

TransitionSystemName (t,e',e) -> activateRule(t,e',e)
   ,{ e' =<E'>.<N'>.<S'>,e=<E>.<N>.<S>};

activateRule (t,e',e) ->
  ,{ e' =<E'>.<N'>.<S'>,e=<E>.<N>.<S>,
     triggerRule1,
     actionrule1,
                 temporalconstraint1(t)};
 ...

 activaterule(t,e',e) ->
  ,{ e' =<E'>.<N'>.<S'>,e=<E>.<N>.<S>,
     triggerRulek,
     actionrulek,
                 timeConstraintk(t)};
```

Fig. 6.26 The Prolog III generic version of a simulation model of the dynamics of complex real-time systems.

This predicate appeals to the predicates of all sub-systems used by the current system (list of formal modules imported).

The main program predicate is the *dynamic* predicate which is independent of the system studied. Its principal task is to design the list or the path of system states for a given simulation horizon. The list is constructed from the initial state. `Dynamic` starts by calling the `machining0` predicate which provides the initial system state, it then calls the `path` predicate to construct the list of states. The `path` predicate has two forms. The first halts recurrence when the length of the path is equal to zero. The second form enables the design by concatenation of the list by adding a new element obtained by the application of the transition rules of the system studied (call to the `machining` predicate) on the current state.

In addition to the construction of the list of states of the path, the `path` predicate also enables time management.

In this way the general form of a Prolog III simulation agent is:

```
      Agent0(0,E) ->
              InitialStateAgent(StateAgent)
              InternalAgent(0,InternalStateAgent)
              ...
      Agent(t,E1, E2) ->
              activateRuleAgent1(t,E1,TP1)
              ...
              activateRuleAgentk(t,E1,TPk)
              InternalAgent1(t,TPk_AG1, E2)
              ...
              InternalAgentn(t,TPk_Agn,E2)
      ,{TPk =<TPk_AG1,…,TPk_Agn>},
   activateRuleAgentk(t,E1,TPk)->
                                                  /*Connection matrix*/
                                         /*Conditions for triggering the rule*/
                              /*Actions of the rule on the state: transformations*/
                                                  /*Temporal constraint*/
               /*Transfer or recopy the rest of the current state which is not affected
                                                  by the transformation*/
   activateRuleAgentk(t,E1,TPk)
                        /*The second form of each rule uniquely involves generating
                                   a new state by simple recopy of the current state*/
   ...
   InternalAgentn(t,TPk_Agn, E2) ->
                                                          /*First form*/
   InternalAgentn(t,TPk_Agn, E2) ->
                                                          /*Second form*/
```

As mentioned above, the departure point for the generation process of the Prolog III code is the graphic description or the textual description obtained from the graphic description.

For reasons of clarity and simplicity, the following section presents the description of the hierarchical sub-system (or arborescence) MACHINING which is composed of two internal agents MILLING and TURNING. The extension of the description of the example as a whole is easy, the principle being the same: instantiation of the generic model above.

```
/*******************************************************/
/* PROGRAM PROLOG III TO SIMULATE THE DYNAMICS */
/* OF THE MODELLING OF DISCRETE EVENT SYSTEMS  */
/*******************************************************/
dynamic(t,<E>,L) ->          /*Prolog rule which enables the system path to be designed
                                       / *from the initial state, for a t horizon*/
MACHININGO(0,E)
     Path(t,<E>.L,t);
Path(0,<E>,T) ->;
Path(t,<E1>.<E2>.L,T) ->
     MACHINING(T-t+1, E1, E2)
     Path(t-1, <E2>.L,T)
,{t>1};
/*******************************************/
/* MA Agent                                */
/*******************************************/
MACHININGO(0,<e0>) ->
     InitialstateMACHINING(<C_MA>)
     MILLINGO(1,<C_MI>)
     TURNINGO(1,<C_TU>)
,{e0=<C_MA>.<C_MI>.<C_TU>,
C_MA=<E_MA>.<N_MA>.<S_MA>.<P_M_MA>.<P_E_MA>,
C_MI=<E_MI>.<N_MI>.<S_MI>.<P_M_MI>.<P_E_MI>,
C_TU=<E_TU>.<N_TU>.<S_TU>.<P_M_TU>.<P_E_TU>,
E_MA=<a_inputMA>,N_MA=<b_stateMA>,<S_MA>=<c_inputAJ_B,d_inputMI>,
P_M_MA=<>,P_E_MA=<>,
E_MI=<e_inputMI>,N_V_MA=<f_stateMI>,<S_MI>=<g_inputTU>,
P_M_MI=<h_Mitaking_place>,P_E_MI=<>,
E_TU=<i_inputTU>,N_V_TU=<j_stateTU>,<S_TU>=<k_outputTU>,
P_M_TU=<l_Tutaking_place>,P_E_TU=<>,

/************CONNECTION MATRIX************/
     e_inputMI = d_inputMI,
     in_inputTU = g_inputTU
/*******************************************/
                         };
initialstateMACHINING(<1,EMPTY,0,0>) ->;
MACHINING(t, E1, E2) ->
     activateruleMACHINING1(t,E1,E3)
     activateruleMACHINING2(t,E3,E4)
     MILLING(t,F4,F2)
     TURNING(t, T4,T2)
,{E1=<U1,F1,T1>, E2<U2,F2,T2>,E4=<U4,F4,T4>, U2=U4, t>0 };
activateruleMACHINING1(t,<<a, b, c, d>,<e, f, g, h>,<i, j, k, l>>,
<<m, n, o, p>,<q, r, s,t_1>,<v, x, y ,w>>) ->
,{

/************CONNECTION MATRIX************/
          q = p
          v = s
/*******************************************/
/*triggerruleMA1*/
a = t, b = empty,
/*actionruleMA1*/
  n = occupied, p = t,
/*timeconstraintruleMA1(t)*/
```

```
/*no constraint*/
/* transfer to the rest of the environment*/
m=a, /*n=b,*/ o=c, /*p=d,*/
/*q=e,*/ r=f, s=g, t_1=h,
/*v=i, */x=j, y=k, w=1,
t>0};
activateruleMACHINING1(t,<<a, b, c, d>,<e, f, g, h>,<i, j, k, l>>,
  <<m, n, o, p>,<q, r, s,t_1>,<v, x, y ,w>>) ->
,{
/************CONNECTION MATRIX************/
            q = p
            v = s
/*******************************************/
/*Transfer Context*/
m = a, n=b, o=c,p=d, /*q=e,*/ r=f, s=g,t_1=h, /*v=i,*/ x=j, y=k,
w=1,
t>0};

activateruleMACHINING2(t,<<a, b, c, d>,<e, f, g, h>,<i, j, k, l>>,
<<m, n, o, p>,<q, r, s,t_1>,<v, x, y ,w>>) ->
,{
/************CONNECTION MATRIX************/
            q = p
            v = s
/*******************************************/
/*triggerruleMA2*/
g = t, b =occupied,
/*actionruleMA2*/
  n = empty, o = t+1,
/*timeconstraintruleMA2(t)*/
/*no constraint*/
/*transfer to the rest of the environment*/
m=a, /*n=b,*/ /*o=c,*/ p=d,
/*q=e,*/ r=f, s=g, t_1=h,
/*v=i,*/ x=j, y=k, w=1,
t>0};
activateruleMACHINING2(t,<<a, b, c, d>,<e, f, g, h>,<i, j, k, l>>,
  <<m, n, o, p>,<q, r, s,t_1>,<v, x, y ,w>>) ->
,{
/************CONNECTION MATRIX************/
            q = p
            v = s
/*******************************************/
/*Transfer Context*/
m = a, n=b, o=c,p=d, /*q=e,*/ r=f, s=g,t_1=h, /*v=i,*/ x=j, y=k,
w=1,
t>0};
/*******************************************/
/* MI Agent                                */
/*******************************************/
MILLING(0,<e, F, G, H>) ->
InitialstateMILLING(<e, f, g, h>);

MILLING(t, e1, e2) ->          activateruleMILLING1(t,e1,e3)
                               activateruleMILLING2(t,e3,e2) ,{ t>0};
InitialstateMILLING(<0,empty,0,0>) ->
```

```
InitialstateMILLING1(t,<e, f, g, h>,<q, r, s,t_1>) ->
,{
/*triggerruleMI1*/
e = t, f = empty,
/*actionruleMI1*/
r =occupied, t_1= t,,
/*timeconstraintruleMI1(t)*/
/*no constraint*/
/*transfer context*/
q = e, s = g,
t>0};
activateruleMILLING1(t,<e, f, g, h>,<q, r, s,t_1>) ->
,{
q=e, r=f, s=g, t_1=h,
t>0};
 activateruleMILLING2(t,<e, f, g, h>,<q, r, s,t_1>) ->
,{
/*triggerruleMI2*/
h = T, f =occupied,
/*actionruleMI2*/
r =empty, s = t+1,
/*timeconstraintruleMI2(t)*/
T= t-3, T>0,                                          /*during(3)*/
/*transfer context*/
q = e, t-1= h,
t>0};

activateruleMILLING2(t,<e, f, g, h>,<q, r, s,t_1>) ->
,{
q=e, r=f, s=g, t_1=h,
t>0};

/********************************************/
/*          TU Agent                        */
/********************************************/

TURNING(0,<i, j, k, l>) ->
InitialstateTURNING(<i, j, k, l>);

TURNING(t,e1,e2) ->activateruleTURNING1(t,e1,e3)
                    activateruleTURNING2(t,e3,e2)
 ,{ t>0};
InitialstateTURNING(<0,empty,0,0>) ->;
activateruleTURNING1(t,<i, j, k, l>,<v, x, y ,w>) ->
,{
/*triggerruleTU1*/
i = t, j = empty,
/*actionruleTU1*/
x = occupied, w = t,
/*timeconstraintruleTU1(t)*/
/*no constraint*/
/*transfer context*/
v = i, y = k,
t>0};
activateruleTURNING1(t,<i, j, k, l>,<v, x, y ,w>) ->
,{
```

```
v=i, x=j, y=k, w=1,
t>0};
 activateruleTURNING2(t,<i, j, k, l>,<v, x, y ,w>) ->
,{
/*triggerruleTU2*/
l = T, j =occupied,
/*actionruleTU2*/
x =empty, y = t,
/*timeconstraintruleTU2(t)*/
T= t-2, T>0,                                            /*during(2)*/
/*transfer context*/
v = i, w= 1,
t>0};
activateruleTURNING2(t,<i, j, k, k>,<v, x, y, w>) ->
,{
v=i, x=j, y=k, w=1,
t>0};
```

The fundamental idea to study the behaviour or dynamics of a real-time multi-agent system, and to manage the causality and communication via messages and events, is to associate a *list of states* to the system, which represents its configuration. For each system agent, it contains the list of input events, the list of output events, the list of state variables visible from the outside (simulation of the transmission of data by the exchange of messages), the list of private state variables and lists of internal events called service events. The following Prolog lists represents the configuration of the above machining unit example:

```
C_MA=<E_MA>.<N_MA>.<S_MA>.<P_M_MA>.<P_E_MA>, /*state of the MACHINING
agent*/
C_MI=<E_MI>.<N_MI>.<S_MI>.<P_M_MI>.<P_E_MI>, /*state of the MILLING agent*/
C_TU=<E_TU>.<N_TU>.<S_TU>.<P_M_TU>.<P_E_TU>, /*state of the TURNING agent*/
E_MA=<a_inputMA>,            /*input messages and events for the MACHINING agent */
N_MA=<b_stateMA>,                         /*state variables of the MACHINING agent*/
<S_MA>=<c_inputAJ_B,d_inputMI>,/*the output messages and events for the
MACHINING agent*/
P_M_MA=<>,                  /*private internal messages for the MACHINING agent*/
P_E_MA=<>,                    /*private state variables for the MACHINING agent*/
E_MI=<e_inputMI>,N_V_MA=<f_stateMI>,<S_MI>=<g_inputTU>,
P_M_MI=<h_MItaking_place>,P_E_MI=<>,
E_TU=<i_inputTU>,N_V_TU=<j_stateTU>,<S_TU>=<k_outputTU>,
P_M_TU=<a2_TUtaking_place>,P_E_TU=<>,
```

C_MA represents the configuration or the true environment of the agent (unit) MACHINING. It is composed of a list of E_MA input events, the list of N_MA state variables and so on. Because it integrates two agents, TURNING and MILLING, their respective environments are also included in the global environment of the MACHINING agent: e0=<C_MA>.<C_MI>.<C.TU>.

6.4.4.3 *The Implementation of Interactions and Temporal Limitations*

The fundamental idea for the exchange of events between agents is to date stamp the events. An event is only valid during Δt, that is to say, it is available during this time interval. Outside of this interval it becomes obsolete, except for certain situations, such as the management of temporal constraints. For example, the instruction: `n2_outputTU=t`, in the second rule of the TURNING agent, indicates that this event has been generated and carries the date stamp or the date *t*. It is therefore available in the global configuration, and can be intercepted and processed in the interval $t + \Delta t$ (next path on the arborescence of the system). In contrast, the following condition of the second rule of the TURNING agent: `a1_Tutaking_place=T, T=22, T>0`, relies on an event which has been triggered in the past. It has effectively been generated by the first rule of the agent and expresses that the agent has started the machining operation. This operation lasts 22 time units, hence it is necessary to refer to the instant the operation started, in the time constraints of the rule which expresses the duration of the transition or the triggering of the rule.

To express a transition duration limit (`during(s))`), it is generally sufficient to write a condition on the triggering event of the action:

```
EV_START = T, T = t-s, T>0
```

We leave it up to the reader to express other types of temporal constraints such as:

- EVERY(s) : which expresses a period of *s* units of time;
- BEFORE(s): which expresses the date limits to trigger an event;
- AT(s): which represents the instant of an event being triggered.

Finally, it is important to remember that time management is carried out exclusively at the level of the recursive predicate *dynamic*. This recurrence enables it to construct the system path until horizon *T*. Each e_i state contains the last date it occurred for each message, if the occurrence took place, otherwise 0. It also contains the last value of each state variable.

The simulation program for the dynamics of the discrete event systems above can be easily rewritten in any programming language supporting recurrence, such as C, C++, ADA, PASCAL and so on.

6.4.4.4 Implementation of a Validation Scenario

The principal use of the preceding program is to study the development of the system state to check:

- The periodicity of the system. System development presents cyclic sequences conforming to the specifications:

  e0.e1.e3.e4.e5.e0.e1.e3.e4.e5.e0.e1.e3.e4.e5.e0.e1.e3.e4.e5

  The sequence e0.e1.e3.e4.e5 represents a schedule or a sequence for the manufacture of a part or a set of parts in a production unit for example. The e_i state contains the different events occurring in the system during this stage, as well as the value of the different state variables of the system;
- The effect of a faulty system component (agent) on overall functioning, to improve the degree of reliability and resistance to faults: functioning in reduced mode.

- Detection of a deadlock in the system. This situation is easily detectable: the development of the system state is no longer possible from a specific e_j state. This state provides the elements necessary to locate the error and detect the faulty developed component(s).
- The study of the effect of the transition time of each rule or transition in the system on the development of the system and its performance.

The first use for the model is to check the initial state of the system. The variable p is instanced by Prolog and gives the initial configuration of each system agent:

```
>dynamic(1,p);
{p =
<<<0>,<empty>,<0,0>,<>,<>>,<<0>,<empty>,<0>,<0>,<>>,<<0>,
<empty>,<0>,<0>,<>>>}
>
```

The program can then be asked for the path of the system for a $t = 8$ horizon for example:

```
>dynamic(8,p);
{p =
<<1,empty,0,0>,<0,empty,0,0>,<0,empty,0,0>>,              /*e0*/
<<1,occupied,0,1>,<1,occupied,0,1>,<0,empty,0,0>>,        /*e1*/
<<1,occupied,0,1>,<1,occupied,0,1>,<0,empty,0,0>>,        /*e2*/
<<1,occupied,0,1>,<1,occupied,0,1>,<0,empty,0,0>>,        /*e3*/
<<1,occupied,0,1>,<1,empty,5,1>,<0,empty,0,0>>,           /*e4*/
<<1,empty,6,1>,<1,empty,5,5>,<5,occupied,0,5>>,           /*e5*/
<<1,empty,6,1>,<1,empty,5,5>,<5,occupied,0,5>>,           /*e6*/
<<1,empty,6,1>,<1,empty,5,5>,<5,empty,7,5>>,              /*e7*/
<<1,empty,6,1>,<1,empty,5,5>,<5,empty,7,5>>,              /*e8*/
<<1,empty,6,1>,<1,empty,5,5>,<5,empty,7,5>>,              /*e9*/
<<1,empty,6,1>,<1,empty,5,5>,<5,empty,7,5>>,              /*e10*/
>}
```

In this scenario, we have restricted the milling time limit to 3 units, and the turning operation to 2 units. Note that in the e4 state the constraint has been satisfied and rule number two of the MILLING agent has been triggered. This is the same for the constraint for rule number two of the TURNING agent which was triggered after two time units (E7).

We leave the reader to discover the different possibilities of the program and its use for the study of diverse situations, notably the determination of temporal constraint values.

6.5 CONCLUSION

The approach presented in this chapter has the advantage of generating formal specifications from graphical descriptions. It integrates different stages of the development cycle of multi-agent systems with the important ability to control their properties and evaluating their performance.

The specification process is based on the theory of formal systems. It respects certain principles of the object-oriented approach. The distributed configurations are formed from communicating agents and messages. The system studied is described in terms of hierarchical agents, messages between agents and rules of behaviour: compound agents.

Control and validation involves carrying out a syntactical reduction by using the PROLOG III system. From a configuration or an initial fact base which represents the instantiation of different system objects, the definition of the initial state by initializing their traits, and the creation of messages which form part of the initial stable state of the system (stimuli), the reduction process aims to develop the system state towards another stable state. If this process does not succeed, the system description and its logic must be re-examined.

6.6 PROJECT 1: MODELLING DISTRIBUTED SYSTEMS

To end this chapter we give another more standard example of distributed system specification: a distributed file management system.

Presentation

In this example (Fig. 6.27), we use the approach given in the preceding paragraphs for the specification of a banking transaction system. On each site, there are *N* servers dedicated to the management of and access to the local bank files. To send a command, a client (workstation in an agency), whatever its location on the network, must reserve a server on the file site. The communication protocol between clients and servers is based on a two-phase client–server model:

- The initialization phase, where a client sends a request to locate and open a file. If the server is free on the file site it confirms its services.
- The dialogue phase, in which the client sends reading or writing requests to the server.

Two types of commands can be used. The first type of command (debtor and creditor) corresponds to asynchronous coupling between the client and the server. It is implemented by using a zero phase validation protocol (rules R2 and R4 of the Client module for example). The second type of command (transfer) requires strong synchronization between the two active entities. In this situation we use a single phase validation protocol (rules R5, R6, R7, R8, R9 of the Client module and rules R5 and R6 of the Server module).

In the Client module, rule R5 is used to transform the message (*transfer S from C to CV*) into two other messages: (connection to the server of C for M) and (*connection to the server of CV for M*) which are necessary to establish a connection with the servers C and CV. The message (*await transfer of S from C to CV*) is used to indicate that the rule has been triggered; in this way no conflict can occur with another parallel activation of the same rule. Rules R6 and R7 guarantee synchronization of validation execution of remote transactions. Rules R8 and R9 are used to manage the potential cancellation of the two remote transactions.

In the Server module, rules R4 and R5 enables the immediate execution of the corresponding operation without a validation phase. Rule R6 clearly shows that on

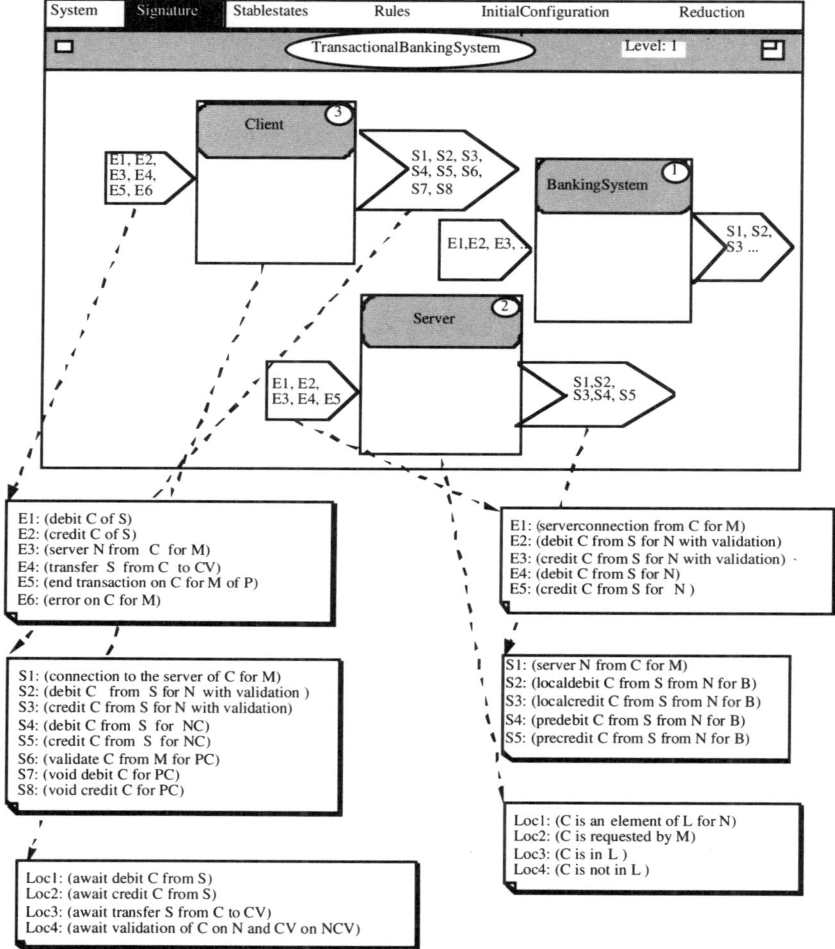

Fig. 6.27a Overall model of a bank transfer system.

reception of the message (*debtor C of S for N*), this addresses a local *pre-debtor* command to the file server. It then creates a new protocol type object (process) to continue the dialogue with the client and ensure the validation phase of the transaction. Rules R6 and R7 are necessary for transactions which involve several remote transactions (debited or credited). The validation of the overall transaction requires the synchronization of local validation procedures.

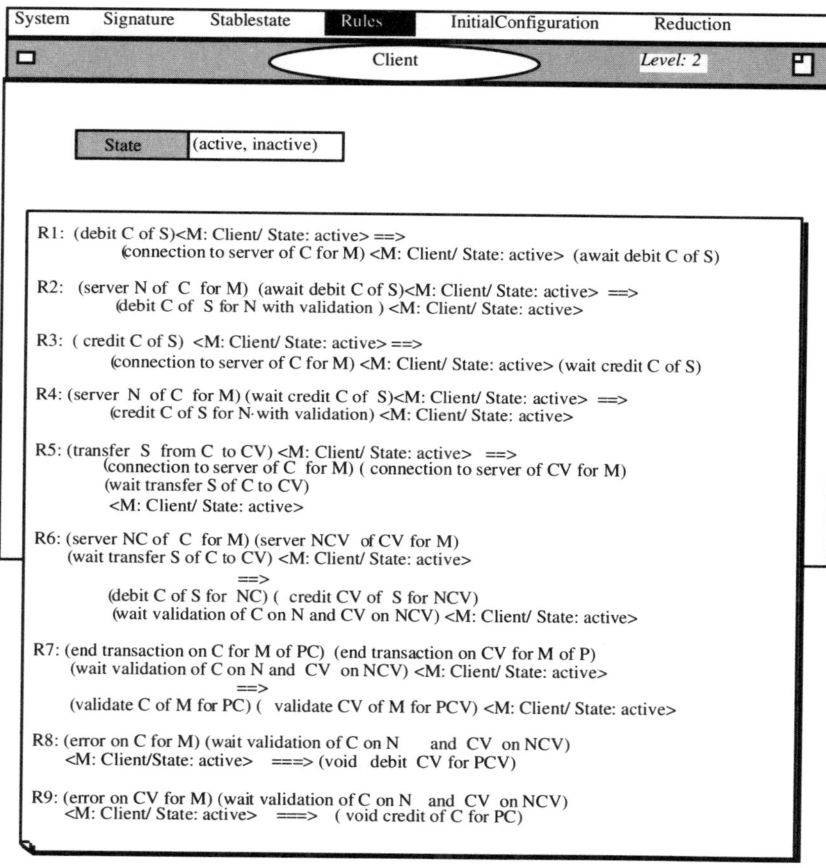

Fig. 6.27b Model of the client object.

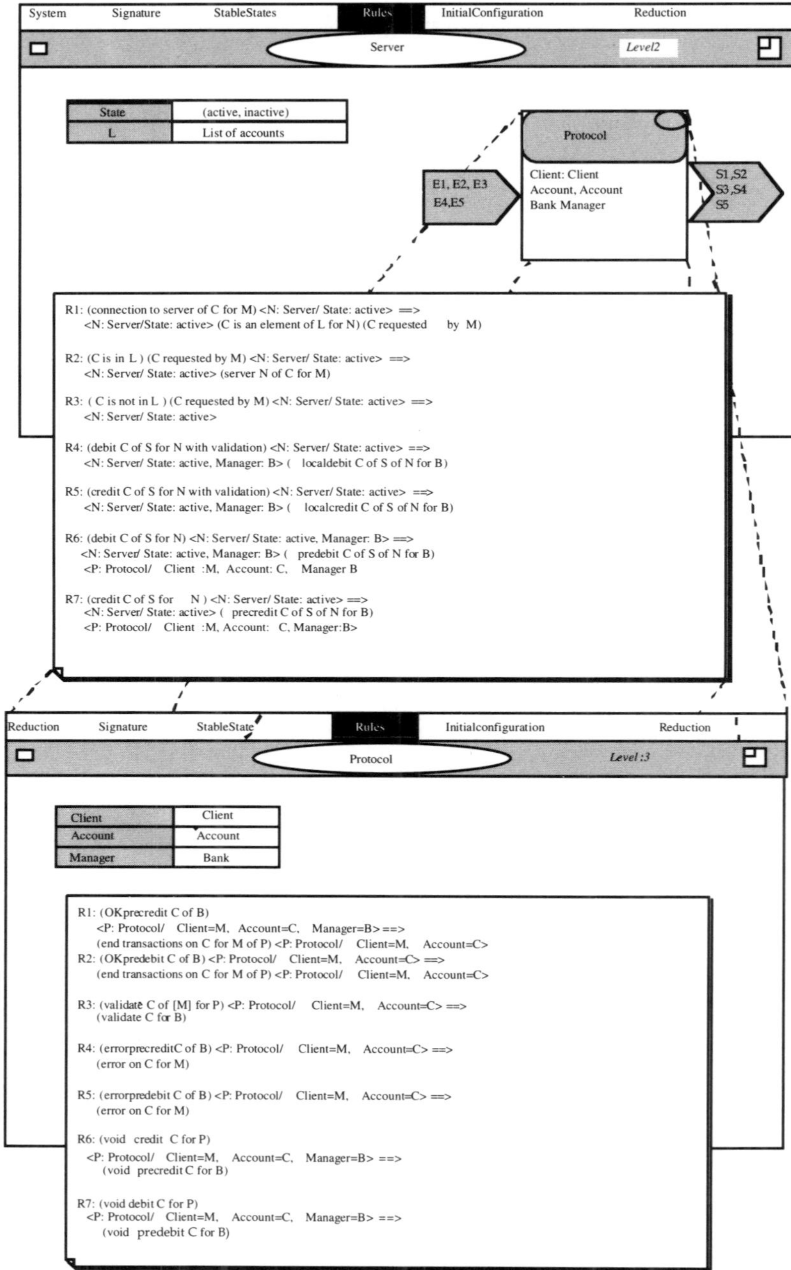

Fig. 6.27c Models for server and protocol objects.

From these descriptions, the editor can automatically manage the formal module for each part of the system. Figure 6.28 gives the formal module corresponding to the Client agent.

```
FormalModule Client {
  Signature{
      Type Client, Id.Client, ObjectId, Msg.Client,Msg, Value,
Configuration;
      Subtype Id,Client < ObjectId < value;
      Subtype Msg.Client < msg;
      Subtype Msg, Client < Configuration;

      Op <_: Client /state:_> : Id.Client Nat -> Client;
      Op(contents of_of_value for_) ObjectId.Client ObjectId
      Op(contents of_is_for__) Objectid Value ObjectId -> Msg;
      Op(Place_of_to_) : ObjectId Id.Client Value->Msg.Client

      Op(debit_from_): ObjectId Nat -> Msg.Client;
      Op(connection server of_for_) : ObjectId Id.Client -> Msg;
      Op(await debit_from_) : ObjectId Nat -> MsgClient;
      Op(server_of_for_) : ObjectId ObjectId Id.Client ->
                           Msg.Client;
      Op(debit_from_for_with validation): ObjectId Nat ObjectId
                           -> Msg;
      Op(await credit_from_) : ObjecttId Nat -> Msg.Client;
      Op(Credit_from_for_with validation): ObjectId Nat ObjectId
                           -> Msg;
      Op(transfer_from_into_): Nat ObjectId ObjectId ->Msg,Client;
      Op(await transfer_from_into_): Nat ObjectId ObjectId
                           -> Msg,Client;
      Op(debit_from_for_): ObjectId Nat ObjectId -> Msg;
      Op(credit_from_for_): ObjectId Nat ObjectId -> Msg;
      Op(await validation of_on_and of_on_): ObjectId ObjectId
                           ObjectId ObjectId -> Msg.Client;
      Op(end operation of_for_of_): ObjectId.Client ObjectId
                           -> Msg.Client;
      Op(Validate_from_for_): ObjectId Id.Client ObjectId -> Msg;
      Op(error on_for_): ObjectId Id.Client -> Msg.Client;
      Op(cancel debit_for_): ObjectId ObjectId -> Msg;
      Op(cancel credit_for_): ObjectId ObjectId -> Msg;
      Op_ _ : Configuration Configuration -> Configuration[Assoc,
                           Comm, Ident=Nil];
            };
Rules{
      Var M: id.Client
      Var C, CV, NC, NCV, PC, PCV,A,O : ObjectId
      Var S,V : Value;

R01: (contents of A of C for 0) <C: Client/ A=V,…> ==>
                   <C: Client/ A=V,...> (contents of A is V for 0)
R02: (Place A from C to V) <C: Client/ A=S,..> ==> <C: Client/
A=V,.>
R1: (debit C from S) <[M]: Client/State: active> ==>
  (server connection from C for [M] <[M]: Client/state: active>
await debit C from S)
R2: (server [N] from C for [M]) (await debit C from S)<[M]: Client/
State: active> ==>
(debit C from S for [N] with validation ) <[M]: Client/ state:
active>
R3:   (credit C from S) <[M]: Client/ state: Active> ==>
```

```
   (server connection from C for [M]) <[M]: Client/ state: active>
 (await credit C from S)
 R4: (server [N] of C for [M] ) (await credit C from S)<[M]: Client/
 state: active> ==>
  (credit C from S for [N] with validation) <[M]: Client/ state:
 active>
 R5: (transfer S from C to CV) <[M]: Client/ state: active>
  (server connection from C for [M]) (server connection from CV for
 [M])
 (await transfer of S from C to CV)
 <[M]: Client/ state: active>
 R6: (server [NC] from C for [M]) (server [NCV] from CV for [M])
 (await transfer S from C to CV) <[M]: Client/ state: active> ==>
 (debit c from S for [NC]) (credit CV from S for [NCV])
 (await validation from C on [PN] and from CV on [PCV]) <[M]:
 Client/ state: active>
 R7: (end operation of C for [M] of [PC]) (end operation on CV for
 [M] from [PCV])
 (await validation from C on [PC] and from CV on [PCV])<[M]: Client/
 state: active> ==>
 (validate C from [M] for [PC]) (validate CV from [M] for [PCV})
 <[M]: Client/ state: active>

 R8: (error on C for [M]) (await validation of C on [PC] and of CV
 on [PCV])
  <[M]: Client/ state: active> ==> (cancel debit CV for [PCV])
 R9: {error on CV for [M]) (await validation of C on [PC] and of CV
 on [PCV])
  <[M]: Client/ state: active> ==> (cancel credit C for [PC])
        }
 }
```

Fig. 6.28 Example of a formal model generated automatically by the editor.

The reader will have certainly understood the necessity for the use of variables in messages!

Principle of the Automatic Generation of a Distributed Program

The process for the generation of a distributed program from a description carried out using the graphics environment VALID, uses an anonymous communication model. This communication module uses the client–server approach to implement a communication model and distributed execution prototype. There is one channel manager per site. In the distributed case, the sites are organized according to virtual ring architecture. The manager is composed of two dedicated servers: an intrasite communication server, and possibly a network server for intersite communication. For more details see Chapter 2.

The generated rewriting system for each formal module essentially acts to implement an agent. A generated rewriting system is composed of a certain number of agents or communicating processes following the communication and distributed execution model presented in Chapter 2. The execution platform can, depending on the case, be a mono-processor system, a multi-processor system or a network of Unix stations.

1. *Transposition of the signature of a formal module*

The transposition of the static part of a formal module is a simple operation. Each module object designer represents the "static data" part of the corresponding management process ("stat" attribute in Figure 6.27 of the client processes for example). The different actions to be carried out are:

- associate a "father" process to the module;
- for each complex component or attribute whose module is imported, create the corresponding processes depending on the number of instances indicated;
- associate a global variable to each elementary attribute;
- connect the son processes to the father process using the channel associated to the local configuration;
- for each local message designer (its scope is the current level, this is the case for Frame Content_A_C_O of the client process in Figure 6.29), associate a Frame object to the server of the local channel. In the opposite case, the frame will be sent to the server of the superior level channel (this is the case for Frame Debtor_C_S_I in Figure 6.29).

2. *Transposition of the rules of re-writing a formal system*

This stage involves the following actions:

- For each visible attribute, associate a son process which integrates a *handler* for the interception of the updating messages. This handler is activated upon each reception of a message of this type. In this solution, the updating operations are considered higher priority than the reading operations.
- To each rule, associate a son process whose role is to wait until the messages which figure in the left part are present and that the conditions which rely on the attributes of objects in the right part are satisfied (process R1 in Figure 6.29). In the case where at least one condition is not satisfied, the messages are replaced in the channel server file.

```
#include <Channel.h>
#include <Process.h>
#include <Event>
#include <Handler>
....
Channel NFS;     /*Global channel to the objects of the NFS system*/
     ...
Process BankBase[N_BankBase]{
      Channel Bankbase;
```

```
       Do::{..};
       }

Client Process[i: 1..N_Client]{

/*static part of the process (given variables)*/
       enum state =(active, inactive);
       Channel Client;     /*channel back-up of the local
configuration*/
/*an interceptor frame corresponds to each extrenal message*/
Frame Content_A_C_O; Client.Filter("content of 'A' of Client[i] for
'O'", content_A_C_O);
Frame Place_A_C_V; Client.Filter("place 'A' of Client[i] to
'V'",place_A_C_V);
Frame Debit_C_S_I; NFS.Filter("debit 'C' from 'S' for Client[i]",
'Debit_C_S_I);
Frame Server_N_C_M; NFS.Filter("server 'N' of 'C' for'M'");
Frame AwaitDebit_C_S; Client.Filter("await debit 'C' from 'S');
Frame Credit_C_S; NFS.Filter("credit 'C' from 'S' for Client[i]");
Frame AwaitCredit_C_S; Client.Filter("await credit 'C' from 'S' for
Client[i]")
Frame  Transfer_S_C_CV; NFS.
Frame End_C_M_PC;
Frame Error_C_M;
Frame Await_C_PC_CV_PCV;


/*management process of visible attributes*/
Process R0
 {Item *msg;
   Handler R01
    {Item *msg;
     Place_A_C_V.Fifo.get(msg);
     Client.stat= msg[3];
     };
   ON Place_A_C_V.event R01;
   DO::{
       Content_A_C_O.Fifo.get(msg);
       Client.Put("content of" msg[1] "is" Client.state
"for" msg[3],



      };
    };

/*Execution process of re-writing rules*/
Process R1
 {Item *msg, *,msg1;
   DO::{Debit_C_S_I.Fifo.get(msg);
      Client.put("contents of state of Client [i] "for Client[i]");
      me.Fifo.get(msg1);
      if(msg1[2]=='active')
      {NFS.put("connection of server" msg[1] "for Client[i]"};
      Client.put("await debit" msg[1] "of" msg [2])}
Else NFS.put(msg);
```

```
        };
        }

        Process R2 {...};
        Process R3 {...};
        Process R4 {...};
        Process R5 {...};
        Process R6 {...};
        Process R7 {...};
        Process R8 {...};
        Process R9 {...};
};                                        /*end of client process*/
```

Fig. 6.29 System rewriting code for the bank transaction system.

It is important to note that all of the synchronization and parallelism problems are resolved by the use of two concepts: communication by the exchange of messages using channels, and Fifo files. The problems with concurrent access to common resources are also solved by the exchange of messages. This involves a totally distributed solution. Figure 6.30 gives the architecture of the execution model for the system associated to the bank transaction system.

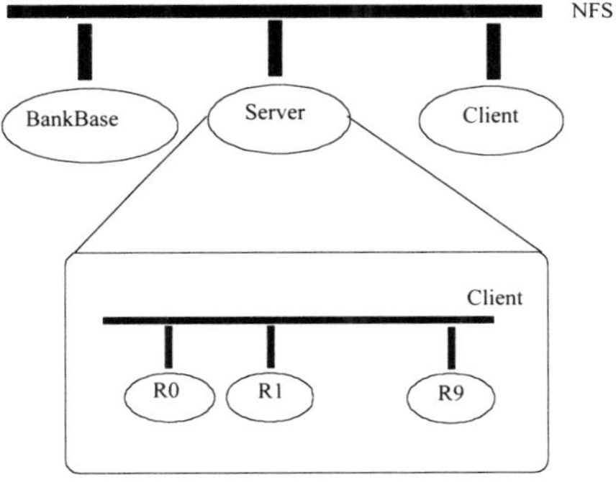

Fig. 6.30 Architecture of the rewriting system of the bank transactional system.

7. Parallel Image Processing

7.1 Presentation

This example is an illustration of the possibilities of distributing complex processes between different agents to substantially reduce the overall execution time of the application, especially in image processing and multimedia applications. The example in Chapter 3 shows how to implement a communication between several agents, the processing of which depends on the results of neighbouring agents. In addition, to this *horizontal communication* between slave agents, there still exists *vertical communication* between the master agent and the slave agents according to the master–slave model supported by PVM.

7.1.1 Function of the Master Agent

In this application, the role of the master agent can be summarized as follows:

1. cut the image to be generated into blocks of almost identical size;
2. create a matrix of $N \times N$ slave agents;
3. transmit the dimensions of the block of image to be generated to each slave agent;
4. collect the different blocks of slave agents and display them in an Xwindow.

The fundamental idea is to divide the Xwindow generated by the master agent into a matrix of $N \times N$ blocks. Each slave agent will therefore have the task of generating the contents of the corresponding block and transmitting it to the master for display. There is a bijection between the window zones and the agent slaves (Fig. 7.1). The master agent plays the role of a client process compared to the server X of the host system.

This application displays two types of interactions:

- client–server: the master demands the services of the server X to manage the display window for the image to be generated;
- master–slave: the master creates a set of agent slaves. Each slave will be responsible for the management and generation of part of the image (Fig. 7.1). The slaves are then destroyed.

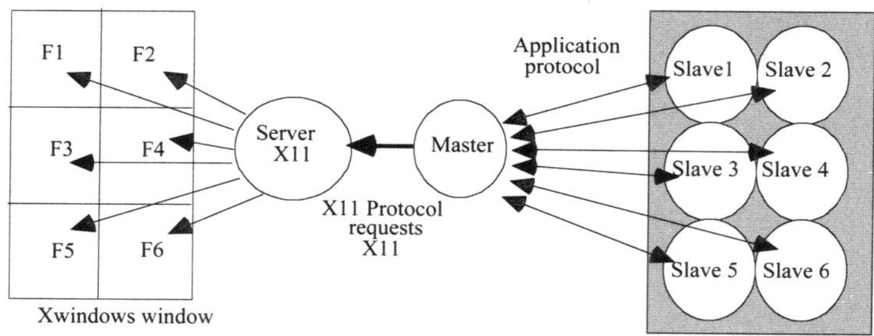

Fig. 7.1 Generation of an image by a set of agents.

7.1.2 Functions of Slave Agents

Each slave agent has the single role of generating the contents of the part of the window that is associated to it, following logical cutting. It must, in fact, generate the colour at each point (pixel) of its block. Calculation of the colour at each point depends on the nature of the image processing application. Where we are concerned, the processing of each agent is limited to calculating the colour of each point by using a simple calculation function which will be explained later. In this way, the processing generally carried out by a slave can be symbolized by the following simple algorithm:

```
Agent_i
     Somuchas Active Do
          Generate dialogue between the neighbouring agents to
     calculate Ψ(t);
          For each point x_j of my block b_i do
             x_j(t) = colour(Ψ(t), t);
          endfor
          transmit B_i(t) to the master;
     Endsomuchas
Endagent;
```

The "colour" function calculates the value (colour) of the pixel x_j at instant t depending on the Ψ context vector. This vector takes into account the initial conditions at the borders of the block at instant t (this relates to the example of heat propagation along a wire in Chapter 2 (Section 2.3.5) to be able to calculate the colour of the internal points of the block at instant t. The vector of the Ψ context generally requires communication with neighbouring agents to update itself before calculating the new values of the internal points. The colour function represents the *progression* or *development law* of any phenomenon: direction and displacement speed of an object in an animation image, simulating the progression of a natural phenomenon (clouds, desertification of certain regions, illness etc.). We have introduced the notion of time into the "colour" function because the image needs refreshing over time. The time interval is chosen depending on the nature of the application. These points will not be discussed any further as they fall outside the scope of this book.

What concerns us is that each agent uses a simple colour function which does not take account of either time (generation of a single image), or the Ψ context vector. The colour of a point corresponds to a value randomly determined in the following manner:

- Consider a polynomial function: `F(x) = x^3-1;`
- Use the Newton method to calculate the roots of F(x):

$$X_{n+1} = X_n - F(X_n)/F'(X_n)$$

- The colour(x) function calculates towards which root the Newton method converges for each initial x0 found in the definition field. The colour of point x corresponds to the number of the root approached by the method:

```
R1 = 1; r = (-1 + sqr(3)i)/2; r3 = (-1 -sqr(3)i)/2
```

The reader can question why we have chosen such a method to generate the colour of a point in a random manner. The answer is easy. In Chapter 1, we insisted on the fact that communication between the different agents of a distributed application is an exception compared to processing. In other words, it is essential that the communication time between agents is noticeably less than the agent's calculation time.

```
Σ time(communication) << Σ time(calculation)
```

If this rule is not respected, a distributed solution for a given problem loses all of its interest:

> The agent will spend more time managing communications instead of executing their processes.

The overall time used by the application (calculation time) becomes insignificant compared to the overall communication time. In this case, the distributed multi-agent approach becomes very detrimental compared to the centralized solution.

To conclude, we have used the Newton method in place of a simple random number generator to make the processes executed by the agents more significant (complex), and to therefore avoid any imbalance between the calculation time and the communication time.

The reader can replace them with any other process according to the needs of the application. The following corresponding program was written in C with PVM.

7.2 Implementation

7.2.1 The Master Agent Code

```
#include "pvm3.h"
#include <X11/Xlib.h>
```

```
#include <X11/Xutil.h>
#include <X11/Xkeysym.h>
#include <stdio.h>

#define SLAVE "newton.fjd"
#define MSGTYPE 0

/*-----------------------------------------------*/
/*          Function protocols                   */
/*-----------------------------------------------*/
void init_dist(void);
void recv_img(void);
/*----------------------------------------------------------*/
/*          Global variables concerning PVM                 */
/*----------------------------------------------------------*/
int nproc, ne;
int tids[100];
/*----------------------------------------------------------*/
/*          Global variables concerning the image           */
/*----------------------------------------------------------*/
static int dimx=240, dimy=240;
static int debx, deby, dx, dy;
static char * tab;
int       flag_cal=0;                /*flag for the image calculation*/
/*-----------------------------------------------*/
/*          Xwindow variables                    */
/*-----------------------------------------------*/
char             *tit_root = "Newton";
Display *display;
Window           root;               /*mother window of all other windows*/

GC               cg_cp;              /*graphical context for the definitive design*/
Colormap         cmap;               /*default table of colours */

                                     /*the indices of colour cells allocated in the cmap*/
unsigned long val_pixels[6];

int make_col = {DoRed | DoGreen | DoBlue};
unsigned long black, white;
int              nb_cell_def;        /*black and white colours */
int              depth_def;          /*number of colour cells by default*/
Xcolour colour
Drawable         image;              /*drawable content of the Pixmap*/
main(int argc, char ** argy)         /*start of master*/
{
 int i, j;

int                     screen;
XEvent           event;
unsigned long    mask_value;
XGCValues               values_gc;

XsizeHints              indic;
Char                    character[10];
KeySym           touch;

Int                     again;
Char                    rep;
```

```
/*------------------------------------------------------*/
/*          Connection to the server                    */
/*------------------------------------------------------*/
display = XopenDisplay(NULL);
if (!display) {
 fprintf(stderr, "impossible to open the display.\n");
 fprintf(stderr, "check that the variable display is initialized.\n");
 fprintf(stderr, "it must contain, for example: \"termx:0\"\n");
 exit(1);
}

printf("Grill[NxN] N = ");
scanf("%d", &nproc);

ne = pvm_spawn(SLAVE, (char**)0, 0, "", nproc*nproc, tids);
if( ne < nproc*nproc ){
 printf("trouble spawning slaves. Aborting. Error codes are:\n");
 for ( i=ne ; i<nproc*nproc ; i++) {
  printf("TID %d %d\n",i,tids[i]);
}
for( i=0 ; i<ne ; i++ ){
 pvm_kill( tids[i] );
}
pvm_exit();
exit();
}

                                  /*Distribution of image blocks*/

init_dist();

/*------------------------------------------------------------------------*/
/*          Consultation of some server X Characteristics                 */
/*------------------------------------------------------------------------*/
screen = DefaultScreen(display);
White = WhitePixel(display, screen);
Black = BlackPixel(display,screen);

/*---------------------------------------------------*/
/*          Allocation of colours                    */
/*---------------------------------------------------*/
/*consultation of certain information concerning the colour*/
depth_def = defaultDepth(display, screen);
printf("Work on a screen in %d bits \n", depth_def);

if (depth_def == 8) {
 nb_cell_def = DisplayCells(display, screen);
 cmap = DefaultColourmap(display, screen);

/*allocation of red, green and blue colours*/
if (XallocColourCells(display, cmap, False, NULL, 0, val_pixels, 4)){
/*if the allocation of colour cells is carried out easily*/
 if (!XParseColour(display, cmap, "indian red", &colour))
 {
  fprintf(stderr, "The IndianRed colour is not supported\n");
  val_pixels[0] = black;
}
```

```
else XStoreNamedColour(display, cmap, "indian red", val_pixels[0],
make_col);

if (!XparseColour(display, cmap, "navy blue", &colour))
 {
  fprintf(stderr, "The NavyBlue colour is not supported\n");
  val_pixels[1] = white;
}
else XstoreNamedColour(display, cmap, "navy blue", val_pixels[1],
make_col);

if (!XParseColour(display, cmap, "forest green", &colour))
 {
  fprintf(stderr, "The ForestGreen colour is not supported\n");
  val_pixels[2] = black;
}
else XstoreNamedColour(display, cmap, "forest green", val_pixels[2],
make_col);
 }
}

/*-----------------------------------------------------------------------------------------------*/
/*          Creation of the top-level window of the "Newton" name                               */
/*-----------------------------------------------------------------------------------------------*/
indic.x = 200; indic.y = 300;
indic.width = dimx; indic.height = dimy;
indic.flags = PPosition | PSize;
root = XCreateSimpleWindow(display, DefaultRootWindow(display),
indic.x, indic.y, indic.wdth,indic.height,
1, black, white);
/*definition of the standard properties of the top-level window for window management*/
XsetStandardProperties(display, root,
tit_root, tit_root, None, ergv, ergc,
&indic);
/*selection of interesting events for the top-level window*/
 XselectInput(display, root,
                        KepPressMask | ButtonpressMask
                        ExposureMask | StructureNotifyMask);

/*-------------------------------------------------------------- */
/*          Creation of a graphics design context                */
/*-------------------------------------------------------------- */
values_gc.foreground = black;
values_gc.backgroumd = white;
values_gc.line_width = 1;
values_gc.function = GXcopy;
mask_value - GCForeground | GCBackground | GCLineWidth | GCFunction;
cg_cp = XcreateGC(display, root, mask_value, &values_gc);

XMapRaised(display, root);

/*Creation of a Pixmap*/
image=XCreatePixmap(display,root,dimx,dimy,depth_def);
XSetForeground(display,cg_cp, white);
XFillRectangle(display,image,cg_cp,0,0,dimx,dimy);
```

```
Puts("press the end button to terminate");
Again = 1;
While (again)
{
 XNextEvent(display, &event);
 Switch (event,type)
 {
 case KeyPress :
  i = XLookupString(&(event.xkey), character, 10, &touch, 0);
  if (touch == XK_End) {
   again = 0;
   pvm_initsend(PVMDataRaw);
   pvm_pkint(&again, 1, 1);
   pvm_mcast(tids, nproc*nproc, MSGTYPE);
  }
  break;
 case Expose :
  if (event.xexpose,count==0)
   {
    if (flag_cal == 0) {          /*reception of the image generated if it is the first time*/
          recv_img();
          flag_cal = 1;
          }
          else
           XCopyArea(display, image, root, cg_cp,0,0,dimx,dimy,0,0);
       }
       break;
  case ConfigureNotify :
       if (event.xconfigure.window == root)
        {
         if ((dimy != event.xconfigure.height) ||
               (dimx != event.xconfigure.width) {
              dimy=indic.height = event.xconfigure.height;
              dimx=indic.width = event.xconfigure.width;

              XFreePixmap(display,image);
              Image=XcreatePixmap(display,root,dimx, dimy,depth_def);
              XSetForeground(display,cg_cp,white);
              XFillRectangle(display,image,cg_cp,0,0,dimx,dimy);

              init_dist();
              recv_img();
         }
     }
  }
}

pvm_exit();

XDestroyWindow(display,root);
XFreeGC(display, cg_cp);
XFreePixmap(display,image);
XCloseDisplay(display);
Return 0;
}
```

```
/*-----------------------------------------------------------------------------*/
/* 1. Distribution of window dimensions                                        */
/* 2. Dividing the image into nproc*nproc blocks                               */
/* with the calculation of co-ordinates of the top left corner                 */
/* and the size (which can be different) of each block                         */
/*-----------------------------------------------------------------------------*/
void init_dist()
{
 int divx, divy, restx, resty;
 int i, j;

/*Broadcast of general info*/
pvm_initsend(PvmDataRaw);
pvm_pkint(&nproc, 1, 1);
pvm_pkint(&dimx, 1, 1);
pvm_pkint(&dimy, 1, 1);
pvm_mcast(tids, nproc*nproc,MSGTYPE);

/*Calculation and broadcast of data for each block*/
divx = dimx / nproc; restx = dimx & nproc;
divy = dimy / nproc; resty = dimy & nproc;

for (i=0 ; i<nproc ; i++) {
 if (i<restx) {
  dx= divx+1; debx = i * dx;
}
else {
 dx = divx; debx = restx*(divx+1) + (i-restx)*divx;
}

for (j=0 ; j<nproc ; j++)
 {
  if (j < resty) {
        dy = divy+1; deby = j*dy;
        }
        else {
         dy = divy; deby = resty*(divy+1) + (j-resty)*divy;
        }
        pvm_initsend(PvmDataRaw);
        pvm_pkint(&debx, 1, 1);
        pvm_pkint(&deby, 1, 1);
        pvm_pkint(&dx, 1, 1);
        pvm_pkint(&dy, 1, 1);
        pvm_send(tids[i*nproc+j], MSGTYPE);
        }
 }
}

/*---------------------------------------------------------------*/
/*         Reception and display of the new image                */
/*---------------------------------------------------------------*/
void recv_img()
{
 char *pt;
 int xe, ye;
 int i, j;
```

```
 for (i = 0; i<nproc; i++)
  for (j=0; j<nproc; j++)
   {
/* Reception of an image block*/
       pvm_recv(-1, MSGTYPE);
       pvm_upkint(&debx, 1, 1);
pvm_upkint(&deby, 1, 1);
pvm_upkint(&dx, 1, 1);
pvm_upkint(&dy, 1, 1);

tab = (char *) malloc (dx*dy*sizeof(char));
pvm_upkbyte(tab, dx*dy, 1);
/*Displaying the received block*/
pt = tab;
for (xe=debx ; xe<debx+dx ; xe++)
 for (ye=deby ; ye<deby+dy ; ye++)
  {
       xSetForeground(display, cg_cp, val_pixels[*pt++]);
       XdrawPoint(display, root, cg_cp, xe,ye);
XdrawPoint(display, image, cg_cp, xe.ye);
        }
       /*       XcopyArea(display,image root,cg_cp,
    debx,deby,dx,dy,debx,deby);*/
       free(tab);
       }
}
```

7.2.2 The "newton.fjd" Agent Code

```
/*-----------------------------------------------------------------*/
/*      NEWTON method to calculate the roots of a function:        */
/*                     f(x)=x^3-1 */                               */
/*                     xn+1 = xn - f(xn)/f'(xn)                    */

/*-----------------------------------------------------------------*/

#include <stdio.h>
#include <errno.h>
#include <X11/Xlib.h>
#include <X11/Xutil.h>
#include <X11/X.h>
#include <X11/keysym.h>

#include "complex.h"
#include "functions.h"
#include "pvm3.h"

int master;

static char * tab;
static int dimx, dimy;

/*-----------------------------------------------------------------*/
/*      "Main" function of the Newton program                      */
/*-----------------------------------------------------------------*/
```

```
main(int argc, char **argv)
{
 int      debx, deby;
 int   dx, dy;
 int   nproc;
 int   msgtype = 0;
 unsigned int          xe, ye;                    /* screen coordinates*/
 unsigned int          c;                                   /* colour*/
 complex_t             x;

master = pvm_parent();

while (1) {
/*Reception of general information*/
        pvm_recv(master, msgtype);
        pvm_upkint(&nproc, 1, 1);
        pvm_upkint(&dimx, 1, 1);
        pvm_upkint(&dimy, 1, 1);

        /* nproc = 0 : end of execution*/
        if (nproc == 0) break;

/*Reception of the start co-ordinates and the size of my block*/
        pvm_recv(master, msgtype);
        pvm_upkint(&debx, 1, 1);
        pvm_upkint(&deby, 1, 1);
        pvm_upkint(&dx, 1, 1);
pvm_upkint(&dy, 1, 1);

/*calculation of the image block */
        tab = (char*) malloc(dx*dy*sizeof(char));
        c=0;
        for (xe=debx; xe<debx+dx; xe++)
         for (ye=deby; ye<deby+dy; ye++) {
        x.re = (double)XMIN + ((double)xe*(XMAX-XMIN))/((double)dimx);
x.im = (double)YMAX - ((double)ye*(YMAX-YMIN))/((double)dimy);
        tab[c++] = colour(x, 0, 1, 2);
         }

/*send the data of my block of the image to the master*/
pvm_initsend(PvmDataRaw);
pvm_pkint(&debx, 1, 1);
pvm_pkint(&deby, 1, 1);
pvm_pkint(&dx, 1, 1);
pvm_pkint(&dy, 1, 1);
pvm_pkbyte(tab, dx*dy, 1);
pvm_send(master, msgtype);

free (tab);
 }

 pvm_exit();
 return 0;
}
```

7.2.3 Manipulation Modules for Complexes

```
#include "complex.h"

/*-------------------------------------------------------------------*/
/* mult_comp  : calculate the product of two complexes              */
/*      input : "a", "b" and the address of "c"                     */
/*      output: "c" = a*b                                           */
/*-------------------------------------------------------------------*/
void mult-comp( complex_t a, complex_t b, complex_t *c)
{
       c->re = a.re * b.re - a.im * b.im;
       c->im = a.re * b.im + a.im * b.re;
}
/*-------------------------------------------------------------------*/
/* mult_scal    : calculate the product of a scalar and a complex  */
/*      input  : the scalar "a", "b" and the address of "c"         */
       /*      output : "c" = a*b                                   */
/*-------------------------------------------------------------------*/
void mult-scal(double a, complex_t b, complex_t *c)
{
       c->re = b.re * a;
       c->im = b.im * a;
}


/*-------------------------------------------------------------------*/
/*  sum    : add the two complexes together                         */
/*  input  : "a", "b" and the address of "c"                        */
/*  output : "c" = a+b                                              */
/*-------------------------------------------------------------------*/
void sum(complex_t a, complex_t b, complex_t *c)
{
       c->re = a.re * b.re;
       c->im = a.im * b.im;
}

/*-------------------------------------------------------------------*/
/* norm2    : calculate the norm of the square of a complex         */
/*   input  : the address of "a",                                   */
/*   output : ||a||^2                                               */
/*-------------------------------------------------------------------*/
double norm2(complex_t a)
{
       return (a.re * a.re + a.im * a.im);
}

/*-------------------------------------------------------------------*/
/* division :divide the two complexes                               */
/*    input : the address of "a", "b" and "c"                       */
/*   output : "c"=a/b                                               */
/*-------------------------------------------------------------------*/
void division(complex_t a, complex_t b, complex_t *c)
{
       double n;
       b.im = -b.im;
```

```
        n = norm2(b);
        mult_comp(a,b,c);
        c->re = c->re / n;
        c->im = c->im / n;
}
```

7.2.4 Implementation of the Calculation Function for the Colour of a Pixel (x,y)

```
#include "complex.h"
#include "function.h"

/*-------------------------------------------------------------*/
/* colour   :calculate towards which root the Newton method     */
/*           converges for each initial x0 found in the         */
/*           definition field                                   */
/*    input : the address of "x=x0"                             */
/*   output : colour of "x" corresponding to the number         */
/*            of the root approached by the method              */
/*            r1 = 1; r2 = (-1 + sqrt(3)i) / 2;                  */
/*            r3 = (-1 - sqrt(s)i) / 2                          */
/*-------------------------------------------------------------*/
unsigned int colour
            (complex_t x, unsigned long c1, unsigned long c2,
unsigned long c3)
{
 complex_t              x2, x3. Xd;
 double          err;
 unsigned int    iter;
 char            c;

 iter = 0;
 do {
        mult_comp(x, x, &x2);
        mult_comp(x, x2, &x3);
        x3.re = x3.re - 1;
        err = norm2(x3);

        xd.re = 1.0; xd.im = 0.0;
        division(xd, x2, &x3);                  /*x3 = 1/x^2*/
        mult_scal(2./3., x, &x2);               /*x2 = 2x/3 */
        mult_scal(1./3., x3, &xd);              /*xd = 1/3x^2*/
        sum(x2, xd, &x);
        iter++;
  } while (err > EPSILON);
  if (x.re >0) return (c1);
  else if (x.im > 0) return (c2);
  else return (c3);
}
```

8. *Client–Server Applications under Unix*

8.1 Presentation

This involves developing tools to facilitate the implementation of real-time applications under UNIX. This example, which is a solid illustration of the notions and concepts introduced in the preceding chapters, presents the implementation of a library of primitives enabling the easier description of the temporal limitations in *soft real-time applications*. These primitives must authorize the following operations:

- limit the execution time of a task or agent;
- trigger an agent on a specific date;
- trigger an agent periodically.

Incidentally, the program in Figure 8.1 gives a very simplistic example of the use of these primitives to describe, with an elevated abstraction level, the complex temporal limitations in an interception system control program, and in the control program for the protection of space in a protected area.

This example presents the main forms of temporal constraints, and proposes a primitive for each:

- EVERY: enables the periodic execution of a process;
- AT and BEFORE: defines the instant of execution of an action;
- WITHIN: associated to the three preceding primitives and enables the substitution of one task whose duration exceeds a certain limit, with another task.

The principal loop in this program represents a periodic task whose period is fixed by the "`period`" variable. It is woken at the start of each new period. It starts by requesting the position, direction and speed of an unidentified flying object by the call to methods (in the object-oriented programming sense) of the remote logic intelligent sensor (`radar`). In the case where radar provides non-empty co-ordinations, which is the affirmation of the existence of an object which is unidentified and unauthorized to fly in the protected airspace, it calculates the point of firing t of the missile before proceeding to direct the firing gun to minimize the risk of missing the object. This last operation must be carried out before instant t.

```
PROGRAM missileInterception;
{
     Time firingInterval;            /* interval of firing*/
     time period;                /* period of radar polling*/
     radar SystemDetection;      /* object radar */
     missile canon;               /* objet canon             */
     coordinates r;               /* coordinates of the object*/
     direction d;                 /* current direction of the object */
     float v;                     /* speed of the flying object */
      ........;
     EVERY(period)                /* polling cycle */
     {
          r = SystemDetection.object_position;
          d = SystemDetection.object_direction;
          v = SystemDetection.object_speed;
          if(r<>nil)

               time t;                       /* instant of firing*/
               t = InstantTir(r,d);
               BEFORE (t, cannon.orientation, alarm);
               AT(t, canon.ActiveMissile)
                         WITHIN(IntervalFire, alarm);
               }
          }
     }
```

Fig. 8.1 Example of a real-time application subjected to strong temporal constraints.

If it misses, an alarm signal is triggered. The last system realized by the principal task in a period, asks the host system to trigger the `Active Missile` mode of the `canon` object to fire at instant *t*. The execution of this operation (method) must be carried out in a time interval that takes account of the technological limitations of firing a missile. If the missile is not fired then an alarm signal is generated.

In this way, these high-level primitives considerably simplify setting up temporal limitations in a real-time application. The designer does not have to manipulate a large number of temporizers and counters, which are often the source of fatal errors in this context. There is a perfect analogy between these temporal constraint management primitives and monitors. These primitives effectively represent the same abstraction level compared to low-level time management tools (timers etc), which represent monitors, and parallel access and synchronization management tools ("Test and Set" (TAS) instruction of 680×0, semaphores etc.).

In the following sections, we give a detailed description of the different parts of the temporal constraint management system in a standard context: UNIX. It can be partly applied to VxWorks, or any other real-time executive, to act as a basic tool for the design of *critical real-time applications.*

8.1.1 Functional Architecture of the System to be Implemented

Figure 8.2 gives the functional architecture of the temporal constraints management system following the design rules of distributed applications according to the client–server model presented in Chapter 4.

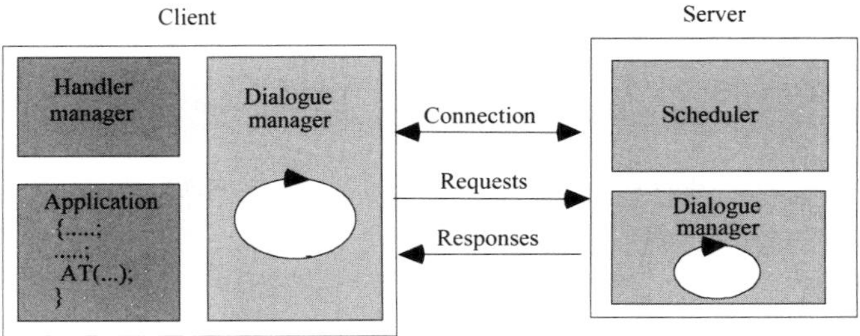

Fig. 8.2 Functional architecture of the system.

The role of the server is to generate specific events and instants near to the clients, which are the system service program users. The arrival of an event must trigger the execution of a precise task at the client end. When an application requests that at instant *t* the $\mathtt{op}_1$ task be executed, it transmits the data *t* to the server. The server must then give a response at instant *t*. It is the arrival of this response which triggers the execution of the $\mathtt{op}_1$ task within the application. This is a solution which can also be used with mono-processor as well as multiprocessor hardware architecture (a transputer machine for example).

8.1.2 Client–Server Communication Protocol

This is a three-phase protocol:

1. *The connection phase:* this is triggered by the client on receipt of the first call to a real-time primitive. A connection request is inserted into the connection file awaiting a server. This file will be regularly checked by the server which accepts each connection in this way.

2. *The dialogue phase:* it relies on two types of exchanges which are the transmission of a request and the transmission of a response. The information transmitted by a client upon dispatching a request indicates the point at which the client must execute a particular task. It is at this point that the server must transmit the response to the client. The response transmitted by the server plays the role of an alarm for the client to enable the imperative execution of a task. It is necessary that the changes between the clients and the server be carried out asynchronously in order to avoid time loss, which would compromise the validity of the system.

    - *AT and BEFORE:* the server transmits the response to the client and then suppresses the request.
    - *EVERY:* The server must periodically transmit the responses (the elements related to this primitive are indefinitely kept by the server).

3. *The termination phase:* this enables the suppression of the connection. Termination can be normal or abnormal. The client sends a specific request to the server. Having been warned in this way, the server can then close the connection and eventually suppress the client's requests.

8.2 Implementation

8.2.1 Scheduling Temporal Constraints

The semantic analysis of the `AT`, `BEFORE` and `EVERY` primitives reveals that these functions rely on a more elementary operation: `IN(instant_min, instant_max, action)`. This involves triggering the action task in a time interval [instant_min, instant_max]. The correspondences can be written as follows:

- `AT(instant, action);` ⇔ `IN(instant, instant, action);`
- `BEFORE(instant, action)` ⇔ `IN(0,instant, action);`
- `EVERY(instant, action)` ⇔ `repeater {wait(instant); IN(0,0, action); };`
- `BEFORE(instant1, action1) WITHIN(instant2, action2);` ⇔ `IN (0,instant1, action1); or IN(instant2, instant2, action2);`

It is important to note that the two final IN instructions are *exclusive* because `action1` is triggered before `instant1` or `action2` is executed to `instant2`.

This refinement simplifies the implementation of the system insofar as the requests received and processed by the server are all identical. This enables the standardization of the exchanges between the client and server. In addition, the behaviour of the server must be unique.

It is necessary to use a tool that is able to choose between the temporal constraints expressed with IN, which must be satisfied in priority. This choice is purely deterministic since it affects the constraint which has the nearest fault. However, we must acknowledge the eventuality where, subjected to a strong charge, the scheduler cannot meet certain requests in the required time. This situation is predictable if at the same instant too many temporal constraints take effect. It is necessary to integrate a new parameter within the IN primitive, which enables a particular operation to be triggered when the predicted task cannot be executed in time.

On the other hand, it is possible that within a program the respect of temporal constraints is particularly important. It would therefore be interesting for the user to be able to effect *a degree of priority* to the constraints expressed.

> In Unix or OS2 type systems, the scheduling policies are generally aimed at making the system user-friendly. The scheduling algorithms used for this are very sophisticated, with progressive policies according to the utilization context. These are very time consuming processor algorithms, which can under no circumstances be used in real-time systems. Among the most widely used scheduling techniques there are the circular (tourniquet) scheduler, the priority scheduler, the multiple queue priority scheduler etc. The scheduler used in this example is the priority scheduler, with several possible limitations for a same level priority.

8.2.2 The Structure of Data Used

The structure of data used for the management of limitations is the chain list (Fig. 8.3).

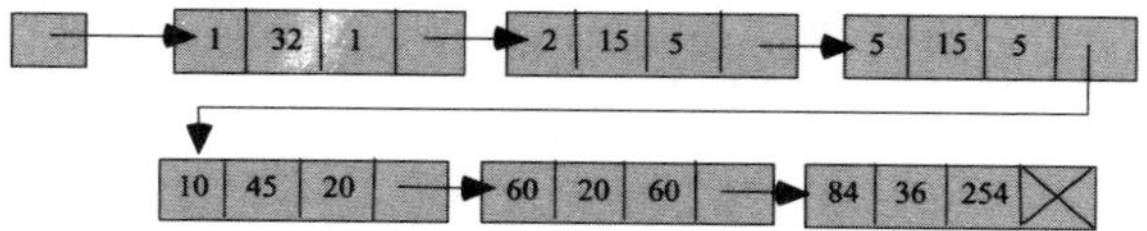

Fig. 8.3 Internal representation of temporal limitations.

Figure 8.4 gives the structure of data used for the requests. The handler_index_table zone corresponds to the indexes of the element of a table containing the addresses of the tasks related to the request. The type_constraint field enables the calls to `AT`, and `BEFORE` to be distinguished from calls to `EVERY`. It also enables the distinction of `WITHIN` constraints which aim to limit the execution time of a task. The two preceding fields are of no use to the server. They are retransmitted to the client at the time of sending the response, to enable it to find the addresses of tasks in the handler table and to take account of the type of limitation.

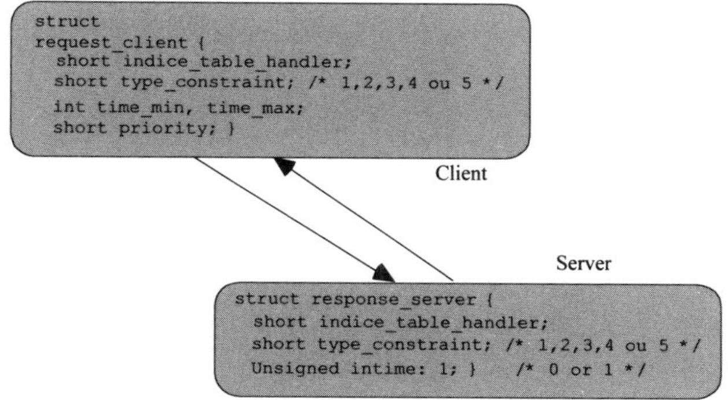

Fig. 8.4 Structure of data used for requests.

8.2.3 An Exchange Scenario between a Client and the Server

Figure 8.5 gives an exchange scenario between an application and the temporal constraint manager.

In this exchange, it must be remembered that:

- the addresses of different tasks are stored at the 0 indexes of the handler table;
- the time scale is in seconds;
- the response provided by the scheduler for the first request is : 1 0 1;

- the request having been processed in time, the client saves its context and launches the task: task 1;
- ten seconds later the client receives the response to the second request: 2,0,1;
- the client recognizes in this situation a second type request. If taskl is terminated, an indicator placed at index 0 in the handler table tells it to follow its normal execution. Otherwise, the client restores the context that it saved and executes task 3.

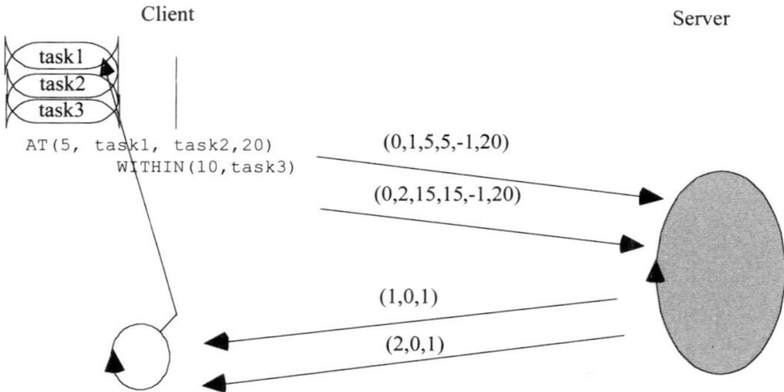

Fig. 8.5 Example of an exchange scenario.

8.2.4 Implemented Primitives

The interface or signature of implemented primitives is slightly different from those used in the example in Figure 8.1. This difference comes from the fact that we wanted to standardize the requests exchanged between the clients and the server by using correspondences displayed previously between these primitives and the "IN" primitive.

A simple method of carrying out the path of the form used in Figure 8.1 and that presented below is to use C language macro-definitions.

```
AT(instant_f1, ptrf1, ptrf2, duration_f1, prtf3, priority)
EVERY(periodicity_f1, ptrf1, ptrf2, duration_f1, priority)
BEFORE(instant_f1, ptrf1, ptrf2, duration_f1, prtf3, priority)
```

with

```
timer * instant_f1, duration_f1, periodicity_f1;
void(*) () ptrf1, ptrf2, prtf3;
short period;
```

the definition of the timer type is:

```
struct timer {
                unsigned int hours;
                unsigned int minutes;
                unsigned int seconds
           }
```

Conforming to that described above, `WITHIN` has not been directly implemented but fused with other primitives by inserting supplementary parameters. This is a valid decision insofar as these implemented primitives are the base level, the user can use the micro-definitions of the C language pre-processor to be able to use them in their initial format.

We also note that function pointers reference the different tasks:

```
ptrf1==> task1, ptrf2==> task2; prtf3==> for the third.
```

The other parameters are:

- `instant_f1:` instant at which task 1 must be executed. If this constraint is not respected task 2 is executed;
- `duration_f1:` specifies a duration for the execution of task 1. If the specified time is exceeded, task 3 is launched;
- `priority:` depicts the importance of the limitations expressed.

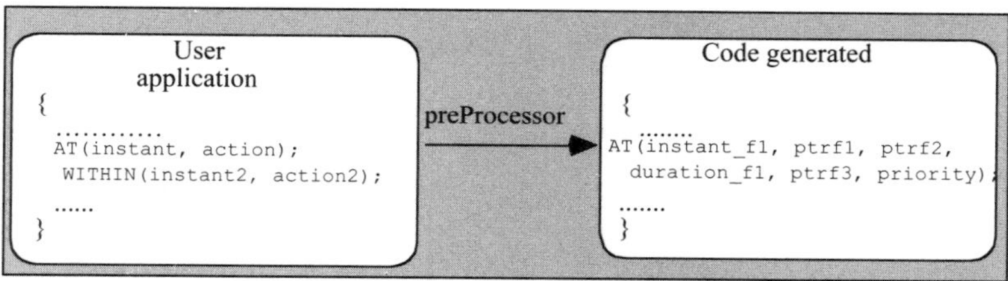

Fig. 8.6 Transformation principle of the initial limitations.

8.2.6 The Function of the Client

Client functioning adheres to the following rules:

1. During the first call to one of the real-time primitives, a procedure is launched to create the socket and transmit a connection demand to the server. This then sets up the interception of signals which can receive a Unix process during an abnormal termination. This is done using the `signal` primitive and, on reception of one of these signals, will enable a specific request to be sent to the server and the socket to be closed. The same principle will be used for `SIGUSR1`and `SIGUSR2` signals. These signals, which will be emitted by the dialogue manager on the arrival of a response from the server, will trigger the execution of the handler manager. Finally, it is important to note that the dialogue manager is triggered as the son process of the application.
2. Upon a call to a real-time primitive, the addresses of tasks are stored in a table called the handler table, a first request is then sent. If the parameters with a type `WITHIN` constraint are expressed, then a second request is then transmitted to the server.

3. When the response from the server arrives, the handler manager is called. According to the data received, this latter executes the predicted task.
4. The process enabling the cessation of execution of a task at the end of a certain time, in order to trigger another remains to be defined. The principle is simple. The manager saves the context of the application before triggering a process whose duration must not exceed a certain limit. This save is enabled using the Unix `setjmp` primitive. When the server returns the response indicating that the time is exceeded, two possible situations occur. Either the task concerned is terminated, in which case an indicator has been placed in the handler table, or it is too long. In this latter case, the context of the application is restored and another process can potentially be launched. Context restoration is carried out using the `longjmp` primitive.
5. For the `EVERY` primitive the principle is the same, except the scheduler takes control of the iterative mechanism by automatically regenerating the request as soon as a response is sent.

8.2.7 The Function of the Server

The server which ensures the scheduling of requests expressed by the different applications, uses an independent program. This program is triggered as a daemon process, that is to say, detached from any terminal. It belongs to the real-time process class which has a high priority within the Unix system.

The server is composed of an actual dialogue and scheduling manager. The dialogue manager is the server body. It ensures the establishment of connections, the receipt of requests and the sending of responses. Multiplexing with the `poll` primitive enables the interception of the arrival of requests on the sockets. The requests are temporarily stored in a table on their arrival. It is the scheduler which ensures that the requests are inserted into the list of requests being processed. Another table is used by the scheduler to temporarily store the responses to be sent. This latter is consulted by the dialogue manager which in this way transmits each waiting response.

The dialogue manager is constantly interrupted to enable request scheduling. Upon launching, the server asks the kernel to send it a signal every second. This is installed by a call to the `setitimer` function. The handler of the `SIGALARM` signal is redefined with `signal` by a particular function. This function increases a global variable and sends a signal triggering the execution of the scheduler.

The Scheduling Algorithm

Figure 8.7 gives the scheduling algorithm used by the server.

The principle of the algorithm is very simple. We leave the reader to read and understand it.

```
Function CLOCK()            /* executed every second*/
{
 Clock = clock + 1;     /* global variable */
 Send signal for SCHEDULER();
}


Function SCHEDULER()      /* activated by the CLOCK() function */
{
        Mask scheduler signa;
        Place it at the start of the list;
        As long as no end list, do
      {
            request.time_min = request.time_min - clock;
            request.time_max = request.time_max - clock;
            if ( request.time_min < 1)
                  if ( request.time_max >=0)
                        response.at time = 1;
                  else
                        response.at time=0;
            response.type = request.type;
            response.num_request = request.type;
               Move to the next request;
      }
        Clock = 0;
        Restore scheduler signal;
}
```

Fig. 8.7 The server scheduling algorithm.

8.3 Mini Project 1: "An Event Management System"

In return for several minimal modifications, the above system can also be used to act as a basis for user event management. Figure 8.8 gives an example of the use of a real-time application for user events.

For this the following primitives must be realized:

- `DeclareEvent(nameEvent, ptr_handler, codeReturn)`

  This primitive enables the user to declare a user event to the system which can be used for synchronization or communication. A single process is authorized to declare an event and become its unique owner. Consequently, it is the only one authorized to suppress it. `nameEvent` is the name of the event, `ptr_handler` is a pointer towards a handler which will be activated when the event occurs. In this case this involves asynchronous communication between tasks. This parameter is optional. If a process has not declared a *handler*, this signifies that it specifically wants to await the event (the process is blocked until this event arrives). This latter case expresses a type of synchronous communication between processes.

- `SendEvent(nameEvent, codeReturn)`

  This primitive will be used by processes to generate the event whose name is provided in a parameter. On receipt of this event, the server must transmit it or activate the interception *handlers* of the set of processes which await it, or which have declared an interception handler.

- `InhibeEvent(nameEvent, codeReturn)`

  This primitive will be used by a process which does not wish to temporarily receive the event provided in the parameter.

- `RestoreEvent(nameEvent, codeReturn)`

  This primitive is the dual primitive of InhibeEvent which enables the user process to retake the direct or indirect interception *via* a *handler* for the event indicated.

- `WaitEvent(nameEvent, codeReturn)`

  This primitive enables the implementation of synchronous communication between tasks. A process which calls this primitive will be blocked until the server activates it again following generation of the blocking event by another process.

```
Object Class ControlSystem
 { time fireInterval;       /* interval of missile firing    */
    time period;           /* period of radar polling        */
    radar detectionSystem; /* class radar                    */
    missile cannon;         /*firing method : launch missile  */
    Event alert_ev;         /* internal event                 */

Private fireInstantComputation(coordinates r, direction d)
 {
 /* calculate the instant the missile was fired using             */
 /* the current coordinates of the object aimed and its direction */
 };

Private critical_situation();
 {  /* retry procedure for critical situations*/
 };

ON alert_ev critical_situation;
    while(1)
    {
        coordinates r;
        direction d;
        EVERY(me.period)
        {
            r = me.detectionSystem.objectPosition();
            d = me.detectionSystem.objectDirection();
            if (r<> nil)
            {
                time t;
                t = fireInstantComputation(r,d);
                me.cannon.orientation() BEFORE(t, alert_ev);
                AT(t) me.cannon.missileFire();
            };
        };
    };
 };
```

Fig. 8.8 Example of the use of user events.

8.4 Mini Project 2: "A VxWorks Version of the Temporal Constraints Manager"

Readers interested in this form of real-time context management can try to design an equivalent version with their own real-time executive or with VxWorks. The advantage of this system is that it considerably increases the design of real-time applications subjected to complex time constraints by being user-friendly and minimizing the risk of errors.

8.5 The Sources of the Temporal Constraint Management System

8.5.1 The Include File

```
/*Timer class header file*/
#include <sys/types.h>
#include <sys/socket.h>
#include <sys/ioctl.h>
#include <sys/fcntl.h>
#include <sys/netinet/in.h>
#include <sys/netdb.h>
#include <sys/signal.h>
#include <sys/setjmp.h>
#include <sys/unistd.h>
#include <sys/stdio.h>

#define SERVER_NAME "gisun01"                    /*name machine server*/
#define PORT 2226                                /*service port*/
#define MAX_SIZE 20                              /*size handler table*/

/*Structure of past function pointer storage*/
/*in parameters on a call to a real-time primitive*/
typedef struct functions_request {
            unsigned inhibe : 1;                 /*call inhibiter*/
            void (*ptrf1)();                     /*task1 pointer*/
            void (*ptrf2)();                     /*task2 pointer*/
            void (*ptrf3)();                     /*task3 pointer*/
} func_req;

/*table of handlers where past functions pointers are stored */
/* in parameters for all calls to real-time primitives*/
func_req * TABLE_REQUESTS [MAX_SIZE];

/*Table of potential safeguard of the application context*/

jmp_buf * TABLE_CONTEXTS [MAX_SIZE];
int sock;                                        /*application socket*/
char *host                                       /*name of server machine*/
struct hostent *hp;                              /*address of server machine*/
struct sockaddr_in srever;                       /*server address*/
```

/*Timer structure*/
```
typedef struct data_timer {
      unsigned int hours;                    /*number of hours*/
      unsigned int minutes;                  /*number of minutes*/
      unsigned int seconds;                  /*number of seconds*/
}timer;
```

/*Structure of client request*/
```
typedef struct data_request {
      short number;                          /*storage index in the table of handlers*/
      short type;                            /*type of constraint*/
pid_t num_process;                           /*number of client process*/
      int time_min,time_max;                 /*interval of time constraint*/
      int periodicity;                       /*periodicity for EVERY*/
      short priority;                        /*constraint priority*/
} request;
```

/*Structure server response*/
```
typedef struct data_response {
      short type_request;                    /*type of constraint */
      short num_request;                     /*storage index in the handler table*/
unsigned atime:1;                            /*service indicator*/
}response;
```

/*Internal Functions*/
```
int conver_seconds();                        /*conversion of atimer data in seconds*/
int storage_request();                       /*storage of past function pointers in*/
                                             /*parameters during the first call to a*/
                                             /*real-time primitive*/
```

/*Dialogue manager*/
```
void hand_termination();                     /*termination of a connection*/
void connection();                           /*establishing a connection*/
void send();                                 /*send a request*/
```

/*Handler manager*/
```
void hand_timer1();                          /*for AT, BEFORE and EVERY type constraints*/
void hand_timer2();                          /*for WITHIN type constraints*/
```

/*Real-time primitives*/
```
void at();
void every();
void before();
```

8.5.2 Internal Service Function File

/*File of internal functions and real-time primitives*/
```
#include "timer.h"
int conver_seconds(atimer)                   /*function of conversion of atimer data
                                               in seconds. RESULT: seconds*/

      timer *atimer;                         /*atimer type data*/
{
        return(atimer->hours*3600 + atimer->minutes*60 + atimer-
>seconds);
};
```

```
void hand_termination()                    /*function of connection termination*/
{
        request req;                       /*request transmitted to a server*/
        req.type=5;
                                           /*send an end request to the server*/
        write(sock,&req,sizeof(request));
                                 /*wait, close the socket and client termination*/
        sleep(5);
        close(sock);
 kill(getpid(), SIGKILL);
}
```

/*Function of establishing the connection with the server*/

```
void connection() {
 strcpy(&host, SERVER_NAME);
        if((hp=(struct hostent *) gethostbyname(&host))==NULL) {
        fprintf(stderr,"%s : SITE UNKNOWN\n", SERVER_NAME);
                return; )
        if((sock=socket(AF_INET,SOCK_STREAM,0))==-1{
                perror("SOCKET CREATION IMPOSSIBLE");
                return; }
        bzero(&server,sizeof(server));
        bcopy((char *) hp->h_addr, (char *) &server.sin_addr,hp-
>h_length);
        server.sin_family=AF_INET;
if(connect(sock,&server,sizeof(server))==-1) {
        perror("CONNECTION IMPOSSIBLE");
        }
```

/*Place the server socket in non-blocking mode */

```
fcntl(sock,F_SETFL,O_NDELAY | fcntl(sock,F_GETFL,0));
```

/*Interception of abnormal termination signals */

```
        signal(SIGHUP,hand_termination);
        signal(SIGINT,hand_termination);
signal(SIGQUIT,hand_termination);
signal(SIGILL,hand_termination);
signal(SIGABRT,hand_termination);
signal(SIGEMT,hand_termination);
        signal(SIGFPE,hand_termination);
signal(SIGBUS,hand_termination);
        signal(SIGSEGV,hand_termination);
signal(SIGIO,hand_termination);
signal(SIGSYS,hand_termination);
signal(SIGPIPE,hand_termination);
signal(SIGTERM,hand_termination);
signal(SIGVTALRM,hand_termination);
        signal(SIGPROF,hand_termination);
signal(SIGXCPU,hand_termination);
        signal(SIGXFSZ,hand_termination);
```

/*Interception of activation signals of the handler manager*/

```
signal(SIGUSR2,hand_termination);
signal(SIGUSR1,hand_termination);
}
```

/*Handler manager for type AT, BEFORE and EVERY limitations*/

```
void hand_timer1()
{
        response rep;                                    /*server response*/
 jmp_buf *new_context;                                   /*application context*/
 read(sock,&rep,sizeof(response));
 if (rep.atime==1) {
                    /*if the request is carried out in time by the server the context*/
                            /*of the application is saved and task1 is executed */
                new_context=(jmp_buf *) malloc(sizeof(jmp_buf));
        TABLE_CONTEXTS[rep.num_request]=new_context;
                if(setjmp(*TABLE_CONTEXTS[rep.num_request]==0)
                 (*TABLE_REQUESTS[rep.num_request]->prtf1)();
                else {
/*Process constraint type within*/
                 (* TABLE_REQUESTS[rep.num_request]->prtf3)();
                if(rep.type_request==2) {
                        free(TABLE_REQUESTS[rep.num_request]);
                         free(TABLE_CONTEXT[rep.num_request]); }
                }
        }
        else {
                            /*if the request is not carried out in time by the */
                                       /*server task2 is executed if it exists*/
        if(TABLE_REQUESTS[rep.num_request]->prtf2)
                (* TABLE_REQUESTS[rep.num_request]->prtf2)();
        }
        if(TABLE_REQUESTS[rep.num_request]->prtf3)
                  /*if task3 exists then the call concerned is inhibited. Task 1 being terminated
                                    it is necessary to cancel the execution of task 3*/
        TABLE_REQUESTS[rep.num_request]->inhibit=1;
                        Else     /*if it is not a call to EVERY all of the data is suppressed*/
        if(rep.type_request==1) {
                        free(TABLE_REQUESTS[rep.num_request]);
                        free(TABLE_CONTEXTS[rep.num_request]); }
/* Signal interception is re-established*/
        signal(SIGUSR1,hand_timer1);
 }

/*Management of handlers for WITHIN type constraints*/
void hand_timer2()
{
        response rep;                                    /*server response*/
 jmp_buf *new_context;
read(sock,&rep,sizeof(response));                  /*read response to the server */
 if (!TABLE_REQUESTS[rep.num_request]->inhibit)
             /*if call non-inhibited restore the application context => return to hand_timer1*/
                longjump(* TABLE_CONTEXTS[rep.num_request],1);
                   if(rep.type_request==4)              /*if this is a call to EVERY
                                                         re-initialize the inhibitor*/

                 (*TABLE_REQUESTS[rep.num_request]->inhibit=0;
                else {
                        free(TABLE_REQUESTS[rep.num_request]);
                         free(TABLE_CONTEXTS[rep.num_request]);
                }
 signal(SIGUSR2,HAND_TIMER2);                      /*re-establish signal interception*/
```

```
}
```

/*Storage function of in the table of handlers of function pointers related to a call to a real-time primitive. RESULT: table index or -1*/

```
int stor_request(prtf1,prtf2,prtf3)
        void(*prtf1)();
        void(*ptrf2)();
void(*ptrf3)();
{
int num_request;                        /*the storage index in the handler table*/
funct__req * func_new_request;                               /*storage element*/
num_request=0;
                                      /*search for an available place in the table*/
while(num_request<SIZE_MAX && TABLE_REQUESTS [num_request])
                num_request=num_request+1;
if (num_request==SIZE_MAX)                                          /*no place*/
        return -1;
                                     /*otherwise storage of function pointers*/
funct_new_request=(func_req *) malloc (sizeof(func_req));
TABLE_REQUESTS [num_request]=func_new_request;
TABLE_REQUESTS [num_request]->ptrf1=ptrf1;
TABLE_REQUESTS [num_request]->ptrf2=ptrf2;
TABLE_REQUESTS [num_request]->ptrf3=ptrf3;
TABLE_REQUESTS [num_request]->inhibit=0;
Return num_request;                                   /*return the storage index*/
}
```

/*Sending a request to the server function */

```
void send(type,num_process,num_request,time_min,time_max,
        periodicity,priority)
short type;                                                /*constraint type*/
id_t num_process;                                /*application process number*/
short num_request;                          /*storage index in the handler table*/
int time_min;      int time_max;                              /*time interval*/
int periodicity;                                      /*periodicity for EVERY*/
short priority;                                         /*constraint priority*/
{
request req;                                                       /*request*/
        int code;
        req.type=type;
        req.nu_process=num_process;
        req.number=num_request
        req.time_min=time_min;
        req.time_max=time_max;
        req.periodicity=periodicity;
        req.priority=priority;
        if(!sock)
                connection();
 write(sock,&req,sizeof(request));
}
```

/*Real-time primitives*/

```
void at(instant_f1,prtf1,ptrf2,duration_f1,prtf3,priority)
        timer *instant_f1;                                  /*point constraint*/
        void(*prtf1)();                                         /*task1 pointer*/
        void(*ptrf2)();                                         /*task2 pointer*/
        timer *duration_f1;                                   /*duration of task1*/
        void(*ptrf3)();                                         /*task3 pointer*/
```

```
        short priority;                                      /*priority constraint*/
{
int num_request;
 if (instant_f1 && prtf1)
                                              /*if instant_f1 parameter informed */
        if ((num_request=stor_request(ptrf1,ptrf2,ptrf3))>-1) {

/*If the handler table is not full then store the tasks in the handler table and transmit the first request*/
        send(1,getpid(),num_request, conver_seconds(instant_f1),
        conver_seconds(instant_f1),-1,priority);
if (duration_f1)                    /*if duration_f1 informed then send second request*/
        send(2,getpid(),num_request, conver_seconds(instant_f1)+
                        conver_seconds(duration_f1),0,-1,priority);
}
}
void every(periodicity_f1,prtf1,ptrf2,duration_f1,prtf3,priority)
        timer *periodicity_f1;
        void(*prtf1)();
        void(*ptrf2)();
        timer *duration_f1;
        void(*ptrf3)();
short priority;
{
int num_request;
 if (instant_f1 && prtf1)                       /*if periodicity_f1 parameter informed*/
        if ((num_request=stor_request(ptrf1,ptrf2,ptrf3))>-1) {

/*If the handler table is not full then store the tasks and transmit the first request*/
send(3,getpid(),num_request, conver_seconds(periodicity_f1),
conver_seconds(peridicity_f1),priority);
if (duration_f1)                         /*if duration_f1 informed then send second req*/
send(4,getpid(),num_request, conver_seconds(periodicity_f1)+
conver_seconds(duration_f1),0,
conver_seconds(periodicity_f1),priority);
        }
}

void before(instant_f1,prtf1,ptrf2,duration_f1,prtf3,priority)
        timer *instant_f1;
        void(*prtf1)();
        void(*ptrf2)();
        timer *duration_f1;
        void(*ptrf3)();
short priority;
{
int num_request;
 if (instant_f1 && prtf1)                       /*if periodicity_f1 parameter informed*/
if ((num_request=stor_request(ptrf1,ptrf2,ptrf3))>-1) {
send(1,getpid(),num_request,0,
 conver_seconds(periodicity_f1),
conver_seconds(instant_f1),-1,priority);
if (duration_f1)
send(2,getpid(),num_request, conver_seconds(instant_f1)+
conver_seconds(duration_f1),0,-1,priority);
        }
}
```

8.5.3 Server Code

/*File server*/

```
#include <signal.h>
#include <fcntl.h>
#include <errno.h>
#include <sys/itypes.h>
#include <sys/socket.h>
#include <netinet/in.h>
#include <netdb.h>
#include <sys/un.h>
#include <fnctl.h>
#include <sys/ioctl.h>
#include <sys/time.h>
#include <stropts.h>
#include <poll.h>
#include <stdio.h>
#define NULL 0
#define PORT 2226                         /*server port*/
#define MAX_CONNECTIONS 5                 /*number of clients*/
#define MAX_NUMSOCKET 10                  /*table size of client sockets*/
#define MAX_RESPONSE 10                   /*table size of responses awaiting*/
define MAX_NEWREQUESTS 10
```

/*Structure of client requests*/

```
typedef struct {
        short number;                     /*storage index in the table of handlers*/
        short type;                       /*type of constraint*/
pid_t num_process;                        /*number of client process*/
        int time_min,time_max;            /*interval of time constraint*/
        int periodicity;                  /*periodicity for EVERY*/
        short priority;                   /*constraint priority*/
} request;
```

/*List of client requests*/

```
/typedef struct request_received {
        request req;                      /*client request*/
        int num_stor;                     /*socket client*/
struct request_received *following;       /*following pointer request*/
} list_requests;
```

/*Structure of server responses*/

```
typedef struct {
        short type_request;               /*temporal constraint type*/
        short num_request;                /*storage index in the handler table*/
              unsigned intime : 1;        /*indicator service*/
} response;
```

/*Table of response to transmit*/

```
typedef struct {
              unsigned toprocess:1;       /*response state*/
              response rep;               /*response to transmit*/
} response_toprocess;
typedef struct {
              pid_t num_process;          /*client process number*/
response_toprocess responses[MAX_RESPONSES];  /*response table*/
```

```
} responses_client;
list_requests header_list_requests=NIL;         /*header list of requests to process*/
int num_process_server;                          /*number of the server process*/
int clock=0;                                     /*the clock increases every second*/
struct sockaddr_in server;                       /*server socket address*/
struct pollfd table_sockets[MAX_CONNECTIONS];    /*table of client sockets*/
responses_client table_responses[MAX_NUMSOCKET]; /*table of responses*/
list_requests * table_new_requests[MAX_NEWREQUESTS]; /*table of new requests*/
int nmbr_new_requests=0;                         /*number of waiting requests*/

/*Sigalrm handler signal to call to the scheduler*/
void handler_clock()
{
        clock=clock+1;

/*Scheduler call*/
        kill(num_process_server,SIGUSR1);
 signal(SIGALRM,handler_clock);
}

/*Sigusr1 handler signal ensuring scheduling*/
void handler_service()
{
        int code,i;                              /*table index*/

/*Request list element pointers */
        list_requests *current,*preceding,*old,*new;
        signal(SIGUSR1,SIG_IGN);                 /*mask signal*/

/*Path of the request list*/
        preceding=NIL;
        current=header_list_requests.following;
        while(current) {
             current->req.time_min=current->req.time_min - clock;
             current->req.time_max=current->req.time_max - clock;
             if(table_responses[current->num_sock].num_process==-1){

/*Suppress request if client terminates*/
                  old=current;
                  if(!preceding)
                  header_list_requests.following=current->following;
                  else
                  preceding->following=current->following
                  current=current->following;
                  free(old);
             }
             else {
                       if (current->req.time_min < 1) {

/*If an instant is missed then store the response in the table of responses to be transmitted*/
                       for(i=0;i<MAX_RESPONSES &&
table_responses[current->num_sock].responses[i].toprocess=1++;
                       if(i<MAX_RESPONSES) {

/*If table not full, store the response*/
table_responses[current->num_sock].responses[i].toprocess=1;
```

```
table_responses[current>num_sock].responses[i].rep.type_request=
current->req.type;
table_responses;current>num_sock].responses[i].rep.num_request=
current-.req.number;
                        if (current->req.time_max>=0)
```

/*If request served in time*/

```
table_responses[current->num-sock].responses[i].rep.intime=1;
                 else
        table_responses[current->num_sock].responses[i].rep.intime=0;
                        old=current;
```

/*Suppression of the request in the list*/

```
                             if(!preceding)
                 header_list_requests.following=current->following;
                      else
                 preceding->following=current->following;
                           current=current->following;
                           if(old->req.periodicity == -1)
```

/*If it is not an every type request destroy it*/

```
                 free(old);
                      else {
```

/*Otherwise store the request in the table of waiting requests */

```
        old->req.time_min=old->req.periodicity+clock;
        old->req.time_max=old->req.periodicity+clock;
table_new_requests[nmbr_new_requests++]=old;
                      }
                 else {                           /*pass to the new request*/
                      preceding=current;
                      current=current->following; }
        }
        else {                                    /*pass to the next request*/
             preceding=current;
             current=current->following; }
                 }
        }
        for(i=0;i<nmbr_new_requests;i++) {
```

/*Path to the request table and insertion into the list of requests to process*/

```
                table_new_requests[i]->req.time_min - = clock;
                table_new_requests[i]->req.time_max - = clock;#
                new=table_new_requests[i];
                current=header_list_requests.following;
                preceding=NIL;
                        while(current && (current->req.time_min<new-
>req.time_min
                || (current->req.time_min=new->req.time_min
                && current->req.priority>=new->req.priority)))
                {
        preceding=current;
        current=current->following;
                }
                if (!preceding)
        header_list_requests.follwoign=new;
                else
```

```
        preceding->following=new;
                new->following=current;
        }
/*Reinitialization*/
  number_new_requests=0;
  clock;
/*Return interception of the signal for the scheduler call */
        signal(SIGUSR1,handler_service);
]

/*Principal program*/
main{}
{
        int sock_listen,sock_service;             /*service and listening socket*/
        int d,i,j;                                /*index tables*/
        list_requests *new;                       /*pointer on new request*/
        struct interval period;                   /*SIGALRM signal period*/
        request req;                              /*new request*/
/*Initializations*/
num_process_server=getpid();
for(i=0;i<MAX_CONNECTIONS;i++)
                table_sockets[i].fd=-1;
for(i=0;i<MAX_NUMSOCKET;i++)
                table_responses[i].num-process=-1;
/*Creation of the listen socket*/
if((sock_liste=socket(AF_INET,SOCK_STREAM,0))==-1 {
        perror("CREATION OF SERVER LISTEN SOCKET IMPOSSIBLE");
        exit(1); }
        bzero(&server,sizeof(server));
        server.sin_family=AF_INET;
        server.sin_port=htons(PORT);
        server.sin_addr.s_addr-INADDR_ANY;
/*Attach a socket to an address*/
if(bind(sock_listen, (struct sockaddr *)&server,sizeof(server))) {
        perror("NAMING OF SERVER SOCKET IMPOSSIBLE");
        exit(2); }
/*Installation of handler for the sigalrm signal*/
period.it_value.tv_sec=1;
period.it_value.tv_usec=0;
period.it_interval.tv_sec=1;
period.it_interval.tv_usec=0;
signal(SIGALRM,handler_clock);
setitimer(ITIMER_REAL,&period,NIL);
/*Installation of handler for the sigusr1 signal*/
signal(SIGUSR1,handler_service);
/*Terminal detaching*/
                        close(0);
                close(1);close(2);
        if((d=open("/dev/tty",O_RDWR))>0) {
                ioctl(d,TIOCNOTTY,0);
                close(d);
        }
/*Creation of the hanging connections file*/
        listen(sock_listen,5);
/*Acceptance loop of a connection*/
        while(1) {                                /*processing of responses to transmit*/
```

```
                for(i=0;i<MAX_NUMSOCKET;i++) {             /*for each client socket*/
                                if(table_responses i].num_process!=-1;
for(j=0;j<MAX_RESPONSES;j++) {                          /*for each response to transmit*/
                if(table_responses[i].responses[j].toprocess) {
                 /*If response for request type AT, BEFORE or EVERY then send a sigusr1 signal*/
        if(table_responses[i].responses[j].rep.type_request==1 ||
table_responses[i].responses[j].rep.type_request==3)
                        kill(table_responses[i].num_process,SIGUSR1);
                else                        /*otherwise send signal SIGUSR2 to the client*/
kill(table_responses[i].num_process,SIGUSR2);
 write(i,&table_responses[i].responses[j].rep.sizeof
(response));
         table_responses[i].responses[j].toprocess=0;
                }
                        }
                }
/*Acceptance of connection requests*/
                sock_service=accept(sock_listne, (struct sockaddr *) 0,
(int *) 0);
                if (sock_service!=1) {
/*If socket created place in non-blocking mode */
                fcntl(sock_service,F_SETFL,O_NDELAY |
fcntl(soxk_service,F_GETFL,0));
                for(i=0;i<MAX_CONNECTIONS && table_socket[in].fd!=-
1;i++);
{
                                  /*if table of client sockets not full then insert the new socket and
                                                       the initialization of the response table*/
table_sockets[i].fd=sock_service;
table_sockets[i].events=POLLOUT;
table_sockets[i].revents=0;
                        for(j=0;j<MAX_RESPONSES;)
table_responses[sock_service].responses[j++].toprocess=0;
        }
 }
 /*Polling of writing on the client sockets*/
  if(poll(table_sockets,MAX_CONNECTIONS,0)>0) { /*if writing is
detected*/
        for(i=0,i<MAX_CONNECTIONS;) {                          /*for each client socket*/
        if(table_sockets[i].fd!=-1) { {                        /*if i is a client socket*/
                        req.type=0;
if(read(table_sockets[i].fd,&req,sizeof(request))>0 && req,type) {
                        /*if a request has arrived on in */
                        if(req.type==5) { /*if termination request then reinitialize
table response for this socket and close the socket*/
        table_responses[table_sockets[i].fd].num-process=-1;
                for(j=0;j<MAX_RESPONSES;j++)
        table_responses[table_sockets[i].fd].responses[j].toprocess=0;
        close(table_sockets[i].fd);
        table_sockets[i].fd=-1;
        }
        else {
         new=(list_requests *) malloc (sizeof(list_requests));
                              new->num_sock=table_sockets[i].fd;
                              new->req.number=req.number;
                              new->req.type=req.type;
```

```
                    new->req.num_process=req.num_process;
                         new->req.time_min=req.time_min;
                         new->req.time_max=req.time_max;
                         new->req.periodicity=req.periodicity
                         new->req.priority=req.priority;
if(table_responses[table_sockets[i].fd].num_process==-1)
table_responses[table_sockets[i].fd].num_process=new->req.num_process;
table_new_requests[nmbr_new_requests++]=new;
                         }
          }
                          /*reset the table for the socket undergoing processing*/
                    table_sockets[i].events=POLLOUT;
                    table_sockets[i].revents=0;
                         }
                    i++;                                  /*following socket*/
                    }
          }
     }
};
```

8.5.4 Sample Data

Triggering the server can be done using a background terminal. In a working situation, it will be declared in the inetd.conf services file to be triggered automatically by the Unix system during the system start up.

Triggering the server:

```
% server&
[3] 30702
%
```

Any application or program using temporal constraints can then be launched. The following program uses type AT and WITHIN constraints:

```
#include "timer.h"
void f11()
{
      printf("\nAT : CLIENT SERVI…");
      while(1);
}
void f12()
{
      printf("\nAT : CLIENT NON SERVI…");
}
VOID F2()
{
      printf("\nAT : CLIENT TRAP…");
}
main()
`{
      timer test1,test2;
      test1.hours=0;
      test1.minutes=0;
      test1.seconds=2;
```

```
        test2.hours=0;
        test2.minutes=0;
        test2.seconds=0;
        at(&test1,f11,f12,&test2,f2,10);
         while(1);
};
```

Once launched, it gives the following result:

```
%tets1
AT; CLIENT SERVI...
AT: CLIENT TRAP...^Ckilled
```

9. *Control of a Product Processing Chain*

Figure 9.1 outlines a product processing chain. It involves didactic equipment adopted and used mostly by national education for teaching industrial sciences in preparatory classes of competitive-entry higher-education establishments, particularly in technical subjects (science, physics and engineering), and engineering schools. This system was designed and commercialized by the Didactic de Festo France unit.

This chain has three functions: the transfer, identification and sorting of photographic film. Identification relies on reading the bar codes on the wrapping. The films are sorted according to their sensitivity, the number of photographs, etc.

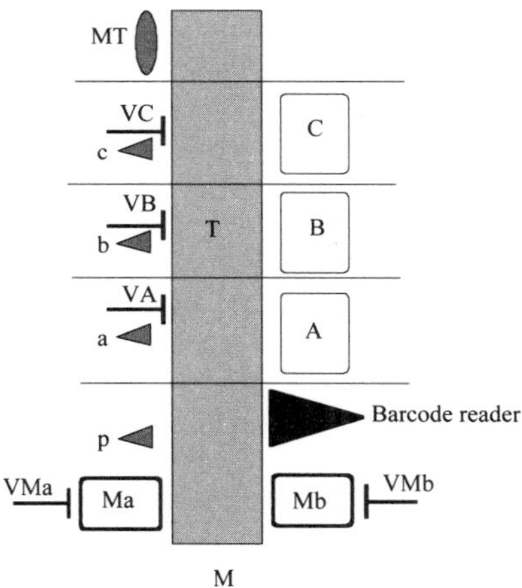

Fig. 9.1 Automated distribution system (ADS).

9.1 Functioning

The films are first placed in a vertical store M which is composed of two columns: Ma and Mb. A supply system sends them along conveyor T. After, identification, they are directed towards one of the three output channels A, B or C. Those which do not conform remain on conveyor T and are discarded when they reach the end.

9.1.1 Description of the Operating Part

- Conveyor T is driven by the reduction motor RM;
- The feeding device is controlled by the pneumatic jack PJ;
- Shunting is controlled by rotating pneumatic jacks PA, PB and PC;
- Sensors a, b, c and p are proximity detectors;
- The identification sensor is a continuous bar code reader.

9.1.2 Specifications

This involves studying and implementing the *command* part conforming to the specifications below. The solution required must enable the implementation of the following global function:

> After feeding the films into the unit or continuous cycle, and identifying the bar codes, each film must be guided towards the output channel corresponding to its code. The limitation is that only one film at a time must be processed in a continuous cycle.

9.2 Analysis and Specification Using the SA/RT Method (SA/SD)

Before giving a detailed presentation of the approach used to understand the study of this and similar systems, we start first by justifying our choice concerning the use of the SA/RT (SA/SD) method. The design and analysis methods used in the field of industrial automation, and the digital control of systems can be ascending or descending. Ascending methods favour the analysis and ascending design of systems studied. The design process is an iterative process. Each stage consists of studying the functions and means required for the design of superior layer functions. Processes stop when the global function is clearly defined. In contrast, with methods based on the abstraction and descending analysis of systems, it starts with functional refinement by abstraction level starting with the general (global function) towards the particular components. It is currently known that using both approaches considerably improves the study and design of complex systems.

In this case study, we propose the SA/RT method which uses knowledge acquired on the application field to render the analysis process more deterministic.

The fundamental differences which exist between standard data processing applications and real-time applications, conditions the use of tools and methods in the different stages of their lifecycle (analysis, specification, design, tests and checks, etc.). For standard data processing applications, the analysis stage must lead to the design of a *static model* which reflects as accurately as possible the true structure of the system in terms of the objects or entities, and the structural relations which exist between these objects (composition, generalization, specialization, etc.). A degree of very fine modelling is therefore necessary as it involves achieving, as successfully as possible, the projection of the real world or the reality perceived on an abstract data processing model. It is the level of accuracy, completeness and semantic wealth of this abstract model (again called the conceptual or static model) that the quality of computer processing (dynamic model) implemented around this model depends on. The analyst must show proof of an adequate abstraction ability to clearly identify the different entities of the system and the relationship between them.

In comparison to data processing applications, two cases are possible to understand the study of automated systems and real-time applications in general:

1. either the operative part already exists, in which case the designer will concentrate specifically on the analysis and design of the command part;
2. or the operative part does not exist, and it is necessary to carry out the global analysis of the requirements which will result in the design of a complete functional model in which the future system is seen in terms of functional processes and interactions between processes.

In the second case, depending on technological constraints, utilization limitations, wait performances, stability and degree of reliability required, etc., the functional model will act as a basis for the construction of the final system architecture and the definition of the hardware and software required to implement the different functional processes. The distribution of functional processes between the operative part and the command part must be carried out during this second stage. In every case, it is the dynamics of these systems, which constitutes the guideline for the different stages of the development process.

The SA/RT (SA/SD) method can be found among the methods best adapted to the analysis and design of real-time systems which propose a particularly global approach from the analysis phase to the design phase. It suggests a consistent approach, from the analysis of system requirements to be installed independently of any technological consideration, to the specification of the final architecture and the technological choices necessary to implement the functions, and system input and output data or control flows. This is a global method which is appropriate for the analysis and design of software or hardware systems. These are the same reasons which led us to choose SA/RT to lead the different analysis and design phases of the *command part* of the automated distribution system (ADS). We provide several technological details, which will enable the reader to appreciate better the completeness and coherence of the different stages of the method when it involves designing an entire complex automated system: the operative part and the command part. [1]

As we have already pointed out in Chapter 5, the second stage of the SA/RT method involving the different architectural diagrams, is not favoured by the users as it involves a rather laborious phase which intervenes relatively late in the development process. To make up for the disadvantages, we propose a variation of SA/RT (SA/SD) in which the details relating to the methods and components able to intervene in the implementation of the system, are taken into consideration very early on, in order to effectively direct and guide the analysis and specification process.

9.2.1 The Analysis Approach

The use of a static model can considerably facilitate the identification of certain processes of the requirements model. The approach is less pragmatic and relies on a more *deterministic* process of analysis. It aims to render the method more accessible by proposing sufficiently clear references and rules for use to enable a beginner to understand better the identification stage of functional processes.

Moreover, the reader is warned that in the rest of this study, we indifferently use the term agent or transformation process which is used initially in the SA/RT method. The aim is the design of the digital command part (software) of a process. Consequently, replacing the term "transformation process" by that of "agent" is unlikely to bring any harm to the SA/RT method or to denature its general philosophy and basic concepts. On the other hand, as will be shown in the following sections, the variant that we suggest involves first unloading the *reactive control agents* from the system which constitutes the innermost layer of the system to be designed. In contrast to the original method, the first stage of analysis is primarily an ascending analysis which identifies base level agents. These reactive agents are the control agents for the different parts of the physical process. It is for these reasons that we will favour the term "agent" more than the term "transformation process", which lends itself better to the analysis of the overall function or the objective installation function.

In the second stage of our study, we will present the different stages and choices possible to construct the final architecture of the system. This architecture must take into account a certain number of limitations (technological, performance related, reliability, stability, etc.). We will try our best to simplify the different stages of the method in order to render them more accessible to the reader via the study of this system.

Finally, we end this study by giving an implementation of the solution. The execution platform and programming language will depend largely on the choices which will be made in the preceding stage.

---

[1] At this point we would like to thank FESTO for giving us the authority to present certain technological details of its automated film sorting and distribution system.

9.2.1.1 The Static Model of the Operative Part

The static model (Fig. 9.2) must clearly indicate the different *logical entities* necessary for the construction of the *operative part.* This latter will be used to implement the overall function which is the "automatic sorting and distribution of films". When the operative part is already defined, as is the case here, we advise the reader to construct a static model as detailed as possible. This model must be independent of any technological considerations (explicit and definitive designation of the technological components), especially in the case where the operative part is not yet defined. The definitive choice of components will be made in the second stage of the method, as will be specified later.

Using this method, we adopt an *ascending* approach, first, to try to identify the components required for the implementation of the overall function. In a second stage, the descending analysis approach will be used to define the overall function. It is a compromise between object-oriented analysis and design methods and the *descending* analysis methods such as SA/RT.

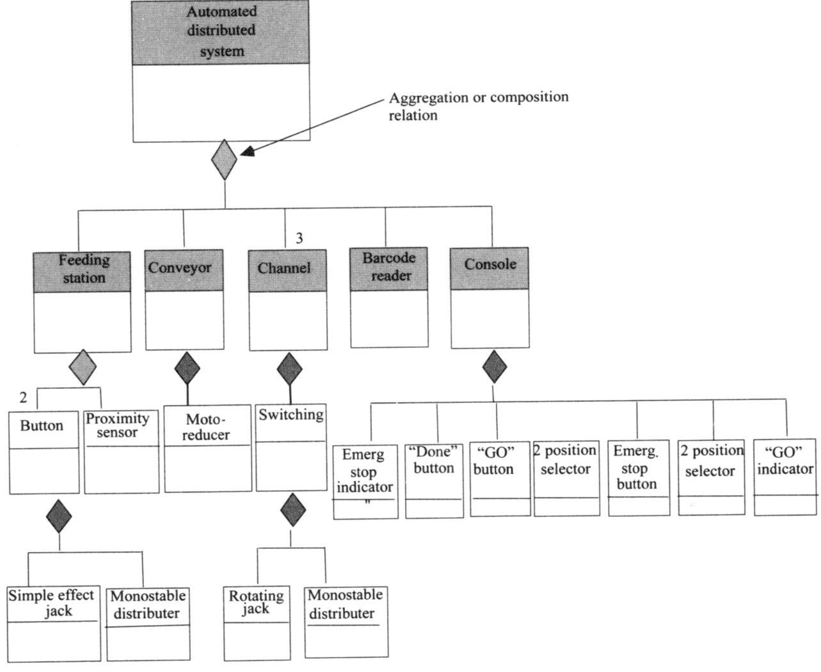

Fig. 9.2 The static model of the automated distribution system.

The static model in Figure 9.2 represents a logical division of the physical process in terms of smaller logical entities. These entities represent smaller operative parts and, consequently, it is this which will considerably facilitate the analysis, specification and design of their control. In this figure, we have kept the following logical entities:

- The *part feeder store* which is composed of two columns, Ma and Mb which are passive entities. Data flows are associated to this entity to control the two button jacks: *exit button (A/B), end course (A/B).* The *PPM* control flow, which is a signal generated by a proximity sensor on exit of each part from one of the stores Ma or Mb, is also associated to this.
- The *channel* A (B/C) (passive entity) used for guiding the films depending on their type. The following are associated to this logical entity: (1) the position sensor which sends the *PPA (PPB/PPC)* signal when a film passes at its level; (2) a rotating jack which is controlled by the signal *GUIDE.A (B/C)*. The *GUIDE.A (B/C) rest position* is generated when the jack finds its rest position again.
- The *conveyor* (passive entity) to which is associated the control of the reduction motor: *Motor M1* to start the motor.
- The *bar code reader* (active entity) which is the only displaced logic entity. It produces the data flow: code read. It is controlled by a set of orders gathered in a metaflow: *characters.* A bar code reader is effectively connected to a data processing system (microcomputer, automaton) via a serial link or local industrial network, and reacts in the same way as a keyboard. The "character" flow represents the communication and communication protocol via the communication support used between the reader and the data processing system.
- The *console* (passive entity) for introducing instructions. It enables the operator to produce one of the following flows:
    - *start/stop* the program;
    - *place under tension* and start the system;
    - select the *continuous cycle* functioning mode;
    - select the *cycle/cycle* functioning mode;
    - *perform* an emergency stop.

  The console entity also enables action on the controller using an "indicator" flow.

It is important to note that this division is not unique. Division where the sensors of positions PPM, PPA, PPB and PPC are associated to the logical entity "conveyor" is another possible alternative. This new division does not profit from the possibilities offered by real-time executives in terms of re-entry and code sharing between tasks. In the division shown, the three channels can be generated by tasks which share the same code. The address of the I/O ports will be transmitted to them during the start of the system. This division also enables the appearance of an identical GRAFCET if the execution platform is the automaton. It is the same for the control of the two stores.

9.2.1.2 Data and Control Context Diagrams (DCD and CCD)

Figure 9.3 gives the data and control context diagrams. The "GUIDE", "GUIDE RST POSITION", "PP", BUTTON RETURN", "EXIT BUTTON" and "PPM" flows are metaflows and are defined later on.

9.2.1.3 Data and Control Flow Diagrams

The DFD0 "Automated Distributed System Guide" which corresponds to the command part to be implemented will be constructed from the DCD and CCD in Figure 9.3 using input and output data and control flows. In this construction process, the nature of the sources and sinks will also be taken into account (deported logic or passive entities). The passive entities effectively represent the elementary operative parts. In DFD0, it is necessary to give them a functional control process called the *command agent*. In contrast, a functional agent or process will be given to entities with deported logic to manage the dialogue and communication according to a protocol specific to the entity in question.

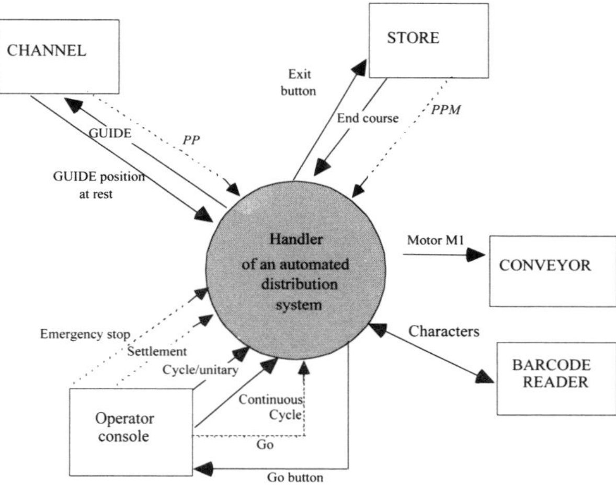

Fig. 9.3 Data and control context diagram (DCD + CCD).

Starting with the classification of logical entities displayed in the static model, we suggest the following approach to easily find the components of the data flow diagram.

9.2.2 "Construction of an Initial DFD" Stage

This stage is manifested by associating a *reactive control agent* to each passive entity. In this way, the modularity and distribution of the guide function, and the overall control of the physical process in a set of *highly specialized elementary agents* is favoured, as they are easy to study and to implement. The following stage involves associating a communicating agent to each deported logic intelligent entity. This specialized agent will act as an interface between the other application agents and the component. The main interest of such an approach is to encapsulate in this second type of agents, the specificity and details of communication dialogue with these intelligent components. It is also necessary to add the following agents to this initial set of specialized agents, which take into account the specifics of the application field (the list provided below is not exhaustive and depends on the application field):

- *An emergency stop processing agent* whose role is to execute a special automated system control procedure when a serious event challenges the normal functioning of the system. Such an event can be external (produced by the operative part or generated from an emergency stop button on the console) or internal (triggered by an agent which, for various reasons, is no longer able to carry out its normal functions: error detection, preventative tests, etc.). The simplest emergency stop procedure involves *stopping the system*. It is then the operator's responsibility to restart the procedure. Other more complex procedures are able to locate and even diagnose and analyze the cause of faults and take adequate measures to place the system back into a state of functional consistency.
- *A supervision agent* whose role is to display in real-time the development of the different variables of the physical process.
- *An agent for the management of dialogue and operator instruction interpretation.*
- *A specialized expert agent* which has the role of implementing the overall function, which is the group's objective and reason for being. This agent is generally subject to other levels of refinement depending on the nature of the production function to be implemented.

The application of this first stage of the approach to the system studied gives the DFD0 and the DFC0 in Figure 9.4. Given the relative simplicity of our system, the supervision agents and operator dialogue management agents have been excluded.

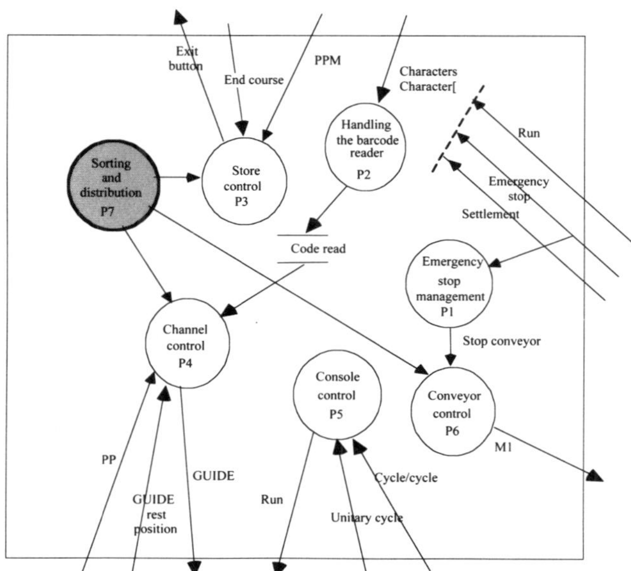

Fig. 9.4 Initial DFD0 and DFC0 "guiding an automated distribution system".

9.2.3 The "Elimination of Superfluous Agents and the Regrouping of Communicating Agents" Stage

The aim of this stage is to try to eliminate certain superfluous control agents. They do not carry out any transformation on the input data and control flows, and are therefore simple intermediaries indifferent to input flows. This is the case with the "`control the conveyor`" agent, and the "`control the console`" agent. The M_1 flow which controls the start or stop of the reduction motor can be directly activated (1) or deactivated (0) by the other agents. This is the same for the "unitary cycle" and the "continuous cycle". They can be directly intercepted and exploited by the principal function agent "`control the stores`", rather than the overall function agent. These two flows effectively indicate to the "`control the stores`" agent that they must only sort one film at a time, or otherwise function in a continuous cycle. In this application, there are no communicating agents to group together. The only agents capable of fulfilling the regrouping condition have already been encapsulated in a unique abstract logical entity in the static model, because they are identical: this is the case for internal "`control the stores`" and "`control the channel`" agents.

The application of this second stage at the initial DFD0 gives the new DFD0 in Figure 9.5:

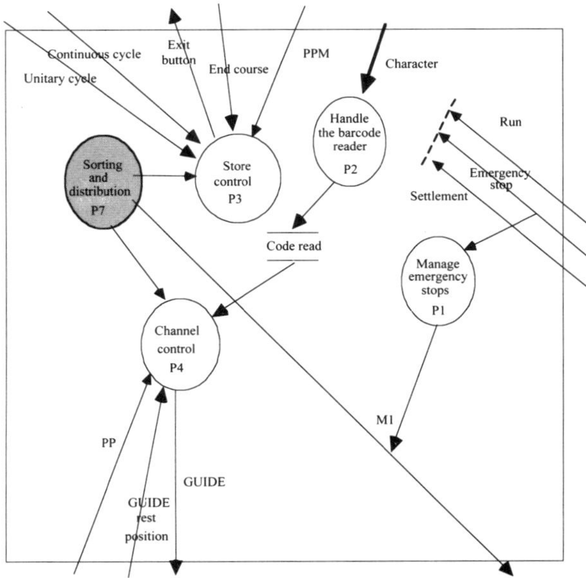

Fig. 9.5 DFD0 and DFC0 "guiding an automated distribution system".

9.2.4 Updating the Data Dictionary Stage

From this stage, it is necessary to update the data dictionary.

> Each dictionary entry contains a clear, precise definition of the data and control flows displayed. This definition must gradually be improved and refined as the analysis, specification and design of the system advances.

Figure 9.6 gives the first version of the dictionary.

Flow	Nature	Flow type
Exit button: 1-exit button A 2-exit button B	Action	Discrete data of type TOR (1 or 0,true or False)
End of course 1- end of course A 2- end of course B	Information	Discrete data of type TOR (1 or 0, True or False)
PPM	Information	Discrete data of type TOR (1 or 0,true or False)
Characters	Information	Discrete data of type TOR (1 or 0,true or False)
Run	Control	Discrete data of type TOR (1 or 0,true or False)
Emergency Stop	Control	Discrete data of type TOR (1 or 0,true or False)
Settlement	Control	Discrete data of type TOR (1 or 0,true or False)
M1	Action	Discrete data of type TOR (1 or 0,true or False)
GUIDE 1- GUIDE A 2- GUIDE A 3- GUIDE A	Action	Discrete data of type TOR (1 or 0,true or False)
PP 1- PPA 2- PPA 3- PPA	Information	Discrete data of type TOR (1 or 0,true or False)
Unitary cycle	Information	Discrete data of type TOR (1 or 0,true or False)
Continuous cycle	Information	Discrete data of type TOR (1 or 0,true or False)
Work indicator	Information	Discrete data of type TOR (1 or 0,true or False)

Fig. 9.6 Data dictionary.

The reader has probably asked how the nature of a flow can be determined as a data flow or a control flow. There is generally no strict rule. It is, however, currently understood that flows with continuous values (values obtained from a pressure or temperature sensor for example), because they represent the values of sampled physical wealth, are data flows. Data flows can also take on discrete values ("unitary cycle" flow, "exit button" flow, "PPM" flow, etc.) The flows which take on discrete values over time, can be indifferently considered as data or control flows. However, we maintain that a flow which has a direct impact on the system's internal state changes has a good chance of being a control flow ("emergency stop" flow, "performance" flow, etc.).

9.2.5 Elementary Agent Behaviour Specification Stage

The transformation agents or processes judged elementary must be the object of a description using a specification file called PSPEC. This file gives a clear description of the agent's logic: the generation principles of the output data and control flows compared to the input data and control flows. There is no restriction on the formalism used to describe agent behaviour.

Analysis of the DFD0 shows that the "`manage the emergency stops`" agent is an elementary agent. According to specifications, when the operator presses on the emergency stop button, the system must immediately stop, especially the conveyor motor. When the operator ceases the stop by pushing the necessary button, the system must return to a stable state. This system possesses one stable state only:

the start of the transfer cycle.

Under these conditions, the role of the "`manage the emergency stops`" agent is limited to stopping the conveyor motor only, and forcing a restart from the stable state: system restart. The recovery of system functions enforces the manual intervention of the operator to remove the film found on the conveyor when it stopped.

In other more complex systems, the onus is on the "`manage the emergency stops`" agent to automatically return the system to a stable state by trying to find a logical issue to the current production (the parts are declared bad and redirected towards an exit store used to this end).

It generally involves making the system function in reduced mode until it returns to a stable state. According to the operator's instructions, the system can continue to function in this mode if the event that started the emergency stop does not severely affect the security of the personnel and the equipment. Under these conditions, the "`manage the emergency stops`" agents must eventually be refined into several specialized sub-agents.

1. **PSPEC P1:** Manage Emergency Stops.

```
     /**************************************************/
     /*Actions to be carried out in the case of an emergency*/
     /*-a1 : stop motor M1*/
     /*-a2 : switch off the controller*/
     /*-a3 : initialize the communication buffer*/
     /*-a4 : Initialize the internal variables */
     /**************************************************/
     Input: ;
     Output: M1, Work, Buffer;
Start P1
     M1 ← 0;                                        /* a1 */
     Work ← 0;                                      /* a2 */
     Buffer ← 0;                                    /* a2 */
     Init();                                        /* a4 */
End P1
```

2. **CSPEC:** Control of an Automated Distribution System.

Remember that the control process represents the command part of the data flow diagram to which it is associated (Fig. 9.7).

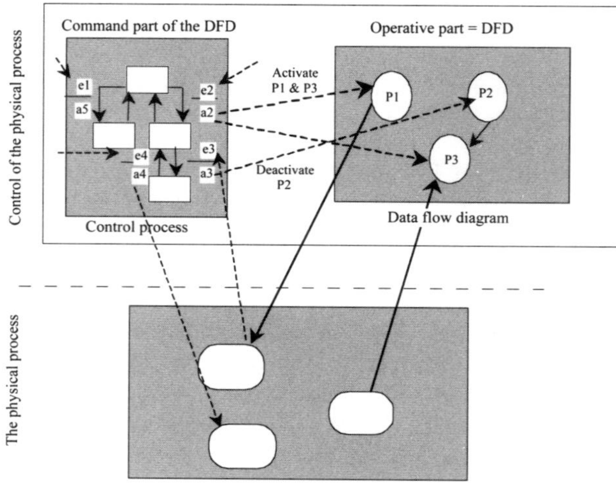

Fig. 9.7 Nature of coupling between the control process and its DFD.

Its role is to manage the activation and deactivation of the DFD transformation agents or processes according to events and its internal state. The different states of the control process are defined following the observable system states to control, which represent a particular configuration of the states of DFD agents. There are only three observable states for this system, as the state transition diagram in Figure 9.8 shows. This diagram is the CSPEC of DFD "Control of an Automated Distribution System". The states of this system are outlined in the following paragraphs.

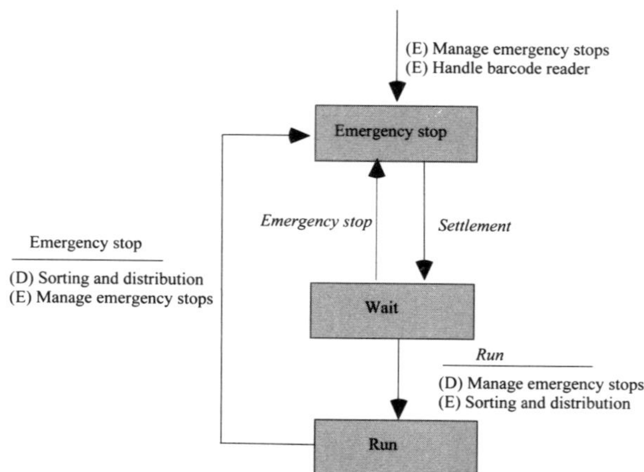

Fig. 9.8 CSPE: Film sorting and distribution.

1. The "Emergency Stop" State

    This state represents one of two stable states within the system.

    > A state is called the stable state of a system if all of the variables of the operative part remain constant and if the global state of the system is consistent.

    The system passes into this state when it is placed under tension, or when the operator specifically requests it by pushing the stop button. Note that if the system passes into this state after being placed under tension, the "`manage the emergency stops`" agent is systematically activated (E) to initialize the system. This is the same for the "`control bar code reader`" agent. The fact that this latter is activated at this instant, and that it has not been deactivated or activated in the rest of the state-transition diagram, indicates that this agent remains constantly active despite the events which can occur, until the system is taken out of tension.

    The system passes from this stability state to the second stability state "Wait" if the "performance" event occurs. The "Wait" state is the only output state to come from the "*Emergency Stop*" state to which it can return if another emergency stop occurs. The system passes into the "Work" state if, and only if, the "work" event is generated.

2. The "Work" State

    This is the normal functioning state. It corresponds to the implementation of the overall "sorting and distribution" function. The system remains in this state as long as the "*emergency stop*" event does not occur, in which case, the "sorting and distribution" state is suspended and the "`manage the emergency stops`" agent is reactivated.

    The reader will have understood that the "cyclic/unitary" event and the "cyclic/continuous" event essentially involve the "`control the stores`" agent, and not the DFD control process "Control of an Automated Distribution System". The control process state of a given DFD effectively represents a particular situation or configuration in the states of DFD transformation agents or processes in which some agents are active and others suspended. The passage of one configuration to another is conditioned by the appearance of internal or external events coming from the physical process.

9.2.6 The Hierarchical Refinement Stage of DFD0 Agents

The preceding stage enabled us only to retain important agents or processes in the general DFD. This stage studies the possibility of breaking them down into sub-agents. This refinement process generally involves agents judged sufficiently complex at this level that they form the object of a simple and concise description with the help of a specification file "PSPEC". The following agents become involved in this category.

The Global Function Agent (Sorting and Distribution)

The refinement of this global function is dependent on the objectives to be met, and the complexity of the tasks required to implement them. In this system, its role is limited to co-ordinating the activation over time of the different control agents: "Store Control Agent" and "Channel Control Agent". The PSPEC of this global function is:

```
PSPEC P7 : Sorting and Distribution
     /********************************/
     /* Overall function: Supply; Identification; Sorting*/
     /********************************/
Input: ;
Output: , (E) Store control, (E) Channel control;
Start P1
     As long as Active
          Make          M1 ← 1;
            Indicator ← 0;
            "E" Store Control;          /* E=Enable : Activate */
            "E" Channel Control;
          End Make;
End P1
```

Note that this specification file displays a cause and effect type relationship between the agent of the overall "sorting and distribution" function and the two agents activated by it.

The coupling is strong between this function and the two agents. The deactivation of the overall function leads to deactivation of the two agents. When this type of coupling is encountered, it is preferable to return directly to the level of the control process which controls the global function. In this way the association of its own control process to the function is avoided. One must not lose sight of the fact that the control process represents the control part of a DFD. The interest of this approach is, particularly, to avoid forgetting to control the composite agents (Fig. 9.9).

In other applications, the support agent of the global function is usually complex and involves several specialized sub-agents in different tasks (Fig. 9.10). For example, one agent for production planning and scheduling, which can be a specific algorithm or an existing tool which will need to be integrated into the production line; a journal agent which has the role of managing the statistics and traces of the physical process variables; a quality control agent to maintain a journal of production and significant events (manufacturing faults, number of rejects, production halts, etc.).

Finally, it is important to note that the complexity of this main agent has a direct impact on the choice of execution platform as will be detailed in the following sections.

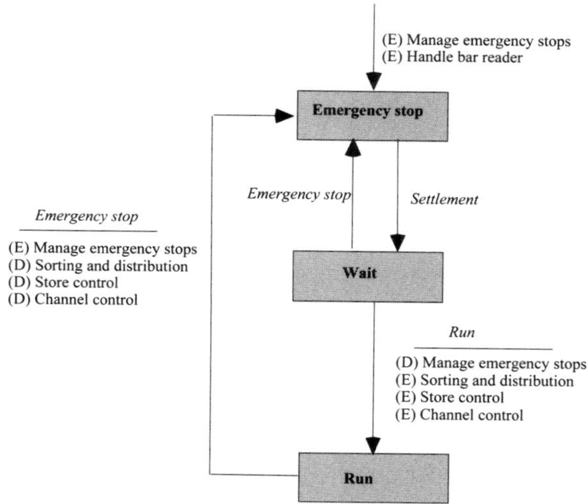

Fig. 9.9 Repercussions of the strong coupling relationship between agents on the CSPEC.

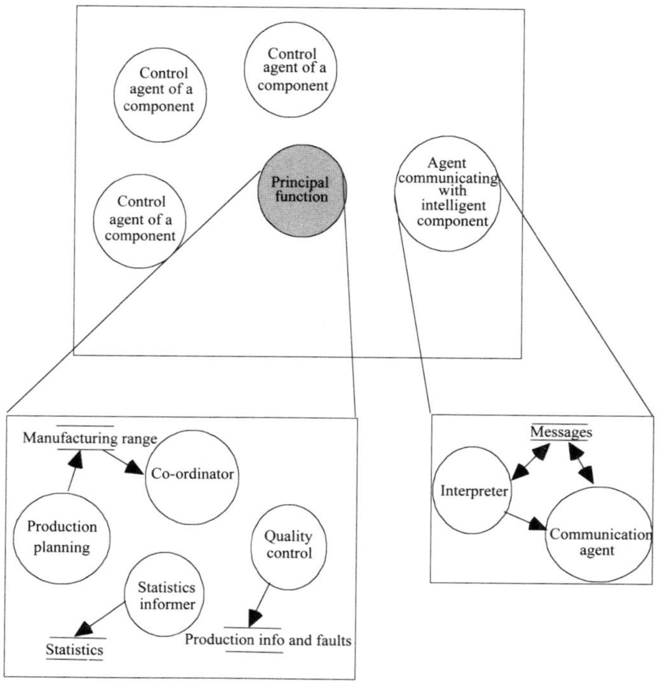

Fig. 9.10 Example of the overall complex function.

Communicating Agents

The agents must manage the dialogue with intelligent deported logic components. Such agents are generally composed of at least one specialized communication agent which uses a protocol to manage the exchanges with the component via a communication means (serial line, parallel line, local industrial network: FIP, PROFIBUS, etc.). A second agent, which ensures the interface between the communication agent and the other agents using its services, is also part of this agent. Where our system is concerned, this agent is composed of a communication sub-agent specialized in the management of the RS232 line. As the bar code reader behaves as a simple computer keyboard, a second sub-agent is used to wait and transfer the codes read from the reception buffer used by the communication agent into a zone accessible to other application agents. The “Bar code reader control” DFD is given in Figure 9.11.

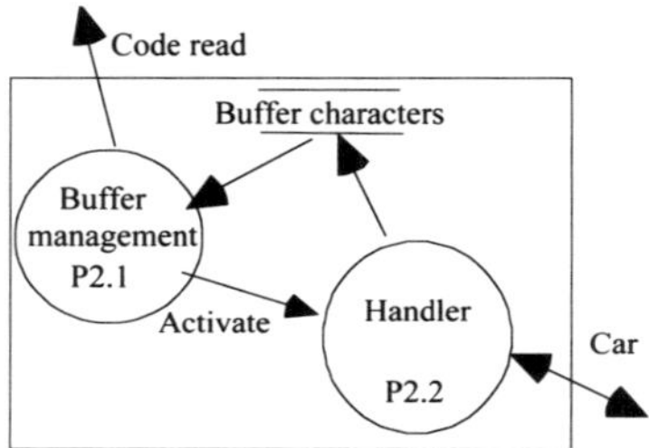

Fig. 9.11 " Bar code reader control " DFD.

Below is the specification file for the P2.1 agent “Buffer Management”:

```
PSPEC P2.1 :Buffer Management
      /*******************************************/
      /*manage the interception of characters coming */
      /*from the serial link                        */
      /*******************************************/
Input:        buffer;
Output:       read code;
Start P1
              Make
              "wait" the reception of the read code;
              read code <-- character buffer;
              End Make;
End P1
```

The PSPEC of agent P2.2 is not given because it is directly dependent on the hardware specifications of the host data processing system, especially the possibilities concerning interrupt management. In the case where the mechanism of interrupt management and interrupt handlers is not available, implementation of this pilot requires the use of the periodic polling technique of the registers of the serial link controller.

The "Store Control" Agent

This is the control agent of a composed logic entity, and consequently must be associated with a DFD (Fig. 9.12).

Specifications state that the first stage of the sorting and distribution cycle corresponds to the intervention of the "`Store Control`" agent which must follow the following stages:

1. Always start by trying to take a film from the Ma store;
2. *If* after 4 seconds the proximity detector PPM does not react, *then* the Ma store is declared empty (synchronization between the two columns is compulsory) *else* A must be deactivated and the process restarts with store B;
3. *If* operator's instruction is the continuous cycle, *then* restart from 1 after a 1 second delay.

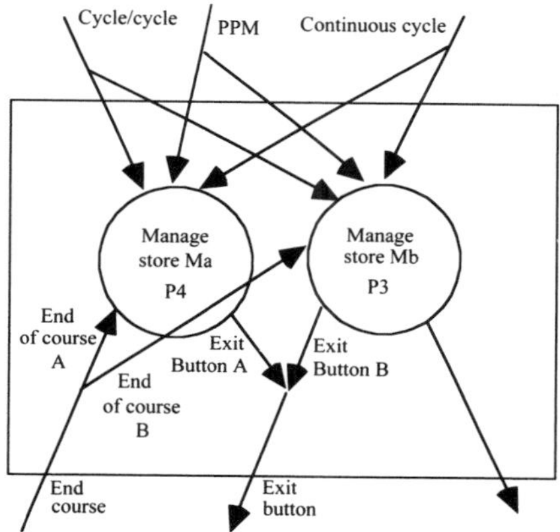

Fig. 9.12 "Store control" DFD.

On the other hand, note that the output flows generated by the "`Store Control`" agent are simple TOR type flows. There is no useful specific process which necessitates the use of the two specialized sub-agents for the encapsulation of these processes. The control process can directly use them. In contrast, if the output flows request a specific logic and process to manage them, it is essential to maintain the two sub-agents "`Manage Store A`" and "`Manage Store B`". In addition, synchronization must be guaranteed between them using a control process which adheres to the rules laid out in the specifications. In our system the generation of output flows comes down to a simple activation or deactivation action of the TOR signals. The maintenance of the two sub-agents necessitates the use of a control process to control them and guarantee their synchronization (if store A is empty or faulty then store B must be used). To suppress them implicates the transfer of output flow generation actions to the control process. Consequently, this latter becomes the direct control part of the physical components (parts of the physical process which represent the logical entity) to which it is attached, and no longer the control part of the two suppressed sub-agents. The "store control" DFD will simply be replaced by a CSPEC: "store control" (Fig. 9.13).

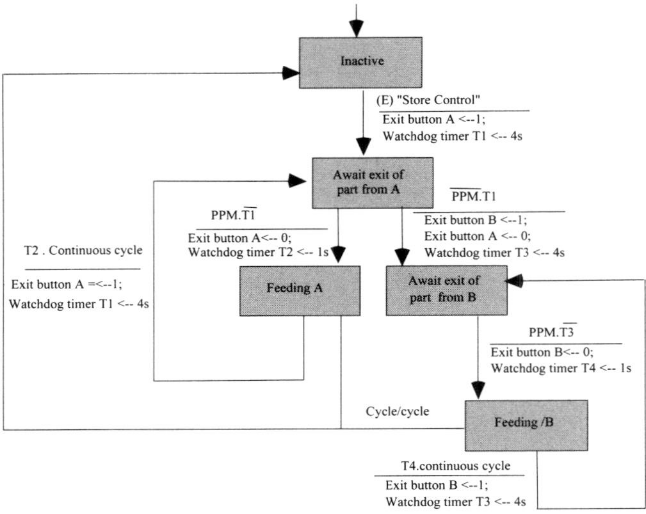

Fig. 9.13 "Store control" CSPEC.

The CSPEC in Figure 9.13 needs some explanation. At each activation, the agent passes into the "await part exit from A" state where it must await the passage of a part in front of the PPM proximity detector. By passing into this state, it activates the button jack of store A by placing at 1 the flow "exit button A". The agent remains in this state until one of the two following conditions are attained:

1. If the proximity detector sends the PPM signal and the temporizer is not triggered, then the agent passes into the "supply from store A" state by deactivating the A jack and activating the T2 temporizer with a value of 1 second. From the "supply from store A" state, the agent can pass into the "inactive" state if the functioning mode is the "cycle by cycle" mode, because in this version one film at a time is allowed on the conveyor. Or, when the T2 temporizer is triggered and the functioning mode is the "continuous cycle" mode, then the agent passes into the "await the exit of part A" state by activating the A jack again and arming the T1 temporizer.

2. If the proximity detector has not generated the PPM signal because the store is empty or one of its components is faulty, and the T1 temporizer is triggered (exactly 4 seconds have passed), then the agent passes into the "await the exit of part B" state. By passing into this state, it deactivates the A jack and activates that of B. It then activates a 4 second delay.

From the point at which the time constraints have been displayed, and involving the data or control flows, or even the causality of events originating from the operative part (observe a delay of one second after the occurrence of the PPM flow), it is necessary to inform two data dictionary appendix tables which must contain the definition of all of the time constraints related to the system studied. Table 9.1 gives each output flow the event trigger and the maximum time for its generation by the command part. Table 9.2 gives the relations explaining the constraints between the events generated by the operative part.

Table 9.1 Command part response times.

Input flow	Event	Output flow	Event	Response time
(E)	Activation	Exit button A<-- 1	Exit of a part	1 sec maximum
PPM	Exit of a part from store A and its passage in front of the sensor	Exit button A<-- 0	Button returned to the rest position	1 sec maximum
...	...	...	...	...

Table 9.2 Causality for events of the operative part.

Flow 1	Event 1	Flow 2	Event 2	Limitation
Exit button A<-- 1	Activation of Ma store button	PPM	Exit of a part from store Ma and its passage in front of the sensor	The maximum time separating the activation of the Ma store jack button and the effective exit of a part is: 4 sec
Exit button A<-- 1	Activation of the Ma store button	Exit button A<-- 0	Button returned to the rest position	1 sec is required to allow the jack to return to its rest position to be able to reactivate it.
...	...	...	...	...

It is clear that Table 9.2 is mainly used to express the time limitations separating the events originating in the operative part, by taking into account the technological limitations. We leave the reader to complete these two tables.

The "Channel Control" Agent

The role of this agent is to manoeuvre the film on the conveyor belt according to its code. Channel A collects 100 ASA films and forms sets of three films. Channel B is specialized for 200 ASA films and channel C for 400 ASA films. Figure 9.14 gives the DFD of this agent which is easily extracted from the static model.

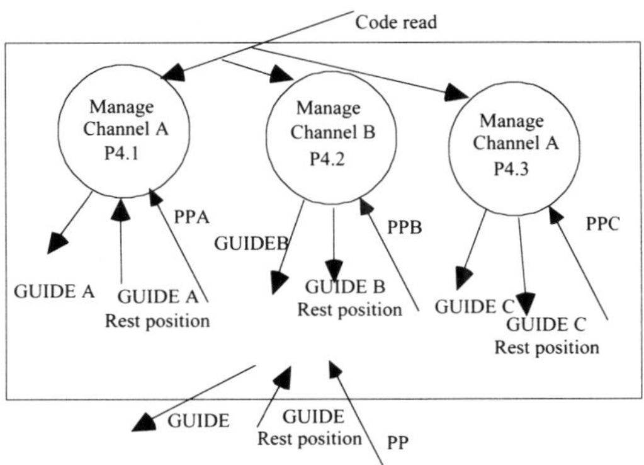

Fig. 9.14 "Channel control" DFD.

In contrast to the above case, the sub-agents of this DFD are independent and require no time co-ordination. The "`manage channel A`" sub-agent will guide the film towards channel A when it passes in front of the PPA proximity sensor, and its code corresponds to the code representing the 100 ASA value. No specific activation order is required to trigger this agent. The same occurs for sub-agents "`manage channel B`" and "`manage channel C`" which have the same behaviour. A direct consequence of this functioning autonomy between the three sub-agents is that they do not require a control process to co-ordinate their actions. Below is the PSPEC for the "`manage channel A`" agent. The PSPECS for the two other agents are similar.

```
PSPEC P4.1 : Manage Channel A
             /**************************************/
             /* manage the guidance of the film present */
             /*in front of the proximity sensor */
             /**************************************/
     Input:  read code, GUIDE A rest position, PPA;
     Output:        GUIDE A;
Start P4.1
     As long as ACTIVE
       Make
        If ( GUIDE A in rest position = 0)
         Then
             If (PPA = 1)                      /*PPA passes from 0 to 1*/
               Then
                 If (read code = "100 ASA value")
                  Then
             GUIDE A <-- 1;                     /*activate rotating jack*/
             Wait 2 seconds;                          /*guide delay*/
             GUIDE A <-- 0;                   /*deactivate rotating jack*/
                        EndIf
                    EndIf
               EndIf
             End Make;
End P1
```

9.3 Design and Implementation of the Command Part

In this section we attempt to overcome the design and implementation problems of the command part. It is a question of discussing the *choice criteria of a target hardware architecture*, which depends finally on the choice of implementation techniques, especially the choice of the execution platform for each agent. The principle of the analysis approach of the requirements and specifications of real-time systems is the SA/RT method as described by D.J. Hatley and I.A. Pirbhai. However, there exists a substantial difference between our approach, which involves the appearance of agents (which constitute the interface with the environment) from the first stages of the analysis, and the philosophy of the original method which aims to free the system functions in terms of the transformation processes, and then study the problems of interfacing with the outside world.

In the following sections, we discuss the various solutions and possible architectures and their impact on the performance, flexibility and adaptability as described above. This raises the remark: we are in the process of studying the command part of an already existing physical process. By its very nature, this considerably simplifies the second stage of the method. Furthermore, it is this that was at the origin of the use of the static model to clarify the physical structure of the operative part and the choice of its division into logical entities. As we have already indicated at the start of this study, this logical division is an efficient means of facilitating the analysis and design of the command part of a physical process. If the physical process does not, however, exist, it is imperative to strictly respect the different stages of the SA/RT (SA/SD) method. In the following text, our discussion will be informal, without adhering to the symbols and the different diagrams which can be used at this stage, principally the context architecture diagrams, the architecture flow diagrams, etc.

9.3.1 Choice of Architecture for the Command Part

At this stage it is necessary to decide on the type of hardware platform required, which will support the control of the film sorting and distribution system, and study the type of physical support to be used for each flow or interaction displayed in the first stage of the analysis. The approach to be followed involves:

- studying the problems of technological choice and the physical limitations which follow for the implementation of context diagram flows (type of physical support necessary to indicate the different flows in Figure 9.3). When this involves a study concerning a new system whose operative part needs to be designed, it is also necessary to study the implementation problems of the logical entities of the static model. Figure 9.16b gives a technological overview of the “Channel” logical entity. It is at this stage that it will be necessary to choose a particular technology to implement each logical entity. Incidentally, we will decide if it is necessary to use monostable or bistable distributors, single effect or double effect jack, etc. to implement the logical entity button.
- studying the target execution platform and the necessary technology to implement the different DFD agents and the implementation of internal interactions between these agents.

In the following section, only the second point will be discussed, the first has been resolved by the fact that the operative part already exists.

9.3.1.1 Data and Control Flow Context Diagrams

Figure 9.15 gives a version of the data dictionary (the three points represent the columns in Figure 9.6) completed with the technological choice concerning the nature, type and origin of data and control flows. The physical support technology is equally as precise.

Flow	...	Designation of component concerned	Communication protocol
Exit Button: 1-exit button A 2-exit button B		Monostable store jack distributor : MYH 5/2M5-L-Led	TOR electric link (24v)
End course 1- end course A 2- end course B		Magnetic sensor: SMTO-1-PS=LED-24	TOR electric link (24v)
PPM		Optical sensor: SOE-RT/L-M18-PS-K-Led	TOR electric link (24v)
Characters		Barcode reader: SCANTEAM 2000	Serial link : normal V24
Run		Push button	Simple link
Emergency stop		Push button	TOR electric link (24v)
Settlement		Push button	TOR electric link (24v)
M1		Continuous current motoreducer	TOR electric link (24v)
GUIDE 1- GUIDE A 2- GUIDE A 3- GUIDE A		Monostable guide jack distributor : MYH 5/2M5-L-Led	TOR electric link (24v)
PP 1- PPA 2- PPA 3- PPA		Optical sensor: SOE-RT/L-M18-PS-K-Led	TOR electric link (24v)
Unitary cycle		2 position selector	Simple link
Continuous cycle		2 position selector	Simple link
Work indicator			TOR electric link (24v)

Fig. 9.15 Data dictionary complete with information on flow implementation.

With the exception of the serial link used to connect the bar code reader to the command part, the other interactions are supported by simple 24v wire links.

Figure 9.16 gives a simplified electronic overview of the system, taking into account the technological choices of the components and their connection to the system, conforming to the existing physical system.

In the case where this latter is to be designed, it is essential to study the technological choices to be made concerning input and output flow supports, as well as the intended components or sources of these flows as indicated in Figure 9.16a, and to complete the data dictionary with the information relating to these choices.

A precise description of the architecture of each entity of the static model and the technological choices of its components must, of course, be carried out at this stage. The final file must contain the technological outline of each logical entity, accompanied by electrical and pneumatic diagrams etc. An exact nomenclature of the components must also figure in this material.

9.3.1.2 Internal Flows and Agents

At this stage, either we know the nature and technology of the physical back up of data and control flows because the operative part exists, or the choices have been made in the preceding stage. The same is true where logical entities are concerned.

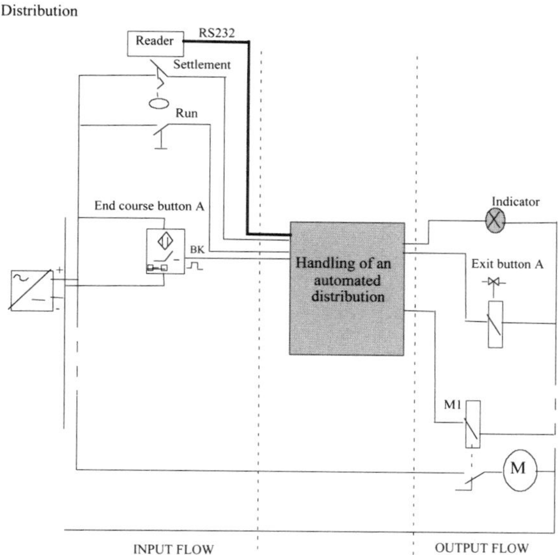

Fig. 9.16a Electrical diagram of the system.

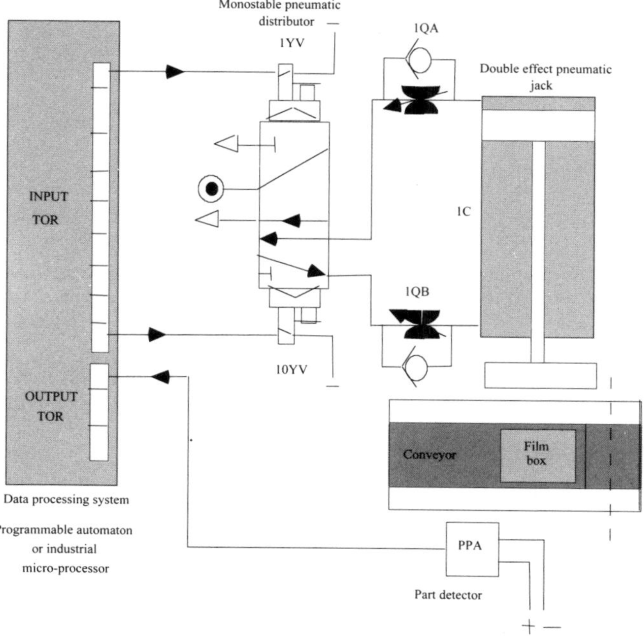

Fig. 9.16b Technological outline of channel logic entity according to our modelling.

Their components are identified as well as their technology and, consequently, the rules of interfacing and use of these components are completely understood. It is clear that the technological choice concerning the flows largely depends on the technological choices of the components.

> The best way of interfacing each logical entity with its command part, indicated by a command agent which was linked to it in the DFD0 remains to be studied.

It is now necessary to take into account the limitations of performance, adaptability, flexibility etc. Taking account of these constraints, which are often contradictory, can lead to certain choices made in the previous stage being challenged, especially where the type and technology of the support of a data, control or component flow is concerned. Depending on the nature of each agent, the type of interaction with the logic entity and its complexity, and the limitations to adhere to, it is necessary to decide on the technology of the host execution platform.

The table in Figure 9.17 gives an overview of the different choices open to the DFD0 agents. It clearly shows that the type of host data processing system is defined according to several criteria, notably the complexity of the logic and processes of each agent, the distance separating the process from the host system, the type of support links, the flows exchanged between the agent and the operative part, etc.

Agent	Complexity	Type of link with process	Distance from the process	Control support	Links with other agents
Store control	Simple	Electric wire or earth bus	Very short	Wired automaton	With P7: activation signal
Channel control	Simple	Electric wire or earth bus	Very short	Wired automaton	With P7: activation signal
Code reader handler	Simple	RS232	Very short	Embedded control automaton	With P4: means of intermediary Storage : register
Emergency stop manager	Simple	Electric wire or earth bus	Very short	Automaton	No direct internal links
Sorting and distribution	Simple	No link		Automaton	With P3et P4: activation signal
Control process	Simple	Electric wire or earth bus	Very short	Automaton	With the whole: signals

Fig. 9.17 Selection table of the host data processing system of the different agents.

The overall function of our system is relatively simple. This led us to opt for a programmable automaton solution as an execution platform. Consequently, the application development chain will be a standard chain using GRAFCET as a design tool. Figure 9.20 gives the different GRAFCETs for the control of an automated distribution system.

This table must be followed by a precise description of the characteristic techniques of each execution platform held (technology, manufacturer, range, execution speed, hardware configuration, type of operating system, characteristics of the operating system, application development environment, etc.).

In the study of complex industrial systems (production lines) which use several interconnected automated systems (or modules), this function is too complex (Fig. 9.18) to have an automaton platform. In general, the choice will be concerned with the programmable automaton for command and control agents, and one or more industrial micro-computers (industrial PC) to support the complex functions such as the global function, supervision, planning etc. Here again, the choice is not definitive if the global function must use software or package services which require more extensive configurations than a simple industrial PC, for example a real-time scheduling and planning tool, or any other software of the same nature involved in the implementation of the function. It is essential therefore to deport specific "expert" agents of the principal function on more powerful platforms (mini or large computers) as indicated in Figure 9.18.

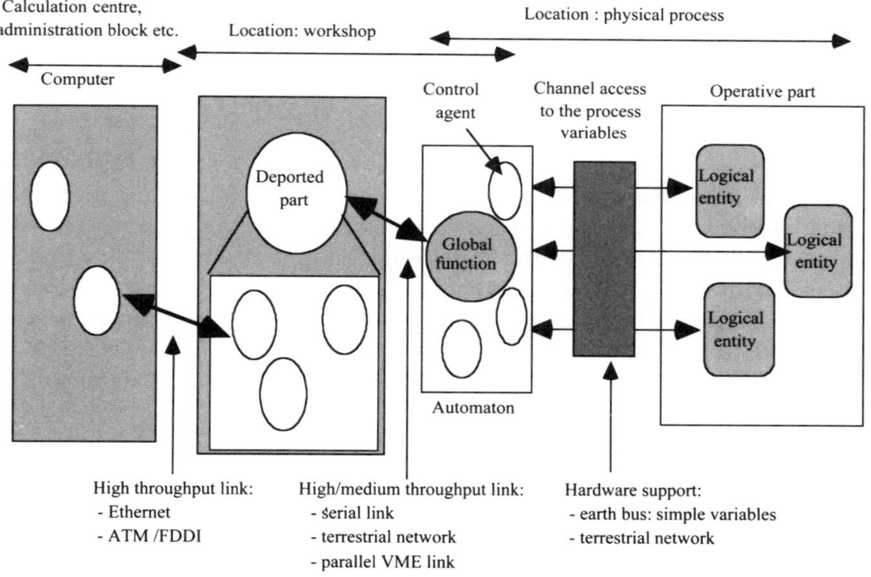

Fig. 9.18 Possible geographical installation of the agents of an industrial application.

The distance between the operative part and the command part, the nature of the exchange flows (simple: TOR or analogue, complex: structured data or messages), the dynamics of the physical process etc. are important criteria for the choice of execution platform for each agent. The choice of programming language and the corresponding development tools depends on the technology of the execution platform.

In the case where the distance between the command and the operative part is very short, it involves an embedded command. Under these conditions, the possible solutions are:

1. A microprocessor-based embedded card with the command and the micro-programmed or remote loading real-time executive. This choice depends on the external environment of the automated system (photocopier, printer,

vehicle on-board computer etc.). In an aggressive industrial environment, *VME technology* (parallel bus) and real-time executives (see Chapter 5) have the advantage of enabling the replacement of automaton when agent processing and logic, especially the global function agent, is highly complex. In certain situations, this solution enables the system to manage without coupling the command automaton with the supervision PC. The possibilities of the extension and development of the solution are also improved.

2. A dedicated automaton. Reduced size automatons are now available on the market, which have a large capacity from the point of view of available resources and execution speeds, which accept the remote loading of programs to be executed via a serial link. The development chain of these programs is found deported on standard micro-computers. This type of automaton constitutes an interesting alternative (quality/price ratio and adaptability of use) to the VME solutions in industrial applications.

9.3.1.3 Choice and Interfacing of a Data Processing System with the Physical Process

At this stage, we establish the correspondence card between the physical communication means available on the host data processing system, and the communication supports used to direct the input/output application flows. Our choice depends on the automaton. Under these conditions, it is necessary to determine the allocation of process variables to the input/output addresses of the automaton. The indications and information related to the allocation must be directly transferred to the data dictionary. Figure 9.19 gives the new version of the dictionary, following the choices that have been made.

9.3.2 Implementation of Agents

The first stage of the phase involves deciding on the form and nature of the internal coupling to be carried out between the agents of the same execution platform (Fig. 9.18). Isolated agents which have been allocated to different platforms will be directly implemented on these platforms with their development tools. All of the digital command agents in the automated distribution system are allocated to an automaton. Consequently, this stage is essential. They have the role of specifying the means that will be used to indicate an agent and to establish a priority relationship between the different agents. There are two ways of implementing an agent:

1. *A task, an autonomous computing process or an independent GRAFCET* depending on the platform. The agents, deemed priority agents because they are subject to demands of performance and stability, also form part of this category. They ensure that the principal vital functions take place, such as the coordination and supervision of the activities of other agents; the immediate consideration of external events originating from a rapid dynamic process etc. The coupling of these agents with the rest of the application is *asynchronous*. They are therefore autonomous where the execution of their processes is concerned.

Flow	Nature	Flow type	...	Sense	@port/variable
Exit button: 1-exit button A 2-exit button B	Action	Discrete data of the type TOR (1 or 0, True or False)		 Input Output	 O 0,1 / VERA O 0,2 / VERB
End of course 1-end of course A 2-end of course B	Information	Discrete data of the type TOR (1 or 0, True or False)		 Input Input	 I 1,0 /FCA I 1,1 / FCB
PPM	Information	Discrete data of the type TOR (1 or 0, True or False)		Input	I 1,2 / PPM
Characters	Information	Discrete data of the type TOR (1 or 0, True or False)		Input	Diagnostic port of the automaton
Run	Control	Discrete data of the type TOR (1 or 0, True or False)		Input	I 0,1 / START
Emergency stop	Control	Discrete data of the type TOR (1 or 0, True or False)		Input	I 2, 7 / BP_AU
Settlement	Control	Discrete data of the type TOR (1 or 0, True or False)		Input	I 0,7/ACQ
MI	Action	Discrete data of the type TOR (1 or 0, True or False)		Output	O 1,0 / M1
GUIDE 1-GUIDEA 2-GUIDEA 3-GUIDEA	Action	Discrete data of the type TOR (1 or 0, True or False)		 Output Output Output	 O 0,5 / GUIDEA O 0,6 / GUIDEB O 0,7 / GUIDEC
PP 1-PPA 2-PPA 3-PPA	Information	Discrete data of the type TOR (1 or 0, True or False)		 Input Input Input	 I 2,3/PPA I 2,4 PPB I 2,5 PPC
Unitary cycle	Information	Discrete data of the type TOR (1 or 0, True or False)		Input	I 0,2 / CU
Continuous cycle	Information	Discrete data of the type TOR (1 or 0, True or False)		Input	I 0,3 / CC
Work indicator	Information	Discrete data of the type TOR (1 or 0, True or False)		Output	O 0,0 / INDICATOR

Fig. 9.19 Updating of the data dictionary to take into account the I/S allocations.

2. *A handler, a sub-handler or a micro-stage,* because the processes implemented by this agent are either too short to form the object of an independent process, or are not critical, and the agent is considered a lower priority than the others. Consequently, the processing of this agent can be grouped with the processing of other agents of the same nature to form a module whose execution will be supported by a single process. This process will look after the co-ordinated execution of processing each agent (problem of the logical link of the processing of a module and the causality between trigger events). Implementation of each agent in the form of an independent process requires the implementation of co-ordination and synchronization between these agents, according to the global communication protocol of the application. Grouping them into a single process gives it responsibility over the co-ordination and activation over time processing problems. This process will be called “master agent” or “superior agent”.

At this stage, it is advisable to rely on the execution diagrams to clarify the different links of agents of the module, and their activation conditions. The global function agent of our system can fill this master agent role. Table 9.3 gives the nature and module of each digital command agent of the SAD system.

Table 9.3

Agent	Type	Module
P1 : Manage emergencies	Autonomous	
P2.1: Manage the buffer	Autonomous	
P2.1: Control port series	Autonomous	
P3.1: Manage store A	Grouped	Sorting and distribution
P3.2: Manage store B	Grouped	Sorting and distribution
P4.1: Manage channel A	Grouped	Sorting and distribution
P4.1: Manage channel B	Grouped	Sorting and distribution
P4.1: Manage channel C	Grouped	Sorting and distribution

9.3.2.1 Solution Based on Programmable Automaton

For an industrial programmable automaton implementation, Figure 9.20 gives the command GRAFCETs which are the result of the translation of the system specifications using the SA/RT method, in this formalism.

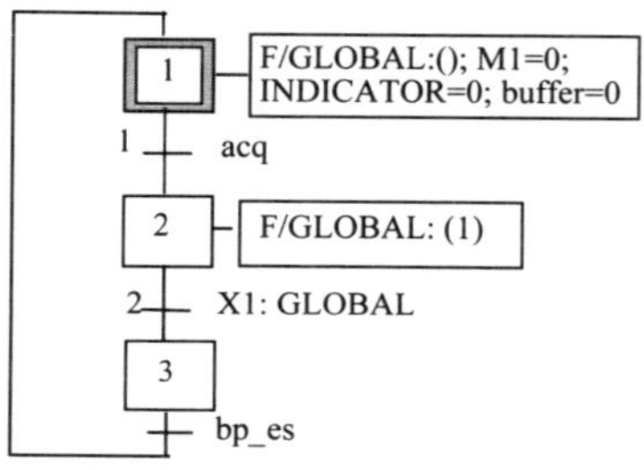

Fig. 9.20a GRAFCET of the "manage emergency stops" agent: EMER_ STOP.

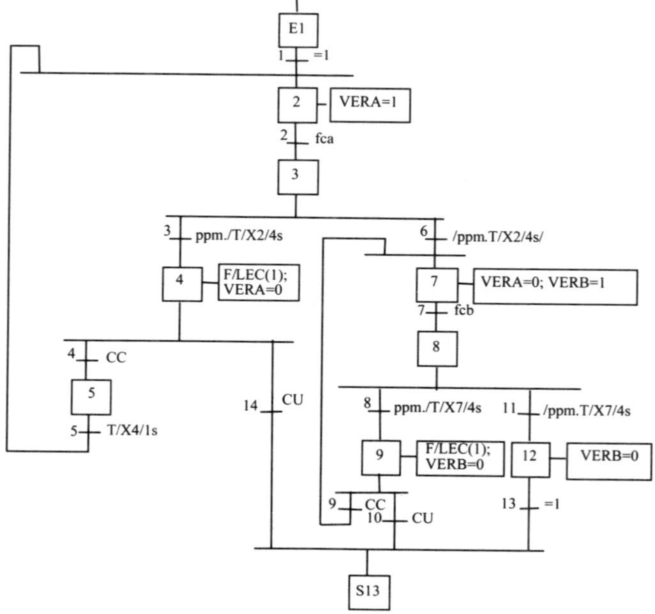

Fig. 9.20b GRAFCET of the "control the stores" agent: STORE.

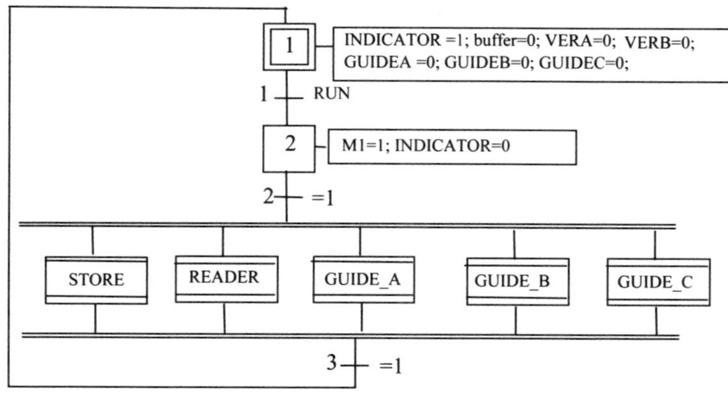

Fig. 9.20c GRAFCET of the "sorting and distribution" agent: GLOBAL.

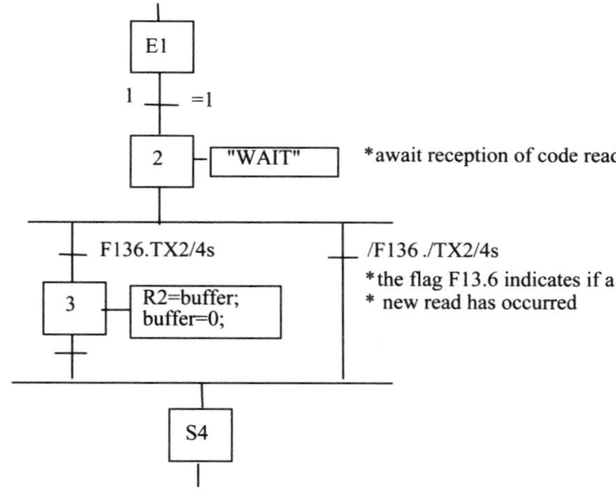

Fig. 9.20d GRAFCET of the "manage buffer" agent: READ.

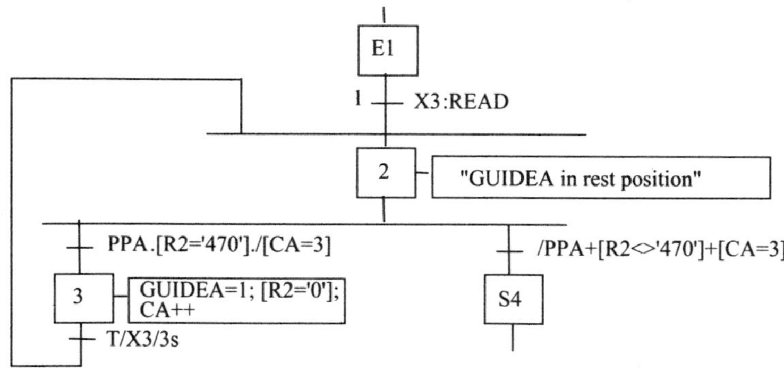

Fig. 9.20e GRAFCET of the "manage channel A" agent: GUIDEA.

The GRAFCETs of the GUIDEB and GUIDEC agents are identical to that of the GUIDEA agent. Figure 9.21 clearly shows the relationships and the existing hierarchy between the different graphs in Figure 9.20.

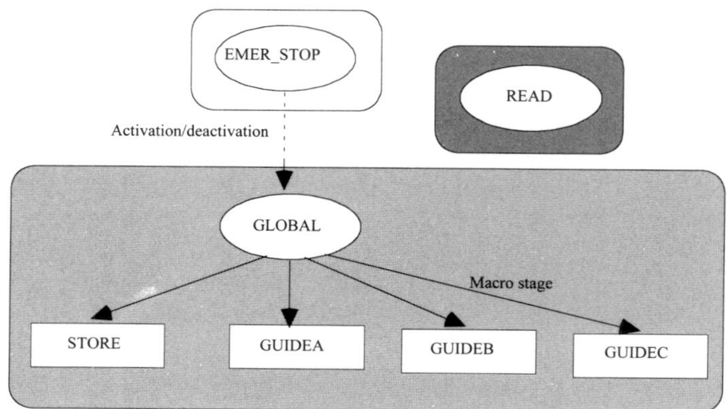

Fig. 9.21 Hierarchy of GRAFCETs of the digital command SAD.

To conclude, we have presented a global approach for the analysis and design of automated systems specifically, and real-time systems in general, which is an adaptation of the SA/RT method. In contrast to the SA/RT method, this approach aims to take into account the knowledge already acquired on the application field (on the architectural plan and the usable functional means) from the first phases of the development cycle in order to render the analysis process more deterministic. The support system is an automated distribution system widely used in the different National Education Establishments in France.

9.3.2.2 *Solution Based on the VxWorks Real-Time Executive*

Finally, we present the main lines of an implementation of the agents of this application with the real-time executive VxWorks. In this solution, we have deliberately opted for a totally distributed solution where each agent displayed in the analysis phase is supported by a process.

```
#define CPU              MC68020
#include "vxWorks.h"
#include "sigLib.h"
#include "semLib.h"
#include "control1.h"                /*direct mode version of the I/O card controller*/
/*******************************************************/
/*Allocation table of the process variables to the bits        */
/*of the I/O register of the card used                          */
/*******************************************************/
/*Actuator variables*/
#define VERA actuator1
#define VERB actuator2
#define M1 actuator3
#define GUIDEA actuator4
```

```
#define GUIDEB actuator5
#define GUIDEC actuator6
#define INDICATOR actuator7

/*Sensor variables*/
#define FCA sensor1()
#define FCB sensor2()
#define PPM sensor3()
#define WORK sensor4()
#define BP_AU sensor5()
#define ACQ sensor6()
#define PPA sensor7()
#define PPB sensor8()
#define PPC sensor9()
#define CU sensor10()
#define CC sensor11()
void READ();
void EMER_STOP();
void STORE();
void GUIDEA();
void GUIDEB();
void GUIDEC();

/*Global variable positioned by the READ agent when a new data arrives*/
/*The film type is stored in this variable*/

short Buffer_full='0' char R2[3]= '0';
int CA = 0;                                          /*channel A lot counter*/
int CB = 0;                                          /*channel B lot counter*/
int CC = 0;                                          /*channel C lot counter*/
launchTask()
{ Init_control();                  /*card initialization depending on the sequences
                                          recommended by the manufacturer */

tid1= taskSpawn("READ",100,0,2000,READ);          /*creation of the ALARM agent*/
tid2= taskSpawn("EMER_STOP",100,0,2000,EMER_STOP);          /*creation of the
                                                  STORE EMER_STOP agent*/
tid3= taskSpawn("STORE",100,0,2000,STORE);      /*creation of the STORE agent*/
tid4= taskSpawn("GUIDEA",100,0,2000,GUIDEA);    /*creation of the GUIDEA agent*/
tid5= taskSpawn("GUIDEB",100,0,2000,GUIDEB);    /*creation of the GUIDEB agent*/
tid6= taskSpawn("GUIDEC",100,0,2000,GUIDEC);    /*creation of the GUIDEC agent*/
                    /*only the EMER_STOP and READ agents are active at the start*/
        taskSuspend(tid2);

/*From this point the master task takes on the CSPEC role of the DFD0*/
for(;;)
        {
        S_EMER_STP :                                  /*Emergency Stop state*/
        taskSuspend(tid3);
        taskSuspend(tid4);
        taskSuspend(tid5);
        taskSuspend(tid6);
        taskResume(tid2);
        while (not (ACQ))                                  /*await the stop*/
taskdelay(sysClkRateGet()*50);        /*suspend the master task for a short time */
         S_WAIT :                                          /*wait STATE*/
        While (not (WORK))
```

```
        taskdelay(sysClkRateGet()*50); /*suspend the master task for a short time */
        taskSuspend(tid2);    /*suspend the emergency stop management agent and activate
                                                                         the others */
taskSuspend(tid3);
        taskSuspend(tid4);
        taskSuspend(tid5);
        taskSuspend(tid6);
         S_WORK :
        While (not (BP_AU))
Taskdelay(sysClkRateGet()*50);                /*suspend the master task for a short time */
        }  /*end loop for (;;)*/
}                                                                    /*end control agent*/
void GUIDEA()
{
  for (;;)
  {
GUIDEA (FALSE);                                  /*force GUIDEA into the rest position*/
While (not Buffer_full) taskdelay(sysClkRateGet()*10);
 If (PPA)
{
if (R2 == '470' & CA <3)
{ GUIDEA(TRUE);
 CA++;
 R2 = '0';
 Taskdelay(sysClkRateGet()*300)              /*wait 3 secs, the time to guide the film*/
};
};
}
void READ ()                                                           /*read agent code*/
 {
 }
void EMER-STOP()                                 /*emergency stop management agent code*/
 {
 }
void STORE()                                                /*store management agent code*/
 {
 }
void GUIDEB()                                                        /*GUIDEB agent code*/
 {
 }
void GUIDEC()                                                        /*GUIDEC agent code*/
 {
 }
```

10. *Management of Persistent Objects*

The aim of this case study is to outline the main points and basic principles of implementing a persistent objects manager. The reader will be inspired to implement a true manager adapted to the needs of these applications. Emphasis will be placed on the system structure in terms of specialized processes or agents, and on the communication protocols of the application as a whole.

10.1 Presentation

The object-oriented model (O2M) is a prototype of SGBDOO that we have developed within the scope of our research. It is aimed at principally supporting "real-time" databases called *active databases*. Its model effectively enables modelling static relations between objects the same as the standard SGBDs and modelling dynamic interactions as in real-time systems. Figure 10.1 gives the functional architecture of the O2M.

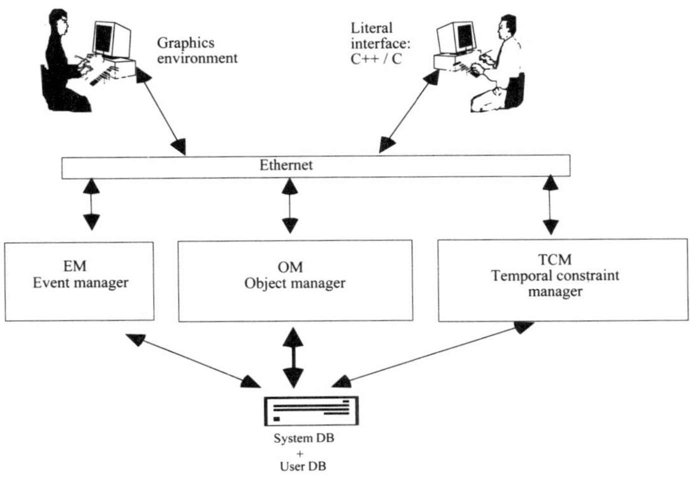

Fig. 10.1 The functional architecture of O2M.

The user interface of the O2M is made up of the VALID editor, presented in Chapter 6, and the standard textual interfaces for the development of applications using C++ and C.

In this chapter, we pay particular attention to the design and implementation of the object manager "OM". The two other components of O2M, the temporal constraint manager, "TCM" and the event manager, "EM", have already been described in detail in Chapter 8.

10.2 The Object Manager (OM)

An object manager must generally provide an abstraction level for representation and access to data. Besides the persistence of objects, it must ensure memory and disk management, data distribution with location transparency, the presence of the mechanism of transaction management and resistance to fault (see Chapter 1), and the management of the supported database schema, etc.

The prototype presented below integrates the following functions:

- *Persistence management:* OM enables the transfer of objects from the central memory on the disk by implementing a mechanism for the management of the virtual memory;
- *Interaction management:* the communication protocols between the different agents or processes of the user's applications and O2M, and the access primitives to OM.

An extension to this prototype, taking into account the set of object manager functions, is easily attainable.

10.2.1 A Multi-Agent Application with OM Persistent Objects

In this section, we give a very simple introductory example, which shows the use of the notion of persistence in multi-agent distributed applications, and its transparency to the developer (*implicit persistence*). This example represents the description of a real-time system. It describes the functioning of a robot which moves in stages following an action plan. A specific control card controls each organ of transport, which will be crudely called a "foot". The robot has two feet. One stage of displacement involves individually displacing each foot and ends when both feet are stationary on the ground. First, foot 1 can be displaced when the second is in a stable stop position on the ground. Once foot 1 has found its position of stability, the second can be triggered. If the overall equilibrium of the robot is challenged by violating this last rule, an urgent *recovery* action must be undertaken to rapidly bring the system back into a stable state of equilibrium; for example, forcing the immobilization of the two feet on the ground. It is also necessary that the displacement action of each foot must not exceed time T, to avoid eventual overloads on the other foot which could render the robot in a state of imbalance.

Conforming to the methodology presented in Chapter 6, this application can be structured using two types of agents; an overall supervision agent called "Robot" and two identical agents called "Foot control". According to the definition given in Chapter 1, the "Robot" agent is a transformation agent, while the two "Foot control" agents are reactive control agents. Figure 10.2 gives a specification of this system with the approach presented in Chapter 6. Note that the broken lines are control flows and the continuous lines are data flows.

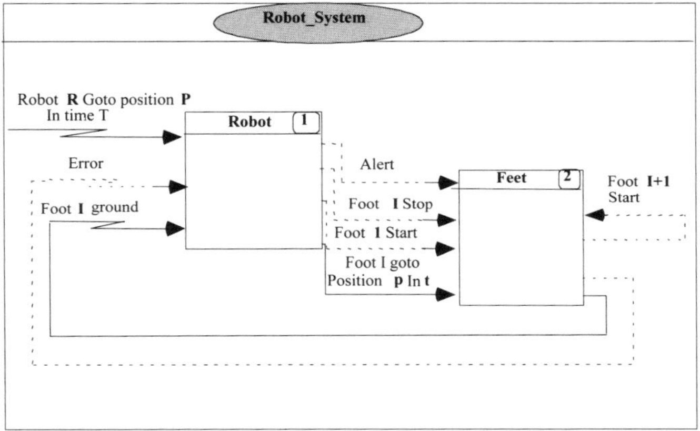

Fig. 10.2a The structure of the mobile robot system.

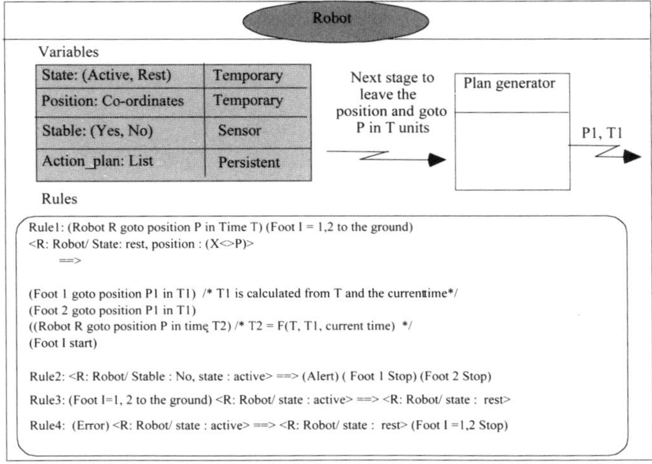

Fig. 10.2b The specification of the robot agent.

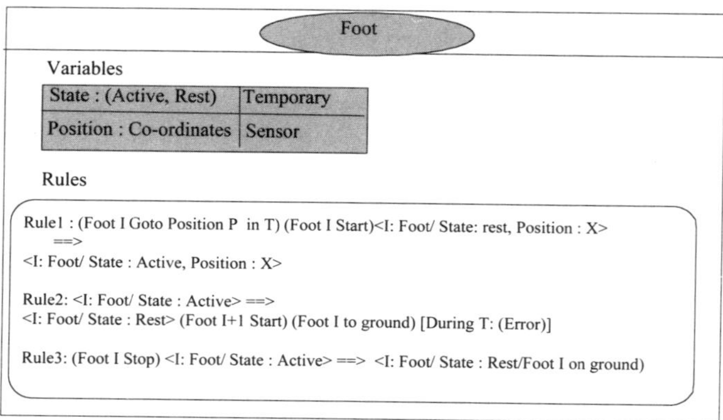

Fig. 10.2c The specification of the foot agent.

The synchronization of robot movements is provided by the exchange of messages between the two "foot" control agents and the "robot" control agent: (Foot 1 Start) in rule 1 of the "robot" agent and (Foot I+1 start) in rule 2 of the "foot" agent. As there are only two "foot" agents, only the "foot 1" agent will generate the message (Foot 1+1 start). Agent two does not have a successor. This hypothesis guarantees that only one foot is activated at a time. This specification is also characterized by control and synchronization distributed by the exchange of messages. The "robot" controller must specifically await the arrival of these messages (foot I = 1,2 on the ground) to trigger a new displacement order. Finally, note that the temporal constraint in rule 2 expresses that the duration of the transition of the rule corresponding to the duration of the elementary displacement action of a foot, must be carried out in a time lapse equal to *T*. If for any reason the action cannot take place (loss of balance, faulty organ, etc.) the "error" message is generated.

This message is essential to ensure recovery after a fault. In this example the recovery procedure is simple. It consists of stopping and immobilizing the whole if this is still possible. The "robot" control agent integrates a planning sub-agent which enables a plan of action to be generated and enables the "robot" agent to determine the co-ordinates of each elementary stage (P2). This sub-agent can be a processing agent if it uses a heuristic to determine the next position (P2), or a cognitive agent (an expert system) if it uses an inference motor to generate an action plan. The description of this agent is not important and falls outside the scope of this book. In this book we are more interested in the implementation of agents and interactions than the internal logic of each agent which depends on the semantics of each application.

From this example we see that the knowledge of an agent is indicated by one of the objects or by the variables. The variables can be:

- *physical variables* of the environment (actuators and sensors), access to the contents of this type of variable is carried out using digital or analogue I/O cards (see Chapter 5);
- *temporary work variables;*

- *persistent variables* whose contents must be saved on a non-volatile back-up. This is precisely the role of the object manager which must guarantee the safety and the restoration of the contents of these types of objects or variables in a way that is more or less *transparent* to the user. It must also guarantee the availability of this data in the central memory at any point, especially when this data is used repeatedly and under temporal limitations. For this, the data manager must use a technique for replacing and updating the data reception field in the central memory (CM) according to an adapted strategy, such as the Last Ready Used (LRU) strategy which guarantees that the most frequently used data remains present in the CM. The manager must provide a set of easy to use primitives which enable the objects to be loaded into the central memory, modified and saved onto disk.

In Figure 10.2b we have deliberately omitted the description of the "plan generator" agent because, as we have already indicated, it can be either a cognitive or processing type of agent. It requires a sufficiently complex logic to be the object of a simple and concise description in this chapter. In the case of a system expert implementation, this agent will use a *rule base* and a *fact base* which are *persistent objects*. Upon each request by the "robot" agent, it generates the co-ordinates of the next position, *P1*, where the robot must go, and the time, *T1*, necessary to accomplish this action. Each new stage is stored in a persistent object "action_plan" which holds the list of stages since the start (the history). In Chapter 5 we showed that the global environment of the agents of an application (Figure 5.41) is composed of:

- physical objects or variables of the process if it is an industrial real-time application;
- temporary work variables which are internal and whose life duration is equal to that of the agent which declared them and uses them;
- persistent variables which are stored on a non-volatile back-up (hard disk). Their life duration does not depend on that of the agent who created them.

The following program outlines the implementation of the control of the "robot" application. Note that only the body of the agent "foot1" has been more or less explained. This implementation assumes that the three modules of the O2M system are available under VxWorks; the object manager, the event manager and the temporal constraints manager.

In this application, we start by declaring the global variables, the communication messages and the events.

The "robot" agent starts by loading the persistent objects it requires before executing its processes.

The "foot1" agent contains a control handler which is activated on the occurrence of the "`Foot1_Start`" event. The `StopAll` handler is activated on the arrival of the "`Alert`" event or the "`Foot1_Stop`" event. The association between these events and the handlers in question is carried out in the body of the agent with the help of the "`ON`" clause. This involves the asynchronous processing of events. The "foot" agent is in a position to execute a process or fundamental task in parallel with the execution of its handlers.

```
#define CPU                    MC68020
#include "vxWorks.h"
#include "sigLib.h"
#include "semLib.h"
#include "control1.h"                /*control of the TOR I/O card used for the
                                       control of the foot motors */
#include "OMclass.h"                 /*file of object manager declarations*/
void robot(1);
void foot1();
void foot2();

/*Declaration of the temporary support variables of the messages exchanged between the agents*/
struct Foot_go_Finto_T {
        int position[2];
        short time;
                } Foot1_F_T, Foot2_F_T;
...;
/*Declaration of events and control signals and of the synchronization between agents*/
Event Foot1_Stop, Foot2_Stop; /*Stop order issued by the robot agent to the feet agents */
Event Foot1_Start, Foot2_Start;                 /*order of movement*/
Event Alert;                                    /*general alert*/

/*Declaration of classes of persistent objects */
_persistentClass        Basic_Rules;
_persistentClass        Basic_Facts;
_persistentClass        Action_Plan;
...;

/*Creation of application agents*/
launchTask()
launchTask()
{ Init_control();                   /*card initialization depending on the sequences
                                      recommended by the manufacturer */
tid1= taskSpawn("ROBOT",100,0,2000,ROBOT);      /*creation of the ROBOT agent*/
tid2= taskSpawn("FOOT1",100,0,2000,FOOT1);      /*creation of the FOOT1 agent*/
tid2= taskSpawn("FOOT2",100,0,2000,FOOT2);      /*creation of the FOOT2 agent*/

/*Creation of a Basic_Rules object pointer and its reception zone*/
Action_Plan *p = new Basic_Rules (param);

/*Creation of a Basic_Facts object pointer and its reception zone*/
Action_Plan *p = new Basic_Facts (param);

/*Creation of an Action_Plan object pointer and its reception zone*/
Action_Plan *p = new Action_plan (param);
}
void robot()
        { position co-ordinates;              /*current position of the robot*/
/*load the object identified by ident into the CM*/
O2M_getobject(Action_Plan,&p,&AP);      /*now P points the persistent object of the 'AP'
                                          identifier*/
O2M_getobject(Basic_Rules,&p1,&BR);     /*now P points the persistent object of the 'BR'
                                          identifier*/
O2M_getobject(Basic_Facts,&p,&BF);      /*now P points the persistent object of the 'BF'
                                          identifier*/
                ...;
```

```
                                                    /* robot agent processing /
                    ...;
                    }
void foot1();
position co-ordinates   /*temporary variable which contains the current position of the foot */

/*Declaration of the interception handlers of synchronization and control events*/
controlFoot (F, T)                          /*principal handler for the control of the foot*/
{

/* Change direction to follow new co-ordinates*/
ActivateActuatorDirection(F, POSITION);                      /*Intelligent Actuator*/

/* Start the displacement motor for T units of time*/
ActivateActuatorDisplacement (TRUE) DURING (t, Alert);
ActivateActuatorDisplacement (FALSE);
 POSITION = p;                              /*update of the variable co-ordinates of the foot*/
};
StopAll()
{              /*when this event arrives during a current movement, the motor must be stopped*/
       ActiveActuatorDisplacement (FALSE);
};
 Task_Fund()
{
          /*Fundamental processing which has a lower priority than event processing handlers*/
};
{                                                         /*Behaviour of the foot1 agent*/
ON Foot1_Start ControlFoot(Foot1_F_T.position, Foot1_F_T.time);
ON alert StopAll();
ON Foot1_Stop StopAll();
 Task_fund();
}
void foot2()
    {                                                     /*behaviour of the foot2 agent*/
       }
```

When an application wants to manipulate objects of a persistent class,[1] such as the `Action_Plan` class, it indicates this by the use of the key word "`persistent Class`" in the declaration of the corresponding variable. The structures of persistent classes (`action_plan.h`) are stored and managed by the *schema manager*. Consequently, any application using persistent classes must be the object of precompiling with the OM pre-processor, aimed at carrying out all the modifications, or add the code necessary for the functioning of the application. Among other things, this pre-processor has the task of removing all of the declarations of the persistent class "class", and for each one of them adding the instruction "#include" from the corresponding class.h source. This source contains the C++ description of the class, and is managed by the schema manager. Figure 10.3 gives the development chain of a real-time application using persistent objects managed by OM.

[1] We assume that the reader is familiar with the notion of objects, classes of objects and C++ object oriented programming in particular.

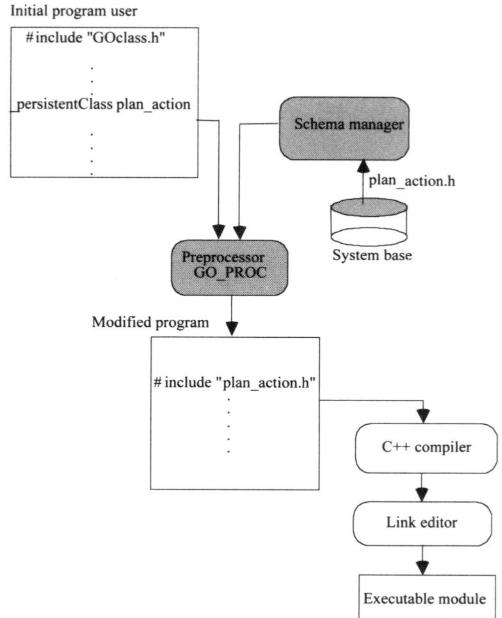

Fig. 10.3 The chain of development of an application using OM.

The "OM_PROC" pre-processor produces sources directly usable by the C++ or C compiler. It is responsible for including, in the place of the programmer, the description of persistent classes, the objects of these can therefore be used in the same way as temporary objects. The schema manager, as well as its own functions, stores the name of the source.h containing the description of the class for each class of object. This latter is therefore available to the pre-processor. The implementation of the OM manager that we give below has been implemented under Unix. Nevertheless, it can easily run under VxWorks.

10.2.2 Client–Server Architecture

OM is responsible for establishing a link between the C or C++ program users, which are executed on different sites (stations), and the shared database. Every user process constitutes a potential client, and a dedicated server (Fig. 10.4) generates each class of objects stored in the base.

User programs which manipulate the classes of a database managed by O2M, create a *client processor* at the start of their execution, which provides all of the dialogues with the class servers, as soon as a primitive is used.

The "listener" process is a lookout process which is on a fixed site known by all the other processes. It is activated when the system is launched and knows the location of the shared object classes as well as the load on all of the network sites. The "listener" process has the task of activating the servers, establishing "client–server" connections, managing the location of servers and balancing the load on the network. There are as many active servers in the system as there are classes being used by active applications. A server can communicate with one or more clients, the same as a client can request the services of several servers.

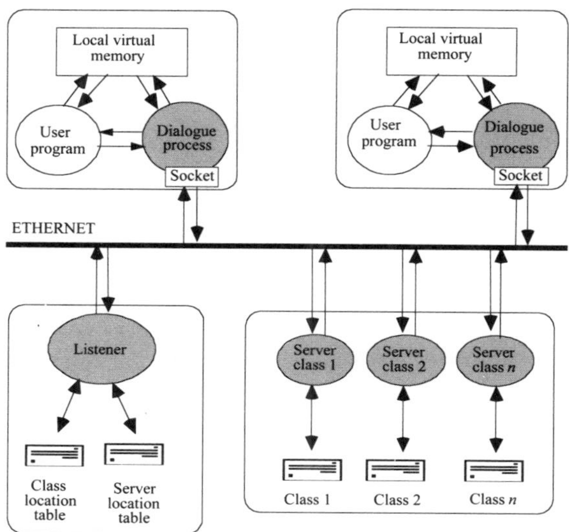

Fig. 10.4 The general architecture of a O2M system.

To establish a dialogue, a client must first ask the "listener" for the location of the server managing the object class concerned. The client and the server then communicate directly via their sockets.

OM uses a specific number of tables to render transparent to the programmer the management of the location of the different servers and classes on the network. The tables are as follows:

- *Table of the Location of Classes* (TLC): This contains the persistent classes which are implemented in the system, and their respective sites. The schema manager carries out the upgrading of this table;
- *Table of the Location of Servers* (TLS): this is local to the listener process. It is from this table that the process will be able to control whether or not a server is active, and find the corresponding site. The listener gradually activates the server processes following the demands of the clients, and therefore upgrades the TLS;
- *The Table of Sites* (TS): this contains all of the network sites on which one or more servers can be activated. It also gives each site its load which corresponds to the number of active servers on the site;
- *The Client–Server Communication Table* (CSCT): this table is local to the client dialogue processes. It holds the set of persistent classes used by the client, and for each class, the location site and address of the server.

Figure 10.5 gives the different stages necessary to a C or C++ program to connect and use the services of the object manager OM:

1. creation of the dialogue client process by the C or C++ user program, and sending the names of the classes concerned to the client;
2. send n class server location messages corresponding to the n classes used in the user program to the listener;
3. activation of the n servers by the listener;
4. sending n synchronization messages to the listener;
5. sending the locations of the n servers to the dialogue client process;

6,7. dialogue between the dialogue client process and the class servers;

8 send the data requested by the program user.

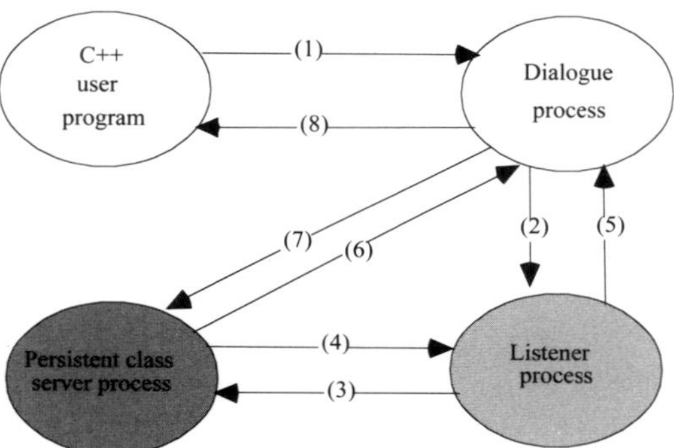

Fig. 10.5 Protocol for the use of a persistent class.

It is important to note that this schema is simplified and is only aimed at showing the overview during a session course of the use of the services of the persistent class manager OM. In the following paragraphs, we are interested in the interactions which exist between the different processes: the process supporting the execution of the user program, the dialogue client process which is dedicated to it, and the Listener process.

10.2.3 Course of an OM User Session

First Phase: Launching the Listener

The activation of the listener follows the stages indicated by Figure 10.6. This phase corresponds to an initialization of the listener. After reading the table of persistent classes and the table of declared sites, we create sockets which allow the dialogue process and the class servers to communicate with the listener. The execution of the listener process occurs on a specific site known to the other processes. The site chosen is the machine with the name “gisun01”.

Communication is carried out via two ports whose numbers are also known to the other processes:

- the port for communicating with the clients is port 1050;
- the port for communicating with the servers is 1051.

The communications are carried out in *datagram mode.*

The sources of the listener process are provided at the end of this section. It is sufficiently documented for us to leave it up to the reader to read up on it, without giving any other explanations. The sources of the other OM modules and primitives are provided on the Web page.

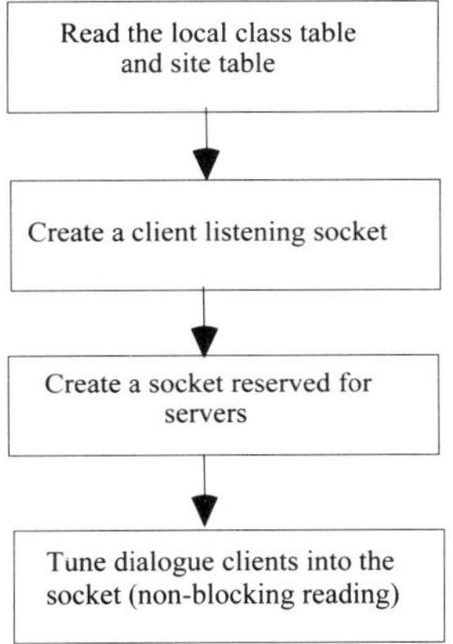

Fig. 10.6 The different stages of activation of the listener.

Second Phase: Interaction between the User Program and the Client Process

This phase enables the user program to be launched, and the dialogue client process to be created. The C++ user program uses two primitives:

- O2M_initclient() which enables the creation of the client process;
- O2M_endclient() which triggers the termination of the same process. This primitive also enables the memory field to be created which accommodates the virtual memory where the data will be stored.

Communication between the C++ or the C program and the client process will be made using two communication pipes. Figure 10.7 gives the different stages of communication between the user process and the corresponding client process.

Third Phase: Interaction between the Client Process and the Listener Process

In this section we pay particular attention to the protocol of communication between the user process and the listener process. Nevertheless, we recall that several sessions of communication can exist simultaneously between the listener and the dialogue process of active user programs at the same time. Figure 10.8 outlines the communication between the listener and a user process.

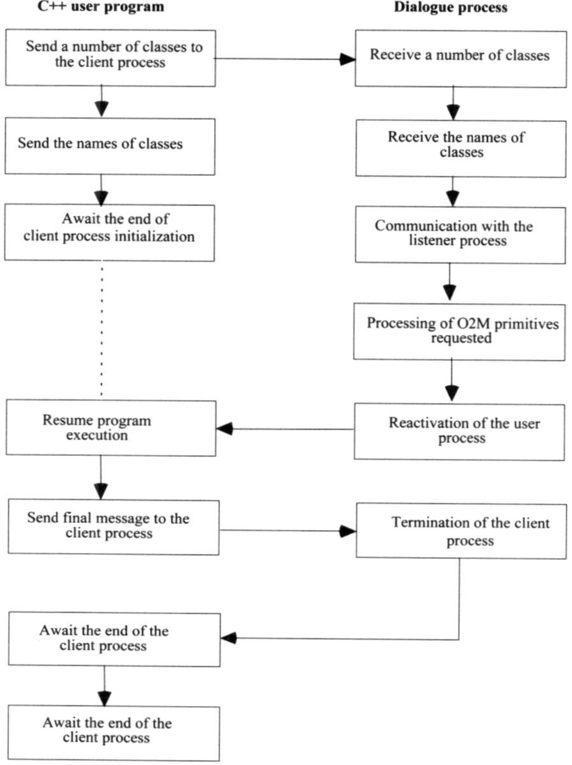

Fig. 10.7 Protocol of communication between the user process and the dialogue process.

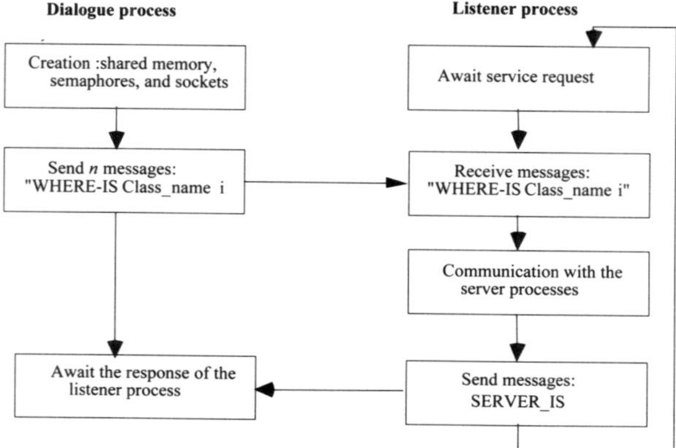

Fig. 10.8 Interaction between the dialogue process and the listener.

This involves a request for the location of the server of a class which is taking place. In the case where the server of the class requested cannot be located, the listener sends a "CLASSERROR" message to the client who then takes it on board.

Fourth Phase: Interaction between a Class Server Process and the Listener

This phase occurs each time a "WHERE-IS" message, sent by the client, is received by the Listener (where the server process requested is inactive) (Fig. 10.9).

Fifth Phase: Termination of the Listener Process and the Server Processes

The "O2M_STOP" primitive is dedicated to stopping the system. It sends an end message to the listener process. This will then force the different server processes to enter into a termination phase. Once it has collected all of the end messages from the server processes, it terminates.

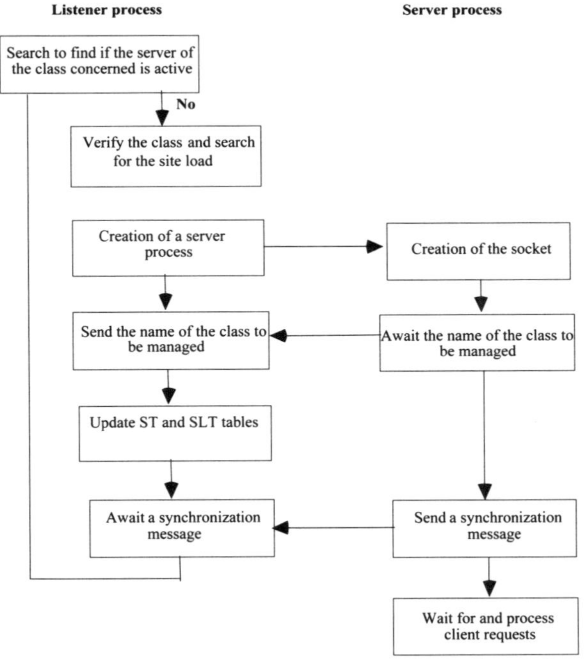

Fig. 10.9 Interaction between a class server process and the listener.

10.2.4 O2M Tools

This section provides a brief presentation of the main tools necessary to render the management of the persistence of O2M object classes transparent to the reader.

10.2.4.1 The "O2M_PROC" Pre-processor

O2M_PROC is a tool which enables the transformation of a user program into a directly executable program. Figure 10.10 illustrates this transformation with the robot control application example.

```
   ...;

   /* creation of an Action_plan object pointer and its
Reception field*/
       Plan_Action *p2 = new Plan_Action (param);
}

void robot()
    { Position co-ordinates;  /* current position of robot */
                /* load into the CM the object identified by ident */
        O2m_getobjet(Plan_Action, &p, &PA);    /* now p
 Point the persistent object of the identifier'PA'*/
...;
```

O2M_PROC

```
   ...;
   /**********PART ADDED BY THE PRE-PROCESSOR ******/

/* Table of persistent classes used in the application*/
char O2M_CLASS[ MAXNBCLASS] [ LGCLASSNAME] ;

short O2M_NBCLASS;   /* number of classes used*/

/*pointer on the address translation table in the storage space
Managed by the manager: Virtual Memory*/
void *MAPADR;
strcopy(OM2_CLASE[ 0] , " Action_Plan ");
strcopy(O2M_CLASS[ 0] , "Base_Rules");
strcopy(O2M_CLASS[ 0] , "Base_Facts");
O2M_NBCLASS = 3;

/*Initialization of the dialogue management agent associated with the application */
O2M_initclient(O2M_CLASS, O2M_NBCLASS, &O2M_MAPADR);

/********************END PART*****************************/

/* Creation of a Action_Plan object type pointer and its reception field*/
 Action_Plan *p2 = new Action_Plan (param);
}

void robot()
     { Position Co-ordinates;  /*current position of the robot*/
                /* load into the CM the object identified by ident */
        O2M_getobjet(Action_Plan, &p, &PA);    /* now p points the persistent object
                                                   Of the identifier 'PA'*/

          /* process the robot agent*/
          ...;
          O2M_endclient(O2M_MAPADR);   /* destroy the dialogue agent and end the
                                          interaction with the servers*/
```

Fig. 10.10 O2M_PROC functioning principle.

The O2M_PROC pre-processor allows the implementation of the following functions:

- *location of classes used* by the program and addition of the file header `include` (class.h) which contains the description of these classes;
- *triggering the initialization protocol* of the client–server interaction by adding the O2M_initclient() primitive;
- *triggering the disconnection protocol* for the client–server interaction by adding the O2M_endclient primitive.

10.2.4.2 Management of the Database Schema

The O2M database is composed of object classes. In order to manage the persistence of each class, O2M must manage its storage space on the disk and its *schema*. The schema of a class is an internal representation belonging to O2M of the external description of the classes as given in program C++: the name of the class, the list of attributes with their type (whole, true, etc.). This description will act as a basis for formatting the file which will receive the class instances. Each instance will be identified by an external identifier to distinguish it from the others ("AP" identifier which designates an Action_Plan object for the Action_Plan class). This identifier will be used by the O2M_getobject() primitive to carry out access direct to the object. At each access, O2M_getobject() checks if the reference object is found in the reception field of the CM. If it is not available, it takes it from the disk and updates the translation of addresses table for objects present in the CM. When the reception field is full, O2M_getobject() proceeds to replace an object in the CM with the object taken from the disk following an acceptable replacement strategy which guarantees a wider availability of the most frequently used objects: for example, the LRU strategy.

The schema manager backs up a *descriptor* with the information related to each class in a file called "class.d". This descriptor is obtained from the C++ description of the class (see the system sources for the contents of the descriptor). From the descriptor, it creates and formats a file with the same name as the class to contain the class instances: persistent file. Figure 10.11 gives the main outline of such a utility. Note that this utility is composed of two modules. The first SCHEMAD (design) module, for the design and generation of the class descriptor with the information relevant to the management of class data. The second SCHEMAC (creation) module which is responsible for creating the class file and formatting it according to the first description taken into account by the SCHEMAD. Finally, SCHEMAC inserts the name of the new class into the local class table, TLC.

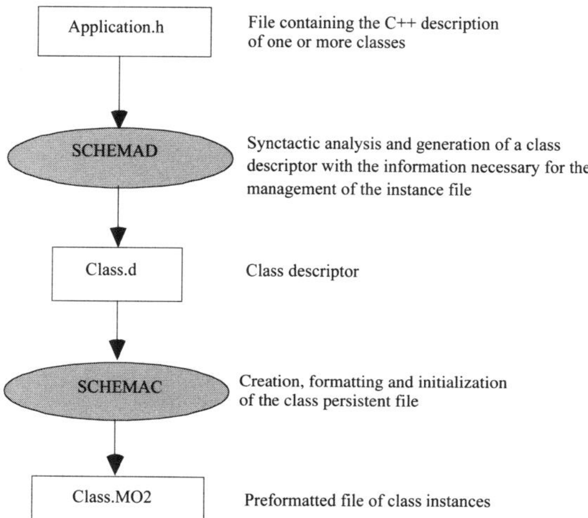

Fig. 10.11 Principle of the functioning of the schema manager.

The following program gives the code for the "listener" process, described above, given its importance in the system.

10.2.4.3 The "Listener" Process Code

```
/****************************************************************/
/*                                                              */
/*LISTENER.C: the listener process = global server, indicating the location of the   */
/*class server to the client process which requests it , and activating the inactive servers  */
/*                                                              */
/****************************************************************/

#include <string.h>
#include <stdio.h>
#include <sys/types.h>
#include <sys/socket.h>
#include <sys/ioctl.h>
#include <unistd.h>
#include <fcntl.h>
#include <errno.h>
#include <sys/un.h>
#include <bstring.h>
#include <netdb.h>
#include <netinet/in.h>
#include <stdlib.h>

#include <typmo2.h>                  /*parameters of implementation of the application*/
#define PORT1 1050
#define PORT2 1051
#define MACHINE_LISTENER        "gisun01"
#define USER                    "nugeyre"

/***********************************************************/
/*PROTOTYPES                                               */
/***********************************************************/

void readfile (STLC s_tabstlc[MAXNBCLASS], STS s_tabsts[MAXNBSITE],
short *s_nbclass,short *s_nbsite);

connection_listener1();

connection_listener2();

void searsite0 (STS e_tabstlc[MAXNBSITE], short e_nbsite, char
s_site0[LGSITENAME], short *s_isite0);

void sendserveris (char e_class[LGCLASSNAME], char
e_siteserver[LGSITENAME], struct sockaddr_in client);

void sendclasspb (char e_class[LGCLASSNAME], char
e_siteserver[LGSITENAME], struct sockaddr_in client);
```

```
void createserver (char e_siteserver[LGSITENAME], char
e_class[LGCLASSNAME], struct sockaddr_in server);

void whereisprocess (STLS s_tabstls[MAXNBCLASS], STLC
E_tabstLC[MAXNBCLASS], STS e_tabsts[MAXNBSITE], short  *e_nbserver,
short *e_nbclass, short *e_nbsite, char e_class[LGCLASSNAME], char
s_siteserver[LGSITENAME], u_short s_port, int *s_cr);

void disconnection();

void endserver(STLS e_tabstls[MAXNBCLASS],short e_nbserver);

/***************************************************************/
/*VARIABLES                                                    */
/***************************************************************/

struct hostent *hp;
struct hostent *gethostbyname();
                         /*socket reserved for messages exchange with clients*/
int sock_clients;
                         /*socket reserved for server synchronization messages*/
int sock_servers;
                                  /*listener address; connection to client*/
struct sockaddr_in listener1;
                                  /*listener address; connection to server*/
struct sockaddr_in listener2;

/***************************************************************/
/*READFILE                                                     */
/***************************************************************/
/*                                                             */
/* - role: memory loading of tables                            */
/*         TLC (class location)                                */
/*         TS (Site tables)                                    */
/*                                                             */
/* - exit: TLC and TS tables                                   */
/*         number of classes in the TLC                        */
/*         number of sites in the TS                           */
/***************************************************************/

void readfile (STLC s_tabstlc[MAXNBCLASS], STS s_tabsts[MAXNBSITE],
short *s_nbclass,short *s_nbsite)
{
int in;
FILE *ftlc;
FILE *fts;

/*Place table TLC in the memory*/
*s_nbclass = 0;
ftlc = fopen(TLCNAME, "r");
if  (!ftlc) {
        ftlc = fopen(TLCNAME, "w");
        if  (!ftlc ) {
                print f ("Listener. Problem with the creation of the
TLC/n file");
                exit(1);
```

```
        }
        fclose (ftlc);
}
else {
        in = 0;
        while (fread((char *)&s_tabstlc[in++],sizeof(STLC),1,ftlc) !=
0)
(*s_nbclass)++;
        fclose (ftlc);
        printf ("\nListener. %d persistent classes found in TLC\n",
*s_nbclass);
}
```

/*Load site table (table system managed by the administrator of the network and simulated by the TS file)*/

```
fts = fopen(TSNAME, "r");
if (!fts) {
        printf ("Listener. Problem: system tabel of sites
inexistent\n");
        exit(1);
}
in = 0;
*s_nbsite = 0;
while (fread((char *)&s_tabsts[in++],sizeof(STS),1,fts) !=0)
(*s_nbsite)++;
fclose (fts);
if (*s_nbsite == 0) printf ("Problem : system table of sites (TS)
empty\n");
else printf ("Listener.%d sites available on the network (TS
table)\n",
*s_nbsite);
}

/*************************************************************/
/*CONNECTION_LISTENER1                                       */
/*************************************************************/
/*                                                           */
/*-role: creation of the socket destined for client communication */
/*                                                           */
/*************************************************************/

connection_listener1()
{
printf("Listener. Creation of the listener-client socket \n");
if ((hp = gethostbyname(MACHINE_LISTENER)) == NULL) {
        perror("Name of listener site : ");
        exit(2);
}
if((sock_clients = socket(AF_INET,SOCK_DGRAM,0)) == -1) {
        perror("SOCKET CREATION IMPOSSIBLE ");
}
bzero(&listener1, sizeof(listener1));
listener1.sin_family = AF_INET;
listener1.sin_port = htons(PORT1);
bcopy(hp->h_addr, &listener1.sin-addr, hp->h_length);
```

```
if ((bind(sock_clients,(struct sockaddr *)&listenr1,
sizeof(listener1)))
== -1) {
        perror("IMPOSSIBLE CLIENT CONNECTION ");
}
}

/*****************************************************************/
/*CONNECTION_LISTENER2                                           */
/*****************************************************************/
/*                                                               */
/*  - role: creation of a specific socket for the reception of synchronization  */
/*     messages sent by from the servers to the Listener.         */
/*                                                               */
/*****************************************************************/

connection_listener2()
{
printf("Listener. Creation of the listener-server socket \n");
if ((hp = gethostbyname(MACHINE_LISTENER)) == NULL) {
        perror("Name of listener site : ");
        exit(2);
}
if((sock_server = socket(AF_INET,SOCK_DGRAM,0)) == -1) {
        perror("SOCKET CREATION IMPOSSIBLE ");
}
bzero(&listener2, sizeof(listener2));
listener2.sin_family = AF_INET;
listener2.sin_port = htons(PORT2);
bcopy(hp->h_addr, &listener2.sin-addr, hp->h_length);
if ((bind(sock_servers,(struct sockaddr *)&listener2,
sizeof(listener2)))
== -1) {
        perror("IMPOSSIBLE CLIENT CONNECTION ");
}
}

/*****************************************************************/
/*SEARCHSITE0                                                    */
/*****************************************************************/
/*                                                               */
/* - role: search for the least loaded site on the network in the site table (TS)  */
/*              (site having the least number of process to support             */
/*                                                               */
/*  - input: TS table                                            */
/*                   number of sites in the TS                   */
/*                                                               */
/*  -ouput:  site found                                          */
/*                   position of site found in the TS table      */
/*                                                               */
/*****************************************************************/

void searchsite0(STS e_tabsts[MAXNBSITE],short e_nbsite,char
s_site0[LGSITENAME],short *s_isite0)
{
                                                /*local variables*/
```

```
short load0;                          /*lightest load of all the sites on the network*/
int i;
load0 = 9999;
in = 0;
while (in < e_nbsite) {
        if (e_tabsts[i].load < load0) {
                load0 = e_tabsts[i].load;
                strcpy(s_site0,e_tabsts[i].site);
                *s_isite0 = i;
        }
        i++
}
}

/**************************************************************/
/*SENDSERVERIS                                                */
/**************************************************************/
/*                                                            */
/* - role: send SERVERIS message to the client to indicate the location of */
/*          the server of the class processed                 */
/*                                                            */
/* - input: class concerned                                   */
/*            name of the server site                         */
/*            address of the client                           */
/*                                                            */
/**************************************************************/

void sendserveris(char e_class[LGCLASSNAME],char
e_siteserver[LGSITENAME], struct sockaddr_in client)
{
MSG mess;
Int code, len;
Printf("Listener. SERVERIS message. Class : %s, site %s \n", e_class,
E_siteserver);
Mess.code = SERVERIS;
Strcpy(mess.body,MSGSERVERIS.class,e_class);
Strcpy(mess.body,MSGSERVERIS.siteserver,e_siteserver);
Len = sizeof(client);
Printf ("Listener. Message server-is %d send to client \n",
mess.code);
Printf ("Listener. Number of client port %d \n",client.sin_port);
Printf ("Listener. Client field %d \n",client.sin_family);
If ((code = sendto(sock_clients, (char *)&mess, sizeof(mess),
0,(struct sockaddr *)&client, len)) == -1 {
        Perror("Client problem : ");
        Exit(1);
}
printf ("Listener. Message server-is sent to the client %s for class
%s \n", e_siteserver, e_class);
}
/**************************************************************/
/*SENDCLASSPB                                                 */
/**************************************************************/
/*                                                            */
/* - role: send CLASSPB message to the client to indicate the class whose */
/*          location it requested is unknown in the system    */
```

```
/*                                                              */
/* - input: class concerned                                     */
/*                name of the server site                       */
/*                address of the client                         */
/*                                                              */
/****************************************************************/

void sendclasspb (char e_class[LGCLASSNAME],char
e_siteserver[LGSITENAME], struct sockaddr_in client)
{
MSG mess;
Int code, len;
Mess.code =CLASSPB;
Strcpy(mess.body,MSGCLASSPB.class,e_class);
Len = sizeof(client);
Code = sendto(sock_clients, (char *)&mess, sizeof(mess), 0,(struct
sockaddr *)&client, len);
Printf ("Listener. Message server-is %d send to client \n",
mess.code);
Printf ("Listener. Class-pb message sent to client %d for the class %s
\n",e_siteserver[LGSITENAME], e_class);
}

/****************************************************************/
/*CREATESERVER                                                  */
/****************************************************************/
/*                                                              */
/* - role: creation of the server process on the determined site */
/*            (use of the creatproc function of the ppgm.c)     */
/*                                                              */
/* - input: site determined                                     */
/*                class to be managed by the server             */
/*                                                              */
/* - output: address of the server                              */
/*                                                              */
/****************************************************************/

void createserver(char e_siteserver, char e_class[LGCLASSNAME], struct
sockaddr_in server);
                                                   /*LGSITENAME*/
{
char command[50];                         /*intermediate buffer*/
struct servant *servant;     /*structure used for the port number */
// int sd;                                /*rexec socket descriptor*/
int sockerr;                           /*control socket sent by rexec*/
// int nbcar;                          /*number of characters read*/
int port;                                          /*port buffer*/
char message[100];
char *siteserver;
int len, code;
Printf("Listener. Start CREATESERVER. site server : %s, class : %s
\n", e_siteserver, e_class);

/*The name of the program is placed in a buffer*/
Printf("Listener. Name of program placed in a buffer \n");
Sprintf(command, "/home3/attoui/o2m/nugeyre/o2m/server");
```

/*Search for the port number associated to rexec*/

```
Printf("Listener. Search for the port number associated with
rexec\n");
Servant = getservbyname("exec","tcp");
```

/*Call rexec*/

```
Printf("Listener. Call rexec \n");
Siteserver = e_siteserver;
Rexec(&siteserver, servant->s_port, USER, USER, command, &sockerr);
Printf("Listener. Launch server \n");
Close(sd);
close(sockerr);
printf("Listener. Await server response \n");
len = sizeof(server) + sizeof(port);
code = recvfrom(sock_servers, (char *)&port, sizeof(port), 0, (struct
sockaddr *)&server, &len);
printf("Listener. Launch server on the port %d \n",port);
```

/*Send the class to be managed by the server*/

```
if ((hp = gethostbyname(e_siteserver)) == NULL) {
        perror("Name ofsiteserver : ");
        exit(2);
}
server.sin_family = AF_INET
server.sin_port = htons(port);
bcopy((char *)hp->h_addr, (char *)&server.sin_addr, hp->h_length);
len = sizeof(server);
code = sendto(sock_servers, (char *)&e_class, sizeof(e_class),
0,(struct sockaddr *)*server, len);
If ((code = -1 {
        Perror("send name of the class to be managed to the server :
");
        Exit(2);
}
else printf ("Listener. Message server-is sent to the server %s for
class %s \n", e_siteserver, e_class);
}
/*************************************************************/
/*WHEREISPROCESS                                             */
/*************************************************************/
/*                                                           */
/* - role:   processing of type 1 message                    */
/*           search for the location of the class server     */
/*           activation of the server if not active          */
/*                                                           */
/* - input: TLS, TLC and TS tables                           */
/*           number of classes in the TLC                    */
/*           number of classes in the TS                     */
/*           class processed                                 */
/*                                                           */
/* - I/O :  number of servers in the TLS                     */
/*           (increase by 1 if the server is active)         */
/*                                                           */
/* - output: site of residence of the server                 */
/*           return code (class correct or unknown --> Class-pb) */
/*                                                           */
/*************************************************************/
```

```
void whereisprocess (STLS e_tabstls[MAXNBCLASS], STLC
e_tabstlc[MAXNBCLASS], STS e_tabsts[MAXNBSITE], short *e_nbserver,
short e_nbclass, short e_nbsite, char e_class[LGCLASSNAME], char
s_siteserver[LGSITENAME], u_short s_port, int *s_cr)
{
int in;
int ok;                                                          /*flag qcq*/
int serverfound;                                        /*presence in the TLS*/
int classfound;                                         /*presence in the TLC*/
char sitestorage[LGSITENAME];          /*resident site of the persistent class*/
short loadsitestorage;   /*load (in number of processes) on the storage site of the class*/
short s_isiteserver;       /*memorizing the site server place in the TS, for later update*/
MSG msgsynch;   /*synchronization message sent by the server, after its creation by the Listener*/
Struct sockaddr_in server;
Int code, len;
Char message[100];
*s_cr = 0;

/*Find out if the class server concerned is active*/
serverfound = 0;
i = 0;
while (i < *e_nbserver) {
     if (strcmp ((e_tabstls[i].class),(s_class)) == 0) {
          serverfound = 1;                              /*server is already active*/
          strcpy(s_siteserver,e_tabstls[i].site);       /*site location of server */
          s_port = e_tabstls[i].number_port;
          i = *e_nbserver;
     }
     i++;
}
/*If a server of the nonexistent class (TLS) then create server
process of the class* /
if (serverfound == 1) {
        printf ("Listener. Server of the class %s already active on the
site : %s \n", e_class, s_siteserver);
        printf("Listener. Port number : %d \n", s_port);
}
else {
printf ("Listener. Srver of %s not active\n",e_class);
                                                /*check class known to O2M (TLC)*/
classfound = 0;
i = 0;
while (i < e_nbclass) {
if (strcmp ((e_tabstlc[i].class),(e_class)) == 0) {
               classfound = 1;                  /*persistent class known to O2M */
               strcpy(sitestorage,e_tabstlc[i].site);     /*class storage site */
               s_isiteserver = i;                /*position of the site of the future
                                                server in the TS (is storage site chosen)*/
i = *e_nbclass;
        }
        i++;
}
/*Create the server process*/
printf("Listeber. Check class known (yes = 1) : %d \n",
classefound);
if (classfound == 1) {
```

```
/*Find storage site load in the table of sites (TS)*/
printf("Listener. Find storage site load in the TS \n",
ok = 0;
i = 0;
while (i < e_nbsite) {
            if (strcmp ((e_tabsts[i].site),(sitestorage)) == 0) {
                ok = 1;
                loadsitestorage = e_tabsts[i].load;
                i = e_nbsite;
        }
        i++;
}
printf("Listener. Storage site found (yes = 1) : %d \n", ok);
if (ok == 0) {
printf("listener. Problem : cstorage site of class %s unknown in TS
\n",e_class);
exit(1);
}
printf("Listener. Storage site : %s \n", sitestorage);
printf("Listener. Load : %d \n", loadsitestorage);

/*Determine resident site of the server process*/
/*If storage site too loaded --> least laden sight in the network (site0)*/
if (loadsitestorage > 3)
findsite0(e_tabsts,e_nbsite,s_siteserver,&s_isiteserver);
else strcpy)s_siteserver,sitestorage);
printf("Listener. Await message1 server \n");
code = recvfrom(sock_servers, message, sizeof(message), 0, 0, &len);
printf("Listener. Message 1 received \n");
printf("Listener. Message 1 : &s \n", message);

/*Update the TLS table*/
printf("Listener.Update the TLS table \n");
i = *e_nbserver;
strcpy(e_tabstls[i].class,e_class);
strcpy(e_tabstls[i].site,s_siteserver);
e_tabstls[i].port_number = s_port;
(*e_nbserver)++;

/*Update the TS table*/
printf("Listener.Update the TS table \n");
i = s_isiteserver;              /*position of the site server in the TS previously memorized */
e_tabsts[i].load++;

/*Wait server process synchronization*/
len = sizeof(listener2);
printf("Listener. Await server message 2 \n");
code = recvfrom(sock_servers, message, sizeof(message), 0, 0, &len);
printf("Listener. Message 2 received \n");
printf("Listener. Message 2 : %s \n", message);
printf("Listener. Await server process synchronization \n");
code = recvfrom(sock_servers, (char *)&msgsynch, sizeof(msgsynch), 0,
0, &len);
printf("Listener. Message of type %d received \n", msgsynch.code);
if (msgsynch.code !=SUNCH1){
      printf ("Listener. Problem: Bad synchro\n");
```

```
        exit(1)
}
}
else {                                          /*case where class - new persistent class*/
        printf("Listener. Class %s not present in TLC \n", e_class);
        *s_cr = 1;
}
}
}

/****************************************************************/
/* DISCONNECTION                                                */
/****************************************************************/
/*                                                              */
/*  - role: close a socket                                      */
/*                                                              */
/*  - input:  number associated to a socket                     */
/*                                                              */
/****************************************************************/

void disconnection()
{
printf("Listener. Disconnection \n");
close(sock_clients);
close(sock)servers);
}
/****************************************************************/
/*ENDSERVER                                                     */
/****************************************************************/
/*                                                              */
/*  - role: send end message to all of the class servers        */
/*                                                              */
/*  - input: TLS table (server locations                        */
/*               number of active servers                       */
/*               handle the listener ball                       */
/*                                                              */
/****************************************************************/

void endserver(STLS e_tabstls[MAXNBCLASS], short e_nbserver)
{
int in, code, len;
MSG mess;
Struct sockaddr_in server;
Int socket;

/*Send an end message to each of the servers*/
i = 0;
while (i < e_nbserver) {
        mess.code = ENDSERV;
        server.sin-family = AF_INET;
        hp = gethostbyname(e_tabstls[i].site);
        bcopy((char *) hp->h_addr, (char *) &server.sin_addr, hp-
>h_length);
        server.sin-port = htons(e_tabstls[i].port_number);
        printf("Listener. End on site %s. Port number %d \n",
e_tabstls[i].site, e_tabstls[i].port_number);
```

```
        if((bind(socket, (struct sockaddr *)&server, sizeof(server)))
== -1) {
                perror("Listener. END - IMPOSSIBLE SERVER CONNECTION
");
        }

        len = sizeof(server);
        if ((code = sendto(sock_servers, (char *)&mess, sizeof(mess),
0,(struct sockaddr *)&server, len)) == -1) {
                perror("Listener. End error message ");
        }
        printf ("Listener. Messge Endserv sent to the server %s for the
class %s \n", e_tabstls[i].site, e_tabstls[i].class);
        i++;
}
printf ("Listener. Send an end message towards each server \n");
}
/***************************************************************/
/*MAIN                                                         */
/***************************************************************/

main ()
{
int end;
short nbserver;
short nbclass;
short nbsite;
MSG messread;
Char siteserver[LGSITENAME];
STLS tabstls[MAXNBCLASS];
STLC tabstlc[MAXNBCLASS];
STS tabsts[MAXNBSITE];
Char class[LGCLASSNAME];
Int cr, code;
U_short port;
Struct sockaddr_in client;

/*Initializations*/
end = 0;
nbserver = 0;                   /*no server active on system initialization*/
int len;
/*Load the TLC and TS files in the memory, and calculate the number of posts on each table*/
readfile(tabstlc,tabsts,&nbclass,&nbsite);
connection_listener1();                          /*client LISTENER socket*/
connection_listener2();                  /*socket for server synchro messages*/
while (end == 0) {
        printf("\nLISTENER awaiting message ......\n");
        len = sizeof(client) + sizeof(messread);
        code = recvfrom(sock_clients, (char *)&messread,
sizeof(messread), 0, (struct sockaddr *)&client, &len);
        if (messread.code == WHEREIS) {
        strcpy(class,messread.body.MSGWHEREIS.class);
        printf("Listener. Processing the Whereis message \n");
        processwhereis (tabstls, tabstlc, tabsts, &nbserver, nbclass,
nbsite, class, siteserver, port, &cr);
```

/*Send SERVERIS or CLASSPB message to the client of the messread.address address*/

```
        messread.address = client;
        if (cr == 1) sendclasspb(class,siteserver,messread.address);
        else sendserveris(class,siteserver,messread.address);
        }
        else {
                if (messread.code == END) {
```

/*Send message at end of all the servers*/

```
                endserver(tabstls,nbserver);
                disconnection();
                printf ("stop LISTENER process\n");
                end = 1;
                }
else {
                printf("Listener. Message received unknown\n");
                exit(1);
                }
        }
}
}
```

Appendix 1

Problems with Hardware–Software Layer Coupling in a Data Processing System

A1.1 The Target Machine

An operating system is software which has the role of *managing* and *optimizing* the use of the different hardware and software machine resources. From the user's angle (user interface), an operating system is the set of software tools which provide the facilities and ease necessary to develop and execute its programs. From the machine angle (system kernel) this is the control part of the hardware layer.

The operating system is a complex real-time control application for the operative part of the different components of the machine. It reacts to internal events, such as input/output requests, the blocking of processes behind semaphores or on a particular resource such as the CPU, and external events such as interrupts originating from the peripherals (keyboard, printer, hard drive, network card, etc.).

An operating system is itself an extreme example of a complex real-time system. The development of the digital command of a process with a real-time executive, especially on embedded real-time systems, often requires an advanced knowledge of the operating system. This appendix is aimed at presenting the reader unfamiliar with operating systems, with a concise introduction of the lower layers across the Unix multi-task, multi-user system. The aim is to make the reader aware of the necessity to integrate the study and the comprehension of the fundamental aspects of this system into his/her knowledge base. Real time first encompasses multi-task operating systems. Recall that a real-time executive is an optimized operating system (see Chapter 5).

To study operating systems first, it is essential to understand the mechanisms used to carry out the interaction between the operating system kernel and the hardware components of the machine. In order to do this, *a choice must be made concerning the target machine* (operative part). Figure A1.1 gives a general simplified view of a machine constructed around Intel 386 and upward microprocessors (PC or compatible). We assume that the integration of all of the components of the machine is carried out using a *bus system.* This is the main component of the system which provides communication between the different elements of the machine. This main bus is composed of three buses:

- *The data bus* with 16, 32 or 64 lines. This is used to carry out data exchange between the different components of the system (microprocessor, central memory circuits, input/output couplers etc);
- *The control bus* which is composed of a variable number of lines depending on the manufacturer, and acts as a vehicle for command or control signals;
- *The address bus* (20 lines) enables one cell in the central memory (one octet, a word), or an input/output port (a register of input/output couplers) to be addressed.

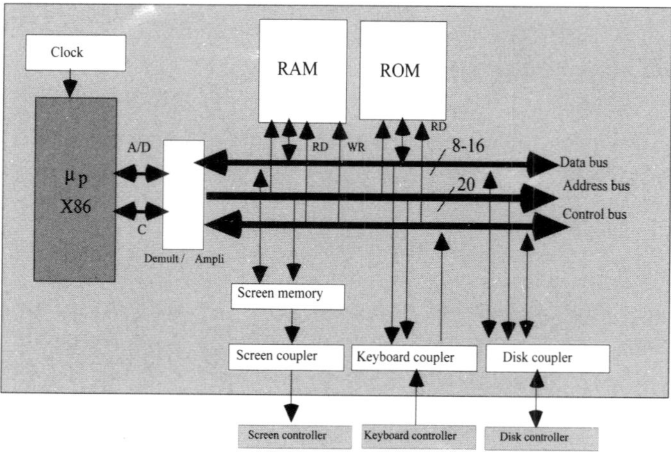

Fig. A1.1 Simplified structure of an IBM-PC microcomputer.

The X86 family uses the data bus multiplexing technique: A/D. The space which can be addressed to the machine is 1Moctet (2^{20}).

A1.1.1 The Internal Organization of the X86

The "noble" component of the system is the microprocessor. This is an *active and reactive component* which provides program execution and the control of other components on the machine (input/output couplers, interrupt controller, etc.).

To ensure these functions, the microprocessor uses a set of registers. Some of these registers are standardized and can be accessed by the programmer. Others are specialized and consequently are not accessible to the programmer. The Intel X86 family has four sets of registers.

1. Operational registers

AX	AH	AL	Accumulator
BX	BH	BL	Base
CX	CH	CL	Counter
DX	DH	DL	Data

2. Address registers

SP	Head of stack pointer
BP	Basic stack address
SI	Index source
DI	Index destination

3. Segment registers

CS	0000	Code segment
DS	0000	Data segment
SS	0000	Stack segment
ES	0000	Supplementary data segment

4. Special registers

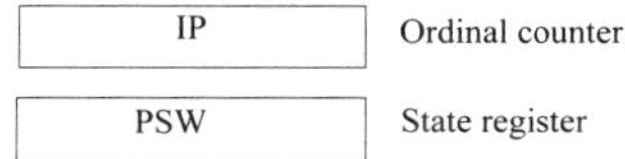

A1.1.1.1 The Processor Status Word

The processor has a status word each bit of which indicates a situation or a particular event. It enables the processor to know its current state, its functioning mode and to make appropriate decisions as a result. Figure A1.2 gives the structure of the status word of a microprocessor from the X86 family, and the semantics or significance of each bit.

A1.1.1.2 Addressable Space and Memory Organization

The addressable space of a data processing system is determined from the size of the address bus (20 lines). It is made up of logically accessible positions or memory cells (2^{20} positions). The address of a cell is a combination of the values and lines of the address bus. This set of logic addresses can be separated to constitute particular specialized fields. Figure A1.3 shows the organization of a PC machine memory for the DOS system. The addresses which fall between 0000 and 00 400 (in Hexa) are reserved for interrupt vectors, and the field whose addresses fall between FE 000 and FF FFF is used to hold the different BIOS (Basic Input Output System) functions. The middle partition can be used by the user's programs.

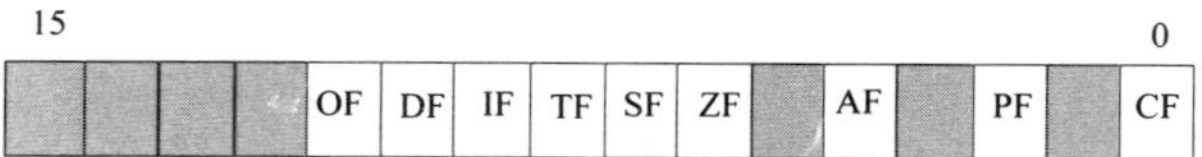

CF, PF, AF, ZF, SF: Condition bits

TF: Trace function

IF: Interrupt function
- realization of exchanges between the CU and the peripherals
- essential for the implementation of the multi-user OS
- CLI assembler instruction: set to zero
- STI assembler instruction STI: set to 1

DF: Character string manipulation

OF: Overflow

Fig. A1.2 Structure of the status word of X86 microprocessors.

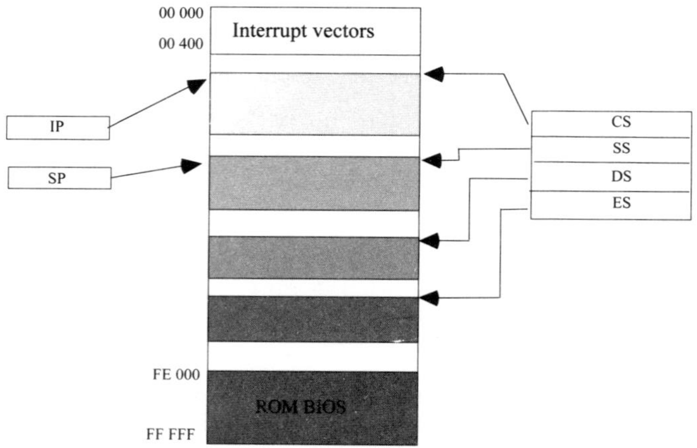

Fig. A1.3 Organization of the addressable space of systems based on the X86 family.

BIOS contains the sub-programs for:

- read and write characters to the hard drive;
- display characters on the screen;
- other I/O operations.

The BIOS sub-programs are not managed by interrupts. Consequently, it is difficult to use it as a base kernel (lower layer) to implement a multi-task operating system. The main characteristic of this type of operating system is asynchronization between the processes and input/output operations, which follows from the exploitation of possibilities in terms of the management of external interrupts coming from the peripherals, which will be described at a later stage.

A direct consequence of this is that Unix on a PC does not use BIOS. It requires a different organization (Fig. A1.4).

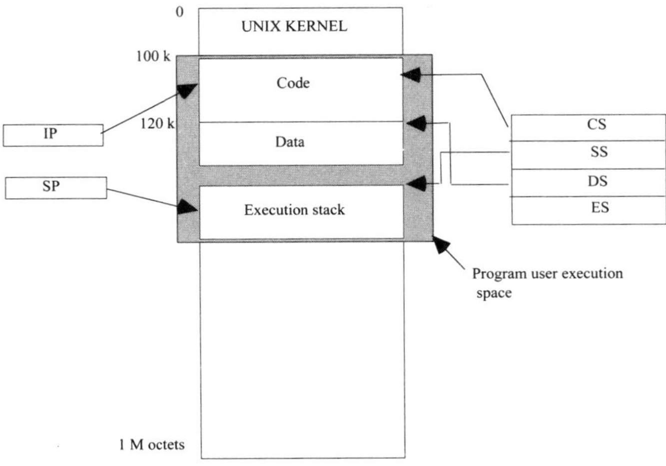

Figure A1.4 Organization of addressable space for Unix.

We assume that this time, the space is composed of two parts:

1. 0-100 Koctets: contains a Unix kernel;
2. 101 - 1 Moctets: space reserved for the user programs. The execution space of a user program is made up of:
   - a code segment (executable program code) pointed by the CS register;
   - a data segment whose start address is found in the DS register;
   - a program execution file segment pointed by SS.

In this way the following assembler instruction: `mov AX, 25 000,` which enables the transfer of the contents of the 25 000 address in the microprocessor accumulator is equivalent to:

```
AX <- (DS + 25 000)
```

And the jump instruction `jmp 101 k` cannot be realized by addressing immediately because the registers of the machine are on 16 bits. It is therefore necessary to use related addressing compared to the CS register:

```
(CS = 100) => jmp 1
```

The following two situations are also often encountered:

1. For the majority of programs, the code and data are stored in the same segment (instruction space = data space):

```
CS = DS ==> addressable space :0 ---> 64 K
```

2. For large programs : (Space I ≠ Space D):

```
CS ≠ DS ==> CS : 0 ---> 64 K ---> 64K
```

The assembler instruction `mov AX, 0` will therefore be executed in a different manner whether or not the two spaces are separate:

- Space I ≠ Space D ==> Place the contents of the first D word into AX;
- Space I = Space D ==> `mov AX, 20480`: calculated by the link compiler and editor.

Finally, this summary addressing PC-type platforms finishes by highlighting the fact that program segments must start with a multiple 16-octet address.

20 bits

CS	0000
SS	0000
DS	0000
ES	0000

The addressing modes available are:

- addressing by register;
- indirect addressing;
- immediate addressing ==>address belongs to (0, 64K);
  ==>access to global variables;
  ==>address known at the compilation point.
- indexed addressing ==>access to the local procedure variables.

A1.1.2 Procedure Call and Context Changing

Figure A1.5 summarizes the different actions to be carried out in order to realize a procedure or function call, and changing the execution context which follows.

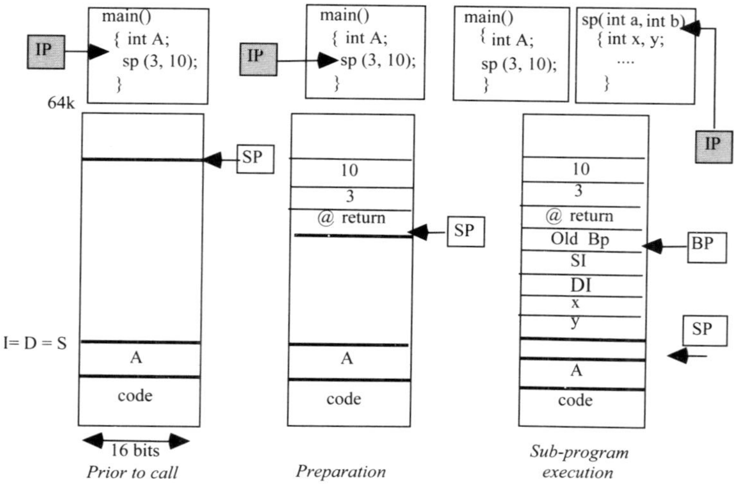

Fig. A1.5 Procedure call and context changing.

Two assembler handlers, CSV (Context SaVe) and CRET (Context REsTore) are generally used to carry out these actions as indicated in Figure A1.6.

The compiler must also insert the following instructions to prepare the call:

1. AX = number of octets necessary for the local variables,
2. Call the CSV procedure.

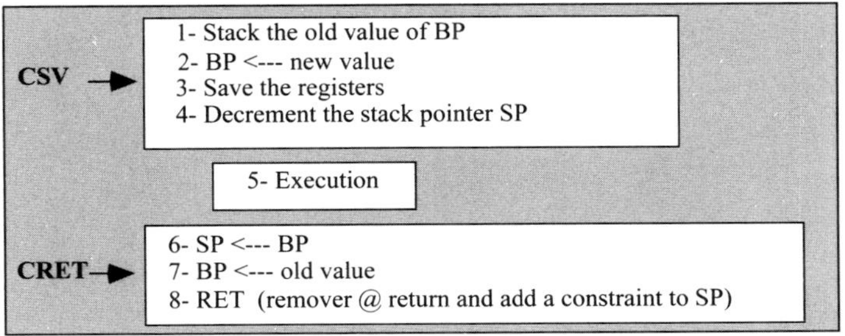

Fig. A1.6 Actions carried out at the instant of the call.

A1.1.3 Co-ordination between the Processor and the Peripheral Controllers

The co-ordination and communication between the microprocessor and the different peripheral controllers can be carried out using two techniques:

- *The status word technique* (POLLING). This is the microprocessor which must regularly *poll* and read the contents of the status register (Fig. A1.7) of each controller to determine their status, particularly if they request to be served by the microprocessor (input/output operation request). There is strong coupling between the microprocessor and the couplers. The time used by the microprocessor to carry out the polling loop is deducted from the total processing time. This technique is particularly applicable to systems which contain a *limited number of couplers.*
- *The interrupt technique.* In this technique, the coupler must notify the microprocessor it requests to be served by, or to which it signals that it is going to terminate an input/output operation. This involves weak coupling between the processor and the couplers. This coupling is essential to implement a multi-task operating system.

Figure A1.7 clearly indicates that the addressable space of the microprocessor is in reality composed of two sub-spaces:

- The memory space, which contains addressable memory cells (RAM + ROM);
- The input/output space, which is composed of the physical addresses of the registers of different controllers.

The RAM (random access memory) cells are accessible by reading and writing. Those of the ROM (read only memory) are only accessible by reading. The ROM mostly contains the boot program (system loading) and the resident part of the operating system kernel. Every time the machine is subjected to tension, the 'RESET' interrupt is generated. It is immediately intercepted by the microprocessor and triggers it to execute the corresponding interrupt handler which is always found at a fixed address (set by the microprocessor manufacturer: 00 000 or FF FFF). The ROM is always interfaced to the system in such a way that call addresses start from 00 000 or FF FFF addresses. The design of the card system (motherboard) always starts by the *definition of the card installation memory* (memory MAP). This indicates the addresses in the logic space which are reserved for each system circuit (memory circuits, input/output couplers, interrupt controllers, etc.).

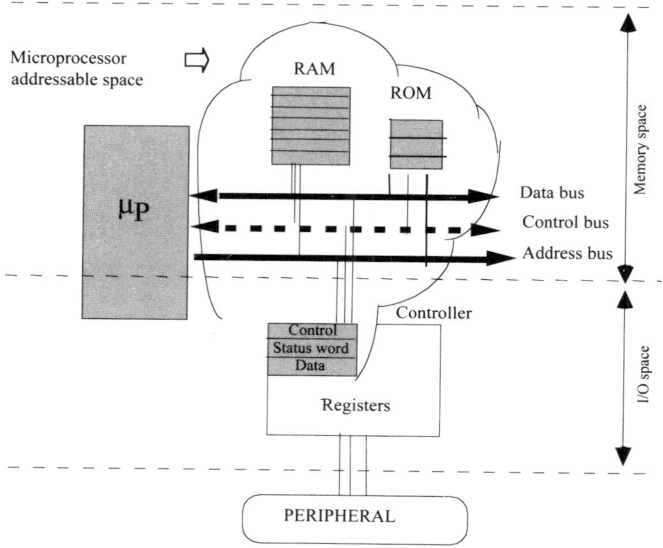

Fig. A1.7 Interactions between the microprocessor and couplers.

The two spaces are usually separated. This avoids the reduction in addressable space for programs. A specific line from the control bus (I/O) indicates the space occupied by the current address on the address bus.

The use of this line requires the use of a specific I/O assembler instruction (IN, OUT for the X86 family), because the standardized memory access instructions are no longer valid for the I/O space (this involves two different spaces). Figure A1.8 gives an example of the interfacing of an input/output coupler "the controller of disk 8272" and the format of several commands. Recall that a coupler can be considered as a specialized microprocessor.

Figure A1.9 shows how the technique of polling the status word "POLLING" can be used to control a coupler, and consequently its peripheral.

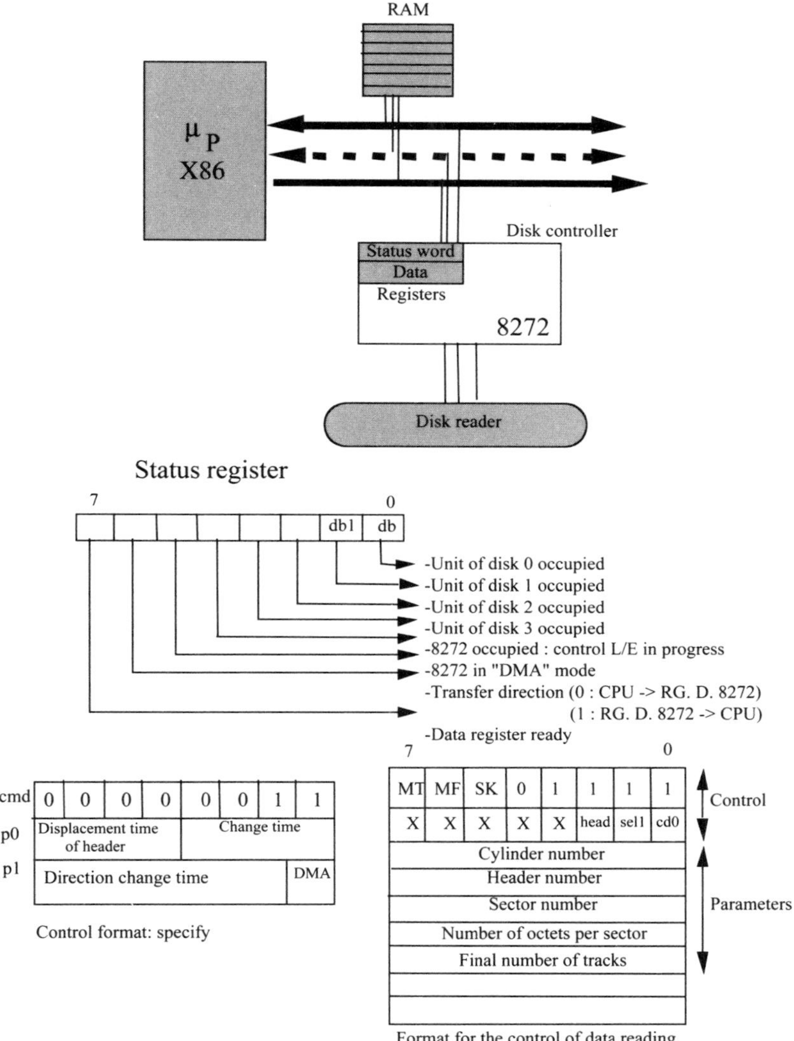

Fig. A1.8 Example of CPU coupling CPU-coupler.

A1.1.4 Interrupts

At each end of an assembler instruction execution, the microprocessor checks the level of the INT pin (connected to the interrupt line of the control bus). A change in level (high or low depending on the technology of the microprocessor) indicates the arrival of an interrupt. When an interrupt is detected, the microprocessor is re-routed to execute a service *handler*. Before executing the handler, it saves the

The CPU manages CPU-Controller exchanges

Example of the co-ordination between le CPU and the MC6850

Limited use: small embedded systems

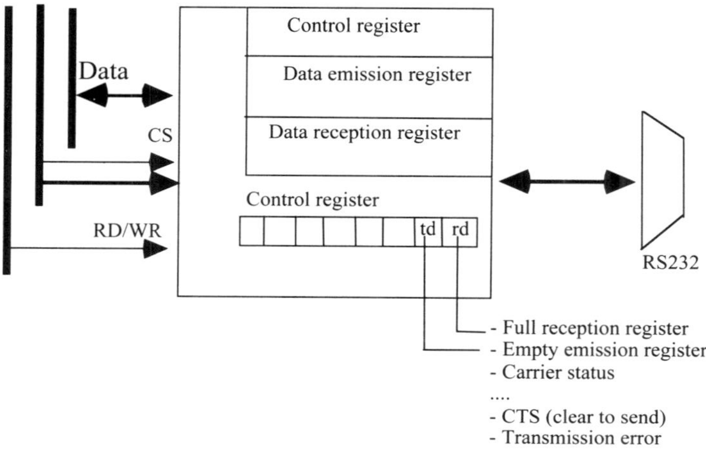


```
#define ADRACIA 0x80                    /* port address of the MC6850 controller*/
#define ADRBFR 0x500                                   /* buffer start address */

main ()
  { char data;                                                /* data to read*/
    struct { union                            /* control ( write), state (read) */

{              int control ;                  /* we are not interested in details*/

struct {              : 6;                                          /* jump 6
bits */  int td: 1;    /* transmission
data */               int rd: 1;  /* receive
data  */             }
status;          }
contstat;        int buffer; /* data register
*/          } * ACIA;    /* asynchronous series transmission controller */
    char *buffer = ADRBFR;

/*              'ACIA initialization and programming;

*/ while (1)
        { while (not ACIA -> contstat.status.rd) ; /* wait until it can read*/
         (*buffer ++) = ACIA->buffer;  /* writing of character read in the  buffer*/
```

Fig. A1.9 Example of the use of POLLING mode.

context of the execution of the current program. Upon termination of the execution of the handler, it takes up the execution of the suspended program again at the place where it had been interrupted (Fig. A1.10).

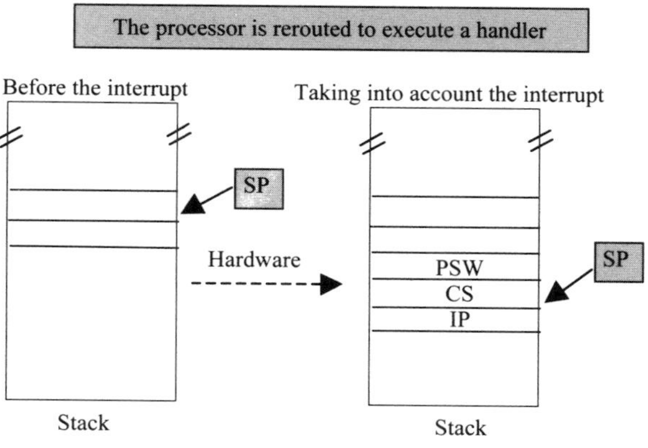

Fig. A1.10 Re-routing of the microprocessor to execute a service handler.

There are two techniques for the management of *handler* addresses:

- the vectored interrupt technique;
- the interrupt *dispatcher* technique.

> It is clear that the interrupt notion is directly linked to the external peripheral control notion. The speed of this latter is largely inferior to that of the microprocessor.

In contrast to the status word technique, the microprocessor will only be requested to serve a peripheral coupler if the latter generates an interrupt. The processor therefore continues to execute programs as long as there are no interrupts coming from a peripheral coupler. Coupling is asynchronous between the CPU and the peripherals.

> A handler is a sub-program that is composed of three parts if written in a higher level language, for example C (Fig. A1.11).

Figure A1.12 gives an overview on the use of the vectorized interrupt technique. In a data processing system, there are several peripherals of differing speeds. As the microprocessor only has one available interrupt pin (line), there are two ways of serving the peripherals:

- All of the peripheral coupler interrupt lines are connected to the INT line of the bus system. When an interrupt arrives, the processor is obliged to consult *all of the coupler status registers* to identify the peripheral which requests to be served. It is clear that the time given to this search is time lost to the processor;
- Unload interrupt management and the identification of peripherals which generated the interrupts from the processor. An interrupt handler is used to do

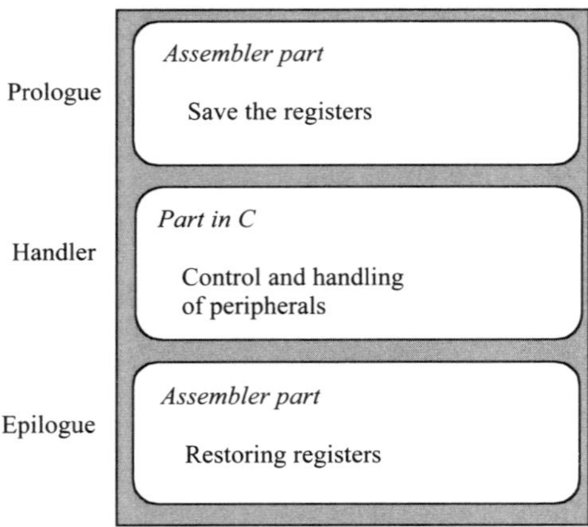

Fig. A1.11 Structure of the service handler of a peripheral.

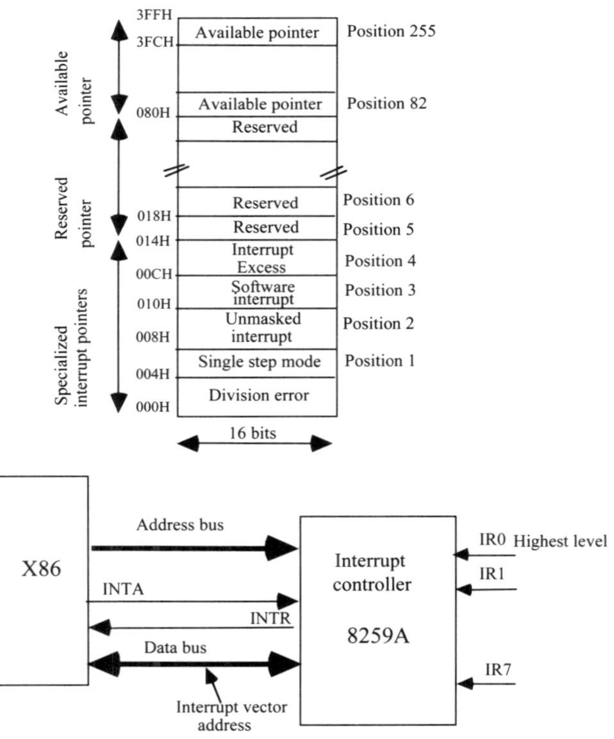

- JCW control ==> provide to 8259: the address at the start of the table (system initialization phase)
- OCW controls==>mask the interrupts, specify the end mode, the special interrupt modes
- IBM/PC ==>I/O port associated to 8259A : 020H
- prevent interrupts==> position the bits concerned in the 8259A control register: port 021H

Fig. A1.12 Use of a programmable interrupt controller (PIC).

this which programs itself and interfaces onto the bus system the same as a peripheral coupler (Fig. A1.12). The use of an interrupt handler enables *priority levels* to be introduced between the peripherals. When a peripheral coupler generates an interrupt, this is received by an interrupt handler which in turn generates an interrupt to the processor, and transmits to it the address of the service handler of the peripheral concerned, on the data bus. It transmits the index of the entry into a particular table called the Interrupt Vector Table. Each entry in the table contains the physical address of a service handler.

Figure A1.13 gives the main points of another interrupt management technique. It is mostly used with processors which automatically save the status word and the register segment in the execution file, and loads the new values of these two registers from the interrupt vector. The value of the status word loaded from the interrupt vector contains the peripheral *handler number*. We draw the reader's attention to the fact that this involves a specific handler entry point and not the handler as a whole. In this technique, all of the interrupts are associated to a single handler called the "dispatcher". This is written on the assembler and its role is to:

- save the registers in the file;
- identify the controller at the origin of the interrupts and call its handler;
- restore the registers.

This technique is mainly used in systems which, when an interrupt occurs:

- save the CS and PSW registers in the file;
- load the new CS and PSW values from the interrupt vector.

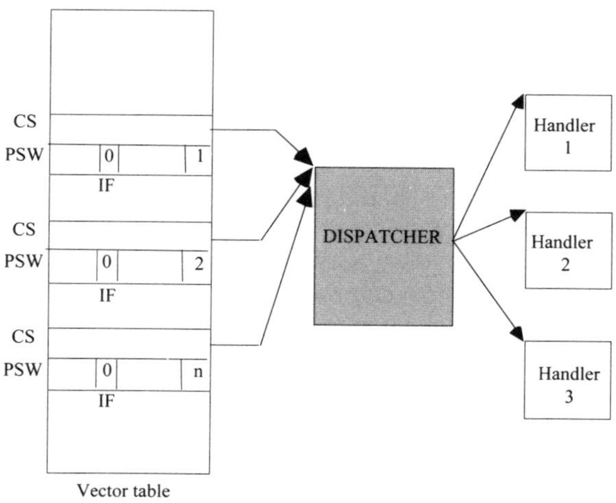

Fig. A1.13 Principle of the dispatcher technique.

Appendix 2 concentrates on an introduction to handlers using Unix Handlers.

Appendix 2

Basic Principles of Peripheral Handlers

A2.1 Presentation

A peripheral handler is a set of functions (primitives) which are called handler entry points: *open(), close(), write(), ioctl(), init(), halt(), poll(), start(), intr(), start()*. These are functions which are written in C and which can be called by the operating system kernel.

There are four types of handlers:

- character mode handlers;
- block mode handlers;
- stream mode handlers;
- terminal handlers.

Figure A2.1 shows the type of interaction between the program user, the kernel and a character mode handler. In a character mode handler, the unit of transfer between the coupler and the peripheral is the character. *Communication is direct* between the user program and the handler primitives (no intermediate means of storage).

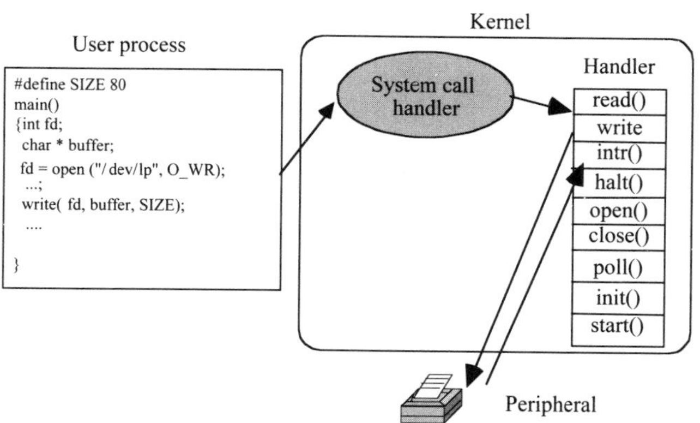

Fig. A2.1 Structure of a handler in character mode.

The implementation of a block mode handler is more complex. The unit of transfer between the coupler and the peripheral is the block (a multiple of 2, generally 512 or 1024 octets). The interaction between the program user and the handler is more complex. The handler must integrate a set of functions to *manage intermediate storage buffers* at the peripheral. They are first stored in the handler buffers which are found in the kernel space: transfer is carried out at the rate of the processor. An internal service handler is responsible for managing the transfer between the handler buffers and the peripheral, at the rate of the peripheral (Fig. A2.2).

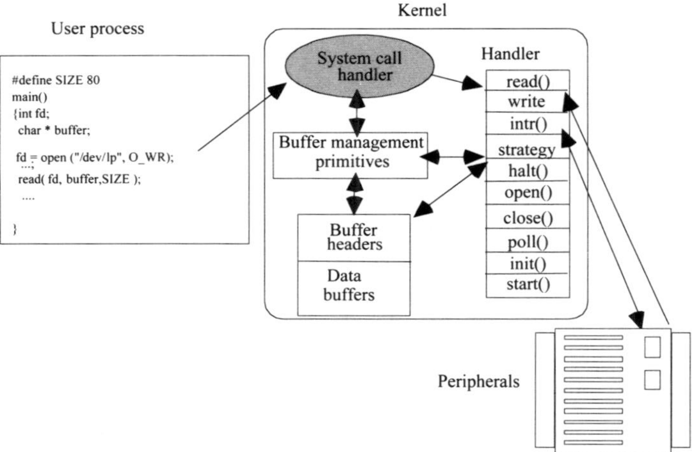

Fig. A2.2 Structure of a handler in block mode.

The reader will have assumed that a minimum of co-ordination and synchronization between the two transfers must be achieved!

Although the terminals are character type peripherals, the implementation of their handler often differs slightly from that of the other peripherals of this type. There are several terminals of differing technology, especially those which use different control sequences (control characters), depending on the manufacturer. To enable the connection of different terminals to the same data processing system, a *virtual terminal protocol* is used, which is independent of the characteristics of each physical terminal, to communicate with the user programs. The conversion and adaptation of dialogue to each physical terminal is carried out in the specific protocol of each terminal (Fig. A2.3).

Recall that virtual terminal protocol is situated at the layer 6 level of the ISO model (see Chapter 1).

Finally, the fourth type of handler concerns access to the communication network (Ethernet, etc) and the management of communication protocols.

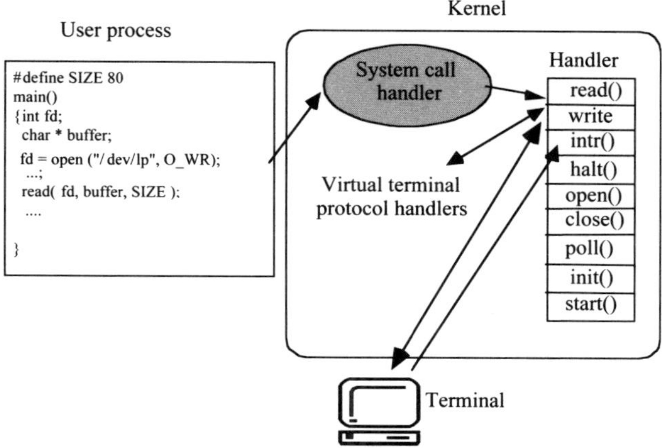

Fig. A2.3 Structure of a terminal handler.

> This type of handler must manage the different layers implicated in a communication session between two remote communicating entities. They are called character flow handlers.

Depending on the protocols of the different layers of the ISO model involved in a communication session, dialogue is effectively carried out in the form of the exchange of a character string. Error management and the recovery of communications must also be integrated into the different layers of the handler.

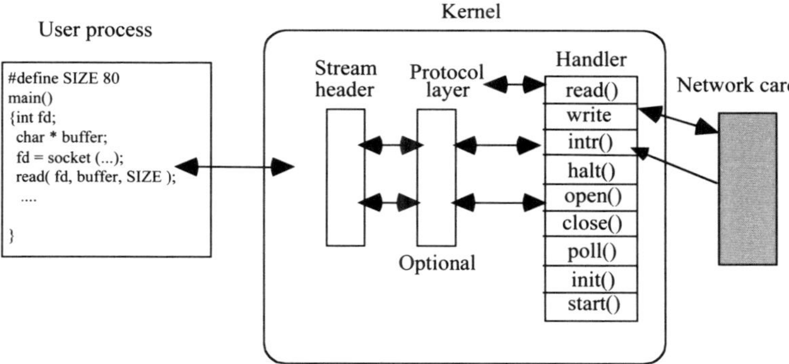

Fig. A2.4 Structure of a stream handler.

A2.2 General Notes on Programming

A handler is a set of C primitives, except potentially the interrupt handler (see Section A2.1). These primitives must be *linked* to the kernel.

The usual functions of the standard C library cannot be used to write handler primitives. The functions accepted are described in the peripheral controller manual: they can carry identical names to the standard functions (print(), copyout(), copyin(), etc.).

The main rules to follow when writing a handler are:

- Limit the use of the file: no recurring functions, no array declarations etc;
- No floating calculations;
- To each Unix system handler must be associated:
  - a special file (for example crw--------2 bin bin 6, 0 Dec 1995/dev/lp);
  - the major (6) and the minor (0).
- Avoid blocking waits (active loop).

The design of the handler must as far as possible respect the structuring model of the following programs:

- *Prologue*: reference to the header files of the other kernel modules used by the handler (the files #include), the definitions and declarations of the constants and the local variables of the handler.
- *The entry points code:* open(), close(), write(), ioctl(), init(), halt(), poll(), start(), intr().

Each operating system manages the handlers installed using tables. There is generally one table for each type of handler or peripheral (handler in character mode, handler in block mode etc). Figure A2.5 gives the structure of the table for handlers in character mode for the Unix operating system.

```
struct cdevsw                /*table entry of handlers in character mode*/
{ int (*d_open) ();          /*entry point to open the peripheral*/
  int (*d_close) ();         /*entry point to close the peripheral*/
  int (*d_read) ();          /*entry point to read the character*/
  int (*d_write) ();         /*entry point to write the character*/
  int (*d_ioctl) ();         /*entry point to carry out I/O control operations*/
  struct streamtab *d_str;
  char *d_name
};
extern int lpopen, lpclose(), lpread, lpwrite, lpioctl();
struct cdevsw [] = { lpopen, lpclose, lpread, lpioctl, NULL, NULL, "lp",...};

                dev_major => cdevsw[dev_major].d_open(...)
```

Fig. A2.5 Structure of the table of handlers in character mode for the Unix system.

A2.3 Communication between the Kernel and the Handler

In a multi-task, multiple user system, the kernel must guarantee minimum user security for the peripherals and their handler to avoid data loss and potential access conflicts. Unix uses data structures which facilitate the development of handlers (Fig. A2.6). The kernel associates a structure to each task or user, which contains the information necessary to implement I/O operations on a given peripheral.

Access to a peripheral follows the chain given in Figure A2.7. Note that the peripheral is declared in the user program in the same way as a file (manipulated with a file descriptor).

Unix associates a file descriptor (*inode*) to a peripheral which contains information relating to its location and access management. It involves a special device type file descriptor or peripheral. The special Unix file descriptor contains the "minor" (the number of the handler version if the peripheral has several) and the "major" (entry into the table of character mode handlers associated to the handler) of the handler.

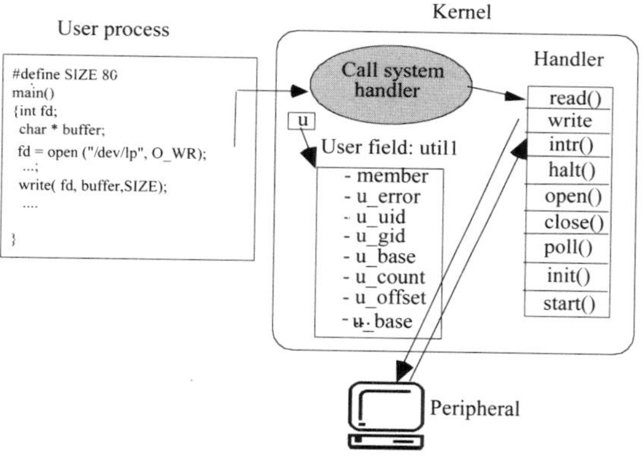

Fig. A2.6 Management of handler-program communications under Unix.

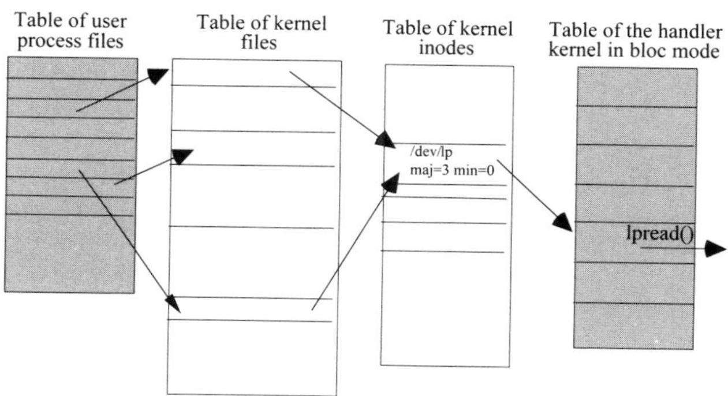

Fig. A2.7 Handler access chain.

A2.4 Installation Procedure of a New Handler under Linux

In this section we show the different stages in the installation of a new handler in block mode under Linux (PC version of Unix). The installation procedure of a handler in character mode is identical to this in its overview, maybe even simpler. This handler category does not use the `strategy()` entry point. Consequently, they are easier to write and install.

Stage 1: Choose a free major number for the block mode handler. The file `/usr/src/Linux/major.h` contains the major declarations for the different handlers. Edit this file and choose an entry (entry 7 is free) for the new handler called test:

```
assignments
devices are as follows (same as minix, so we can use the minix fs):

    character      block        comments
    -----------    ---------    --------------
    ...
    7 -            test         new handler with major = 7
```

Once the table has been modified (this table only serves to inform the user of the numbers already used), the major number of the new handler must be declared. This can be done by adding the `TEST_MAJOR` constant into the `major.h` file:

```
#define TEST_MAJOR
```

Stage 2: Creation of the inode associated to the handler in the `/dev:` repertoire (type of handler, number of major and minor) under the repertoire `/dev(cd /dev`. The inode test can be created with the command:

```
Mknod [inode_name] [handler_type] [major_number] [minor_number].

    Mknode test b 7 1
```

Stage 3: Modification of the `blk.h` file.

The `/usr/src/linux/drivers/block/blk.h` file must be edited to add the declaration of the handler initialisation function prototype:

```
...
#ifdef CONFIG_TEST
extern long test_init(long mem_start);
#endif
...
#elif )major_NR == test_major)
/* test */
#define DEVICE_NAME "handler test"
#define DEVICE_REQUEST do_test_request
#define DEVICE_NR(device) ((device) & 7)
#define DEVICE_OFF (device)

#elif ...
...
```

Stage 4: Modification of the `11_rw_blk.c` file to reserve the size of the buffer of the new handler, within the kernel space. The size of this buffer is decided by the `test_init()` initialization function. This initialization will be made just before that of ramdisk.

```
...
#ifdef CONFIG_TEST
     mem_start += test_init(long mem_start);
#end #CONFI_TEST

     if (ramdisk_size)
     mem_start += rd_init(mem_start, ramdisk_size*1024);
     return mem_start
...
```

Stage 5: Modification of the Makefile file of the block mode handler repertoire. This requires the `/usr/src/linux/drivers/block/ Makefile` file to be edited.

It is then necessary to add test.c and test.o of the new handler to the list of source and object files required for the generation of the kernel (kernel recompilation).

```
...
#ifdef CONFIG_TEST
OBJS := $ (OBJS) test.0
SRCS := $ (SRCS) test.c
Endif
...
```

Stage 6: Modification of the `config.in` file to enable the selection or not of the handler during `make config`. The following file must be edited for this:

```
/usr/src/linux/arch/i386/config.in
```

and to add the following lines:

```
...
'How will you install the handler test?'

Bool 'handler test?' CONFI_TEST n
If [ "$CONFIG_TEST" = "Y" ]; then
     How 'the handler test will be installed'.
Else
     How 'the handler test will not be installed'
End
...
```

Now the test.c file must be created which contains the blocking mode handler sources. This file must be stored in the `/usr/src/linux/ drivers/block` file.

```
/*Handler prologue*/

#include<linux/sched.h>
#include<linux/minix_fs.h>
#include<linux/ext2_fs.h>
#include<linux/fs.h>
#include<linux/kernel.h>
#include<linux/string.h>
```

```
#include<linux/mm.h>

#include<asm/system.h>
#include<asm/segment.h>

#define MAJOR_NR        TEST_MAJOR                  /*major number of handler*/
#include "blk.h"

/*declaration of constants*/
/*declaration of variables*/

/*handler entry points*/

static do_test_request (void)
{/*********** to complete************/}
static struct file_operations test_fops = {
        NUL,    /* 1seek        -default        */
        ...     /*********** to complete************/
        };

long test_init (long mem_start)
{/*********** to complete************/}
```

This is a brief introduction to handlers, the interested reader can study the technical documentation of the operating system used.

Appendix 3

Process Management

A3.1 Introduction

The scheduler plays a determining role in a multi-task, multiple user operating system. It is this which guarantees the efficient use of the system resources and the consistent development of the status of each process or each task active in the system, despite the events which occur. Its principal task involves moving the processes from one queue into another (Fig. A3.1).

Each of these files represents a *stage* in the life of the process:

- queue of processes in the *ready* state;
- queue of processes in *blocked* behind an event (I/O, semaphore);
- queue of processes in the *suspended* state.

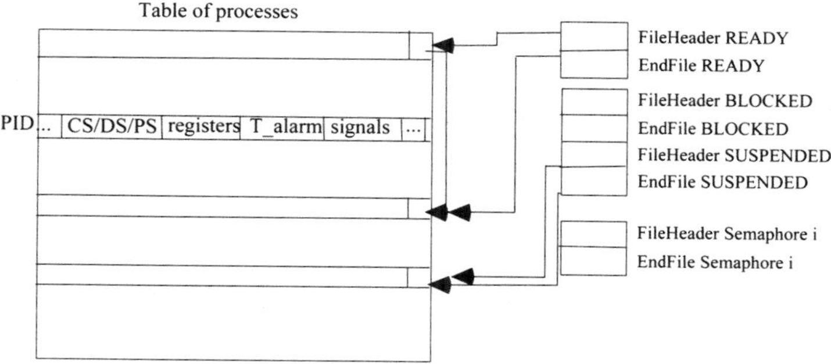

Fig. A3.1 The different queues used by the scheduler.

The information stored in these queues is limited to only the PID of each process.

The PID (process identification) is a pointer on an entry into the process table. Each entry in this table is a process descriptor. It holds the information necessary for the location of the process in the CM (addressable space of the process: CS, DS,

SS, ES) (Fig. A3.1), the external name of the process, its priority, its affiliation, its state (active, blocked) etc.

The lists managed by the scheduler do not all have the same characteristics:

- some are managed using the FIFO strategy;
- some are sorted according to the priority of the process;
- others are scheduled according to the time remaining for the process to be activated.

A3.2 Scheduler Implementation Principle

One of the main functions of the scheduler in a multi-task system is the *management of execution time for each process.* In the absence of significant events (end of an input/output operation, the current process blocked behind a semaphore or the initialization of an input/output operation, the arrival of an interrupt, etc) which enables the scheduler to take control and choose a new process, the scheduler must intervene to choose a process from those found in the "READY" state, they have all of the resources available except the CPU. It is the same principle as the multi-task: *avoid the monopolization of the CPU by a process or class of processes.* For this, a *quantum* (credit) of time is associated to each process. Once the process is activated (it is found in the "CHOSEN" state, it possesses all of the resources including the CPU), it continues to be executed as long as an event does not come along to help the scheduler, or that its quantum of time expires. The expiration of time of a process is seen as an event on which the scheduler must intervene to elect another process.

The processes can ask to be suspended for a certain time: a delay. They ask the scheduler to watch and manage the term of each suspended process. A list scheduled on the time remaining to the processes is used: the DELTA list for the management of terms (Fig. A3.2).

We recall that:

- The pre-emption of the current process to the benefit of another avoids the monopolization of the CPU by the latter, especially in the absence of external events (I/O);
- The use of real-time clocking is necessary for the implementation of the scheduler;
- Pre-emption enables all processes of equal priority to access the CPU ==> a *quantum* or credit of time is given to each process that it can use as long as it is not blocked or does not request an input/output operation;
- The scheduler provides a global variable called PRE-EMPTION that initializes to QUANTUM each time a new process passes into the CHOSEN state;

- The PRE-EMPTION variable is reduced at each clocking interrupt;
- The clock *handler* calls the scheduler as soon as the PRE-EMPTION variable reaches zero, to elect another process;
- The value of QUANTUM must be carefully chosen to avoid:
  - *a value too small* which leads to frequent changes in context which trigger an system overload;
  - *a value too big* which is the cause of the monopolization of the CPU by a process which generated processes of the same priority.

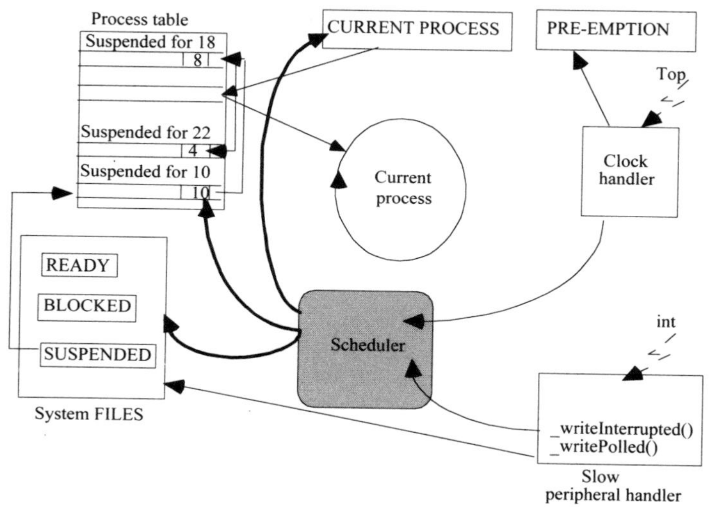

Fig. A3.2 The interaction of the scheduler with its environment.

At each clock stroke, the DELTA list enables processes to be awakened whose term has ended, without having to carry out a costly search into the long list.

The processes in the DELTA list are scheduled according to the date of awakening: the key field of the list in each process descriptor gives the number of clock strokes which differentiate it from the processes which precede it in the list (Fig. A3.2). The head of the list gives access to the first processes on the list.

The intervention of the clock handler is limited to reduce the key field of the first processes. The keys of the other processes are related to those of the first.

In a multiple process system, the most expensive resource which flaws the set of processes, except the ELECTED (current) process, is the central unit. The READY list groups processes in possession of all of the resources they need except the CPU. They are eligible for the CPU.

The change in context can be summarized in two main actions:

1. select one process from those in the READY list;
2. pass the control of the CPU over to the processes selected.

> The scheduler is the component of the operating system responsible for carrying out a selection strategy. The most frequently used strategy involves "choosing at any instant the processes which possess the highest priority level among the READY and ELECTED list of processes". Processes of equal priority are selected in turn (use of the execution quantum).

The selection operation of a new process must *be extremely rapid*. This requirement is easily met by classing the processes in order of priority in the READY list.

A3.3 The Scheduler and the Internal Synchronization of Handlers

We emphasized in Section A3.2 that it was necessary to provide co-ordination and synchronization between the handler primitives which carry out data transfer from the user program space (process) to the handler buffers in the kernel space, and the handler primitives which manage the transfer of data to the registers of the peripherals controller. This synchronization is essential because of the considerable difference between speed of data production (data transfer from the user space to the handler buffers) which is equal to that of the CPU, and the speed of data consumption (data transfer from the handler buffers towards the controller registers) which is equal to that of the peripheral. Figure A3.3 shows how this synchronization is implemented in the printer handler (lp) of Unix on a PC (Linux).

In this system, a queue is linked to each handler. The printer handler (lp) is composed of the standard entry points which make up its user interface (see part 2): `Lp_open()`,`Lp_init()`,`Lp_interrupt()`,`Lp_read()` and `Lp_ write()`. It also contains the following internal points (service handlers):

- `lp_write_interrupt()`: this is used by the handler to transfer the buffer data towards the controller. It is used (by `lp_write()` primitive) only in cases where the printer controller is able to manage an interrupt (functioning in interruptible mode). This enabled the interrupt handler `lp_interrupt()`: to be used every time an interrupt occurs.
- `Lp_polled()`: this is also used to transfer data from the buffers towards the controller. It is used by the pilot (`Lp_write()`) in cases where the controller is incapable of generating an interrupt. It also involves a handler which uses the status word technique (see part 1).

We leave the reader to try to understand the synchronization mechanism implemented, and the link which exists between the handler and the scheduler. Note that the `schedule()` function is the Linux scheduling algorithm. The synchronization problem of the different parts of the handler is a standard problem known as the producer–consumer problem, for which there are several solutions (see Chapter 2) in the literature.

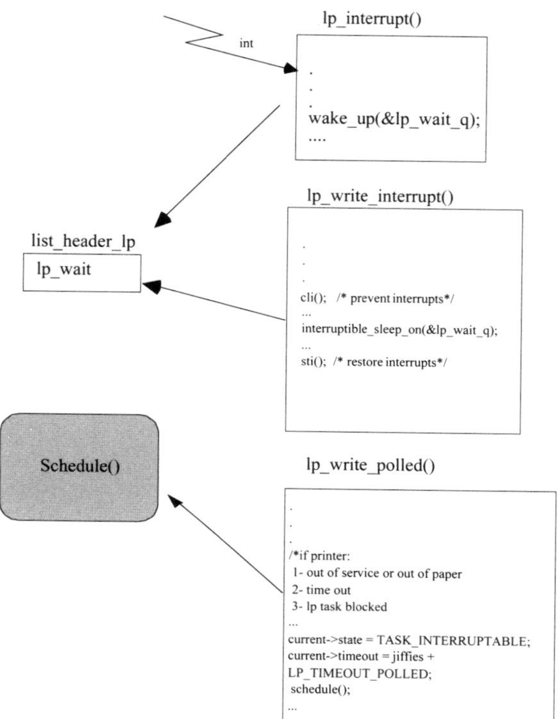

Fig. A3.3 Scheduler–handler interaction.

Appendix 4

Management of the Central Memory

The management of the central memory is partly undertaken by the hardware layer and partly by the operating system kernel.

A4.1 The Part Supported by Hardware

A virtual address (logic) specified by an instruction is first transformed into a linear address by the mechanism of microprocessor (X86) integrated segmentation.

The linear address is then transformed into a physical address by the paging mechanism.

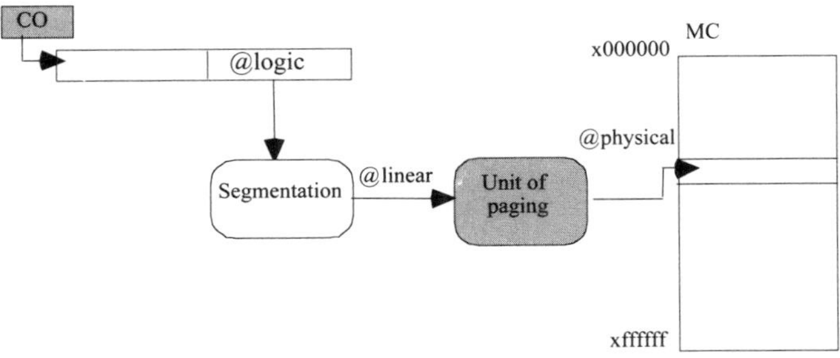

Structure of a linear address

31 22	21 12	11 0
@DESCRIPTIVE	@Table	Movement

Fig. A4.1 Transformation mechanism of logic addresses into physical addresses.

A4.2 The Paging Mechanism

A page is the unit of transfer between the central memory and the hard drive. A segment can be divided into pages.

Figure A4.2 gives the principle of the paging mechanism for the X86 family.

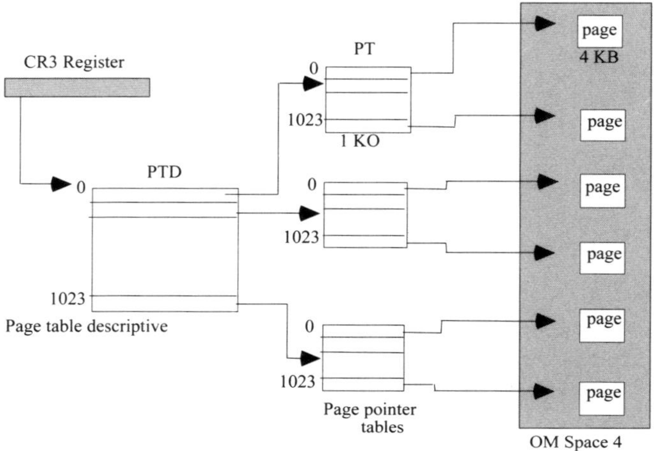

Fig. A4.2 The paging mechanism.

Note that the CR3 register is part of the task (process) context. It is saved and restored in the execution stack.

The content of the specification of the page tables is:

31 12	11 9	8	7	6	5	4	3	2	1	0
Address	OS	0	0	D	A	0	0	U/S	R/W	P

D : 1 ==> not empty
R/W: 0 ==> read only for users
U/S : 1 ==> page user
P : 1 ==> page is present in the CM
A : 1 ==> access to the page has occurred
OS : bits available for the operating system (Last Ready Used...)

When a page is swapped (transferred from the hard drive to the central memory), bits 1-31 of the page descriptor contain the physical address of the page on the hard drive (the bit 0 must be equal to 0). The paging mechanism is activated when the most significant bit of the CRO register equals 1. At each stage of the address transformation process, the mechanism carries out the following checks which trigger a "lack of page" event:

- access rights;
- presence of pages in the CM;
- security violation.

The "lack of page" event handler has the role of guaranteeing the linear address which caused the last lack of page. A cache (TLB) for the most recently used virtual physical addresses is operated by the microprocessor at each transformation of a virtual address into a physical address (Fig. A4.3).

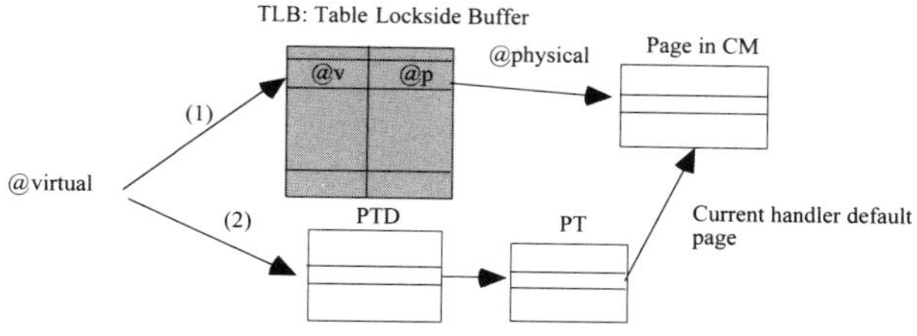

Fig. A4.3 The use of a cache to accelerate the transformation process.

TBL is updated each time the CR3 register is loaded, or specifically by updating the bits of the CR0 registers.

A4.3 The Segmentation Mechanism

A segment is the logic unit of management of the space addressable to the processes. A linear address is a set address:

Linear_address = base_segment + virtual_address

Each segment in the system is described by an 8-octet descriptor which contains the information necessary for its management (base, limit, privilege...).

There are two types of segment:

- regular segments (code and data segments);
- system segments (TSS: Task State Segment and LDT: Local Descriptor Table).

A4.4 Characteristics of Segment Systems

A TSS (descriptor) is associated to each task in the system. The LDT segments contain the descriptors of regular segments lacking system tasks. In Linux, there is one LDT per task, their size is 24 octets and they contain:

- LDT[0] NULL (obligatory);
- LDT[1] segment code descriptor;
- LDT[2] data/stack segment descriptor.

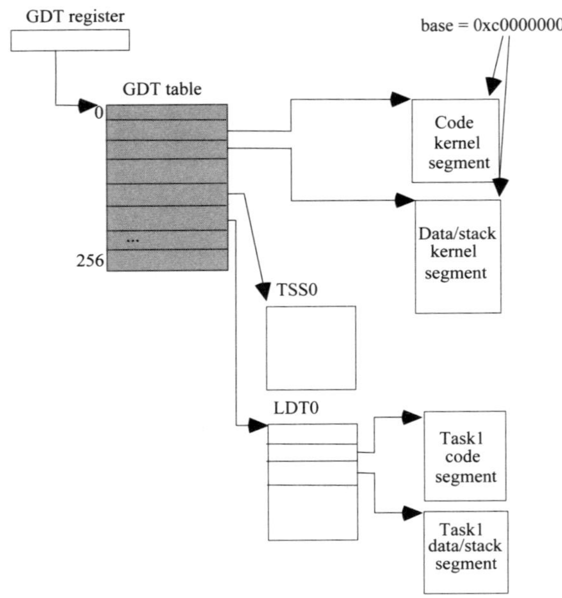

Fig. A4.4 The different segmentation mechanism tables.

For the user segments:

```
Base_segment = 0x000 ==> linear address = virtual address
```

The 386 microprocessor uses a global descriptive called GDT for Global Descriptor Table (Fig. A4.4) which is created by the system in the CM: pointed by the GDT register. GDT contains one segment descriptor for each TSS, LDT and the regular segments. For the Linux system, GDT contains only two entries:

- GDT[0]: the NULL descriptor;
- GDT[1]: the kernel segment code descriptor;
- GDT[2]: the kernel segment stack/data descriptor.

The other entries are attributed to the TSS and LDT descriptors:

- GDT[4] = TSS0, GDT[5] = LDT0;
- GDT[6] = TSS1, GDT[7] = LDT1, etc.

A segment can only be used if its descriptor has been changed in the corresponding register segment.

The 386 possesses a set of register access criteria. Consequently, the programmer cannot load a descriptor into a register. Furthermore, only one part of the segments (the selector) is visible to the programmers: CS, DS, FS, GS and SS.

The programmer loads one of these registers with a value of 16-bits "SELECTOR". The selector only enables the identification of a segment descriptor in one of the tables.

A4.5 386 Selectors

A segment selector is loaded into a register (CS, DS, etc.) to select one of the regular segments in the system. Its structure is as follows:

15	3	2	1	0
Index		TI		RPL

TI Table Indicator
0: ==> GDT
1: ==> LDT

RPL Privilege level (Linux uses 2 privilege levels)
0 ==> Kernel
1 ==> User

The following table gives the selectors used in Linux:

TI	Index	RPL	Selector	Segment	
0	1	0	0x08	Kernel code	GDT[1]
0	2	0	0x10	Data/stack code	GDT[2]
0	3	0			GDT[2]
1	1	3	0x0F	User code	LDT[1]
1	2	3	0x17	Data/stack user	LDT[2]

System segment selectors can not be directly loaded in segment registers. Only TR and LDTR can be. Each system call (system primitive) starts by:

- updating DS and ES ==> system data segment (0×10);
- FS points on the user data segment (0×17) which will be used to obtain data pointed by the call arguments of the system primitive;
- the stack segment and pointers are automatically set to ss0 and esp0 by the interrupt. The old values are restored when the system primitive is left.

A4.6 Segment Descriptors

One segment descriptor exists for each segment used in the system. There are regular descriptors and system descriptors. A segment descriptor contains the following fields:

63-54	55	54	53	52	51-48	47	46	45	44-40	39-16	15-0
Base	G	D	R	U	limit	P	DPL	S	Type	Base segment	End segment
31–24					19–16					23–0	15–0

R : reserved (0)
DPL : 0 ==> kernel, 1 ==> user
G : 1==> 4k granularity (always used by Linux)
D : 32 bits by default
U : to define by programme
P : 1 ==> present in the memory
S : 0 ==> system segment, 1 ==>normal code or data segment
TYPE : used indifferently for descriptors or users.

The structure of registers associated to segmentation is the following (only the selector is accessible by the programmer):

16-bits	32-bits	32-bits	
Selector	Base @ physical	Segment limit	Attributes

Finally, we end this part by giving a brief presentation of the software part of the segmentation mechanism, supported by the kernel.

A4.7 The Part Supported by the Kernel

Following a `fork()` (creation of a son process), a process inherits from the page pointer table (PPT). The management strategy is as follows:

- *Copy-on-write:* the page is physically copied in the space of the process during the first access to this writing page (Fig. A4.5).

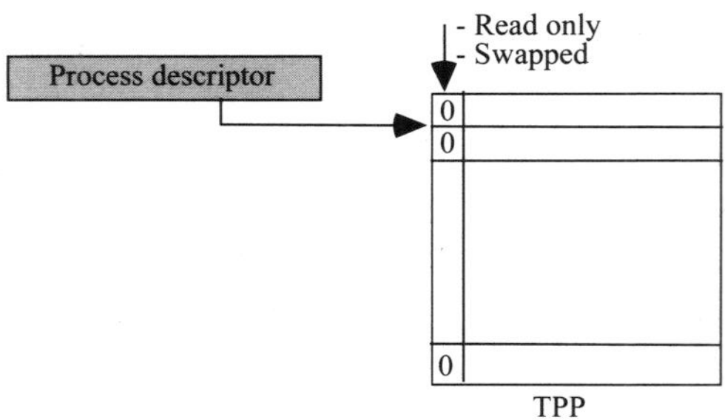

Fig. A4.5 The page pointer table.

Each process possesses an LDT table. In the user space:

- @linear(0==> 4 GB) = @ logic (selector segment + displacement);
- CS and DS of the kernel are privileged segments defined in GDT;
- CS and DS of the kernel occupy the 3GB ==> 4GB part of the logic space.

The system table Swapper_page.dir ==> enables translations to be carried out (Fig. A4.6):

@logic ==>@physical in the kernel space

To process a system call (`fork()`, `exec()`, `lpread()`, etc) the user process moves into supervisor mode with its current context. In supervisor mode, it reaches the kernel space from its "*page directory*" table which contains pointers towards the system table *Swapper_page_table.*

Only task[0] (the NULL process) directly uses the Swapper_page_table table.

If @linear above 3 GB ==> uses the same translation table:

Swapper_page_table (kernel space).

The user stack starts from the summit of the data segment and increases towards the base. *Kernel_stack_frame(a page)* ==> is associated to each new process. It is used each time a kernel operates from the process context.

In the user translation table (Page Directory), only the pages filled can be swapped.

We stop here as there are several publications which cover the architecture of x86 microprocessors and the mechanisms which support them. There is also much literature on the Linux operating system.

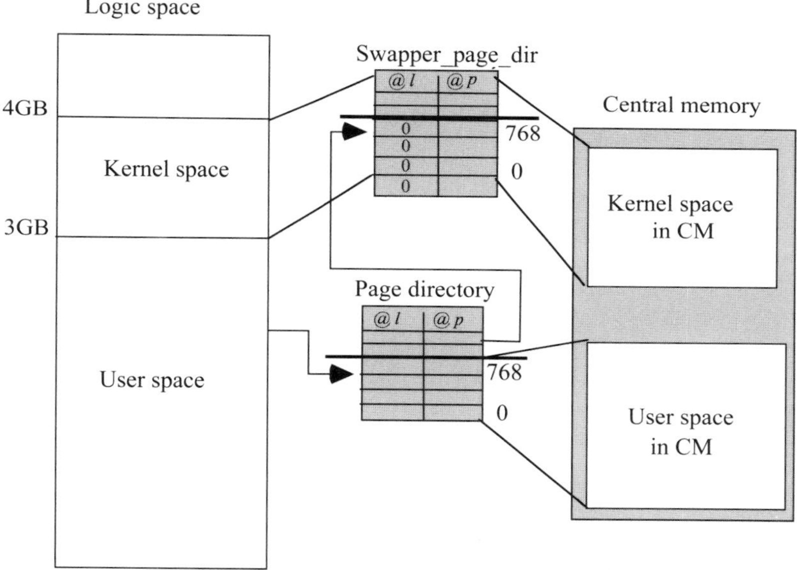

Fig. A4.6 Space addressable to a process.

Appendix 5

Logic Programming and Constraints

J.-L. Imbert

The 1970s saw the birth of a new generation of programming languages based on logic. The first of these was called *Prolog*, a contraction of *logic programming*, and is the product of Alain Colmerauer and Philippe Roussel (1993). These languages have been improved by the contribution of constraint towards the middle of the 1980s, and parallel technologies during the last few years. There are an increasing number of industrial logic programming with constraint applications: production planning, protoyping, simulation, configuration of high security keys, configuration of assembly lines, optimization, wood cutting, stock management, transport, telecommunications, aerial traffic and equipment rotation, to name but a few.

Over the next pages, our aim is to succinctly provide the basics of this type of programming necessary for the understanding of some passages in this book.

Languages of this type have the ability to express problems clearly. A problem processed by this type of language must be described, modelled. In contrast to procedural languages, the calculation method must never be described. A logic program with constraints is therefore a model describing a problem (Fig. A5.1). A program is formed from rules such as:

$$A <== R_1, A_0, A_1, \ldots, A_k$$

where A, A_0, $A_1, \ldots, A_k$ are predicates and R a constraint system. R can be empty as can the following A, A_0, $A_1, \ldots, A_k$. One such rule reads: *A is satisfied if the system R is soluble and all predicates A_0, $A_1, \ldots, A_k$ are satisfied.* A is called the rule header, and R, A_0, $A_1, \ldots, A_k$ the rule queue. When the rule queue is empty, A is a *fact* as it is satisfied without condition.

A5.1 Functioning of a Logic Program

A logic program can be considered a database describing a knowledge, to which questions called *requests* can be posed. A request takes the form of:

$$S_0, B_0, B_1 \ldots, B_n$$

where S_0 is a soluble constraint system, and B_0, $B_1 \ldots, B_n$ a suite of predicates for which we want to know if they are simultaneously satisfied (controlled). For this:

1. the language chooses a rule

$$A <== R_l, A_0, A_1, \ldots, A_k$$

2. checks if the constraint system $S_1 = S_0, R, \{B_0{=}A\}$ is soluble,
3. if yes, obtains a new request

$$S_1, A_0, A_1 \ldots, A_k\, B_1 \ldots, B_n$$

Proving that the original request is satisfied, also proves that this new request is satisfied.

If not, or if the new request cannot be proved, another rule is tried. If there is not another rule, the initial request can be proved (we say that it has failed), and we return to the earlier state to try another rule.

Logic programming with constraints

The following program describes the sum of the positive elements of a set of numbers.

A suite of numbers is noted in square brackets. The numbers are separated by commas. [x11] signifies that x is the first element in the set, and 1 the rest of the set ([x|l]=[2,3,4,5] signifies x=2, l=[3,4,5]). The empty set is represented by the symbol [ ]. The program is composed of the three following logic rules:

```
sum([ ], 0) <== .
```

Which confirms that the sum of the positive elements of an empty set is 0.

```
sum([x|l], x+s) <== {x >= 0}, sum(l, s).
```

reads: the sum of the positive elements of a set [x11] is x+s on condition that x is positive and that s is the sum of the positive elements of set l.

```
sum([x|l], s) <== {x< 0}, sum(l, s).
```

reads: the sum of a set [x|l] is s on condition that x is negative and that s is the sum of the positive elements of set 1.

The following questions can be asked

```
sum([3,-1,2], r).
```

And the answer is r=5. Or

```
sum([a,3,b], 10).
```

With 3 answers : a+b=7, a >= 0, b>= 0 ;
a=7, b<0 ;
b=7, a <0.

Fig A5.1 A logic program.

If the program includes facts, we can hope that successive requests will have a suite of predicates growing smaller. If a request is reached whose suite of predicates is empty, this is a success: the initial request is checked (like intermediary requests). The final system (which is soluble) is the result. It provides conditions so that initial requests (as well as all of the derived requests) are satisfied.

$\underline{S_0, R, \{B_0{=}A\},}$ $\quad A_0,\ldots,A_k\, B_1\ldots,B_n$

$\Downarrow$

S_1

.

.

$S_2, B_1\ldots,B_n$

.

.

S_0, B_n

.

.

S_{final}

This functioning is illustrated in Figure A5.2.

There are different types of constraints: arithmetic, linear, non-linear, boolean, list, etc. The designers of these languages must therefore display the constraint solutions capable of incrementally processing these according to their specifications. By incremental, we mean integrate at the least cost the constraints which arrive in small groups, without being obliged to reprocess the system as a whole (Imber, 1995).

Prolog III and Prolog IV (Colmerauer, 1987) are among the most well-known pioneered languages which possess constraint solutions on booleans, rational and real linear constraints, lists, intervals and non-linear arithmetic, CLP® (Jaffar and Machaylov, 1987) which process linear and non-linear constraints on floaters, CHIP (Dincbas *et al.*, 1988) which can work on the finished sets, booleans, rational linear constraints and floaters.

Take the program in Figure A2.1.

```
sum([ ], 0) <==
sum([x/l],x+s) <== {x >= 0}, sum( l,s).
sum([x|l], s) <== {x< 0}, sum( l,s).
```

Initial request:

```
{ },  sum([3, -1, 2], r);
{x1 =3, x1  >= 0 , r = x1 +s1 },  sum([-1,2],s1 ) ;
{x1 =3, x1  >= 0 , r = x1 +s1 , x2 = -1, x2  < 0 , s1 = s2 }, sum([2],s2) ;
{x1 =3, x1  >= 0 , r = x1 +s1 , x2 = 5, x2  < 0 , s1 = s2 , x3 = 2, x3 >= 0, s2 = x3  + s3}, sum([ ],s3) ;
```

Final request:

```
{x1 =3, x1  >= 0 , r = x1 +s1 , x2 = 5 , x2  < 0 , s1 = s2 , x3 = 2, x3 >= 0, s2 = x3  + s3 , s3  = 0},  0 ;
```

The final system can be simplified as:

```
{ r = 5};
```

Fig. A5.2 An example.

A5.2 Prolog III

In the Prolog III language, a rule such as:

$$<== R_1\ A_0, A_1,\ldots,A_k..$$

where A_0, $A_1,\ldots,A_k$ are predicates and R a constraint system, is written:

$$A\text{->}\ A_0, A_1,\ldots,A_k..\{R\};$$

The constraint system R must be written after the predicates. A predicate is written as a suite of characters (uppercase and lowercase unaccented letters, numbers, and the underline character:_) beginning with at least two letters and if there are arguments, they must be in brackets. The arguments can either be predicates, constants or authorized expressions, or variables. Variable identifiers follow the same syntax as predicate identifiers, except that they must start with a single letter.[1] A predicate is never a variable. Following this syntax, the program example in Figures A5.1 and A5.2 is written in Prolog III.

```
Sum([ ], 0) -> ;
Sum([ x] L_list], x+s) -> sum(L-list,s), { x>= 0} ;
Sum([ x] L_list], s) -> sum(L-list,s), { x< 0} ;
```

The initial request is written: `Sum([3, -1,2],r);`

Each response found is shown inside curly brackets. For example, the solution for the above request is:

{r=5}

but for the initial request: sum{[a,3,d],7);

there are three responses : {7 > = a > = 0, b = -a + 7}
{a = 7, b < 0}
{a < 0, b = 7}

to complete all of the functions of Prolog III used in this book, a second form of list remains to be introduced: *tuples*. Prolog III understands two types of lists: binary lists written between square brackets, and tuples between <> (Fig. A5.3).

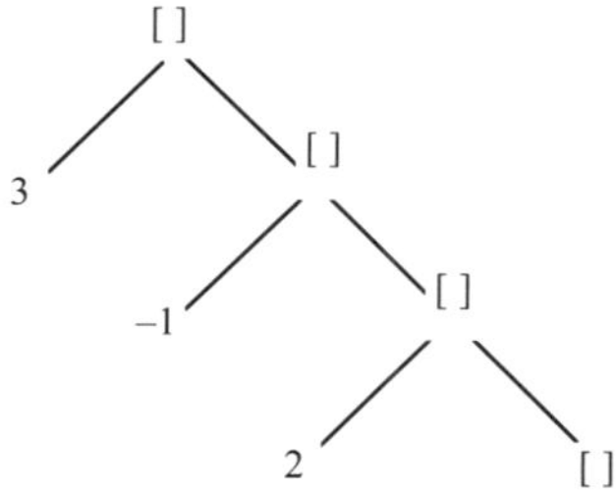

Fig. A5.3a Binary list [3, -1, 2].

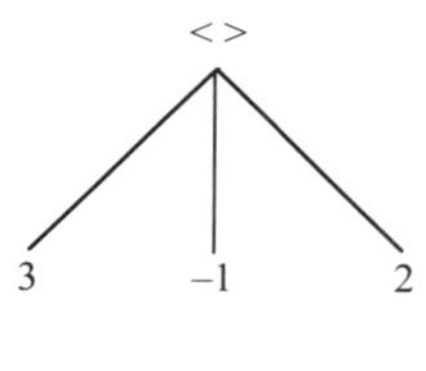

Fig. A5.3b Tuple list <3, -1, 2>.

[1] Sum(x,[1,2,35]), profits, union(intersection(A,B),X124) are three predicates.
X,A,B,X124, P_product, n12_number_of_people, q1234suite are eight variable identifiers.

An interesting function of tuples is the concatenation operator represented by a point. For example, the tuple list <2,3,4> concatenated to the list <8,9> can indifferently be written:

<2,3,4>.<8,9> or <2,3,4,8,9>

Note also the existence of the relation '::' which gives the length of the <> list. This operator is actually more general, it gives the number of sons of the root of a tree. Supposing that `L` is the list <1,2,3,8,9>, then the constraint `L::n` will give `n=5`. If, on the other hand, `L` is a binary list, then the constraint `L::n` will give `n=2`.

Example

Take *s*, a suite of numbers to the power of two, classed in descending order.

Such a suite is modelled by the following Prolog III program:

```
Suite(<1>) -> ;
Suite(<2x, x>.1) ->. Suite(<x>.1);
```

To obtain the suite of the nine first powers of two, the following request can be launched:

```
Suite(1),              {1::9};
```

The response given by Prolog is:

```
{1 = <256, 128, 64, 32, 16, 8, 4, 2, 1>};
```

A5.3 Accepted Expressions

Prolog III enables linear expressions to be processed on rational (of unlimited size), on floaters, on boolean expressions and on tree format expressions.

Trees

These are predicates with or without arguments. Each argument is also formed from a predicate with or without arguments, and so on. We have already seen several tree functions.

Mathematical Expressions

The mathematical expressions accepted are those formed from integers, rationale, floaters, variables and the operators +, –, * and /.

The arithmetical constraints accepted are those formed from authorized arithmetical expressions and the relations <, <=, =, >, >= and # (for <>). Only linear arithmetical constraints are immediately taken into account and processed, the other expressions are delayed until they become linear by knowing the value of several variables that they contain. A classic example is that modelled on a financial calculator:

Take a loan of K pounds borrowed at a rate of i per cent to be repaid in a set of instalments A_1,A_2... Note `L` the list of these instalments. This gives the following model:

- If K is nil, there is nothing to repay and therefore the set is empty;
- Otherwise, during the first period the capital due is accrued at i per cent and is worth $K(1 + i)$ at the end of this. Repaying the value of $A1$ at the end of this period means that the remaining capital due will be $K(1 + i) - A1$.It follows that the remaining capital must be repaid by the set of instalments formed in list L taken from $A1$.

The model is therefore composed of the two following rules:

```
borrow(0, i, <>) -> ;
borrow(K, i, <A>.L) -> borrow ((K*(1+i)-A, i, L);
```

Although the expression of the remaining capital due is not linear, it can become linear. This is the case with the following request which gives the value of each instalment if a sum of £1000 is repaid in ten equal instalments at 8 per cent.

```
borrow(1000, 0.08, L), (L::10, };
```

Note that `<A>.L=L.<A>` is the same as saying that all elements of L are equal.

The Prolog III response is therefore:

```
{A=1.49029488697075e+03, L=<1.49029488697075e+03,...,1.49029488697075e+03>};
```

That is to say: A = £149.02, and L = <149.02,..,149.02>;

On a final note, the process which enables the rational mode to pass to the floating mode, is finding a decimal point (floating mode) or not.

Boolean Expressions

The boolean expressions accepted are expressions formed from variables, constant booleans (0' which signifies *false* and 1' which signifies *true*), and connectors ~ (*no*), | (*yes*), & (*and*), => (*implies*) and <=> (*equivalent*).

The boolean constraints accepted are those formed from authorized boolean expressions and relations =, # and =>. There are several other relations which are not needed in order to read this book. The interested reader can study the *Manuel d'Utilisation de Prolog III.*

An example which figures in this book and which uses booleans is that of a binary adder:

```
Adder(1, m, n) ->
     {
               l=<x1,x2,x3>;
               m=<y1,y2>;
```

```
            n=<u1,u2,u3>;
            u1=x1 + x3;
            u2=x2 + u3;
            y1=u1 | u2;
            u3= ~(x1 <=> x3);
            y2= ~(x2 <=> u3)
      }
```

where l, m and n are vectors of boolean values.

A5.4 Conclusion

Logic languages and their extensions have led a rapid development in program design methods. They enable us to concentrate directly on analysing problems without having to worry about how the calculations are made; in fact it involves the modelling of problems. They have a great range of expression to offer; in this context, $x = x + y$ retains its mathematical sense and can also be written $x + y = x$. $x = x + 1$ no longer makes sense as this equation cannot be solved. The qualities of this type of program are such that a wide range of industrial and other applications are able to use it.

Bibliography

Agha, G and Hewitt, C. (1987) *Concurrent Programming using Actors,* OOCP87, Yonezama, MIT Press.

Airau, R. (1987) *VHDL du Langage de la Modélisation,* Presses Polytechniques et Universitaires Rornandes Press, Lausanne.

Andrews, G.R. (1991) "Paradigms for Process Interaction in Distributed Programs", *ACM Computing Surveys,* Vol. 23, No. l; March.

Arnold, A. (1990) "Systèmes de Transitions Finis et Sémantique des Processus", *Technique et Science lnformatiques,* Vol. 9, No. 3.

Arnold, A. (1992) *Systémes de Transitions Finis et Sémantique des Processus Communicants,* Masson editions.

Asch, G. *et al.* (1991) *Les Capteurs en L'Instrumentation Industrielle,* Dunod editions, Paris.

Attoui, A. *et al.* (1996) "A Formal Approach for the Specification and the Behavior Validation of Real-Time Systems Based on Rewriting Logic", *Real-Time Systems Journal,* Vol. 10, No. l; January.

Audureau, E. *et al.* (1989) *Logique Temporelle, Sémantique et Validation de Programmes Parallèles,* Masson editions, Paris.

Ayel, J. (1994) "Concurrent Decisions in Production Management", *Journal Integrated Computer-Aided Engineering* Special Issue "AI in Manufacturing and Robotics".

Baillet, P. (1994) *Contribution à l'amélioration de la réactivité dans les systmèmes de production, notamment par la mise en oeuvre des concepts de décentralisation des fonctions de décisions.* Thèse de doctorat en Sciences, Université d'Aix-Marseille; 3 November.

Bal, H.E. *et al.* (1989) "Programming Languages for Distributed Systems", *ACM Computing Surveys,* Vol. 21, No. 3; September.

Balter, R. (1985) *Maintien de la Cohérence dans les Systèmes d'Information Répartis,* Thèse es-Science Mathématiques, Institut National Polytechnique, Grenoble.

Banatre, J.P., Coutant, A. and Metayer, D. (1988) *Parallel Machine for Multi-Set Transformation and its Programming Style*, Future Generation Computer Systems 4, North-Holland.

Baptiste, P. and Manier, H. (1993) *Pilotage d'un anneau flexible de production: une approche définissant un comportement autonome par station*, GS14 : Quatrième Congrès Internationale de Génie Industriel, Marseille; 15–17 December.

Barbier, F. and Jaulent, P. (1992) *Techniques Orientées Objet et CIM*, Eyrolles editions.

Barbuceanu, M. and Fox, M.S. (1994) *The Information Agent: An Infrastructure Agent Supporting Collaborative Enterprise Architectures*, 3rd Workshop on Enabling Technologies: Infrastructure for Collaborative Enterprises, Morgantown, West Virginia.

Baude, F. (1991) *Utilisation du Paradigme Acteur pour le Calcul Parallèle*, Thèse d'Informatique, Université Paris XI Orsay.

Belina F. and Hogrefe D., "Introduction to SDL", *in Proceedings FOR*- TEE'88, Stirling, Scotland, September 1988.

Bernard, J.M., Hugon, J. and LeCorve, C.R. (1979) *De la Logique Cablée aux Microprocesseurs*, Volumes 1–4; Eyrolles editions.

Berry, G. and Boudol, G. (1990) "The Chemical Machine", *Proc. of POPL90 ACM.*

Bert, D. *et al.* (1988) "LPG: A Generic Logic and Functional Programming Language", *Proceedings 4th Software Engineering Conference/Exhibition (CGL4)*, AFCET, Paris.

Bestougeff, H., Ligozat, G. (1989) *Outils Logiques pour le Traitement du Temps*, Masson editions, Paris.

Binding, C., Saria, H. and Nirschi, H. (1991) "Mixing LOTOS and SDL Specifications", in Verrijn and Stuart (eds.), *Proceedings FORTE'91*, Sydney, 12-22 November 1991, North Holland Publishing Company, IFIP.

Bisiere, E.C. (1988) *Simulation des Systèmes Socio-économiques en Prolog III.*, Mémoire DEA, option I.A., Faculté des Sciences de Luminy, Groupe d'intelligence Artificielle, Marseille.

Black, A.P. (1985) "Supporting Distributed Applications: Experience with Eden, Proceedings of the 10th ACM Symposium on Operating Systems Principles", *SIGOPS Operating Systems Review*, Vol. 19, No. 5, pp. 181-93; December.

Black, A.P. (1986) "Distributed and Abstract Types in Emerald", *IEEE Transaction on Software Engineering*, Vol. SE-12; December.

Blanchard, M. (1979) *Comprendre, Maitriser et Appliquer le GRAFCET*, CEPADUES editions, Toulouse.

Bowen, J. *et al.* (1989) "An IA Approach to Loading Workshop Resources in a Distributed Job Shop Controller", *CIMS*, pp. 21-28.

Bratko, I. (1988) *Programmation en PROLOG pour l'Intelligence Artificielle*, InterEditions, Paris.

Brissaud, F. (1990) "Des Associations pour un Modèle à Objets, 4èmes Journées Pratique des Méthodes et Outils Logiciels d'Aide à la Conception de Systèmes d'Information", Nantes; 25–27 September.

Broy, M. *et al.* (1992) *The Requirement and Design Specification Language SPECTRUM: An Informal Introduction, Version 0.3 tech. Rep.*, Universität München, TUM-19140.

Bruno, G. and Marchetto, G. (1986) "Process Translatable Petri nets for the Rapid Prototyping of Process Control Systems", *IEEE Transactions on Software Engineering*, SE-12; February.

Bulter, R.M. *et al.* (1993) *Monitors, Messages, and Clusters. The P4 Parallel Programming System*, Technical Report, College of Computing Sciences and Engineering, University of North Florida.

Busttard, D.W, Norris, M.T, Orr, R.A and Winstanley, A.C. (1992) "An Exercise in Formalising the Description of Concurrent Systems", *Software Practice and Experience*, Vol. 22, No. 12; December.

Calvez, J.P. (1990) *Spécification et Conception des Systèmes: Etudes de Cas*, Masson editions.

CFIP'91 (1991) *Ingenierie des Protocoles*, Hermes edition.

Chandy, M. and Gelerntner, D. (1988) *Parallel Programming Design, A Foundation*, Addison-Wesley, Amsterdam.

Chauvet, J.M. (1997) *Corba, Activex and Java Beans*, Eyrolles Editions.

Choppy, C. *et al.* (1994) *Rapid Prototyping Algebraic Specification: A Case Study*, Rapport de Recherche L.R.RI., INRIA.

Clerment, L. (1983) *Systèmes à Microprocesseurs*, Volumes 1, 2, 3, 5, 6, Cabay editions.

Codognet, P. (1995) "Programmation Logique avec Contraintes: Une Introduction", *RAIRO, Technique et Science Informatiques*, Vol. 14, No. 6; June.

Colette, J.M. (1996) "Vers l'Analyse de l'Ordonnancement des Systèmes", *Mensuel Electronique*, No. 55; January.

Colmerauer, A. (1987) "Opening the Prolog III Universe", *BYTE*; August.

Colmerauer, A. (1990) "An Introduction to Prolog III", *Communications of the ACM*, Vol. 33, No. 7, July.

Colmerauer A. and Roussel P. (1993) "The Birth of Prolog", in *Proceedings of HOPLII*.

Comer, D. (1992) *TCP/IP: Architecture Protocoles, Applications*, Inter-Editions, Paris.

Cornafion (1981) *Systèmes Informatique Répartis: Concepts et Techniques,* Dunod.

Cosnard, M. *et al.* (1993) *Algorithmes et Applications Parallèles,* Inter-Editions, Paris.

Coulouris, G. *et al.* (1993) *Distributed Systems: Concepts and Design,* 2nd edition, Addison-Wesley, Amsterdam.

Courtiat, J.P. *et al.* (19989) "Estelle, un Langage ISO pour les Algorithmes Distribués et les Protocoles", *Technique et Science Informatique,* Vol. 6, No. 2.

David, R. and Alla H. (1992) *Du GRAFCET aux Réseaux de Petri,* Hermés editions, Paris.

Delahaye, J.P. (1987) *Systèmes Experts : Organisation et Programmation des Bases de Connaissance en Calcul Propositionnel,* Eyrolles editions, Paris.

Diaz, M. (1993) "Conception Formelle des Protocoles et Services dans les Systèmes Distribuées", *Génie Logiciel et les Systèmes Expert,* No. 30; March.

Dijsktra (1974) "Self Stabilizing Systems of Distributed Control", *CACM*; November.

Dincbas, M. *et al.* (1988) "The Constraint Logic Programming Language CHIP", in *Proceedings of the International Conference on Fifth Generation Computer Systems*, Tokyo, Japan; December.

Dombre, E. and Khahil W. (1988) *Modélisation et Commande des Robots*, Hermés editions, Paris.

Dorseuil A. and Pillot P. (1991) *Le TEMPS REEL en Milieu Industrial. Concepts, Environnements, Multitàches*, Dunod Editions.

Dzierzgowski, D. (1990) "Quatre Exemples de Langages ou Environnements pour le Développement de Programmes où le Temps Intervient", *Technique et Science lnformatiques,* Vol. 9, No. 4.

Erceau, J. and Barat, M. (1993) "Système Distribuée Homme-Machines, l'IA Distribuée et la Conception Coopérative des SystèmesComplexes du Future", *INFAU-TOM'93, du traitment réparti aux systèmes multi-agents et à l'autonomie des systèmes,* Toulouse; 18–19 February.

Farreny, H. *et al.* (1987) *Eléments d'lntelligence Artificielle,* Hermés editions, Paris.

Fayad, M.E. (1994) "Objects Modelling Technique (OMT): Experience Report" *Journal of Object-Oriented Programming;* November-December.

Ferber, J. (1993) "Modèle des Systèmes Multi-agents - Du réactif au cognitif", *INFAU-TOM'93, du traitement réparti aux systèmes multi-agents et à l'autonomie des systèmes*, Toulouse; 18–19 February.

Ferreny, H. (1985) *Les Systèmes Experts Principes et Exemples,* CEPA-DUES editions, Toulouse.

Festo (1996) *Documentations Techniques du Système Automatisé de Distribution et de Tri*, Festo Didactic, Paris.

Finin, T., *et al.* (1992) Specification of the KQML Agent Communication Language, the DARPA Knowledge Sharing Initiative, External Interfaces Working Group.

Fraser, M.D. *et al.* (1994) "Strategies for Incorporating Formal Specifications", *Communications of the ACM,* Vol. 37, No. 10; October.

Gabassi, M. and Dupuoy, B. (1992) *L'informatique Répartie sous Unix,* Eyrolles editions.

Gaubert, S. (1994) "Discrete Event Systems and (Max,+) Automata", *MOVEP"94,* Modélisation et Vérification des Processus parallèles: Application aux Systèmes à Evénements Discrets, Nantes; 21–24 June.

Gehani, N.H. and Roome, H.D. (1992) Implementing Concurrent C, *Software Practice and Experience,* Vol. 22, No. 3; March.

Genesereth, M.R. and Fikes, R.E. (eds.) (1992) *Knowledge Interchange Format, Version 3.0, Manuel de Référence,* Computer Science Department, Stamford University, Technical report Logic-92-1.

Genesereth, M.R. and Ketchpel, S.P. (1994) "Software Agents", *Communications of the ACM,* Vol. 37, No. 7, pp. 48-53; July.

Germain-Renaud and Sansonnet, J.P. (1991) *Les Ordinateurs Massivement Parallèles,* Armand Colin edition.

Gesit, A. *et al.* (1994) *PVM 3 User's Guide and Reference Manual,* Oak Ridge National Laboratory, Tennessee.

Ghernaouti, S. (1990) *Réseaux: Applications Réparties Normalisées,* Eyrolles editions. Paris.

Giannesini, F. *et al.* (1985) *PROLOG,* Inter-Editions, Paris.

Ginsburg, D. (1992) *ATM Strategies and Implementations,* Addison-Wesley, Amsterdam.

Goguen, J. and Meseguer, J. (1988) "Software for the Rewrite Rule Machine", *Proceedings of the International Conference of Fifth Generation Computer Systems,* Edited by ICOT, Tokyo.

Gross, C. (1996) "La Cosimulation Matériel-Logiciel", *Mensuel Electronique,* No. 60; June.

Harel, D. (1987) "Statecharts: A Visual Formalism for Complex Systems", *Science of Computer Programming,* Vol. 8, No. 3; June.

Harmon, P. (1995) "Software Agents", *Intelligent Software Strategies,* Vol. XI, No. 1; January.

Hatley, D.J. and Pirbhai, P.A. (1990) *Real-Time Specification Strategies (SA-RT),* Masson editions, Paris.

Helios Technical Guides (1990) *The HELIOS Parallel Programming Tutorial*, Distributed Software Limited; January.

Henri, E *et al.* (1992) "Orca: A Language for Parallel Programming of Distributed Systems", *IEEE Transactions on Software Engineering*, Vol. 18, No. 3; March.

Herrmann, F. (1987) "Chorus: Un Environnement pour le Développement et l'Execution d'Applications Répartis", *Technique et Sciences Informatiques*, Vol. 6, No. 2.

Hirsch, B.E. *et al.* (1994) "Intelligent Application Integration for Distributed Production", *IMSE, European Workshop on Integrated Manufacturing Systems Engineering*, Grenoble; 12–14 December.

Hoare, C.A.R. (1974) "Monitors: An Operating System Structuring Concept", *Communications of the ACM*, Vol. 17, No. 10; October.

Hoare, C.A.R. (1985) *Communicating Sequential Processes*, Prentice-Hall, Englewood Cliffs.

Imber, J.-L. (1995) "Linear Constraint Solving in CLP Languages", in A. Podelski (ed.), *Constraint Programming: Basics and Trends: Selected Papers*, Lecture Notes in Computer Science, Vol. 910, Springer.

Inmos Limited (1988) *OCCAM2 Reference Manual*, Prentice-Hall International Series in Computer Science.

International Workshop on Timed Petri Nets (1985) *IEEE Computer Society Press*, Torino, ltaly, 1–3 July.

Ishikawa, Y. *et al.* (1990) "Object-oriented Real-time Language Design Constructions for Timing Constraints", *ECOOP/OOPSLA'90 Proceedings*; October.

ISO 8807 (1988) *SLOTOS, A Formal Description Technique Based on the Temporal Ordering of Observational Behavior;* December.

ISO 9074 (1989) Information Processing systems – OSI, *Estelle: A Formal Description Technique Based on an Extended State Transition Model.*

Jaffar, J. and Machaylov, S. (1987) "The Methodology and Implementation of a CLP System", in *Proceedings of the Logic Programming Conference*, Melbourne, MIT Press.

Jahanian, F. and Stuart, D.A. (1988) "A Method for Verifying Properties of Modechart specifications", *IEEE Real-Time Systems Symposium*, Huntsville, Alabama; December.

Jones, B.C. (1993) *VDM une Méthodologie Rigoureuse pour le Développement du Logiciel*, Masson editions.

Kautz, H.A., Bart, S. and Coen, M. (1994) "Bottom-up design of software agents", *Communication of the ACM*, Vol. 37, No. 7, pp. 143-47;July.

Kowk, A. and Norrie, D. (1994) "A Development System for Intelligent Agent Manufacturing Software", *Integrated Manufacturing Systems*, Vol. 5, No. 4/5, pp. 64-76.

Krakowiak, S. *et al.* (1990) "Design and Implementation of an Object-oriented Strongly Typed Language for Distributed Applications", *Joop*, Vol. 3, No. 3, September/ October.

Lalement, R. (1990) *Logique Réduction Résolution*, Masson editions, Paris.

Lamport (1978) "Time, Clocks and the Ordering of Events in Distributed Systems", *CACM*.

Lauriere, J.L. (1987) *Intelligence Artificielle, Résolution de Problémes par l'Homme et la Machine*, Eyrolles, Paris.

LeBeux, P. (1984) *Introduction à ADA*, SYBEX editions.

LeMarie, S. (1992) "Etude et Réalisation d'un Système Réparti Fondé sur les Acteurs", Thèse d'infomatique, Université Paris VI.

LePage, F. *et al.* (1992) *Les Réseaux des Drivers UNIX*, Addison-Wesley editions, Paris.

Les Automates Programmables (1988) CEPADUES editions, Toulouse.

Lightfoot, D. (1991) *Formal Specification Using Z*, Macmillan Press.

Lightfoot, D. (1994) *Spécification Formelle avec Z*, Teknea editions.

Liskov, B.H. (1985) "The Argus Language and System, in Distributed Systems Methods and Tools for Specification", *Lecture Notes in Computer Science*, Springer-Verlag.

Lui and Layland, *A Practitioner's Handbook for Real-Time Analysis*, Kluwer Academic Publishers.

Manuel d'Utilisation de Prolog III, Prolog1A, Parc Technologique de Luminy - Case 919, 13288 Marseilles Cedex 9.

Marca, D., MacGowan, A. and Clement, L. (1988) *SADT: Structured Analysis Systems, Edit and Design Technique*, McGraw Hill.

McGuire, J.G. *et al.* (1993) "SHADE: Technology for Knowledge-Based Collaborative Engineering", *Journal of Concurrent Engineering: Research and Applications (CERA)*, Vol. 1, No. 2; September.

Menga, G., Moriso, M., Lo Russo, G. (1989) "A Framework for Object Oriented Design and Prototyping of Manufacturing Systems", *TOOL'89*, Paris, France.

Meseguer, J. (1990) "A Logical Theory of Concurrent Objects", in *Proceedings Concur 90 Conference*, Springer-Verlag, Amsterdam; August.

Milner, R. (1980) "A Calculus of Communicating Systems", *Lecture Notes in Computer Science.*

Mowbray, T. and Zahavi, R. (1995) *The Essential CORBA: System Integration Using Distributed Objects*, Wiley.

Mullender, S. (1985) "Principles of Distributed Operating Systems Design", Academisch Profschrift, Vrije Universitieit, Amsterdam, Mathematisch Centrum; October.

Object-Oriented Concepts Inc. (1998) *Object-Oriented Concepts*, Billeria, MA (www.ooc.com).

Orfali, R., Harkey, D. and Edwards, J. (1996) *Objets Repartis, Guide de Survie*, Thomson Publishing.

Parunak, H.V.D. (1993) "Industrial Applications of Multi-agent Systems", INFAUTOM'93 du traitement réparti aux systèmes multi-agents et à l'autonomie des systèmes, Toulouse; 18–19 February.

Perez, J.P. (1990) *Systèmes Temps Réel: Méthodes de Spécification et de Conception*, Dunod editions.

Peterson, J.L. *Petri Nets Theory and the Modelling of Systems*, Prentice Hall.

Rangarajian, S. *et al.* (1991) "Efficient Synchronization of Clocks in Distributed Systems", in *Proceedings of the IEEE Real-Time Systems Symposium*, San Antonio.

Raynal, M. (1983) *Synchronisation de Programmes Parallèles*, Dunod editions, Paris.

Raynal, M. (1991) *La Communication et le Temps dans les Systèmes Répartis*, Eyrolles editions.

Raynal, M. (1992) *Synchronisation et Etat Global dans les Systèmes Répartis*, Eyrolles edition.

Rifflet, J.M. (1990) *La Communication sous Unix*, McGraw Hill edition.

Rumbaugh, J. *et al.* (1995) *Modélisation et Conception Orientées Objet*, Masson and Prentice-Hall, Paris.

S-DOS (1990) *Manuel Utilisateur, Manuel de Programmation*, Microprocess, Software Systemes Speciaux.

Sessions, R. (1996) *Object Persistence*, Prentice–Hall.

Sibertin-Blanc, C. (1975) "High-level Petri Nets with Data Structures", in *Proceedings 6th European Workshop on Applications and Theory of Petri Nets*, Helsinki; June.

Sijelmassi, R. and Strausser, B. (1991) *NIST Integrated Tool Set For Estelle, Formal Description Techniques*, Quemada (ed.), North-Holland.

Sinha, A. (1992) "Client-Server Computing", *Communications of the ACM*, Vol. 35, No. 7; July.

Sommerville, I. (1993) *Le Génie Logiciel*, Addison-Wesley.

Spivey, J.M. (1990) "Specifying a Real-Time Kernel", *IEEE Software Journal,* September.

Sun Microsystems (1996) *Java FAQ List and Tutorial: A Work in Progress.*

Tanenbaum, A.S. and Renese, R.V. (1985) "Distributed Operating Systems", *ACM Computing Surveys,* Vol. 17, No. 4; December.

Thorin, M. (1990) *Parallélisme: Génie Logiciel Temps Réel,* Dunod edition.

Tschirhart, D. *Commande en Temps Réel: Conception et Mise en Oeuvre d'un Exécutif Multitàche,* Dunod edition.

Valette, R. and Paludetto, M. (1988) "Designing Real Time Software with the Object Oriented HOOD Approach and Petri Nets", in *International Workshop on Software Engineering and its Applications,* Toulouse, France; December.

Vidal-Naquet, G. and Choquet-Geniet, A. (1992) *Réseaux de Petri et Systèmes Paralléles,* Armand Colin Editions, Paris.

Vigder M. (1991a) "Using VDM within Object Oriented Framework", in *Proceedings VDM91 Formal Software Development Methods,* Noordwijkerhout, the Netherlands; 21–25 October.

Vigder, M. (1991b) "Using LOTOS in a Design Environment", in *Proceedings FORTE'91,* Sidney, 12–22 November.

VXWorks Programmers' Guide (1992) Wind River Systems, Inc.

Ward, P.T. and Mellor, S.J. (1985) *Structured Development for Real Time Systems,* Yourdon Press, NY.

Ward, P. (1989) "How to Integrate Object Orientation with Structured Analysis and Design", *Software,* Vol. 6 No. 2, pp. 74-82; March.

Wirsing, M. (1990) "Algebraic Specification", in Van Leeuwen (ed.), *Handbook of Theoretical Computer Science,* Vol B, Amsterdam, North-Holland.

Wirsing, M. (1993) "Développement de Logiciel et Spécifications Formelles", *TSI,* Vol. 12, No. 4.

WorldFIP (1995a) *Guide de la Technologie WorldFIR,* WorldFIP Europe, Nancy.

WorldFIP (1995b) *Le Protocole WorldFIP,* WorldFIP Europe, Nancy.

Index

abstract type 246
accept 149
actor 72, 110, 120
actuator 176, 207, 226
ADA 282, 288
addressing
  immediate 408
  indexed 408
  indirect 408
  network 132
  by register 408
ADEPA 182
AF_INET 147
AF_UNIX 147
AFCET 182
agent
  cognitive 3, 378
  co-operating 349
  natural 3
  processing 3
  reactive control 346, 349, 377
  specialised 375
  superior 52, 369
algebra 246
analysis
  ascending 346
  composite 241
  descending 241, 344
anonymous communication 76
API 184
April 209
ARP 130
artificial intelligence 199
ASCII 157
ASIC 265
asynchronism 139
asynchronous 70, 162, 230, 321
AT 321
ATM 22, 62
atomicity 47, 51
automaton 276, 368
  industrial 370
  programmable 178
auto-validation 53

barcode 240
BEFORE 321
bind 162
BIOS 406

causality 294
CCD 348
certification 346
CFD 188
CFDO 349
chain list 323
channel 303, 363
CICS 42
class 79
  persistent 381
client–server 19, 77, 125
close 148
co-design 56
combinatorial 4
communication 166, 327
  asynchronous 327
  horizontal 307
  synchronous 327
  vertical 307
completeness 243
configuration 355
connect 148, 157, 162
consistence 243
constraint
  technological 361
  temporal 319, 361
controller 409
  interrupt 415
conveyor belt 240, 361
co-ordination 188
co-ordinator 188
couplers 179
coupling
  asynchronous 368
  strong 138
  weak 138
coverification 232
critical section 221
CSPEC 189, 360

data dictionary 351, 352, 363, 364, 369
data transmission 9
database
  active 375
  shared 382
datagram 130, 133, 148
DBMS 55, 57, 375
DCD 348
DDBMS 20
deadlocking 22, 39, 41, 50
deamon 32, 64, 84, 104, 106, 142
DES 32, 39, 104
descriptor 109, 142, 389, 432, 433
detection-recovery 188
device 142
DFD 187, 188
DFD0 349, 351
DIE-WAIT 44
Direct Access 389
dispatcher 229, 413, 415
dynamic 244
  rapid 368

eagle design 232
emergency stop 179, 184, 350
Ethernet 10, 15, 49, 62, 128, 129
EVERY 322, 362
exceptions 205
exec 136
execution
  asynchronous 29
  synchronous 29

fact base 278, 288
FACTOR 208
FDDI 62
FIFO 101
file 75, 362
  wait 425
FIP 211, 358
flexible production unit 192
fork() 136
FPGA 56
free() 84
FTP 33
function
  global 344
  objective 345

gethostbyname 156
GOTO 35
GRAFCET 183, 185, 188, 366, 368, 370
granularity 18

handler 141, 200, 204, 221, 271
  blocking mode 420, 422
  character mode 420
HiPPI 62
htons 157, 168

inetd.conf 340
inference motor 288
inference rules 278
information warehouse 18
inheritance 247
inode 421
instance 389
interaction 187
Internet 127
interoperability 119, 125
interoperables 1
interrupt handler 4, 113
interrupt technique 409
interrupt vectors 206
IP/X25 131
IPC 101

jack 363
JNET 209

Kermit 33
kernel
  MMS 213
  real-time 185, 201

Lex 306
Linux 422
Lisp 249
listen 149
Listener 385
log 47, 49, 51
logic
  displaced 186
  predicate 245
  proposition 245
longjmp 326
loop
  closed 177
  open 177

maintenance 192, 277
major 421
Makefile 423
malloc() 83

management
  event 376
  object 376
  schema 381
  temporal constraints 376
MAP 208
master 109
master-slave 65, 120
Max-Plus 252, 256
Memory MAP 410
Mentor Graphics 232
method
  Newton 309
  VDM 245
methodology 67
micro-processor 409
migration 26, 48
minor 421
missile 320
mode
  command 177
  connected 151, 154, 156, 160, 170
  datagram 163, 166
  operator guide 177
  reduced 353
  surveillance 177
  synchronous 27
  XDR connected 172
model 285
  abstract informatics 345
  communication 57
  conceptual 345
  dynamic 345
  functional 345
  ISO 12, 21, 34, 68
  static 345
modelling 264
modem 7
modularity 14, 192
modules 269
monitors 35, 150, 320
monolithic 55, 191, 192
mono-processor 192
monostable distributors 363
mosaic 106
multiple copies 21, 30
multiple processor 321
multi-process 320
multi-programming 5
multi-task 55, 191
mutual exclusion 80, 221

Netscape 106
network
  computer 9
  form 162
  format 113
  local 16, 62
Neumann 60
NFS 134
nomenclature 364
ntohs 168

object-oriented 19
OMT 66
operative part 347, 403
order relation 193
OS2 56, 57
OS-9 57
overload 427

paging mechanism 431
Parallel Access 35, 45, 47
passive entities 347
periodic task 195, 320
persistence, implicit 376
peripherals 403
pipe 143, 220, 385
  communication 385
  named 147
pipeline 60, 67
planning 367, 378
poll 142
POLLING 207, 222, 409
popen 136
port 148
predicate 259, 289
pre-emption 192, 193, 195
prevention-avoidance 43
priority 193, 322
process
  communicating 35
  concurrent 35, 100
  filter 72
  light 75
  lookout 382
  placing 75
  reactive 64
  transformation 176
producer-consumer 428
production unit 295
PROFIBUS 358
programming
  concurrent 14
  modular 241
  object-oriented 319
  structured 241
  systematic 241
progression law 308

Prolog III 297
proof 250
Protocol
  communication 270, 375
  dialogue 270
  disconnection 388
  initialization 388
  validation 297
prototyping 197
proximity detector 345
PSPEC 355, 362
PVM 103
pvm_addhost 111
pvm_bcast 120
pvm_bufinfo 116
pvm_config 112
pvm_exit 111
pvm_gettid 120
pvm_gsize 120
pvm_init 110
pvm_initsend 109
pvm_joingroup 120
pvm_kill 111
pvm_lvgroup 120
pvm_mcast 113
pvm_mkbuf 112
pvm_mstat 111
pvm_mytid 110
pvm_notify 117
pvm_nrecv 109
pvm_parent 111
pvm_pkstr 110
pvm_precv 114
pvm_pstat 111
pvm_recv 109
pvm_send 113
pvm_sendsig 117
pvm_spawn 111
pvm_tasks 111
pvm_tidtohost 112
pvm_trecv 115
pvmd 107

quantum 427

radar 319
RAM 409
RARP 131
reactivity 1, 76, 175, 221
reader 144
  barcode 348, 358
real-time executive 368, 372
recovery 376, 378
recvfrom 149
reduction 277
re-entry 204, 348
registers 405
regulation 188, 193, 197
remote events 253
rendezvous 78
restart 353
resource 403
  active 270
  passive 270
RMA 195
robot 376
ROM 409
round-robin 202
routing 131
RPC 27
RS232 358
rule base 379

SA/RT 344
SA/SD 344
sampling 192
schedulable 195, 196
scheduler 23, 30, 189, 193
scheduling 36, 43-44, 196, 201
schema 389
scientific computation 56
semaphore 22
sensor 176
  intelligent 319
  proximity 362
sequencers 180
sequential 4
serialization 45
setitimer 326
setjmp 326
SGBD 55, 57, 375
signal 79
simulation horizon 290
simulation 256, 258, 261
site
  substitute 53
  superior 50
slave 65, 121
SLIP 131
SMTP 134
socket 153
software engineering 241
SONET 62
special file 420
specification 345
  algebraic 247
sporadic server 197
SQL 19

state
  observable 354
  stable 355
storage space 389
strategy
  FIFO 426
  LRU 379
stream 72
supervision 369
  overall 376
synchronization 369, 376
  distributed 378
synchronous 69
system bus 403
system
  banking 305
  distributed xiii
  expert 278
  heterogeneous 59
  multi-agent 4
  operating 14
  production 269
  reactive 269
  remote 264
  reservation 14
  transactional 14

TCP 129, 133
TCP/IP 129
TELNET 133
temporal referential 24
temporization 204
temporizer 320, 360
termination point 35
threads 73
time
  critical real 320
  shared 15
  soft real 319
time stamp 43, 44
timer 221, 320
token 40
  circulating 38, 40
TOP 209
transactional co-operator 9
transactions 19
transcoder 306
transformation 187
TRANSPAC 22
transputers 60

UDP 133
Unix 33, 103, 150, 322, 403

validation 1
  0-phase 50, 51
  1-phase 51
  2-phase 52
  overall 25
validation point 46-48
VHDL 282
virtual 150
virtual address 151
virtual channel 148
virtual machine 103, 108
virtual memory 376, 385
virtual ring 37, 40, 77
virtual terminal 418
VME 368
VxWorks 372

wait 29
WAIT_DIE 44
wait graph 39
watchdog timer 195
WINDOWS-95 56, 57
workshop 282
WOUND-WAIT 44

XDR 113, 134, 168
xdrmem_create 169
Xelinx 57
X-WINDOW 57, 134

yacc 306

Z language 244